Third Edition

Rexford E. Santerre
Professor of Finance and Healthcare
*   Management*
Center for Healthcare and Insurance
*   Studies*
University of Connecticut

Stephen P. Neun
Professor of Economics
Dean of Social Sciences and
*   Management*
Utica College of Syracuse University

HEALTH ECONOMICS

Theories, Insights, and Industry Studies

THOMSON

SOUTH-WESTERN

Australia · Canada · Mexico · Singapore · Spain · United Kingdom · United States

To Our Wives:

Laurie

&

Joan

THOMSON

SOUTH-WESTERN

Health Economics: Theories, Insights, and Industry Studies   Third Edition

Rexford E. Santerre
Bentley College

Stephen P. Neun
Utica College of Syracuse University

**Vice President/
Editorial Director:**
Jack Calhoun

Editor-in-Chief:
Mike Roche

Publisher of Economics:
Michael B. Mercier

Senior Acquisitions Editor:
Peter Adams

Developmental Editor:
Andrew McGuire

Marketing Manager:
Janet Hennies

Production Editor:
Cliff Kallemeyn

Manufacturing Coordinator:
Sandee Milewski

Media Developmental Editor:
Peggy Buskey

Media Production Editor:
Pam Wallace

Compositor:
Cover to Cover Publishing, Inc.

Printer:
Phoenix Color
Hagerstown, MD

Designer:
Bethany Casey

Library of Congress
Control Number:

2002115010

ISBN: 0-324-17186-2 (package)
ISBN: 0-324-27366-5 (core book)

The health care sector, now representing nearly one-seventh of the U.S. economy in terms of economic activity, continues to change in unimaginable ways. Wide-sweeping transformations in the organizational arrangements of health care providers, newly developed medical technologies, the creation of new health insurance products, and the development and evaluation of various public policy initiatives all make the health care sector a dynamic and exciting area for applying the lens and tools of economic analysis. Indeed, not a day goes by without the unfolding of some medical event that requires the insights of economics to unravel the depths of its implications.

Our textbook, now in its third edition, is written expressly to capture the excitement generated by the health care field. Like in the earlier editions, we take a fresh, contemporary approach to the study of health economics. We present the material in a lively and inviting manner by providing numerous and timely real-world examples throughout the text. At the same time, we resist the temptation of becoming overly encyclopedic and avoid purely technical issues that interest only academics and not students.

As a result of the approach taken, our book has wide appeal. Many business schools; liberal arts colleges; medical schools; and schools of public health, pharmacy, and health administration; at both the undergraduate and graduate levels, have chosen to use our textbook. In addition, the national Certified Employee Benefits Specialist (CEBS) program, cosponsored by the International Foundation of Employee Benefit Plans and the Wharton School of the University of Pennsylvania, has chosen our book for their program. The mix of adopters attests to the relevance and practicality of the material and the consistent and inviting manner in which the principles and concepts of health economics are presented.

WHAT'S NEW IN THE THIRD EDITION?

Several changes have been made in this third edition in response to the suggestions of readers and reviewers. First, some reorganization of chapters has been made. The chapters titled "Health and Medical Care" and "Cost and Benefit Analysis" are now Chapters 2 and 3, respectively. By moving the material on health and medical care to the front, students will understand the factors behind the production of health and the relative importance of medical care early on in the course. Also, the students will gain an early understanding of what efficiency entails by moving the cost and benefit discussion to Chapter 3.

We have also consolidated the material on competitive and noncompetitive market theory into one chapter and expanded our discussion on oligopoly. We eliminated the chapter on "Not-for-Profit Objectives" but dispersed the material into the industry chapters where appropriate. For example, the hospital chapter now includes a discussion of various models of not-for-profit behavior as applied to a hospital setting. Many instructors felt that this change provides a more integrated perspective, and we think you'll find this a positive change too. In addition, a new industry chapter titled "Long-Term Care" has been added to the book for the obvious reason.

As requested by a former student, an important pedagogical feature has been introduced in the text. We now include a caption under each graph to explain the theory being offered. Given that the presentation of the graphical model is now relatively self-contained, it is less necessary for students to inconveniently and repeatedly flip pages back and forth to understand the graphical exposition. We believe ours is the only health economics textbook on the market presently possessing this important pedagogical feature.

In addition to the reorganization of chapters, adding a new chapter, and the inserted captions, we have also updated and expanded the discussion on various topics. As one example, we have added more discussion on medical malpractice and defensive medicine in the physician chapter. You will also notice in the physician chapter that we have included McGuire's quantity-setting model of physician behavior. Thus, our text may be the first to provide an explicit model that describes the physician decision-making process with respect to the price and quantity of care. As other examples, we have added material on pharmaceutical benefit management companies in the pharmaceutical chapter and the insurance chapter now addresses if HMOs possess monopsony power.

SUPPLEMENTS

Web Site   The support site for *Health Economics* can be accessed at http://santerre. swlearning.com and contains chapter-by-chapter web links, term paper tips, instructor's resources, and other teaching and learning resources.

Web-based Instructor's Manual   The *Health Economics* support site (http://santerre. swlearning.com) contains password-protected material for instructors only, including answers to end-of-chapter questions in the text, a sample syllabus with web links, a list of readings for each chapter, and ideas for course projects.

PowerPoint Slides   PowerPoint slides are also located on the support site, and are available for use by students as an aid to note-taking, and by instructors for enhancing lectures. These slides include a lecture outline, key tables and graphs, and a brief summary.

InfoTrac College Edition   InfoTrac College Edition is packaged with every copy of the textbook. It is a fully searchable online university library containing complete articles and their images. Its database allows access to hundreds of scholarly and popular publications—all reliable sources, including magazines, journals, encyclopedias, and newsletters.

ACKNOWLEDGMENTS

Our goal is to create the best possible learning device for students and teaching tool for professors. We are profoundly grateful to all of the reviewers for helping us bring this goal to fruition. For reviewing this third edition and providing numerous comments and suggestions, we thank Jay Bae of Georgia State University, Sewin Chan of New York University, Diane Dewar of the University of Albany, Alfredo Esposto of Eastern Michigan University, Irene Powell of Grinnell College, and Jeffrey Rubin of Rutgers University. Most of their suggestions have been incorporated into the text. We also thank the reviewers of past editions and others who have provided us with comments for improving the text, including Steven Andes, Mary Ann Bailey, Laurie Bates, Sylvester Berki, Bruce Carpenter,

Partha Deb, Randall Ellis, Andrew Foster, A. Mark Freeman, Glenn Graham, Dennis Heffley, Robert Jantzen, Donald Kenkel, Frank Musgrave, Albert Oriol, James Thornton, Kay Unger, Gary Wyckoff, and Donald Yett. The time-consuming and exhaustive review and appraisal of the original manuscript by Steven Andes, Mary Ann Bailey, and Gary Wyckoff continues to receive our deepest appreciation.

At South-Western we thank Andrew McGuire, our developmental editor. Not only has Andy keenly and expertly orchestrated the revision from beginning to end, but he has also been an understanding and collegial individual to work with. Our thanks are also extended to all of the production staff and marketing personnel who face the important and overwhelming task of packaging and selling the final product. We are very appreciative for their professional support. Lastly, we thank our families for their understanding and love.

As mentioned in the previous editions, if any of our readers, students, or colleagues have any comments or suggestions for improving the text, please bring them to our attention. We are only an email message away. We thank you in advance.

Rex Santerre
Rexford.Santerre@business.uconn.edu

Stephen Neun
sneun@utica.edu

THE CERTIFIED EMPLOYEE BENEFIT SPECIALIST® (CEBS) PROGRAM

The International Foundation of Employee Benefit Plans (IFEBP), located in Brookfield, Wisconsin, and The Wharton School of the University of Pennsylvania cosponsor the CEBS Program. Founded in 1954 the IFEBP is a not-for-profit educational association, dedicated to the education of and exchange of information among individuals responsible for the administration of employee benefits. The Wharton School, the world's first collegiate school of management, was founded in 1881 and is today widely regarded as a leader in preparing students to succeed in a globally competitive business environment. The IFEBP and Wharton established the CEBS Program in 1974 by creating a ten-course curriculum in health and welfare and retirement employee benefit programs. The curriculum covers fundamental concepts and principles of insurance, law, accounting, finance, human resources management, and economics and their applicability to the employee benefits field.

Candidates can earn three designations: two specialty designations—Group Benefit Associate (GBA) and Retirement Plan Associate (RPA)—and the CEBS designation. The CEBS designation is earned by successfully completing an exam after studying each of the ten following courses:

Course 1   Employee Benefits: Concepts and Health Care Benefits
Course 2   Employee Benefits: Design, Administration, and Other Welfare Benefits
Course 3   Retirement Plans: Basic Features and Defined Contribution Approaches

Course 4   Retirement Plans: Defined Benefit Approaches and Plan Administration
Course 5   Contemporary Legal Environment of Employee Benefit Plans
Course 6   Financial Concepts and Practices
Course 7   Asset Management
Course 8   Human Resources and Compensation Management
Course 9   Health Economics
Course 10   Contemporary Benefit Issues and Practices, or PFP 1: Personal Financial
            Planning 1: Concepts and Principles

GBA Designation: Complete Courses 1, 2, 9 plus Course 8 or PFP 1
RPA Designation: Complete Courses 3, 4, 7 plus Course 8 or PFP 1

The candidate can prepare for the exams by selecting to do self-study, participate in on-line courses, or enroll in classes that are offered at over 80 educational institutions including The Wharton School.

CEBS candidates are a diverse group representing all sectors of the employee benefit industry—plan sponsors, consulting firms, managed care organizations, banks, hospitals, law, investment and accounting firms, labor organizations, and professional associations. The CEBS designation is the most widely recognized and respected designation in the employee benefits field and has been earned by about 9,300 individuals as of September 2002. CEBS graduates combine academic education with professional experience to fulfill, at the highest level, employers, and clients, needs. Upon completing the CEBS Program, graduates continue their professional development by joining the International Society of Certified Employee Benefit Specialists and participating in educational activities sponsored by local chapters. As members of the Society, graduates can build on their employee benefits knowledge through continuing education courses and examinations on emerging benefit issues and statutory changes.

A CEBS Program Catalog of Information can be obtained by contacting the IFEBP or The Wharton School at the following addresses:

CEBS Program
IFEBP
18700 W. Bluemound Road
P.O. Box 1270
Brookfield, WI 53008-1270
(262) 786-6710, Ext. 8579
cebs@ifebp.org
http://www.ifebp.org

CEBS Program
The Wharton School
St. Leonard's Court, Suite 217
3819-33 Chestnut Street
Philadelphia, PA 19104-3106
(215) 898-2678

The **Review Questions and Problems** sections of selected chapters in the textbook include sample Questions on Subject Matter from the CEBS Study Manual for Course 9 and sample CEBS Exam Questions.

PART 1

BASIC HEALTH CARE ECONOMIC TOOLS AND INSTITUTIONS

1

INTRODUCTION

Like millions of Americans at some point in their lives, Joe awoke one night feeling a crushing weight on his chest. As the pain spread down his arm, he realized he was experiencing his worst dread: a heart attack. His wife, Angela, called the paramedics. While the ambulance was rushing Joe to the hospital, she anguished over the kind of care he would receive. Angela's anxiety starkly illustrates the basic questions any health care system faces:

1. Who should receive the medical goods and services? Would a person like Joe receive care merely because he is a citizen, or would he receive care only if he worked for a large company that provides health insurance for its employees?

2. What types of medical goods and services should be produced? Should the most expensive tests (such as angiograms) be performed without regard to cost? What treatments (such as balloon angioplasties) should be provided?

3. What inputs should be used to produce the medical goods and services? Should the hospital use high-tech medical equipment, a large nursing staff, or both?[1]

This chapter examines these fundamental questions. In addition, the chapter

> Introduces the discipline of health economics.

> Discusses the design and purpose of models and analysis in health economics.

> Explains how economic decisions are typically driven by a cost-benefit calculation.

> Examines the X and Y theories of health economics.

---

[1]We are indebted to Gary Wyckoff of Hamilton College for providing us with this example.

WHAT IS HEALTH ECONOMICS?

For many of you, this textbook provides your first exposure to the study of health economics. Perhaps the ongoing controversy regarding health care reform or the prospect of a career in the health care field motivated you to learn more about health economics. Or perhaps you need only three more credits to graduate. Whatever the reason, we are sure you will find health economics to be challenging, highly interesting, and personally rewarding.

The study of health economics involves the application of various microeconomics tools, such as demand or cost theory, to health issues and problems. The goal is to promote a better understanding of the economic aspects of health care problems so that corrective health policies can be designed and proposed. A thorough understanding of microeconomic analysis is essential for conducting sound health economics analyses. If you lack a background in microeconomics, don't worry. This textbook is intended to help you learn and apply basic microeconomic theory to health economic issues. Before long, you will be thinking like a health economist!

The tools of health economics can be applied to a wide range of issues and problems pertaining to health and health care. For example, health economics analysis might be used to investigate why 47 of every 1,000 babies born in Turkey never reach their first birthday, whereas all but 4 of every 1,000 babies born in Japan live to enjoy their first birthday cake. The tools of health economics analysis might also be used to examine the economic desirability of a hotly contested merger between two large hospitals in a major metropolitan area. The burning question is: Will the merger of the two hospitals result in lower hospital prices due to overall cost savings or higher prices due to monopoly power?

Health economics is difficult to define in a few words because it encompasses such a broad range of concepts, theories, and topics. *The Mosby Medical Encyclopedia* (1992, p. 361) defines *health economics* as follows:

> **Health economics** . . . *studies the supply and demand of health care resources and the impact of health care resources on a population.*

Notice that health economics is defined in terms of the determination and allocation of *health care resources*. This is logical, because medical goods and services cannot exist without them.[2] Health care resources consist of *medical supplies*, such as pharmaceutical goods, latex rubber gloves, and bed linens; *personnel*, such as physicians and lab assistants; and *capital inputs*, including nursing home and hospital facilities, diagnostic and therapeutic equipment, and other items that provide medical care services. Unfortunately, health care resources, like resources in general, are limited or scarce at a given time, and wants are limitless. Thus, trade-offs are inevitable and a society, whether it possesses a market-driven or a government-run health care system, must make a number of fundamental but crucial choices. These choices are normally couched in terms of four basic questions, discussed next.

---

[2]Even health care services produced in the home, such as first aid (therapeutic services) or home pregnancy tests (diagnostic services), require resources.

THE FOUR BASIC QUESTIONS

As just noted, resources are scarce. Scarcity means that each society must make important decisions regarding the consumption, production, and distribution of goods and services as a way of providing answers to the four basic questions, which are:

1. What combination of nonmedical and medical goods and services should be produced in the macroeconomy?
2. What particular medical goods and services should be produced in the health economy?
3. What specific health care resources should be used to produce the final medical goods and services?
4. Who should receive the medical goods and services?

How a particular society chooses to answer these four questions has a profound impact on the operation and performance of its health economy.

The first two questions deal with **allocative efficiency**: What is the best way to allocate resources to different consumption uses? The first decision concerns what combination of goods and services to produce in the overall economy. Individuals in a society have unlimited wants regarding nonmedical and medical goods and services, yet resources are scarce. As a result, decisions must be made concerning the best mix of medical and nonmedical goods and services to provide, and this decision-making process involves making trade-offs. If more people are trained as doctors or nurses, fewer people are available to produce nonmedical goods such as food, clothing, and shelter. Thus, more medical goods and services imply fewer nonmedical goods and services, and vice versa, given a fixed amount of resources.

The second consumption decision involves the proper mix of medical goods and services to produce in the health economy. This decision also involves trade-offs. For example, if more health care resources, such as nurses and medical equipment, are allocated to the production of maternity care services, fewer resources are available for the production of nursing home care for elderly people. Allocative efficiency in the overall economy and the health economy is achieved when the best mix of goods is chosen given society's underlying preferences.

The third question—what specific health care resources should be used?—deals with **production efficiency**. Usually resources or inputs can be combined to produce a particular good or service in many different ways. For example, hospital services can be produced in a capital- or labor-intensive manner. A large amount of sophisticated medical equipment relative to the number of patients served reflects a capital-intensive way of producing hospital services, whereas a high nurse-to-patient ratio indicates a labor-intensive process. Production efficiency implies that society is getting the maximum output from its limited resources because the best mix of inputs has been chosen to produce each good.

Production and Allocative Efficiency and the Production Possibilities Curve

The most straightforward way to illustrate production and allocative efficiency is to use the **production possibilities curve (PPC)**. A PPC is an economic model that depicts the various combinations of any two goods or services that can be produced efficiently given the stock of resources, technology, and various institutional arrangements. Figure 1–1 displays a PPC. The quantities of maternity services, M, and nursing home services, N, are shown on the vertical and horizontal axes, respectively.[3] Points on the bowed-out PPC depict the various combinations of maternity and nursing home care services that can be efficiently produced within a health economy assuming the amounts of health care resources and technology are fixed at a given point in time.

FIGURE 1–1

Production Possibilities Curve for Maternity and Nursing Home Services

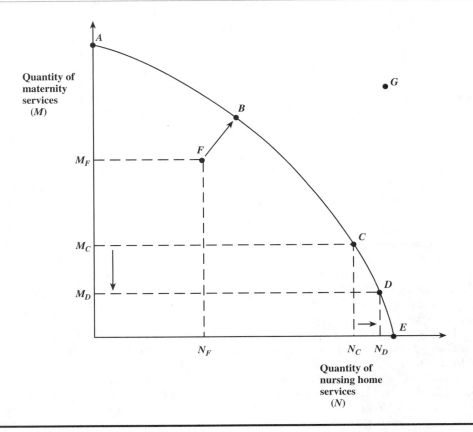

The PPC shows the trade-off between any two goods given a fixed stock of resources and technology. Any point on the PPC, like points A through E, reflect efficiency because units of one good must be given up to receive more of the other. A point in the interior, such as F, reflects inefficiency because more of one good can be attained without necessarily reducing the other. A point outside the PPC such as G, is not yet attainable but can be reached with an increase in resources or through any institutional or technological changes that improve productivity.

---

[3]We assume society has already made its choice between medical and nonmedical goods.

Every point on the PPC implies production efficiency, since all health care resources are being fully utilized. For example, notice points A, B, C, D, and E on the PPC. At each of these points, medical inputs are neither unemployed nor underemployed (e.g., a nurse involuntarily working part time rather than full time) and are being used in the most productive manner so that society is getting their maximum use. If a movement along the curve from one point to another occurs, units of one medical service must be forgone to receive more units of the other medical service.

Specifically, assume the health economy is initially operating at point C with M_C units of maternity care services and N_C units of nursing home services. Now suppose health care decision makers decide that society is better off at point D with one more unit of nursing home services, $N_D - N_C$. The movement from point C to point D implies that $M_C - M_D$ units of maternity care services are given up to receive the additional unit of nursing home services. Because medical resources are fully utilized at point C, a movement to point D means that medical inputs must be drawn or reallocated from the maternity care services market to the nursing home services market. As a result, the quantity of maternity care services must decline if an additional unit of nursing home services is produced. The forgone units of maternity care services, $M_C - M_D$, represent the **opportunity cost** of producing an additional unit of nursing home services.[4] Generally, opportunity cost is the value of the next best alternative that is given up.

The bowed-out shape of the PPC implies that opportunity cost is not constant but increases with a movement along the curve. Imperfect substituability of resources is one reason for this so-called **law of increasing opportunity cost**. For example, suppose the nursing home services market expands downward along the PPC. To produce more nursing home services, employers must bid resources away from the maternity care services market. Initially, the least productive inputs in the maternity care services market are likely to be bid away, because they are available at a lower cost to nursing home employers. Consequently, very few maternity care services are given up at first. As the nursing home services market continues to expand, however, increasingly productive inputs in the maternity care services market must be drawn away. The implication is that society gives up ever-increasing units of maternity care services. Thus, the law of increasing opportunity cost suggests that ever-increasing amounts of one good must be given up to receive successively more equal increments of another good.

If medical inputs are not fully utilized because some inputs are idle or used unproductively, more units of one medical service can be produced without decreasing the amount of the other medical service. An example of an underutilization of resources is indicated by point F in the interior of the PPC. At point F, the health care system is producing only M_F units of maternity services and N_F units of nursing home services. Notice that by moving to point B on the PPC, both maternity care services and nursing home services can be increased without decreasing the other. The quantities of both goods increase only because some resources are initially idle or underutilized at point F. Health care resources are inefficiently employed at point F.

A point outside the current PPC, such as G, is attainable in the future if the stock of health care resources increases, a new, productivity-enhancing technology is discovered, or various economic, political, or legal arrangements change and improve productive

---

[4]As economists are fond of reminding noneconomists, "There is no such thing as a free lunch!"

relationships in the health economy. If so, the PPC shifts out and passes through a point like *G*. For example, technological change may enable an increased production of both maternity and nursing home services from the same original stock of health care resources. Alternatively, a greater quantity of maternity and nursing home services can be produced and the PPC shifts outward if more people enter medical professions (possibly at the expense of all other goods and services).

Production efficiency is attained when the health economy operates at any point on the PPC, since medical inputs are producing the maximum amount of medical services and no unproductive behavior or involuntary unemployment exists. Allocative efficiency is attained when society chooses the best or most preferred point on the PPC. All points on the PPC are possible candidates for allocative efficiency. The ideal, or optimal, point for allocative efficiency depends on society's underlying preferences for the two medical services.

The Distribution Question

The answer to the fourth question—who should receive the medical goods and services?—deals with *distributive justice*, or *equity*. It asks whether the distribution of output is equitable, or fair, to everyone involved. In a pure market system, the marketplace distributes output based on willingness and ability to pay. It follows that in a pure market system those individuals without sufficient income face a financial barrier to obtaining goods and services. On the other hand, in a perfect egalitarian system the government ensures that everyone receives an equal distribution of the output produced.

In the mixed-capitalistic system of the United States, many goods and services are distributed by both the market and the government. Yet many allege that an unfair distribution of output remains. For example, on an average day, about 14 percent of the U.S. population lacks public (e.g., Medicare or Medicaid) or private health insurance coverage. The uninsured typically face a financial barrier when obtaining medical services and often are forced to acquire the needed medical care, usually after it is too late and more costly, in the emergency room of a public hospital. As a result, equity advocates argue that health insurance coverage should be made available for all U.S. residents.

In contrast, nearly all individuals have health insurance coverage or free access to medical care services in the health care systems of Canada, the United Kingdom, and some other nations. Regardless of willingness and ability to pay, all people essentially pay a zero out-of-pocket price for medical treatment because medical costs are financed through taxes. This does not mean that medical services are not rationed. Any good that is scarce must be rationed in some manner. The difference between a market-directed system and a system that provides free medical care, like the Canadian system, lies in *how* medical services are rationed. In a market system, price rations scarce goods among consumers. In a system where price to consumers is essentially zero at the point of access, medical services must be rationed on some nonprice basis, such as the amount of waiting time, age, or severity of illness.

Implications of the Four Basic Questions

Given a scarcity of economic resources, a society generally wishes to produce the best combination of goods and services by employing least-cost methods of production. Trade-offs are inevitable. As the production possibilities curve illustrates, some amount of one good or service must be given up if the production and consumption of another good or service increases. As a result, each society must make hard choices concerning consumption and production activities because scarcity exists. Choices may involve sensitive trade-offs, for example, between the young and the old, between prevention and treatment, or between men (prostate cancer) and women (breast cancer).

In addition, some individuals lack financial access to necessary goods and services like food, housing, and medical care. Because achieving equity is a desirable goal, a society usually seeks some redistribution of income. Normally, the redistribution involves taxation. However, a tax on labor or capital income tends to create a disincentive for employing resources in their most efficient manner.[5] Inefficient production suggests that fewer goods and services are available in the society (production inside the PPC). Thus, a trade-off often exists between equity and efficiency goals, and, consequently, hard choices must be made between the two objectives. The design of a nation's health care system normally reflects the way the society has chosen to balance efficiency and equity concerns.

A simple example will help to clarify how a trade-off might occur between efficiency and equity. In any classroom, some people learn more easily than others. The teacher can give every student the same amount of personal attention, or she or he can spend most of the time with the slow learners and leave the others to manage on their own. The second strategy will probably result in less variation in final performance across class members, but might mean a smaller increase in knowledge and skills for the class as a whole. That is because the faster learners may have learned much more with additional personal attention from the teacher. If efficiency is defined in relation to the total increase in knowledge and equity is defined in relation to variation in final knowledge levels, the efficiency and equity goals can be in conflict.[6]

ECONOMIC MODELS AND ANALYSIS

Economic Models

As mentioned earlier, the production possibilities curve is an example of an **economic model**. Models are abstractions of reality and are used in economics to simplify a very complex world. Economic models can be stated in descriptive (verbal), graphical, or mathematical form. Usually an economic model like the PPC describes a hypothesized relation between two or more variables. For example, suppose the hypothesis is that health care expenditures, E, are *directly* (as opposed to *inversely*) related to consumer income, Y. That hypothesis simply means that expenditures on health care services tend to rise when consumer income increases. Mathematically, a health care expenditure function can be stated in general form as

(1–1) $$E = f(Y).$$

Equation 1–1 implies that health care spending is a *f*unction of consumer income. In particular, health care expenditures are expected to rise with income.

---

[5]This point is discussed in more detail in later chapters after we develop the appropriate tools of economic analysis.
[6]We thank Mary Ann Baily of George Washington University for providing this insightful example.

An assumption underlying economic models is that all factors, other than the variables of interest, remain unchanged. For example, our hypothesis that health care expenditures are directly related to income assumes that all other likely determinants of health care spending, such as prices, tastes, and preferences, stay constant. As another example, notice in the previous analysis that the stocks of resources and technology are held constant when constructing the PPC. Indeed, economists normally qualify their hypotheses with the Latin phrase *ceteris paribus*, meaning "all other things held constant." By holding other things constant, we can isolate and describe the pure relation between any two variables.

The expenditure function in equation 1–1 is expressed in general mathematical form, but a hypothesis or model is often stated in a specific form. For example, the following equation represents a linear expenditure function for health care services:

(1–2) $$E = a + bY,$$

where a and b are the fixed parameters of the model. This equation simply states that health care expenditures are directly related to consumer income in a linear (rather than nonlinear) fashion. Mathematically, the parameter a reflects the amount of health care expenditures when income is zero, whereas b is the slope of the expenditure function. The slope measures the change in health care expenditures that results from a one-unit change in income, or $\Delta E/\Delta Y$.

For example, let us assume the parameter a equals $1,000 per year and b equals one-tenth, or .1. The resulting health care expenditure function is thus

(1–3) $$E = 1,000 + .1Y.$$

Equation 1–3 implies that health care expenditures rise with income. In fact, the slope parameter of .1 suggests that each $1,000 increase in consumer income raises health care spending by $100.

The health care expenditure function in equation 1–3 is represented graphically in figure 1–2. Yearly consumer income per household is shown on the horizontal axis, and annual health care spending per household is shown on the vertical axis. According to the function, health care spending equals $3,000 when household income is $20,000 per year. Consumers earning $50,000 per year spend $6,000 per year on health care services. Note that the expenditure function clearly represents our hypothesis concerning the direct relation between income and health care spending.

Now suppose some other determinants of health care expenditures change. Although this assumption violates our implicit *ceteris paribus* condition, we can incorporate changes in other factors into the health care expenditure model fairly simply. For example, suppose people generally become sicker than before, perhaps because households have become older on average. Obviously, this change tends to increase health care spending. Assuming the "aging" effect influences only the intercept term and not the value of the slope parameter, the expenditure function shifts upward by the yearly increase in health care spending due to the aging population. Figure 1–3 (page 12) shows an example of this effect.

Yearly medical costs are assumed to increase by $500 for the typical household. Thus, the health care expenditure function shifts upward at each level of income by $500 to E_1. If the aging effect also influences the percentage of additional income that people spend on

FIGURE 1–2
Health Care Expenditure Function

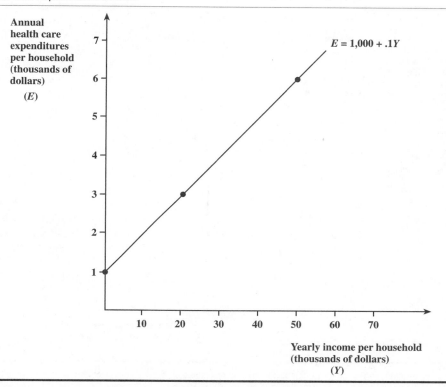

According to the expenditure function, health care spending increases with income. For example, health care spending equals $3,000 when household income equals $20,000 per year and $6,000 when household income equals $50,000 per year.

health care services, the slope of the function changes as well. An increase (decrease) in the marginal propensity to spend out of income raises (lowers) the slope and rotates the expenditure function to the left (right).[7]

In sum, models are used in economics to simplify a complex world and to isolate the relation among a few important variables. Models can be stated descriptively, mathematically, or graphically.

Empirical Testing of Health Economic Theories

Health economists often use statistical methods to test their theories. Statistical tests are conducted either to verify the theories or to quantify the magnitude of the relation among economic variables. For example, empirical methods might be used to estimate values for

[7]A problem at the end of the chapter asks you to complete an exercise of this type.

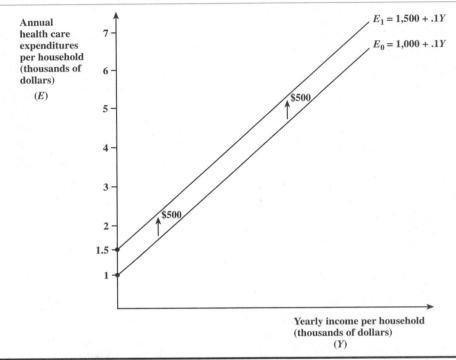

Yearly health care spending is assumed to increase by $500 for a reason other than a change in income. Thus, the expenditure function shifts upward at each level of income by $500 to E_1.

---

the parameters a and b in equation 1–2. A statistical study of this type could lend support for our hypothesis that income and health care expenditures are directly related by finding empirically that the slope parameter, b, has a positive value. In addition, an empirical study could provide some useful information concerning how strongly income affects health care spending. Is b equal to .1 or 1.2?

Throughout this book, we refer to a host of empirical studies using multiple regression analysis. In the simplest terms, **multiple regression analysis** is a statistical technique used to estimate lines or curves such as equation 1–2. The only difference is that a number of independent variables are specified on the right-hand side of the equation—hence *multiple* regression. Reviewing multiple regression studies should give you a better understanding of the underlying theories and also help you learn how to interpret multiple regression findings. Most of you have probably studied multiple regression analysis in your statistics classes; an elementary discussion of regression analysis is provided in an appendix at the end of this chapter. For those desiring a more advanced treatment of regression analysis, an additional appendix is provided at http://santerre.swcollege.com. The material provides a general overview of the technique and some pitfalls commonly encountered in multiple regression studies.

INSIGHT 1–1

We Should Address Some Basic Questions

Following is an excerpt from an opinion piece written by Samuel J. Tibbitts in 1988, well before the National Health Security Act of 1993 was proposed by the Clinton administration. Tibbitts was inducted into the Health Care Hall of Fame in 1997. When he wrote this article, Tibbitts was chair of the board of Unihealth of America, a health care company that owned 14 hospitals. In this essay, he expands on the four basic questions and offers some normative insights into health care policy in the United States.

We are in a health-care crisis that has never before been seen in this country. The public has come to believe that health care is a basic right. The government has fostered this belief. But neither government, employers, insurance carriers nor the people themselves are willing to pay the cost.

While it is not legally guaranteed, as a society we have come to expect access to health care as something highly desirable and important to our well-being. Without health we have nothing. But no one in this country has ever identified a national policy that describes how much health care should be everyone's right, how should it be provided and who should pay for it.

We must have state and national health policies. A top-level, knowledgeable and bipartisan commission should be formed to address some very weighty and politically sensitive health care issues:

- *Is health care a right for all Americans?*
- *Is there a limit on the resources that our society is willing to pay for health care?*
- *Is the financial responsibility for health care properly proportioned among government, employers, health-care providers and the individual citizen?*
- *Should health services be the same for all people regardless of income?*
- *If resources are limited, where should the money be spent in terms of health education, preventive health services, acute health care, home health care, mental health care, skilled nursing facilities and hospice?*
- *Should there be age limits or other criteria to ration the provision of highly expensive health services such as open heart surgery or liver transplants to those who would benefit the least? Bioethical issues such as the individuals' right to die must also be addressed.*

This nation certainly has the capability to handle the health-care crisis. However, we have not yet found the political will to solve it. If we don't solve it soon, issues such as the national debt and trade imbalances will pale by comparison. The people without adequate access to needed health care will become weak and demoralized; an unhealthy nation will be a weak nation. We simply cannot afford the consequences.

SOURCE: Excerpt from Samuel J. Tibbitts, "Health Care Denied Makes a Weak Nation," *Los Angeles Times*, August 21, 1988, part 5, p. 5. Reprinted by permission of Audrey Tibbitts (widow of Samuel J. Tibbitts).

Positive and Normative Analysis

Health economists perform two types of analysis. **Positive analysis** uses economic theory and empirical analysis to make statements or predictions concerning economic behavior. It seeks to answer the questions "What is?" or "What happened?" For example, we might investigate the exact relation between income and health care spending. Because positive analysis provides explanations or predictions, it tends to be free of personal values.

Normative analysis, on the other hand, deals with the appropriateness or desirability of an economic outcome or policy. It seeks to answer the questions "What ought to be?" or "Which is better?" For example, an analyst might conclude that households with incomes below $30,000 per year should be subsidized by the government because they are unable to maintain a proper level of health care spending. Naturally, this implies that the analyst is making a value judgment. Because opinions vary widely concerning the desirability of any given economic outcome and the role government should play in achieving outcomes, it is easy to see why normative statements generally spark more controversy than positive ones. For instance, when 518 health economists were asked whether the Canadian health care system is superior to the U.S. system, there was much disagreement. Fifty-two percent of the economists agreed and 38 percent disagreed with the statement. The remaining 10 percent had no opinion or lacked the information needed to respond to the question (Feldman and Morrisey, 1990).

The following sets of positive and normative economic statements should give you a better understanding of the difference between the two. Notice that the positive statements deal with what is or what will be, whereas the normative statements concern what is better or what ought to be.

Positive: According to Becker and Murphy (1988), a 10 percent increase in the price of cigarettes leads to a 6 percent reduction in the number of cigarettes consumed.
Normative: The government should increase the tax on cigarettes to prevent people from smoking.

Positive: A study by Hellinger (1991) estimates that the average yearly cost of treating someone with AIDS is $38,300, while the lifetime costs equal $102,000.
Normative: It is in our country's best interests that the federal government take a more active role in the prevention of AIDS.

Positive: National health care expenditures per capita are higher in the United States than Canada.
Normative: To control health care expenditures, the United States should adopt a national health insurance program similar to Canada's.

THE NET BENEFIT CALCULUS

As we saw from the PPC analysis, resource scarcity forces society to make choices. For example, an entire economy must collectively decide how much medical care to produce and who is to receive it, while each health care provider must determine the most appropriate method to produce health care services. Even the consumer who has complete medical insurance coverage faces scarcity and choices because time is a finite commodity. In this situation, the consumer must consider the opportunity cost of time. The consumer must decide whether the time needed to make a doctor's appointment, travel to the physician's office, and receive medical services is worth the value of forgone activities. Thus, scarcity necessitates choice, and economics is the social science that analyzes the process by which society makes these choices.

Economists treat people as *rational* decision makers. **Rationality** means people know how to rank their preferences from high to low or best to worst. It also means people never purposely choose to make themselves worse off. Consequently, it stands to reason that people will make choices based on their self-interests and choose those activities they expect will provide them with the most net satisfaction. Pursuing self-interests does not mean people are always selfish, however. For example, giving money to charity or volunteering one's time at a local hospital gives even the most devout good samaritan a considerable amount of pleasure.

The decision rule people follow when choosing activities is straightforward and involves an assessment of the expected benefits and costs associated with each choice. If expected benefits exceed expected costs for a given choice, it is in the economic agent's best interest to make that choice. In formal terms, the optimizing rule looks like this:

(1–4)
$$NB^e(X) = B^e(X) - C^e(X)$$

where X represents a particular choice or activity under consideration, B^e stands for the expected benefits associated with the choice, C^e equals the expected costs resulting from the choice, and NB^e represents the expected net benefits.

Expected values take both the probability of occurrence and the magnitude of the loss or gain into consideration. For example, the expected benefit of activity X can be expressed in the following manner:

(1–5)
$$B^e(X) = Pr(X) \times B(X), \text{ where } 0 \le Pr(X) \le 1.$$

$Pr(X)$ measures the probability or degree of certainty that activity X will provide actual benefits, and $B(X)$ reflects the dollar magnitude of the actual benefits. If $Pr(X)$ equals 1, the actual benefits of activity X are known with perfect certainty. Oppositely, if $Pr(X)$ equals zero, the true benefits of X are completely unknown. Intermediate values for $Pr(X)$ mean the benefits of X are uncertain to some degree. For example, in deciding whether to purchase an over-the-counter cold remedy, a person implicitly considers both the probability that the cold remedy will be effective and the benefit of being relieved of cold symptoms.

Expected costs are calculated in an analogous manner. In the decision to purchase a cold remedy, the monetary costs are known, a priori, so the probability of occurrence is 100 percent, or 1. In that case, the expected cost equals the actual cost of the cold remedy. In some instances, however, the true costs may be unknown when the activity initially takes place, so expected costs are either implicitly or explicitly estimated. For example, actual physician charges are never known until after the episode of care is completed. One office visit may result in numerous tests and many follow-up visits.

If NB^e is larger than zero, the economic agent's well-being is enhanced by choosing the activity. Your reading of this textbook indicates that the book's expected benefits outweigh its expected costs (unless, of course, your professor forced you to buy and read it). That is, you expect this book to provide benefits in excess of the money you spent on it, plus the forgone use of your time. Nonreaders of this book obviously believe the costs outweigh the benefits.

Health care providers, government agencies, and individual consumers employ cost-benefit analysis on either an informal or a formal basis to guide them in the decision-making process. The formal approach is to estimate the monetary value of the expected costs and benefits associated with a policy proposal. If the benefits exceed the costs, the policy may warrant adoption. More likely, however, several proposals are under consideration, so the best proposal is associated with the highest net benefit or payoff. Chapter 3 discusses formal cost-benefit analysis in detail.

Medical care providers use cost-benefit analysis when deciding whether to produce an additional unit of medical services. For example, the expected benefits to a physician of performing one more office visit are the added revenues plus the psychic value that she or he places on helping an additional person. The incremental expected costs equal the amount of money and time needed to perform the additional office visit. The difference between the two is the net benefit generated from the office visit. Naturally, if incremental net benefits are expected to be positive, it is in the physician's best interest to treat the patient.

Consumers also use cost-benefit analysis to make allocation decisions, although they generally do not go to the trouble of calculating the monetary value of the expected benefits and costs associated with the various choices. Consider the individual who is deciding whether to visit a physician for an annual physical exam. The cost equals the direct out-of-pocket expense the consumer incurs after the impact of health insurance has been taken into account, plus the opportunity cost of the individual's time spent in making the appointment, traveling to and from the doctor's office, and receiving the physical exam. Although difficult to quantify, the benefits equal the potential decrease in out-of-pocket medical care costs that result from preventing an illness, plus the monetary value attached to any increase in life-years or restoration of good health that the visit generates. If the benefits exceed the costs, it is in the consumer's best interest to have the physical exam.

Equation 1–4 can also be used to illustrate how government policies sometimes attempt to alter behavior by manipulating the expected costs or benefits associated with a health care decision. For example, the primary purpose of "sin taxes" on cigarettes and alcohol is to discourage the consumption of both products by increasing their actual costs. Government warnings on cigarette packages and alcoholic beverages aim to lower the expected benefits associated with these consumption practices and thereby reduce the amount of medical care services directed toward alcohol- and tobacco-induced illnesses.

THE THEORIES X AND Y OF HEALTH ECONOMICS

Discussions concerning health economics often spark considerable debate. Controversy abounds because people tend to have different views about such matters as the primary determinants of good health, the practice of medicine, the uniqueness of medical care, and the proper role of economics and government in health care affairs. Musgrave (1995) provides a useful conceptual framework in which different views can be contrasted. He refers to the framework as the theories X and Y of health economics. Table 1–1 summarizes Musgrave's dichotomy, presenting theories X and Y as they pertain to five dimensions of health economics. Notice the essential differences.

On the one hand, theory X views illnesses as occurring randomly. That is, some people get sick or become involved in accidents, and others do not, some live long and healthy

TABLE 1–1

The X and Y Theories of Health Economics

View of	Theory X	Theory Y
Health	Health and disease occur randomly	Health is determined by people's lifestyles choices
Medical care	Special	No different than any other good or service
The practice of medicine	A science	An art
Economics	Financial rewards reduce the quality of caring	Financial rewards are responsible for generating high-quality medicine
Policy	Regulations are needed to mitigate economic forces	Reduce regulations and encourage market forces
	Tax the healthy; subsidize the sick	Tax the sick, not the healthy
	Discourage new medical technologies	Encourage new medical technologies

SOURCE: Based on Gerald L. Musgrave, "Health Economics Outlook: Two Theories of Health Economics," *Business Economics* (April 1995), pp. 7–13.

lives, whereas others live abnormally short lives plagued with illness. On the other hand, theory Y treats illnesses and accidents as being determined largely by lifestyle choices. Choices concerning cigarette smoking, excessive drinking, safe sex, wearing safety belts, occupation, and the like can affect the probability of entering a state of sickness or suffering a harmful accident. Those individuals who choose healthy lifestyles enjoy long lives free of sickness, according to theory Y.

Theory X treats medical care as being special. Necessity, consumer ignorance, the dominance of nonprofit hospitals and other medical institutions, highly inelastic demand, and the preponderance of government intervention all make medical care unique. Theory X says that because of uniqueness, medical care "is not and cannot be treated in the same fashion as other economic commodities whose allocation is left to relatively unregulated markets" (Aaron, 1991, p. 6). In fact, greedy, profit-oriented doctors, insurance companies, and pharmaceutical companies as well as the unfettered forces of the marketplace are the root cause of rising health care costs, according to theory X.

Theory Y, in contrast, perceives medical care to be no different from any other good or service. Health care is not more important than food, clothing, or shelter. Consumers probably know more about health care than they do about the engines in their cars, Musgrave asserts, because the benefit of possessing information is greater. Just as no one blames carpenters for homelessness, according to theory Y, health care providers should not be held responsible for the failure of the U.S. health care system. High profits in the health care sector reflect success, not failure. Theory Y'ers believe that markets have not been allowed to work because of excessive government regulations.

Theory X also views medicine as a science. Someday experts will arrive at the best way to treat each and every illness. Conversely, theory Y treats medicine as an art. Health care

INSIGHT 1–2

The Opportunity Cost of 1 Million Medical Dollars

Economists generally prefer to look at opportunity costs when judging whether a given medical expenditure is generating the maximum amount of output. Recall that the opportunity cost of any medical good or service equals the benefits forgone from not pursuing the next best alternative. If the opportunity cost, or benefits forgone, is compared with the benefits generated from a particular medical intervention, a decision can be made concerning the appropriateness of the expenditure. For example, if the benefits generated from a medical program exceed its opportunity cost, medical expenditures enhance net welfare. If the opposite occurs, net benefits can be increased by adopting the alternative medical program.

Table 1 illustrates the opportunity cost of $1 million spent on various medical interventions.[1] For example, $1 million spent on monitoring low-risk patients in coronary units buys 3 life-years, while a Pap smear every three years for women between 20 and 75 years of age buys 52 life-years.[2] Bypass surgery for middle-aged men with symptoms of left-main coronary artery disease buys the greatest number of life-years (134).

TABLE 1
Years of Life Purchased per $1 Million (1990 Dollars)

Procedure	Life-Years
Monitoring low-risk patients in coronary care units	3
Pap smear every 3 years	52
Bypass surgery for left-main coronary artery disease in middle-aged men	134

Based solely on the results presented, the opportunity cost of spending $1 million to monitor low-risk heart patients is 134 life-years. This represents the life-years that could be saved if this $1 million were spent on bypass surgery rather than on monitoring low-risk heart patients. If the objective is to maximize the number of life-years saved, the results indicate that more money should be spent on bypass surgery and less on monitoring low-risk patients. Information such as this helps decision makers spend medical care dollars more wisely.

SOURCE: Based on Louise B. Russell "Opportunity Costs in Modern Medicine," *Health Affairs* (summer 1992), pp. 162–69.

[1]The estimates consider the number of units of a medical service that $1 million can buy and the effectiveness, in terms of life-years saved, of an individual unit, or medical procedure.
[2]A Pap smear is a medical procedure that tests for cervical cancer.

providers will never find the best cure for a given illness, especially because many illnesses are patient specific and newer, less painful, and lower-cost treatments will always be in demand.

Regarding economics, theory X proposes that financial rewards diminish the quality of care. Economics and medicine, like oil and water, do not mix. Profit seeking gets in the way of proper patient care. For example, theory X'ers claim that personal investments in MRI facilities create an incentive for physicians to overprescribe their diagnostic services to patients. Theory Y, in contrast, views financial rewards as the reason for high-quality medicine in the United States. Health care providers are in the best position to determine the true needs for health care capital. Ownership provides health care providers with an incentive to ensure that needed capital is supplied.

Given the difference between the two views regarding health, medical care, the practice of medicine, and the role of economics, it should not be surprising that theories X and Y take a different stance on policy as well. Table 1–1 lists three policy stances. According to theory X, because financial rewards are the source of system failure, further regulations are needed to curb the profit appetites of health care providers. Government planning is necessary to control the number of hospitals, physicians, and other health care providers and establishments. Government requires more information on health care markets for planning purposes.

Theory Y asserts that health care markets are already overregulated as mentioned earlier. Excessive regulations are partly accountable for some of the observed health care problems. Competitive economic forces should be allowed to function such that health care providers have incentives to produce with least-cost methods and satisfy consumer wants. Consumers need information to make more informed decisions.

Theory X further proposes that taxes should be levied on healthy individuals to pay for the health care costs of unhealthy ones. Because bad health or illness occurs randomly, it is fair to tax the lucky and not the unlucky. In contrast, theory Y argues that subsidizing sickness rewards it. Taxing health reduces the number of people who will remain healthy. It is not efficient to tax the healthy to subsidize the unhealthy.

Finally, theories X and Y differ on their positions concerning medical technology. New technology and health care spending are undesirable, according to theory X. Global budgets and other spending controls are necessary to curb technologies offering high-cost, low-benefit medicine. Theory Y asserts just the opposite. New technologies advance medical care. More health care services, just like more clothing or food, are good. When expenditures rise in the computer or automobile industry, for example, people point to success, not failure.

Given these two extreme views, it should not be surprising that many issues pertaining to health economics are hotly debated. Of course, it is constructive to remember that most issues, especially as they pertain to a social science field like health economics, are never truly black or white, but, as Billy Joel reminds us, are only different "shades of grey."[8] Hence, many people adopt an intermediate view of health economics somewhere in the XY theory plane. Indeed, you may wish to return to this section as your understanding of health economics progresses for some introspection to determine where your overall perspective falls in the XY theory plane of health economics.

---

[8]"Shades of Grey" written by Billy Joel © 1992 Impulsive Music (ASCAP).

INSIGHT 1-3

A Growing Economy Can Pay Its Health Care Bills

Health care spending grew from slightly over 5 percent of GDP in 1960 to over 13 percent more recently. Not suprisingly, many people have expressed alarm over the rapid growth of health care costs. The overriding concern appears to be that other goods will be less available if more GDP is siphoned off to pay for health care products over time. In a *Wall Street Journal* article, William Baumol pointed out the fallacy behind this line of reasoning. The fallacy deals with the difference between an increase in health care costs at a point in time (a movement along the production possibilities curve) and an increase in health care costs over time (a shifting out of the PPC).

Based on his cost-disease of the service sector theory, Baumol pointed out that productivity stagnation of the service sectors has led to persistent rises in their costs. He notes, however, that increasing productivity in the rest of the economy means that a society can afford more of everything, including more health care services. That is because fewer resources are needed to maintain the same level of output as before in sectors of the economy where productivity is rising. The extra resources can be transferred and used to produce more services, such as health care, in the stagnant sector.

The production possibilities curves in figure 1 can be used to clarify Baumol's view. To simplify things, constant opportunity costs are assumed so that the PPCs are drawn as straight lines. The quantity of all other goods, Z, is shown on the horizontal axis, and units of health care services, Q, are given on the vertical axis. Assuming initially that a society operates at point A on the PPC curve labeled MN with Z_A and Q_A units of all other goods

FIGURE 1
Rising Productivity Growth in the Rest of the Economy and Rising Health Care Costs

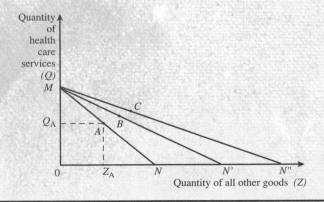

and health care products, an increase in the quantity of health care services results in a movement upward along the initial PPC at a point in time. The implication is that some amount of all other goods must be given up to receive more units of health care services *at a point in time*.

Now assume productivity growth in the rest of the economy rises but productivity growth remains stagnant in the health care sector over time. The rising productivity in the rest of the economy can be shown by pivoting the PPC at point M and rotating the PPC to the right. Following this procedure, we derive two other PPCs labeled MN' and MN''. Notice that due to the productivity growth in the rest of the economy, health care expenditures can increase over time without causing a decrease in the quantity of all other goods. For example, suppose a society adopts positions B and C on curves MN' and MN'' in the future, implying that the quantities of both health care services and other goods increase over time. That is possible because the rising productivity in the rest of the economy means that some resources can be transferred to the relatively stagnant health care sector. More medical inputs imply more medical output despite a low or zero productivity growth. As Baumol notes, "To achieve greater abundance of everything, society must change the *proportion* of its income that it devotes to the different products but not the *total amount* of labor or products it gives up in exchange."

SOURCE: William J. Baumol, "A Growing Economy Can Pay Its Bills," *The Wall Street Journal,* May 18, 1992, p. A16.

SUMMARY

Health economics is concerned with the determination and allocation of health resources and distribution of medical services in a society. Because resources are scarce, society must determine what amounts of medical services to produce, what kinds of medical services to produce, what mix of health resources should be used, and who should receive the output of health care services. Answering these four basic questions involves tough trade-offs.

Essential to the study of health economics is the use of microeconomic models. Economic models are necessary to simplify a very complex world. Models or hypotheses can be expressed in descriptive, mathematical, or graphical form and can be used to conduct positive analysis or draw normative conclusions.

A major assumption in economics is that people are rational; that is, people are able to rank their preferences from high to low and never purposely make themselves worse off. People choose activities that offer the greatest benefits at the lowest possible cost.

Most health economics issues are sharply debated, in part because people adopt different views concerning, for example, the uniqueness of medical care and whether economics and medicine mix in practice. These alternative views were couched in terms of the theories X and Y of health economics.

REVIEW QUESTIONS AND PROBLEMS

1. Draw a bowed-out production possibilities curve (PPC) with an *aggregate* measure of medical services, Q, on the horizontal axis and an *aggregate* measure of all other goods (and services), Z, on the vertical axis. Discuss the implications of the following changes on the quantities of medical services and all other goods.

   A. A movement down along the curve.

   B. A movement from the interior of the curve to a northeasterly point on the curve.

   C. An increase in the quantity of labor in the economy.

   D. A technological discovery that increases the production of Z.

   If it were your choice, where would you choose to produce on the PPC? Why?

2. Determine whether the following statements are based on positive or normative analysis. Be sure to substantiate your answers.

   A. Prices of physician services should be controlled by the government because many citizens cannot afford to pay for a visit to a physician.

   B. According to Tosteson et al. (1990), a 25 percent drop in the number of people who smoked in 1990 would reduce the incidence of coronary heart diseases by .7 percent by the year 2015.

   C. Rising health care costs have forced numerous rural hospitals to close their doors in recent years.

   D. According to government statistics, in 1989 7.2 deaths per 100,000 residents were alcohol induced. To decrease this number, the government should impose higher taxes on alcohol.

3. According to Louise B. Russell (1992), $1 million spent on two medical interventions yield the following life-years for elderly persons:

Pneumococcal pneumonia vaccine	100 life-years
Influenza vaccine	11,100 life-years

   Given this information, what is the opportunity cost of $1 million spent on the pneumococcal pneumonia vaccine? What is the opportunity cost of $1 million worth of influenza vaccine? If $1 million were available to spend on medical care for elderly persons, how should it be spent based on the data provided if the goal is to save the greatest number of life-years?

4. Suppose a health expenditure function is specified in the following manner:

$$E = 500 + .2Y,$$

   where E represents annual health care expenditures per capita and Y stands for income per capita.

   A. Using the slope of the health expenditure function, predict the change in per capita health care expenditures that would result from a $1,000 increase in per capita income.

   B. Compute the level of per capita health care spending when per capita income takes on the following dollar values: 0; 1,000; 2,000; 4,000; and 6,000.

   C. Using the resulting values for per capita health care spending in part B, graph the associated health care expenditure function.

    D. Assume the fixed amount of health care spending decreases to $250. Graph the new and original health care functions on the same graph. What is the relation between the original and new health care expenditure functions?

    E. Now assume the fixed amount of health care spending remains at $500 but the slope parameter on income decreases to .1. Graph both the original and new health care expenditure functions. Explain the relation between the two lines.

5. Assume the following facts at a particular point in time:

    A. There is a 20 percent, or .20, probability that the appropriate dosage of a painkiller will relieve your headache.

    B. Headache relief provides you with $30 worth of actual benefits.

    C. The monetary cost of the appropriate dosage is $7.50. Would you purchase the painkiller? Why or why not?

    D. Would you purchase the painkiller if headache relief provides you with $50 of actual benefits because of an important job interview? Why or why not?

6. Victor Fuchs (1996) lists the following questions in an article in *The Wall Street Journal*. Identify whether the following questions involve positive or normative analysis. All the questions deal with a Republican plan to reform Medicare, the public health insurance program for the elderly.

    A. How many Medicare beneficiaries will switch to managed care?

    B. How much should the younger generation be taxed to pay for the elderly?

    C. Should seniors who use less care benefit financially, or should they subsidize those who use more care?

    D. How many Medicare beneficiaries will switch to medical savings accounts (see Chapter 16)?

    E. What effect will these changes have on utilization?

    F. How much should society devote to medical interventions that would add one year of life expectancy for men and women who have already passed the biblical "three score and ten"?

    G. Will senior citizens' choices about types of coverage depend on their health status?

    H. If the rate of spending growth is reduced to 6 percent from 10 percent a year, what will happen to the growth of medical services? To physician incomes?

7. At this early juncture in the learning process, would you consider yourself more of a theory X'er or theory Y'er? What are the main reasons why you are leaning toward that particular theory? Are your cited reasons based on gut instincts or sound empirical analysis?

ONLINE RESOURCES

To access Internet links related to the topics in this chapter, please visit our web site at http://santerre.swcollege.com.

REFERENCES

Aaron, Henry J. *Serious and Unstable Condition: Financing America's Health Care.* Washington, D.C.: The Brookings Institution, 1991.

Baumol, William J. "A Growing Economy Can Pay Its Bills." *The Wall Street Journal*, May 18, 1992, p. A16.

Becker, Gary S., and Kevin M. Murphy. "A Theory of Rational Addiction." *Journal of Political Economy* 96 (August 1988), pp. 675–700.

Feldman, Roger, and Michael A. Morrisey. "Health Economics: A Report on the Field." *Journal of Health Politics, Policy and Law* 15 (fall 1990), pp. 627–46.

Fuchs, Victor R. "The Tofu Triangle." *The Wall Street Journal*, January 26, 1996, p. A16.

Hellinger, Fred J. "Forecasting the Medical Care Costs of the HIV Epidemic: 1991–1994." *Inquiry* 28 (fall 1991), pp. 213–25.

Musgrave, Gerald L. "Health Economics Outlook: Two Theories of Health Economics." *Business Economics* (April 1995), pp. 7–13.

The Mosby Medical Encyclopedia. New York City: C. V. Mosby, 1992.

Russell, Louise B. "Opportunity Costs in Modern Medicine." *Health Affairs* 11 (summer 1992), pp. 162–69.

Tibbitts, Samuel J. "Health Care Denied Makes a Weak Nation." *Los Angeles Times*, August 21, 1988, part 5, p. 5.

Tosteson, Anna, et al. "Long-Term Impact of Smoking Cessation on the Incidence of Coronary Health Disease." *The American Journal of Public Health* 80 (December 1990), pp. 1481–86.

CEBS QUESTIONS*

CEBS Sample Question on Subject Matter from CEBS Course 9 Study Manual

1. Using the mathematical terminology in the text and the model, $E = a + bY$, how much will health care expenditures change when income increases from \$30,000 to \$50,000 if when income is zero, health care expenditures equal \$2,000 and the slope is .05? (pages 10–11)

CEBS Sample Exam Questions

1. The "XY theory plane" of health economics refers to:
   A. The "excellent income" hypothesis
   B. The level of production that could be achieved if both labor and capital were utilized perfectly
   C. A theory of health economics that considers illnesses as not being solely determined by lifestyle choices
   D. The level of theory that is too theoretical to be of practical value
   E. The opposite of the "YX" theory of health economics
2. Which of the following statements regarding a production possibilities curve is (are) correct?
   I. Points on the curve show the combinations of production that can be efficiently produced.

---

*The CEBS designation stands for the Certified Employee Benefit Specialist program.

II. Points under the curve illustrate combinations with the highest opportunity cost.

III. Points above the curve can be achieved in the future with better technology.

    A. I only

    B. II only

    C. I and II only

    D. I and III only

    E. I, II, and III

3. All the following statements regarding regression analysis are correct EXCEPT:

    A. The purpose of regression analysis is to isolate the cause and effect among variables.

    B. The "ordinary least squares" is a popular method of fitting a line to data in a scatter diagram.

    C. t-statistics identify the fraction of the variation in the dependent variable that is explained by the independent variable.

    D. Multiple linear regression has more than one independent variable.

    E. A rule of thumb is that when the t-statistic is 2 or more we can place about 95 percent confidence in the estimated average value of the estimated parameter.

Answer to Sample Question from Study Manual

At an income level of $30,000 expenditures will be: ($2,000 + .05 ($30,000)) or $3,500. At an income level of $50,000, expenditures will be ($2,000 + .05 ($50,000)) or $4,500. The difference, or increase, is $1,000, i.e., $4,500 − $3,500.

Answers to Sample Exam Questions

1. C. See pages 16–19 of the text.

2. D. See pages 5–8 of the text.

3. C. The coefficient of determination, R^2, shows the percentage of the variation in the dependent variable that is explained by the independent variable. See pages 28–29 of the text.

APPENDIX TO CHAPTER 1

Regression Analysis

As mentioned in Chapter 1, empirical testing of economic theories is important for two reasons. First, economic hypotheses require empirical validation, especially when there are a number of competing theories for the same real-world occurrence. For example, those who prescribe to the theory X of health economics believe medical illnesses occur randomly whereas theory Y'ers believe medical illness is largely a function of lifestyle. The "random" and "lifestyle" explanations represent two competing theories for medical illnesses. Empirical studies can potentially ascertain which theory does a better job of explaining illnesses.

Second, even well-accepted theories are unable to establish the magnitude of the relation between any two variables. For example, suppose we accept the theory that lifestyle is a very important determinant of health status. A question remains about the magnitude or strength of the impact lifestyle has on health status. Does a young adult who adopts a sedentary lifestyle face a 10, 20, or 50 percent chance of dying prematurely than an otherwise comparable individual? Empirical studies can help provide the answer to that question.

There are many different ways for researchers to conduct an empirical analysis. The method we emphasize in this book, which most economists also use, is **regression analysis**. Regression analysis is a statistical method used to isolate the cause-and-effect relation among variables. Our goal in this appendix is to provide the reader with an elementary but sufficient understanding of regression analysis so the regression results discussed in this book can be properly interpreted. Regression analysis is explained through an example.

The example used concerns the relation between health care expenditures, E, and consumer income, Y, which was briefly introduced in Chapter 1. Suppose we hypothesize that health care expenditures rise with household income and want to test our theory. Health care expenditures represent the dependent variable, and income is the independent variable. Furthermore, suppose we expect a linear (or straight-line) relationship between income and health care expenditures, or

(A1–1) $$E = a + bY,$$

where a is the constant or intercept term and b is the slope parameter. If you recall, the slope parameter in this case identifies the change in health care expenditures that results from a one-unit change in income.

Because we are interested in the actual or real-world magnitudes of the parameters a and b, we now collect a random sample of observations relating information on both medical expenditures and income. The data might be series observations on income and expenditures for a particular household over time or cross-sectional observations on income and expenditures across different households at a particular point in time. In this case we collect cross-sectional data on income and medical expenditures from a random survey of 30 households.

Exhibit A1–1 shows a scatter diagram illustrating our random sample of observations (only 5 of the 30 observations are illustrated for easier manageability). Notice that the scatter diagram of observations does not automatically show a linear relation between income and health care expenditures because of omitted factors that also influence spending on health care, some randomness to economic behavior, and measurement error. Our objective is to find the line that passes through those observations and provides the best explanation of the relation between Y and E. One can imagine numerous lines passing through the set of observations. What we want is the line that provides the best fit to the data.

A criterion is necessary to determine which line constitutes the best fit. One popular criterion is ordinary least squares, or OLS. OLS finds the best line by minimizing the sum of the squared deviations, e_i, from the actual observations and a fitted line passing through the set of observations, or

(A1–2)   Minimize $\Sigma e_i^2 = \Sigma (E_a - E_f)^2 = \Sigma (E_a - \hat{a} - \hat{b}Y)^2,$

where E_a is the actual observation on medical expenditures and E_f is fitted (or predicted) expenditures from the estimated regression line, $\hat{a} + \hat{b}Y$. In exhibit A1–2, we show an example of a fitted line and the resulting deviations between actual and fitted expenditures. Based upon the sample of observations, a computer program (such as SAS, SPSS, or TSP) searches for the best line using the OLS procedure. In the process of finding the best line,

E X H I B I T   A 1 – 1

Scatter Diagram of Income and Health Care Expenditures

Health Care
Spending
(E)

Income *(Y)*

E X H I B I T   A 1 – 2

Fitted Line

Health Care
Spending
(E)

e_1

e_2

$\hat{a}$

Slope $= \hat{b}$

Income *(Y)*

the intercept and slope are determined, and thus we estimate the best magnitudes for a and b that minimize the sum of the squared deviations from the actual observations.

Let's suppose the following results are obtained from the regression analysis:

(A1–3) $E = 2,000 + .2Y.$

The results would tell us that the best fitted line to the data has an intercept of $2,000 and a slope of .2. Although the fitted or estimated regression line provides the "best" fit compared to all other lines, we do not know yet whether it represents a "good" fit to the actual data. Fortunately, the computer estimation procedure also provides us with some goodness of fit information that we can use to determine if the best fit is also a reasonably good one.

The two most common and elementary goodness of fit measures are the coefficient of determination, R^2, and the t-statistic, t. The coefficient of determination identifies the fraction of the variation in the dependent variable that is explained by the independent variable. Thus, the R^2 ranges between 0 and 1. Researchers tend to place more faith in a regression line that explains a greater proportion of the variation in the dependent variable.

The values for the parameters $\hat{a}$ and $\hat{b}$ are average estimates rather than true values because they are based on a sample instead of all possible observations; thus, they are associated with some error. Accordingly, there will be some deviations around the average estimate for a and also around the average estimate for b. In fact, if the deviations are very large, we cannot place much faith in the estimated value for the parameters. Indeed, the true value for b may be zero. If so, no relationship exists between income and health care expenditures.

The computed t-statistic helps us identify how much deviation occurs around the estimated average value for the parameters of the model. A t-statistic of 2 or more means that the value of the estimated parameter was at least twice as large as its average deviation. A rule of thumb is that when the t-statistic is 2 or more, we can place about 95 percent confidence in the estimated average value for the parameter, meaning that only a 5 percent likelihood exists that the relationship could have occurred by chance. Another rule of thumb is that when the t-statistic is 3 or more, we can place 99 percent confidence in our estimated value for the parameter. In this case, only a 1 percent likelihood exists that the relation occurred by chance.

Regression results are generally reported similar to the following:

(A1–4) $E = 2,000 + .2Y.$ $R^2 = .47$
                              (2.52)   (3.40) $N = 30$

The t-statistics are reported in parentheses below the parameter estimates. Because the t-statistic associated with income is greater than 3, we can place a high degree of confidence in the parameter estimate of .2. Also, according to the regression results, income explains about 47 percent of the variation in health care expenditures. The number of observations, N, is 30.

Before we move on we need to interpret the parameter estimates for equation A1–4. The intercept term of 2,000 tells us the level of health care expenditures when income is zero. The parameter estimate of .2 on the income variable is much more telling and suggests that expenditures on health care will increase by twenty cents if income increases by one dollar. If the estimated parameter was instead –.2, it would mean that a one dollar increase in income causes health care expenditures to decrease by twenty cents. Thus, both the sign and value of the parameter estimate convey important information to the researcher.

The regression analysis we have been discussing thus far is an example of a simple regression because there is only one independent variable. Multiple regression refers to an analysis when more than one independent variable is specified. For example, theory might tell us that price or tastes and preferences should also be included in an expenditure equation. The OLS procedure behind multiple regression is the same as that for simple regression and finds the best line that minimizes the squared deviations between the actual and fitted values. The computed R^2 identifies the variation in the dependent variable, say, health care expenditures, explained by the set of independent variables, which in our example would be price, income, and tastes and preferences. Each independent variable would be associated with an estimated parameter and t-statistic. For example:

$$\text{(A1–5)} \qquad E = 1{,}000 \; - \; .2P \; + \; .13Y \; + \; .8A \qquad\quad R^2 = .75$$
$$\phantom{\text{(A1–5)} \qquad E = 1{,}000 \;} (2.32) \quad (.42) \quad (3.23) \quad (4.00) \qquad\quad N = 30$$

where P represents the price of medical services and A represents the average age in the household as a proxy for tastes and preferences. According to the regression results, the independent variables explain 75 percent of the variation in health care expenditures. Also, the regression results suggest that income and age both have a statistically significant direct impact on health care expenditures. Price, on the other hand, has no impact on health care expenditures according to the regression findings.

HEALTH AND MEDICAL CARE: AN ECONOMIC PERSPECTIVE

Some time ago, a newspaper article reported that the residents of Glasgow, Scotland, pursue such an unhealthy lifestyle that their average life expectancy is one of the lowest in the Western world (Horwitz, 1992). Their diets generally lack fruits and vegetables and consist primarily of high-fat foods, such as "greasy cannonballs" (deep-fried, hard-boiled eggs wrapped in sausage). In addition, the per capita consumption of cigarettes and alcohol is extremely high. For example, 83 percent of all middle-aged men in Glasgow have regularly smoked cigarettes at some time in their lives.

Economic and environmental factors also contribute to the low life expectancy rate in Glasgow. A lack of job opportunities over the years has forced many residents to live in unhealthy surroundings, including crowded, damp tenements and heavy smog. At one point, the smog was so bad and the "slums so foul that a parliamentarian branded Glasgow earth's nearest suburb to hell" (Horwitz, 1992).

The situation in Glasgow illustrates the important roles lifestyle, socioeconomic conditions, and the environment play in the overall health of a community. This chapter explores these relationships by establishing the theoretical and empirical connection between health and various factors such as medical care. In particular, this chapter

> Discusses the concepts of health and medical care.

> Introduces utility analysis to explain why people desire health.

> Utilizes production theory to explain the making of health.

> Reviews the empirical results concerning the factors that influence health.

WHAT IS HEALTH?

The *Mosby Medical Encyclopedia* (1992, p. 360) defines **health** as "a state of physical mental and social well-being and the absence of disease or other abnormal condition." Economists take a radically different approach. They view health as a durable good, or type of capital, that provides services. The flow of services produced from the stock of health "capital" is consumed continuously over an individual's lifetime (see Grossman, 1972a, 1972b). Each person is assumed to be endowed with a given stock of health at the beginning of a period, such as a year. Over the period, the stock of health depreciates with age and may be augmented by investments in medical services. Death occurs when an individual's stock of health falls below a critical minimum level.

Naturally, the initial stock of health, along with the rate of depreciation, varies from individual to individual and depends on a great many factors, some of which are uncontrollable. For example, a person has no control over the initial stock of health allocated at birth, and a child with a congenital heart problem begins life with a below-average stock of health. However, we learn later that medical services may compensate for many deficiencies, at least to some degree. The rate at which health depreciates also depends on many factors, such as the individual's age, physical makeup, and lifestyle; environmental factors; and the amount of medical care consumed. For example, the rate at which health depreciates in a person diagnosed with high blood pressure is likely to depend on the amount of medical care consumed (is this person under a doctor's care?), environmental factors (does he or she have a stressful occupation?), and lifestyle (does the person smoke or have a weight problem?). All these factors interact to determine the person's stock of health at any point in time, along with the pace at which it depreciates.

Regardless of how you define it, health is a nebulous concept that defies precise measurement. In terms of measurement, health depends as much on the quantity of life (i.e., number of life-years remaining) as it does on the quality of life. Quality of life has become an increasingly important issue in recent years due to the life-sustaining capabilities of today's medical technology. The issue gained national prominence in 1976 when, in a landmark court decision, the parents of Karen Ann Quinlan were given the right to remove their daughter, who was in a persistent vegetative state, from a ventilator. Because the quality of life is a relative concept that is open to wide interpretation, researchers have wrestled with developing an instrument that accurately measures health. As we will see, health economists often use the inverse of mortality or morbidity rates as a measure of health.

WHY GOOD HEALTH? UTILITY ANALYSIS

Now that we have a working definition of health, the next step is to introduce some fundamental economic principles to illustrate why an individual desires health. As mentioned earlier, the stock of health generates a flow of services as other durable goods do. The services yield satisfaction, or what economists call **utility**. Your television set is another example of a durable good that generates a flow of services. It is the many hours of programming, or viewing services, that your television provides that yield utility, not the set itself.

As a good, health is desired for consumption and investment purposes. From a consumption perspective, an individual desires to remain healthy because she or he receives utility from an overall improvement in the quality of life. In simple terms, a healthy person feels great and thus is in a better position to enjoy life. The investment element concerns the relation between health and time. If you are in a positive state of health, you allocate less time to sickness and therefore have more healthy days available in the future to work and enhance your income or to pursue other activities, such as leisure. Economists look at education from the same perspective. Much as a person invests in education to enhance the potential to command a higher wage, a person invests in health to increase the likelihood of having more healthy days to work and generate income.

The investment element of health can be used to explain some of the lifestyle choices people make. A person who puts a high value on future events is more inclined to pursue a healthy lifestyle to increase the likelihood of enjoying more healthy days than a person who puts a low value on future events. A preference for the future explains why a middle-aged adult with high cholesterol orders a salad with dressing on the side instead of a steak served with a baked potato smothered in sour cream. In this situation, the utility generated by increasing the likelihood of having more healthy days in the future outweighs the utility received from consuming the steak dinner. In contrast, a person who puts a much lower value on future events and prefers immediate gratification may elect to order the steak dinner and ignore the potential ill effects of high cholesterol and fatty foods.

Naturally, each individual chooses to consume that combination of goods and services, including the services produced from the stock of health, that provides the most utility. The isolated relation between an individual's stock of health and utility is captured in figure 2–1, where the quantity of health, H, is measured on the horizontal axis and the level of utility, U, is represented on the vertical axis.[1] The positive slope of the curve indicates that an increase in a person's stock of health directly enhances total utility. The shape of the curve is particularly important because it illustrates the fundamental economic principle of the **law of diminishing marginal utility**. This law states that each successive incremental improvement in health generates smaller and smaller additions to total utility; in other words, utility increases at a decreasing rate with respect to health.

For example, in figure 2–1 an increase in health from H_0 to H_1 causes utility to increase from U_0 to U_1, while an equal increase in health from H_2 to H_3 generates a much smaller increase in utility, from U_2 to U_3. In the second case, the increase in utility is less when the stock of health is greater because of the law of diminishing marginal utility. The implication is that a person values a marginal improvement in health more when sick (i.e., when having a lower level of health) than when healthy. This does not mean that every individual derives the same level of utility from a given stock of health. It is possible for two or more people to receive a different amount of utility from the same stock of health. The law of diminishing marginal utility requires only that the addition to total utility decreases with successive increases in health.

Another way to illustrate the law of diminishing marginal utility is to focus on the marginal utility associated with each unit of health. Marginal utility equals the addition to total utility generated by each successive unit of health. In mathematical terms,

(2–1) $$MU_H = \Delta U / \Delta H,$$

where MU_H equals the marginal utility of the last unit of health consumed and Δ represents the change in utility or health. In figure 2–1, equation 2–1 represents the slope of a tan-

---

[1] To simplify matters, we ignore the intermediate step between the health stock, the services it provides, and the utility received from these services and assume that the stock of health directly yields utility.

F I G U R E   2 – 1
The Total Utility Curve for Health

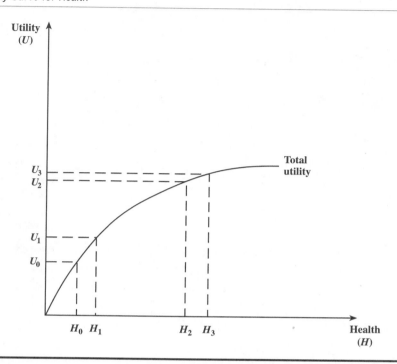

The total utility curve is upward sloping and depicts the relation between an individual's stock of health and utility. The positive slope indicates that total utility increases as an individual's stock of health improves while the bowed shape of the curve captures the impact of the law of diminishing marginal utility. This law is a fundamental principle of economics that states each additional improvement in health generates an ever smaller increase in utility. Notice that the increase in health from H_0 to H_1 causes utility to increase from U_0 to U_1, while an equal increase in health for H_2 to H_3 results in a smaller increase in utility from U_2 to U_3.

gent line at each point on the total utility curve. The bowed shape of the total utility curve implies that the slope of the tangent line falls as we move along the curve, or that MU_H falls as health increases.

Figure 2–2 captures the relation between marginal utility and the stock of health. The downward slope of the curve indicates that the law of diminishing marginal utility holds because each new unit of health generates less additional utility than the previous one.

WHAT IS MEDICAL CARE?

Medical care is composed of myriad goods and services that maintain, improve, or restore a person's physical or mental well-being. For example, a young adult might have shoulder surgery to repair a torn rotator cuff so that he can return to work, an elderly woman may have hip replacement surgery so that she can walk without pain, or a parent may bring a

FIGURE 2-2
The Marginal Utility Curve for Health

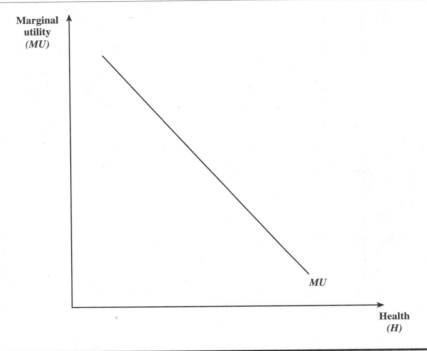

The *MU* curve illustrates the relation between marginal utility and the stock of health, and it is downward sloping because of the law of diminishing marginal utility. The shape of curve reflects the notion that each additional improvement in health results in a smaller increase in utility than the previous one.

child to the dentist for an annual cleaning to prevent future medical problems. Prescription drugs, wheelchairs, and dentures are examples of medical goods, while surgeries, annual physical exams, and visits to physical therapists are examples of medical services.

Because of the heterogeneous nature of medical care, units of medical care are difficult to measure precisely. Units of medical care are also hard to quantify because most represent services rather than tangible products. As a service, medical care exhibits the four *I*s that distinguish it from a good: intangibility, inseparability, inventory, and inconsistency (Berkowitz, Kerin, and Rudelius, 1989).

The first characteristic, **intangibility**, means a medical service is incapable of being assessed by the five senses. Unlike a new car, a steak dinner, or a new CD, the consumer cannot see, smell, taste, feel, or hear a medical service.

Inseparability means the production and consumption of a medical service take place simultaneously. For example, when you visit your dentist for a checkup, you are consuming dental services at the exact time the dentist is producing them. In addition, a patient often acts as both producer and consumer. Without the patient's active participation, the medical product is likely to be poorly produced.[2]

Inventory is directly related to inseparability. Because the production and consumption of a medical service occur simultaneously, health care providers are unable to stockpile or maintain an inventory of medical services. For example, a dentist cannot maintain an inventory of dental checkups to meet demand during peak periods.

Finally, **inconsistency** means the composition and quality of medical services consumed vary widely across medical events. Although everyone visits his or her physician at some time or another, not every visit to a physician is for the same reason. One person may go for a routine physical, while another may go because she or he needs heart bypass surgery. The composition of medical care provided or the intensity at which it is consumed can differ greatly among individuals.

The quality of medical services may also be inconsistent. Quality differences are reflected in the structure, process, and/or outcome of a medical care provider (Donabedian, 1980, 1988). **Structural quality** is reflected in the physical and human resources of the medical care provider, such as the facilities (level of amenities), medical equipment (type and age), personnel (training and experience), and administration (organization structure). **Process quality** reflects the specific actions health care providers take on behalf of patients in delivering and following through with care. Process quality might include access (waiting time), data collection (background history and testing), communication with the patient, and diagnosis and treatment (type and appropriateness). **Outcome quality** refers to the impact of care on the patient's health and welfare as measured by patient satisfaction, work time lost to disability, or postcare mortality rate. Because it is extremely difficult to keep all three aspects of quality constant for every medical event, the quality of medical services, unlike that of physical goods, is likely to be inconsistent.

As you can see, medical care services are extremely difficult to quantify. In most instances, researchers measure medical care in terms of either availability or use. If medical care is measured on an availability basis, such measures as the number of physicians or hospital beds available per 1,000 people are used. If medical care is measured in terms of use, the analyst employs data indicating how often a medical service is actually delivered. For example, the quantity of office visits or surgeries per capita is often used to represent the amount of physician services rendered, whereas the number of inpatient days is frequently used to measure the amount of hospital or nursing home services consumed.

THE PRODUCTION OF GOOD HEALTH

Health economists take the view that the creation and maintenance of health involves a production process. Much as a firm uses various inputs, such as capital and labor, to manufacture a product, an individual uses medical inputs and other factors, such as lifestyle, to produce health. The relation between medical inputs and output can be captured in what economists call a production function. A **production function** is simply a

---

[2]Educational services, like medical services, require the consumer's active participation; that is, education is likely to be poorly provided when the student plays a passive role in the process.

mathematical expression that shows how the level of output (in this case, health) depends on the quantities of various inputs, such as medical care. A generalized health production function for an individual takes the following form:

(2–2)   Health = H(Profile, Medical Care, Lifestyle,
                                          Socioeconomic Status, Environment),

where *health* reflects the level of health at a point in time; *profile* captures the individual's mental and physical profile as of a point in time; *medical care* equals the quantity of medical care consumed; *lifestyle* represents a set of lifestyle variables, such as diet and exercise; *socioeconomic status* reflects the joint effect of social and economic factors, such as education, income, and poverty; and *environment* equals a vector of environmental factors, including air and water quality.

To focus on the relation between health and medical care, we assume initially that all other factors in the health production function remain constant. Figure 2–3 depicts this re-

FIGURE 2–3
The Total Product Curve for Medical Care

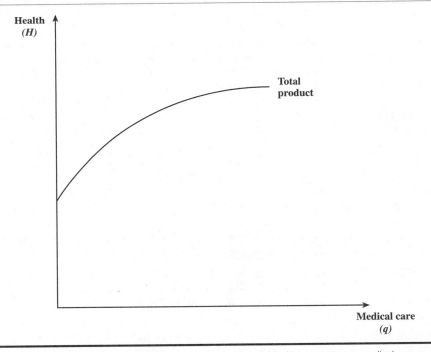

The total product curve is upward sloping and indicates that as an individual consumes more medical care, overall health improves. The positive intercept term represents the individual's level of health when no medical care is consumed and is a function of other factors such as lifestyle and the environment. The law of diminishing marginal productivity accounts for the bowed shape of the curve. This law is a fundamental principle of production theory and it implies health increases at a decreasing rate when additional units of health care are consumed, holding all other inputs in the health production process constant.

lation with the quantity of medical care, q, measured on the horizontal axis and the level of health, H, measured on the vertical axis. The intercept term represents the individual's level of health when zero medical care is consumed. As drawn, the **total product curve** implies that an individual's level of health is positively related to the amount of medical care consumed.[3] The shape of the curve is very similar to that in figure 2–1 and reflects the **law of diminishing marginal productivity**. This law implies that health increases at a decreasing rate with respect to additional amounts of medical care, holding other inputs constant. For example, suppose an individual makes an initial visit and several follow-up visits to a physician's office for a specific illness or treatment over a given period of time. It is very likely that the first few visits have a more beneficial impact on the individual's stock of health than the later visits. Thus, each successive visit generates a smaller improvement in health than the previous one.

The relation between health and medical care can also be viewed from a marginal perspective, where the marginal product of medical care represents the incremental improvement in health brought about by each successive unit of medical care consumed, or

(2–3)
$$MP_q = \Delta H / \Delta q,$$

where MP_q equals the marginal product of the last unit of medical care services consumed. The law of diminishing marginal productivity holds that the marginal product of medical care diminishes as the individual acquires more medical care. A graph of this relationship appears as a negatively sloped curve in figure 2–4.[4]

The other variables in the health production function can also be incorporated into the analysis. In general terms, a change in any of the other variables in the production function shifts the total product curve. The slope of the total product curve may also change if the marginal product of medical care has been affected.

The profile variable in equation 2–2 depends upon a host of variables and controls for such items as the person's genetic makeup, mental state, age, gender, and race/ethnicity as of a given point in time (e.g., the beginning of the year). Any change in the profile variable affects both the intercept term and the slope of the health production function. For example, an individual's genetic makeup may make him or her a candidate for prostate or breast cancer. If this individual gets cancer for that reason, then his or her total product curve shifts downward. That is because overall health has decreased regardless of the amount of medical care consumed. The total product curve is also likely to rotate downward at the same time because the marginal product of medical care should decrease as profile worsens. The total product curve rotates downward because an otherwise healthy person is likely to respond more favorably to medical treatments *for a given medical complication* than one who is less healthy. Both of these changes are represented in figure 2–5, where the total product curve shifts and rotates downward at the same time from TP_0 to TP_1. The

---

[3]However, we should not rule out the possibility that poor health status or an illness might be created by additional medical services. An illness created by a medical care encounter is referred to as an *iatrogenic disorder*, "a condition caused by medical personnel or procedures or through exposure to the environment of a health-care facility" (*Mosby Medical Encyclopedia*, p. 401). For example, a physician may accidentally harm a patient by prescribing the wrong medicine for a given medical condition.

[4]As in utility analysis, the marginal product of medical care equals the slope of a tangent line drawn to every point on figure 2–3.

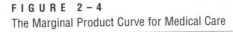

FIGURE 2–4
The Marginal Product Curve for Medical Care

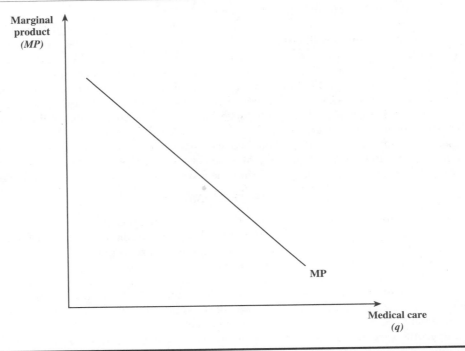

The *MP* curve establishes the relation between the marginal product of medical care and the amount of medical care consumed. The curve is downward sloping because the marginal product of the last unit of medical care consumed decreases as the individual consumes more medical care, reflecting the law of diminishing marginal productivity.

marginal product curve for medical services also shifts to the left, because each incremental unit of medical care now brings about a smaller improvement in health.

The effect of age on the production of health is relatively straightforward. Age affects health through the profile variable. As an individual ages and deteriorates physically, both health and the marginal product of medical care are likely to fall. In addition, the rate at which health depreciates over the period is also likely to increase with age. This causes the total product curve to shift downward and flatten out. The decrease in the marginal product of medical care also causes the marginal product curve to shift to the left.[5]

Lifestyle variables consider the impact of personal health habits on the production of health. Personal habits include such things as whether the person smokes, drinks excessively, leads a sedentary lifestyle, is overweight, or has an improper diet. For example, con-

---

[5]The impact of gender on the total and marginal product curves is left to the reader and is the focus of a review question at the end of this chapter.

FIGURE 2-5

A Shift in the Total Product Curve for Medical Care

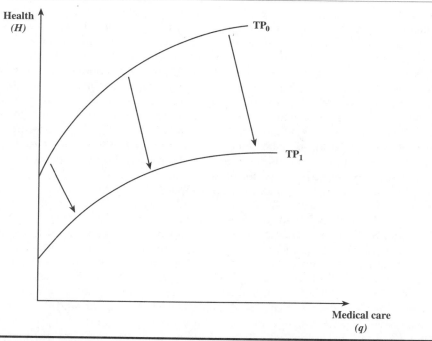

The graph illustrates what happens to the total product curve when an individual gets an illness such as cancer for a reason other than improper medical care. The curve shifts downward because at each level of medical care consumed the individual is less healthy than previously was the case. The curve also rotates downward and becomes flatter, reflecting the likelihood that the now ill individual is going to respond less favorably to a given amount of medical care consumed, such as an office visit, than previously was the case when she was healthy.

sider a newly health-conscious individual who decides that a change in lifestyle is in order. After a regimen of diet and exercise, this person loses some weight and improves his physical conditioning. As a result of this change in lifestyle, the individual's level of health and the marginal product of medical care should increase. This causes the total product curve to shift and rotate upward.

As is the case with improvements in personal habits, improved socioeconomic conditions cause the intercept term and the marginal product of medical care to increase. For example, since education is likely to make the individual a more efficient producer of health independently of the amount of medical care consumed, the total product curve shifts upward. An individual with more education is likely to better understand the positive impact of a healthy diet on health. The total product curve also steepens, or the marginal product of medical care increases, because education allows the person to utilize each unit of medical care consumed more effectively. For example, an educated individual may be more inclined to understand and follow a physician's advice concerning diet and exercise after undergoing a heart bypass operation. In addition, she may be able to recognize a medical problem early and seek medical care quickly when the effectiveness of medical treatment is generally at its maximum.

Some analysts have hypothesized that the relation between education and health is far more complex. For example, Fuchs (1979) has argued that the acquisition of education and health depends on the value people place on future events, or the rate at which they discount future events. Individuals who place a high value on future benefits and are willing to postpone gratification are inclined to acquire more education and pursue a healthier lifestyle when they are young. This is because they want to reap the rewards of a higher income and a longer life that more education and a healthier lifestyle can bring. On the other hand, individuals who place a low value on future events and desire immediate gratification are not likely to acquire significant amounts of education or to follow a healthy lifestyle because they have adopted a "live for today" attitude. Thus, according to Fuchs, higher levels of education may be associated with better health not because there is a direct link between the two variables but because both variables are directly correlated with a third factor, the degree to which future events are valued.

The impact of income on health is also complex and is referred to as the "income gradient" in the literature "to emphasize the gradual relationship between the two: health improves with income throughout the income distribution" (Deaton 2002, p. 14). Income is likely to indirectly impact health through a number of pathways. An increase in income provides the individual the means to consume more medical care. In addition, a more affluent individual is likely to be more educated, pursue a healthier lifestyle, and live in a safer environment, all of which contribute to improved health.[6] For example, a more affluent individual may live in an urban setting where the crime rate is low, access to drugs and alcohol is limited, and quality health care is available just around the corner. Income may also have a direct impact on health, although the net effect is far from clear. On the one hand, a wealthier individual may be employed in a safer work environment where the risk of a work-related accident or illness is slim. On the other hand, a wealthier individual may be employed in a more stressful occupation, which can adversely impact health.

A number of recent studies indicate that the distribution of income may also impact health through what is referred to as the relative income hypothesis. According to Kawachi and Kennedy (1999), the literature has offered three ways by which income inequality may impact health. First, income inequality may create an incentive for government to limit educational spending. As income inequality becomes more pronounced, the interests of the wealthy begin to diverge from the rest of the population and they become more interested in limiting their tax liabilities rather than expanding public educational spending especially if their children are enrolled in private schools. As a result, they begin to exert economic and political pressure to cap public spending and decrease taxes. With a decrease in spending on public education comes poorer educational outcomes for lower income classes, which translates into poorer health for all the reasons previously illuminated concerning the relationship between education and health.

Next, income inequality may lead to an erosion of social capital that is defined as "those features of social organization—such as the extent of interpersonal trust between citizens, norms of reciprocity, and vibrancy of civic organizations—that facilitate cooper-

---

[6]For a more detailed look at the relationship between income and health consult Deaton (2002) and Marmot (2002). These authors do an excellent job reviewing the literature on the connection between income and health.

ation for mutual benefit" (Kawachi and Kennedy 1999, p. 221). When the income differential between the rich and poor increases, greater distrust develops between income classes. The poor, which are the most vulnerable members of society under any circumstances, become disenfranchised. As a result, the poor find their public health needs are largely ignored by government officials because of a lack of representation. Finally, there is the problem of the psychosocial impact of relative comparisons. When the distribution of income becomes skewed, those at the bottom of the income scale may become frustrated and feel left behind by the "American dream" despite the fact that they have enough income to live in reasonable housing and receive adequate health care. Out of a sense of discouragement the tendency may be for these people to give up and pursue a lifestyle detrimental to one's health that could involve increased alcohol consumption, smoking, and obesity.

An adjustment in a person's physical environment is also likely to affect the total product curve. For example, an individual with an asthmatic condition might move from Los Angeles, where smog is intense, to a community on the far outskirts of the city. Or the person's spouse may give up smoking to decrease the level of secondhand smoke in the home. As a result, the probability that this person will succumb to a respiratory ailment diminishes. Both of these changes cause the total product curve to shift and rotate upward.

In short, health production theory suggests that a variety of factors, such as the individual's profile, medical care, lifestyle, socioeconomic status, and environment, interact to determine health. The theory also suggests that health increases at a diminishing rate with respect to greater amounts of medical care consumed, provided all other inputs remain constant. If any other inputs in the production process change, the impact of medical care on health is also likely to change.

Before we conclude this section, you should be aware that recently Jacobson (2000), Bolin, Jacobson, and Lindgren (2002), and others have extended the Grossman model and developed a number of sophisticated mathematical models that focus on the family rather than the individual as the main producer of health. While these models are beyond the scope of this book, they represent a valuable addition to the literature. The common theme is that individual decisions to invest in health are made within the context of a family and that any decision on the part of one family member regarding investments in health impacts the health investment decisions of others in the family. For example, a learning disabled child may provide an incentive to a mother to invest more in her own health to ensure that she will have the time to aid her child. These theoretical developments provide a number of challenges to researchers as they strive to understand the complex relationships that exist between family members and individual health-related decisions.

EMPIRICAL EVIDENCE ON THE PRODUCTION OF HEALTH IN THE UNITED STATES

The production of health has been the focus of numerous empirical studies. In most instances, a formula similar to equation 2–2 is estimated using multiple regression analysis. Health is usually represented by the inverse of an age-, gender-, and race-adjusted mortality rate. Using the literature as our guide, we will review the empirical evidence concerning the characteristics associated with the production of health for adults and infants.

The Determinants of Health Among Adults

To no one's surprise, the literature has found that the consumption of medical care has a positive impact on the production of adult health. However, the results also indicate that quantitatively, the impact is relatively small. For example, Hadley (1982) found that a 10 percent increase in per capita medical care expenditures results in only a 1.5 percent decrease in the adult mortality rate. These estimates confirm those of an earlier study conducted by Auster, Leveson, and Sarachek (1969), who estimated that a 10 percent increase in medical services leads to a 1 percent drop in the age-adjusted mortality rate. Enthoven (1980) has referred to the small marginal impact of medical care services on the health status of adults as "flat-of-the-curve" medicine. In the context of figures 2–3 and 2–4, this means that the typical adult consumes medical services at the point where the slope of the total product curve or marginal product of medicine is near zero.

If, as the empirical evidence indicates, the overall contribution of medical care to health is rather modest at the margin, what determines marginal improvements in health? The answer lies in the other factors associated with the production of health, with education, income, lifestyle, and the environment, being the major contributing factors.

The positive relation between education and health has been well documented in the literature. For example, Guralnik et al. (1993) found education positively impacted life expectancy among older adults. Those adults 65 years of age with at least 12 years of education had a life expectancy approximately three years longer than those of similar age with less than 12 years of education. Elo and Preston (1996) found that education had a significant impact on mortality for both men and women in the United States during the early 1980s, with the impact of education greater for men and those of working age than woman and the elderly. Finally, Lleras-Muney (2001) found a significant relation between education levels and health. In particular, she found that one more year of schooling decreases the probability of dying within 10 years by 3.6 percent.

Empirical studies have also documented a positive connection between income and health. Ettner (1996) found increases in income enhanced both mental and physical health while Lantz et al. (2001) found that income and education were both associated with improved health. More specifically, they found that people with less than a high school education and incomes below $10,000 were between two and three times more likely to have functional limitations and poorer self-rated health than their more advantaged counterparts.

The impact of income inequality and health is far from clear. On the one hand, a number of studies including Lynch et al. (1998) and McLaughlin and Stokes (2002) have found greater income inequality to be associated with poorer health. On the other hand, Blakely, Lochner, and Kawachi (2002), Muller (2002), and Gravell, Wildman, and Sutton (2002) found little or no relation between income inequality and health. Clearly, more research needs to be done in this area before we can arrive at a definitive answer concerning the connection between the distribution of income and health status.

The literature abounds with studies that illustrate the important role lifestyle plays in determining health. Among the risky lifestyle behaviors found to negatively impact health are smoking, excessive alcohol consumption, lack of physical activity, and poor diet. For example, Leigh and Fries (1992) estimated that the typical one-pack-a-day smoker experiences 10.9 more sick days every six months than comparable nonsmokers, while a person who consumes two or more drinks a day has 4.6 more sick days than a comparable light drinker (one or fewer drinks a day). Strum (2002) analyzed the impact of obesity, being overweight, smoking, and problem drinking on health and the consumption of health care for a sample of adults between the ages of 18 and 65 in 1997–1998. He found that all four risk behaviors impacted health to some degree, with obesity having the greatest impact. In fact, Strum estimated that obesity has the same impact on health as 20 years of aging when health status was measured by the number of 17 common chronic conditions present. The impact increased to 30 years when health was measured by a quality of life index. Strum also found a correlation between the four risky behaviors and the level of medical care consumed. For example, obesity was related to an average increase in expenditures on inpatient and ambulatory care of $395 a year. In the context of figure 2–5, these results suggest that obesity causes the total product curve for medical care to shift downward and possibly flatten out. To partially compensate for the loss in health, an obese person slides up the total product curve by consuming more medical care.

Taken together theses studies illustrate the fundamental role lifestyle plays in the production of health for adults. Such information is important if we are to develop appropriate public policies to improve health.

INSIGHT 2–1

It's the Economy, Stupid!

"It's the economy, stupid" was a phrase used by James Carville, political advisor to the Democratic Party, to keep the Clinton campaign focused on the economy during the 1992 presidential election. During much of the campaign the economy was in a recession with real GDP contracting by –0.06 percent in 1991 and unemployment hovering between 6 and 7 percent. The strategy worked as a dissatisfied electorate voted George Bush out of office and elected Bill Clinton the forty-second president of the United States.

Clearly, cyclical, or temporary, fluctuations in the level of economic activity have the power to impact the outcome of presidential elections. But how does the business cycle impact overall health? Or put in other terms, what is the relationship between cyclical changes in the macro economy and overall health? Your first inclination is to assume a procyclical relationship between the state of the economy and health. In other words, as the economy emerges from a recession and the unemployment rate begins to fall, overall health should improve. Clearly, higher per capita incomes should translate into improved health as people have more discretionary income to spend on medical care. Coupled with the income effect there should also be a price effect. As more people acquire jobs with employer-financed health insurance, the out-of-pocket price for health care should drop, causing people to consume more health care. An improved economy may also be associated with healthier lifestyles because as unemployed workers find employment, stress levels are likely to fall along with alcohol consumption and smoking.

Ruhm (2000) argues just the opposite may occur: an improved economy may be linked to poorer health. He cites four reasons why health may decline during an economic expansion. First, the opportunity cost of time is likely to increase with an improved economy. As workers find employment, the amount of leisure time they have to perform what Ruhm refers to as health-producing activities diminishes. For example, employed workers have less time to exercise, eat right, and schedule appointments with health care providers. The result should translate into poorer health.

Second, the actual act of work may adversely impact the production of health. As the economy improves and more workers find employment, the number of work-related accidents and work-related stress increases. All of these factors contribute to an overall reduction in health. Third, an economic expansion may cause an increase in other types of unintentional injuries such as traffic fatalities, homicides, and suicides.

Finally, an increase in economic activity may result in migration flows between states because economic expansions generally do not occur evenly across the country. Those states that grow the fastest are likely to experience a surge in population. With that influx of new workers may also come poorer health because migrants may import disease or be unfamiliar with the availability of medical services. In contrast, the surge in migrants may cause death rates to fall because the new residents may be younger and healthier than the general population.

To test the relationship between macroeconomic conditions and health, Ruhm estimated the impact various economic indicators such as unemployment and personal income have on a number of health indicators. The author utilized a state-based data set for the years 1972 through 1991 and estimated a number of equations utilizing a variety of health measures. Among the measures of health included in the analysis were overall mortality rates, age-based mortality rates, and deaths due to specific causes such as cardiovascular diseases, chronic liver disease and cirrhosis of the liver, motor vehicle accidents, and suicide.

The results are illuminating and suggest an inverse relationship between the strength of the economy and health. Overall, Ruhm found that a 1 percent drop in the unemployment rate, relative to the state historical average, resulted in an increase in the total mortality rate of between 0.5 and 0.6 percent. In addition, Ruhm found the impact of changes in the unemployment rate on mortality rates appears to be concentrated among the relatively young, between the ages of 20 and 44. This makes intuitive sense given that they are the ones likely to be hit hardest by temporary changes in economic conditions. The author also found fluctuations in state unemployment rates to be inversely related to a number of specific causes of death. For example, Ruhm found decreases in state unemployment rates to be associated with increased fatalities from auto accidents, others types of accidents, homicides, cardiovascular disease, and influenza.

Ruhm's empirical results are compelling because they suggest that cyclical, or temporary, changes in economic activity inversely impact health. Thus, it appears that as a particular region of the country rebounds from a recession and the unemployment rate drops so does health. Now when you hear the old saying, "what this country needs is good old-fashioned recession," you will have to ask yourself whether it is an economist or a health care provider talking.

SOURCE: Ruhm, Christopher. "Are Recessions Good for Your Health?" *Quarterly Journal of Economics* 115 (May 2000), pp. 617–650.

The relation between environmental factors and health is mixed and, as a result, it is difficult to draw overall conclusions from the literature. Auster, Leveson, and Sarachek (1969) included two variables in the regression equation to capture the impact of environmental factors on health: an index of industrialization and a variable that measured the extent of urbanization. Both measures were hypothesized to be positively associated with

INSIGHT 2 – 2

A Look at the Major Causes of Death in the United States in 2000

As mentioned in the text, lifestyle factors play a significant role in the production of health. If so, one might suspect that national disease-specific mortality rates would reflect the importance of lifestyle. That is, mortality rates should be high for diseases that are more sensitive to adverse lifestyle behavior. With this in mind, table 1 lists the top 12 causes of death in the United States for 2000. Over the course of the year, more than 2.4 million individuals died in the United States from all causes. Of this number, approximately 81 percent succumbed to the 12 most common causes of death listed in the table. By far the number one cause of death was diseases of the heart. It accounted for almost 30 percent of all deaths in the United States in 2000. Although researchers are still unclear as to what determines an individual's risk for heart disease, they are certain that the blood level of cholesterol, smoking, level of physical activity, stress, and obesity play a major role in determining the risk of heart disease. Each one of these factors is influenced by lifestyle to a large degree.

The second leading cause of death is malignant neoplasms, or cancers. Lifestyle choices often have an impact on this type of illness as well. For example, Edlin and Golanty (1988, p. 26) point out that approximately 80 percent of all lung cancer deaths, the most common form of cancer, can be attributed to smoking. The remaining 20 percent may result in part from environment factors such as air pollution. The third leading cause of death is stroke and the medical community is in agreement that lifestyle, such as whether or not a person follows a proper diet and exercises, impacts the chances of having a stroke.

It is interesting to note that 2 of the 12 categories, accidents and suicide, deal with deaths related to individual behavior rather than natural causes. A total of 121,924 people died violent deaths in 2000 and together these two causes of death accounted for slightly more than 5 percent of all deaths in the United States in 2000.

Chronic liver disease and cirrhosis was the twelfth leading cause of death. Social factors also play a role here as cirrhosis can be alcohol induced and brought about by years of heavy drinking. Finally, the list is interesting for what is does not include. In 1995 the human immunodeficiency virus (HIV) disease was the eighth leading cause of death, accounting for 42,506 deaths; by 2000 that number had dropped to 14,370. This dramatic drop in the number of deaths can be attributed to a series of factors including improved therapies and changes in lifestyle brought about by greater public awareness of the disease.

Clearly, these data point to the importance of lifestyle in determining deaths in the United States. Of course, some social scientists would argue that lifestyle itself is strongly influenced by environment and socioeconomic conditions. That is a topic beyond the scope of this book.

TABLE 1
The Leading Causes of Death in the United States in 2000

Cause	Number	Rate*
1. Diseases of the heart	709,894	257.9
2. Malignant neoplasms (cancerous tumors)	551,833	200.5
3. Cerebrovascular diseases (stroke)	166,028	60.3
4. Chronic lower respiratory diseases	123,550	44.9
5. Accidents	93,592	34.0
6. Diabetes mellitus	68,662	24.9
7. Influenza and pneumonia	67,024	24.3
8. Alzheimer's disease	49,044	17.8
9. Nephritis, nephritic syndrome, and nephrosis (kidney disease)	37,672	13.7
10. Septicemia	31,613	11.5
11. Suicide	28,332	10.3
12. Chronic liver disease and cirrhosis	26,219	9.5
TOTAL—All Causes	2,404,624	873.6

*This equals deaths per 100,000 population.

SOURCE: Arialdi Minino, and Betty L. Smith. "Deaths: Preliminary Data for 2000." *National Vital Statistics Reports. U.S. Department of Health and Human Services* 49 (October 9, 2001).

such factors as air and water pollution, and therefore negatively related to health. The index of industrialization was found to cause higher mortality, but the level of urbanization had no influence.

Hadley (1982) undertook one of the more comprehensive assessments of the impact of environmental factors on health. Included in the regression analysis were variables representing water quality, air quality, climate, and occupational hazards. The results were inconclusive, which Hadley attributed mainly to "the lack of good quality data" (p. 73). Clearly more refined data must be analyzed before any definitive conclusions can be drawn regarding the importance of environmental factors on the production of health.

Other variables found to contribute to health are age and marital status. The impact of marital status on health is interesting and merits a brief discussion. Married adults appear to experience better health than their single counterparts, everything else held constant. Most likely, this is because a spouse augments the production of health within the home. Marriage may also have a positive effect on health by altering preferences for risky behavior. Manor, Eisenbach, Israeli, and Friedlander (2000) found the mortality rate of married women to be lower than unmarried women for a sample of Israeli adult women, while more recently Kravdal (2001) found that married people had a higher chance of survival from 12 common forms of cancer in Norway than their unmarried counterparts.

INSIGHT 2–3

The Impact of Drug Use on Number of Newborns with Low Birthweight in New York City

A study by Joyce et al. (1992) illustrates in rather dramatic fashion the impact of lifestyle on health. Realizing that birthweight is one major predictor of neonatal and infant morbidity and mortality, the authors examined the causes of the dramatic increase in low-birthweight infants in New York City during the mid-1980s. In particular, they used regression analysis to focus on the impact of prenatal illicit substance abuse on the proportion of low-birthweight infants in various districts across New York City from 1980 through 1986.

The dependent variable in the regression equation was the proportion of low-birthweight infants across districts in New York City. The dependent variables included, among other items, the proportion of births from unmarried women, the proportion of mothers who smoked, the proportion of women who received inadequate medical care, and, most important, the proportion of women who used illicit substances during pregnancy.

The authors ran separate regressions for blacks, Hispanics, and whites and found that the impact of illegal drug use on the proportion of low-birthweight infants varied significantly across race. They found almost no impact for whites and only some impact for Hispanics. They found a much stronger relation between illicit drug use and the proportion of low-birthweight babies among blacks. In fact, the authors estimated that illicit drug use accounted for between 1,500 and 3,400 low-birthweight babies, which equaled between 3.2 and 7.3 percent of all low-birthweight infants in New York City from 1980 to 1986. They also estimated the neonatal costs of these births to be between $18 million and $41 million over the period in question.

This study clearly points out that the lifestyle of pregnant women plays a critical role in determining the initial endowment of health for newborns.

The Determinants of Health Among Children

Numerous studies have investigated the factors that influence health among children. The literature is extensive and for the sake of brevity the discussion concentrates on two studies by Corman and Grossman (1985) and Case, Lubotsky, and Paxson (2002).

Employing county-level data, Corman and Grossman regressed the nenonatal mortality rates for blacks and whites on a host of factors including education of the mother, the prevalence of poverty (a measure of income), and the availability of public programs.[7] Some of the public programs included in the analysis were the existence of neonatal intensive care facilities, the availability of abortion services, organized family planning,

---

[7]The infant mortality rate equals the number of deaths from the first to the 364th day of life per 1,000 live births. The neonatal mortality rate represents the number of deaths from the first to the 27th day of life per 1,000 live births.

and Medicaid. Overall, the results are robust and enlightening. Lack of schooling and the existence of poverty were found to raise the neonatal mortality rate for both white and black infants. Together, they accounted for an increase in neonatal mortality rates by .950 and .786 per 1,000 live births for whites and blacks, respectively. Access to health care also played a role, as the presence of neonatal intensive care caused the neonatal mortality rate to fall by .631 and .426 per 1,000 live births for white and black infants, respectively. Moreover, the results indicate that various government programs were associated with a reduced mortality rate for black as well as white infants. For example, Medicaid accounted for a decrease in the mortality rate by .632 per 1,000 live births for white children and .359 per 1,000 live births for black children.

Case, Lubotsky, and Paxson (2002) focus on the impact of socioeconomic status on children's health.[8] To no one's surprise, the authors found a strong positive relation between the education of the parents and the health of their children. For example, the health of children was positively related to the education of mothers for those children living with a mother. Education, in this case, was measured by whether the mother did not complete high school, had a high diploma, or had more than a high school education. The education of fathers was also found to positively contribute to improved health among children, implying that parental education positively impacts the production of child's health at all age levels.

The study also found that household income was a strong predictor of children's health. More specifically, the authors found that when household income doubled, the probability that a child 3 years old or younger was in excellent or very good health increased by 4 percent. Comparable improvements for children between the ages of 4 and 8, 9 and 12, and 13 and 17 were 4.9 percent, 5.9 percent, and 7.2 percent, respectively. Just as interesting, the authors found that permanent income was a strong determiner of children's health. In particular, they found that family income before a child is born was positively related to the child's health for all ages.

Finally, the authors found that healthier parents tend to have healthier children. Why that is the case, however, remains to be determined. However, the authors did estimate a series of equations for children with adoptive and biological parents and found the impact of income on health was not significantly different across the two populations. While this evidence is not definitive, it does suggest that genetics may explain only part of the reason why healthier parents have healthier children. Could it be that the production of health takes place at the household level and that healthier parents are simply more efficient producers of health for all members of the household? Clearly, more research needs to be done before we fully understand how parental behavior coupled with socioeconomic factors impact children's health.

In summary, health production studies have left little doubt that at the margin, socioeconomic conditions and lifestyle factors play a greater role in determining health than medical care does. These results have some rather interesting policy implications. They suggest that any public policy aimed at improving health should be directed toward raising education levels, reducing the amount of poverty, or improving lifestyles rather than simply providing additional medical care. Naturally, the specifics of any policy should be based on sound cost-benefit analysis.

---

[8]Consult Case and Paxson (2002) for a nontechnical overview of the study.

SUMMARY

Health, like any other good or service, is desired because it generates utility. Also like other goods and services, health is subject to the law of diminishing marginal utility. This law stipulates that each additional unit of health provides less marginal utility than the previous unit.

The making, or production, of health is influenced by a variety of factors, including the amount of medical care consumed. The positive relation between health and medical care, however, is nonlinear due to the law of diminishing marginal productivity. This law underlies a fundamental production relation stating that health increases at a decreasing rate with additional amounts of medical care, holding other inputs constant. Some of the other factors determining health are the individual's initial health profile, socioeconomic status, lifestyle, and environmental factors.

The empirical evidence for both infants and adults indicates that good health depends only moderately on the consumption of medical care. Socioeconomic status and lifestyle appear to play a much greater role in the production of good health.

REVIEW QUESTIONS AND PROBLEMS

1. Describe the factors that make it difficult to measure output in medical care markets.
2. As mentioned at the beginning of the chapter, the life expectancy rate for Glasgow is low primarily because of the residents' lifestyle. Use health production theory to explain what would happen to the relationship between good health and medical care for those residents of Glasgow who improved their lifestyle. Provide a graph to illustrate your explanation.
3. Use health production theory to explain the role gender plays in the production of health during pregnancy. Provide a graph to illustrate your answer.
4. In your own words, use utility analysis to explain why people demand health. How does the law of diminishing marginal utility fit into the analysis?
5. Explain how an increase in income would affect the level of health in a relatively affluent country like the United States compared to a relatively poor country like Haiti.
6. You have just been appointed to the post of surgeon general of the United States. The president wants you to develop an advertising campaign called "A Healthy America by the Year 2010" that encourages Americans to lead a healthier lifestyle. What types of behavior would you try to influence? Why?
7. You have just been hired by a major metropolitan city as a health policy analyst. Your assignment is to devise a plan that city authorities could implement to lower the infant mortality rate. Based on the results cited in this chapter, what types of policies would you recommend? Substantiate your answer.
8. Explain how a change in each of the following factors would alter the shape of the total product curve for medical care.
   A. An increase in education.
   B. An improvement in lifestyle.
   C. An improvement in the environment.

9. Some people believe cigarette and alcohol advertisements should be banned completely in the United States. If this were the case, what would likely happen to the shapes of the total and marginal product curves for medical care?

ONLINE RESOURCES

To access Internet links related to the topics in this chapter, please visit our web site at http://santerre.swcollege.com.

REFERENCES

Auster, Richard, Irving Leveson, and Deborah Sarachek. "The Production of Health: An Exploratory Study." *Journal of Human Resources* 9 (fall 1969), pp. 411–36.

Berkowitz, Eric N., Roger A. Kerin, and William Rudelius. *Marketing*, 2d ed. Homewood, IL: Richard D. Irwin, 1989.

Blakely, Tony A., Kimberly Lochner, and Ichiro Kawachi. "Metropolitan Area Income Inequality and Self-Rated Health—A Multi-Level Study." *Social Science and Medicine* 54 (2002), pp. 65–77.

Bolin, Kristian, Lena Jacobson, and Bjorn Lindgren. "The Family as the Health Producer—When Spouses Act Strategically." *Journal of Health Economics* 21 (May 2002), pp. 475–95.

Case, Anne, Darren Lubotsky, and Christina Paxson. '"Economic Status and Health in Childhood: The Origins of the Gradient." *Working Paper*, Center for Health and Well-being, Princeton University, February 2002.

Case, Anne, and Christina Paxson. "Parental Behavior and Child Health." *Health Affairs* 21 (March/April 2002), pp. 164–78.

Corman, Hope, and Michael Grossman. "Determinants of Neonatal Mortality Rates in the U.S." *Journal of Health Economics* 4 (September 1985), pp. 213–36.

Deaton, Angus. "Policy Implications of the Gradient of Health and Wealth." *Health Affairs* 21 (March/April 2002), pp. 13–30.

Donabedian, Avedis. *The Definition of Quality and Approaches to Its Assessment*. Ann Arbor, MI: Health Administration Press, 1980.

———. "The Quality of Care: How Can It Be Assessed?" *Journal of the American Medical Association* 260 (September 23–30, 1988), pp. 1743–48.

Edlin, Gordon, and Eric Golanty. *Health and Wellness: A Holistic Approach*. Boston: Jones and Bartlett Publishers, 1988.

Elo, Irma T., and Samuel H. Preston. "Educational Differentials Immortality: United States, 1979–1985." *Social Science and Medicine* 42 (1996), pp. 47–57.

Enthoven, Alain C. *Health Plan*. Reading, MA: Addison-Wesley, 1980.

Ettner, Susan L. "New Evidence on the Relationship between Income and Health." *Journal of Health Economics* 15 (1996), pp. 67–85.

Fuchs, Victor R. "Economics, Health and Post-Industrial Society." *Millbank Memorial Fund Quarterly* 57 (1979), pp. 153–82.

Gravelle, Hugh, John Wildman, and Matthew Sutton. "Income, Income Inequality and Health: What Can We Learn from Aggregate Data." *Social Science and Medicine* 54 (2002), pp. 577–89.

Grossman, Michael. *The Demand for Health: A Theoretical and Empirical Investigation.* New York: National Bureau of Economic Research, 1972a.

———. "On the Concept of Health Capital and the Demand for Health." *Journal of Political Economy* 80 (March–April 1972b), pp. 223–55.

Guralnik, Jack M., et al. "Education Status and Active Life Expectancy among Older Blacks and Whites." *New England Journal of Medicine* 329 (July 8, 1993), pp. 100–16.

Hadley, Jack. *More Medical Care, Better Health.* Washington, D.C.: The Urban Institute Press, 1982.

Horwitz, Tony. "Lethal Cuisine Takes High Toll in Glasgow, West's Sickest City." *The Wall Street Journal,* September 22, 1992, p. A1.

Jacobson, Lena. "The Family as Producer of Health—An Extended Grossman Model." *Journal of Health Economics* 19 (September 2000), pp. 611–37.

Joyce, Theodore, Andrew D. Racine, and Naci Mocan. "The Consequences and Costs of Maternal Substance Abuse in New York City." *Journal of Health Economics* 11 (1992), pp. 297–314.

Kawachi, Ichiro, and Bruce P. Kennedy. "Income Inequality and Health: Pathways and Mechanisms." *Health Services Research* 34 (April 1999, Part II), pp. 215–27.

Kravdal, Oystein. "The Impact of Marital Status on Cancer." *Social Science and Medicine* 52 (2001), pp. 357–68.

Lantz, Paula M., et al. "Socioeconomic Disparities in Health Change in a Longitudinal Study of US Adults: The Role of Health-Risk Behaviors." *Social Science and Medicine* 53 (2001), pp. 29–40.

Leigh, Paul J., and James F. Fries. "Health Habits, Health Care Use and Costs in a Sample of Retirees." *Inquiry* 29 (spring 1992), pp. 44–54.

Lleras-Muney, Adriana. "The Relationship Between Education and Adult Mortality in U.S." *Working Paper*, Center for Health and Wellbeing, Princeton University, May 2001.

Lynch, J.W., et al. "Income Inequality and Mortality in Metropolitan Areas of the United States." *American Journal of Public Health* 88 (1998), pp. 1074–80.

Manor, Orly, Zvi Eisenbach, Avi Israeli, and Yechiel Friedlander. "Mortality Differentials Among Women: The Israel Longitudinal Mortality Study." *Social Science and Medicine* 51 (2000), pp. 1175–88.

Marmot, Michael. "The Influence of Income on Health: Views of an Epidemiologist." *Health Affairs* 21 (March/April 2002), pp. 31–46.

McLaughlin, Diane K., and C. Shannon Stokes. "Income Inequality and Mortality in US Counties: Does Minority Racial Concentration Matter?" *American Journal of Public Health* 92 (January 2002), pp. 99–104.

Minino, Arialdi, and Betty L. Smith. "Deaths: Preliminary Data for 2000." *National Vital Statistics Reports. U.S. Department of Health and Human Services* 49 (October 9, 2001).

Mosby Medical Encyclopedia. New York City: C. V. Mosby, 1992.

Muller, Andreas. "Education, Income Inequality and Mortality: A Multiple Regression Analysis." *British Medical Journal* 324 (January 5, 2002), pp. 23–25.

Ruhm, Christopher. "Are Recessions Good for Your Health?" *Quarterly Journal of Economics* 115 (May 2000), pp. 617–50.

Strum, Roland. "The Effect of Obesity, Smoking, and Drinking on Medical Problems and Costs." *Health Affairs* 21 (March/April 2002), pp. 245–53.

COST AND BENEFIT ANALYSIS

Every day decisions are made in the health care sector concerning the best, or most efficient, amount of medical care to provide. At some juncture in the decision-making process, the all-important question becomes: At what point do the added costs of providing more medical care outweigh the benefits in terms of improved health? In practice, the answer to this question is complex because costs and benefits depend on such factors as the availability of medical resources, patient preferences, and the severity of illnesses.

Consider an adult who complains to her physician about chest pains during an annual physical exam. The first thing the physician must do is determine the seriousness of the problem. The pain could simply be the result of stress or could be a sign of more serious trouble, such as an impending heart attack (remember Joe at the beginning of Chapter 1?). When confronted with a patient's chest pains, a physician faces several options. For example, one clinical professor of medicine says,

> *To assess chest pain, . . . we can take a history and a physical examination for $100; do an exercise test for $500; perform a nuclear stress test for $1,500; or do coronary angiography for $5,000. Each escalation in diagnostic approach improves the accuracy of diagnosis from 50 percent to 60 to 80 to 100 percent. (Rubenstein, 1994)*

Basically, the best medical procedure is chosen by comparing the incremental costs of progressively more expensive medical tests with the benefits of additional medical information provided by greater diagnostic capabilities.

This chapter examines how costs and benefits affect medical decisions from the point of view of a health policymaker who is attempting to make informed choices concerning the production or allocation of medical care services. The information provided will make you more knowledgeable about such important concepts as costs, benefits, and efficiency. Specifically, this chapter:

> Introduces cost identification analysis.

> Reviews the theory underlying cost-benefit analysis.

> Illustrates how cost-benefit analysis can be used to make health care decisions.

> Explains the concept of discounting to take into account those costs and benefits resulting from health care decisions that occur over time.

> Discusses the monetary value of a life using the human capital and willingness-to-pay approaches.

> Introduces cost effectiveness analysis as an alternative to cost-benefit analysis.

COST IDENTIFICATION ANALYSIS

The first type of analysis we will consider is cost identification. Generally speaking, **cost identification** studies measure the total cost of a given medical condition or type of health behavior on the overall economy. The total cost imposed on society by a medical condition or a health behavior is generally one of three major types:

1. Direct medical care costs
2. Direct nonmedical costs
3. Indirect costs

Direct medical care costs encompass all costs incurred by medical care providers, such as hospitals, physicians, and nursing homes. They include such costs as the cost of all necessary medical tests and examinations, the cost of administering the medical care, and the cost of any follow-up treatments.

Direct nonmedical costs represent all monetary costs imposed on any nonmedical care personnel, including patients. For the patient, direct nonmedical costs include the cost of transportation to and from the medical care provider, in addition to any other costs borne directly by the patient. For example, the patient may require home care or have specific dietary restrictions. Others may also be influenced by the treatment. For example, the cost of instituting a substance abuse program in the workplace includes not only the direct medical costs of drug and alcohol rehabilitation but also any nonmedical costs the firm incurs while implementing and overseeing the program. Family members may be financially affected as well.

Indirect costs consist primarily of the time costs associated with implementation of the treatment. Indirect costs include the opportunity cost of the patient's (or anyone else's) time that the program affects, especially because many health behaviors and medical conditions result in lost productivity due to injury, disability, or loss of life. Consider the substance abuse program previously discussed. Costs should reflect the opportunity costs of the time needed to educate workers about the potential dangers of substance abuse. The time cost is borne by the employer and equals the value of forgone production.

By and large, cost identification studies consider the direct and indirect costs associated with medical actions or adverse medical behavior. For example, Druss et al. (2001) estimated the total economic cost of five chronic medical conditions—mood disorders, diabetes, heart disease, asthma, and hypertension—in 1996. In their estimates, the authors considered medical costs as well as work loss. Out of the five conditions, hypertension was by far the most costly medical condition with a total cost of $121.8 billion annually, of which slightly more than 90 percent was accounted for in health care costs. The next largest was mood disorders, $66.4 billion, followed by diabetes, $57.6 billion, heart disease, $42.4 billion, and asthma, $31.2 billion. In another study, Meltzer, Cox, and Fukuda (1999) estimated that an influenza pandemic in the United States would result in 89,000 to 207,000 deaths, 314,000 to 734,000 hospitalizations, 18 to 42 million outpatient visits, and 20 to 47 million other illnesses. The economic impact of such an outbreak would be between $71.3 and $165.5 billion.

Other cost identification studies provide yearly cost estimates on a per-case basis. For example, Ernst and Hay (1994) estimated the total costs of Alzheimer's disease to equal $173,932 per case in 1991. Waitzman, Romano, and Scheffler (1994) estimated the per-case cost of 18 different birth defects in the United States for 1988. Among other results, they found that the per-case costs of cerebral palsy and Down's syndrome equaled $445,000 and $410,000, respectively.

Cost identification studies like these are enlightening because they provide us with a sense of the total costs associated with various medical conditions or health behaviors. However, they provide little guidance for decision making. For example, what is the best, or most efficient, method to treat Alzheimer's disease? To answer questions like this, we must turn to other types of decision-making techniques, such as cost-benefit and cost effectiveness analysis.

COST-BENEFIT ANALYSIS

In Chapter 1, we introduced the net benefit calculus or decision rule that economic actors utilize when making rational decisions. In a nutshell, it is in the economic agent's best interests to make a particular choice when the decision's expected benefits exceed its expected cost. Recall that the equation looks like the following:

(3–1)
$$NB^e(X) = B^e(X) - C^e(X),$$

where NB^e represents the expected net benefits, X equals the individual decision or choice under consideration, B^e stands for the expected benefits from that choice, and C^e equals the expected costs resulting from that choice.

Formal cost-benefit analysis utilizes the same net benefit calculus to establish the monetary value of all the costs and benefits associated with a given health policy decision. Such information is invaluable to policymakers who are under pressure to utilize scarce resources to generate the most good for society. To illustrate this point, let's suppose that an all-knowing benevolent dictator, called the "surgeon general," is responsible for ensuring the economic happiness of the people in some hypothetical society. The surgeon general realizes that people possess unlimited wants and that numerous goods and services, such as food, clothing, housing, medical care, and automobiles, provide them with satisfaction. The surgeon general also knows that scarcity of resources involves trade-offs; that is, more of one good means less of the others.

The surgeon general's task is to maximize the social utility of the population by choosing the best aggregate mix of goods and services to produce and consume.[1] To accomplish this objective, the surgeon general has the power to allocate land, labor, and capital resources to any and all uses. Consistent with the maximization of the social utility received

---

[1]In the context of the production possibilities curve, the surgeon general is trying to find the specific point that maximizes the collective well-being of the population. The surgeon general is assumed to accept the current distribution of income.

from all goods and services, we can think of the surgeon general as trying to maximize the **total net social benefit (TNSB)** from each and every good and service produced in the economy. The total net social benefit derived from a good or service is the difference between the total social benefit (TSB) in consumption and the total social cost (TSC) of production. It represents the net benefit, or gain, that the society receives from producing and consuming a particular amount of some good or service. The total social benefit can be treated as the money value of the satisfaction generated from consuming the good or service. The total social cost can be looked at as the money value of all the resources used in producing the good or service.

For example, the total net social benefit from medical services can be written as

(3–2) $$\text{TNSB}(Q) = \text{TSB}(Q) - \text{TSC}(Q).$$

Equation 3–2 allows for the fact that the levels of benefits, costs, and net social benefit depend on the quantity of medical services, Q. The surgeon general maximizes TNSB by choosing the quantity of medical services at which the difference between total social benefit and total social cost reaches its greatest level. Figure 3–1 presents a graphical representation of this maximization process.

FIGURE 3–1
Determination of the Efficient Level of Output

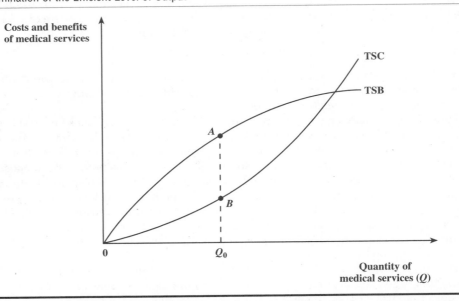

The TSB curve represents the monetary value of the total social benefit generated from consuming medical care. The curve is positively sloped to reflect the added monetary benefits that come about by consuming more medical care. The curve bows downward to capture the fact that society experiences diminishing marginal benefit with regard to medical care. The TSC curve represents the total social cost of producing medical care and is upward sloping because total costs increase as more medical care is produced. The curve bows toward the vertical axis because the marginal cost of producing medical care increases as more medical care is produced. Total net social benefit is maximized when the vertical distance between the two curves is greatest and that occurs at Q_0 level of medical services.

Notice in the figure that total social benefits increase at a decreasing rate with respect to the quantity of medical services. This shape reflects an assumption that people in society experience diminishing marginal benefit with respect to medical services and indicates that successive incremental units generate continually lower additions to social satisfaction. Total social costs increase at an increasing rate and reflect the increasing marginal costs of producing medical services.

The slope of the TSB curve can be written as

(3–3) $MSB(Q) = \Delta TSB/\Delta Q,$

where MSB stands for the marginal social benefit from consuming a unit of medical services. Obviously, MSB decreases with quantity since the slope of the TSB curve declines due to diminishing marginal benefit. Similarly, the slope of the TSC curve is

(3–4) $MSC(Q) = \Delta TSC/\Delta Q,$

where MSC represents the marginal social cost of producing a unit of medical services. MSC increases with output as the slope of the TSC curve gets steeper due to increasing marginal cost.

Total net social benefit is maximized where the vertical distance between the two curves is the greatest at distance AB. A common principle in geometry is that the distance between two curves is maximized when their slopes are equal. That condition holds at output level Q_0 and implies that allocative efficiency, or the best quantity of medical services, results where

(3–5) $MSB(Q) = MSC(Q).$

Thus, the surgeon general chooses output Q_0 because it maximizes TNSB.

To illustrate this point in a slightly different manner, figure 3–2 graphs the MSB and MSC curves. Notice that the negatively sloped MSB and the positively sloped MSC reflect diminishing marginal benefit and increasing marginal costs, respectively. The efficient amount of medical services is at Q_0 in figure 3–2 because MSB equals MSC. Let us consider why Q_0 is the efficient or best level of medical services by examining the figure more closely.

In the figure, units of medical services to the left of Q_0 such as Q_L, imply that too few medical services are being produced because MSB (point E) is greater than MSC (point F). At Q_L, an additional unit of medical services generates positive additions to TNSB because the marginal net social benefit, the difference between MSB and MSC, is positive. Society is made better off if more medical services are produced. At Q_0, where MSB equals MSC, the marginal net social benefit is equal to zero and TNSB is maximized.

In contrast, output levels to the right of Q_0 suggest that too many medical services are being produced. For example, at Q_R, MSC (point G) exceeds MSB (point H) and marginal net social benefit is negative, subtracting from maximum total net social benefit. The cost of producing unit Q_R exceeds the benefits at the margin, and society is made better off by not producing this unit. This same argument applies to all units of medical services to the right of Q_0.

TNSB is represented by the area below the MSB curve but above the MSC curve in figure 3–2. This is because TNSB is equal to the sum of the marginal net social benefits, or the difference between MSB and MSC for every unit of medical services actually produced.

FIGURE 3–2

Under- and Overprovision of Medical Services

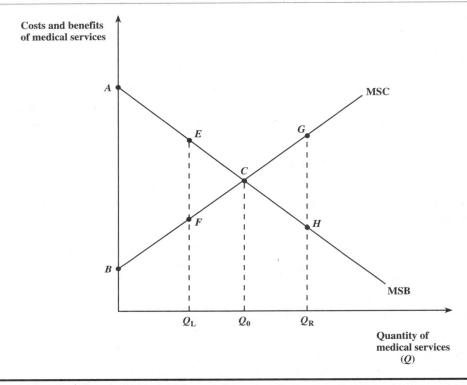

The MSB curve stands for the marginal social benefit generated from consuming medical care and is downward sloping because of the notion of diminishing marginal benefit. The MSC curve stands for the marginal social cost of producing medical care and is upward sloping because of increasing marginal costs. Total net social benefit is maximized at Q_0 level of medical care where the two curves intersect. At that point, the marginal social benefit of consuming medical care equals the marginal social cost of production. If Q_L amount of medical care is produced, then the MSB exceeds the MSC and society would be better off if more medical services were produced. If Q_R amount of medical care is produced, then the MSB is less than the MSC and too much medical care is produced.

Thus, in figure 3–2, the area ABC represents the maximum TNSB that the society receives if resources are allocated efficiently. (Conceptually, this area is equal to the vertical distance AB in figure 3–1.)

    If the surgeon general decides to produce Q_L instead of Q_0 units of medical services, society fails to receive the part of the TNSB indicated by area ECF. In economics, the lost amount of net social benefits is referred to as a **deadweight loss**. In this example, it measures the cost associated with an underallocation of resources to medical services. Similarly, if the surgeon general chooses to produce Q_R units of medical services, a deadweight loss of area GCH results. Area GCH indicates the net cost to society from producing too many units of medical services and too few units of all other goods and services.

The preceding discussion can be easily couched in terms of the net benefit calculus in equation 3–1. For example, if we solve equation 3–5 for the difference between the marginal social benefit and the marginal social cost, we get

(3–6) $\text{NMSB}(Q) = \text{MSB}(Q) - \text{MSC}(Q),$

where NMSB equals the **net marginal social benefit** the society derives from consuming a unit of the good. If NMSB is larger than zero, total net social benefit increases if an additional unit of the good is consumed. Naturally, if NMSB is negative, the society is made worse off if an additional unit of the good is consumed.

The Practical Side of Using Cost-Benefit Analysis to Make Health Care Decisions

Public policymakers concerned with formulating health policies that affect the overall well-being of society, or total net social benefit, must wrestle with the problem of operationalizing equation 3–6. That is no easy task, as it requires that they establish the monetary value of all the costs and benefits associated with a given health policy decision. The problem is complicated by the fact that some of the costs and benefits may be of an indirect nature and therefore difficult to quantify. For example, suppose you are responsible for estimating the net benefits associated with a rehabilitation program that requires one hour of exercise a day for people who recently had a heart bypass operation. One of the costs you will have to measure is the opportunity cost of the patients' time. Your first inclination may be to base your estimate on the average hourly wage of the people in the program. But what if the people conduct their daily exercise regime on their own time rather than while at work? You now face the problem of determining the opportunity cost of leisure time.[2] As you can see, indirect costs or benefits may be hard to quantify. The benefits, or diverted costs of a medical intervention, fall into four broad categories:

1. The medical costs diverted because an illness is prevented.
2. The monetary value of the loss in production diverted because death is postponed.
3. The monetary value of the potential loss in production saved because good health is restored.
4. The monetary value of the loss in satisfaction or utility averted due to a continuation of life or better health or both.

The first benefit is usually the easiest to calculate and involves estimating the medical costs that would have been incurred had the medical treatment not been implemented. The next two benefits involve projecting the value of an individual's income that would be lost due to illness or death.

The last benefit is the most subjective and therefore the most difficult to quantify, because it involves estimating the monetary value of the pleasure people receive from a longer life and good health. For example, how does one attach a dollar value to the decrease in pain and suffering an individual may experience after hip replacement surgery? Or what is the monetary value of the satisfaction a parent receives from watching a child

---

[2]Although no hard-and-fast rule exists, the opportunity cost of leisure time is most often estimated at some fraction, usually one-half, of the average hourly wage.

grow up? Given the difficulty involved in measuring the pleasure of life, many studies simply calculate the other three types of benefits. The resulting figure is considered to reflect a lower bound estimate of total benefits.[3]

Discounting

The costs and benefits of any medical decision are likely to accrue over time rather than at a single point in time. For example, the benefits of a polio vaccination are felt primarily in terms of allowing children who might otherwise have been afflicted with polio to lead normal, healthy, active lives. The benefits in this case accrue over many decades. Therefore, an adjustment must be made to account for the fact that a benefit (or a cost) received today has more value than one received at a future date. That is, the net benefit of an activity yielding a stream of future returns must be expressed in **present value** terms before proper comparisons can be made.

In simplest terms, present value means that an individual prefers $100 today rather than a year from now. Even if the individual wants to spend the money a year from now, she or he is still made better off by accepting the money today. For example, $100 deposited in a savings account offering a 4 percent annual return yields $104 a year later. We say that the present value of $104 to be received a year from now at a 4 percent rate of interest equals $100. In more formal terms, we can state present value, PV, using the following equation:

$$(3\text{--}7) \qquad\qquad PV = \frac{F}{(1 + r)}$$

where F equals a fixed sum of money and r represents the annual rate of interest, or the rate at which the sum is discounted. In our example, F equals $104 and r is 4 percent, or .04, so PV equals $100. Notice that a higher interest rate means the present value of a fixed sum falls. For example, if the rate of interest increases to 5 percent, the present value of $104 decreases to $99.05. Thus, the present value of a fixed sum is inversely related to the rate at which it is discounted.

When referring to sums of money received over a number of periods, the present value formula becomes slightly more complicated. If different sums of money, or net benefits, are to be received for a number of years, n, at the close of each period, the formula looks like the following:

$$(3\text{--}8) \qquad PV = \frac{F_1}{(1 + r)^1} + \frac{F_2}{(1 + r)^2} + \frac{F_3}{(1 + r)^3} + \ldots + \frac{F_n}{(1 + r)^n}$$

---

[3] In this simple example, we considered the costs and benefits associated with a new medical treatment where one never existed before. As a result, we considered the total costs and benefits experienced by society. In some instances, however, that approach is not appropriate. Consider a new medical treatment that potentially displaces, or complements, an existing one. In this situation, the appropriate practice is to focus on the incremental, or marginal, costs and benefits associated with the new treatment rather than the total costs and benefits. As such, only the added costs and benefits of the new treatment are considered.

where F_i ($i = 1, 2, 3, \ldots, n$) equals the payment, or net benefit, received annually for n years. For simplicity's sake, we normally assume the discount rate is fixed over time. Each annual payment is expressed in today's dollars by dividing it by the discounting factor. The discounting factor equals 1 plus the rate of interest raised to the appropriate power, which is the number of years in the future when the payment is to be received. The sum total, or PV, represents the present value of all annual payments to be received in the future.

If equation 3–8 is rewritten in summation form and specifically in terms of benefits and costs over time, it looks like the following:

$$(3\text{–}9) \qquad\qquad NB = \sum_{i=1}^{n} \frac{(B_i - C_i)}{(1 + r)^i}$$

where NB equals the present value of net benefits.

In every cost-benefit study in which the effects of a medical treatment or project occur over time, careful consideration must be given to choosing the discount rate. That is because the rate at which future payments are deflated can profoundly affect the present value of a project, especially when the costs or benefits do not accrue until far into the future. The earlier polio vaccination example is a case in point. A cost-benefit analysis of a polio vaccination project involves taking the present value of benefits potentially received 70 years into the future (the average American can expect to live about 75 years). Selecting an interest rate that is too high results in the choice of medical interventions that offer short-term net benefits. Conversely, choosing an interest rate that is too low leads to the choice of medical projects that provide long-term net benefits.

Theoretically, the chosen interest rate should equal the rate at which society collectively discounts future consumption, or society's time preference. In an industrial economy, however, there are many interest rates to choose from, including the prime business lending rate, the residential mortgage rate, and the U.S. government bond or T-bill rate. So naturally, the "correct" interest rate is open to interpretation. Most studies choose a discount rate of between 3 and 5 percent or look to private financial markets for guidance. In the latter instance, the interest rate on government bonds is the typical choice. The T-bill interest rate is chosen because it supposedly represents a risk-free rate of return and therefore reflects the rate at which the private sector discounts future streams of income in the absence of risk. Some studies circumvent this problem by presenting a range of estimates based on alternative rates of interest. It is then left to the ultimate decision maker to choose the appropriate rate of discount.

The Value of Life

To properly estimate the total benefits of a medical intervention, we must be able to measure the value of a human life, because many medical interventions extend or improve the quality of life. The most common method used to determine the monetary worth of a life is the human capital approach.[4] The **human capital approach** essentially equates the value of a life to the market value of the output produced by an individual during his or her

---

[4]Economists view expenditures on education and health as personal investments that enhance an individual's ability to command a higher salary in the marketplace; hence the term *human capital*.

expected lifetime. The technique involves estimating the discounted value of future earnings resulting from an improvement in or an extension of life.

Figure 3–3 provides some average estimates of the present value of lifetime earnings (including fringe benefits) by age and gender, discounted using a 2.5 real discount rate. Notice that the discounted value of lifetime earnings initially increases with age and then decreases. The present value figures increase at first because as an individual ages beyond infancy, the value of lifetime earnings that accrue mainly in the middle adult years are discounted over a shorter period of time. For both males and females the discounted value of lifetime earnings peak between the ages of 20 and 24 years, $1.16 million for males and $644 thousand for females. Eventually, lifetime earnings decrease with age as productivity and the number of years devoted to work decrease.

FIGURE 3–3
Present Value of Lifetime Earnings for Males and Females, 1994

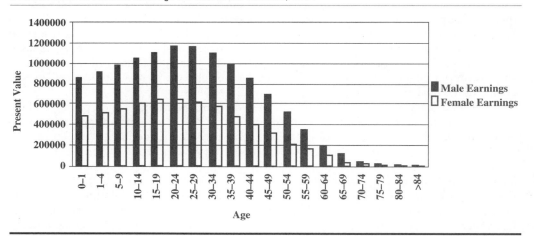

SOURCE: Ted R. Miller, et al. *The Consumer Product Safety Commission's Revised Injury Cost Model.* Calverton, Maryland: U.S. Consumer Protection Safety Commission, 2000, table 15.

Although the human capital approach is the most widely accepted method for determining the value of a life, the technique is not without shortcomings. One concern is that the approach is unable to control for labor market imperfections. For example, from figure 3–3, it is apparent that the discounted value of lifetime earnings for males is substantially greater than that for females. Gender discrimination in the workplace may account for part of the difference. As a result, women may be penalized and assigned a lower value of life because of their gender. Also, racial and other forms of discrimination may result in an inappropriate estimate of the value of life when the human capital approach is used.

The human capital approach can also be criticized because it fails to consider any nonmarket returns the individual might receive from other activities, such as leisure. As such, it does not take into account the value of any pain and suffering averted because of a medical treatment, nor does it consider the value an individual receives from the pleasure of life itself. For example, take an extreme view. According to the human capital approach, a chronically unemployed person has a zero or near-zero value of life.

An alternative approach used to measure the value of a life is the willingness-to-pay approach. The **willingness-to-pay approach** is based on how much money people are willing to pay for small reductions in the probability of dying. This kind of information is revealed when, for example, people install or fail to install smoke detectors in their homes, wear or do not wear automobile seat belts, or smoke or do not smoke cigarettes. For example, assume that people in society choose to spend $100 per person per year on some device that improves environmental quality and reduces the probability of a person dying by 1 in 10,000. In this case, the imputed value of the average person's life equals $1 million ($100 ÷ 1/10,000).

To understand how the willingness-to-pay approach works, consider a person who is deciding whether to purchase a potentially life-saving medical service. The benefit of the life-saving medical service equals the reduced probability of dying, Pr, times the value of the person's life, V. Using a cost-benefit approach, the "marginal" person purchases the medical service if the benefit, Pr × V, just compensates for the cost, C, or

(3–10) $$\text{Pr} \times V = C,$$

although "inframarginal" consumers might perceive greater benefits because they value their lives more highly. Dividing both sides by Pr results in

(3–11) $$V = C/\text{Pr}.$$

Equation 3–11 implies that a lower bound estimate can be calculated for the value of a human life by dividing the cost of a life-saving good or service by the reduced probability of dying.

The advantage of the willingness-to-pay approach is that it measures the total value of life and not just the job market value. The imputed value of life generated by the willingness-to-pay approach includes the value of forgone earnings plus the nonmarket value received from life and good health. As a result, the willingness-to-pay approach generally estimates the value of a life to be higher than that generated by the human capital approach. For example, based on a survey conducted in 1999, Alberini, Cropper, Krupnick, and Simon (2002) estimated the mean value of a statistical life to equal $933,000 in Canada and $1.5 million in the United States for a 5 in 1,000 reduction in risk. The mean estimates jumped to $3.7 million in Canada and $4.8 in the United States for a 1 in 1,000 reduction in risk. In addition, Viscusi (1993) found the willingness-to-pay estimates to range between $3 and $7 million in 1990 dollars. All indications are that the willingness-to-pay estimates are considerably higher than the human capital estimates.

Keeler (2001) recently illustrated how the human capital approach can be reconciled with the willingness-to-pay approach by estimating the discounted value of life and considering the monetary value of all time, not just work time. As such, he estimated the value of life by assuming that all time is valued at the market wage rate and controlling for the total number of hours remaining for an individual at a given age, rather than simply the remaining number of work hours. Given that the average worker under 50 years of age is likely to spend only between one-tenth and one-fifth of future hours working, you can imagine how this increased the discounted value of a remaining life. For a 30-year-old male, Keeler estimated the value of all future hours to equal slightly more than $2.6 million in 1990 dollars, which is more than five times the discounted value of future earnings, and in line with willingness-to-pay estimates. While his figures are crude, they do illustrate that people place a significant monetary value on the amount of time spent outside of work, and that researchers need to consider that when estimating the value of a life.

INSIGHT 3–1

"Mother, How Much Is the Health and Welfare of Your Child Worth?"

Based on a survey conducted in 1995, Lui, Hammitt, Wang, and Lui (2000) utilize the willingness-to-pay approach to see how much mothers would be willing to pay for themselves and their children to prevent a minor illness, namely a cold in Taiwan. The median estimates indicate that mothers would be willing to pay $37 to avoid suffering from a cold and $57 to prevent their child from having a cold. The authors also consider that the average cold generally lasts longer for an adult than a child and is more severe. After taking this into account, they estimate that the average mother is willing to pay almost $75 for her child to avoid a cold as severe as she might get. Thus, it appears that the representative mother is willing to pay almost twice the amount for her child to avoid a minor illness than she is for herself to avoid that same illness.

Carlin and Sandy (1991) used the willingness-to-pay approach to estimate the value of a young child's life based on the mother's decision to buy and and use a child's car seat. By purchasing and using a safety seat, the mother reveals how much she is willing to pay for a small reduction in the risk of her child dying in an auto accident. The benefits of using a childcare seat were expressed in terms of a decrease in the probability of a child dying in an automobile accident. According to the authors, a child who uses a safety seat faces a reduction in the probability of dying in an automobile accident of approximately 4 in 10,000. Based on those estimates and other considerations, the authors determined that the imputed value of a young child's life as revealed by the decision to use a safety seat equals $418,597. The authors added to that figure the discounted cost of raising a child to arrive at a total figure of $526,826. The final figure represents the total value of a young child's life as determined by the mother's willingness to purchase and use safety seats and raise her child.

An Application of Cost-Benefit Analysis— Should College Students Be Vaccinated?

An increase in the number of reported cases of meningococcal disease in the United States has prompted a discussion as to whether college students should be vaccinated for the disease. Jackson et al. (1995) utilize cost-benefit analysis to determine if such a policy would be an appropriate use of scarce health care resources. That is done by comparing the benefits that would result from a decrease in the number of cases of meningococcal disease to the cost of implementing a vaccination program for all college students.

The cost of this medical intervention equals the cost of the vaccine multiplied by the number of doses needed plus the estimated cost of any side effects occurring because of the vaccine. The total cost of the vaccine was assumed to equal $30 per dose, which accounted for the actual cost of the vaccine plus the cost of administering the vaccine. The authors also assumed that 2.3 million freshmen would enter college every year and that 80 percent of those would receive the vaccine. Regarding side effects, the authors assumed that there would be one severe reaction to the vaccine per 100,000 students vaccinated, which would cost $1,830 per case. Based on these factors, the authors calculate that it would cost $56.2 million a year to administer a vaccination program among college students.

The benefits include the medical costs diverted plus the estimated value of the lives saved because of the vaccine. Treatment costs per case were assumed to equal $8,145, which included seven days of hospitalization and one physician visit per day, and costs for cases occurring in the second, third, and fourth years of college were discounted at a rate of 4 percent. Because there is no way of knowing the rate at which college students contract meningococcal disease, the authors used varying multiples of the baseline rate (the national average for that age group) to calculate the benefits. A total of 58 cases would be prevented at 2 times the baseline rate for a savings of $500,000 in direct medical costs. The cost savings equal $3.1 million at 15 times the baseline rate.

The human capital approach was used to determine the value of lost earnings, and it was assumed that each life saved was worth $1 million. The total benefit from lives saved was $8.8 million for 2 times the baseline rate and $60.7 million for 15 times the baseline rate.

Table 3–1 summarizes the findings for the scenarios where students contract meningococcal disease at 2 times and 15 times the national average. According to the estimates, the net benefit for vaccinating college students is –$46.9 million, assuming a baseline rate of 2 times the national average for that age group. In other words, the estimated costs of this program outweigh the benefits by more than $46 million. Under the assumption that students contract the disease at 15 times the national average, the net benefits equal $7.6

T A B L E   3 – 1

Estimated Benefits and Costs for the Vaccination of College Students Against Meningococcal Disease (in millions of dollars)

	Baseline times 2	Baseline times 15
Cost of the Vaccination Program	$ 56.2	$56.2
Total Benefits	9.3	63.8
Direct Medical Benefits	0.5	3.1
Indirect Benefits—Value of Lives Saved	8.8	60.7
Net Benefits—(Benefits – Cost)	–46.9	7.6

SOURCE: Lisa Jackson, et al. "Should College Students Be Vaccinated against Meningococcal Disease? A Cost-Benefit Analysis." *American Journal of Public Health* 85 (June 1995), table 1.

million. In fact, a student rate of 13 times the national average must be employed before the estimated benefits generated by a vaccination program equal the costs. Using a rate of 2.6 times the national average for that age group, which the authors feel is the maximum possible rate for students, Jackson et al. conclude that the costs of any vaccination program are likely to far outweigh the benefits. Thus, while one cannot ignore the fact that lives would be saved through a vaccination policy, the estimates indicate that such a policy may not be the most efficient way to spend scarce medical care dollars.

INSIGHT 3 – 2

The Cost and Benefits of Medical Technologies

Some believe that the scientific method of medicine is responsible for the exorbitant cost of medical care in the United States. New expensive technologies are developed and adopted with little regard to whether the benefits justify the costs. While that is clearly a debatable premise, Cutler and McClellan (2001) analyze the costs and benefits associated with technological change in five specific health conditions: heart attack, low-birthweight infants, depression, cataracts, and breast cancer. In four out of the five cases (breast cancer being the lone exception), they found that the benefits of technological change have outweighed the costs. For example, in the case of low-birthweight infants, the net benefits equal $200,000 per infant with a pay-off of approximately 6 to 1. In the case of technological advances in the treatment of breast cancer, the costs appear to equal the benefits.

While one needs to be cautious and not overgeneralize from the results, it is fair to say that Cutler and McClellan develop a compelling case for technological change. In most cases, the benefits of technological change in recent years appear to justify the costs. The authors conclude their article with a word of caution concerning cost containment policies. While everyone benefits when resources are used efficiently in the production of health care, any policy change that halts or slows down the rate of technical innovation should be examined with a skeptical eye. Technological change is a dynamic process and any "policies that eliminate waste and increase the incremental value of treatment may also retard the technological progress" (p. 25).

COST EFFECTIVENESS ANALYSIS

The difficulty of measuring benefits is one major drawback of cost-benefit analysis. The problem is even more pronounced in the health care field because the benefits associated with the adoption of a technology or a medical intervention are often in terms of intangible long-term benefits, such as the dollar value of a prolongation of life or an enhancement in the quality of life. As we learned earlier, considerable debate surrounds the most appropriate way to determine the value of a human life. When the health benefits that accrue from a particular policy are clearly defined and deemed desirable, cost effectiveness analysis (CEA) is often employed.

McGuigan and Moyer (1986, pp. 562–63) suggested that the primary difference between cost-benefit and cost effectiveness analysis lies in the basic question being asked: "Cost-benefit analysis asks the question: What is the dollar value of program costs and benefits, and do the benefits exceed the costs by a sufficient amount, given the timing of these outcomes to justify undertaking the program?" In contrast, the question asked in cost effectiveness analysis is: "Given that some prespecified object is to be attained, what are the costs associated with the various alternative means for reaching that objective?"

With CEA, the analyst estimates the costs associated with a particular technology or treatment in achieving a given health care objective. The objective is normally specified in terms of life-years saved.[5] Other objectives, such as reducing cholesterol levels or blood pressure, may also be specified. Cost effectiveness analysis enables decision makers to make informed choices concerning the use of scarce medical resources by comparing the cost of saving a life-year for different types of medical interventions (e.g., review Insight 1–2 in Chapter 1).

For example, Lindfors and Rosenquist (1995) examined the cost effectiveness of breast cancer screening using mammography. According to their estimates, the cost of breast cancer screening per year of life saved varies between $16,000 and $31,900, with the most cost-effective strategy being a biennial mammogram for women between the ages of 50 and 59. The most costly strategy ($31,900 per life-year saved) is an annual screening for high-risk women between the ages of 40 and 49, a biennial screening for low-risk women in the same age bracket, and an annual screening for all women between 50 to 79 years of age. These results are similar to other findings in the literature and are part of an ongoing debate as to whether women in their forties should have a regular mammogram.

Even cost effectiveness analysis is not without its critics. For example, some argue that life-years saved are not homogeneous. Sometimes a medical intervention is associated with a significant number of life-years saved but a reduced quality of life. Conversely, a medical intervention may result in few life-years saved but an enhanced quality of life. For example, some analysts claim that coronary bypass operations do little to extend the lives of elderly men but do permit them to live out their remaining years more comfortably.

As a result, another technique, called *cost-utility analysis*, has been used frequently in recent years. **Cost-utility analysis** considers the number of life-years saved from a particular medical intervention along with the quality of life. As such, it adjusts the number of life-years gained by an index (a scale between zero and 1) that reflects health status, or quality of life (Drummond, Stoddart, and Torrance, 1987). For example, the index may be a weighted average of various health indicators, such as death, pain, or a disability. The difficulty in using utility analysis lies in developing the appropriate index to measure utility.

According to Drummond, Stoddart, and Torrance, two basic methods are used to construct the index. The first method asks people who have the same health condition to assess the quality of their lives. The second describes the condition to a group of people who do not have the condition and asks them to gauge the quality of life, or utility. Those consulted might include a group of individuals who are knowledgeable about the medical

---

[5]For a comprehensive review of cost-benefit and cost effectiveness analysis, consult Drummond, Stoddart, and Torrance (1987), Mishan (1982), or Warner and Luce (1982).

outcome, such as physicians and nurses. Once the index has been established, it is multiplied by the number of life-years saved to determine quality-adjusted life-years saved (QALYs). For example, a year of life with an amputed leg may be worth .5 QALYs.

Cost-utility analysis has emerged as an accepted and common form of analysis in recent years. As an example, Neumann, Sandberg, Bell, Stone and Chapman (2000) examined the results of almost 230 studies that used cost-utility analysis to see if prescription drugs are a cost-effective means of improving overall health. According to their study, pharmaceutical studies have generated a mean ratio of $11,000 per quality-adjusted life-year. As a category, immunization had the lowest mean ratio of $2,000 per QALY, while medical procedures had the highest ratio at $140,000 per QALY. Other categories included surgery at $10,000 per QALY and screening at $12,000 per QALY. Although these results only pertain to average outcomes, they illustrate the importance of conducting sound research to determine whether any medical advancement, such as a new drug, offers a viable treatment option.

An Application of Cost Effectiveness Analysis: Autologous Blood Donations—Are They Cost Effective?

Since the rise in the number of cases of acquired immunodeficiency syndrome (AIDS), there has been a growing concern about the safety of the U.S. blood supply. Many are worried that they may receive tainted blood through a transfusion and contract an infectious disease, such as HIV or hepatitis C. This has led to an increase in the number of autologous blood donations.[6] Although more costly than traditional community blood donations, autologous donations are safer because the risk of receiving any contaminated blood is zero. Unfortunately, autologous blood donations are also more costly because they involve more administrative and collection expenses and have higher discarding costs than allogeneic donations. The question now becomes whether the increase in safety brought about by using autologous blood donations is worth the additional costs.

Using cost effectiveness analysis, Etchason et al. (1995) estimate the cost per quality-adjusted life-year saved through autologous blood donations for four different surgical procedures: total hip replacement, coronary-artery bypass grafting, abdominal hysterectomy, and transurethral prostatectomy. The added, or marginal, costs of using autologous blood donations are provided in the first row of table 3–2. As you can see, the marginal cost of autologous blood donations varies from $68 to $4,783 per unit. The difference results mostly from the disposed cost of discarded units of blood. The second row of table 3–2 provides the quality-adjusted life-years gained from using autologous donated blood for each of the four procedures. The authors arrived at these figures by first estimating the probabilities of acquiring a number of infections, such as hepatitis C and HIV, through transfusions of allogeneic blood and then estimating the number of disease outcomes that would result from those infections. These figures were used to determine changes in life expectancy for each of the four surgical procedures. Finally, the authors consulted the medical literature and adjusted their life expectancy figures to arrive at estimates for quality-adjusted life-years (QALY). For example, using autologous blood donations for a hip replacement would result in .00029 quality-adjusted life-years saved, or approximately 2.5 hours.

---

[6]An autologous blood donation is one in which the donor and the recipient of the blood are the same person. An allogeneic donation is one in which the donor and the recipient are different people.

TABLE 3 – 2
Estimated Cost Effectiveness of Autologous Blood Donations

	Total Hip Replacement	Coronary-Artery Bypass Grafting	Abdominal Hysterectomy	Transurethral Prostatectomy
Additional cost per unit of autologous blood transfused	$68	$107	$594	$4,783
QALY per unit transfused	.00029	.00022	.00044	.00020
Cost effectiveness (row one/row two)	$235,000	$494,000	$1,358,000	$23,643,000

SOURCE: Jeff Etchason, et al. "The Cost Effectiveness of Preoperative Autologous Blood Donations." *New England Journal of Medicine* 332 (March 16, 1995), table 4.

The cost effectiveness per unit of autologous blood for each procedure can be arrived at by dividing the marginal cost of using autologous blood by the QALY saved per unit. For example, according to table 3–2, the costs effectiveness for using autologous blood for a hip replacement equals $235,000 per quality-adjusted life-year, or $68/.00029.

As you can see, the cost effectiveness per unit of autologous blood runs from $235,000 per quality-adjusted life-year saved for a total hip replacement to over $23 million for a transurethral prostatectomy. Although there is no rule concerning what constitutes a cost-effective expenditure for a medical intervention, the estimates generated by Etchason et al. (1995) are high and suggest that the use of autologous blood donations represents a costly way of saving a life.

INSIGHT 3 – 3

The Monetary Value of Improvements in Health from 1970 to 1990: Was It Worth the Cost?

Using a variety of data sources, Cutler and Richardson (1998, 1997) measure the monetary value of improvements in health in the United States from 1970 to 1990. The authors begin by taking a simple years-of-life approach and assume that each added year of life is worth $100,000 with a discount rate of 3 percent. Under this scenario, the authors estimate that the value of health for a newborn between 1970 and 1990 increased by $77,000, while the value of health for a person aged 65 over the same period increased by $159,000. Under a second scenario the authors calculated the improvement in health in terms of quality-adjusted life-years. In this case, they estimate the improvement in health for newborns to equal $95,000 and that for someone 65 years of age to equal $169,000.

Using cross-sectional data, Cutler and Richardson (1997) also calculate that medical costs increased by $19,000 for infants and $34,000 for a 65-year-old individual from 1970 to 1987 in 1987 dollars. Since the monetary value of the increase in health far outweighs the added cost of medical care, the authors conclude that the rate of return on medical care expenditures from 1970 through 1990 was very high. Thus, while medical care expenditures increased rather dramatically throughout the 1970s and 1980s, they appear to have generated a much greater increase in the value of health capital.

SUMMARY

Because resources are limited, allocation decisions must be made based on cost-benefit analysis. If the benefits resulting from a health care decision exceed the costs, it is in the economic agent's best interests to pursue that decision. One problem that frequently arises when utilizing formal cost-benefit analysis is that of determining the monetary worth of a human life. The human capital approach is the most common method used to translate the value of a life into dollars. It involves estimating the discounted value of earnings gained through an extension of life. The willingness-to-pay approach is an alternative method that has been gaining wider acceptance in recent years. With the willingness-to-pay approach, the monetary value of a life is based on the amount people are willing to pay for small reductions in the probability of dying. The advantage of this approach is that it captures the total value of a life rather than simply the market value, as is the case with the human capital approach. Unfortunately, data limitations preclude the widespread use of the willingness-to-pay approach.

Cost effectiveness analysis is another method commonly used to determine the merits of health care policy options. Because the benefits of improved health are difficult to quantify, many analysts elect to use cost effectiveness analysis. The analysis involves estimating the cost of achieving a given health care objective, usually a life-year saved. More sophisticated analyses consider quality-adjusted life-years saved.

The various techniques discussed in this chapter represent a sampling of the tools health care economists have at their disposal for analyzing the economic aspects of resource allocation. These tools provide policymakers with the information they need to make informed decisions concerning the allocation of scarce health care resources across competing ends.

REVIEW QUESTIONS AND PROBLEMS

1. We have learned that production efficiency is achieved when society is receiving the maximum amount of output from its limited resources. Explain how cost-benefit analysis can be used to achieve that outcome.

2. You have just been hired by your city's department of health. Your first task is to use cost-benefit analysis to evaluate a smoking awareness program that the department has been promoting for two years. Under the smoking awareness program, the department of health sends a team of health care professionals to various private firms free of charge to lecture to employees about the risks of smoking. The lecture takes one hour and is given during the workday. Describe the costs and benefits you should consider in your analysis.

3. In your own words, describe the difference between cost-benefit and cost effectiveness analysis.

4. According to a study by Boyle et al. (1983), it costs $2,900 per life-year gained and $3,200 per quality-adjusted life-year gained to use neonatal intensive care to increase the survival rates of low-birthweight infants weighing from 1,000 to 1,499 grams. For newborns weighing between 500 and 999 grams, the figures are $9,300 and $22,400, respectively. Based on these figures, for which group of low-birthweight infants does neonatal intensive care have the most cost effectiveness results? Why?

5. Think of a situation in which cost effectiveness analysis and cost-utility analysis would give you contrary results. Substantiate your answer.

6. As of March 1, 1994, children riding bicycles in New York must wear safety helmets. Assuming the decision to enact this law was based on cost-benefit analysis, what types of costs and benefits do you think were included in the study?

7. The commissioner of health is concerned about the increasing number of reported cases of preventable childhood diseases, such as polio and rubella. It appears that a growing number of young children are not being vaccinated against childhood diseases as they should be. Two proposals to address the problem are sitting on the commissioner's desk. The programs have equal costs, but the commissioner has funding for only one. The first proposal involves providing free vaccinations at clinics around the country. The benefits from a free vaccination program are likely to be experienced immediately in terms of a drop in the number of reported cases of illness. The second program calls for educating young married couples about the benefits of vaccination. The benefits in this instance will not be felt for some years. The commissioner wants to use cost-benefit analysis to determine which proposal should be implemented. Explain to the commissioner the critical role the discount rate plays in determining which program is chosen. In particular, which program is more likely to be chosen if a relatively low discount rate is selected? Why?

8. Distinguish between the human capital and willingness-to-pay approaches for determining the value of a life. Why does the willingness-to-pay approach generally estimate the value of a life to be higher than the human capital approach does?

9. According to Chase (1993), TPA, a heart drug produced by Genentech Inc., costs 10 times more at $2,200 a dose than streptokinase, an alternative heart drug sold by Astra AB and Kabi Farmacia AB of Sweden and by Hoechst AG of Germany. A trial of 41,000 heart attack patients found that the TPA treatment saves 1 more life out of 100 than streptokinase does. Assume a person pays full cost for either drug and chooses TPA over streptokinase. Another otherwise identical person makes the opposite choice. Use the willingness-to-pay approach to calculate the difference in the value of their lives (assume dosage requirements are the same).

10. Read the following passage from an article in *The Wall Street Journal* (October 3, 1995, p. B1) and answer the following questions.

Diabetic Toby Warbet quit her secretarial job last year because of physical problems, including blurred vision and a general loss of sensation. Such was her desperation that when she heard about an unproven treatment that might help her, she decided to borrow $20,000 from relatives to pay for it. . . . "Even if the chances are one in a million, I was hoping I would be the one," says the Livingston, NJ resident.

   A. Use the human capital approach to provide a monetary estimate of the value of Toby Warbet's life as of October 3, 1995. Explain.
   B. Use the willingness-to-pay approach to estimate the value of Toby Warbet's life. Explain.
   C. Provide a reason for the discrepancy between the two approaches.
   D. How might you measure the value of Toby Warbet's life using the human capital approach and attain a figure close to the willingness-to-pay approach?

ONLINE RESOURCES

To access Internet links related to the topics in this chapter, please visit our web site at http://santerre.swcollege.com.

REFERENCES

Alberini, Anna, Maureen Cropper, Alan Krupnick, and Nathalia B Simon. *Does the Value of a Statistical Life Vary With Age and Health Status? Evidence From the United States and Canada*. Resources of the Future. Washington, D.C., April 2002.

Boyle, H. Michael, George W. Torrance, John C. Sinclair, and Sargent P. Horwood. "Economic Evaluation of Neonatal Intensive Care of Very-Low-Birth-Weight Infants." *New England Journal of Medicine* 308 (June 2, 1983), pp. 1330–37.

Carlin, Paul S., and Robert Sandy. "Estimating the Implicit Value of a Young Child's Life." *Southern Economic Journal* 58 (July 1991), pp. 186–202.

Chase, Marilyn. "Genentech Drug Raises Question of a Life's Value." *The Wall Street Journal*, May 3, 1993, p. B1.

Cutler, David M., and Elizabeth Richardson. "The Value of Health 1970–1990." *American Economic Association Papers and Proceedings* 88 (May 1998), pp. 97–100.

———. "Measuring the Health of the U.S. Population." In *Brookings Papers on Economic Activity: Microeconomics 1997*, eds. by Martha Gottron et al., Washington, D.C.: Brookings Institution, 1997.

Cutler, David M., and Mark McClellan. "Is Technological Change in Medicine Worth It?" *Health Affairs* 20 (September/October 2001), pp. 11–29.

Drummond, Michael F., Greg L. Stoddart, and George W. Torrance. *Methods for Economic Evaluation of Health Care Programmes*. Oxford: Oxford University Press, 1987.

Druss, Benjamin, et al. "Comparing the National Economic Burden of Five Chronic Conditions." *Health Affairs* 20 (November/December 2001), pp. 233–41.

Ernst, Richard L., and Joel W. Hay. "The U.S. Economic and Social Costs of Alzheimer's Disease Revisited." *American Journal of Public Health* 84 (August 1994), pp. 1261–64.

Etchason, Jeff, et al. "The Cost Effectiveness of Preoperative Autologous Blood Donations." *New England Journal of Medicine* 332 (March 16, 1995), pp. 719–24.

Jackson, Lisa A., et al. "Should College Students Be Vaccinated against Meningococcal Disease? A Cost-Benefit Analysis." *American Journal of Public Health* 85 (June 1995), pp. 843–46.

Keeler, Emmett B. "The Value of Remaining Lifetime is Close to Estimated Values of Life." *Journal of Health Economics* (January 2001), pp. 141–43.

Lindfors, Karen K., and John Rosenquist. "The Cost-Effectiveness of Mammographic Screening Strategies." *Journal of the American Medical Association* 24 (September 20, 1995), pp. 881–84.

Lui, Jin-Tai, James K. Hammitt, Jung-Der Wang, and Jin-Long Lui. "Mother's Willingness to Pay for Her Own and Her Child's Health: A Contingent Valuation Study in Taiwan." *Health Economics* 9 (2000), pp. 319–26.

McGuigan, James R., and R. Charles Moyer. *Managerial Economics*, 4th ed. St. Paul, MN: West, 1986.

Meltzer, Martin J., Nancy J. Cox, and Keiji Fukuda. "The Economic Impact of Pandemic Influenza in the United States: Priorities for Intervention." *Emerging Infectious Diseases* 5 (September/October 1999), pp. 659–71.

Miller, Ted R., et al. *The Consumer Product Safety Commission's Revised Injury Cost Model*. Calverton, Maryland: U.S. Consumer Protection Safety Commission, 2000.

Mishan, E.J. *Cost-Benefit Analysis: An Informal Introduction*. 3d ed. London: George Allen and Unwin, 1982.

Neumann, Peter J., Eileen A. Sandberg, Chaim M. Bell, Patricia W. Stone, and Richard H. Chapman. "Are Pharmaceuticals Cost-Effective: A Review of the Evidence." *Health Affairs* 19 (March/April 2000), pp. 92–109.

Rubenstein, Joel L. "The High Cost of Marginal Benefits." *Boston Globe*, May 12, 1994, p. 70.

Viscusi, W. Kip. "The Value of Risks to Life and Health." *Journal of Economic Literature* 31 (December 1993), pp. 1912–46.

Waitzman, Norman J., Patrick S. Romano, and Richard M. Scheffler. "Estimates of the Economic Costs of Birth Defects." *Inquiry* 31 (summer 1994), pp. 188–205.

Warner, Kenneth, and Bryan R. Luce. *Cost-Benefit and Cost-Effectiveness Analysis in Health Care: Principles, Practice, and Potential*. Ann Arbor, MI: Health Administration Press, 1982.

CHAPTER 4

PPOs, HMOs, and DRGs are just a few of the many health care acronyms bandied around in the popular press. To the uninformed, they are simply the ingredients in an alphabet soup. Those familiar with them know they stand for preferred provider organizations, health maintenance organizations, and diagnosis-related groups. They, like many other health care institutions, have evolved over the last several decades and have greatly contributed to the ongoing and wide-sweeping transformation of the U.S. health care system.

This chapter introduces and explains the structure and purpose behind various institutions and payment systems that typically comprise a health care system. The knowledge you gain will help you better understand how the different parts of a health care system are interrelated. In addition, the material will provide you with a greater appreciation for the remaining chapters of the book and help make you a more informed consumer or producer of health care services. Specifically, this chapter:

> Constructs a general model of a health care system.

> Discusses the reasoning for and responsibilities of third-party payers.

> Introduces and explains some of the different reimbursement methods used by third-party payers.

> Identifies some structural features associated with the production of medical services and the role of health care provider choice.

> Uses the general model to describe the health care systems in Canada, Germany, and the United Kingdom.

> Provides an overview of the U.S. health care system.

ELEMENTS OF A HEALTH CARE SYSTEM

A **health care system** consists of the organizational arrangements and processes through which a society makes choices concerning the production, consumption, and distribution of health care services. How a health care system is structured is important because it determines who actually makes the choices concerning the basic questions, such as what medical goods to produce and who should receive the medical care. At one extreme, the health care system might be structured such that choices are decided by a centralized government, or authority, through a single individual or an appointed or elected committee. At the other extreme, the health care system might be decentralized. For example, individual consumers and health care providers, through their interaction in the marketplace, may decide the answers to the basic questions.

From a societal point of view, it is difficult to determine whether a centralized or decentralized health care system is superior. A normative statement of that kind entails value judgments and trade-offs are inevitably involved. On the one hand, a centralized authority with complete and coordinated control over the entire health care system may be more capable of distributing output more uniformly and have a greater ability to exploit any economies associated with large size. At the same time, a single centralized authority may lack the competitive incentive to innovate or respond to varied consumer-voter demands. A central authority may also face high costs of collecting information about consumer needs.

On the other hand, a health care system with a decentralized decision-making process, such as the marketplace (or a system of local governments), may provide more alternatives and innovation but may result in high costs in the presence of economies of size, nonuniformity, or lack of coordination. Determining the best structure for a health care system involves quantifying the value society places on a number of alternative and sometimes competing outcomes, such as choice, innovation, uniformity, and production efficiency, among other things. A study of that kind is difficult at best because it involves so many normative decisions. Indeed, alternative health care systems exist throughout the world because people place different values on each of the various outcomes (Reinhardt, 1996). Reflecting the trade-offs involved, most health care systems today are neither purely centralized nor decentralized but rather take on elements of both systems of decision making. In any case, as we discuss the elements of various health care systems, it is important to keep in mind that understanding how and at what level decisions are made is critical to grasping how any health care system works.

Health care systems are huge, complex, and constantly changing as they respond to economic, technological, social, and historical forces. For example, the structure of the U.S. health care system involves a seemingly endless list of participants, some of which were foreign to us only a decade ago, such as preferred provider organizations. The list includes over 800,000 physicians and dentists, about 2 million nurses, nearly 7,000 hospitals, and over 80,000 nursing homes and mental retardation facilities, not to mention the many millions of people who purchase medical care, the thousands of health insurers, and the multitude of government agencies involved in health care issues.

Because of the vastness and complexity of health care systems, many people have trouble understanding how they function. With that problem in mind, figure 4–1 presents a general model of a health care system. Notice that the diagram possesses a triangular shape

FIGURE 4–1
A Model of a Health Care System

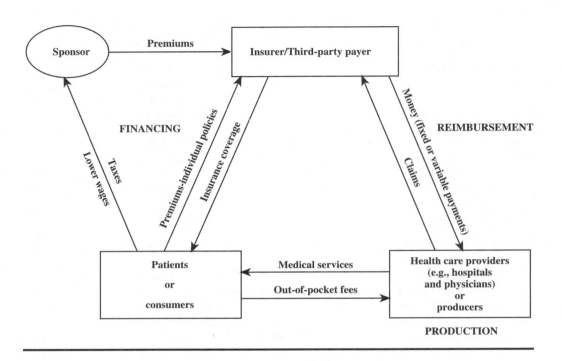

reflecting the three major players in any health care system: patients or consumers, health care providers or producers, and insurers or third-party payers. Sponsors, such as employers or the government, are also included in the general model because they act as intermediaries or brokers. As brokers, sponsors structure coverage, manage enrollment, contract and negotiate risk-sharing arrangements, and collect and submit the contributions of insured (Van de Ven and Ellis, 2000). Contributions show up as foregone wage income resulting from either taxes or premium payments. The figure also illustrates the three elements common to all health care systems: financing, reimbursement, and production or delivery.

For a typical market transaction, the individual consumer and producer are the only ones involved in the exchange as shown in the bottom flow of the diagram. In that instance, the consumer's out-of-pocket price equals the full cost of the service provided. Buyer and seller are equally well informed, and the buyer pays the seller directly for the good or service. For example, the purchase of a loaf of bread at a local convenience store involves a normal market transaction. Both consumer and seller have the same information regarding the price and quality of the bread, and the transaction is anticipated and planned by the consumer. An unexpected outcome is not likely to occur, and, if it did, it could be easily rectified (for example, stale bread can be easily returned).

In a medical market, the corresponding situation is a prespecified patient fee paid directly to a doctor or a hospital for some predetermined and expected quantity and quality of medical services. In the case of medical services, however, the transaction is often not anticipated, and the price, quantity, and quality of medical services are unknown until after the medical event occurs. The transaction is unanticipated because medical illnesses occur irregularly and unexpectedly (Arrow, 1963). The price, quality, and quantity of medical services are not known initially because much uncertainty surrounds the diagnosis and proper treatment of a medical problem. In addition, health care providers possess a greater amount of information relative to patients regarding the provision of medical services, giving rise to an asymmetry of information. Because no simple relation exists between diagnosis and treatment, and much is left to the discretion of health care providers, possibilities for opportunistic behavior arise. That is, health care providers may produce more treatments or a higher-quality treatment than economic considerations warrant.[1]

THE ROLE AND FINANCING METHODS OF THIRD-PARTY PAYERS

Because the timing and amount of medical treatment costs are uncertain from an individual consumer's perspective, third-party payers, such as private health insurance companies or the government, play a major role in medical care markets. Third-party payers often serve as intermediaries between the consumer and the health care producer and monitor the behavior of health care providers as a means of controlling medical costs.

Also, third-party payers are responsible for managing the financial risk associated with the purchase of medical services. A third-party payer faces a much lower level of risk than does an individual consumer because it can pool its risk among various subscribers by operating on a large scale. The law of large numbers implies that whereas single events may be random and largely unpredictable, the average outcome of many similar events across a large population can be predicted fairly accurately. For example, it is difficult for one individual to predict whether he or she will experience a heart attack. An insurance company, on the other hand, can be reasonably sure about the heart attack rate by judging from past experiences involving a large number of individuals. Third-party payers can use indicators such as occupational and demographic averages to forecast expected medical claims for a large group of individuals. A risk-averse consumer is made better off by making a certain preset payment to an insurer for coverage against an unforeseen medical event rather than facing the possibility of paying some unknown medical costs. Essentially, consumers receive a net benefit from the financial security that third-party payers supply.[2]

Third parties make the health care system much more complex because the source of third-party financing and the method of reimbursement must be worked into the model. If the third-party payer is a private health insurance company, the consumer pays a premium in exchange for some amount of medical insurance coverage. As part of the health insurance plan, the consumer may be responsible for paying a deductible portion as well as a copayment or coinsurance. The deductible provision requires the consumer to pay the first

---

[1]This so-called **supplier-induced demand theory** is explained in great detail in Chapter 12.
[2]Health insurance principles are developed more fully in Chapters 5 and 6.

X of medical costs, after which the health insurance company is responsible for reimbursement. With a coinsurance provision, the consumer pays a fixed percentage of the cost each time he or she receives a medical service. A copayment refers to a fixed amount per service.

When a government agency (or a public health insurance company) acts as a third-party payer, the financing of medical care insurance usually comes from taxes. Premiums and taxes differ in the way risk is treated and the voluntary nature of the payment.[3] Premiums are paid voluntarily and often depend on the risk category of the buyer of health insurance. Tax payments are mandatory and represent a single fee without reference to risk category.

Some alternative ways to finance health care can be gleaned by examining the different methods used in Canada, Germany, and the United Kingdom.[4] We chose these particular countries because their health care systems possess highly unique features. In addition, most proposals for health care reform in the United States are based to some extent on the health care systems of these three countries.

Canada has a compulsory **national health insurance (NHI)** program administered (somewhat differently) by each of its 10 provinces. The NHI program provides first-dollar coverage, and no limit is imposed on the level of medical benefits an individual can receive during his or her lifetime. **First-dollar coverage** means complete health insurance coverage in that the health insurer reimburses for the first and every dollar spent on medical services (i.e., there is no deductible or copayment amount). For all practical purposes, taxes finance the NHI program in each province.[5] In addition, the Canadian government provides up to 40 percent in direct cost sharing and makes hospital construction grants available to provinces. Private insurance is available for some forms of health care in Canada, although private coverage is prohibited for services covered by the NHI plan. Because the public sector rather than the private sector insures against medical costs, there are no marketing expenses, no administrative costs of estimating risk status or determining whom to cover, and no allocation for profits.

The **socialized health insurance (SI)** program in Germany is based on government-mandated financing by employers and employees. The premiums of unemployed individuals and their dependents are paid by former employers or come from various public sources (the Federal Labor Administration and public pension funds). Private not-for-profit insurance companies, called **Sickness Funds,** are responsible for collecting funds from employers and employees and reimbursing physicians and hospitals. The statutory medical benefits are comprehensive, with a small copayment share for some services. Affluent and self-employed individuals are allowed to go outside the system and purchase private health insurance coverage.

Mechanic (1995) and others refer to the health care system in the United Kingdom (UK) as a **public contracting** model because the government contracts with various

---

[3]See Bodenheimer and Grumbach (1992) for an in-depth comparison of taxes and premiums for financing universal health insurance.
[4]See Raffel (1997) for discussion on the health care systems in various industrialized countries. For manageability, we confine the discussion to the insurance, physician, and hospital services industries. No mention is made of the existing systems in the pharmaceutical and long-term care markets, for example.
[5]Three provinces charge insurance premiums that are related to family size rather than risk. These premiums are not compulsory for coverage and will be paid by the province if individuals are unable to pay. Because these premiums are not adjusted for risk, they are essentially taxes.

providers of health care services on behalf of the people. The UK health care system, under the auspices of the National Health Service (NHS), offers universal health insurance coverage financed through taxation. The NHS provides global budgets to district health authorities (DHAs). Each DHA is responsible for assessing and prioritizing the health care needs of about 300,000 people and then purchasing the necessary health care services from public and private health care providers. Hospital services are provided by nongovernmental trusts, which compete among themselves and with private hospitals for DHA contracts. Community-based primary care givers also contract with the DHAs. In addition, general practitioner (GP) fundholders apply for budgets from the DHAs, and, with the budgets, service a minimum group of 5,000 patients by providing primary care and purchasing elective surgery, outpatient therapy, and specialty nursing services. There is some limited competition among GP fundholders for patients.

RISK MANAGEMENT, REIMBURSEMENT, AND CONSUMER COST SHARING

Another important element of a health care system concerns the manner in which health care providers are reimbursed and the share of medical costs paid by consumers. Reimbursement is important because some payment methods shift much more financial risk onto health care providers than others. As figure 4–1 indicates, insurers may reimburse health care providers with either a fixed or variable payment, although in practice the payment methods are sometimes combined. A fixed payment is set independent of the amount of medical services actually provided to patients for a given and defined treatment episode. If the actual costs of delivering services to patients are less than the level of the fixed payment, health care providers are normally allowed to keep the surplus. However, health care providers also face the possibility that actual costs are greater than the fixed payment. Thus, some financial risk is shifted to health care providers when reimbursement takes place on a fixed-payment basis. A prospectively set fixed annual budget to a hospital or nursing home or a fixed annual salary for an employee are examples of fixed-payment systems. Regardless of how many resources a hospital or nursing home employs, or the number of hours an employee works during a given period, the payment remains the same.

Under a variable-payment system, the reimbursement amount varies with the quantity of services actually delivered to patients. Retrospective reimbursement, in which the health care provider bills for actual costs incurred, and fee-for-service, in which a price is paid for each unit of a medical service, are two common examples of a variable-payment system. A few state governments still reimburse nursing homes on a retrospective basis for caring for Medicaid patients. The price paid for each physician office visit is an example of a fee-for-service payment. When reimbursement takes on a variable-payment basis, health care providers face much less risk from cost overruns.

Similarly, the share of medical costs paid by consumers is important because a greater amount of cost sharing puts more financial risk on them. For example, take the extreme cases. The typical consumer faces very little financial incentive if any to care about the costs associated with his or her medical treatment if fully insured with no out-of-pocket expenses. Even if the medical costs equal $100, $1,000, or $10,000, the consumer pays a zero out-of-pocket price if fully insured. Conversely, that same consumer faces much more financial incentive to be concerned with the cost if they are required to pay the entire bill (i.e., 100 percent out-of-pocket price) associated with the medial treatment. No one disagrees that the opportunity cost of paying $200 for an office visit is much greater than paying $100.

The matrix in figure 4–2 helps to illustrate the importance of risk sharing. The matrix shows how the two reimbursement schemes just discussed and the consumer's out-of-pocket price interact and affect the likelihood that a large volume of medical services will be supplied and demanded. The probability of a high volume of medical services is given inside each cell of the matrix for each combination of reimbursement method and consumer out-of-pocket price.

FIGURE 4–2

The Likelihood of a Large Volume of Medical Services for
Different Reimbursement and Consumer Copayment Schemes

		Type of reimbursement scheme	
		Fixed payment	Variable payment
Out-of-pocket price to consumer	Low	Low likelihood (1)	High likelihood (2)
	High	Very low likelihood (3)	Moderate likelihood (4)

We can identify the opportunity for a large volume of medical services per patient by considering how the different provider reimbursement schemes and consumer payment plans affect the incentives of health care providers and consumers. For example, a health care provider that is reimbursed on a fixed-payment basis is very unlikely to supply a large volume of medical services to a patient unnecessarily. The cost of additional medical services immediately subtracts from the fixed payment and puts the health care provider at risk for cost overruns. In contrast, for the variable-payment schemes, health care providers do not absorb the financial risk of the higher costs associated with additional services.

We can conduct a similar analysis for the consumer. Consumers who face a low out-of-pocket price of obtaining medical services are more likely to seek out additional medical services (this is referred to as the moral hazard problem in Chapter 5). On the other hand, consumers who face a high out-of-pocket price are less inclined to seek out medical services given the greater opportunity cost of their money.

Combining the reimbursement and out-of-pocket payment schemes, the likelihood of a large volume of medical services per patient is the greatest in cell 2, where a variable-payment scheme interacts with a low consumer out-of-pocket plan. Neither party loses much financially in the exchange of dollars for medical services. Conversely, a large volume of medical services is least likely in cell 3, where a fixed-payment plan coexists with a large consumer out-of-pocket scheme. Both parties in the exchange lose financially. Cell 4 offers a moderate likelihood of a large volume of medical services, since the provider is not made financially worse off by providing additional services. For this to happen, however, either the consumer's out-of-pocket price must not be too high or the consumer must be relatively insensitive to price (i.e., highly inelastic demand). Finally, in cell 1, the health care provider is made worse off while the consumer is relatively unaffected by additional medical services, so the probability of a large volume of medical services is low.

A major current concern of health care policymakers is that a variable reimbursement system, when combined with a modest consumer out-of-pocket plan, results in excessive medical services that provide low marginal benefits to patients but come at a high marginal cost to society. For example, medical care providers may offer expensive diagnostic tests to low-risk patients. The tests come at a high marginal cost to society but yield only small marginal benefits to patients given their low-risk classification. Small marginal medical benefits coincide with the "flat-of-the-curve" medicine observed in several empirical studies, as discussed in Chapter 2.

As a result, many health policy analysts believe that fee-for-service or retrospective payments and small consumer out-of-pocket payments are responsible for high-cost, low-benefit medicine. Policymakers typically argue that some cost sharing is needed on the supply and/or demand side of the market to reduce the potential for excess medical services (Ellis and McGuire, 1993). That is, they believe fixed-payment reimbursement plans and nontrivial consumer payments are required to control unnecessary medical services.

We can appreciate the importance of the reimbursement method by examining and contrasting the countrywide reimbursement schemes practiced in Canada, Germany, and the United Kingdom. In Canada, everyone is eligible for the same medical benefits, and there are no copayments for most medical services. Patients essentially drop out of the reimbursement picture, and reimbursement exclusively takes place between the public insurer (the government) and the health care provider. In terms of figure 4–1, this means that the monetary exchange is virtually nonexistent between patient and health care provider. The ministry of health in each province is responsible for controlling medical costs. Cost control is attempted primarily through fixed global budgets for hospitals and predetermined fees for physicians. Specifically, the operating budgets of hospitals are approved and funded entirely by the ministry in each province, and an annual global budget is negotiated between the ministry and each individual hospital. Capital expenditures must also be approved by the ministry, which funds the bulk of the spending.

Physician fees are determined by periodic negotiations between the ministry and provincial medical associations (the Canadian version of the American Medical Association). With the passage of the Canada Health Act of 1984, the right to **extra billing** was removed in all provinces. Extra billing or balance billing refers to a situation in which the physician bills the patient some dollar amount above the predetermined fee set by the third-party payer. For the profession as a whole, negotiated fee increases are implemented in steps, conditional on the rate of increase in the volume of services. If volume per physician rises faster than a predetermined percentage, subsequent fee increases are scaled down or eliminated to cap gross billings—the product of the fee and the volume of each service—at some predetermined target. The possible scaling down of fee increases is supposed to create an incentive for a more judicious use of resources. Physicians enjoy nearly complete autonomy in treating patients (e.g., there is no mandatory second opinion for surgery) because policymakers believe there is no need for intrusive types of controls given that the hospital global budgets and physician expenditure targets tend to curb unnecessary services.

The Sickness Funds in Germany, which collect employer and employee insurance premiums, pay negotiated lump-sum funds equal to the product of a capitation (per-patient) payment and the number of insured individuals to regional associations of ambulatory care physicians. These regional associations, in turn, reimburse individual physicians for services on the basis of a fee schedule. The fee schedule is determined through negotiation between the regional associations of Sickness Funds and physicians. To determine the fee schedule, each physician service is assigned a number of points based on relative worth. The price per point is established by dividing the lump-sum total budget by the actual number of points billed within a quarter by all physicians. The income to an individual physician equals the number of points billed times the price per point.

The Sickness Funds that operate in a given state also negotiate fixed prices for various procedures (based on the diagnosis-related group, or DRG) with local hospitals. Because hospitals can make profits or incur losses because of the fixed prices, there is an incentive for hospitals to save resources and specialize in certain procedures. For some procedures, hospital accommodations are reimbursed on a per diem basis but funds are limited by an overall budget. Hospital-based physicians are paid on a salary basis. Most of the hospital funds for capital acquisitions come from state and local governments and are reviewed and approved through a state planning process.

In the UK, the district health authorities are allocated funds by the NHS on a weighted capitation basis, which considers age, sex, and health-risk factors as well as geographical cost differences. Independent community-based family practitioners contract with the NHS and are uniformly paid throughout the UK, primarily on a capitation basis. The DHAs

INSIGHT 4–1

Physician Utilization Rates in Salary- and Fee-Based Reimbursement Systems

As discussed in this section, the reimbursement method influences the quality of services supplied to patients. Because a fee-for-service reimbursement scheme pays a set amount for each unit of services, physician income increases with a greater number of services provided. Thus, a fee-for-service reimbursement system may create an incentive for physicians to deliver more services, some of which may be excessive or wasteful (column 2 in figure 4–2). In contrast, if physicians are paid on a salary basis, they receive a predetermined amount of income that is independent of the amount of services provided. In this type of reimbursement system, physicians could actually face the opposite incentive: to discourage offices visits and reduce workloads as a way to receive on-the-job leisure time (column 1 in figure 4–2).

Most empirical studies attempting to sort out any behavioral differences between salary- and fee-for-service-based reimbursement systems have compared medical utilization rates in the salaried physician practices of health maintenance organizations to conventional fee-for-service practices. These studies may have been flawed, however, because the results could have been affected by other factors, such as the organizational form of the practice setting, types of physicians, and patient behavior. In particular, observed medical utilization rates depend on both the provider net benefits and the patient costs associated with additional services. Because consumer out-of-pocket costs are typically higher in a fee-for-service setting than in a prepaid practice, it is difficult to compare any utilization differences that arise solely from the health care provider reimbursement scheme.

A study by Hickson, Altemeier, and Perrin (1987) overcomes this problem. Specifically, nine pairs of closely matched medical residents at a Vanderbilt pediatric clinic were randomly assigned to a fee-for-service or salary-based reimbursement group over a nine-month period. The common clinic setting and random assignment of physicians controlled for the organizational form, patient payment methods, and physician characteristics, so any utilization differences could be attributed solely to the method of reimbursing physicians. Residents in the fee-for-service group received $2 per patient visit, while the others received a monthly salary of $20. At the end of the nine months, records were consulted to determine the utilization rates of the residents in the two groups.

Although the average number of patient visits per physician did not differ significantly between the fee-for-service (111.6) and salaried (104.8) physician groups, the results show that fee-for-service patients are more likely to see their regular physicians. In the study, almost 87 percent of fee-for-service visits were attended by the primary physician, whereas the comparable figure for the salaried group was only about 78 percent. In addition, fee-for-service patients were less likely to visit the emergency room than those patients assigned to salaried physicians, supporting the contention that fee-for-service physicians direct their patients away from the emergency room to their offices, where it is easier for them to personally treat their patients. Thus, Hickson, Altemeier, and Perrin noted that a fee-for-service reimbursement scheme may provide more "continuity" of care given that patients are more likely to see their regular doctors.

The results also suggest that fee-for-service physicians schedule and attend more visits than salaried physicians. In fact, there were 22 percent more visits per capita amount patients assigned to fee-for-service physicians than for salaried physicians. The difference was due to well-child visits and not initial or follow-up visits. Further investigation by Hickson, Altemeier, and Perrin found that the number of well-child visits was higher because fee-for-service physicians miss fewer recommended visits (due to financial incentive) and make more visits in excess of the American Academy of Pediatrics' guidelines.

Interestingly, the authors found that patient satisfaction did not differ significantly in the two groups, although for some unknown reason, parents in the salary group perceived that they had better access to their physicians. From an economic perspective, Hickson, Altemeier, and Perrin concluded that the potential benefits from greater continuity of care and fewer emergency room visits must be weighed against the likely higher costs associated with excessive services under a fee-for-service reimbursement scheme.

prospectively reimburse individual hospital trusts based on the actual cost of providing the services. All hospital-based physicians and consultants are paid on a fixed salary basis by the trusts. Trusts are required to earn a 6 percent return on assets and the residual is returned to the DHA. Capital funding for the trusts is determined by the DHA and is based on its regional allocation.

Any funds allocated to GP fundholders are deducted from the DHA's allocation. GP fundholders annually negotiate funds to purchase elective and nonemergency services for their subscribers. About 41 percent of the population in England is served by GP fundholders. Any savings made by a fundholder may be reinvested in the practice or new services but cannot directly increase the GP's personal income. GP fundholders are not at personal financial risk as they are protected against any legitimate cost overruns by the DHAs.

In sum, these three countries have shied away from relying on an uncontrolled fee-for-service reimbursement scheme because of the concern that it creates incentives for high-cost, low-benefit medicine. The payment is on either a per diem, per-person, or negotiated fee-for-service basis. In addition, the payment for medical services is determined by a single payer—the government in Canada and the United Kingdom and representatives of the Sickness Funds in Germany. Policymakers in these countries believe that a single-payer, controlled-payment system can reduce the incentive to provide high-cost, low-benefit medicine and better contain health care costs.

THE PRODUCTION OF MEDICAL SERVICES

The mode of production also differs across health care systems. Several distinguishing features of production are worth mentioning. We normally think of health care services as being produced on an inpatient care basis in hospitals or nursing homes or on an outpatient (ambulatory) care basis at physician clinics or in the outpatient department of a hospital. However, health care services are also produced in the home. Preventive care (e.g., exercise, dieting, and flossing) and first aid are two prime examples of home-produced health care services. In addition, long-term or chronic care services are often produced in the home rather than in an institution, such as a nursing home. Although acute care services can also be produced in the home, the cost of producing these services is usually prohibitive for the individual consumer because of the high per-person labor and capital expenses.[6] As a result, it is almost always cheaper for the individual consumer to purchase acute care services at a hospital because such an organization can exploit various economies associated with large size.

Outside the home, health care providers may be organized in a number of ways. For example, a hospital may be a freestanding, independent institution or part of a multihospital chain. Similarly, a physician may operate in a solo practice or belong to a group practice. Usually the size and scope of the medical organization depend on whether any economies exist from operating on a small or large scale. In addition, some physicians,

---

[6]According to the *Mosby Medical Encyclopedia*, long-term care is "the provision of medical care on a repeated or continuous basis to persons with chronic physical or mental disorders" (p. 471). Acute care is "treatment for a serious illness, for an accident, or after surgery. . . . This kind of care is usually for only a short time" (p. 11).

such as radiologists and anesthesiologists, may be employees of the hospital. In contrast, some physicians on the medical staff may not be employees of the hospital but instead are granted admitting privileges.

Health care services may be produced in the private or public sector by health care providers in the medical services industry. If produced in the private sector, the health care provider may offer medical services on a not-for-profit or a for-profit basis. A not-for-profit organization is required by law to use any profits exclusively for the charitable, educational, or scientific purpose for which it was formed. For example, a hospital may use profits to lower patient prices or finance medical equipment or hospital expansion.

Institutional Differences Between For-Profit and Not-for-Profit Health Care Providers

Because not-for-profit institutions are so prevalent in the health care sector, it is important that we examine the institutional differences between for-profit and not-for-profit firms. There are five basic institutional differences between these two classes of organizations.

First, when for-profit firms are established, they acquire initial capital by exchanging funds for ownership with the private sector. Ownership gives the private sector a claim on future profits. Not-for-profit firms must rely on donations for their initial capital because they are not privately owned. In a broad sense, they are owned by the community at large. Second, for-profit providers are capable of earning accounting profits and distributing cash dividends to their owners, where as not-for-profit firms face a non-distribution constraint and are prohibited from distributing profits. Third, for-profit organizations can easily be sold or liquidated for compensation by their owners, where as it is very difficult to sell a not-for-profit organization. Fourth, not-for-profit providers are exempt from certain types of taxes and are eligible to receive subsidies from the government. In fact, it has been argued that the tax exemption and subsidies give not-for-profit firms an unfair advantage over for-profit firms. Finally, not-for-profit providers are restricted by law in the types of goods and services they can provide.

Why Are Not-for-Profit Health Care Providers So Prevalent?

Now that we understand the differences between for-profit and not-for-profit providers, the next item to address is why not-for-profit providers are so prevalent in the health care sector. Weisbrod (1988) discusses the issue in general terms, but his analysis can easily be applied to the health care sector. Not-for-profit firms exist primarily as a result of market failure in the private sector. The market failure results from three factors.

First, the private sector works best when all market participants are perfectly informed. However, given the complexity of medical technology and the difficulty of assessing the appropriateness of medical care, consumers typically possess imperfect information about the health care sector. As a result, many consumers believe they are in a vulnerable situation and can easily be exploited by medical providers for the sake of profits. For that reason, they prefer to deal with not-for-profit providers, which presumably are driven by more altruistic motives.

The second reason for market failure concerns equity. Society as a whole believes each citizen has a right to some minimum level of medical care that would not be provided if health care resources were allocated by the for-profit sector. The profit motive ensures that health care is allocated based on the ability to pay and not on need. As a result, some argue that not-for-profit providers are necessary to meet the needs of those who cannot pay for medical care.

The third reason for market failure involves the presence of externalities as discussed further in Chapter 9. When externalities exist, resources are not efficiently allocated because the for-profit sector does not consider all the costs and benefits associated with production. Thus, for these three reasons, the for-profit sector may fail to address the collective need for health care.

The next question that comes to mind is why the public sector does not simply take over the allocation of health care resources in the presence of market failure. The answer, Weisbrod contends, is that consumer needs are heterogeneous. When needs are widely diverse, the government has difficulty developing an appropriate overall policy that meets the desires of all consumers in a cost-effective manner. For example, "one-size-fits-all" medicine most likely would not appeal to everyone. Hence, a multitude of not-for-profit health care providers, such as hospital and nursing homes, are required to satisfy heterogeneous demands. Each institution can be tailored to fit the individual demands of its constituents. For example, the Shriners run not-for-profit hospitals aimed at orthopedic pediatric care, while some religious organizations operate nursing homes specifically for elderly members of their own religion.

One last question deserves some discussion. If theses market failures are in fact substantial, why is the for-profit sector allowed to operate at all in the health care field? Consumer knowledge and preferences provide the answer to this question. Although some consumers may lack the information they need to make informed decisions, others are much more informed. Informed consumers may "have no institutional preferences" and "prefer to deal with any organization, regardless of ownership form, that provides the wanted outputs at the lowest price" (Weisbrod, 1988, p. 124). Thus, the for-profit sector exists in the health care market primarily to satisfy the demands of these types of consumers.

INSIGHT 4-2

Medical Technology in Canada, Germany, the United Kingdom, and the United States

The availability of medical technologies undoubtedly has a powerful impact on the production of medical care services and health care costs. Medical technologies, such as drugs, medical devices, and procedures, may offer cost savings or higher-quality services.

Four stages are associated with the development and diffusion of medical technology. According to the National Science Foundation, the first stage, *basic research*, is defined as "original investigation for the advancement of scientific knowledge without specific commercial objectives." Basic medical research produces new knowledge about various biological mechanisms or malfunctions involving the human body. In the second stage, *applied research*, the basic knowledge is applied to yield solutions for the prevention, treatment, or curing of diseases. At the *clinical investigation and testing* stage, new medical technologies are tested on human subjects. The benefit and safety of the medical technology are usually demonstrated at this point. The final stage, *diffusion* (or imitation), involves the commercial introduction, adoption, and spreading of medical technologies.

Health policy analysts (e.g., Aaron, 1991) have expressed concern that unconstrained health care markets result in medical technologies that offer low benefits at high costs. As a result, many countries have adopted policies to either directly or indirectly control the adoption and diffusion of medical technologies to contain costs. Public control may occur at any one or all four of the stages associated with the invention and diffusion of medical technology (Banta and Kemp, 1982).

For example, hospital budgets are limited in Canada and Great Britain partly to indirectly control the proliferation of expensive medical technologies. It is argued that the limited budgets create a financial incentive for hospital administrators to economize on medical technologies offering low benefits at a high cost. At the other extreme, the adoption and diffusion of technology are determined more by market forces in the United States. Germany, on the other hand, has taken a middle position between these two extremes with some limited control over the proliferation of new medical technologies (Rublee, 1989).

Reinhardt, Hussey, and Anderson (2002) provide some evidence on the relative availability of different medical technologies in Canada, Germany, United Kingdom, and the United States (among other countries). Listed in their study are data for five different medical technologies: magnetic resonance imagers (MRIs) per million population, CT scanners per million people, coronary bypass surgeries per 100,000 population, coronary angioplasty procedures per 100,000 people, and the number of patients undergoing dialysis per 100,000 population. Several implications can be drawn from the data in their study.

First, as one might expect given the greater reliance on market forces, the data show a greater availability of medical technologies in the United States than in the three other countries. For example, the United States has nearly 50 percent more MRIs per million people than the United Kingdom and more than four times the amount of MRIs in Canada. In addition, only Germany had more CT scanners per million people than the United States. There is also a much greater prevalence of coronary bypass procedures, coronary angioplasty procedures, and patients undergoing dialysis in the United States than in the other three countries.

Second, the data suggest to some degree that the relative availability of medical technologies in Germany tends to fall somewhere between the United States and the other two countries. Besides having the most CT scanners, Germany has the second greater number of MRIs and persons undergoing dialysis and coronary angioplasty. Germany, however, is last among the four countries in terms of coronary bypass procedures.

Third, it is difficult to conclude from the information available whether medical technologies are overprovided in the United States or underprovided in the other three countries. In fact, a different level of medical technology could be optimal for each country because of differing social values (Rublee, 1994). Cost-benefit analysis, cost effectiveness studies, or outcomes research would be necessary to draw any definitive conclusions on this issue. Finally, the availability of medical technology in itself indicates little about the overall effectiveness of the health care system. To determine overall health care system effectiveness, a host of factors must also be considered, including the quantity and quality of other medical inputs.

Production of Health Care in the Three Systems

The organization of production in the three health care systems we have been discussing have some slight differences. In Canada, medical services are produced in the private sector. Most hospitals in the private sector are organized on a not-for-profit basis and are owned by either charitable or religious organizations. In Germany, medical services are produced primarily in the private sector, because most physicians operate in private practices. Public hospitals control about 51 percent of all hospital beds in Germany. The remaining beds are managed by not-for-profit (35 percent) and for-profit hospitals (13 percent). Office-based physicians are normally prohibited from treating patients in hospitals, and most hospital-based physicians are not allowed to provide ambulatory care services in Germany.

The structure of production in the UK now largely takes place in the private, although mostly not-for-profit, sector. The present situation in the UK is in stark contrast to the method of production that prevailed before the passage of the National Health Service and Community Act of 1990. Up to 1990, almost all hospitals were publicly owned and operated and most doctors were employees of the NHS. Even before 1990, however, family practitioners were community-based in solo or small group practices and simply contracted with the NHS.

PHYSICIAN CHOICE AND REFERRAL PRACTICES

Important differences in the availability and utilization of medical services can also result from the degree of physician choice the health care consumer possesses and the types of referral practices used within the health care system. More choice typically provides consumers with increased satisfaction (Schmittdiel et al., 1997). However, greater choice may come at a cost if it leads to a large number of fragmented health care providers that are unable to sufficiently coordinate care or exploit any economies that come with large size (Halm et al., 1997).

In some health care systems, patients have unlimited choice of and full access to any physician or health care provider within any type of setting (e.g., clinic or hospital). For example, at one time in the United States, insured individuals could directly seek out any general practitioner or specialist without financial penalty. Moreover, at one time in the United States, it was not unusual for a general practitioner to review the care of a patient referred for hospital services. We will see later that conditions regarding physician choice and referral practices have changed a great deal in the United States.

Other countries have adopted different referral practices. Although the Canadian and German health care systems allow free choice of provider, general practitioners in the UK act as "gatekeepers" and must refer patients to a specialist or a hospital. Once the patient is referred to a hospital, the patient–general practitioner relationship is severed for any particular illness in both the UK and Germany. Unlike in Germany, however, patients are allowed to go directly to a family practitioner or a hospital for primary care in the UK, unless they are registered with a GP fundholder.

THE THREE NATIONAL HEALTH CARE SYSTEMS SUMMARIZED

Based on our generalized model of a health care system, table 4–1 provides a capsulized summary of the current national health care systems in the three countries we have been

TABLE 4-1

A Comparison of Health Care Systems

Feature	COUNTRY (TYPE OF SYSTEM)			
	Canada (NHI)*	Germany (SI)†	United Kingdom (PC)‡	United States (Pluralistic)
Health insurance coverage	Universal	Near universal	Near universal	84 percent
Financing	General taxes	Payroll and general taxes	General taxes	Voluntary premiums or general taxes
	Single-payer system	Single-payer system§	Single-payer system	Multipayer system
Reimbursement	Global budgets to hospitals	Fixed payments to hospitals	Global budgets to hospitals	Mostly fixed payments to hospitals
	Negotiated fee-for-services to physicians	Negotiated point-fees-for-service to physicians	Salaries and capitation payments to physicians	Mostly fee-for-service to physicians
Consumer out-of-pocket price	Negligible	Negligible	Negligible	Positive, but generally small
Production	Private	Private	Private but public contract	Private
Physician choice	Unlimited	Unlimited	Limited	Relatively limited

*NHI = national health insurance program.
†SI = socialized insurance.
‡PC = public contracting.
§Multiple third-party payers are responsible for paying representatives of the health care providers, but the universal fees are collectively negotiated by the third-party payers.

discussing. Each national health care system is differentiated according to the degree of health insurance coverage, type of financing, reimbursement scheme, consumer out-of-pocket price, mode of production, and degree of physician choice. The essential features of the Canadian health care system are national health insurance, free choice of health care provider, private production of medical services, and regulated global budgets and fees for health care providers. The dominating features of the German health care system include socialized health insurance financed through Sickness Funds, negotiated payments to health care providers, free choice of provider, and private production of health care services. In the case of Great Britain, the distinguishing characteristics include restrictions on choice of provider, public contracting of medical services, global budgets for hospitals, fixed salaries for hospital-based physicians, and capitation payments to family practitioners.

The U.S. health care system is discussed in detail in the next section, and the last column in table 4-1 gives a quick preview. The pluralistic U.S. health care system contains some structural elements found in most of the other three systems (e.g., private production) but relies more heavily on a fee-for-service reimbursement scheme. In addition, health care providers are reimbursed through multiple payers, including the government and thousands of private insurance companies, in contrast to the single-payer system in Canada (government), Germany (Sickness Funds), and the UK (government).

AN OVERVIEW OF THE U.S. HEALTH CARE SYSTEM

Some analysts argue that the multifaceted nature of the health care system accounts for the relatively high expenditures devoted to medical care in the United States. Although this may be true and is a topic of discussion throughout this book, it most certainly is true that this diversity makes it very difficult to describe the U.S. health care system in sufficient detail. This section presents a brief overview of the current system in the United States based on the generalized model of a health care system. The remainder of the book discusses the operation and performance of the U.S. health care system in much greater detail, albeit on a piecemeal basis.

Financing of Health Care in the United States

The United States has no single nationwide system of health insurance. Health insurance is purchased in the private marketplace or provided by the government to certain groups. Private health insurance can be purchased from various for-profit commercial insurance companies or from nonprofit insurers, such as Blue Cross/Blue Shield. About 86 percent of the population is covered by either public (24 percent) or private (72 percent) health insurance.[7]

Approximately 64 percent of health insurance coverage is employment related, largely due to the cost savings associated with group plans that can be purchased through an employer. Employers voluntarily sponsor the health insurance plans. Nearly all privately insured individuals belong to some type of managed care plan. As discussed in Chapter 6, managed care plans are designed to practice cost effective medicine and place varying degrees of restrictions on consumer choices.

In addition to private health insurance, nearly 24 percent of the U.S. population is covered by public health insurance. The two major types of public health insurance, both of which began in 1966, are **Medicare** and **Medicaid**.[8] Medicare is a uniform, national public health insurance program for aged and disabled individuals (e.g., those with kidney failure). Administered by the federal government, Medicare is the largest health insurer in the country, covering about 13 percent of the population and is primarily financed through

---

[7]U.S. Census Bureau, "Health Insurance Data," http://www.census.gov/hhes/www/hlthins.html (accessed June 10, 2002). The figures for private and public insurance coverage do not sum to 86 percent because of double-counting. For example, some people receiving public insurance coverage also purchase private health insurance.

[8]See Chapter 10 for a more detailed discussion on the Medicare and Medicaid programs. The federal government is also responsible for providing health insurance to individuals in the military and to federal employees.

taxes. The Medicare plan consists of two parts. Part A is compulsory and provides health insurance coverage for inpatient hospital care, very limited nursing home services, and some home health services. Part B, the voluntary or supplemental plan, provides benefits for physician services, outpatient hospital services, outpatient laboratory and radiology services, and home health services.

The second type of public health insurance program, Medicaid, provides coverage for certain economically disadvantaged groups. Medicaid is jointly financed by the federal and state governments and is administered by each state. The federal government provides state governments with a certain percentage of matching funds ranging from 50 to 83 percent, depending on the per capita income in the state. Individuals who are elderly, blind, disabled, or members of families with dependent children must be covered by Medicaid for states to receive federal funds. In addition, although the federal government stipulates a certain basic package of health care benefits (i.e., hospital, physician, and nursing home services), some states are more generous than others. Consequently, in some states individuals receive a more generous benefit package under Medicaid than in others. Medicaid is the only public program that finances long-term nursing home care. Approximately 10 percent of the population is covered by Medicaid.

In summary, the financing of health care falls into three broad categories: private health insurance, Medicare, and Medicaid. However, another category of individuals exists: those who are uninsured. Approximately 14 percent of the U.S. population is estimated to lack health insurance coverage at any point in time. This does not mean these individuals are without access to health care services. Many uninsured people receive health care services through public clinics and hospitals, state and local health programs, or private providers that finance the care through charity and by shifting costs to other payers. Nevertheless, the lack of health insurance can cause uninsured households to face considerable financial hardship and insecurity. Furthermore, the uninsured often find themselves in the emergency room of a hospital, sometimes after it is too late for proper medical treatment.

Reimbursement for Health Care in the United States

Unlike in Canada and Europe, where a single-payer system is the norm, the United States possesses a multipayer system in which a variety of third-party payers, including the federal and state governments, commercial health insurance companies, and Blue Cross/Blue Shield, are responsible for reimbursing health care providers. Naturally, reimbursement takes on various forms in the United States, depending on the nature of the third-party payer. The most common form of reimbursement is fee-for-service, although most health care providers accept discounted fees from private health insurance plans.

Physician services under Medicare (and most state Medicaid plans) are also reimbursed on a fee-for-service basis, but the fee is set by the government based on the time and effort involved in providing the care. Since 1983, the federal government has reimbursed hospitals on a prospective basis for services provided to Medicare patients. This Medicare reimbursement scheme, called the **diagnosis-related group (DRG)** system, contains 500 or so different payment categories based on the characteristics of the patient (age and sex), primary and secondary diagnosis, and treatment.[9] A prospective payment is established for

---

[9]The DRGs are based on 23 major diagnostic groups centered on a different organ of the body.

each DRG. The prospective payment is claimed to provide hospitals with an incentive to contain costs (cells 1 and 3 of figure 4–2).

Beginning in the early 1980s, many states, such as California, instituted **selective contracting**, in which various health care providers competitively bid for the right to treat Medicaid patients. In fact, much of the favorable experience with selective contracting in the United States led to the adoption of the public contracting model in the United Kingdom (Mechanic, 1995). Under selective contracting, recipients of Medicaid are limited in the choice of health care provider. In addition, to better contain health care costs and coordinate care, the federal government and various state governments have attempted to shift Medicare and Medicaid beneficiaries into Managed Care Organizations (MCOs). As of 1997, about 48 percent of all Medicaid recipients and roughly 15 percent of all Medicare beneficiaries were enrolled in MCOs.

Production of Health Services and Provider Choice in the United States

Like the financing and reimbursement schemes, the U.S. health care system is very diversified in terms of production methods. Government, not-for-profit, and for-profit institutions all play an important role in health care markets. For the most part, primary care physicians in the U.S. function in the private for-profit sector and operate in group practices, although some physicians work for not-for-profit clinics or in public organizations. In the hospital industry, the not-for-profit is the dominant form of ownership. Specifically, not-for-profit hospitals control about 70 percent of all hospital beds. The ownership structure is the reverse in the nursing home industry, however. More than 70 percent of all nursing homes are organized on a for-profit basis. One should also keep in mind that mental retardation facilities, dialysis facilities, and even insurance companies possess different ownership forms. The variety of ownership forms helps to make health care a very difficult, but challenging and interesting, industry to analyze.

In addition, we previously mentioned that provider choice matters. Consumers typically receive greater satisfaction from facing more choices. We also discussed, however, that more choices may come at greater costs if small, differentiated providers are unable to fully exploit any economies associated with size. Hence, it is important to know how much choice consumers have over health care providers in the United States.

Up to the early 1980s most insured individuals had full choice of health care providers in the United States. Consumers could choose to visit a primary care giver or the outpatient clinic of a hospital, or see a specialist if they chose to. The introduction of restrictive health insurance plans and such new government policies as selective contracting have limited the degree to which consumers can choose their own health care provider. For example, some health care plans require that patients receive their care exclusively from a particular network, otherwise they are fully responsible for the ensuing financial burden. Furthermore, the primary care giver acts as a gatekeeper and must refer the patient for additional care. Of course, the lower premiums of a restrictive plan compensate consumers at least to some degree for the restriction of choice. There are arguments for and against free choice of provider and once again trade-offs are involved. This issue will be discussed throughout the text in more depth. For now let us just say that these trade-offs must be given serious thought when determining what degree of consumer choice is best from a societal point of view.

INSIGHT 4–3

Consumer Satisfaction with the Health Care System in Canada, Germany, United Kingdom, and the United States

We mentioned in Chapter 1 how any health care system must concern itself with the allocation of medical resources and distribution of medical services because economic resources are so scarce. The people in various nations count on their governments to choose and support the health care system that best promotes efficiency and equity given their historical background, cultural system, and political beliefs. One interesting question is whether people in various nations are satisfied with their current health care system. In an attempt to answer this question, a number of public opinion polls have tried to estimate the degree of consumer satisfaction with the present health care system in a number of nations.

Recently Blendon, Kim, and Benson (2001) cited various opinion polls involving interviews of a random sample of households in various countries, including Canada, Germany, the United Kingdom, and the United States. The households were asked if they were satisfied with the present health care system in their country. The poll findings on this topic yielded some interesting insights. Several findings are worth noting.

In terms of overall satisfaction, the German health care system proved superior, holding a slight edge over the health care system in the United Kingdom with 58 percent of Germans satisfied with their system compared to a 57 percent satisfaction rating in the United Kingdom. Recall that Germany has a health care system characterized by a universal social insurance program. The comparable rates for Canada and the United States are 46 percent and 40 percent, respectively, suggesting that people in the United States are least satisfied with their current health care system.

However, if the poll results are only considered for those individuals considered to be poor, the relative ranking changes with the United Kingdom on top with a 67 percent satisfaction rate and the rate in Germany falling to 52 percent. Among the poor, the U.S. health care system fares a bit better with 45 percent of the poor satisfied compared to 40 percent of the poor in Canada satisfied with their own health care system.

Finally, if the poll results are confined to the elderly, the poll rankings change once again. The UK health care system comes out on top with 69 percent of the elderly satisfied with their own health care system. Interesting enough, the United States ranks second with 61 percent of the elderly satisfied with their health care system. Recall that Medicare, a universal health insurance program for the elderly, exists in the United States. The comparable percentages are 57 and 48 percent in Germany and Canada, indicating that the elderly in Canada are least satisfied with their own health care system.

Of course, public opinion polls may not accurately reflect the success or failure of a health care system or provide a complete representation of the quality of life in a nation. For example, low levels of education and income may cause individuals to be generally dissatisfied with their environment. How people feel about the operation of the health care system relative to the functioning of the overall economic system (or job market) might provide a more accurate indicator of public satisfaction. In addition, unknown to the public, the structure of the health care system may not account for the poor performance of

(continued)

the medical sector. Instead, the poor performance of the health care sector may be due to insufficient resources and income or adverse lifestyles. Finally, from a general welfare perspective, consumer dissatisfaction with the health care system may be sufficiently balanced by high levels of satisfaction with other sectors of the economy. These trade-offs should be considered when assessing the general quality of life across nations.

SUMMARY

Every health care system must answer the four basic questions concerning the allocation of medical resources and the distribution of medical services. Some systems rely on centralized decision making whereas others answer the basic questions through a decentralized process. Health care systems are complex largely because third-party payers are involved. Third-party payers help to reduce the financial risk associated with the irregularity and uncertainty of many medical transactions. Third-party payers also help monitor the behavior of health care providers.

The financing, reimbursement, and production methods and the degree of choice over the health care provider are important elements that make up a health care system. Medical care is financed by out-of-pocket payments, premiums, and/or taxes. Medical care providers are reimbursed on a fixed or variable basis. The production of medical care may take place in a for-profit, a not-for-profit, or a public setting, and medical care providers may operate in independent or large group practices. Choice of provider may be limited. All these features are important because they often influence the operation and performance of a health care system. For example, many economists predict that fee-for-service insurance plans provide an incentive for medical care providers to produce a large volume of services.

The U.S. health care system is very pluralistic. For instance, considerable variation exists in the financing, reimbursement, and production of medical care. The remainder of this book provides a better understanding about how each of these elements affects the functioning of the U.S. health care system.

REVIEW QUESTIONS AND PROBLEMS

1. Answer the following questions pertaining to health care systems.
   A. Why isn't the market for health care services organized according to a typical consumer (patient) and producer (health provider) relationship?
   B. What are the basic differences between insurance premiums and taxes as sources of medical care financing?
   C. How might the reimbursement method differ among health care providers? Why might the reimbursement method make a difference?

    D. Identify the four basic kinds of health care systems discussed in the chapter.

    E. Point out some unique institutions (compared to the United States) associated with the health care systems of the various countries discussed in the chapter.

2. Suppose you had the opportunity to organize the perfect health care system. Explain how you would organize the financing method, reimbursement scheme, mode of production, and physician referral procedure.

3. Which of the following reimbursement and consumer copayment schemes would have the greatest and lowest likelihood of producing high-cost, low-benefit medicine? Explain your answers.

    A. Fee-for-service plan with 40 percent consumer copayment.

    B. Prepaid health plan with 40 percent consumer copayment.

    C. Fee-for-service plan with no consumer cost sharing.

    D. Fixed-salary plan with no consumer cost sharing.

    E. Prepaid health plan with no consumer cost sharing.

    F. Fixed-salary plan with 40 percent consumer cost sharing.

4. Answer the following questions regarding the U.S. health care system.

    A. What are the basic differences between conventional health insurance and managed-care health insurance in terms of type of insurance offered and reimbursement practice?

    B. What is the difference between Medicare and Medicaid? How is Medicare financed? How is Medicaid financed?

    C. What is the DRG system? How are physicians currently reimbursed under the Medicare system?

ONLINE RESOURCES

To access Internet links related to the topics in this chapter, please visit our web site at http://santerre.swcollege.com.

REFERENCES

Aaron, Henry J. *Serious and Unstable Condition: Financing America's Health Care.* Washington, D.C.: The Brookings Institution, 1991.

Arrow, Kenneth J. "Uncertainty and the Welfare Economics of Medical Care." *American Economic Review* 53 (December 1963), pp. 941–73.

Banta, H. David, and Kerry Britten Kemp, eds. "Introduction." In *The Management of Health Care Technology in Nine Countries.* New York: Springer, 1982, pp. 1–9.

Blendon, Robert J., Minah Kim, and John M. Benson. "The Public Versus the World Health Organization on Health System Performance." *Health Affairs* 20 (May/June 2001), pp. 10–20.

Bodenheimer, Thomas, and Kevin Grumbach. "Financing Universal Health Insurance: Taxes, Premiums and the Lessons of Social Insurance." *Journal of Health Politics, Policy and Law* 17 (fall 1992), pp. 439–62.

Ellis, Randall P., and Thomas G. McGuire. "Supply-Side and Demand-Side Cost Sharing in Health Care." *Journal of Economic Perspectives* 7 (fall 1993), pp. 135–51.

Halm, Ethan A., Nancyanne Causino, and David Blumenthal. "Is Gatekeeping Better Than Traditional Care?" *Journal of the American Medical Association* 278 (November 1997), pp. 1677–81.

Hickson, Gerald B., William A. Altemeier, and James M. Perrin. "Physician Reimbursement by Salary or Fee-for-Service: Effect on Physician Practice Behavior in a Randomized Prospective Study." *Pediatrics* 80 (September 1987), pp. 344–50.

Mechanic, David. "Americanization of the British NHS." *Health Affairs* 14 (summer 1995), pp. 51–67.

Mosby Medical Encyclopedia. New York: C. V. Mosby, 1992.

Raffel, Marshall W., ed. *Health Care and Reform in Industrial Countries*. University Park, PA: Pennsylvania State University Press, 1997.

Reinhardt, Uwe E., Peter S. Hussey, and Gerard F. Anderson. "Cross-National Comparisons of Health Systems Using OECD Data, 1999." *Health Affairs* 21 (May/June 2002), pp. 169–81.

Reinhardt, Uwe. "Economics." *Journal of the American Medical Association* 275 (June 1996), pp. 23–25.

Rublee, Dale A. "Medical Technology in Canada, Germany, and the United States: An Update." *Health Affairs* 13 (fall 1994), pp. 113–17.

———. "Medical Technology in Canada, Germany, and the United States." *Health Affairs* 8 (fall 1989), pp. 178–81.

Schmittdiel, Julie, Joe V. Selby, Kevin Grumbach, and Charles P. Quesenberry. "Choice of Personal Physician and Patient Satisfaction in a Health Maintenance Organization. *Journal of the American Medical Association* 278 (November 1997), pp. 1596–99.

Van de Ven, Wynund, P.M.M., and Randall P. Ellis. "Risk Adjustment in Competitive Health Plan Markets." In *Handbook in Health Economics,* eds. A.J. Calger and J.P. Newhouse. Amsterdam: North Holland, 2000, Chapter 14, pp. 755–845.

Weisbrod, Burton A. *The Nonprofit Economy*. Cambridge, Massachusetts: Havard University Press, 1988.

CEBS QUESTIONS

CEBS Sample Question on Subject Matter from CEBS Course 9 Study Manual

1. Why does a third-party payer face a much lower level of risk than an individual health care consumer does? (page 77)

CEBS Sample Exam Questions

1. In the Canadian health care system, cost containment is accomplished primarily through:
   A. Copayments
   B. High deductibles

    C.   Cost sharing with the government
    D.   Voluntary restraint in raising prices
    E.   Fixed budgets for hospitals and predetermined fees for physicians

2. Which of the following statements regarding health insurance systems in foreign countries is (are) correct?

    I. Canada has a national health insurance program that provides first-dollar coverage with no limit on lifetime benefits.

    II. Germany has socialized health insurance financed by employers and employees.

    III. The primary health service in the United Kingdom is much the same as the Medicaid program in the United States.

    A. II only
    B. III only
    C. I and II only
    D. II and III only
    E. I, II, and III

3. The four stages associated with the development and dissemination of medical technology include all the following EXCEPT:

    A. Basic research
    B. Applied research
    C. Clinical investigation and testing
    D. Comparative analysis
    E. Diffusion

Answer to Sample Question from Study Manual

Third-party payers face much lower risk than individual consumers because of the law of large numbers. That is, third-party payers can pool the experience of many individuals and use indicators such as occupational and demographic averages to predict aggregate medical costs.

Answers to Sample Exam Questions

1. E is the correct answer. See page 81 of the text.
2. C is the correct answer. The primary health care system in the United Kingdom is not only for the economically disadvantaged. See pages 75–79 of the text.
3. D is the answer. See pages 86–87 of the text.

CHAPTER 5

THE DEMAND FOR MEDICAL SERVICES

Many people have the misconception that economic theory has little relevance to the demand for medical care because economic factors are not important when an individual needs urgent medical attention. Recall Joe in Chapter 1, who awoke one night with a pain in his chest and realized he was having a heart attack. It is highly unlikely that he and his wife considered the price of medical care as Joe was rushed to the hospital.

However, most visits to a physician's office and the majority of visits to a hospital emergency room are not of a life-threatening nature. Thus, for many medical care transactions, there is sufficient time to make conscious choices, and price often plays an important role in the determination of choices. Results of a survey of various types of health care providers and insurers substantiate the critical role price plays in determining the demand for medical care (Winslow, 1994). According to the survey, price was ranked as more important than patient satisfaction or access to doctors, among other factors, in determining the economic success of health care providers.

This chapter explores the demand side of the medical care market. The chapter highlights:

> The theoretical derivation of the demand curve for medical services.

> Economic and noneconomic variables that influence the demand for medical services.

> The impact of health insurance on the demand for medical services.

> The concept of elasticity of demand.

> A review of the empirical literature concerning the factors that determine the demand for medical care.

> An examination of health spending in the United States.

> A review of the sources and uses of health care funds in the United States.

THE DEMAND FOR HEALTH CARE SERVICES AND THE LAW OF DEMAND

To derive the demand curve for medical services, we must first establish the relation between the quantity of medical services and utility. Recall from Chapter 2 that the stock of health can be treated as a durable good that generates utility and is subject to the law of diminishing marginal utility.[1] This means that each incremental improvement in health generates successively smaller additions to total utility. We also know that medical services are an input in the production of health because a person consumes medical care services for the express purpose of maintaining, restoring, or improving health. However, the law of diminishing marginal productivity causes the marginal improvement to health brought about by each additional unit of medical care consumed to decrease.

From this discussion, it follows that medical care indirectly provides utility. Specifically, medical care helps to produce health, which in turn generates utility. Consequently, utility can be specified as a function of the quantity of medical care. Figure 5–1 depicts the relation between the level of medical care consumed and utility. Utility is specified on the vertical axis, and the quantity of medical care (q) is measured on the horizontal axis. The shape of the total utility curve indicates that utility increases at a decreasing rate with respect to medical care, or that medical care services are subject to diminishing marginal utility. Marginal utility decreases because (1) each successive unit of medical care generates a smaller improvement in health than the previous unit (due to the law of diminishing marginal productivity) and (2) each increase in health, in turn, generates a smaller increase in utility (due to the law of diminishing marginal utility).

The Utility-Maximizing Rule

Given market prices at a point in time, consumers must decide which combination of goods and services, including medical care, to purchase with their fixed incomes. According to microeconomic theory, each consumer chooses the bundle of goods and services that maximizes utility. Without working through the mathematics underlying the process, logic dictates that consumer utility is maximized when the marginal utility gained from the last dollar spent on each product is equal across all goods and services purchased.[2] This condition is known as the **utility-maximizing rule**, and it basically states that total utility reaches its peak when the consumer receives the maximum "bang for the buck" in terms of marginal utility per dollar of income from each and every good. In mathematical terms, the rule states that utility is maximized when

(5–1)
$$MU_q/P_q = MU_z/P_z,$$

where MU_q represents the marginal utility received from the last unit of medical care purchased, q, and MU_z equals the marginal utility derived from the last unit of all other

---

[1]As a reminder, note that we continue to ignore the intermediate step between the stock of health, the services it provides, and utility.

[2]That is, assuming all prices are known, income is spent over the period in question, and all products are subject to the law of diminishing marginal utility.

FIGURE 5–1

The Relationship between Utility and Medical Services

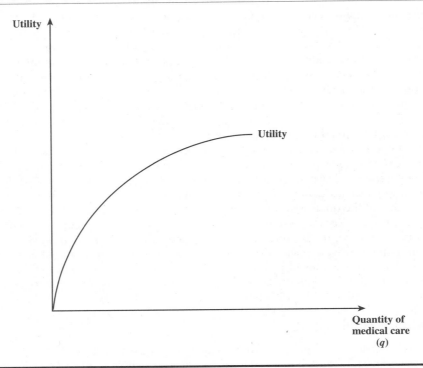

The shape of the utility curve illustrates that total utility increases at a decreasing rate with respect to the level of medical care consumed. The curve has a bow shape for two reasons. First, each additional unit of medical care consumed results in a smaller increase in health than the previous unit because of the law of diminishing marginal productivity. Second, each additional improvement in health generates a smaller increase in utility because of the law of diminishing marginal utility.

goods, z. The latter good is often referred to as a *composite good* in economics. To illustrate why the utility-maximizing rule must hold, suppose that

(5–2) $$MU_q/P_q > MU_z/P_z.$$

In this case, the last dollar spent on medical care generates more additional utility than the last dollar spent on all other goods. The consumer can increase total utility by reallocating expenditures and purchasing more units of medical care and fewer units of all other goods. As the consumer purchases more medical services at the expense of all other goods (remember that the consumer's income and the composite good's price are fixed), the marginal utility of medical care falls and the marginal utility of other goods increases. This, in turn, causes the value of MU_q/P_q to fall and the value of MU_z/P_z to increase. The consumer purchases additional medical services until the equality in equation 5–1 again holds, or the last dollar spent on each product generates the same amount of additional satisfaction. At this point, total utility is maximized and any further changes in spending patterns will negatively affect total utility.

The Law of Demand

The equilibrium condition specified in equation 5–1 can be used to trace out the demand curve for a particular medical service, such as physician services. For simplicity, assume the prices of all other goods and income remain constant and initially the consumer is purchasing the optimal mix of physician services and all other goods. Now assume the price of physician services increases. In this case, MU_q/P_q is less than MU_z/P_z (where MU_q and P_q represent the marginal utility and price of physician services, respectively). Consequently, the consumer receives more satisfaction per dollar from consuming all other goods. In reaction to the price increase, the consumer purchases fewer units of physician services and more units of all other goods. This reallocation continues until MU_q/P_q increases and MU_z/P_z decreases and the equilibrium condition of equation 5–1 is again in force such that the last dollar spent on each good generates an equal amount of utility. Thus, an inverse relation exists between the price and the quantity demanded of physician services.

If the price of physician services continually changes, we can determine a number of points representing the relation between the price and the quantity demanded of physician services. Using this information, we can map out a demand curve like the one depicted in figure 5–2, where the horizontal axis indicates the amount of physician services consumed (as measured by the number of visits, for example) and the vertical axis equals the price of physician services. The curve is downward sloping and reflects the inverse relation between the price and the quantity demanded of physician services, *ceteris paribus*. For example, if the price of physician services equals P_0, the consumer is willing and able to purchase q_0. Notice that if the price falls to P_1, the consumer purchases q_1 amount of physician services.

In this case, price represents the per-unit out-of-pocket expense the consumer incurs when purchasing medical services from a physician. As such, it equals the amount the consumer must pay after the impact of third-party payments has been taken into account. Naturally, if the visit to the physician is not covered by a third party, the actual price of the visit equals the out-of-pocket expense.

Another way to illustrate the inverse relation between price and the quantity demanded of physician services is with the substitution and income effects of a price change. Both of these effects predict that a higher price will lead to a smaller quantity demanded and, conversely, a lower price will result in a greater quantity demanded. According to the substitution effect, a decrease in the price of physician services causes the consumer to substitute away from the relatively higher-priced medical goods, such as hospital outpatient services, and purchase more physician services. That is, lower-priced services are substituted for higher-priced ones. As a result, the quantity demanded of physician services increases as price decreases.

According to the income effect, a lower price also increases the real purchasing power of the consumer. Because medical care is assumed to be a normal good (i.e., the quantity demanded of medical services increases with income), the quantity demanded of physician services increases with the rise in purchasing power. That also generates an inverse relation between price and quantity demanded because as price falls, real income increases

FIGURE 5-2
The Individual Demand Curve for Physician Services

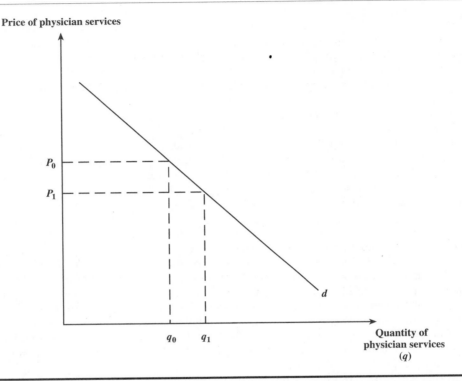

The individual demand curve for physician services is downward sloping, illustrating that quantity demanded increases as the price of physician services drops. Utility analysis, or the income and substitution effects, can be used to derive this inverse relationship, which is called the *law of demand*.

and quantity demanded rises. Taken together, the substitution and income effects indicate that the quantity demanded of physician services decreases as price increases.

In summary, figure 5–2 captures the inverse relationship between the price the consumer pays for medical care (in this instance, physician services) and the quantity demanded. The curve represents the amount of medical care the consumer is willing and able to purchase at every price. Utility analysis, or the income and substitutions effects, can be used to generate this relationship. This inverse relationship is sometimes referred to as the **law of demand**. It is important to note that the demand for medical care is a *derived* demand, because it depends on the demand for good health. A visit to a dentist illustrates this point. An individual receives no utility directly from having a cavity filled. Rather, utility is generated from an improvement in dental health.

Of course, other economic and noneconomic variables also influence the demand for health care. Unlike price, which causes a movement along the demand curve, other factors influence quantity demanded by altering the position of the demand curve. These other economic and noneconomic determinants of demand are the topic of the next section.

Other Economic Demand-Side Factors

Real income is another economic variable that affects the demand for medical services. Because medical care is generally assumed to be a normal good, any increase in real income, which represents an increase in purchasing power, should cause the demand for medical services to rise. Figure 5–3 illustrates what happens to the demand for physician services when real income increases. The increase in income causes the demand curve to shift to the right, from d_0 to d_1, because at each price the consumer is willing and able to purchase more physician services. Similarly, for each quantity of medical services, the consumer is willing to pay a higher price. This is attributable to the fact that at least some portion of

FIGURE 5–3

Shifts in the Individual Demand Curve for Physician Services

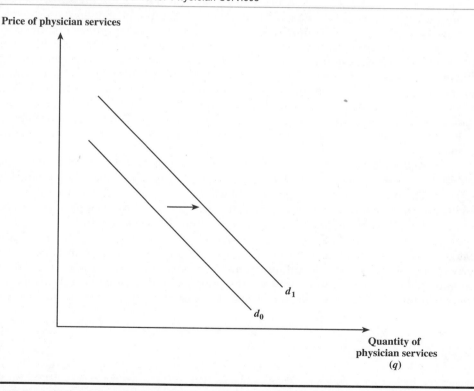

Medical care is assumed to be a normal good, which means that as real income increases the consumer spends at least a portion of the increase in purchasing power on additional physician services. As a result, the individual demand curve for physician services shifts to the right, from d_0 to d_1, when income increases. At each price, the consumer is now willing and able to purchase more physician services.

the increase in income is spent on physician services. Conversely, a decrease in real income causes the demand curve to shift to the left.[3]

The demand for a specific type of medical service is also likely to depend on the prices of other goods, particularly other types of medical services. If two or more goods are jointly used for consumption purposes, economists say that they are *complements* in consumption: Because the goods are consumed together, an increase in the price of one good inversely influences the demand for the other. For example, the demand for eyewear (i.e., glasses or contact lenses) and the services of an optometrist are likely to be highly complementary. Normally, an individual has an eye examination before purchasing eyewear. If these two goods are complements in consumption, the demand for optometric services should increase in response to a drop in the price of eyewear. As a result, the demand curve for optometric services shifts to the right. Another example of a complementary relation exists between obstetric and pediatric services. An increase in the price of pediatric services should inversely influence the demand for obstetric services. If, for example, a woman postpones pregnancy because of the high cost of pediatric services, her demand for obstetric services also falls. The demand curve for obstetric services shifts to the left.

It is also possible for two or more goods to satisfy the same wants or provide the same characteristics. If that is the case, economists say that these goods are *substitutes* in consumption: The demand for one good is directly related to a change in the price of a substitute good. For example, suppose physician services and hospital outpatient services are substitutes in consumption. As the price of outpatient services increases, the consumer is likely to alter consumption patterns and purchase more physician services because the price of a visit to the doctor is cheaper in relative terms. That causes the demand curve for physician services to shift to the right. Generic and brand-name drugs provide another example of two substitute goods. The demand for brand-name drugs should decrease with a decline in the price of generic drugs. If so, the demand curve for brand-name drugs shifts to the left. Finally, eyeglasses and contact lenses are likely to be substitutes in consumption.

Time costs also influence the quantity demanded of medical services. Time costs include the monetary cost of travel, such as bus fare or gasoline, plus the opportunity cost of time. The opportunity cost of an individual's time represents the dollar value of the activities the person forgoes when acquiring medical services. For example, if a plumber who earns $50 an hour takes two hours off from work to visit a dentist, the opportunity cost of the time equals $100. The implication is that the opportunity cost of time is directly related to a person's wage rate. Given time costs, it is not surprising that children and elderly people often fill doctors' waiting rooms. Time costs can accrue while traveling to and from a medical provider, waiting to see the provider, and experiencing delays in securing an appointment. In other words, travel costs increase the farther an individual has to travel

---

[3]Some goods are referred to as *inferior* goods. This is because the demand for these goods decreases as income increases. A classic nonmedical example is hamburger. As real income increases, the consumer may prefer to buy more expensive cuts of meat and purchase less hamburger. In the medical sector, hospital outpatient services may be an example of an inferior good. As income increases, the consumer may prefer to visit a private physician to receive individual care rather than outpatient services. As a result, the demand for outpatient services may decrease as income increases. Some researchers have found that tooth extractions represent an inferior dental service.

to see a physician, the longer the wait at the doctor's office, and the longer the delay in getting an appointment. It stands to reason that the demand for medical care falls as time costs increase (i.e., the demand curve shifts to the left).

The Relationship Between Health Insurance and the Demand for Medical Services

The growth of health insurance coverage is one of the most significant developments in the health care field over the past several decades. It has had a profound influence on the allocation of resources within the medical care market, primarily through its impact on the out-of-pocket prices of health care services. Insight 5–6 illustrates how dramatic this change has been. Out-of-pocket payments for health care dropped from almost half of total expenditures in 1960 to approximately one-sixth in 2000. Even more striking, out-of-pocket payments for hospital care fell from 20.7 percent in 1960 to a mere 3.2 percent in 2000. Given that various features are associated with health insurance policies, it is impossible to discuss the economic implications of each one. Here we will focus on three of the more common features of health insurance policies: coinsurance, indemnity insurance, and deductibles.

Coinsurance.   Many health insurance plans, particularly private plans, have a **coinsurance** component. Coinsurance is different than a copayment. A copayment represents a fixed amount paid by the consumer. Under a coinsurance plan, the consumer pays some fixed percentage of the cost of health care and the insurance carrier picks up the other portion. For example, under a plan with a coinsurance rate of 20 percent (a common arrangement), the consumer pays 20 cents out of every dollar spent on health care and the carrier picks up the remaining 80 cents. As you can imagine, an insurance plan like this one has a significant impact on the demand for health care because it effectively lowers the out-of-pocket price of health care by 80 percent.

Let's begin our discussion of coinsurance coverage by looking at the demand curve for medical care from an alternative perspective. We normally think of the demand curve as revealing the amount of a good that a consumer is willing and able to buy at various prices. However, a demand curve also shows the consumer's willingness to pay (or marginal benefit) for each unit of a good. The negative slope of the curve indicates that the willingness to pay falls as more of the good is consumed due to the law of diminishing marginal utility.

For example, the demand curve d_{WO} (WO = without insurance) in figure 5–4 stands for the consumer's demand or willingness-to-pay curve without insurance coverage. This demand curve reveals that the consumer is willing to pay $50 for the fifth unit of physician services. If $50 is the actual price paid for physician services, the consumer purchases five visits in the process of maximizing utility. Notice, however, that the consumer's willingness to pay for the first four units, as revealed by the demand curve, exceeds the actual price of $50. The difference is referred to as **consumer surplus** and reflects the net benefits received from consuming the physician services.

Now suppose the consumer acquires a health insurance plan that calls for her to pay a certain fraction, C_0, of the actual price, P, of physician services. In this case, the insurance coverage drives a wedge between the willingness to pay and the actual price paid for the physician services. Because this utility-maximizing consumer determines the appropriate amount of physician services to buy by equating her willingness to pay (marginal benefit)

FIGURE 5-4

The Demand Curve for Physician Services with Coinsurance

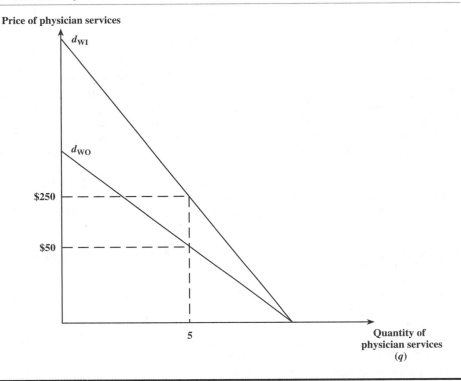

The graph illustrates how a coinsurance health plan impacts the individual demand curve for physician services. The demand curve labeled d_{WO} is the individual's demand without coinsurance while the demand curve labeled d_{WI} is with coinsurance. The demand curve d_{WI} traces out the total price for various quantities of physician services and captures that portion paid by consumers as out-of-pocket payments as well as that portion paid by the insurance carrier. If you draw a vertical line from any point on the d_{WI} curve to the horizontal axis, you can break down the amount paid by consumers (from the horizontal axis to the d_{WO} curve) and the amount paid by the insurance carrier (the wedge between the d_{WI} and d_{WO} curves). As the coinsurance rate falls, d_{WI} rotates upward and pivots off the point where the two curves cross the horizontal axis.

to the out-of-pocket price (marginal cost), the relationship between the actual and out-of-pocket price can be specified by the following equation:

(5–3) $$P_w = C_0 P.$$

Here P_w stands for the consumer's willingness to pay for the last unit, and C_0 represents the coinsurance amount. If we solve equation 5–3 for the actual price, we get

(5–4) $$P = P_w / C_0.$$

Because the coinsurance, C_0, is less than 1, it follows that the actual price paid for medical services is greater than the out-of-pocket price the consumer pays. For example, if she is willing to pay $50 for five visits to a doctor and the coinsurance is 20 percent of the full price, the actual price equals $250 per visit, or $50/.2.

The demand curve labeled d_{WI} (WI = with insurance) in figure 5–4 reflects the total demand curve for medical services that takes into account the coinsurance paid by the insured. The vertical distance between d_{WI} and the horizontal axis represents the total price for units of medical services. That can be broken down into the amount the consumer pays and the amount the insurance carrier pays. The portion of the total price the consumer pays as an out-of-pocket payment equals the distance between the horizontal axis and the d_{WO} demand curve. The remaining distance between the two curves represents the amount the insurance carrier pays. It represents the wedge that coinsurance drives between the consumer's willingness to pay and the total price for medical services.

It is easy to see from this analysis that a reduction in the coinsurance rate causes d_{WI} to rotate clockwise and pivot off the point where d_{WO} crosses the horizontal axis. At a zero willingness-to-pay price, insurance has no bearing on quantity demanded because medical care is a free good to the individual. In addition, d_{WI} becomes steeper as the coinsurance, C_0, decreases in value as indicated by equation 5–4. That makes intuitive sense, because we expect the consumer to become less sensitive to changes in the total price as the coinsurance declines.

In the case where the consumer has full coverage ($C_0 = 0$), the demand curve d_{WI} rotates out to its fullest extent and becomes completely vertical. This is shown in figure 5–5. Because the consumer faces a zero price, she consumes medical care as though it were a free good, when in reality it has a nonzero price. Equation 5–4 can be used to illustrate that point. As C_0 approaches zero, the total price is potentially infinity even when P_w equals zero.

Indemnity Insurance.   With **indemnity insurance**, the insurance carrier pays a fixed amount for each type of medical care purchased. For example, the insurer may pay $150 for each overnight visit to a hospital. If the bill exceeds this amount, the consumer picks up the difference in the form of an out-of-pocket payment. Figure 5–6 shows the impact of indemnity insurance on the demand for health care. Let d represent a linear noninsured demand curve for hospital services and $X the fixed payment received for each overnight stay. The indemnity insurance shifts the demand curve for hospital services upward in a parallel fashion by the amount $X. The new demand curve, d_*, considers the impact of indemnity insurance on the demand for hospital services. An increase in the level of payment, $X, causes the demand curve to shift upward even farther.

Deductibles.   Many insurance policies have a deductible whereby the consumer must pay out of pocket a fixed amount of health care costs per calendar year before coverage begins. For example, the plan may call for the individual to pay the initial $100 of health care expenses with a limit of $400 per family per year. Once the deductible is met, the insurance carrier pays all or some portion of the remaining medical bills, depending on how the plan is specified. From the insurance carrier's perspective, the purpose of a deductible is to lower costs. This is accomplished in two ways.

First, the deductible is likely to lower administrative costs because fewer small claims will be filed over the course of a year. Second, the deductible is likely to have a negative impact on the demand for health care. The extent to which this is true, however, is difficult to determine and depends on such factors as the cost of the medical episode, the point

FIGURE 5–5
The Demand Curve for Physician Services with 100 Percent Coverage

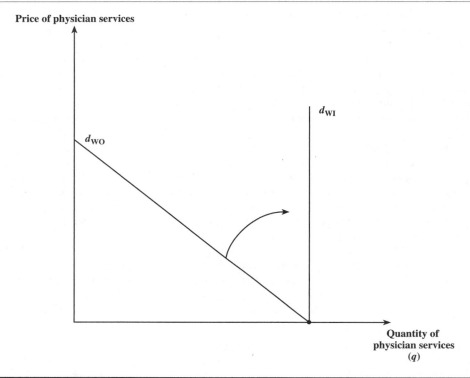

The graph illustrates the situation where the individual has complete medical coverage and the coinsurance rate is zero. Notice that the d_{WI} curve is vertical because the individual faces a zero out-of-pocket price and consumes physician services as if they were free.

in time when the medical care is demanded, and the probability of needing additional medical care for the remainder of the period. To illustrate, assume a new deductible is put in place at the beginning of each calendar year and once the deductible is met, the consumer has full medical coverage. It is easy to see that the extent to which a deductible influences the demand for medical services for any one medical episode is likely to be inversely related to the cost of the medical services involved. For example, if the consumer faces a potentially large medical bill for an operation, the existence of a deductible is likely to have little impact on demand. This is because in relative terms, the deductible represents very little money. On the other hand, a deductible may play a crucial role in the decision to purchase medical care if the cost of such care is relatively inexpensive. In this case, the out-of-pocket cost is substantial relative to the total cost, and the consumer may elect not to purchase the medical care or postpone the purchase to a later date.

It is slightly more difficult to understand how the health of the individual, along with the time of the year, influences the impact of a deductible on demand. The best way to explain this is with an example. Consider a normally healthy individual who contracts the flu

---

F I G U R E   5 – 6

The Demand Curve for Hospital Services with Indemnity Insurance

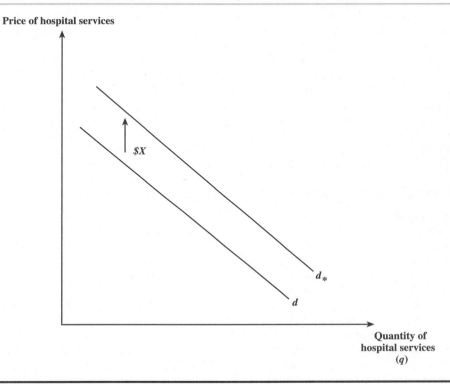

The individual demand curve shifts upwards in a parallel fashion, from *d* to *d**, with indemnity insurance of $X. The vertical distance between the two curves of amount $X represents the fixed payment received for hospital services purchased.

---

late in November and has incurred no medical expenses up to this point. Under these circumstances, he may be less inclined to visit the doctor. This is because he will have little opportunity to take advantage of the fact that health care is a free good after he makes his initial visit to the physician and fulfills the deductible. On the other hand, this same individual is much more likely to visit the physician if he catches the flu early in February and his overall health is such that he can expect to visit the physician three or four more times over the remainder of the year. By visiting the doctor and meeting the deductible, he lowers the cost of any future visits to zero for the rest of the year. Therefore, a deductible is likely to have the greatest negative impact on the demand for medical care when the cost of the medical episode is low, the need for care is late in the calendar year, and the probability of needing future care is slight because the person is in good health.

Moral Hazard

Before we leave the subject of the impact of insurance on the demand for medical care, we need to introduce the concept of moral hazard. **Moral hazard** refers to the situation where consumers alter their behavior when provided with health insurance. For example, health insurance may induce consumers to take fewer precautions to prevent illnesses or to shop very little for the best medical prices. In response to health insurance, consumers may act in a way that leads to an increase in the consumption of medical care. Let's illustrate this point by referring to figure 5–4. According to the graph, a consumer without insurance purchases five units of medical services at a price of $50 per unit. If that consumer acquires full medical coverage such that the insurer's coinsurance rate, C_0, equals zero, the quantity demanded of medical care increases to the point where the demand curve crosses the horizontal axis. At this point, the consumer consumes medical care as though it were a free good because she faces a zero price. Thus, any extension of medical insurance coverage has the potential to increase the consumption of medical care because consumers no longer pay the full price. The availability and extensiveness of health insurance may have a profound effect on medical care expenditures. Chapter 11 examines the implications of moral hazard in more detail in a discussion of the private health insurance industry.

Noneconomic Determinants of the Demand for Medical Services

Four general noneconomic factors influence the demand for medical services: tastes and preferences, physical and mental profile, state of health, and quality of care.

Taste and preference factors include such personal characteristics as marital status, education, and lifestyle, which might affect how people value their healthy time (i.e., their marginal utility of health), or might lead to a greater preference for certain types of medical services. Marital status is likely to impact the demand for health care in the marketplace primarily through its effect on the production of health care in the home. A married individual is likely to demand less medical care, particularly hospital care, because of the availability of a spouse to care for him at home, such as when recuperating from an illness.

The impact of education on the demand for medical care in the marketplace is difficult to predict. On the one hand, a consumer with additional education may be more willing to seek medical care to slow down the rate of health depreciation because that consumer may have a better understanding of the potential impact of medical care on health. As an example, an individual with a high level of education may be more inclined to visit a dentist for periodic examinations. Thus, we should observe a direct relation between educational attainment and demand.

On the other hand, an individual with a high level of education may make more efficient use of home-produced health care services to slow down the rate of health depreciation and, as a result, demand less medical care services in the marketplace. For example, such an individual may be more likely to understand the value of preventive medicine (e.g., proper diet, exercise). In addition, the individual may be more likely to recognize the early warning signs of illness and be more apt to visit a health care provider when symptoms first occur. As a result, health care problems are addressed early when treatment has a greater probability of success and is less costly. That means that we should observe an inverse relation between the level of education and the demand for medical care, particularly acute care.

Finally, lifestyle variables, such as whether the individual smokes cigarettes or drinks alcohol in excessive amounts, affect health status and consequently the amount of health care demanded. For example, a person may try to compensate for the detrimental health impact of smoking by consuming more health care services. That translates into an increased demand for medical care.

INSIGHT 5-1

Did Cinderella Have Routine Visits to the Doctor?

In Chapter 2 we learned that family structure plays an important role in the production of health. But, how does family structure impact the demand for medical care? Case and Paxson (2001) provided some answers to this question when they examined whether there was any relationship between the number of routine medical visits for a child and whether that child resided with his or her biological mother. While this is not a demand study in the traditional sense because the authors did not include a price variable in the estimated equation, it is interesting and sheds light on the factors that impact the amount of health care consumed by children. In the analysis, the dependent variable was whether the child had a routine visit with a doctor in the past year. A host of independent variables were included in the analysis to control for the impact of socioeconomic status and other important factors on the consumption of medical care. For example, the authors consider the child's age, household income, and household size, along with the age, education, and work status of the parents. Also included were the age of the mother when she had the child and the gender and race of the child. Most important, the authors included several variables to control for family structure.

The results are intriguing and suggest that family structure impacts medical investments in children's health. The authors found that children living with adoptive mothers or foster parents were more likely to have a routine visit with a physician than those children living with their biological mothers. However, children living with stepmothers were found to be 8 percent less likely to visit a doctor when compared to children residing with their birth mothers. The authors also delved into the issue of whether stepchildren who had regular contact with their birth mothers were more likely to receive routine care than those who did not interact with their birth mothers on a regular basis. The study found that those stepchildren who had regular contact with their birth mothers received routine care at the same level as those living with their birth mothers. The same cannot be said for those stepchildren who did not have regular contact with their biological mothers. Stepchildren without regular contact with their biological mother were found to be significantly less likely to have had a routine visit with a physician, visit a dentist, or have a regular health care provider to acquire regular or sick care. Cinderella was surely lucky to have been swept away by Prince Charming!

The *profile* variable considers the impact of such factors as gender, race/ethnicity, and age on the demand for medical services. For example, females generally demand more health care services than males primarily because of childbearing. In addition, certain diseases, such as cardiovascular disease, osteoporosis, immunologic diseases (e.g., thyroid disease and rheumatoid arthritis), mental disorders, and Alzheimer's disease, are more prevalent in women than men (Miller, 1994). Age also plays a vital role in determining the demand for medical care. As we stated in Chapter 2, as an individual ages, the overall stock of health begins to depreciate. To compensate for this loss in health, the demand for medical care is likely to increase with age, at least beyond the middle years (the demand curve shifts to the right). Thus, we should observe a direct relation between age and the demand for medical care.

State of health controls for the fact that sicker people demand more medical services, everything else held constant. As you might expect, health status and the demand for health care are also likely to be directly related to the severity of the illness. For example, a person who is born with a medical problem, such as hemophilia, is likely to have a much higher than average demand for medical care. In economics jargon, an individual who is endowed with less health is likely to demand more health care in an attempt to augment the overall stock of health.

Finally, although nebulous and impossible to quantify, the *quality of care* is also likely to impact the demand for medical care. Because quality cannot be measured directly, it is usually assumed to be positively related to the amount and types of inputs used to produce medical care. Feldstein (1967, pp. 158–62) defines the quality of care as "a catch-all term to denote the general level of amenities to patients as well as additional expenditures on professional staff and equipment." For example, a consumer may feel that larger hospitals provide better quality care than smaller ones because they have more specialists on staff along with more sophisticated equipment. Or, that same individual may think that physicians who have graduated from prestigious medical schools provide a higher quality of care than those who have not. It matters little whether the difference in the quality of medical care provided is real or illusory. What matters is that the consumer perceives differences in quality actually exist.

With regard to the previous example, it is certainly not the case that larger hospitals provide better care for all types of hospital services. However, if the consumer generally feels that larger hospitals provide better services, the demand for medical services at larger hospitals will be higher than at smaller ones. As Feldstein's definition indicates, quality can also depend upon things that have little to do with the actual production of effective medical care. For example, the consumer may have a preference for a physician who has a pleasant office with a comfortable waiting room along with courteous nurses. Thus, any increase in the quality of care provided is likely to increase that consumer's demand for medical care regardless of whether it affects the actual production of health care.

Before we move on, we must make a distinction between a movement along the demand curve and a shift of the curve. A change in the price of medical services generates a change in the quantity demanded, and this is represented by a movement along the demand curve. If any of the other factors change, such as income or time costs, the demand curve for medical services shifts. This shift is referred to as a change in demand. Thus, a change in the quantity demanded is illustrated by a movement along the demand curve, while a change in demand is illustrated by a shift of the curve.

In summary, let's review the variables we expect to influence an individual's demand for medical care. Economic theory indicates that the demand equation should look something like the following:

(5–5)   Quantity   = *f*(out-of-pocket price, real income, time costs, prices of
          demanded   substitutes and complements, tastes and preferences,
                             profile, state of health, and quality of care)

Equation 5–5 states that the quantity demanded of medical services is a function of, or depends upon, the general factors listed.

The Market Demand for Health Care

Up to now, we have been discussing the individual's demand for medical care services. The market demand for medical care, such as physician services, equals the total demand by all consumers in a given market. In graphical terms, we can construct the market demand curve for medical care services by horizontally summing the individual demand curves. This curve represents the amount of medical services that the entire market is willing and able to purchase at every given price. For example, if the average price of a visit to a doctor is $50 and at this price consumer A is willing to see a physician three times over the course of a year while consumer B is willing to make four visits, the total, or market, demand for physician services is seven visits per year at $50 per visit. The market demand curve is downward sloping for the same reasons the individual demand curves are downward sloping. In addition, the factors that shift the individual demand curves also shift the overall market demand curve, providing the changes take place on a marketwide basis. The market demand curve also shifts if the overall number of consumers in the market increases or decreases. For example, the demand for medical care in a particular community may increase if an influx of new residents occurs. This causes the market demand curve to shift to the right.

The Fuzzy Demand Curve

Up to this point, we have assumed the market demand curve for medical care is a well-defined line, implying a precise relation between price and quantity demanded. In reality this is usually not the case, and we need to refer to the derivation of the demand curve for medical care to see why. Recall that the demand for medical care is a derived demand and depends on the demand for health and the extent to which medical care influences the production of health. The relation between medical care and health, however, is far from exact. That is because there is a considerable lack of medical knowledge concerning the efficacy of certain types of medical interventions. As a result, health care providers disagree about the treatment of some types of medical problems, and the demand for medical services becomes fuzzy. For example, there is debate among physicians concerning when surgery is necessary for elderly males with prostate cancer.

In addition, in some instances consumers may lack the information or medical knowledge they need to make informed choices. Consequently, consumers tend to rely heavily on the advice of their physicians when making such decisions as when a particular medical test or surgery is necessary. The implication is that physicians rather than consumers choose medical services, which makes the demand curve fuzzier. Further complicating matters is the inability to accurately measure medical care, an issue we touched on earlier. For example, how do we measure the quantity of medical care produced during a one-hour therapy session with a psychiatrist?

All these factors combined make it extremely difficult to accurately delineate the relation between the price and the quantity demanded of medical care. In other words, the relation between price and quantity demanded is rather fuzzy (Aaron, 1991). A more accurate depiction of the relation between price and quantity may not be a well-defined line but a gray band similar to the one depicted in figure 5–7.

Two implications are associated with the fuzzy demand curve. First, for a given price, we may observe some variation in the quantity or types of medical services rendered. Indeed, researchers have documented variations in physician practice styles across

FIGURE 5-7
The Fuzzy Demand Curve for Medical Care

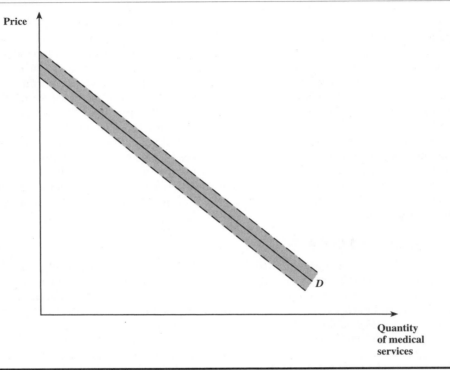

The gray band represents the possible fuzziness of the demand for medical services given uncertainty and the role of the physician.

geographical areas (e.g., Phelps, 1992); we take up that discussion in Chapter 12. Second, for a given quantity or type of medical service, we are likely to witness price differences. For example, Feldstein (1988) reported a substantial variation in physician fees for similar procedures in the same geographical area. We must stress, however, that the existence of the band is unlikely to detract from the inverse relation between the price and the quantity demanded of medical care as suggested by the empirical evidence that follows.

ELASTICITIES

Economic theory gives us insights into the factors that influence the demand for medical care, along with the direction of their influence. For example, we know that if the price of physician services increases by 15 percent, the quantity demanded falls. But by how much does it fall? Is there any way to determine whether the decrease is substantial or negligible? The answer is yes, with the help of a measure economists call an *elasticity*. Elasticity measures the responsiveness of quantity demanded to a change in an independent factor.

INSIGHT 5-2

Substitutes or Complements? The Demand for Traditional and Western Medicine in Taiwan

The price of related goods plays a critical role in establishing the demand for medical goods and services. If two goods are complements in consumption then the cross-price elasticity is negative and an increase in the price of one good will cause a decrease in demand for the other good. On the other hand, if the two goods are substitutes in consumption then the cross-price elasticity is positive and an increase in the price of one product will stimulate an increase in the demand for the other product.

Yen, Tang, and Su (2001) provide an interesting application of the theory of demand when they tested whether modern Western medicine and Chinese medicine are considered substitutes in consumption by Taiwanese. In a nutshell, Western medicine is the application of the scientific method to medicine, while traditional Chinese medicine is best known for "acupuncture and the use of herbal medicine" (p. 221). The data were from a 1992 medical survey in Taiwan and the dependent variable in the estimated equation was the number of visits to a physician practicing Chinese medicine during the month prior to the survey. The estimated equation included a host of explanatory variables that controlled for health, insurance coverage, lifestyle, and demographic attributes. Also included in the equation were two price variables: one measure for the price of Chinese medicine and the other for the price of Western medicine. Demand theory suggests that the parameter estimate for the price of Chinese medicine should be negative because quantity demanded should be inversely related to price. The sign on the parameter estimate for the price of Western medicine is the primary focus of the study. If the parameter estimate is positive, then Chinese and Western medicine can be considered substitutes in consumption; as the price of Western medicine increases so does the demand for more traditional Chinese medicine. On the other hand, if the parameter estimate is negative the two schools of medicine could be considered complements in consumption. An increase in the price of Western medicine causes the demand for traditional Chinese medicine to decrease.

According to the empirical results, the parameter estimate on the price variable for Chinese medicine was negative, as expected, and statistically significant. The authors also found the parameter estimate on the price of Western medicine to be positive and significant, leading one to the conclusion that Chinese and Western medicine are considered substitutes in consumption by Taiwanese. Because the cross-price elasticity is relatively low in magnitude, however, the authors point out that the degree of substitution may be rather small.

Own-Price Elasticity of Demand

The most common elasticity is the **own-price elasticity of demand**. This measure gauges the extent to which consumers alter their consumption of a good or service when its own price changes. The formula looks like this:

(5–6) $$E_D = \%\Delta Q_D / \%\Delta P,$$

where E_D denotes the price elasticity of demand, $\%\Delta Q_D$ represents the percentage change in quantity demanded, and $\%\Delta P$ is the percentage change in price. As you can see from the formula, E_D is a simple ratio that equals the percentage change in quantity demanded divided by the percentage change in price. Because elasticity is specified as a ratio of two percentage changes, it is scale free. This makes it much easier to compare elasticities across different goods. For example, we can compare the price elasticity of demand for physician services with that for nursing home care and not have to concern ourselves with the fact that the demand for physician services is usually measured in terms of the number of visits while the demand for nursing home care is measured in terms of the number of inpatient days.[4]

The value of E_D is negative and reflects the inverse relationship between price and quantity demanded. In economics, the normal practice is to take the absolute value of the price elasticity of demand measure, or $|E_D|$, and eliminate the minus sign. If the price elasticity of demand is greater than 1 in absolute terms ($|E_D| > 1$), the demand for the product is referred to as **price elastic**. In arithmetic terms, $|E_D| > 1$ if the absolute value of the percentage change in price is smaller than the absolute value of the change in the quantity demanded, or $|\%\Delta P| < |\%\Delta Q_D|$. For example, if the price elasticity of demand for dental services equals 1.2, this means the quantity consumed falls by 12 percent if the price of dental care increases by 10 percent, *ceteris paribus*.

The price elasticity of demand is referred to as **inelastic** if $|E_D| < 1$ but greater than zero. In this case, $|\%\Delta P| > |\%\Delta Q_D|$, or the percentage change in price is greater than the percentage in quantity demanded in absolute value terms. For example, if the elasticity of demand for physician services equals .6, a 10 percent decrease in price leads to a 6 percent increase in quantity demanded. If $|E_D|$ happens to equal 1 because $|\%\Delta P|$ equals $|\%\Delta Q_D|$, the price elasticity of demand is **unit elastic**. This implies that a 10 percent decrease in the price of the product leads to a 10 percent increase in the quantity demanded.

A demand curve that is vertical is said to be **perfectly inelastic** because no change occurs in the quantity demanded when the price changes. In mathematical terms, E_D equals zero because $\%\Delta Q_D$ equals zero. At the other extreme, if the demand curve is horizontal, it is referred to as being **perfectly elastic** and $|E_D|$ equals infinity (∞). Any change in price leads to an infinite change in the quantity demanded.

It stands to reason that the more elastic the demand for the product, the greater the response of quantity to a given change in price. Compare the effects of a 10 percent decrease in price on two goods—one with a price elasticity of $-.1$ and another with a price elasticity of -2.6. In the first case, the quantity demanded increases by only 1 percent, while in the second case, it increases by 26 percent. We can also use the elasticity of demand to make inferences regarding the slope of the demand curve. Generally, the more elastic the demand for the product, the flatter the demand curve at any given price. This also means the curve is relatively steep at any given point for an inelastic demand. Consider the two linear demand curves that intersect at point P_0, Q_0 in figure 5–8. If the price of the product increases to P_1, the quantity demanded decreases to Q_a off the flat curve (D_a) and to Q_b off the steep curve (D_b). Therefore, the same percentage increase in price generates a

---

[4]The *point elasticity* formula can be used to actually calculate the elasticity of demand if the changes in the variables are small. The formula equals $(\Delta Q_D/Q_D)/(\Delta P/P)$. For readers with a background in calculus, it equals $(dQ_D/Q_D)/(dP/P)$ if the changes are infinitesimally small.

FIGURE 5 – 8

The Elasticity of Demand and the Slope of the Demand Curve

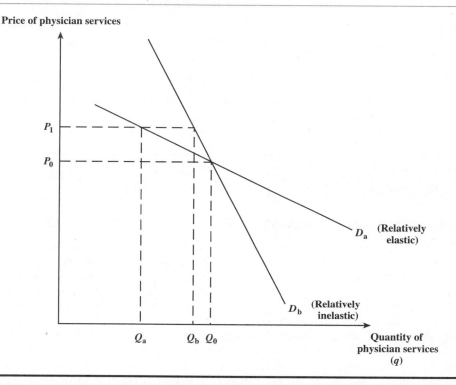

The steep demand curve, D_b, is relatively inelastic and illustrates that an increase in price from P_0 to P_1 generates only a modest decrease in quantity demanded from Q_0 to Q_b. The flatter demand curve, D_a, is relatively elastic and, in this case, the same increase in price for P_0 to P_1 generates a much larger decrease in quantity demanded from Q_0 to Q_a.

smaller percentage decrease in the quantity demanded for the steeper curve D_b than for the flatter curve D_a at a similar price of P_0. This means demand must be more price elastic for curve D_a than for curve D_b over the range P_0 to P_1. Table 5–1 summarizes our discussion thus far on price elasticity of demand.

The own-price elasticity of demand varies greatly across products, and economists point to several factors that determine its value. Among the factors most often mentioned are the portion of the consumer's budget allocated to the good, the amount of time involved in the purchasing decision, the extent to which the good is a necessity, and the availability of substitutes. Briefly, as the portion of a consumer's budget allocated to a good increases, the consumer is likely to become much more sensitive to price changes. Demand should therefore become more elastic. An increase in the decision-making time frame is also likely to make demand more elastic. If the consumer has more time to make informed choices, he or she is likely to react more strongly to price changes. Because the consumer typically pays a small portion of the cost of medical services because of insurance, and

TABLE 5–1
A Summary of the Own-Price Elasticity of Demand

Perfectly Inelastic	Inelastic	Unitary	Elastic	Perfectly Elastic
$\lvert E_D \rvert = 0$	$0 < \lvert E_D \rvert < 1$	$\lvert E_D \rvert = 1$	$1 < \lvert E_D \rvert < \infty$	$\lvert E_D \rvert = \infty$
$\%\Delta Q_D = 0$	$\lvert \%\Delta Q_D \rvert < \lvert \%\Delta P \rvert$	$\lvert \%\Delta Q_D \rvert = \lvert \%\Delta P \rvert$	$\lvert \%\Delta Q_D \rvert > \lvert \%\Delta P \rvert$	$\%\Delta Q_D = \infty$

INSIGHT 5 – 3

Those Pointy-Headed Economists

McMenamin (1990) questions whether the theory of demand can be realistically applied to health care. He asks, "If patients' demand for health care services were responsive to price, at a price sufficiently low such patients should be expected to ask for two or more, say, appendectomies." Because many health care purchases, such as operations, are one-time events, it seems absurd to think that price plays a role in the decision. Do economists deserve their reputation for being pointy-headed?

As McMenamin points out, the idea that consumers respond to the price of health care is not as absurd as you might imagine if you consider the fact that decisions to purchase health care take place at either the intensive or the extensive margin. Most of the time, economists focus on the intensive nature of demand. Thus, as the price of a product falls, consumers purchase more of it, or consume it more intensively. That is basically the approach we have taken in this chapter. For example, as the price of physician services falls, consumers visit their physicians more frequently—that is, use their services more intensively.

To explain many of the "one-shot" purchases that take place on an either-or basis in health care, economists rely on the notion of the *extensive demand* for a product. Although each individual consumer can elect to purchase certain types of health care only once, in the aggregate more consumers may elect to purchase that particular type of health care if its price falls. Therefore, we may still observe an inverse relationship between price and quantity demanded. For example, an individual can have a particular tooth pulled only once. This is a one-shot purchase that either happens or does not happen. If the price of tooth extractions falls, however, we may still observe an inverse relationship between the price and number of teeth extracted. That is because at the extensive margin, more consumers elect to purchase this one-time form of dental service as price falls.

Thus, the notion of using traditional demand theory to explain the role of price in the consumption of health care is less absurd than it first appears. It seems that economists are not as pointy-headed as many imagine.

because medical services are sometimes of an urgent nature, these two considerations suggest that in many cases, the demand for medical services is inelastic with respect to price.

If a good is a necessity, such as a basic foodstuff, the own-price elasticity should be relatively inelastic. The product is purchased with little regard for price because it is needed. Basic phone service might be considered another example of a necessity. Because our society depends so heavily on the phone as a form of communication, it is difficult to imagine a household functioning effectively without one. Naturally, basic health care falls into the same category. If an individual needs a particular medical service, such as an operation or a drug, and if not having it greatly affects the quality of life, we can expect that person's demand to be inelastic with respect to price. In addition, when a person needs a particular medical service in a life-or-death situation, demand is likely to be perfectly inelastic because the medical service must be purchased regardless of price if the person has sufficient income.

Given that many medical services are necessities, we expect the overall demand for medical services to be somewhat inelastic. A word of caution, however: This does not mean the amount of health care demanded does not react to changes in price. Rather, it means a given percentage change in price generates a small percentage change in the quantity demanded of medical services. For some types of medical care, however, demand may be more elastic. Elective medical care, such as cosmetic surgery, may fall into this category, because in most instances it is considered a luxury rather than a necessity. As a result, price may play an important role in the decision to have the surgery. To a lesser degree, dentist services and eyewear might fall into this category. In fact, any medical service that can be postponed is likely to display some degree of price elasticity.

The availability of substitutes is another determinant of price elasticity. As we saw earlier, various types of medical services may serve as substitutes for one another. The larger the number of substitutes, the greater the opportunity to do some comparison shopping. As a result, the quantity demanded of any medical service is likely to be more sensitive to price changes when alternative means of acquiring medical care are available. The own-price elasticity of demand for any given product should be directly related to the number of substitutes available. Stated another way, demand should become more price elastic as the number of substitutes expands. One implication is that the demand for an individual medical service or an individual medical care provider is likely to be more elastic than the overall demand for medical care.

One more point concerning the elasticity of demand needs to be discussed before we leave this subject. The own-price elasticity of demand can be used to predict what happens to total health expenditures if price increases or decreases. Total revenues (or total expenditures, from the consumer's perspective) equal price times quantity. In mathematical notation,

(5–7) $$\text{TR} = PQ_D,$$

where TR represents total revenue. Demand theory tells us that as the price of a product increases, the quantity demanded decreases, or that P and Q_D move in opposite directions. Whether total revenue increases or decreases when the price changes is dictated by the relative rates at which both variables change, or the elasticity of demand. Consider an increase in the price of physician services where demand is inelastic. This means that $\mid \%\Delta Q_D \mid\ <\ \mid \%\Delta P \mid$, or that the percentage increase in price is larger than the percentage decrease in quantity demanded in absolute value terms. In terms of equation 5–7, P increases faster than Q_D falls. This means total revenue must increase with a higher price. If demand happens to be elastic, the opposite occurs: Quantity demanded falls faster than price increases, and, as a result, total revenue decreases. No change occurs in total revenue when demand is unitary because the increase in price is matched by the same percentage decrease in quantity demanded. We leave it to you to work out the implications of a price decrease on total revenue when demand is elastic, inelastic, and unitary.

Other Types of Elasticity

The concept of elasticity can be used to measure the sensitivity of quantity demanded to other demand-side factors as well. The **income elasticity of demand** represents the percentage change in quantity demanded divided by the percentage change in income, or $E_Y = \%\Delta Q_D / \%\Delta Y$, where $\%\Delta Y$ equals the percentage change in real income. It quantifies the extent to which the demand for a product changes when real income changes. If E_Y is positive, the good is referred to as a *normal good* because any increase in real income leads to an increase in quantity demanded. For example, if E_Y equals .78, this means a 10 percent increase in income causes the quantity consumed to increase by 7.8 percent. An *inferior good* is one for which E_Y is negative and an increase in income leads to a decrease in the amount consumed. For most types of medical care, the income elasticity of demand should be larger than zero.

The **cross-price elasticity** (E_C) measures the extent to which the demand for a product changes when the price of another good is altered. In mathematical terms, $E_C = \%\Delta Q_X / \%\Delta P_Z$, where the numerator represents the percentage change in the demand for good X and the denominator equals the percentage change in the price of good Z. If E_C is negative, we can infer that the two goods are complements in consumption. Returning to our earlier example, the cross-price elasticity between the demand for optometric services and the price of eyewear should be negative. If the price of eyewear increases, the demand for optometric services should drop. Two goods are substitutes in consumption when the cross-price elasticity is positive. For example, the cross-price elasticity of the demand for physician services with respect to the price of hospital outpatient services may turn out to be positive. Naturally, if E_C equals zero, the demand for the product is independent of the price of the other product.

EMPIRICAL ESTIMATION

Numerous studies have attempted to empirically quantify how various factors influence the demand for medical care. Although the studies varied widely in terms of methodology and scope of analysis, certain broad conclusions emerged. Generally, some form of equation 5–5 was estimated with the use of regression analysis. Unfortunately, the dependent variable representing the amount of medical services consumed is very difficult to measure. Ideally, quantity demanded should capture both the utilization and the intensity of medical services. Data of these kinds are unavailable, so usually only some utilization measure, such as number of physician visits or hospital patient days, is used to measure the quantity demanded of medical services. Proxy variables are then included as independent variables to control for variations in quality. A failure to properly control for quality biases the results. That is because changes in demand may be attributed to changes

INSIGHT 5 – 4

An International Look at the Relationship Between Income and Health Care Spending

A group of researchers has looked at the relation between real income and health care expenditures to ascertain how economic growth impacts national health care expenditures. This is generally done by regressing real per capita health expenditures on some measure of real per capita income along with a number of other control variables. The samples usually include most of the more developed countries of the world. The estimates are then used to calculate the aggregate income elasticity, which gives the extent to which health care expenditures increase as national income expands.

The intercountry estimates suggest that the aggregate income elasticity generally approaches or exceeds +1.0. For example, Newhouse (1977) finds the income elasticity to range between 1.13 and 1.31, while Parkin et al. (1987) estimate the rate to be slightly below +1. Finally, Leu (1986) and Gerdtham et al. (1992) agree with Newhouse and find the aggregate income elasticity to be above one. The intercountry income elasticity estimates are in direct contrast to intracountry estimates. Income elasticity estimates for the United States are generally well below +1.0. This difference is interesting and deserves explanation. According to Newhouse, the difference exists because, for example, within the United States at any point in time the average consumer pays only a small portion of the price of medical care (approximately 15 percent in 2000), while over time the country as a whole must pay the full price of health care. As the out-of-pocket price of health care falls for the average consumer, the income elasticity should also fall because the consumer is less conscious of price. For example, if the out-of-pocket price of health care falls to zero, then the average individual is going to consume health care regardless of income. The income elasticity in the extreme equals zero. The country as a whole, however, must face the entire burden of the cost of health care and, as a result, is going to be much more sensitive to price and income.

One of the more interesting questions concerning this research has to do with whether health care is a luxury good. Economists define a luxury good as one that has an income elasticity above +1.0. In this case, an increase in income leads to an even larger increase in the quantity consumed of the good. For example, assume that the income elasticity of a good equals 1.5. A 10 percent increase in income leads to a 15 percent increase in consumption of the good. Naturally, this means that the portion of one's budget allocated to the consumption of the good also increases with income.

If the aggregate income elasticity of health care is above +1.0, this may provide a demand-side explanation as to why health care expenditures in the United States as a portion of GDP have increased over the past few decades. As the U.S. economy grew over the past few decades and real per capita income expanded, the nation allocated a greater portion of GDP health care because it is a luxury good. Consequently, the health care sector received a larger and larger slice of the economic pie. A simple example will illustrate that point. Let's assume that a fictitious country with 100 inhabitants has a GDP of $1 million and a per capita income of $10,000. Let's also assume that the aggregate income elasticity equals 1.2, and this country presently spends 10 percent of its income on health care

(continued)

services ($100,000). Now, let's assume that per capita income grows by 20 percent ($12,000) over the next five years and the size of the population remains constant. GDP would equal $1.2 million, while expenditures on health care services would expand to $124,000. That represents 10.33 percent of GDP, or an increase of one-third of a percent in just five years.

in other variables when in fact they are the result of differences in the quality of care provided.

The measurement of the out-of-pocket price of medical care also presents a problem for economists. This problem has become more severe in recent years given the increasing role of third-party payers. In a perfect world, the out-of-pocket price of medical services should equal the amount the consumer pays after the impact of insurance has been considered. Unfortunately, such data are rarely available, and economists often have to resort to using such variables as the average price of medical services rendered. An additional variable is then included in the equation to control for the presence of health insurance. The price variable should negatively affect the demand for medical care, while the presence of insurance should positively influence quantity demanded.

A real income variable is included to capture the impact of purchasing power on demand, while time cost variables control for the effects of travel and waiting costs on demand. We expect the real income variable to have a positive effect on demand and the time cost variables to have a negative impact. The prices of various substitutes and complements in consumption should also be included in the regression equation. This has become even more important in recent years as medical markets have become more interrelated. For example, if we are trying to assess the quantity demanded of inpatient services at a hospital, we should control for the prices of hospital outpatient services (potentially a substitute service) and physician services (potentially a complementary service). The remaining factors (tastes and preferences, rate of health depreciation, stock of health, and quality of care) are referred to as *control variables* and capture the impact that various noneconomic factors may have on the demand for health care services. Theoretically, a change in any one of these independent factors should affect the demand for medical care.

Own-Price, Income, Cross-Price, and Time Cost Elasticity Estimates

In general, the literature has found that the demand for primary care services is price inelastic. For example, Newhouse and the Insurance Experiment Group (1993) found the overall own-price elasticity for medical care to be –.22, while Eichner (1998) estimated it to lie between –.62 and –.75. Although the estimates vary, they tend to be in the –.1 to –.7 range. In more specific terms, Manning et al. (1987) estimated the own-price elasticity of hospital admissions to lie between –.1 and –.2, while Cromwell and Mitchell (1986) found the own-price elasticity for total and elective surgery to be –.14 and –.17, respectively. To round things out, Stano (1985) found the price elasticity of physician visits to equal –.06. Taken as a whole, the estimates suggest that a 10 percent increase in the out-of-pocket price of hospital or physician services leads to a 1 to 7 percent decrease in the quantity demanded. The inelastic estimates also imply that total expenditures on hospital and physician services increase with a greater out-of-pocket price, *ceteris paribus*.[5]

In general, the research indicates that the demand for other types of medical care is slightly more price elastic than the demand for primary care. That is not at all surprising given that the percentage of out-of-pocket payments is the lowest for hospital and physician services (see Insight 5–6). Everything else held constant, consumers should become more price sensitive as the portion of the bill paid out of pocket increases. For example, Manning and Phelps (1979) found the demand for dental services to be slightly more price elastic and to vary by type of service provided and the sex and age of the patient. The price elasticity of demand for dental services by adult females appears to vary between –.5 and –.7, and the demand for dental services by adult males and children seems to be slightly more price elastic. The demand for nursing home services also appears to be more price elastic than primary medical services. Chiswick (1976) found the own-price elasticity for nursing home services to be between –.73 and –2.40, and Lamberton, Ellingson, and Spear (1986) estimated that it equals –.76. Finally, Headen (1993) found the own-price elasticity for the probability of entering a nursing home to be –.7.

Overall, the empirical evidence indicates that health care is a normal good with an income elasticity below +1.0. Time costs also appear to have a significant impact on the demand for medical services. In fact, research indicates that the travel time elasticity of demand is approximately equal to the own-price elasticity of demand. According to Acton (1975) and Phelps and Newhouse (1974), the travel time elasticity of demand ranges from –.14 to –.51. Using a data set generated in the United Kingdom, Gravelle, Dusheiko, and Sutton (2002) found elasticity of admissions with respect to distance to equal –.35. Taken together, these studies suggest that a 10 percent increase in travel time reduces the quantity demanded for medical services by roughly 3 percent. It also appears that consumers place a value on the time spent waiting for medical services. McCarthy (1985) found the wait time elasticity to range from –.36 to –1.14, while Martin and Smith (1999) found it to equal –.20. In addition, Gravelle, Dusheiko, and Sutton (2002) estimated the elasticity of admissions with respect to waiting time to equal –.25. Time costs also influence the decision to acquire medical care; Frank et al. (1995) found the elasticity of travel time costs on the probability of a timely completion of childhood immunization to be roughly –.08.

The extent to which various types of medical services serve as substitutes or complements in consumption is not clear at this time. For example, there appears to be little consensus as to whether inpatient and outpatient hospital services are substitutes or complements. Davis and Russell (1972) found that the cross-price elasticity between the price of inpatient services and number of outpatient visits to vary between .85 and 1.46, indicating that they are substitutes. These results were later qualitatively confirmed by Gold (1984). Thus, as the price of inpatient services at a hospital increases, consumers rely more on outpatient services to save money. Freiberg and Scutchfield (1976), on the other hand, found that no substitution occurs between these two types of hospital services. At the other extreme, Manning et al. (1987) suggested that they are complements in

---

[5]Here is an abbreviated list of selected results from other studies. Davis and Russell (1972) found price elasticity for outpatient visits to equal –1.0 and inpatient visits to vary between –.32 and –.46; Phelps and Newhouse (1974) found the elasticity of demand for physician visits to equal –.14; and Feldman and Dowd (1986) found the price elasticity of demand for patient days to vary between –.74 and –.80 and admissions to equal –1.1.

consumption. A similar debate in the literature concerns whether physician and hospital inpatient or outpatient services are substitutes or complements.

The Impact of Insurance on the Demand for Medical Services

The growth of health insurance, both public and private, has had a profound impact on the demand for health care. Instead of reviewing the results from the many studies that analyzed the impact of insurance on the demand for health care, we will focus on a study conducted by the RAND Corporation (Manning et al., 1987). The RAND Health Insurance Study (HIS) is without doubt the most comprehensive study to date. Families from six sites (Dayton, Ohio; Seattle, Washington; Fitchburg, Massachusetts; Charleston, South Carolina; Georgetown County, South Carolina; and Franklin County, Massachusetts) were enrolled in various types of health insurance plans in a controlled experiment to test the impact of differences in insurance coverage on the demand for medical care.[6]

In one phase of the study, families were randomly assigned to 14 different fee-for-service plans. The plans varied in terms of the consumer coinsurance rate and the upper limit on annual out-of-pocket expenses. Every plan had a *maximum* limit of $1,000 in out-of-pocket expenses per year. Table 5–2 presents selected results for five of the plans: free (0 coinsurance rate), 25 percent coinsurance rate, 50 percent coinsurance rate, 95 percent coinsurance rate, and individual deductible. The individual deductible plan had a 95 percent coinsurance rate for outpatient services, subject to a limit of $150 per person or $450

TABLE 5–2
Sample Means for Annual Use of Medical Services per Capita

Plan*	Face-to-Face Visits	Outpatient Expenses (1984 $)	Inpatient Dollars (1984 $)	Total Expenses (1984 $)	Probability of Using Any Medical Services
Free	4.55	$340	$409	$749	86.8
25%	3.33	260	373	634	78.8
50%	3.03	224	450	674	77.2
95%	2.73	203	315	518	67.7
Individual deductible	3.02	235	373	608	72.3

*The *chi*-square test was used to test the null hypothesis of no difference among the five plan means. In each instance, the *chi*-square statistic was significant to at least the 5 percent level. The only exception was for inpatient dollars.

SOURCE: Willard G. Manning et al. "Health Insurance and the Demand for Medical Care: Evidence from a Randomized Experiment." *American Economic Review* 77 (June 1987), table 2.

---

[6]The present discussion focuses on the results published by Manning et al. (1987). However, a number of other articles analyze the data from the RAND HIS study. Among them are Newhouse et al. (1981), Keeler and Rolph (1983), O'Grady et al. (1985), Manning et al. (1985), Leibowitz, Manning, and Newhouse (1985b), Leibowitz et al. (1985a), and Manning et al. (1986). For a summary of the entire RAND HIS study, consult Newhouse and the Insurance Experiment Group (1993).

per family, and free inpatient care. Essentially, an individual or a family with this plan receives free medical care after meeting the deductible for outpatient expenditures. In table 5–2, face-to-face visits equal the number of per capita visits per year to a medical provider, such as a physician. The category excludes visits for radiology, anesthesiology, or pathology services. The third, fourth, and fifth columns list, respectively, total per capita expenditures for outpatient, inpatient, and all medical services, excluding dental care and psychotherapy. The sixth column indicates the probability of using any medical services over the course of the year.

The results largely confirm our expectations concerning the impact of coinsurance on the demand for health care. As the level of coinsurance rises, or the out-of-pocket price of medical care increases, consumers demand less medical care. The number of face-to-face visits decreased from 4.55 per year when health care was a free good to 2.73 when the consumer paid 95 percent of the bill. This represents a decrease in visits of 40 percent. The largest drop in visits took place between the free plan and the 25 percent coinsurance plan. This overall decrease in visits was matched by an identical drop in outpatient expenses from $340 to $203 per year. According to Manning et al., this indicates that as the out-of-pocket price of medical care increases, consumers reduce medical expenditures largely by cutting back on the number of visits to health care providers and not on the amount spent on each visit. It is interesting to note that the authors reported no significant differences in the amount spent on inpatient services across plans. This, they concluded, was the result of the $1,000 cap put on out-of-pocket expenditures. In 70 percent of the cases where people were admitted for inpatient services, the cost exceeded the $1,000 limit.

The last two columns in table 5–2 also largely support our expectations regarding the impact of insurance on the demand for medical services. In every case, as the level of coinsurance increased, the probability of using any medical services, along with total medical expenditures, diminished. The only exception occurred between the 25 and 50 percent coinsurance rates for total medical expenditures.

Finally, the results from the individual deductible plan illustrate the negative impact of deductibles on the consumption of medical care. In every instance, less medical care was consumed with the deductibles than would have been the case if medical care was a free good. It seems that individuals with this plan consumed medical services at a rate somewhere between the 25 and 95 percent coinsurance rate.

The results also indicate that the own-price elasticity of demand is sensitive to the level of insurance. When the level of coinsurance ranged from 25 to 95 percent, the elasticities of demand for all care and outpatient care were calculated as –.14 and –.21. These numbers decreased to –.10 and –.13 when the level of coinsurance ranged from 0 to 25 percent. This makes economic sense. As the level of coinsurance drops, consumers become less sensitive to price changes due to lower out-of-pocket payments.

In conclusion, the results from the RAND HIS study point to the significant impact of health insurance on the demand for medical care. It is apparent that if either the rate of coinsurance or the deductible falls, the amount of health care consumed increases.

The Impact of Noneconomic Factors on the Demand for Medical Services

The empirical research also indicates that a host of other factors, such as tastes and preferences or the stock of health, affect the demand for medical care. Researchers generally

INSIGHT 5 – 5

Time Is Money: It Was Then and Still Is Now[1]

In the mid-nineteenth century the average income for most physicians in the United States was quite modest and many were forced to find a second income to make ends meet. One major factor that contributed to the low demand for physician services, and therefore the low income, was the high cost of transportation. During the mid-1800s, the United States was primarily a rural society without a modern transportation system. Since most families lived in rural settings and travel was slow, a trip into town to visit a physician was in all likelihood an all-day affair. For a farmer, that meant losing a day's labor, making the opportunity cost of travel very high for most families.

When an individual was ill and could not be moved, it was up to the physician to travel to the individual's house or farm to administer care. Most physician fee schedules at that time reflected the high cost of travel, which included the opportunity cost of the physician's time along with the explicit cost of a horse or horse and buggy. In many cases the transportation costs outweighed the direct cost of medical care. For example, in Addison County, Vermont, in 1843, "the fee for each visit by a doctor was 50 cents at less than half mile; $1.00 between a half mile and two miles; $1.50 between two and four miles; $2.50 between four and six miles and so on" (Starr, p. 67). As you can imagine, physicians did not have to travel far out of town before the proportion of the bill resulting from travel exceeded the direct cost of medical services. The historical evidence clearly indicates the important role time costs played in determining the price of physician services in the mid-1800s.

A study by Whitney et al.[2] illustrates that time costs still play a role in the pricing behavior of medical care providers. In this case, however, the time costs are not related to travel but rather to the time associated with scheduling an appointment and waiting in the reception room to see a dentist. According to the results of the study, the price of dental services "decreased by $4.86 per day wait for a new-patient appointment and by $5.20 per minute wait in the reception room" (p. 783). Anyone who has nervously waited in the dentist's reception room can attest to the willingness of consumers to pay a premium for shorter waiting times.

[1]This insight is based primarily on Chapter 2 of Paul Starr's *The Social Transformation of American Medicine* (New York: Basic Books, 1982).
[2]Coralyn Whitney et al. "The Relationship between Price of Services, Quality of Care, and Patient Time Costs for General Dental Practice." *Health Services Research* 31 (February 1997), pp. 773–90.

agree that age and severity of illness directly influence the demand for medical care, while the overall health of the individual inversely affects the demand for care. There does not, however, appear to be a consensus concerning the impact of education on the demand for health care. This may indicate that the direct impact of education on the demand for medical care (a greater willingness to seek care) is offset by the inverse effect (a greater ability to produce health care at home) or that more research needs to be done in this area.

It is interesting to note that a few researchers have focused specifically on the effect of medical knowledge on the demand for medical care. Unlike the results for general education, a positive relationship appears to exist between consumers' medical knowledge and the demand for medical care. This means that consumers with a more extensive background in medicine tend to consume more medical services. For example, Kenkel (1990) found that consumers' medical knowledge is positively related to the probability of visiting a physician for medical care, while Hsieh and Lin (1997) uncovered that those elderly who had a greater understanding of health were more likely to acquire preventive medical care. Both studies suggest that consumers with a lack of medical knowledge tend to underestimate the impact of medical care on overall health and, as a result, fail to consume an appropriate amount. It may also be the case that more medical information enhances the ability of an individual to effectively consume medical care, causing the marginal product of medical care to increase (consult Chapter 2). As a result, the demand for various types of medical care increases with consumer information.

It is interesting to note that Hsieh and Lin (1997) found that years of schooling, whether the individual worked in the health care field, medical insurance, and income positively influenced the level of health information acquired. They also found that age and whether the individual drank or smoked inversely affected the quantity of health information collected. It appears that older people acquire less new knowledge because they have fewer years to live and reap any reward from that knowledge, while individuals who drink or smoke receive less utility from any good health that may result from added medical knowledge.

HEALTH CARE SPENDING IN THE UNITED STATES

Continually rising health care costs are certainly one of the most glaring problems associated with the U.S. health care system. According to table 5–3, nominal national health care expenditures totaled $26.9 billion in 1960 and by 2000 had grown to $1,299.5 billion. That represents a little more than a forty-seven-fold increase in 40 years.

The annualized rates of growth, also provided in table 5–3, indicate that the increase in medical expenditures was sustained throughout the entire period. The average annual rate of increase topped 10 percent between 1960 and 1970 and increased to 12.9 percent by 1980. In more recent years the annual rate of growth in national medical care expenditures decreased substantially. From 1980 through 1990, the average annual rate of growth was 11.0 percent, and it dropped in the early to mid-1990s. In 1998 the annual rate of growth fell to 5.4 percent. Recently, however, the rate of growth in national health expenditures has begun to increase modestly and by 2000 expenditures increased at a rate of 6.9 percent per year. The rise in total national health care expenditures was accompanied by an increase in per capita national medical expenditures. In 1960 the typical American consumed $141 worth of medical care, and by 2000 per capita consumption grew to $4,637 (see table 5–3). This equals an increase of almost 3,200 percent.

Although these statistics clearly indicate that health care expenditures have risen substantially in the United States over the last four decades, they tell only part of the story, because the U.S. economy also grew over the same period. A more telling statistic is the ratio of medical spending to national income, because it measures the portion of the economic pie allocated to the production of medical care. These figures appear in the bottom

TABLE 5–3

Health Care Expenditures in the United States, 1960–2000

	1960	1970	1980	1990	1998	1999	2000
National Health Expenditures (billions of dollars)	$26.9	73.2	247.3	699.5	1,149.8	1,215.6	1,299.5
Annual Rate of Growth (average annual percent change from previous period shown)	—	10.6%	12.9	11.0	5.4	5.7	6.9
Nominal per Capita Health Expenditures	$141	341	1,052	2,691	4,177	4,377	4,637
Health Expenditures as a Percent of GDP	5.1%	7.1	8.9	12.2	13.1	13.1	13.2

SOURCE: Center for Medicaid and Medicare Services, http://www.hcfa.gov. Accessed October 1, 2002.

row of table 5–3. In 1960, health care expenditures as a percentage of GDP equaled 5.1 percent and by 1980 this number had grown to 8.9 percent.[7] The ratio continued to grow throughout the 1980s and by the 1990s it topped 13 percent. Since that time it has remained relatively constant, suggesting that throughout much of the 1990s, health care expenditures grew at the rate of the overall economy. Prior to that, however, health care expenditures in the United States grew at a much faster pace than the economy as a whole. As a result, the portion of GDP allotted to the production of health care increased significantly.

Sources and Uses of Medical Funds in the United States in 2000

Figures 5–9 and 5–10 provide detailed numbers regarding the sources and uses of health care funds in the United States in 2000. The sources of funds tell us where the health care dollars came from, while the uses indicate how the funds were spent. In 2000, 55 percent of the funds spent on national health care came from the private sector, down from approximately 76 percent in 1960. The bulk of this decrease took place in the mid-1960s when the Medicare and Medicaid programs were first introduced. Since 1990, the share of national health expenditures emanating from the private sector has dropped slightly from 59 percent to about 55 percent.

The mix between private insurance and out-of-pocket payments has also changed in recent years. Private insurance expanded its role as a source of funds and substituted partially for out-of-pocket payments. Specifically, in 1980, private health insurance provided the funding for 29 percent of total national health expenditures, and out-of-pocket payments fell to about 17 percent. By 2000 slightly more than one-third of total national

---

[7]GDP stands for gross domestic product and equals the total value of goods and services produced within a country's borders over a particular time. GDP is measured on an annual basis in this case.

FIGURE   5 – 9

Sources of Health Care Funds in the United States, 2000

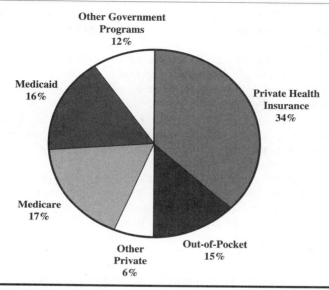

SOURCE: Center for Medicaid and Medicare Services, http://www.hcfa.gov. Accessed October 1, 2002.

FIGURE   5 – 1 0

Uses of Health Care Funds in the United States, 2000

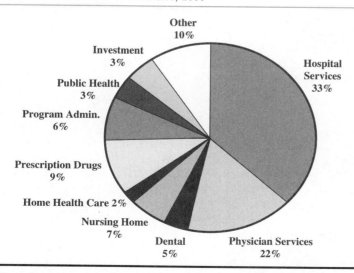

SOURCE: Center for Medicaid and Medicare Services, http://www.hcfa.gov. Accessed October 1, 2002.

health care expenditures came from private health insurance, while out-of-pocket payments fell to about 15 percent. (For a more detailed look at out-of-pocket payments see Insight 5–6) Other private expenditures, which included funds from businesses to provide health care services directly to employees, philanthropic sources, private construction, and nonpatient revenue sources (i.e., revenue from hospital gift shops), accounted for 6 percent of the total in 2000.

Public sources accounted for the remaining 45 percent of total national health care expenditures in 2000. The single largest source of public funds in 2000 was the Medicare program, which provides medical insurance to disabled individuals and those 65 years of age and older, with 17 percent of the total; this was up from 14.6 percent in 1980. The Medicaid program that provides insurance to some segments of the poor accounted for 16 percent of the total, an increase of approximately 6 percentage points since 1980. Other government expenditures, which reflected spending on other state and local public assistance programs, expenditures by the Department of Veterans Affairs, and outlays for state and local hospitals, made up 12 percent of total expenditures in 2000.

The single largest use of medical funds in 2000 was hospital services, which accounted for 33 percent of the total. The next largest use of funds was physician services (22 percent). Together these two uses of medical dollars made up slightly more than one-half of all health care spending. It is interesting to note that this percentage has remained relatively constant over the years. In fact, in 1980 the two categories combined to make up 58 percent of the total national health care expenditures. The next two largest uses of medical funds in 2000 were prescription drugs and nursing home care, accounting for 9 and 7 percent of total medical expenditures, respectively. Expenditures in the remaining smaller categories are also shown in figure 5–10.

INSIGHT 5 – 6

Out-of-Pocket Expenditures in 2000

The figures indicate that the percentage of total health care expenditures financed directly by consumers as out-of-pocket payments has fallen over time in the United States. In 1960 consumers financed almost half (48.7 percent) of total health care expenditures. That percentage dropped continuously throughout the period, and by 2000 consumers financed only 15 percent of total health care expenditures as out-of-pocket expenditures. This decrease can be attributed to a simultaneous growth in private and public health insurance.

Figure 1 presents the portion of health care costs financed by out-of-pocket payments for various categories of expenditures in 2000. The data indicate that the percentage of out-of-pocket payments varied widely across categories. Out-of-pocket payments accounted for only 3.2 percent of hospital expenditures and 11.6 percent of physician and clinical services expenditures. At the other extreme, 44.8 percent of dentist expenditures and 32 percent of prescription drug expenditures were the result of out-of-pocket expenditures.

FIGURE 1
Percent of Out-of-Pocket Payments for Selected Categories, 2000

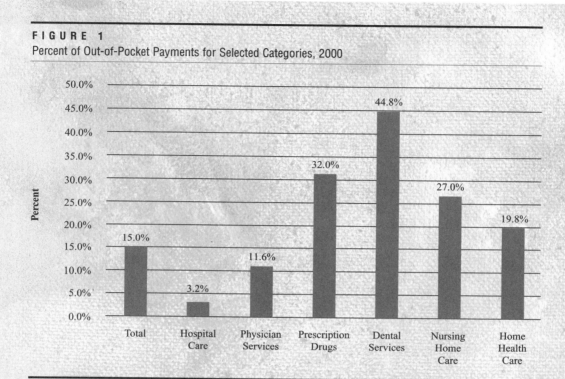

SOURCE: Center for Medicaid and Medicare Services, http://www.hcfa.gov. Accessed October 1, 2002.

Out-of-pocket expenditures accounted for 27 percent of nursing home expenditures and 19.8 percent of home health care expenditures.

It is interesting to note that there appears to be a strong inverse correlation between the amount of spending on health care and the percent financed by out-of-pocket payments. This is true not only over time but also across types of medical expenditures. From 1960 to 2000, when total expenditures on health care grew almost fifty fold, out-of-pocket payments fell from just under 50 percent to 15 percent. Also, the single largest category of medical expenditures in 2000 was hospital care at $412.1 billion, and it had the lowest percent of out-of-pocket payments. Expenditures on physician and clinical services was the next largest category; in this instance only 11.6 percent of the expenditures were directly financed by consumers. Dental services was one of the smaller categories and out-of-pocket payments equaled 44.8 percent. Thus, cursory evidence is consistent with the hypothesis that a lower out-of-pocket price increases the quantity demanded of medical services. However, it could also reflect just the opposite—that the demand for third-party insurance coverage increases with the magnitude of health care costs. This possibility is discussed in the next chapter.

SUMMARY

Economic theory suggests that the demand for medical care is a derived demand because it is but one input in the production of health. As a result, the utility received from consuming medical care is in the form of the satisfaction that accrues from improvements in the stock of health. Utility analysis also indicates that the quantity demanded of health care is inversely related to price because improvements in health are subject to diminishing returns. The demand for medical care, like the demand for many other services, depends on the out-of-pocket price, income, the prices of substitutes and complements, and time costs, along with a host of noneconomic factors, such as tastes and preferences, quality of care, and the state of health.

Economists use the concept of elasticity to measure the degree to which an economic agent, such as a consumer, adjusts to a change in the value of an independent variable. The most common elasticity is the own-price elasticity of demand, which measures the extent to which consumers react to a change in the price of a good or service. In mathematical terms, it equals the percentage change in quantity demanded divided by the percentage change in price. If the demand for a product is elastic, the consumer's willingness to purchase the product is very sensitive to a price change. On the other hand, if the demand for the product is inelastic, price changes play a less significant role in determining overall demand. From a graphical perspective, the more elastic the demand for a product, the flatter the demand curve. Additional types of elasticities, such as the income elasticity of demand, have also been employed to assess how demand reacts to changes in variables other than own price.

The empirical evidence indicates that the demand for medical care is inelastic with respect to price. Medical care also appears to be a normal good in that the demand for medical care increases with real income. In addition, time costs along with many noneconomic variables, such as age, gender, severity of illness, education, and consumer knowledge, influence demand. The evidence from the RAND HIS study verifies that health insurance plays a major role in determining the demand for medical care. As economic theory suggests, when the level of health insurance rises, the amount of medical care demanded increases while the price elasticity of demand becomes more inelastic.

Medical expenditures in the United States have grown rapidly in recent decades. In 1960 nominal per capita health expenditures equaled approximately $140, and overall health expenditures accounted for 5.1 percent of GDP. By 2000 per capital expenditures equaled approximately $4,600, while total health expenditures accounted for 13.2 percent of GDP.

REVIEW QUESTIONS AND PROBLEMS

1. In your own words, use utility analysis and production theory to explain why the demand curve for medical care is downward sloping.

2. After reading the chapter on demand theory, a classmate turns to you and says, "I'm rather confused. According to economic theory, people demand a good or service because it yields utility. This obviously does not apply to medical services. Just last week I went to the dentist and had a root canal, and you can't tell me I received any utility

or satisfaction from that!" Explain to your classmate how utility analysis can be used to explain why she or he went to the dentist.

3. Use a graph to illustrate how the following changes would affect the demand curve for inpatient services at a hospital in a large city.

   A. Average real income in the community increases.

   B. In an attempt to cut costs, the largest employer in the area increases the coinsurance rate for employee health care coverage from 10 percent to 20 percent.

   C. The hospital relocates from the center of the city, where a majority of the people live, to a suburb.

   D. A number of physicians in the area join together and open up a discount-price walk-in clinic; the price elasticity of demand between physician services and inpatient hospital services is −.50.

4. In recent years, many elderly people have purchased Medigap insurance policies to cover a growing Medicare copayment. These policies cover some or all of the medical costs not covered by Medicare. Use economic theory to explain how the growth of these policies is likely to influence the demand for health care by elderly people.

5. If you are covered by a private or a public insurance plan, obtain a pamphlet outlining the benefits provided and the cost of the plan. Are there any copayments or deductibles? If so, use economic theory to explain how they may influence your demand for medical care.

6. In your own words, explain what a fuzzy demand curve is. Why does it exist? What are its implications?

7. In reaction to higher input costs, a physician decides to increase the average price of a visit by 5 percent. Will total revenues increase or decrease as a result of this action? Use the concept of price elasticity to substantiate your answer.

8. You have just been put in charge of estimating the demand for hospital services in a major U.S. city. What economic and noneconomic variables would you include in your analysis? Justify why each variable should be included in the study, and explain how a change in each variable would likely affect the overall demand for hospital services.

9. Define *own-price elasticity of demand*, and explain how it is related to the demand curve. Provide four reasons why the demand for medical services is likely to be inelastic with respect to its price.

10. You are employed as an economic consultant to the regional planning office of a large metropolitan area, and your task is to estimate the demand for hospital services in the area. Your estimates indicate that the own-price elasticity of demand equals −.25, the income elasticity of demand equals +.45, the cross-price elasticity of demand for hospital services with respect to the price of nursing home services equals −.1, and the elasticity of travel time equals −.37. Use this information to project the impact of the following changes on the demand for hospital services.

    A. Average travel time to the hospital diminishes by 5 percent due to overall improvements in the public transportation system.

    B. The price of nursing home care decreases by 10 percent.

    C. Average real income decreases by 10 percent.

    D. The hospital is forced to increase its price for services by 2 percent.

11. A recent study estimates the demand for over-the-counter cough and cold medicines to be:

$$Log\ Q = .885 - .744\ log(P) - .50\ log(INC) + .253\ log(ADV) - .30\ log(PHYSP)$$
$$(5.52)\ (4.92)\qquad (1.40)\qquad\quad (6.64)\qquad\quad (0.99)$$
$$Adj.\ R^2 = .30$$
$$N = 243$$

where Q = Annual dosages demanded of cough and cold medicines

P = Price per dosage of cough and cold medicines

INC = Average income of buyers

ADV = Advertising expenditures on cough and cold medicines

PHYSP = Market price of a physician visit

t-statistics shown in parentheses below the estimated coefficient

All variables expressed in logarithms so the coefficient estimates can be interpreted as elasticities.

A. Which of the estimated coefficients have signs contrary to theoretical expectations? Explain. Be specific in your explanation.
B. Which coefficient estimates are statistically significant from zero at the 5 percent level or better? Explain.
C. What percentage of the variation in dosages demanded remains unexplained? Explain.
D. Suppose the price per dosage increased by 10 percent. By how much would dosages demanded change? Explain. Would total revenues to cold medicine producers increase or decrease? Explain.

ONLINE RESOURCES

To access Internet links related to the topics in this chapter, please visit our web site at http://santerre.swcollege.com.

REFERENCES

Aaron, Henry J. *Serious and Unstable Condition: Financing America's Health Care.* Washington, D.C.: The Brookings Institution, 1991.

Acton, Jan Paul. "Nonmonetary Factors in the Demand for Medical Services: Some Empirical Evidence." *Journal of Political Economy* 83 (June 1975), pp. 595–614.

Case, Anne, and Christina Paxson. "Mothers and Others: Who Invests in Children's Health." *Journal of Health Economics* 20 (May 2001), pp. 301–28.

Chiswick, Barry. "The Demand for Nursing Home Care." *Journal of Human Resources* 11 (summer 1976), pp. 295–316.

Cromwell, Jerry, and Janet B. Mitchell. "Physician-Induced Demand for Surgery." *Journal of Health Economics* 5 (1986), pp. 293–313.

Davis, Karen, and Louise B. Russell. "The Substitution of Hospital Outpatient Care for In-patient Care." *Review of Economics and Statistics* 54 (May 1972), pp. 109–20.

Eichner, Matthew J. "The Demand for Medical Care: What People Pay Does Matter." *American Economic Review Papers and Proceedings* 88 (May 1998), pp. 117–21.

Feldman, Roger, and Bryan Dowd. "Is There a Competitive Market for Hospital Services?" *Journal of Health Economics* 5 (1986), pp. 272–92.

Feldstein, Martin S. *Economic Analysis for Health Services Efficiency*. Amsterdam: North-Holland Publishing Co., 1967.

Feldstein, Paul. *Health Care Economics*. New York: John Wiley & Sons, 1988.

Frank, Richard G., et al. "The Demand for Childhood Immunizations: Results from the Baltimore Immunization Study." *Inquiry* 32 (summer 1995), pp. 164–73.

Freiberg, Lewis, Jr., and F. Douglas Scutchfield. "Insurance and the Demand for Hospital Care: An Examination of the Moral Hazard." *Inquiry* 13 (March 1976), pp. 54–60.

Gerdtham, Ulf-G, et al. "An Econometric Analysis of Health Care Expenditure: A Cross-Section Study of the OECD Countries." *Journal of Health Economics* 11 (1992), pp. 63–84.

Gold, Marsha. "The Demand for Hospital Outpatient Services." *Health Services Research* 19 (August 1984), pp. 384–412.

Gravelle, Hugh, Mark Dusheiko, and Matthew Sutton. "The Demand for Elective Surgery in a Public System: Time and Money Prices in the UK National Health Service." *Journal of Health Economics* 21 (May 2002), pp. 423–49.

Headen, Alvin E. "Economic Disability and Health Determinants of the Hazard of Nursing Home Entry." *Journal of Human Resources* 28 (1993), pp. 80–110.

Hsieh, Chee-ruey, and Shin-jong Lin. "Health Information and the Demand for Preventive Care among the Elderly in Taiwan." *Journal of Human Resources* 32 (1997), pp. 308–33.

Keeler, Emmett B., and John E. Rolph. "How Cost Sharing Reduced Medical Spending of Participants in the Health Insurance Experiment." *Journal of the American Medical Association* 249 (April 22–29, 1983), pp. 2220–22.

Kenkel, Don. "Consumer Health Information and the Demand for Medical Care." *Review of Economics and Statistics* 72 (1990), pp. 587–95.

Lamberton, C.E., W.D. Ellingson, and K.R. Spear. "Factors Determining the Demand for Nursing Home Services." *Quarterly Review of Economics and Business* 26 (winter 1986), pp. 74–90.

Leibowitz, Arleen, et al. "Effects of Cost-Sharing on the Use of Medical Services by Children: Interim Results from a Randomized Controlled Trial." *Pediatrics* 75 (May 1985a), pp. 942–50.

Leibowitz, Arleen, Willard G. Manning, and Joseph P. Newhouse. "The Demand for Prescription Drugs as a Function of Cost-Sharing." *Social Science and Medicine* 21 (1985b), pp. 1063–69.

Leu, Robert E. "The Public-Private Mix and International Health Care Costs." In *Public and Private Health Services*, eds. A.J. Culyer and B. Jonsson. Oxford: Basil Blackwell, 1986.

Manning, Willard G., Howard L. Bailit, Bernadette Benjamin, and Joseph P. Newhouse. "The Demand for Dental Care: Evidence from a Randomized Trial in Health Insurance." *Journal of the American Dental Association* 110 (June 1985), pp. 895–902.

Manning, Willard G., et al. "Health Insurance and the Demand for Medical Care: Evidence from a Randomized Experiment." *American Economic Review* 77 (June 1987), pp. 251–77.

Manning, Willard, et al. "How Cost Sharing Affects the Use of Ambulatory Mental Health Services." *Journal of the American Medical Association* 256 (October 10, 1986), pp. 1930–34.

Manning, Williard G., and Charles E. Phelps. "The Demand for Dental Care." *Bell Journal of Economics* 10 (autumn 1979), pp. 503–25.

Martin, Stephen, and Peter C. Smith. "Rationing By Waiting Lists: An Empirical Investigation." *Journal of Public Economics* 71 (January 1999), pp. 141–64.

McCarthy, Thomas. "The Competitive Nature of the Primary-Care Physicians Service Market." *Journal of Health Economics* 4 (1985), pp. 93–118.

McMenamin, Peter. "What Do Economists Think Patients Want?" *Health Affairs* 9 (winter 1990), pp. 112–19.

Miller, Lisa. "Medical Schools Put Women in Curricula." *The Wall Street Journal*, May 24, 1994, p. B1.

Newhouse, Joseph P. "Medical-Care Expenditures: A Cross-National Survey." *Journal of Human Resources* 12 (winter 1977), pp. 115–24.

Newhouse, Joseph P., et al. "Some Interim Results from a Controlled Trial of Cost Sharing in Health Insurance." *New England Journal of Medicine* 305 (December 17, 1981), pp. 1501–7.

Newhouse, Joseph P., and the Insurance Experiment Group. *Free for All? Lessons from the RAND Health Insurance Experiment*. Cambridge, Mass.: Harvard University Press, 1993.

O'Grady, Kevin F., Willard G. Manning, Joseph P. Newhouse, and Robert H. Brook. "Impact of Cost Sharing on Emergency Department Use." *New England Journal of Medicine* 313 (August 22, 1985), pp. 484–90.

Parkin, David, Alistair Mcquire, and Brian Yule. "Aggregate Health Care Expenditures and National Income: Is Health a Luxury Good?" *Journal of Health Economics* 6 (1987), pp. 109–27.

Phelps, Charles E. "Diffusion of Information in Medical Care." *Journal of Economic Perspectives* 6 (summer 1992), pp. 23–42.

Phelps, Charles E., and Joseph P. Newhouse. "Coinsurance, the Price of Time, and the Demand for Medical Service." *Review of Economics and Statistics* 56 (August 1974), pp. 334–42.

Stano, Miron. "An Analysis of the Evidence on Competition in the Physician's Services Market." *Journal of Health Economics* 4 (1985), pp. 197–211.

Starr, Paul. *The Social Transformation of American Medicine*. New York: Basic Books, 1982.

Whitney, Coralyn W., et al. "The Relationship between Price of Services, Quality of Care, and Patient Time Costs for General Dental Practice." *Health Services Research* 31 (February 1997), pp. 773–90.

Winslow, Ron. "In Health Care Low Cost Beats High Quality." *The Wall Street Journal*, January 18, 1994, p. B1.

Yen, Steven T., Chao-Hsiun Tang, and Shew-Jiuan B. Su. "Demand for Traditional Medicine in Taiwan: A Mixed Gaussion-Poisson Model Approach." *Health Economics* 10 (2001), pp. 221–32.

CEBS QUESTIONS

CEBS Sample Question on Subject Matter from CEBS Course 9 Study Manual

1. What effect does each of the following have on the demand curve for medical services? (pages 105–107)
   a. Coinsurance
   b. Indemnity insurance (defined in the textbook as the insurance carrier pays a fixed amount for various types of medical services)

CEBS Sample Exam Questions

1. When a demand curve for medical care is described as "fuzzy" this refers to the fact that:
   A. Demand is less important than supply
   B. The concept of a demand curve cannot be applied to medical care
   C. It is extremely difficult to accurately delineate the relation between the price and the quantity demanded of medical care
   D. The demand for medical care is a derived demand
   E. The demand curve for medical care, unlike typical demand curves, does not slope downward to the right

2. Which of the following statements regarding a demand curve is (are) correct?
   I. In a demand curve illustration, the vertical axis is "quantity"
   II. A demand curve normally slopes downward to the right
   III. A demand curve shows that a greater quantity will be demanded at a higher income
   A. II only
   B. III only
   C. I and II only
   D. II and III only
   E. I, II, and III

3. All the following statements regarding elasticity are correct EXCEPT:
   A. If elasticity is negative, the good is called a normal good
   B. Total revenue decreases when the price increases and the demand is elastic
   C. When the price elasticity is greater than one, the demand for the product is said to be elastic
   D. A horizontal demand curve is perfectly elastic
   E. The availability of substitutes is a determinant of price elasticity

Answer to Sample Question from Study Manual

a. Coinsurance makes the demand curve for medical services rotate clockwise and become steeper. Coinsurance drives a wedge between what the consumer is willing to pay and the actual price paid for the medical services. At a zero willingness-to-pay, insurance has no bearing on quantity demanded because medical care is a free good to the individual. In the case where the consumer has full coverage (no out-of-pocket expenses), the demand curve becomes completely vertical.

b. The existence of indemnity insurance shifts the demand curve for medical services upward. The greater the amount paid by insurance, the more the demand curve will shift.

Answer to Sample Exam Questions

1. C is the correct answer. The demand curve for medical care is "fuzzy" because the exact relationship between price and quantity demanded is difficult to determine. See pages 113–114 of the text.

2. A is the correct answer. The vertical axis for a demand curve is "price" not quantity. Statement III is incorrect because a demand curve shows the relationship between price and quantity demanded, not income. See pages 101–103 of the text.

3. The correct answer is A. If elasticity is positive, the good is a normal good. All the other statements are correct. See pages 114–120 of the text.

THE DEMAND FOR MEDICAL INSURANCE: TRADITIONAL AND MANAGED CARE COVERAGE

Remember Joe, who suffered a heart attack at the beginning of Chapter 1? Things turned out quite well, both medically and financially, for our friend Joe. You see, Joe's medical bills were covered by a Blue Cross indemnity insurance plan he had obtained through his employer. Joe could thus afford the best and fastest hospital care money could buy, and the triple bypass surgery he received at the prestigious private teaching hospital was highly successful. Angela, his wife, and the two children are tickled pink now that Joe is back to his former self.

But, how might events have differed if Joe had not been covered by medical insurance, or if Joe was enrolled in a managed care plan? Would Joe have been unduly delayed in the busy emergency room of a public hospital? Would Angela be inordinately stressed out because she was concerned about the unknown financial consequences associated with Joe's illness or worried that the managed care plan may not cover the cost of the care because the hospital did not participate in the plan, or because she did not receive prior authorization for the hospital services? These are among the questions for which we search for answers in this chapter.

Specifically, this chapter:

> Looks at the factors influencing the demand for health insurance.

> Examines empirical estimates of the price and income elasticities of the demand for health insurance.

> Discusses the health insurance product, contrasting traditional and managed care coverage.

> Addresses the regulation of managed care organizations.

THE DEMAND FOR PRIVATE HEALTH INSURANCE

Because of imperfect information, many of the choices individuals make as health care consumers or providers involve a substantial amount of uncertainty. For example, for an individual consumer, many medical illnesses occur randomly, and therefore the timing and amount of medical expenditures are uncertain. Likewise, from the health care provider's perspective, patient load and types of treatment are unknown before they actually occur. Because these events are unpredictable, they involve a substantial degree of risk. Because most people generally dislike risk, they are willing to pay some amount of money to avoid it.

For the medical care consumer, health insurance mitigates some of the risk involved in purchasing medical care services. Consumers pay an insurer a certain amount of income (i.e., a premium), and the insurer covers some or all of the medical costs in the event an illness actually occurs. During any given period the actual benefits paid out by an insurer to any single consumer may be higher or lower than the premiums received from that consumer. By operating on a large scale, an insurer pools or spreads the risk among many subscribers so that, on average, the total premiums received *at least* compensate for the total cost of paying for medical services, particularly in the long run. In addition, given some amount of competition in the health insurance market, the difference between total premiums and total benefits paid out to all subscribers (or the loading fee) should approximate a "normal" amount.

Consumers differ in terms of the amounts and types of health insurance coverage they buy, and these differences are reflected in such items as the deductible amount, the coinsurance rate, and the number of events covered. (We will examine the health insurance product more closely later on in the chapter.) In general, a high deductible and a high coinsurance rate reflect less extensive or less complete health insurance coverage. For example, some consumers purchase health insurance plans that offer first-dollar coverage for all types of medical services, including routine care. Others purchase health insurance plans with large deductibles and copayments that cover only catastrophic illnesses. Differences in health care coverage can be explained by a host of factors, including the price of obtaining health insurance, the individual's degree of risk aversion, the perceived magnitude of the loss relative to income, and information concerning the likelihood that an illness will actually occur.

Deriving the Demand for Private Health Insurance

We can get a better understanding about how these factors individually influence the quantity demanded of health insurance by focusing on figure 6–1, where the actual utility, U, associated with different levels of income, Y, is shown for a representative consumer (ignore the chord AB for now). The slope of this utility function at any point is $\Delta U/\Delta Y$ and represents the marginal utility of income. The declining slope, or marginal utility of income, is based on the premise that the individual is risk averse. This means the risk-averse person is opposed to a fair gamble where there is a 50–50 chance of losing or gaining one dollar because a dollar loss is valued more highly than a dollar gain. That is, for any given

FIGURE 6-1
Expected Utility Model

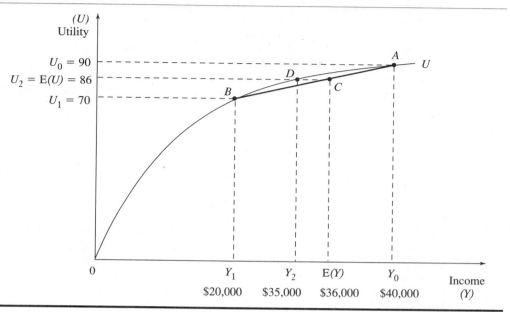

The curve shows the actual utility associated with different levels of income (not drawn to scale). The concavity of the curve illustrates risk aversion. Suppose a person has $40,000 of income and a medical illness costs $20,000. Assuming no health insurance, chord AB represents the expected utility associated with different probability values (Pr) betweens zero and 1 of an illness occurring. Points A and B represent two extreme outcomes for which the illness is not expected to occur (Pr = 0) and the illness is perfectly certain (Pr = 1). Point C reflects an example of an intermediate position where there is a 20 percent chance (Pr = .20) of an illness occurring such that expected income after the loss equals $36,000 and expected utility equals 86. Notice a risk-averse person is indifferent in terms of utility levels between losing a known amount of $5,000 at point D and an expected amount of $4,000 at point C. Thus, the expected utility model suggests that a risk-averse person can be made better off by paying an insurer some amount above the expected loss to be relieved of the associated risk.

level of income, the pain of losing an incremental dollar exceeds the pleasure associated with gaining an additional dollar.[1]

Suppose a person has an income of Y_0 equaling $40,000. As indicated in the figure, this income level yields actual utility of U_0, which amounts to 90 utils.[2] Further, suppose the person faces a choice concerning whether or not to purchase health insurance. The decision is based partly on a belief that if an illness occurs, the medical services will cost $20,000. Consequently, if the illness occurs and the consumer pays the entire medical bill, income declines to $20,000 and the level of actual utility falls to U_1, or 70 utils.

---

[1]If the marginal pain equals the marginal pleasure, the slope of the utility curve is constant (a straight line through the origin) and the person is risk neutral. For a risk lover, the pleasure of an additional dollar gained exceeds the pain of an incremental dollar loss, and the slope is increasing in value.
[2]For expository purposes, we assume utility can be measured directly in units called *utils*.

The two outcomes that can occur if the consumer does not purchase health insurance are represented by points A and B. At point A, no illness occurs and income remains at $40,000 such that actual utility equals U_0. At point B, an illness occurs and (net) income falls to $20,000 such that actual utility equals U_1. Because the resulting outcome is unknown before it actually occurs, the individual forms expectations concerning the probability of each outcome occurring. With these subjective probabilities, the expected (rather than actual) levels of utility and income can be determined. Specifically, the individual's expected level of utility, $E(U)$, can be determined by weighing the actual utility levels associated with the two possible outcomes by their subjective probabilities of occurrence, Pr_0 and Pr_1:

(6–1) $$E(U) = Pr_0 \times U_0(Y_0 = \$40,000) + Pr_1 \times U_1(Y_1 = \$20,000),$$

or

(6–2) $$E(U) = Pr_0 \times 90 + Pr_1 \times 70,$$

where Pr_0 and Pr_1 sum to 1. Based on equation 6–2, the chord AB in figure 6–1 shows the level of expected utility for various probabilities that the illness will occur. As the probability of getting ill increases, expected utility declines, and this outcome is associated with a point closer to B on the chord. The precise probability value that the individual attaches to the illness occurring is based on his or her best personal estimate. It is likely to depend on such factors as the individual's stock of health, age, and lifestyle.

Suppose the consumer attaches a subjective probability of 20 percent to an illness actually occurring. Following equation 6–2, the expected utility is

(6–3) $$E(U) = .8 \times 90 + .2 \times 70 = 86$$

and the expected level of income, $E(Y)$, is

(6–4) $$E(Y) = Pr_0 \times Y_0 + Pr_1 \times Y_1 = .8 \times 40,000 + .2 \times 20,000 = 36,000.$$

Equation 6–4 represents the weighted sum of the two income levels with the probability values as the weights. Thus, expected income equals $36,000 and the expected level of utility is 86 utils if insurance is not purchased (and full risk is assumed) given a perceived probability of illness equal to .2 and a magnitude of the loss equal to $20,000. The levels of expected income and expected utility are also shown in figure 6–1.

Notice in the figure (not drawn to scale) that the person is just as well off in terms of actual utility by paying a third party a "certain" income of $5,000 to insure against the expected loss of $4,000. The certain loss of $5,000 reduces net income to $35,000 and provides the consumer with an actual utility level of 86 utils, which equals the expected utility level without insurance. To the consumer, the $1,000 discrepancy, or distance CD, represents the maximum amount he or she is willing to pay for health insurance above the expected loss. It reflects the notion that a risk-averse consumer always prefers a known amount of income rather than an expected amount of equal value. This preference reflects the value the consumer places on financial security. It is for this reason that the typical person faces an incentive to purchase health insurance.

It is easy to see from this analysis why an insurance company is willing to insure against the risk. Assuming this person is the average subscriber in the insured group and the probability of an illness occurring is correct from an objective statistical perspective, the insurance company could potentially receive premium revenues of $5,000 to pay the expected medical benefits of $4,000 with enough left over to cover administrative expenses, taxes, and profits. The expected medical benefits can also be referred to as the actuarial fair value or "pure premium." To the insurer, the difference between the total premium and medical benefits paid out or pure premium, is referred to as the *loading fee*. In the economics of insurance literature, the loading fee is also referred to as the *price of insurance*.

Factors Affecting the Quantity Demanded of Health Insurance

The model in figure 6–1 can be used to explain how the price of insurance affects the quantity demanded of health insurance. Under normal circumstances, the consumer purchases health insurance if the actual utility with health insurance exceeds the expected utility without it.[3] In figure 6–1, that happens whenever the loading fee leads to an income level associated with a point between D and C on the actual utility curve for the given set of circumstances (i.e., probability values, degree of risk aversion, and magnitude of loss). In terms of the present example, the consumer demands health insurance if the loading fee is less than $1,000 because actual utility exceeds expected utility. If expected utility exceeds actual utility, the consumer does not purchase health insurance coverage because the price is too high (a loading fee producing actual utility between points D and B). This happens if the loading fee exceeds $1,000 in our example. Finally, if actual and expected utility are equal due to the loading fee, the individual is indifferent between buying and not buying health insurance (point D or a loading fee of $1,000). Both options make the consumer equally well off. Therefore, it follows that the loading fee, or the price of health insurance, helps to establish the completeness of insurance coverage and the number of people who insure against medical illnesses. Specifically, as the price of insurance declines, actual utility increases relative to expected utility and the quantity demanded of health insurance increases, *ceteris paribus*.

At this point, it is useful to note that employment-related health insurance premiums, unlike cash income, are presently exempt from federal and state income taxes even though they are a form of in-kind income. For example, if an employer pays cash wages of $800 and provides health insurance benefits equal to $200 per month to an employee, only the $800 is subject to taxes even though total compensation equals $1,000. Assuming a 20 percent marginal tax rate, the individual pays $160 in taxes on $800 of cash income rather than $200 on $1,000 of total compensation.

Thus, relative to cash income (or all other goods purchased out of cash income), health insurance is effectively subsidized by the government because of its tax exemption status. We can view this tax subsidy on health insurance benefits in another way. Each time the employer raises the employee's wage by $1, the employee receives only $100 − t$ percent of that $1 as after-tax income, where t percent is the marginal tax rate. However, if employer health insurance contributions increase by $1, the employee receives the entire dollar as benefits. In effect, the government picks up t percent of the price of the health insurance

---

[3]The theoretically correct comparison is between the expected utility with health insurance and the expected utility without health insurance. Because the amount of the premium payment is perfectly certain with a probability of occurrence equal to one, however, the expected and actual utility with health insurance are equal. We use actual utility here to avoid confusion.

in forgone taxes and the employee pays the remaining $(100 - t)$ percent in forgone wage income (since both wages and in-kind benefits are substitute forms of compensation).[4] Given $t = 20$, the government implicitly pays 20 cents and the employee pays 80 cents of the marginal dollar spent on health insurance. If we allow for the possibility that not all health insurance premiums are tax exempt (e.g., the health insurance premiums of some individuals who purchase individual policies), the user price of health insurance can be written as $(1 - et/100)P_{HI}$, where e is the fraction of health insurance premiums exempted from taxes and P_{HI} is the price of health insurance (the loading fee). The user price of health insurance obviously decreases with a higher marginal income tax rate and tax-exempt fraction.

The model in figure 6–1 can also help explain other factors affecting the demand for health insurance. First, the subjective probability of an illness occurring affects the amount of health insurance demanded. In terms of the figure, as the probability of an illness increases from zero to 1, the relevant point on chord AB moves from A toward B. Given the shapes of the two curves, the horizontal distance between the actual utility curve and the expected utility line, which measures the willingness to pay for health insurance beyond the expected level of medical benefits, at first gets larger, reaches a maximum, and then approaches zero with a movement from A to B. Therefore, all else held constant, including the loading fee, the quantity demanded of health insurance first increases, reaches a maximum amount, and then decreases with respect to a higher probability of an illness occurring. The implication is that individuals insure less against medical events that are either highly unlikely (closer to A) or most probable (closer to B). In the latter case, it is cheaper for the individual to self-insure (i.e., save money for the "rainy day") and avoid paying the loading fee. For example, assume the probability of illness is 1. In this case, the expected and actual levels of utility are equal at point B in figure 6–1. In this situation, it is cheaper for the individual to self-insure than to pay a loading fee above the medical benefits actually paid out. Alternatively stated, there is no need for insurance since the outcome is certain. The probability of an illness occurring is one reason more people insure against random medical events than against routine medical events, such as periodic physical and dental exams, which are expected.

Another factor affecting the amount of insurance coverage is the magnitude of the loss relative to income. Assuming the same probabilities as before, the expected utility line (chord AB) in figure 6–1 rotates down and pivots off point A if the magnitude of the loss increases. In this case, the new expected utility line meets the actual utility curve somewhere below point B. For the same probability values as before, the horizontal distance between the expected and actual utility curves increases. Thus, the willingness to purchase health insurance increases with a greater magnitude of a loss. This implies that a greater number of people insure against illnesses associated with a large loss, at least relative to income. Insurance coverage is also more complete. The potential for a greater loss is one reason more people have hospital insurance than dental or eye care insurance coverage.

The final factor affecting the amount of health insurance demanded is the degree of risk aversion. Obviously, people who are more risk averse have more insurance coverage than otherwise identical people who are less risk averse. Greater risk aversion makes the utility

[4]In other words, the opportunity cost of $100 of nontaxable benefits is $(100 - t)$ dollars of wage income.

curve more concave. In fact, according to the theory, a risk lover does not choose to purchase health insurance coverage because of a convex utility curve.

In sum, we can specify the quantity demanded of health insurance, Q_{HI}, as a function of the following factors:

(6–5) $Q_{HI} = f[(1 - et/100) \times P_{HI}, \text{Degree of risk aversion, Probability}$
             $\text{of an illness occurring, Magnitude of loss, Income}].$

With suitable data, equation 6–5 can be estimated to determine the user price and income elasticities of the demand for health insurance. In practice, however, it is very difficult to measure the user price and quantity demanded of health insurance. Therefore, various proxies are used depending on data availability. For example, the price of health insurance, P_{HI}, is sometimes proxied by the size of the insured group. The expectation is that the loading fee, or the price of health insurance, falls with a larger group size due to administrative and risk-spreading economies. Some studies assume the price of health insurance is the same for all individuals and allow only marginal tax rates, t, and the tax-exempt fraction, e, to vary.

Proxy measures for the quantity of health insurance must also be employed. The quantity of health insurance is usually measured by either total insurance premiums, some measure of insurance coverage completeness, or a coverage option (e.g., less versus more restrictive health insurance plans). Table 6–1 displays some of the estimated price and income elasticities of the demand for health insurance reported in various studies. The studies reveal that individuals possess a price-inelastic demand for health insurance. Furthermore, while health insurance is considered to be a normal good (i.e., an income elasticity greater than zero), the studies found a relatively small income effect. Even the demand for long-term care insurance is found to be inelastic, with price and income elasticities of about –.39 and .18, respectively (Kumar et al., 1995).

However, these studies generally assume the individual is able to make marginal changes in the insurance policy. But employer-sponsored group insurance policies are largely beyond the control of the single individual employee. Typically, the employer or union representatives make decisions concerning the insurance package by taking into consideration the welfare of the overall group rather than that of any one individual employee. See Goldstein and Pauly (1976) or Pauly (1986) for further discussion on this

---

TABLE 6–1

Price and Income Elasticities of the Demand for Health Insurance

Study	Price Elasticity	Income Elasticity
Taylor and Wilensky (1983)	–.21	.02
Farley and Wilensky (1984)	–.41	.04
Holmer (1984)	–.16	.01
Short and Taylor (1989)	–.32	.13
Manning and Marquis (1989)	–.54	.07
Marquis and Long (1995)	–.03	.15
Liu and Christianson (1998)	–.33	.12

INSIGHT 6-1

The Demand for Employer Contributions to Health Insurance Premiums

Voluntary private employer contributions to health insurance premiums as a percentage of total wage and salary compensation grew from 1.47 in 1965 to 6.56 in 1995 but declined to 5.89 in 2000.[1] Economic theory suggests that the proportion of health care benefits in total compensation can be attributed to a variety of factors. First, given the tax-exempt status of employer contributions to health insurance, higher marginal tax rates on wage income reduce the user price of health insurance and lead to a greater quantity demanded of employer contributions to health insurance. Thus, the marginal tax on wage income and, correspondingly, the user price of health insurance partly account for employer contributions to health care benefits.

Second, the size of the insured group affects the price of health care benefits. As the size of the group increases and administrative and risk-bearing costs fall, the price of health care benefits declines. The lower price raises the demand for employer contributions. Therefore, the number of employees at the typical firm may be partly responsible for the amount of employer contributions to health care benefits.

Third, changes in real income can affect the demand for employer-provided health care benefits. The exact relationship depends on the relative income elasticities of the demand for wage and nonwage compensation. Higher income leads to an increased demand for employer contributions to health insurance if the income elasticity of demand for health care benefits is greater than that for wage compensation.

Fourth, health care benefits increase relative to wage compensation as a result of unionization. Unions provide information to employees about the tax and group size advantages of health care benefits, which serves to increase the demand for health care benefits relative to wage income.

Finally, demographic factors, such as the age and gender composition of the workforce and the distribution of job characteristics, cause the demand for employer-provided health care benefits to change given potential differences in risk aversion and medical utilization rates. For example, the labor force participation rate of women has increased significantly over time. Given that women generally consume more medical services than men, it is easy to see why the demand for employer-provided medical insurance changes when the female labor force participation rate adjusts.

Using time series data, a study by Long and Scott (1982) determined how these various factors individually affected the demand for employer-provided health care benefits in the United States over the period 1947 to 1979. The authors specified a linear multiple regression equation linking the percentage of compensation as health insurance (PCTHLTINS) to the average marginal tax rate (MTR), average real family income (RFAMINC), union membership as a fraction of the total labor force (UNION), the percentage of total employees

---

[1] Estimates are drawn from Cowan, McDonnell, Levit, and Zezza (2002).

who are female (PCTFEM), and the percentage of employment found in the service industries (PCTSERV).[2] They obtained the following results (t-statistics in parentheses):

(5–6)

$$PCTHLTINS = -8.64 + .0284\ MTR$$
$$(6.22)\quad (3.98)$$

$$+\ .0498\ RFAMINC - .0094\ UNION$$
$$(1.14)\qquad\qquad (.57)$$

$$+\ .088\ PCTFEM + .1283\ PCTSERV$$
$$(3.72)\qquad\qquad (5.52)$$

$$Adj.\ R^2 = .9968,\ N = 32$$

The coefficient estimate on MTR was found to be positive and statistically significant, lending strong support for the premise that higher marginal tax rates reduce the price and increase the quantity demanded of employer contributions to health insurance. Using sample averages, Long and Scott computed the elasticity to be .41, implying that a 10 percent increase in the marginal tax rate increases the health insurance percentage by 4.1 percent.

The coefficient estimate on real family income, RFAMINC, was found to be positive but statistically insignificant. The result suggests that the income elasticities of demand are approximately equal for wage income and health care benefits. No empirical evidence was found for the expected direct relation between unionization and employer-sponsored health care benefits given that the coefficient estimate on UNION was not statistically different from zero. However, some cross-sectional findings in this same study and a paper by Woodbury (1983) did report a positive relation between the degree of unionization and total fringe benefits. Finally, the last two variables, reflecting demographic (PCTFEM) and employment (PCTSERV) differences over time in the United States, were both shown to lead to a higher percentage of compensation paid as employer contributions to health insurance.

---

[2]Due to limited data availability, Long and Scott were unable to examine the relation between firm size and the demand for health care benefits in a time series context. In their cross-sectional study of total fringe benefits, they found a positive relation between firm size and the demand for total fringe benefits (also see Woodbury [1983]). Long and Scott also specified a variable reflecting the labor turnover rate. Labor turnover did not seem to be a likely determinant of health care benefits, however, and proved to be statistically insignificant; hence, the results for this variable are not discussed.

---

point. When employees can select from multiple similar plans offered by the employer and must pay more for more expensive plans, demand is found to be much more responsive to price. For example, Dowd and Feldman (1994/95) found that the demand for a health plan is highly elastic with respect to price at about –7.9 when multiple similar plans are offered. Strombom, Buchmueller, and Feldstein (2002) estimate elasticities ranging from –2 to –8.4 depending upon the cost of switching plans as measured by age, job tenure, and medical risk category.

THE HEALTH INSURANCE PRODUCT: TRADITIONAL VERSUS MANAGED CARE INSURANCE

Before the 1980s, the health insurance product was fairly easy to define because the consumer, insurer, and health care provider relationship was much less complicated. Most consumers, through their employers, purchased conventional insurance that allowed for free choice of health care provider. Insurance premiums were largely determined by community rating, where the premium is based on the risk characteristics of the entire membership. In contrast, when premiums are determined using **experience rating**, insurers place individuals, or groups of individuals, into different risk categories based on various identifiable personal characteristics, such as age, gender, industrial occupation, and prior illnesses. The main difference among health insurance plans before the 1980s was simply the amount of the deductible and copayment, if any, that the subscriber had to pay for medical services and the specific benefits covered under the plan.

Because physicians typically operated in solo practices, enrollees dealt directly with individual physicians or local hospitals for care rather than with a network of providers before the 1980s. Health care providers had full autonomy and practiced medicine as they deemed appropriate. The main function of the insurer was to manage the financial risk associated with medical care and to pay the usual, customary, or reasonable (UCR) charge for any medical services rendered by physicians. UCR means that the fee is limited to the lowest of three changes: the actual charge of the physician, the customary charge of the physician, or the prevailing charge in the local area.

Since 1980, however, managed care organizations (MCOs) have exploded on the health care scene. The phrase "managed care" has been assigned to these organizations because, by design, they are supposed to emphasize cost-effective methods of providing comprehensive services to enrollees in exchange for a prepaid premium. MCOs integrate the financing and delivery of medical care. The integration often involves such practices as a network of providers, reimbursement methods other than UCR charges, and various review mechanisms. MCOs also rely to a greater degree on experience rating of enrollees because of the price competition that results.

The main types of MCOs are the health maintenance organization, the preferred provider organization, and the point of service plan. A **health maintenance organization (HMO)**, like other MCOs, combines the financing and delivery of care into one organization by providing medical care to enrollees in exchange for a prepaid premium. A distinguishing feature of an HMO is that the assigned or chosen primary care provider acts as a gatekeeper and refers the patient for specialty and inpatient care. Four distinct types of HMOs are generally recognized:

> ***Staff Model.*** *In this type of HMO, physicians are directly employed by the organization on a salary basis. In terms of figure 4–1, a staff HMO merges the insurer and provider functions. Because medical care is not reimbursed on a fee-for-service basis, physicians have little if any incentive to overutilize medical services.*

> ***Group Model.*** *This type of HMO provides physician services by contracting with a group practice. Normally the group is compensated on a capitation basis. As a*

result, physicians in the group face a strong disincentive to overutilize medical services.

Network Model. *The only difference between the group model and the network model is that in the latter case, the HMO contracts with more than one group practice for physician services. As is the case with the group model, compensation is generally on a capitation basis.*

Individual Practice Association (IPA) Model *This form of HMO contracts with a number of physicians from various types of practice settings for medical services. In this situation, physicians generally provide care in a traditional office setting and are normally compensated on a fee-for-service basis, but at a discounted rate. In return, the HMO promises a large and continuous volume of patients.*

A **preferred provider organization (PPO)** is a different type of insurer and health care provider arrangement. A PPO exists when a third-party payer provides financial incentives to enrollees to acquire health care from a predetermined network of physicians and hospitals. The incentive can be in terms of a higher coinsurance or a higher deductible when someone acquires medical care outside the network of health care providers. To participate in a PPO network, physicians agree to accept a lower fee for services rendered. In return for a lower fee, physicians are promised a steady supply of patients. Normally, patients can directly seek out specialty or inpatient care if they belong to a PPO.

Like PPOs, **point-of-service (POS)** plans provide generous coverage when enrollees use in-network services and cover out-of-network services at reduced reimbursement rates. Unlike PPOs but similar to HMOs, POS plans assign each enrollee a primary caregiver who acts as a gatekeeper and authorizes specialty and inpatient care.

Estimates indicate that 93 percent of all privately insured workers in 2001 were covered by MCOs, reflecting a continual decline in conventional insurance coverage, which stood at 73 percent as recent as 1988. Most of the enrollment increase has taken place in the least restrictive managed care plans over the last five years. HMO s witnessed a decline in market share from a high of 31 percent in 1996 to 23 percent in 2001. PPOs, the least restrictive of the MCOs, enjoyed the largest surge in enrollment, from 11 percent in 1988 to 48 percent by 2001. Enrollments in POS plans also increased with its market share growing from 7 percent in 1993 to 25 percent in 1999 but then stabilizing at 22 percent since 2000.[5]

Landon, Wilson, and Cleary (1998), among others, argue that the traditional distinction among health insurance products, such as conventional insurance and MCOs, or even the distinction among MCOs, has become blurred in practice. For example, even the so-called conventional insurance plans now involve some type of utilization review program. Given that the traditional taxonomy of insurance plans may no longer adequately describe the differences among organizations, it is better to differentiate among health insurance products based on the types and restrictiveness of the financial incentives and management strategies facing patients and health care providers. Let us elaborate.

---

[5]The Kaiser Family Foundation and Health Research and Educational Trust. "Employee Health Benefits, 2001 Annual Survey." http://www.kff.org/content/2001/3138/EHB2001—6.pdf. Accessed June 11, 2002.

Financial Incentives and Management Strategies Facing Consumers/Patients

Depending on the precise nature of the health insurance product, consumers/patients face different financial incentives to use medical care. As examined theoretically in Chapter 5, the consumer's out-of-pocket price, as captured by the size of the deductible and coinsurance, inversely affects the quantity demanded of medical care. Some health insurance plans may contain high deductibles and coinsurance as a way of containing medical costs. In addition, some plans may set their premiums on an experience-rated basis as an incentive for subscribers to adopt more healthy lifestyles.

In addition to indirect financial incentives, insurers may also adopt various management strategies to directly affect the consumer's utilization of medical care. First, the insurer may require prior medical screening to avoid insuring high-risk patients or exclude coverage for preexisting conditions. Insurers may also restrict the choice of provider by building provider networks in which the consumer must participate. In addition, the insurer may employ a primary care gatekeeper to determine whether further services are medically warranted. Pre-authorization of medical services, a type of utilization review practice, is another management strategy affecting the consumer's direct use of medical care.

By combining the financial incentives and management strategies facing patients, we can get a better understanding of the underlying health insurance product. For example, a health insurance plan with a high deductible and coinsurance and experience-rated premiums, combined with limits on choice of physician and pre-authorization, offers much less insurance than one with no out-of-pocket costs or pre-authorization, community-rated premiums, and full choice of provider. The latter situation aptly describes the conventional insurance offered by Blue Cross plans back in the 1970s. A POS plan comes close to an example of the former situation as far as financial incentives and management strategies facing consumers are concerned.

Financial Incentives and Management Strategies Facing Health Care Providers

The health insurance product may also contain financial incentives and/or management strategies to affect the delivery of medical care by health care providers. As a result, the health insurance product can also be differentiated based on the types and restrictiveness of the financial incentives and management strategies facing health care providers. In terms of financial incentives, the health insurance product may adopt different provider reimbursement practices, such as fee-for-service, capitation, bonuses, and/or withholds. Withholds occur when the insurer withholds part of the health care provider's reimbursement until after a stipulated period at which the appropriate use of medical care has been evaluated. Inappropriate use of medical care results in the physician not receiving all or part of the withheld money. The prospect of incomplete reimbursement payments presumably acts as an incentive for health care providers to offer the truly medically necessary care.

As we saw in Chapter 4, fixed payment systems, such as capitation, can discourage the delivery of high-cost, low-benefit medicine. Capitation places the health care providers financially at risk for any cost overruns. When properly designed, performance-based measures, such as bonuses and withholds, can accomplish that same goal.

Insurers can also directly influence the delivery of medical care through various management strategies. Selective contracting, deselection of providers, physician profiling, utilization review, practice guidelines, and formularies are among the more common management strategies facing health care providers. **Selective contracting** occurs when managed care plans contract solely with an exclusive set of providers. The selection and **deselection** of providers involves the establishment of the criteria and process by which health care providers will be included in or terminated from the network. For example, insurers may include physicians in their network who are of high quality and/or utilize cost-effective practice patterns. **Physician profiling** may be used to monitor performance in the selection or deselection process. The profiling may only include information, for example, on the primary care physician's track record regarding referrals to specialty and inpatient care as a way to identify high-cost providers, or it may include information on quality of care or patient satisfaction.

Utilization review programs "seek to determine whether specific services are medically necessary and whether they are delivered at an appropriate level of intensity and cost" (Ermann, 1988, p. 683). **Practice guidelines** provide information to health care providers about the appropriate medical practice in certain situations. A **formulary** contains a list of pharmaceutical products that physicians must prescribe whenever necessary. All these management strategies are designed to directly affect how a physician behaves in a specific clinical circumstance.

Consequently, the health insurance product also differs based on the type of provider reimbursement method and the existence and restrictiveness of various management strategies. For example, a capitation reimbursement scheme in conjunction with utilization review and practice guidelines means a much different insurance product than one with a fee-for-service payment system in which the health care provider has full autonomy over patient care. The former situation resembles the staff HMO whereas the latter reflects the traditional BC/BS or commercial insurance of the 1970s.

The first column in table 6–2 provides a summary of the four basic features of any health insurance product: patient financial incentives, consumer management strategies, provider financial incentives, and provider management strategies. Below each feature is a list of specific policies aimed at altering the behavior of either consumers or health care providers. As you can see, health insurance is a complex and multidimensional product. At one extreme lies the perfectly unrestricted health insurance plan, the basic characteristics of which are provided in the second column of table 6–2. With this type of insurance consumers pay no out-of-pocket prices; health care providers are reimbursed based on the usual, customary, and reasonable fee-for-service; and there are no consumer or provider management strategies. At the other extreme, the basic characteristics of a perfectly restrictive insurance plan are shown in the third column of table 6–2. In this case, significant financial incentives and management strategies face both consumers and health care providers. In terms of examples, the traditional Blue Cross/Blue Shield insurance plan of the 1970s compares quite closely to the unrestricted plan described in table 6–2, while the staff HMO, except for the significant out-of-pocket price, fits the insurance plan described in the last column of table 6–2.

Although table 6–2 provides a good framework for defining and conceptualizing the health insurance product, some caveats are in order. It is important to realize that any one health insurer may offer multiple health insurance products. For example, a health insurer may offer both a staff HMO and a traditional indemnity plan. Of course, the prices of the

TABLE 6-2

Spectrum of Health Insurance Products

Basic Features (Examples)	Unrestricted or Complete Insurance Plan	Restrictive Insurance Plan
Patient Financial Incentives Deductibles Coinsurance Premiums	no or low deductible with no coinsurance community rated	significant deductible with a high coinsurance experience rated
Consumer Management Strategies Prior medical screening Restrictions on choice Gatekeeper Pre-authorization	no restrictions	consumers must receive care exclusively from the network of providers
Provider Financial Incentives Risk-sharing and/or bonus arrangements	none—UCR chages	capitation with bonuses or withholds
Provider Management Strategies Selective contracting Deselection Physician profiling Utilization review Practice guidelines Formularies	none	an array of management strategies are employed to control costs

two plans should differ significantly. It is also important to realize that health care providers may deal with various health insurance products. A large physician practice may treat some patients who belong to a PPO plan and others who subscribe to HMO plans, for example. An additional complexity is that a group physician practice may be reimbursed on a capitation basis by the insurer whereas the individual physician within the practice is compensated on a salary basis. It is also important to mention that financial incentives and management strategies may serve as complementary or substitute methods of controlling the behavior of consumers and providers. As Gold et al. (1995, p. 315) point out:

> For example, plans that capitate primary care physicians and place them at risk for specialty referrals and inpatient care through a withholding account may be expected to place particular emphasis on monitoring physicians to ensure that the financial incentives do not result in underservice. On the other hand, plans operating in areas where physicians are resistant to accepting much financial risk may rely particularly heavily on nonfinancial mechanisms such as utilization management to influence practice patterns.

THE REGULATION OF MCOS

There has been considerable debate in the academic literature and the popular press concerning the effect of managed care plans on the cost and quality of medical care. By design, MCOs are supposed to employ cost-effective methods of delivering a comprehensive set of services to enrollees for a fixed premium. The original proponents of managed care thought that MCOs would encourage preventive and coordinated primary care as a way of reducing the need for more expensive specialty and inpatient care. Also, advocates thought that MCOs would eliminate the high-cost, low-benefit medicine associated with traditional fee-for-service indemnity insurance (i.e., the moral hazard problem). As a result, high quality of care and low operating costs were expected from MCOs.

Because lower quality of care translates into lower costs and higher profits, critics claim that MCOs face an incentive to reduce the quality of care, perhaps by denying or skimping on costly but necessary medical treatments. Health care providers have no recourse but to follow the wishes of the MCOs given the restrictive financial incentives and management strategies they face, according to the critics.

Given this controversy which we discuss more fully in later chapters, many states and the federal government have introduced or enacted various regulations to influence the behavior of MCOs. Miller (1997, p. 1102) notes that the regulatory actions taken to control managed care practices have been "referred to as 'patient protection' or 'patient bill of rights' acts by proponents and as 'anti-managed' bills by those opposed." The legislation has attempted to extend the rights of patients and physicians and also improve the patient/physician relationship under managed care. According to Miller, in just six months from January to July 1996, more than 400 bills were introduced in the various states to control managed care practices. Most of the laws concern such issues as anti-gag rules, limits on financial incentives, continuity of care, and expanding the rights of health care professionals. Let's examine each of these issues more closely.

Gag rules prohibit doctors in a managed care plan from discussing treatment options not covered under the plan, from providing information on plan limitations, or from commenting unfavorably upon the plan. Opponents of managed care argue that gag rules cause physicians to deny care by suppressing useful information on alternative treatments that the managed care plan may not find cost-effective to provide. Managed care representatives claim that the so-called gag rules are designed to prevent physicians from disparaging the plan or releasing proprietary information concerning compensation and similar issues.

Critics further argue that managed care payment systems, such as capitation or performance-based systems like bonuses or withholds, create a financial incentive for physicians to deny medically appropriate or useful treatments. Indeed, much mention has been made in the popular press of "drive-through medicine," involving short maternity stays in hospitals or mastectomies taking place in outpatient rather than inpatient facilities because of managed care financial arrangements. Laws limiting financial incentives are designed to prevent denial of care from taking place. Managed care representatives, on the other hand, argue that the financial incentives of MCOs are necessary to control the moral hazard problem.

Miller notes that state policies offer little concrete guidance about how the general prohibition against financial incentives applies to the myriad financial arrangements set by

INSIGHT 6-2

Satisfaction with Managed Care in Switzerland

Not a day goes by, it seems, without a popular press article describing the experience of managed care in the United States. But do we know anything about how managed care has fared in other countries? To some extent we do. Perneger, Etter, and Rougemont (1996) were able to conduct a natural experiment on the effect of switching enrollees from indemnity health insurance to a managed care plan in Switzerland. It all began in the fall of 1992 when the University of Geneva automatically transferred the members of its indemnity plan into a managed care plan. Some of the characteristics associated with the managed care plan were restricted choice of primary care provider, gatekeeper referral to specialty care, gatekeepers paid on a salary basis, and no consumer copayment.

Employees semi-voluntarily joined the managed care program because they had only two choices. One choice was to switch to managed care and receive the benefit of a university-negotiated group insurance premium. The other was to opt out of the university plan and find a new indemnity insurance plan. Because the monthly premium was about 25 percent higher for the indemnity plan than for the managed care plan, 88 percent of the university's former plan members switched to managed care.

Perneger et al. performed a before-and-after evaluation of health status and satisfaction with care in the managed care and indemnity plans. Specifically, they compared three groups of enrollees: 332 managed care joiners, 186 nonjoiners who opted out and purchased an indemnity plan on their own, and a control group of 296 persons who continuously enrolled in other indemnity plans. Health status and satisfaction with care information was collected at the time of the switch and one year later.

The researchers found that health status over the one-year period remained unchanged in the three groups. Satisfaction with health insurance coverage increased for those belonging to the MCO but satisfaction with health insurance coverage declined for both the nonjoiners and the continuous indemnity plan enrollees. In addition, they found that the nonjoiners and the continuous indemnity plan members both experienced an increase in their satisfaction with health care, particularly with continuity of care, whereas the joiners suffered a loss in satisfaction with health care.

The main implication of the study is that the semi-voluntary change from an indemnity plan to a managed care plan had a mixed effect on global indicators of care: health status remained unchanged and satisfaction with insurance coverage increased but satisfaction with health care decreased for those in the managed care plan. While the basic limitation of the study is the one-year follow-up period, the authors point out that their results are consistent with those of the RAND Health Insurance Experiment of the 1970s (see Chapter 5). The RAND study also found that health status remained unchanged but satisfaction with health care worsened for a group of individuals who were randomly assigned to a managed care plan. The general dissatisfaction with health care in MCOs should not come as too much of a surprise given that economic theory predicts that people receive generous amounts of care, perhaps too much care, in a fee-for-service indemnity plan. If MCOs force individuals to consume the appropriate amount of care, obviously some will be disappointed.

MCOs. As a result, she claims that without additional clarification, regulatory actions against managed care financial arrangements will have to be argued on a case-by-case basis, creating much uncertainty for the various parties involved.

Medical experts argue that continuity of care is an important consideration for the patient/physician relationship and for patient well-being, especially for certain groups, such as pregnant women or the severely ill. Critics of MCOs claim that continuity of care is at stake because some employers subscribe to only one managed care plan, because a managed care plan may change its networks of physicians, or because physicians may be deselected. In all these cases, consumers have to pay more to visit a physician of their own choice and the continuity of care is compromised. Although proponents argue that MCOs can only provide the desired health care cost savings for society by directing patients to selected physicians, laws have been introduced in many states to extend the option of continued care from primary care givers.

In addition, numerous laws have been introduced across the states that aim to expand the rights of health care professionals. With the growth of MCOs, many health care professionals feel the pressure from market demands and also the loss of autonomy brought on by contracts with managed care plans. For example, some physicians find themselves unable to participate in or are deselected from managed care plans without being provided with the rationale.

The first laws introduced concerned any willing provider (AWP) or freedom of choice (FOC) laws. According to Hellinger (1995, p. 297), "AWP laws require managed care plans to accept any qualified provider who is willing to accept the terms and conditions of a managed care plan." According to the law, MCOs do not have to contract with all providers but must explicitly state evaluation criteria and ensure "due process" for providers wishing to contract with the plan. Due process rights provide professionals with access to information regarding MCO standards, termination decisions, and physician profiling. FOC laws allow a patient to be reimbursed for medical services received from qualified physicians from outside the network. FOC laws do not guarantee that the patient will incur the same out-of-pocket cost, however. Proponents of AWP and FOC laws argue that they increase the continuity of care by offering a fuller choice of provider. Opponents argue that without selective contracting, managed care plans are unable to obtain volume discounts because they are powerless to channel patients to selected providers. In addition, it is alleged that these laws lead to a diminished quality of care because of the higher monitoring costs brought on by a greater number of health care providers.

In sum, anti-gag laws, laws restricting the financial incentives of MCOs, laws promoting continuity of care, and laws extending the rights of health care professionals are among the various regulations advanced by various states to control the practices of MCOs. The basic hypothesis is that MCOs face an incentive to restrict the quality of care because increased profits can be made. Critics claim that various financial incentives and management strategies help MCOs achieve their objective of maximum profits. Interestingly, all these laws essentially attempt to transform MCOs into indemnity plans. The superiority of indemnity and managed care plans remains a controversial issue and is the subject of ongoing theoretical and empirical debates.

INSIGHT 6 – 3

Increasing the Demand for Private Health Insurance in Australia

The Medicare program in Australia provides universal, compulsory, and tax-financed public insurance to its citizens. The program provides free access to public hospital care with some coverage for certain kinds of physician and pharmaceutical care but with some consumer cost sharing. Under the National Health Act of 1953, private health insurance is allowed to cover services not paid by Medicare such as dentistry and physical therapy. Individuals can also purchase private health insurance to gain access to private hospitals and choice of specialists in both private and public hospitals. Private hospitals are sometimes viewed as a way of getting quick attention and to avoid public hospital waiting lists. About one-third of all health care spending currently comes from the private sector in Australia. Private health insurance is purchased on an individual basis rather than through employers in Australia.

From 1984 to 1998, the percentage of the Australian population with private health insurance declined from 50 to 30.1 percent. The decline in private health insurance coverage apparently occurred because of the free treatment in public hospitals (although hospital doctors are appointed rather than chosen) under Medicare and because the government mandated community rating of private health plans. Community rating made the insurance expensive and unattractive for low-risk individuals such as the young and healthy but attractive for high-risk consumers such as the elderly and unhealthy. In fact, it was believed that many people joined private plans to receive timely treatment, only to withdraw from the plan once the treatment was completed. This opportunistic "hit and run" behavior was not conducive to the proper functioning of the private health insurance market.

To relieve the pressure on the public hospital system brought on by the decline in private insurance coverage, the Australian government instituted three new policies over a three-year period to increase the demand for private health insurance. The Private Health Insurance Incentives Act, implemented in July 1997, introduced a Medicare levy surcharge of 1 percent of income on high-income households if they failed to purchase private health insurance coverage with low deductibles. The Act also instituted a partial refund of insurance premiums to low-income individuals to encourage the purchase of private health insurance. These policies, however, were ineffectual, paradoxically resulting in an almost immediate reduction in the percentage of the population covered by private insurance.

Given the failure of the first policy, the Private Health Insurance Incentives Act was amended in January 1999 to include an across-the-board 30 percent subsidy on both existing and new private health insurance policies. The immediate response to this sizeable rebate was a moderate increase in the percentage of persons covered by private health insurance, from 30.1 percent at the end or 1998 to 31.1 percent at the end of 1999.

Given the relatively small percentage change in enrollment from the second policy, the National Health Amendment Act of 1999 created the Lifetime Health Cover, which took effect in July 2000. The Lifetime Health Cover softened the community rating requirement and allowed insurers to adjust premiums to reflect age. However, the regulatory change allowed anyone who was insured by the cutoff date of June 30, 2000, to pay the base rate regardless of age. For those signing up after the cutoff date the base premium increased by 2 percent for each year the individual was older than 30 when first joining, up to a maximum of 70 percent. In essence, the Lifetime Health Cover allowed people to lock in at a low premium for life.

The program and its promotion in 1999 were so successful that the government extended the sign-up deadline to July 15, 2000. The percentage of people with private health insurance exploded from 31.3 percent at the end of 1999 to 43 percent by the end of June 2001. (As of March 31, 2002, it stood at 44.7 percent.) It is unclear, however, what impact the age rating had on enrollment apart from that of the 30 percent subsidy, given that the subsidy may have taken some time to fully take effect.

Hopkins and Frech (2001) point to a study by Butler (1999) that estimated the demand elasticity of private health insurance in Australia at −.5. Notice the similarity to the elasticity estimates provided in table 6-1. This elasticity explains only 15 percent of the increase in enrollment given the 30 percent subsidy, but enrollment increased by over 40 percent during the period. Therefore, it appears that the Lifetime Health Cover had the greatest impact on increasing the demand for private health insurance in Australia.

This insight is particularly appealing because it demonstrates the important factors underlying the demand for health insurance, such as the price of health insurance. It also shows that with some knowledge of the underlying factors, governments around the world might change incentives to alter the demand for private health insurance if deemed necessary.

SOURCE: This insight is based on Hopkins and Frech (2001) and Wilcox (2001).

SUMMARY

As for any good or service, the demand for private health insurance can be derived theoretically from an expected utility maximization model. As a result, the quantity demanded of health insurance can be specified as a function of user price, income, and other factors. Empirical studies have found that an individual's demand for health insurance is inelastic with respect to both price and income.

The health insurance product is multidimensional and complex because many attributes, such as benefits covered, out-of-pocket payments, choice of provider, and the provider payment scheme, must be considered. Most of the insured in the United States today are covered by some type of managed care plan. Many states have enacted various regulations to control the financial incentives and management strategies adopted by managed care plans.

REVIEW QUESTIONS AND PROBLEMS

1. Joe is currently unemployed and without health insurance coverage. He derives utility (U) from his interest income on his savings (Y) according to the following function:

$$U = 5Y^{1/2}.$$

   Joe presently makes about $40,000 of interest income per year. He realizes that there is about a 5 percent probability that he may suffer a heart attack. The cost of treatment will be about $20,000 if a heart attack occurs.
   A. Calculate Joe's expected utility level without any health insurance coverage.
   B. Calculate Joe's expected income without any health insurance coverage.
   C. Suppose Joe must pay a premium of $1,500 for health insurance coverage with ACME insurance. Would he buy the health insurance? Why or why not?
   D. Suppose now that the government passes a law that allows all people—not just the self-employed or employed—to have their entire insurance premium exempted from taxes. Joe is in the 33 percent tax bracket. Would he buy the health insurance at a premium cost of $1,500? Why or why not? What implication can be drawn from the analysis?
   E. Suppose Joe purchases the health insurance coverage and represents the average subscriber, and his expectations are correct. Calculate the loading fee the insurance company will receive.

2. During the Reagan administration, the marginal tax rate on wage income fell dramatically. For example, the top rate was sliced from 70 to 33 percent. Use the demand theory of health insurance to predict the effect of this change on the quantity demanded of employer-sponsored health insurance.

3. Explain the effect of the following changes on the quantity demanded of health insurance.
   A. A reduction in the tax-exempt fraction of health insurance premiums
   B. An increase in buyer income
   C. An increase in per capita medical expenditures
   D. New technologies that enable medical illnesses to be predicted more accurately
   E. A tendency among buyers to become less risk averse, on average

4. What are the primary differences between the HMO, PPO, and POS plans?

5. Explain the following terms:
   A. Community rating
   B. Experience rating
   C. Selective contracting
   D. Utilization review
   E. Physician profiling
   F. Practice guidelines
   G. Formulary
   H. Gatekeeper
   I. Gag rules
   J. Any Willing Provider law
   K. Freedom of Choice law

6. Briefly summarize the two ways regarding how managed care might affect the cost and quality of medical care.

7. If you had the choice between a traditional unrestricted indemnity plan with a 10 percent copayment and a staff HMO with no copayment, at what percentage difference in premiums (i.e., 10 percent, 20 percent, 30 percent) would you be indifferent between the plans? Do you think your choice of the percentage difference is a function of your age and/or health status? If you were elderly and/or sickly, which plan would you prefer if they cost you the same amount? Why?

8. Would a theory X'er or Y'er want increased regulation of MCOs? Why?

ONLINE RESOURCES

To access Internet links related to the topics in this chapter, please visit our web site at http://santerre.swcollege.com.

REFERENCES

Butler J. "Estimating Elasticities of Demand for Private Health Insurance in Australia." National Centre for Epidemiology and Population Health. Working Paper no. 43, ANU, Canberra, 1999.

Cowan, Cathy A., Patricia A. McDonnell, Katherine R. Levit, and Mark A. Zezza. "Burden of Health Care Costs: Businesses, Households, and Governments, 1987–2000." *Health Care Financing Review* 23 (Spring 2002), pp. 131–59.

Dowd, Bryan, and Roger Feldman. "Premium Elasticities of Health Plan Choice." *Inquiry* 31 (winter 1994/95), pp. 438–44.

Ermann, Dan. "Hospital Utilization Review. Past Experience, Future Directions."*Journal of Health Politics, Policy, and Law* 13 (winter 1988), pp. 683–704.

Farley, Pamela J., and Gail Wilensky. "Household Wealth and Health Insurance as Protection Against Medical Risks." In *Horizontal Equity, Uncertainty, and Economic Well-Being*, eds. David Martin and Timothy Smeeding. Chicago: University of Chicago Press for the NBER, 1984, pp. 323–54.

Gold, Marsha, Lyle Nelson, Timothy Lake, Robert Hurley, and Robert Berenson. "Behind the Curve: A Critical Assessment of How Little Is Known about Arrangements between Managed Care Plans and Physicians." *Medical Care Research and Review* 52 (September 1995), pp. 307–41.

Goldstein, Gerald S., and Mark V. Pauly. "Group Health Insurance as a Local Public Good." In *The Role of Health Insurance in the Health Services Sector*, ed. Richard Rossett. New York: NBER, 1976, pp. 73–110.

Hellinger, Fred J. "Update: Any-Willing-Provider and Freedom-of-Choice Laws: An Economic Assessment." *Health Affairs* 14 (winter 1995), pp. 297–302.

Holmer, Martin. "Tax Policy and the Demand for Health Insurance." *Journal of Health Economics* 3, no. 3 (1984), pp. 203–21.

Hopkins, Sandra, and H. E. Frech III. "The Rise of Private Health Insurance in Australia: Early Effects on Insurance and Hospital Markets." *Economic and Labor Relations Review* 12 (December 2001), pp. 225–38.

Kumar, Nanda, Marc A. Cohen, Christine E. Bishop, and Stanley S. Wallack. "Understanding the Factors Behind the Decision to Purchase Varying Coverage Amounts of Long-Term Care Insurance." *Health Services Research* 29 (February 1995), pp. 653–78.

Landon, Bruce E., Ira B. Wilson, and Paul D. Cleary. "A Conceptual Model of the Effects of Health Care Organizations on the Quality of Medical Care." *Journal of the American Medical Association* 279 (May 6, 1998), pp. 1377–82.

Liu, Chuan-Fen, and Jon B. Christianson. "The Demand for Health Insurance by Employees in a Voluntary Small Group Insurance Program." *Medical Care* 36 (1998), pp. 437–43.

Long, James E., and Frank A. Scott. "The Income Tax and Nonwage Compensation." *Review of Economics and Statistics* (May 1982), pp. 211–19.

Manning, William G., and M. Susan Marquis. "Health Insurance: The Trade-off between Risk Pooling and Moral Hazard." (R-3729–NCHSR) Santa Monica, CA: RAND, 1989.

Marquis, M. Susan, and Stephen H. Long. "Worker Demand for Health Insurance in the Non-Group Market." *Journal of Health Economics* 14 (1995), pp. 47–63.

Miller, Tracy E. "Managed Care Regulation: In the Laboratory of the States." *Journal of the American Medical Association* 278 (October 1, 1997), pp. 1102–9.

Pauly, Mark V. "Taxation, Health Insurance, and Market Failure in the Medical Economy." *Journal of Economic Literature* 24 (June 1986), pp. 629–75.

Perneger, Thomas V., Jean-François Etter, and Andre Rougemont. "Switching Swiss Enrollees from Indemnity Health Insurance to Managed Care: The Effect on Health Status and Satisfaction with Care." *American Journal of Public Health* 86 (March 1996), pp. 388–93.

Short, Pamela F., and Amy K. Taylor. "Premiums, Benefits, and Employee Choice of Health Insurance Options." *Journal of Health Economics* 8 (1989), pp. 293–311.

Strombom, Bruce A., Thomas C. Buchmueller, and Paul J. Feldstein. "Switching Costs, Price Sensitivity and Health Plan Choice." *Journal of Health Economics* 21 (2002), pp. 89–116.

Taylor, Amy K., and Gail R. Wilensky. "The Effect of Tax Policies on Expenditures for Private Health Insurance." In *Market Reforms in Health Care,* ed. Jack Meyer. Washington, D.C.: American Enterprise Institute, 1983.

Wilcox, Sharon. "Promoting Private Health Insurance in Australia." *Health Affairs* 20 (May/June 2001), pp. 152–61.

Woodbury, Stephen A. "Substitution between Wage and Nonwage Benefits." *American Economic Review* (March 1983), pp. 166–82.

MEDICAL CARE PRODUCTION AND COSTS

In December 2000, it was announced that Northeast Georgia Health System, a 338-bed not-for-profit hospital in Gainsville, Georgia, proposed to buy Lanier Park Hospital, a 119-bed for-profit hospital also in Gainsville, for $40 million. The acquisition would result in only one hospital in Gainsville. Executives at the hospitals claim the acquisition would save $2 million annually (Kirchheimer, 2000). Similarly, in May 2002, Anthem proposed an acquisition of Trigon Health Care. Both of these companies are for-profit insurers within the Blue Cross/Blue Shield system. The newly created organization would be the fifth largest publicly traded health benefits company in terms of revenues and membership, with assets of nearly $9 billion, revenues of $13 billion, net income of $458 million, and 10 million members. Spokespersons for the two insurers argued the merger would lead to $40 million in pretax savings in 2003 and $75 million in pretax savings in 2004 (Greenwald, 2002).

These are just two examples of the many mergers that take place in the health care sector. Recent combinations among firms in other health care markets, such as the physician, pharmaceutical, and nursing home industries, also testify to the assertion that larger firm size confers significant cost advantages. But are there any plausible economic reasons to support the claim that cost savings are associated with larger organizational size? If so, sound economic reasoning can justify a merger among two or more firms in the same industry. On the other hand, might operating costs actually increase as a firm gets too large? If that is the case, a merger among firms is not desirable if cost savings are the overriding concern.

This chapter introduces various microeconomic principles and concepts that can be used to analyze the cost structure of medical firms and thereby determine the true relation between firm size and costs of production. In addition, the chapter:

> Discusses various production characteristics, including marginal and average productivity and the elasticity of substitution among inputs.

> Uses the resulting production theory to derive short-run and long-run costs of production.

> Examines economies and diseconomies of scale and scope.

THE SHORT-RUN PRODUCTION FUNCTION OF THE REPRESENTATIVE MEDICAL FIRM

All medical firms, including hospitals, physician clinics, nursing homes, and pharmaceutical companies, earn revenues from producing and selling some type of medical output. Production and retailing activities occur regardless of the form of ownership (i.e., for-profit, public, or not-for-profit). Because these activities take place in a world of scarce resources, microeconomics can provide valuable insights into the operation and planning processes of medical firms. In this chapter, we focus on various economic principles that guide the production behavior of medical firms. We begin by analyzing the short-run production process of a hypothetical medical firm.

To simplify our discussion of short-run production, we make five assumptions. First, we assume the medical firm produces a single output of medical services, q. Second, we initially assume only two medical inputs exist: nurse-hours, n, and a composite capital good, k. We can think of the composite capital good as an amalgamation of all types of capital, including any medical equipment and the physical space in the medical establishment. Third, since the short run is defined as a period of time over which the level of *at least* one input cannot be changed, we assume the quantity of capital is fixed at some amount. This assumption makes intuitive sense, because it is usually more difficult to change the stock of capital than the number of nurse-hours in the short run. Fourth, we assume for now that the medical firm faces an incentive to produce as efficiently as possible. Finally, we assume the medical firm possesses perfect information regarding the demands for its product. We relax the last two assumptions at the end of the chapter.

As we know from Chapter 2, a production function identifies how various inputs can be combined and transformed into a final output. In the present example, the short-run production function for medical services can be mathematically generalized as

(7–1) $q = f(n, k_*)$.

The short-run production function for medical services in equation 7–1 indicates that the level of medical services is a function of a variable nurse input and a fixed (denoted with an asterisk) capital input. The production function identifies the different ways nurse-hours and capital can be combined to produce various levels of medical services. The production function allows for the possibility that each level of output may be produced by several different combinations of the nurse and capital inputs. Each combination is assumed to be **technically efficient**, since it results in the maximum amount of output that is feasible given the state of technology. Later we will see that both technical and economic considerations determine a unique least-cost, or economically efficient, method of production.

We begin our analysis by examining how the level of medical services, q, relates to a greater quantity of the variable nurse input, n, given that the capital input, k_*, is assumed to be fixed. Various microeconomic principles and concepts relating to production theory are used to determine the precise relation between the employment of the variable input and the level of total output. As mentioned in Chapter 2, one important microeconomic principle from production theory is the law of diminishing marginal productivity. This is not really a law; rather, it is a generalization about production behavior and states that total output at first increases at an *increasing* rate, but after some point increases at a *de-*

creasing rate, with respect to a greater quantity of a variable input, holding all other inputs constant.[1]

Figure 7–1 applies the law of diminishing productivity. It shows a graphical relation between the quantity of medical services on the vertical axis and the number of nurse-hours on the horizontal axis. The curve is referred to as the *total product curve*, TP, because it depicts the total output produced by different levels of the variable input, holding all other inputs constant. Notice that the quantity of services first increases at an increasing rate over the range of nurse-hours $0n_1$. The rate of increase is identified by the slope of the curve at each point. As you can see, the slope of the total product curve increases in value as the tangent lines become steeper over this range of nurse-hours.

F I G U R E   7 – 1

The Total Product Curve

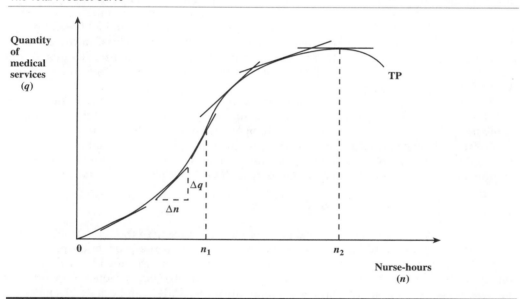

The total product curve shows that output initially increases at an increasing rate from 0 to n_1 nurse-hours, then increases at a decreasing rate from n_1 to n_2 nurse-hours, and finally declines after n_2 nurse-hours as the medical firm employs more nurse-hours. Diminishing marginal productivity provides the reason why output fails to expand at an increasing rate after n_1 nurse-hours.

---

[1]In Chapter 2, we assumed for simplicity that the law of diminishing marginal returns sets in immediately; that is, the marginal product of medical services was always declining. In this chapter, we take a less restrictive approach to allow for the theoretical possibility that the marginal product of the variable input may increase initially. The fundamental idea remains the same, however. Eventually a point is reached where additional units of an input generate smaller marginal returns.

Beyond point n_1, however, further increases in nurse-hours cause medical services to increase, but at a decreasing rate. That is the point at which diminishing productivity sets in. Notice that the slope of the total product curve gets smaller as output increases in the range n_1n_2 (as indicated by the flatter tangent lines). At n_2, the slope of the total product curve is zero, as reflected in the horizontal tangent line. Finally, beyond n_2, we allow for the possibility that too many nurse-hours will lead to a reduction in the quantity of medical services. The slope of the total product curve is negative beyond n_2.

In terms of the production decision at the firm level, we have not yet accounted for the specific reasoning underlying the law of diminishing marginal productivity. Economists point to the fixed short-run inputs as the basis for diminishing productivity. For example, when nurse-hours are increased at first, there is initially a considerable amount of capital, the fixed input, with which to produce medical services. The abundance of capital enables increasingly greater amounts of medical services to be generated from the employment of additional nurses. In addition, a synergy effect may dominate initially. The synergy effect means that nurses, working cooperatively as a team, are able to produce more output collectively than separately because of labor specialization, for example.

At some point, however, the fixed capital becomes limited relative to the variable input (e.g., too little medical equipment and not enough medical space), and additional nurse-hours generate successively fewer incremental units of medical services. In the extreme, as more nurses are crowded into a medical establishment of a fixed size, the quantity of services may actually begin to decline as congestion sets in and creates unwanted production problems.

In general, any physical constraint in production, such as the fixed size of the facility or a limited amount of medical equipment, can cause diminishing productivity to set in at some point. In fact, if it weren't for diminishing productivity, the world's food supply could be grown in a single flowerpot and the demand for medical services could be completely satisfied by a single large medical organization. What a wonderful world it would be! Unfortunately, however, diminishing productivity is the rule rather than the exception.

Marginal and Average Products

We can also use marginal and average product curves rather than the total product curve to illustrate the fundamental characteristics associated with the production process. In general, the marginal product is the change in total output associated with a one-unit change in the variable input. In terms of our example, the marginal product or quantity of medical services associated with an additional nurse-hour, MP_n, can be stated as follows:

(7–2) $$MP_n = \Delta q/\Delta n.$$

The magnitude of the marginal product of a nurse-hour reveals the additional quantity of medical services produced by each additional nurse-hour. It is a measure of the marginal contribution of a nurse-hour in the production of medical services.

In figure 7–1, the slope of the total product curve at every point represents the marginal product of a nurse-hour, since it measures the rise (vertical distance) over the run (horizontal distance), or $\Delta q/\Delta n$. Consequently, we can determine the marginal product of an additional nurse-hour by examining the slope of the total product curve at each level of nurse-hours. Figure 7–2 graphically illustrates the marginal product of a nurse-hour. Initially, the MP_n is positive and increases over the range $0n_1$ due to increasing marginal pro-

FIGURE 7-2

The Marginal Product Curve

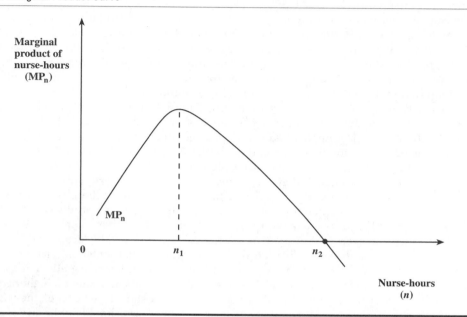

The marginal product of an additional nurse-hour is found by dividing the change in output by the change in the number of nurse-hours and is measured by the slope of the total product curve. Marginal productivity first increases with the number of nurse-hours because of synergy and labor specialization and then falls because of the fixed input that exists in the short run.

ductivity. In the range $n_1 n_2$, the marginal product is positive but decreasing, because diminishing marginal productivity has set in. At n_2, the marginal product of a nurse-hour is zero and becomes negative thereafter. The marginal product curve suggests that each additional nurse-hour cannot be expected to generate the same marginal contribution to total output as the previous one. The law of diminishing marginal productivity dictates that in the short run, a level of output is eventually reached where an incremental increase in the number of nurse-hours leads to successively fewer additions to total output (because some other inputs are fixed).

In addition to the MP_n, the average product of a nurse-hour can provide insight into the production process. In general, the average product equals the total quantity of output divided by the level of the variable input. In terms of the present example, the average product of a nurse-hour, AP_n, is calculated by dividing the total quantity of medical services by the total number of nurse-hours:

(7–3) $AP_n = q/n.$

The average product of a nurse-hour measures the average quantity of medical services produced within an hour. For example, suppose we (crudely) measure total medical services by the number of daily patient-hours at a medical facility. In addition, suppose 200 nurse-hours are employed to service 300 daily patient-hours. In this example, the average product of a nurse-hour equals 300/200 or 1½ patients per hour.

We can also derive the average product of a nurse-hour from the total product curve, as shown in figure 7–3a. To derive the AP_n, a ray from the origin is extended to each point on the total product curve. The slope of the ray measures the AP_n for any given level of nurse-hours, since it equals the rise over the run, or q/n. In figure 7–3a three rays, labeled $0A$, $0B$, and $0C$, emanate from the origin to the total product curve. The slope of ray $0A$ is flatter than that of $0B$ and therefore is of a lower magnitude. In fact, as it is drawn, ray $0B$ has a greater slope than any other ray emanating from the origin. At this level of nurse-hours, the average product is maximized. The slope of ray $0C$ is flatter and of a lower magnitude than that of $0B$. The implication is that average product initially increases over the range $0n_3$ reaches a maximum at n_3, and then decreases, as shown in figure 7–3b. It is the law of diminishing marginal productivity that accounts for the shape of the AP_n.

In figure 7–4, the marginal and average product curves are superimposed to illustrate how they are related. Some characteristics of the relation between these two curves are worth mentioning. First, the marginal product curve cuts the average product curve at its maximum point. In fact, it is a common mathematical principle that the marginal equals the average when the average is at its extreme value.[2] Second, the MP_n lies above the AP_n whenever the AP_n is increasing. This too reflects a common mathematical principle and should come as little surprise to the reader. For example, if your average grade in a course is a B+ until the final and you receive an A on the final exam, this incremental higher grade pulls up your final average grade. Third, the MP_n lies below the AP_n whenever the AP_n is declining. This relation between marginal and average values also should not be surprising. As you know, your course grade slips if you receive a lower grade on the final exam relative to your previous course average.

Putting the grades aside (because learning is more important than grades—right?), we can discuss the relation between the marginal and average product curves in terms of our example concerning nurse-hours and the production of medical services. For this discussion, it helps to think of the marginal product curve as the amount of medical services generated hourly by the next nurse hired. Also, we can think of the average product curve as the average quantity of medical services generated by the existing team of nurses within an hour—that is, the "team" average.

Looking back at figure 7–4, notice that the next nurse hired always generates more services per hour than the team average up to point n_3. Consequently, up to this point, each additional nurse helps to pull up the team's average level of output. Beyond n_3, however, the incremental nurse hired generates less services per hour than the team average;

---

[2]*Proof:* For simplicity, suppose the production function relates the quantity of output, q, to a single input of nurse-hours, n, such that $q = f(n)$. The average product of nurse-hours, AP_n, can be written as $f(n)/n$. To determine where AP_n reaches a maximum point, we can take the first derivative of AP_n and set it equal to zero. Following the rule for taking the derivative of a quotient of two functions (see Chiang, 1984), it follows that

(7–1a) $$f'(n) = \frac{f(n)}{n}.$$

Since $f'(n)$ equals MP_n and $f(n)/n$ equals AP_n, $MP_n = AP_n$ when AP_n is maximized.

FIGURE 7–3

Deriving the Average Product Curve from the Total Product Curve

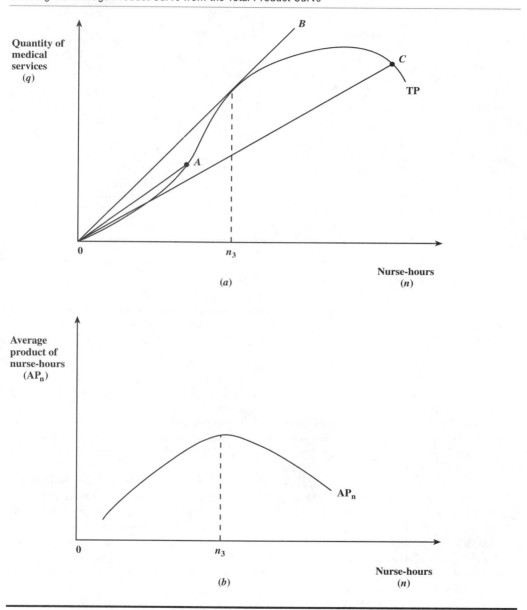

The average product of a nurse-hour is found by dividing total output by the total number of nurse-hours and can be derived by measuring the slope of a ray emanating from the origin to each point on the total product curve. Average productivity first increases with the number of nurse-hours and then declines because of increasing and then diminishing marginal productivity.

FIGURE 7-4
Relation between the Marginal and Average Product Curves

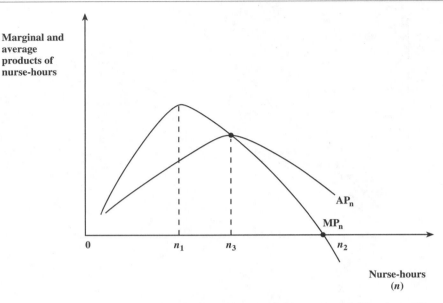

Average productivity rises when marginal productivity exceeds average productivity. Average productivity falls when marginal productivity lies below average productivity. Marginal productivity equals average productivity when average productivity is maximized.

as a result, the team average falls. It is important to realize that any increase or decrease in the marginal product has nothing to do with the individual talents of each additional nurse employed. Rather, it involves the law of diminishing marginal productivity. At some point in the production process, the incremental nurse becomes less productive due to the constraint imposed by the fixed input. The marginal productivity, in turn, influences the average productivity of the team of nurses.

At first glance, it seems logical to assume that a medical firm desires to produce at a point like n_1 or n_3 in figure 7–4. After all, they represent the points at which either the marginal or the average product is maximized. In most cases, however, a medical firm finds it more desirable to achieve some financial target, such as a maximum or break-even level of profits. As a result, we need more information concerning the revenue and cost structures the medical firm faces before we can pinpoint the desired level of production. In later chapters we will see that under normal conditions, the relevant range of production in figure 7–4 is between n_3 and n_2.

Elasticity of Input Substitution

Up to now, we have assumed only one variable input. Realistically, however, the medical firm operates with more than one variable input in the short run. Thus, there may be some possibilities for substitution between any two variable inputs. For example, licensed practical nurses often substitute for registered nurses in the production of inpatient services, and physician assistants sometimes substitute for physicians in the production of ambulatory services. The actual degree of substitutability between any two inputs depends on technical and legal considerations. For example, physician assistants are prohibited by law from prescribing medicines in most states. In addition, licensed practical nurses normally lack the technical knowledge needed to perform all the duties of registered nurses.

In general terms, the elasticity of substitution between any two inputs equals the percentage change in the input ratio divided by the percentage change in the ratio of the inputs' marginal productivities, holding constant the level of output, or

$$(7\text{--}4) \qquad \sigma = \frac{\Delta(I_1/I_2)}{I_1/I_2} \div \frac{\Delta(MP_2/MP_1)}{MP_2/MP_1}$$

I_i (i = 1,2) stands for the quantity employed of each input. The ratio of marginal productivities, MP_2/MP_1, referred to as the *marginal rate of technical substitution*, illustrates the rate at which one input substitutes for the other in the production process, at the margin. For example, suppose the marginal product of a registered nurse-hour is four patients and the marginal product of a licensed practical nurse-hour is two patients. It follows that two licensed practical nurse-hours are needed to substitute completely for one registered nurse-hour.

Theoretically, σ (Greek letter sigma) takes on values between 0 and $+\infty$ and identifies the percentage change in the input ratio that results from a 1 percent change in the marginal rate of technical substitution. The magnitude of σ identifies the degree of substitution between the two inputs. For example, if σ = 0, the variable inputs cannot be substituted in production. In contrast, when $\sigma = \infty$, the two variable inputs are perfect substitutes in production. In practice, it is more common for σ to take on values between these two extremes, implying that limited substitution possibilities exist.

SHORT-RUN COST THEORY OF THE REPRESENTATIVE MEDICAL FIRM

Before we begin our discussion of the medical firm's cost curves, we need to address the difference between the ways economists and accountants refer to costs. In particular, accountants consider only the *explicit costs* of doing business when determining the accounting profits of a medical firm. Explicit costs are easily quantified because a recent market transaction is available to provide an accurate measure of cost. Wage payments to the hourly medical staff, electric utility bills, and medical supply expenses are all examples of the explicit costs medical firms incur because disbursement records can be consulted to determine the magnitudes of these expenditures.

Economists, unlike accountants, consider both the explicit and implicit costs of production. *Implicit costs* reflect the opportunity costs of using any resources the medical firm owns. For example, a general practitioner (GP) may own the physical assets (e.g., clinic and medical equipment) used in producing physician services. In this case, a recent market transaction is unavailable to determine the cost of using these assets. Yet an opportunity cost is incurred when using them because the physical assets could have been rented out for an alternative use. For example, the clinic could be remodeled and rented

INSIGHT 7–1

A Production Function for Hospital Admissions

Jensen and Morrisey (1986) provide one of the more interesting empirical studies on the production characteristics of hospital services. In keeping with equation 7–1, Jensen and Morrisey estimated a production function for admissions at 3,540 nonteaching hospitals in the United States as of 1983 in the following general form:[1]

(7–5) $\begin{aligned} \text{Case-mix-adjusted} \\ \text{hospital admissions} \end{aligned} = f(\text{Physicians, nurses, other} \\ \text{nonphysician staff, hospital beds}, X).$

Notice that hospital admissions serve as the measure of output. Given the heterogeneous nature of hospital services, however, this output measure was adjusted for case-mix differences across hospitals by multiplying it by the Medicare patient index. This index is the weighted sum of the proportions of the hospital's Medicare patients in different diagnostic categories where the weights reflect the average costs per case in each diagnostic group. The number of physicians, nurses (full-time equivalent [FTE] units), and other nonphysician staff (FTE) represented the labor inputs, the number of beds constituted the capital input, and X stood for a number of other production factors not central to the discussion.

To put equation 7–5 in a form that can be estimated with a multiple regression technique, Jensen and Morrisey specified a translog production function. The form and properties of this particular mathematical function are too complex to describe briefly; it suffices to note that the translog is a flexible functional form that imposes very few restrictions on the estimated parameters.[2]

From the empirical estimation, Jensen and Morrisey were able to derive estimates of each input's marginal product. As expected, the marginal products were all positive. Jensen and Morrisey noted that the marginal product of each input declined in magnitude with greater usage, as the law of diminishing marginal product suggests. The estimated marginal product of a physician implied that an additional doctor generated 6.05 additional case-mix-adjusted annual admissions. The nurse input was by far the most productive input. In particular, the marginal nurse was responsible for producing about 20.3 additional case-mix-adjusted annual admissions. The marginal products of other nonphysician staff and beds were found to be 6.97 and 3.04 case-mix-adjusted annual admissions, respectively.

The estimation procedure also generated sufficient information to enable Jensen and Morrisey to measure the input substitution possibilities available to hospitals. Each input was found to be a substitute for the others in production. In particular, the substitution elasticities between physicians and nurses, physicians and beds, and nurses and beds were

---

[1]For the sake of brevity, we do not discuss their results for the sample of teaching hospitals.

[2]In a translog function, (the natural log of) each independent variable enters the equation in both linear and quadratic form. In addition, a cross-product linear term is created between any two independent variables and specified in the function. Similar cross-product terms are eliminated from the specification. To ensure a well-behaved function, restrictions are normally imposed on the parameter estimates.

reported to be .547, .175, and .124, respectively. The relatively large elasticity of .547 between physicians and nurses tells us that the average hospital can more easily substitute between these two inputs. This particular input elasticity estimate can be interpreted to mean that a 10 percent increase in the marginal productivity of a doctor causes a 5.47 percent increase in the ratio of nurses to doctors, *ceteris paribus*. These positive substitution elasticities suggest that hospital policymakers can avoid some of the price (wage) increase in any one input by substituting with the others. For example, to maintain a given level of admissions, a wage increase for nurses might be partially absorbed by increasing the number of hospital beds.

as a beauty salon, and the medical equipment could be rented out to another physician. Thus, the forgone rental payments reflect the opportunity cost of using the physical assets owned by the GP.[3]

Consequently, when determining the economic (rather than accounting) profits of a firm, economists consider the total costs of doing business, including both the explicit and implicit costs. Economists believe it is important to determine whether sufficient revenues are available to cover the cost of using all inputs, including those rented and owned. For example, if the rental return on the physical assets is greater than the return on use, the GP might do better by renting out the assets rather than retaining them for personal use.

The Short-Run Cost Curves of the Representative Medical Firm

Cost theory is based on the production theory of the medical firm previously outlined and relates the quantity of output to the cost of production. As such, it identifies how (total and marginal) costs respond to changes in output. If we continue to assume the two inputs of nurse-hours, n, and capital, k_*, the short-run total cost, STC, of producing a given level of medical output, q, can be written as

(7–6) $$\text{STC}(q) = w \times n + r \times k_*,$$

where w and r represent the hourly wage for a nurse and the rental or opportunity cost of capital, respectively. Input prices are assumed to be fixed, which means the single medical firm can purchase these inputs without affecting their market prices. This is a valid assumption as long as the firm is a small buyer of inputs relative to the total number of buyers in the marketplace.[4]

---

[3]The general practitioner's labor time should also be treated as an implicit cost of doing business if he or she independently owns the clinic. As an entrepreneur, the GP does not receive an explicit payment but instead receives any residual profits that are left over after all other costs are paid. If the physician does not receive an appropriate rate of return, he or she may leave the area or the profession to get a better rate of return.

[4]If the single firm were a large or an influential buyer, it might possess some "monopsony" power and could affect the market prices of the inputs.

Equation 7–6 implies that the short-run total costs of production are dependent on the quantities and prices of inputs employed. The wage rate times the number of nurse-hours equals the total wage bill and represents the total variable costs of production. Variable costs respond to changes in the level of output.[5] The product of the rental price and the quantity of capital represent the total fixed costs of production. Obviously, this cost component does not respond to changes in output, since the quantity of capital is fixed in the short run.

The total product curve not only identifies the quantity of medical output produced by a particular number of nurse-hours but also shows, reciprocally, the number of nurse-hours necessary to produce a given level of medical output. With this information, we can determine the short-run total cost of producing different levels of medical output by following a three-step procedure. First, we identify, through the production function, the necessary number of nurse-hours, n, for each level of medical output. Second, we multiply the quantity of nurse-hours by the hourly wage, w, to determine the short-run total variable costs, STVC, of production, or $w \times n$. Third, we add the short-run total fixed costs, STFC, or $r \times k_*$, to STVC to derive the short-run total costs, STC, of production. If we conduct this three-step procedure for each level of medical output, we can derive a short-run total cost curve like the one in figure 7–5.

Notice the reciprocal relation between the short-run total cost function in figure 7–5 and the short-run total product curve in figure 7–1. For example, when total product is increasing at an *increasing* rate up to point n_1 in figure 7–1, short-run total costs are increasing at a *decreasing* rate up to point q_1 in figure 7–5. This is because the increasing productivity in this range causes the total costs of production to rise slowly. Output increases at a *decreasing* rate immediately beyond point n_1 in figure 7–1 (as shown by the slope of the total product curve), and, as a result, short-run total costs increase at an *increasing* rate beyond q_1 in figure 7–5. Also notice that total costs increase solely because additional nurses are employed as output expands. Figure 7–5 also shows how short-run total cost can be decomposed into its variable and fixed components for the level of output q_2.

Short-Run Per-Unit Costs of Production

Another way to look at the reciprocal relation between production and costs is to focus on the short-run marginal and average variable costs of production. The short-run marginal costs, SMC, of production are equal to the change in total costs associated with a one-unit change in output, or

(7–7) $$\text{SMC} = \Delta \text{STC}/\Delta q.$$

In terms of equations 7–6 and 7–7, the short-run marginal costs of production look like the following:

(7–8) $$\text{SMC} = \Delta(w \times n + r \times k_*)/\Delta q.$$

---

[5]For simplicity, we assume the wage rate represents total hourly compensation, including any fringe benefits.

FIGURE 7-5
The Short-Run Total Cost Curve

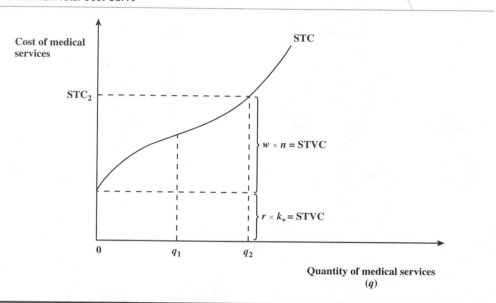

The short-run total cost, STC, of producing medical services equals the sum of the total variable, STVC, and fixed costs, STFC. STC first increases at a decreasing rate up to point q_1 and then increases at an increasing rate with respect to producing more output. STC increases at an increasing rate after q_1 because of diminishing marginal productivity.

Because the wage rate and short-run fixed costs are constant with respect to output, equation 7–8 can be rewritten in the following manner:

(7–9) $$\text{SMC} = w \times (\Delta n/\Delta q) = w \times (1/\text{MP}_n) = w/\text{MP}_n.$$

Notice on the right-hand side of equation 7–9 that short-run marginal costs equal the wage rate divided by the marginal product of nurse-hours.

The short-run average variable costs, SAVC, of production equal the short-run total variable costs, STVC, divided by the quantity of medical output. Because STVC is the total wage bill (i.e., $w \times n$),

(7–10) $$\text{SAVC} = \text{STVC}/q = (w \times n)/q = w \times (1/\text{AP}_n) = w/\text{AP}_n$$

such that SAVC equals the wage rate divided by the average product of a nurse-hour. Notice that the short-run marginal and average variable costs are inversely related to the marginal and average products of labor, respectively. Thus, marginal and average variable costs increase as the marginal and average products fall, and vice versa. Figure 7–6 shows the graphical relation between the per-unit product and cost curves.

The two graphs in figure 7–6 clearly point out the reciprocal relation between production and costs. For example, after point n_1 in figure 7–6a, diminishing productivity sets in and the marginal product begins to decline. As a result, the short-run marginal costs

FIGURE 7 – 6

Relation between the Per-Unit Product and Cost Curves

(a)

(b)

Short-run marginal cost, SMC, equals the change in total costs brought on by a one-unit change in output. Short-run average variable cost, SAVC, equals short-run total variable cost divided by total output. SMC and SAVC are inversely related to marginal and average productivity. For example, marginal costs decline as marginal productivity increases.

$(= w/MP_n)$ increase beyond output level q_1 given a fixed wage. Similarly, the average product of a nurse-hour declines beyond n_3, so the average variable costs of production increase beyond q_3. Obviously, the shapes of the marginal cost and average variable cost curves reflect the law of diminishing marginal productivity. Because of this reciprocal relation, production and costs represent dual ways of observing various characteristics associated with the production process.

It is apparent from equations 7–9 and 7–10 that the maximum points on the marginal and average product curves correspond directly to the minimum points on the marginal and average variable cost curves. Note in figure 7–6b that the short-run marginal cost curve passes through the minimum point of the short-run average variable cost curve. In addition, the SMC curve lies below the SAVC curve when the latter is decreasing and above the SAVC curve when it is increasing.

In simple terms, the graph in figure 7–6b identifies how costs behave as the medical firm alters output in the short run. Initially, as the medical firm expands output and employs more nurse-hours, both the marginal and average variable costs of production decline. Eventually, diminishing productivity sets in due to the fixed inputs, and both marginal and average variable costs increase. It follows that the marginal and average variable costs of production depend in part on the amount of output a medical firm produces in the short run.

Besides the marginal and average variable costs of production, decision makers are interested in the short-run average total costs of operating the medical firm. Following equation 7–6, we can find the short-run average total costs of production by summing the average variable costs and average fixed costs.[6] Short-run average fixed costs (SAFC) are simply total fixed costs (STFC) divided by the level of output, or

$$(7\text{–}11) \qquad\qquad SAFC = STFC/q.$$

Because by definition the numerator in equation 7–11 is fixed in the short run, the SAFC declines as the denominator, medical services, increases in value. Consequently, the average fixed costs of production decline with greater amounts of output because total fixed costs (or overhead costs) are spread out over more and more units.

Figure 7–7 shows the graphical relation among SMC, SAVC, and SATC. Note that the marginal cost curve cuts the average total cost curve at its minimum point. (The minimum SATC lies to the right of the minimum SAVC. Why?) Also, note that the vertical distance between the average total and variable cost curves at each level of output represents the average fixed costs of production. This should not be surprising, since total costs include both variable and fixed costs. The vertical distance between the two curves gets smaller as

---

[6]Equation 7–6 can be rewritten as

(7–6a)   STC = STVC + STFC.

Dividing both sides of equation 7–6a by the level of output gives

(7–6b)   STC/q = STVC/q + STFC/q.

Thus, by definition;

(7–6c)   SATC = SAVC + SAFC.

FIGURE 7–7

Relation among Short-Run Marginal, Average Variable, and Average Total Costs

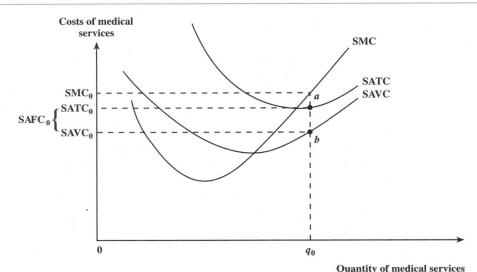

Short-run average total cost, SATC, equals the sum of short-run average variable cost, SAVC, and short-run average fixed cost, SAFC. Hence, SAFC is reflected in the vertical distance between the SATC and SAVC curves at each level of output. SMC cuts both of the average cost curves at their minimum points. SMC lies above the SAVC and SATC curves when they are rising and below them when they are falling.

output increases because the SAFC approaches zero with increases in output. One implication of the model is that average total costs increase at some level of output because eventually the cost-enhancing impact of diminishing productivity outweighs the cost-reducing tendency of the average fixed costs.

The unwitting reader may think that the medical firm should choose to produce at the minimum point on the SATC curve because average costs are minimized. As mentioned earlier, however, the level of output the medical firm chooses depends on the firm's objective (e.g., to achieve maximum or break-even level of profits). Hence, a proper analysis requires some knowledge of the revenue structure in addition to the cost structure. In later chapters, we entertain some alternative objectives that may motivate the production behavior of medical firms. For now, however, assume for pedagogical purposes that the firm has chosen to produce the level of medical output, q_0, in figure 7–7. Let's identify the various costs associated with producing q_0 units of medical output.

The identification of the per-unit cost of producing a given level of output is a fairly easy matter. We can determine the per-unit cost by extending a vertical line from the appropriate level of output until it crosses the cost curves. For example, the average total cost of producing q_0 units of output is $SATC_0$, while the average variable cost is $SAVC_0$. The average fixed cost of producing q_0 units of output is represented by the vertical distance between $SATC_0$ and $SAVC_0$, or distance ab. In addition, SMC_0 identifies the marginal cost of producing one more unit assuming the medical firm is already producing q_0 units of medical services.

Now suppose that instead of the per-unit costs, we want to identify the various total costs (i.e., STC, STVC, and STFC) associated with producing q_0 units of output. We can do this by multiplying the level of output by the per-unit costs of production. For example, the rectangle $SAVC_0$–b–q_0–0 in figure 7–7 measures the total variable costs of producing q_0 units of output, since it corresponds to the area found by multiplying the base of 0–q_0 by the height of 0–$SAVC_0$. Following similar logic, the total fixed costs are represented by rectangle $SATC_0$–a–b–$SAVC_0$, and total costs can be measured by area $SATC_0$–a–q_0–0. The ability to interpret and read these cost curves is useful for the discussion that follows.

Factors Affecting the Position of the Short-Run Cost Curves

A variety of short-run circumstances affect the positions of the per-unit and total cost curves.[7] Among them are the prices of the variable inputs, the quality of care, the patient case-mix, and the amounts of the fixed inputs. Whenever any one of these variables changes, the positions of the cost curves change through either an upward or a downward shift depending on whether costs increase or decrease. For example, if input prices increase in the short run, the cost curves shift upward to reflect the higher costs of production (especially since $SAVC = w/AP_n$ and $SMC = w/MP_n$). If input prices fall in the short run, the cost curves shift downward to indicate the lower production costs.

Furthermore, if the medical firm increases the quality of care or adopts a more severe patient case-mix, the cost curves respond by shifting upward. That is because a higher quality of care or a more severe patient case-mix means that a unit of labor is less able to produce as much output in a given amount of time. In terms of our formal analysis, a higher quality of care or a more severe patient case-mix reduces the average and marginal productivity of the labor input and thereby raises the costs of production. For example, a nurse can care for many more patients within an hour when these patients are less severely ill and quality of care is of secondary importance. Conversely, a reduction in the quality of care or a less severe patient case-mix is associated with lower cost curves.

Finally, a change in the amount of the fixed inputs can alter the costs of production. For example, it can be shown that excessive amounts of the fixed inputs lead to higher short-run costs (Cowing and Holtmann, 1983). We discuss the specific reasoning underlying the relation between fixed inputs and short-run costs when we examine the long-run costs of production later in this chapter.

In sum, a properly specified short-run total variable cost function for medical services should include the following variables:

(7–12)   STVC = f(output level, input prices, quality of care, patient case-mix, quantity of the fixed inputs).

We suspect that these factors can explain cost differentials among medical firms in the same industry. Specifically, output influences short-run variable costs by determining

---

[7]The position of the average and total fixed cost curves is influenced by the price of the fixed input. Fixed costs do not affect the typical marginal decision in the short run. Therefore, we do not discuss the factors affecting the position of the fixed cost curves.

INSIGHT 7–2

Estimating a Short-Run Cost Function for Hospital Services

Cowing and Holtmann (1983) empirically estimated a short-run total variable cost function for a sample of 138 short-term general care hospitals in New York using 1975 data. Along the lines of equation 7–12, they specified the short-run total variable cost (STVC) function in the following general form:

$$(7\text{–}13) \qquad \begin{aligned} STVC = f(&q_1, q_2, q_3, q_4, q_5, \\ &w_1, w_2, w_3, w_4, w_5, w_6, K, A). \end{aligned}$$

Each q_i $(i = 1,5)$ represents the quantity of one of five different patient services—emergency room care, medical-surgical care, pediatric care, maternity care, and other inpatient care—measured in total patient days; each w_j $(j = 1,6)$ stands for one of six different variable input prices for nursing labor, auxiliary labor, professional labor, administrative labor, general labor, and material and supplies; K is a single measure of the capital stock (measured by the market value of a hospital); and A is the fixed number of admitting physicians in the hospital.[1]

Compared to equation 7–12, Cowing and Holtmann's specification of the cost function is more complex and introduces a greater degree of realism into the empirical analysis. First, the hospital is realistically treated as a multiproduct firm, simultaneously producing and selling five different types of patient services. Second, instead of our single variable input price (i.e., hourly nurse wage), six different variable input prices are specified. Finally, Cowing and Holtmann include the number of admitting physicians in the model because they play such a key role in the hospital services production process (see also Insight 7–3).

The authors assumed a multiproduct translog cost function for equation 7–13. We do not discuss the properties associated with this specific functional form; it suffices to note that this flexible form enables us to assess a large number of real-world characteristics associated with the production process.

First, this functional form allows for an interaction among the various outputs so that economies of scope can be examined. **Economies of scope** result from the joint sharing among related outputs of resources, such as nurses, auxiliary workers, and administrative labor. Scope economies exist if the joint cost of producing two outputs is less than the sum of the costs of producing the two outputs separately. For example, many colleges and universities produce both an undergraduate and a graduate education jointly due to perceived cost savings from economies of scope. The same professors, library personnel, and buildings can be used in producing both educational outputs simultaneously.

---

[1]Cowing and Holtmann also specify two dummy variables reflecting for-profit versus nonprofit ownership status and teaching versus nonteaching institution as a way to control for differences in quality and case-mix severity across hospitals. The inadequate control for quality and severity of case-mix is one of the few faults we can find with this paper.

Cowing and Holtmann found some very intriguing results. First, their study reveals evidence of **short-run economies of scale**, meaning that an increase in output results in a less than proportionate increase in short-run total variable costs. Evidence of short-run economies indicates that the representative hospital operates to the left of the minimum point on the short-run average variable cost curve and implies that larger hospitals produce at a lower cost than smaller ones in the short run. They point out that this result is consistent with the view that aggregate hospital costs could be reduced by closing some small hospitals and merging the services among the remaining ones.

Second, in contrast to scale economies, Cowing and Holtmann discovered only limited evidence for economies of scope with respect to pediatric care and other services. They also found limited evidence to support diseconomies of scope with respect to emergency services and other services. In fact, they argued that the results for both scope and scale economies indicate that larger but more specialized hospitals may be more effective given the significance of the scale effects and the general lack of any substantial economies of scope.

Third, Cowing and Holtmann also noted that the short-run marginal cost of each output, $\Delta STVC/\Delta q_i$, declined and then became constant over the levels of output observed in their study. For example, the marginal cost of an emergency room visit was found to be approximately $32 for 54,000 visits per year and about $20 for 100,000 visits per year. For medical-surgical care, marginal cost was found to fall from $255 per patient day for 6,000 annual patient days to around $100 for 300,000 annual total patient days. For maternity care, the evidence suggests that the marginal costs of $540 per patient day for hospitals with 1,500 total annual patient days declined to $75 for hospitals with 20,000 total annual patient days. Eventually each of the marginal costs leveled off.

Finally, Cowing and Holtmann estimated the short-run elasticities of input substitution between all pairs of variable inputs. They reported that the results indicate a substantial degree of substitutability between nursing and professional workers, nursing and general workers, nursing and administrative workers, and professional and administrative labor.

---

where the medical firm operates along the cost curve, whereas the other factors affect the location of the curve. Most likely, high-cost medical firms are associated with either more output, higher wages, increased quality, more severe patient case-mixes, and/or an excessive quantity of fixed inputs.

THE COST-MINIMIZING INPUT CHOICE

A medical firm makes choices concerning which variable inputs to employ. Recognizing that there is usually more than one way to produce a specific output, medical firms typically desire to produce with the least-cost or cost-minimizing input mix. For example, suppose administrators desire to produce some given amount of medical services, q_0, at minimum total cost, TC, using two variable inputs: registered nurses, RN, and licensed practical nurses, LPN. (For ease of exposition, we ignore the capital input in this example.)

These two inputs are paid hourly wages of w_R and w_L, respectively. The medical firm wants to minimize

(7–14) $$TC(q_0) = w_R \times RN + w_L \times LPN$$

subject to

(7–15) $$q_0 = f(RN, LPN)$$

by choosing the proper mix of registered nurses and licensed practical nurses.

Taken together, equations 7–14 and 7–15 mean that administrators want to minimize the total cost of producing q_0 units of medical services by choosing the "right," or efficient, mix of RNs and LPNs so that $TC(q_0)$ is as low as possible and sufficient amounts of the two inputs are available to produce q_0. The efficient combination depends on the marginal products and relative prices of the two inputs. By using a mathematical technique called *constrained optimization*, we can show that the efficient mix of RNs and LPNs is chosen when the following condition holds:[8]

(7–16) $$MP_{RN}/w_R = MP_{LPN}/w_L.$$

Equation 7–16 means that the marginal product to price ratio is equal for both registered nurses and licensed practical nurses in equilibrium. The equality implies that the last dollar spent on registered nurses generates the same increment to output as the last dollar spent on licensed practical nurses. As a result, a rearranging of expenditures on the two inputs cannot generate any increase in medical services, since both inputs generate the same output per dollar at the margin.[9]

To more fully appreciate this point, suppose this condition does not hold such that

(7–17) $$MP_{RN}/w_R < MP_{LPN}/w_L.$$

In that case, the last dollar spent on a licensed practical nurse generates more output than the last dollar spent on a registered nurse. A licensed practical nurse is more profitable for the hospital at the margin, because the medical organization receives a "bigger bang for the buck." But as the organization hires more LPNs and fewer RNs, the marginal productivities adjust until the equilibrium condition in equation 7–16 results. Specifically, the marginal productivity of the LPNs decreases, while the marginal productivity of the RNs increases due to diminishing marginal productivity.

For example, suppose a newly hired RN can service six patients per hour and a newly hired LPN can service only four patients per hour. At first blush, with no consideration of the price of each input, the RN might appear to be the "better buy" because productivity is 50 percent higher. But suppose further that the market wage for an RN is $20 per hour, while an LPN requires only $10 per hour to work at the medical facility. Given relative input prices, the 50 percent higher productivity of the RN costs the medical facility 100 percent more. Obviously, the LPN is the better buy. That is, the last dollar spent on an LPN results in the servicing of .4 additional patients per hour, while a dollar spent on an RN allows the servicing of only .3 more patients per hour.

---

[8]The interested reader can consult Chiang (1984).
[9]The astute reader most likely recognizes that equation 7–16 is similar to the utility-maximizing condition noted in Chapter 5.

INSIGHT 7-3

The Shadow Price of an Admitting Physician

Most physicians are not hospital employees and paid an explicit salary; instead they are granted admitting privileges by the hospitals. The granting of admitting privileges comes at a cost to the hospital, however. For example, the hospital incurs costs when it reviews and processes the physician's application, monitors the physician's performance to ensure quality control, and allows the physician to use its resources. Based on their empirical procedure discussed in Insight 7-1, Jensen and Morrisey (1986) were able to estimate the shadow price, or implicit cost, of a physician with admitting privileges at a representative hospital. They imputed the shadow price of a physician by using the condition for optimal input use. Following the format of equation 7-16, the optimal combination of doctors, doc, and nurses, n, is chosen when

(7-18)
$$MP_{doc}/w_{doc} = MP_n/w_n.$$

By substituting in the estimated marginal products for doctors (6.05) and nurses (20.3) from their study, and the sample average for the annual nurses' salary ($23,526), Jensen and Morrisey solved for the shadow price of a doctor, w_{doc}. The resulting figure implies that the typical hospital in the sample incurred implicit costs of approximately $7,012 per year from granting admitting privileges to the marginal physician.

LONG-RUN COSTS OF PRODUCTION

Up to now, we have focused on the short-run costs of operation and assumed that one input is fixed. The fixed input leads to diminishing returns in production and to U-shaped average variable and total cost curves. In the long run, however, when the medical firm is planning for future resource requirements, all inputs, including capital, can be changed. Therefore, it is also important to analyze the relation between output and costs when all inputs are changed simultaneously in the long run.

Long-Run Cost Curves

The long-run average total cost curve can be derived from a series of short-run cost curves, as shown in figure 7-8. The three short-run average total cost curves in the figure reflect different amounts of capital. For example, each curve might reflect the short-run average total costs of producing units of medical services in physically larger facilities of sizes k_1, k_2, and k_3. If decision makers know the relation among different-size facilities and the short-run average total costs, they can easily choose the SATC or size that minimizes the average cost of producing each level of medical services in the long run.

FIGURE 7–8

The Short-Run Average Cost Curves and the Long-Run Planning Curve

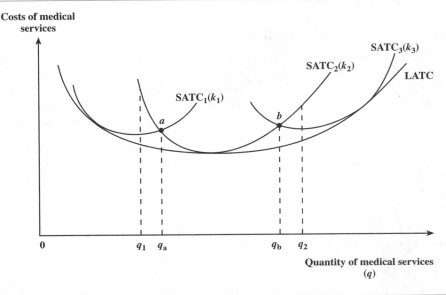

All inputs are variable in the long run. SATC₁, SATC₂, and SATC₃ represent the cost curves for small, medium, and large size facilities, respectively. If decision makers choose the efficiently sized firm for producing output in the long run, a long-run average total cost, LATC, can be derived from a series of short-run average total cost curves brought on by an increase in the stock of capital. The U-shape of the LATC reflects economies and diseconomies of scale.

For example, over the range 0 to q_a, facility size k_1 results in lower costs of production than either size k_2 or k_3. Specifically, notice that at output level q_1, SATC₂ exceeds SATC₁ by a significant amount. Therefore, the administrators choose size k_1 if they desire to produce q_1 units of medical services at least cost in the long run. Similarly, from q_a to q_b, facility size k_2, associated with SATC₂, results in lower costs than either size k_1 or k_3. Beyond q_b units of medical services (say, q_2), a size of k_3 enables lower costs of production in the long run.

The three short-run cost curves in figure 7–8 paint a simplistic picture, since conceptually each unit of medical services can be linked to a uniquely sized cost-minimizing facility (assuming capital is divisible). If we assume a large number of possible sizes, we can draw a curve that connects all the cost-minimizing points on the various short-run average total cost curves. Each point indicates the least costly way to produce the corresponding level of medical services in the long run when all inputs can be altered. Every short-run cost curve is tangent to the connecting or envelope curve, which is referred to as the *long-run average total cost curve (LATC)*. The curve drawn below the short-run average cost curves in figure 7–8 represents a long-run average total cost curve.

Notice that the U-shaped long-run average cost curve initially declines, reaches a minimum, and eventually increases. Interestingly, both the short-run and long-run average cost curves have the same shape, but for different reasons. The shape of the short-run average total cost curve is based on the law of diminishing productivity setting in at some point. In the long run, however, all inputs are variable, so by definition a fixed input cannot account for the U-shaped long-run average cost curve. Instead, the reason for the U-shaped LATC curve is based on the concepts of *long-run economies* and *diseconomies of scale*.

Long-run economies of scale refer to the notion that average costs fall as a medical firm gets physically larger due to specialization of labor and capital. Larger medical firms are able to utilize larger and more specialized equipment and to more fully specialize the various labor tasks involved in the production process. For example, people generally get very proficient at a specific task when they perform it repeatedly. Therefore, specialization allows larger firms to produce increased amounts of output at lower per-unit costs. The downward-sloping portion of the LATC curve in figure 7–8 reflects economies of scale.

Another way to conceptualize long-run economies of scale is through the direct relation between inputs and output, or returns to scale, rather than output and costs. Consistent with long-run economies of scale is increasing returns to scale. **Increasing returns to scale** result when an increase in all inputs results in a more than proportionate increase in output. For example, a doubling of all inputs that results in three times as much output is a sign of increasing returns to scale. Similarly, if a doubling of output can be achieved without a doubling of all inputs, the production process exhibits long-run increasing returns, or economies of scale.

Most economists believe that economies of scale are exhausted at some point and diseconomies of scale set in. **Diseconomies of scale** result when the medical firm becomes too large. Bureaucratic red tape becomes common, and top-to-bottom communication flows break down. The breakdown in communication flows means management at the top of the hierarchy has lost sight of what is taking place at the floor level. As a result, poor decisions are sometimes made when the firm is too large. Consequently, as the firm gets too large, long-run average costs increase. Diseconomies of scale are reflected in the upward-sloping segment of the LATC curve in figure 7–8.

Diseconomies of scale can also be interpreted as meaning that an increase in all inputs results in a less than proportionate increase in output, or **decreasing returns to scale**. For example, if the number of patient-hours doubles at a dental office and the decision maker is forced to triple the size of each input (staff, office space, equipment, etc.), the production process at the dental office is characterized by decreasing returns, or diseconomies of scale.

Another possibility, not shown in figure 7–8, is that the production process exhibits constant returns to scale. **Constant returns to scale** occur when, for example, a doubling of inputs results in a doubling of output. In terms of long-run costs, constant returns imply a horizontal LATC curve, in turn implying that long-run average total cost is independent of output.

Shifts in the Long-Run Average Cost Curve

The position of the long-run average cost curve is determined by a set of long-run circumstances that includes the prices of all inputs (remember, capital is a variable input in the long run), quality (including technological change), and patient case-mix. When these circumstances change on a long-run basis, the long-run average cost curve shifts up or down depending on whether the change involves higher or lower long-run costs of production. For example, an increase in the long-run price of medical inputs leads to an upward shift in the long-run average cost curve. A cost-saving technology tends to shift the long-run average cost curve downward. Conversely, a cost-enhancing technology increases the average costs of production in the long run and shifts the LATC curve upward. Higher quality of care and more severe patient case-mixes also shift the LATC curve upward.

Long-Run Cost Minimization and the Indivisibility of Fixed Inputs

Long-run cost minimization assumes that all inputs can be costlessly adjusted upward or downward. For an input like an hourly laborer, employment adjustments are fairly simple because hours worked or number of workers can be changed relatively easily. Capital inputs cannot always be as easily changed, however, because they are less divisible. As a result, a medical firm facing a sharp decline in demand may be unable to reduce the physical size of its facility. For example, Salkever (1972) found that hospitals realize less than 10 percent of the desired cost savings per year.[10] Therefore, medical firms may adjust slowly to external changes, not produce in long-run equilibrium, and operate with excess capital relative to a long-run equilibrium point.

Figure 7–9 clarifies this point. Suppose that initially a dental clinic produces q_0 amount of output (say, dental patient-hours) with a facility size of 1,200 square feet, as represented by the curve $SATC_2$. This represents a long-run equilibrium point because the efficient plant size is chosen such that $SATC_2$ is tangent to the LATC curve at q_0; that is, q_0 is produced at the lowest possible long-run cost and 1,200 square feet is the efficiently sized facility. Now suppose output sharply falls to q_1 due to a decline in demand. Long-run cost minimization suggests that the dental firm will reduce the size of its facility to that represented by $SATC_1$ and operate at point a on the LATC curve. It might do this by selling the old facility and moving into a smaller one. Because it may take time to adjust to the decline in demand, the dental clinic may not operate on the long-run curve at q_1 (point a) but instead continue to operate with the larger facility as represented by point b on $SATC_2$. The dental clinic incurs higher costs of production as indicated by the vertical distance between points b and a in the figure.

Cowing and Holtmann (1983) derived a test to determine whether firms are operating in long-run equilibrium. Using a simplified version of equation 7–12, we can write a long-run total (LTC) cost function as

$$\text{(7–19)} \qquad\qquad \text{LTC} = \text{STVC}(q, w, k) + r \times k,$$

where all variables are as defined earlier. According to equation 7–19, long-run total costs equal the sum of (minimum) short-run total variable costs and capital costs. The level of short-run total variable costs is a function of, or depends on, the quantity of output, the wage rate, and the quantity of capital (and other things excluded from the equation for simplification).

According to Cowing and Holtmann, a necessary condition for long-run cost minimization is that $\Delta\text{STVC}/\Delta k = -r$.[11] The equality implies that the variable cost savings real-

---

[10]As cited in Cowing, Holtmann, and Powers (1983, p. 265).
[11]This equality can be derived by taking the first derivative of equation 7–19 with respect to k and setting the resulting expression equal to zero.

FIGURE 7–9
Long-Run Disequilibrium of the Medical Firm

A firm may not operate in long-run equilibrium because of the sizeable costs of adjusting to a sharp change in demand. For example, assuming that the dental clinic is initially producing in long-run equilibrium at q_0 and output sharply falls to q_1, it may take time for the dental clinic to downsize its capital facility. As a result, the dental clinic may operate with costs, point b, that are higher than that predicted by long-run equilibrium, point a.

ized from substituting one more unit of capital must equal the rental price of capital in long-run equilibrium. That is, the marginal benefits and costs of capital substitution should be equal when the firm is minimizing the long-run costs of production. A nonnegative estimate for $\Delta STVC/\Delta k$ is a sufficient condition for medical firms to be overemploying capital. A nonnegative estimate implies that the cost of capital substitution outweighs its benefit in terms of short-run variable cost savings.

In their study, Cowing and Holtmann (see Insight 7–2) specified two fixed inputs: capital and the number of admitting physicians. As with capital, hospitals may operate with an excessive number of admitting physicians relative to a long-run equilibrium position. That is because the loss of one admitting physician can mean the loss of many more patients in the future. Cowing and Holtmann estimated the change in short-run total variable costs resulting from a one-unit change in capital and number of admitting physicians. Both estimates were found to be positive rather than negative. Thus, the authors found that the "average" hospital in their New York sample operated with too much capital and too many physicians. Their empirical results suggest that hospitals could reduce their costs by limiting the amount of capital and controlling the number of physicians.

NEOCLASSICAL COST THEORY AND THE PRODUCTION OF MEDICAL SERVICES

The cost theory introduced in this chapter, typically referred to as *neoclassical cost theory* under conditions of perfect certainty, assumes firms produce as efficiently as possible and possess perfect information regarding the demands for their services. Based on the underlying theory, the short-run or long-run costs of producing a given level of output can be determined by observing the relevant point on the appropriate cost curve. However, when applied to medical firms, this kind of cost analysis may be misleading for two reasons.

First, some medical firms, such as hospitals or nursing homes, are nonprofit entities or are reimbursed on a cost-plus basis or both. Therefore, they may not face the appropriate incentives to produce as cheaply as possible and, consequently, may operate above rather than on a given cost curve. Second, medical firms may face an uncertain demand for their services. Medical illnesses occur irregularly and unpredictably, and therefore medical firms like hospitals may never truly know the demand for their services until the actual events take place. Accordingly, medical firms may produce with some amount of reserve capacity just in case an unexpected large increase in demand occurs.

Although these two considerations may pose problems when conducting a cost analysis of medical firms, do not be misled into thinking that the material in this chapter is without value. That is clearly not the case. These two considerations are modifications that can and should be incorporated into the cost analysis when possible. Indeed, a strong grounding in neoclassical cost analysis under conditions of perfect certainty is necessary before any sophisticated analyses or model extensions can be properly conducted and understood.

SUMMARY

In this chapter, we focused on characteristics and concepts pertaining to the costs of producing medical services. First, we examined the underlying production behavior of a single medical firm. The short-run production function that resulted from this examination relates productivity to input usage. Among the more important principles we examined was the law of diminishing marginal productivity, the notion that the marginal and average productivities of a variable input first increase but eventually fall with greater input usage because a fixed input places a constraint on production.

Second, we discussed the inverse relation between productivity and costs. Simply stated, increasing marginal and average productivities translate into decreasing marginal and average variable costs. Conversely, declining productivities imply higher per-unit costs of production. As a result, the average variable cost curve is U-shaped, implying that the average variable cost of production first decreases with greater production but at some point begins to increase as output expands. Taking the property of fixed costs into consideration, we also derived a U-shaped short-run average cost curve, which relates average operating costs to the amount of medical services produced.

Finally, we examined some concepts relating to long-run costs of production, including economies and diseconomies of scale. We also discussed the determinants of the optimal input mix.

REVIEW QUESTIONS AND PROBLEMS

1. Suppose you are to specify a short-run production function for dental services. What inputs might you include in the production function? Which would be the variable inputs and which the fixed inputs?

2. In your own words, explain the law of diminishing marginal productivity. Be sure to mention the reason this law tends to hold in the short run.

3. Explain the difference between technical efficiency and economic efficiency.

4. Discuss the relation between the marginal and average productivity curves and the marginal and average variable cost curves.

5. What does the elasticity of substitution illustrate? How is it expressed mathematically? What two factors affect its magnitude?

6. Explain the difference between the explicit and implicit costs of production. Cite an example of each.

7. Suppose that with 400 patients per year, the SAFC, SATC, and SMC of operating a physician clinic are $10, $35, and $30 per patient, respectively. Furthermore, suppose the physician decides to increase the annual patient load by one more patient. Using short-run cost theory, explain the impact of this additional patient on the SAVC and SATC. Do they increase or decrease? Why?

8. What factors shift the short-run average variable and total cost curves? Explain why these curves would shift up or down in response to changes in these factors.

9. Suppose you are to specify a short-run total variable cost function for a nursing home. Explain the variables you would include in the function. What is the expected relation between a change in each of these variables and short-run total variable costs?

10. What does *economies of scope* mean? Provide an example.

11. Explain the reasoning behind the U shape of the long-run average total cost curve. Why might this cost curve shift upward?

12. You are responsible for hiring one of two hygienists for a dental office. The first dental hygienist has 25 years of experience. Given her record, she is likely to satisfactorily service 16 patients per day. Her hourly wage would be approximately $16 per hour. The other hygienist is new to the industry. He is expected to satisfactorily service 10 patients per day at an hourly wage of $8. Which dental hygienist would be the better hire? Why?

13. Santerre and Bennett (1992) estimated the short-run total variable cost function for a sample of 55 for-profit hospitals in Texas (*t*-statistics are in parentheses below the estimated coefficients).

$$\ln STVC = 1.31 + 0.47\ln q + 0.80\ln w + 0.73\ln QUALITY$$
$$(0.69)\ (3.31)\qquad (4.42)\qquad\quad (2.58)$$

$$+\ 0.11\ln CASEMIX + 0.29\ln k + 0.07\ln DOC$$
$$(1.48)\qquad\qquad\quad (3.16)\qquad (0.88)$$

$$+\ \text{Other factors}$$

Adj. R^2 = .95
   N = 55

where STVC = short-run total variable cost, q = a measure of output (total inpatient days), w = average wage rate or price of labor, QUALITY = a measure of quality (number of accreditations), CASEMIX = an indicator of patient case-mix (number of services), k = a measure of capital (beds), and DOC = number of admitting physicians. All variables are expressed as natural logarithms (ln), so the estimated coefficients can be interpreted as elasticities.

A. How much of the variation in STVC is explained by the explanatory variables? How do you know that?

B. Which of the estimated coefficients are not statistically significant? Explain.

C. Does the estimated coefficient on output represent short-run economies or diseconomies of scale? Explain.

D. What are the expected signs of the coefficient estimates on w, QUALITY, and CASEMIX? Explain.

E. Provide an economic interpretation of the magnitude of the estimated coefficient on w.

F. What do the estimated coefficient on k and DOC suggest about the amount of capital and physicians at the representative hospital?

14. Draw a U-shaped LATC curve. Then draw the related long-run marginal cost (LMC) curve, keeping in mind the geometric relation between marginal cost and average cost (see the discussion on short-run cost curves). What is the relation between LATC and LMC when increasing returns to scale are present? Between LATC and LMC when the production process exhibits decreasing returns to scale? What type of returns to scale holds when LMC equals LATC?

15. Describe the two limitations associated with the cost theory provided in this chapter when it is applied to explain the behavior of medical firms.

ONLINE RESOURCES

To access Internet links related to the topics in this chapter, please visit our web site at http://santerre.swcollege.com.

REFERENCES

Chiang, Alpha C. *Fundamental Methods of Mathematical Economics*. New York: McGraw-Hill, 1984.

Cowing, Thomas G., and Alphonse G. Holtmann. "Multiproduct Short-Run Hospital Cost Functions: Empirical Evidence and Policy Implications from Cross-Section Data." *Southern Economics Journal* 49 (January 1983), pp. 637–53.

Cowing, Thomas G., Alphonse G. Holtmann, and S. Powers. "Hospital Cost Analysis: A Survey and Evaluation of Recent Studies." In *Advances in Health Economics and Health Services Research*, Vol. 4, eds. Richard M. Scheffler and Louis F. Rossiter. Greenwich, CT: JAI Press, 1983, pp. 257–303.

Greenwald, Judy. "Blues Consolidation Continues." *Business Insurance*, May 16, 2002.

Jensen, Gail A., and Michael A. Morrisey. "The Role of Physicians in Hospital Production." *Review of Economics and Statistics* 68 (1986), pp. 432–42.

Kirchheimer, Barbara. "Ga. Hospitals to Combine." *Modern Healthcare*, December 11, 2000.

Salkever, David. "A Microeconomic Study of Hospital Cost Inflation." *Journal of Political Economy* 80 (November 1972), pp. 1144–66.

Santerre, Rexford E., and Dana C. Bennett. "Hospital Market Structure and Cost Performance: A Case Study." *Eastern Economic Journal* 18 (spring 1992), pp. 209–19.

CEBS QUESTIONS

CEBS Sample Question on Subject Matter from CEBS Course 9 Study Manual

1. Explain, in words—not a mathematical formula—the condition that must exist for the most efficient mix of RNs and LPNs. (pages 179–180)

CEBS Sample Exam Questions

1. Economists and accountants treat production costs differently. The difference is that economists consider:
   A. Only the explicit costs
   B. Only verifiable costs
   C. Historical costs
   D. Opportunity costs
   E. Actual costs

2. A medical firm increased all inputs 10 percent and output increased 12 percent. Which of the following statements is (are) correct?
   I. This is an example of an exception to the law of diminishing productivity.
   II. This is an example of increasing returns to scale.
   III. This example must involve the long run, not the short run.
      A. II only
      B. III only
      C. I and III only
      D. II and III only
      E. I, II, and III

3. All the following statements regarding the neoclassical cost theory are correct EXCEPT:
   A. The theory assumes that all firms are operating under conditions of perfect certainty.
   B. The theory assumes that all firms produce as efficiently as possible.
   C. The theory has limited usefulness to medical firms because these organizations usually have short-run cost curves that are not U shaped.
   D. The theory may be difficult to apply to medical firms because some firms may not have the incentive to produce as cheaply as possible.
   E. The theory poses problems for medical firms because the demand for medical services is unpredictable.

Answer to Sample Question from Study Manual

The condition that must exist for the most efficient mix of RNs and LPNs is that the last dollar spent on registered nurses (the marginal cost of nurses) must generate the same increment to output as the last dollar spent on licensed practical nurses. In other words, both inputs will generate the same output per dollar at the margin.

Answers to Sample Exam Questions

1. D is the correct answer. Economists, unlike accountants, consider both the explicit and implicit costs of production. Implicit costs include opportunity costs. See pages 169 and 171 of the text.
2. The correct answer is D. Increasing returns to scale involve the long-run when all inputs are increased. Statement I is incorrect because at least one factor must be held constant to apply the concept of diminishing productivity. See pages 163–164 and 183 of the text.
3. C is the correct answer. The short-run cost curves for medical firms must have a U shape under the assumptions of the theory. See pages 171–177 and 184–186 of the text.

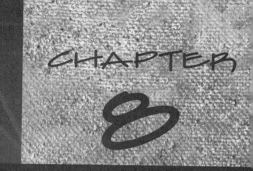

CHAPTER 8

STRUCTURE, CONDUCT, PERFORMANCE, AND MARKET ANALYSIS

"Genentech's Activase Faces Competition from New Set of Blood-Clot Dissolvers" (*The Wall Street Journal*).

"Market Forces Are Starting to Produce Significant Cuts in Health-Care Costs" (*The Wall Street Journal*).

"Price Competition Hits Hospitals" (*Hartford Courant*).

"Yes, the Market Can Curb Health Costs" (*Fortune*).

In Chapter 3 we discussed the efficient allocation of resources in the context of a benevolent surgeon general in a hypothetical economy. We learned, from a theoretical perspective, that an efficient allocation of resources occurs when each good and service is produced at the point where marginal social cost equals marginal social benefit. Taking the discussion a step further, Chapter 4 pointed out that actual decisions in the real world concerning resource allocation may be conducted at a centralized or decentralized level.

Continuing with this line of reasoning, this chapter develops a theoretical framework to examine how resource allocation takes place in a decentralized marketplace. That is, instead of a benevolent dictator, the decisions of individual consumers and producers allocate society's scarce resources among various goods and services. The analysis allows the marketplace to take on varying degrees of competition.

At the top of this page are various headlines from the popular press extolling the existence and virtues of competitive markets for medical services. The belief many people hold in the ability of competitive markets to efficiently allocate resources should not surprise anyone schooled in economics. According to traditional microeconomic theory, perfect competition creates a "survival of the fittest" market mentality and thereby forces firms to satisfy consumer wants and produce with least-cost methods of production. If competition has the power to weave this same magic in medical markets, incentives exist for medical firms to offer high-quality, cost-effective medical products at the lowest possible prices. With health care costs such a significant percentage of national income, competitive behavior among medical firms might be a welcome sight in today's health economy.

But are the various features normally associated with perfect competition applicable to medical care industries? Do the characteristics necessary for a perfectly competitive framework hold in medical markets? If some particular medical industries closely resemble the perfectly competitive model, how are markets expected to behave according to economic theory? What happens to market outcomes if markets are not perfectly competitive? This chapter answers these questions. Specifically, the chapter:

> Introduces the structure, conduct, and performance paradigm of industrial organization.

> Discusses the structural characteristics of perfect competition, monopolistic competition, oligopoly, and monopoly.

> Shows how a perfectly competitive market determines the price and quantity of a good or service, allocates resources, and corrects for shortages and surpluses.

> Examines the characteristics of pure monopoly.

> Compares and contrasts perfect competition and pure monopoly with respect to resource allocation.

> Discusses intermediate market outcomes between the polar extremes of perfect competition and pure monopoly.

STRUCTURE, CONDUCT, AND PERFORMANCE PARADIGM

When conducting an industry study, many economists rely on the structure, conduct, and performance (SCP) paradigm developed in industrial organization (IO), a field of economics interested in the behavior of firms and markets. Figure 8–1 illustrates the SCP paradigm. The first of the three important elements in the IO triad, **market structure**, establishes the overall environment or playing field within which each firm operates. Essential market structure characteristics include the number and size distribution of the sellers and buyers, the type of product offered for sale, barriers to entry, and whether any asymmetry of information exists between buyers and sellers. Entry barriers reflect any increased costs that new firms must incur relative to existing firms when entering a particular market. As we will see in this chapter, high costs may deter entry. Product type considers if firms in the same industry produce standardized or differentiated products. As we will learn, differentiated products are less substitutable and may thereby reduce the level of actual competition observed in an industry. Also notice in figure 8–1 that market structure often differs across industries because of variations in basic conditions, including the underlying technological base, the legal environment, demand conditions, and economies of scale. All of these basic conditions tend to affect the number and size distribution of firms observed in an industry.

Market conduct, the second element, shows up in pricing, promotion, and research and development activities. Whether a firm decides its policies independently or in conjunction with other firms in the market has a crucial impact on the conduct of the industry. The third element, **market performance**, feeds off of conduct and is reflected in the degree of production and allocative efficiencies, equity, and technological progress.

Overall, the IO triad predicts that the structure of an industry, in conjunction with the objectives of firms (see figure 8–1), determines the conduct of the firms, which in turn influences market performance. While significant feedback effects exist among the three el-

FIGURE 8-1
The Industrial Organization Triad

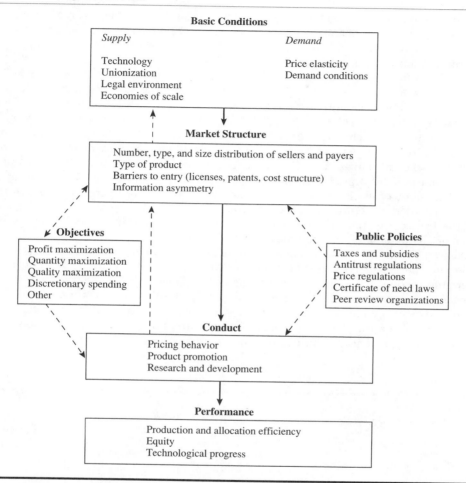

Basic Conditions

Supply

Technology
Unionization
Legal environment
Economies of scale

Demand

Price elasticity
Demand conditions

Market Structure

Number, type, and size distribution of sellers and payers
Type of product
Barriers to entry (licenses, patents, cost structure)
Information asymmetry

Objectives

Profit maximization
Quantity maximization
Quality maximization
Discretionary spending
Other

Public Policies

Taxes and subsidies
Antitrust regulations
Price regulations
Certificate of need laws
Peer review organizations

Conduct

Pricing behavior
Product promotion
Research and development

Performance

Production and allocation efficiency
Equity
Technological progress

ements, the overriding implication of the model is that the structure of the market indirectly affects industrial performance through its impact on market conduct. An underlying belief of the SCP analysis is that society values greater efficiency and technological progress, and fairness in the distribution of income. If unfettered markets do not produce desired levels of performance, the general idea is that public policies should be aimed at correcting this failure of the market. For example, public policies may involve restructuring or regulating an industry. For this reason, public policies also show up in the SCP paradigm of figure 8–1.

Microeconomic theory offers the theoretical connection between market structure and performance. Conventional microeconomic theory assumes that consumers maximize utility and that firms maximize economic profits. These objectives are specified so predictions can be made about the likely response of consumers and firms to changing market conditions. For example, as we learned in Chapter 5, utility maximization leads to downward-sloping demand curves for goods and services. Thus, a higher price means that consumers purchase less of a product, *ceteris paribus*. Likewise, profit maximization allows us to examine how the behavior of firms might adjust in response to changing external circumstances that might influence revenues or costs.

Usually profit-seeking firms are forced by competitive market forces to serve the interests of society by efficiently allocating scarce resources—the so-called invisible hand of Adam Smith. When competitive market forces are absent or weak because firms acquire **market power**, profit seeking may lead to a misallocation of society's resources as discussed later in the chapter. The amount of market power held by an individual firm or a collection of firms is a matter of degree and is dictated by the various characteristics that make up market structure. Table 8–1 presents the various structural characteristics that interact to affect the degree of market power possessed by firms. Across the top of the table, the degree of market power is measured from zero to 100 percent. The next row gives four market structure classifications commonly identified by economists, from the most (perfect competition) to the least (pure monopoly) competitive. Next, the table lists the major characteristics of each type of market structure

According to table 8–1, the characteristics of **perfect competition** are many sellers possessing tiny market shares, a homogeneous product, no barriers to entry, and perfect consumer information. The characteristics of many sellers with tiny market shares and homogeneous products, taken together, mean that a considerable amount of **actual competition** exists in the industry because there exists many substitute firms offering identical products. No barriers to entry suggest that the threat of **potential competition** exists because nothing prevents new firms from entering the industry. For example, a single sup-

TABLE 8–1
Market Structure and Market Power

Characteristics	DEGREE OF MARKET POWER			
	0%		...	100%
	Perfect Competition	Monopolistic Competition	Oligopoly	Pure Monopoly
Number of sellers	Many	Many	Few, dominant	One
Type of product	Homogeneous	Differentiated	Homogeneous or differentiated	Homogeneous by definition
Barriers to entry	None	None	Substantial	Complete
Consumer information	Perfect	Slightly imperfect	Perfect or imperfect	Perfect or imperfect

plier of frozen pizzas may be reluctant to increase price if the resulting higher profits entice new firms offering frozen pizzas to enter the market. The high degree of both actual and potential competition in a perfectly competitive market indicates that one firm's production decision has no meaningful impact on the overall performance of the industry. Hence a single perfectly competitive firm lacks any market power.

Monopolistic competition refers to a market that has many sellers possessing relatively small market shares, a product that is somewhat differentiated across firms, no barriers to entry, and some slight imperfections concerning consumer information. Numerous sellers and no entry barriers imply that a single monopolistically competitive firm's production decision has little impact on overall market performance. However, a monopolistically competitive firm may gain some power over resource allocation in a niche market because of its differentiated product.

A few dominant firms and substantial barriers to entry characterize an **oligopoly**. Given the relatively large size of each firm and protection from new firms because of high barriers to entry, each firm may have the power to negatively influence market outcomes through its production decision. However, competition among the few dominant firms, provided collusion does not take place, has the potential of harnessing each firm's behavior. Finally, the least competitive market structure is a **pure monopoly**, in which one firm is the sole provider of a product in a well-defined market with complete or perfect barriers to entry. These circumstances offer the greatest potential for a single firm to alter market performance in a socially undesirable manner through its production decision.

To gain a better appreciation of the differences among these four market classifications and their impact on performance, we next examine the polar cases of perfect competition and monopoly. After this discussion, the intermediate cases of monopolistic competition and oligopoly are studied.

IS A PERFECTLY COMPETITIVE MARKET RELEVANT TO MEDICAL CARE?

People who have had little exposure to the study of economics tend to have different ideas about what perfect competition entails. To some, perfect competition means that each firm in the marketplace strives to attain the greatest market share by charging low, cutthroat prices. Others believe that perfectly competitive firms compete for customers through advertisements or preferred locations. Perfect competition, however, is an abstract concept—a model—and therefore involves the four conditions specified in table 8–1. It also involves the assumptions of utility and profit maximization that underlie conventional microeconomic analysis. If any one of these characteristics or assumptions is violated, firms and markets are unlikely to behave as the perfectly competitive model predicts.

When applied to medical care industries, many of the assumptions behind conventional microeconomic analysis and characteristics of perfect competition often do not fit well. Several examples highlight this point. First, the not-for-profit status of many medical enterprises means that health care providers may not pursue maximum economic profits. Second, physician licensure creates an occupational barrier to entry and may shield highly salaried physicians from new competition. Finally, consumers typically lack perfect information about the prices and technical aspects of many medical services. Lack of information places physicians in a strong position to practice opportunistic behavior.

While deviations from characteristics of perfect competition and assumptions of microeconomic theory may make it improper to use the model as an evaluative tool of firm and market behavior in many medical markets, the perfectly competitive model fills several important purposes. First, the supply and demand model, which is based on perfect competition, serves as a useful way of explaining or predicting changes in price and output at the market level, often even in medical markets. Second, medical markets are sometimes "reasonably" competitive in the real world so supply and demand analysis remains applicable. Third, the perfectly competitive outcome serves as a valuable benchmark with which to compare market outcomes from other models of medical market behavior. In any case, throughout the text the assumptions of perfect competition are relaxed and alternatives to perfect competition are entertained.

A MODEL OF SUPPLY AND DEMAND

As mentioned previously, perfect competition is based on a model where a large number of consumers maximize their personal utilities and many producers individually maximize their economic profits. The massive number of consumers and producers results in each individual consumer and producer acting as a price taker. To maximize (personal) utility, the typical consumer continues to buy units of a good or service up to the point where marginal private benefit, MPB, as revealed by demand, equals market price. Similarly, the representative profit-maximizing firm continues to produce and sell units of a good or service up to the point where market price equals marginal private cost, MPC. Consequently, a perfectly competitive market clears at the level of output where the marginal private benefit to consumers equals the marginal private costs to producers, with market price serving as a coordinating device. We can use a graphical version of a supply and demand model to illustrate the market-clearing process.

Suppose the supply and demand model in figure 8–2 represents the market for generic aspirin. The per-unit price of generic aspirin, P, is specified on the vertical axis, and the quantity of generic aspirin, Q, is shown on the horizontal axis. The market demand curve, D, is downward sloping, reflecting the substitution and income effects normally associated with a lower relative price for a product, as discussed in Chapter 5. The demand curve also shows the diminishing marginal private benefit that consumers receive from additional tablets of aspirin. The supply curve, S, is upward sloping, indicating that marginal private cost increases with respect to the production of additional tablets of aspirin. Marginal private cost reflects the variable costs of production that individual firms incur from hiring labor and purchasing materials. Marginal private cost typically increases in the short-run because of a capacity constraint caused by a fixed input (e.g., size of the production facility or amount of equipment). Because of the rising marginal cost, a higher price is necessary to encourage producers to produce and sell more aspirin.[1]

The equilibrium, or market-clearing, price and output of aspirin are at the point where demand intersects with supply or where quantity demanded equals quantity supplied. By

---

[1]Recall from ECON 101 that each perfectly competitive firm, as a price taker, faces an infinitely elastic or horizontal demand for its product. Also recall that market supply is derived by horizontally summing across all firms the portion of the marginal cost curve that lies above the minimum point on the average variable cost curve.

FIGURE 8 – 2

The Perfectly Competitive Outcome

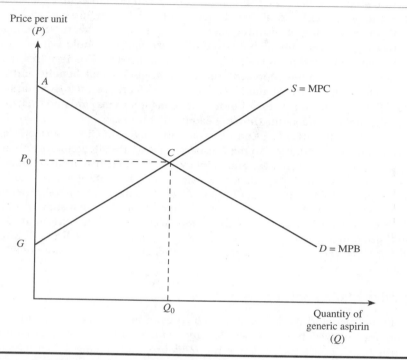

Market demand, *D*, represents the marginal private benefit, MPB, associated with the consumption of various units of a good. MPB is downward sloping to reflect the law of diminishing marginal utility. Market supply, *S*, reflects the marginal private cost, MPC, of production and is upward sloping to reflect the law of diminishing marginal productivity. Equilibrium in a perfectly competitive market occurs at the intersection of supply and demand. The triangular area P_0AC represents consumer surplus and the triangular area P_0CG captures producer surplus. Total social surplus equals the triangle *ACG*.

definition, equilibrium occurs when there is no tendency for further change. At the equilibrium price of P_0, consumers are willing and able to purchase Q_0 tablets of aspirin because that represents the utility-maximizing amount. In addition, manufacturers of aspirin wish to provide Q_0 tablets on the market at this price because that represents the profit-maximizing amount. Thus, both consumers and producers are perfectly satisfied with the exchange because both can purchase or sell their desired quantities at a price of P_0. The area under the demand curve but above price (triangle P_0AC) measures **consumer surplus**, reflecting the net benefit to consumers from engaging in free exchange. Consumer surplus shows the difference between what the consumer would be willing to pay and what the consumer actually has to pay over the relevant range of output. Similarly, the area below market price but above the supply curve (triangle P_0CG) represents **producer surplus**, signaling the net benefit to producers from participating in free trade. Producer surplus measures the difference between the actual price received by the seller and the required price as reflected in the marginal costs of production. The sum of consumer and producer surplus captures the total net gains from trade to both consumers and producers (triangle *ACG*).

Notice the similarity between the market supply and demand curves in figure 8–2 and the marginal social benefit and marginal social cost curves of figure 3–2 where we learned that an efficient allocation of resources occurs in an economy when MSB equals MSC for each and every good. The similarity between the two figures should not be surprising because consumers and producers comprise an important part of society in a market economy. If demand and supply represent the full marginal social benefit and cost of the exchange, that is, if MPB = MSB and MPC = MSC, a perfectly competitive market results in allocative efficiency in the process of individual consumers maximizing their private utilities and individual producers maximizing economic profits.

However, an inefficient allocation of resources may result in a perfectly competitive market when others, in addition to market participates, are affected either beneficially or adversely by a market exchange. Inefficiency results because utility-maximizing consumers and profit-maximizing producers consider only their marginal private benefits and costs and not the full social impact of their choices. It is likely that allocative efficiency results for our generic aspirin example because others besides the consumers and producers of aspirin are normally unaffected by that exchange. We take up externalities and public goods, two situations where a perfectly competitive market may fail to allocate resources efficiently, in Chapter 9. We also learn later in this chapter that a monopoly fails to efficiently allocate resources.

Comparative Static Analysis

The supply and demand model can be used to examine how surpluses and shortages of goods temporarily develop, as well as to study changes in the price and quantity of goods and services in the marketplace. Using the model to study changes in price and quantity is referred to as **comparative static analysis**. Comparative static analysis examines how changes in market conditions influence the positions of the demand and supply curves and cause the equilibrium levels of price and output to change. As the demand and supply curves shift, we can trace out price and output effects by comparing the different equilibrium points. Comparative static analysis can be used to explain the effects of market changes in the past or to forecast future market outcomes.

As discussed in Chapter 5, several factors, such as the number of buyers, consumer tastes, income, and the prices of substitutes and complements, affect the position of the market demand curve. Similarly, various factors, including input prices and technology, determine the position of the supply curve by affecting the costs of production. A change in any one of these factors shifts the corresponding curve and alters the price and output of goods and services in the marketplace.

For example, suppose consumer income increases by a significant amount. Assuming aspirin represents a normal good, the higher income causes the demand curve to shift to the right. In figure 8–3, notice that as the demand curve shifts to the right, a temporary shortage of *EF* is created in the market for aspirin if price remains constant. A shortage develops because at the initial price, the quantity demanded on the new demand curve, D_1, exceeds the quantity supplied of aspirin. However, price does not remain constant in a competitive market and is eventually bid up from P_0 to P_1. The higher price creates an incentive for manufacturers to offer more aspirin in the marketplace, and quantity supplied increases from Q_0 to Q_1. The higher prices also create an incentive for consumers to pur-

Effect of an Increase in Demand

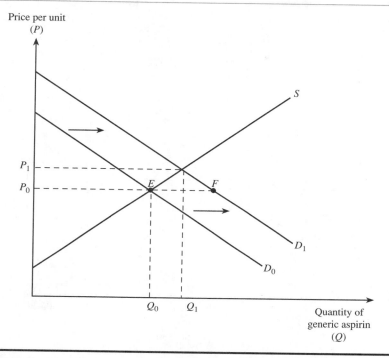

A change in demand causes a change in the equilibrium price and quantity of a good. Here the demand increases from D_0 to D_1 because of an increase in consumer income assuming that generic aspirin is a normal good. As a result, a temporary shortage of horizontal distance EF is created in the market at the existing price of P_0. Eventually price increases in the market from P_0 to P_1 in response to the increase in demand. Quantity also increases from Q_0 to Q_1.

chase less aspirin than originally planned at point F, perhaps by switching to alternative pain killers, consuming only one-half of a tablet per use, or postponing their consumption. Thus, under normal conditions, supply and demand analysis predicts that a higher price and quantity of aspirin are associated with greater consumer income, *ceteris paribus*.

As another example, suppose aspirin manufacturers adopt a cost-saving technology that increases supply. Therefore, the supply of aspirin shifts to the right, as shown in figure 8–4. If the price of aspirin remains at P_0, a surplus of AB results because quantity supplied exceeds quantity demanded. In a competitive market, however, the surplus creates an incentive for the price of aspirin to decline from P_0 to P_1. Consequently, the quantity demanded of aspirin increases from Q_0 to Q_1 as price declines and consumers face an incentive to purchase more aspirin. At the same time, the quantity that producers are willing to supply falls when price declines toward equilibrium. These actions result in a new equilibrium and market-clearing price and quantity. Thus, supply and demand analysis predicts that the adoption of a cost-saving technology causes price to decline and quantity to increase, assuming all else remains constant.

FIGURE 8-4
Effects of an Increase in Supply

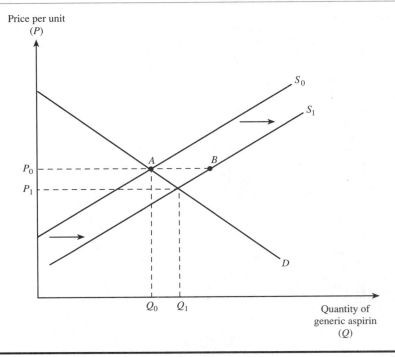

A change in supply causes a change in the equilibrium price and quantity of a good. Here the supply increases from S_0 to S_1 because of the introduction of a cost-saving technology. As a result, a temporary surplus of horizontal distance *AB* is created in the market at the existing price of P_0. Eventually price decreases in the market from P_0 to P_1 in response to the increase in demand. Quantity increases from Q_0 to Q_1.

Notice in the previous discussion that price serves several important functions. First, price provides useful information to both consumers and producers regarding the relative availability and value of a good or service in the marketplace. Second, price serves as a co-ordination device, bringing the actions of consumers and producers into harmony and helping to clear markets. Third, price serves as a rationing device, distributing the good or service to the consumers who value them the most. Fourth, price acts as an incentive mechanism, encouraging more resources to markets with shortages and less resources to markets with surpluses of goods.

A Note on Long-Run Entry and Exit in a Perfectly Competitive Market

The analyses thus far have concerned short-run adjustments because the number of firms has remained unchanged. But entry and exit of firms may take place in the long run as sellers take advantage of changing profit opportunities in various markets. For example, since there are no barriers to entry in a perfectly competitive marketplace, excess profits create an incentive for new firms to enter an industry as they strive to make a higher than normal rate of return. Conversely, economic losses create an incentive for firms to leave an industry as they try to avoid an unusually low rate of return on their investment. Finally, when normal profits exist in a perfectly competitive industry, the market is in long-run

INSIGHT 8 – 1

Explaining Rising Health Care Costs

Supply and demand analysis offers many reasons why national health care expenditures in the United States exploded from 5.1 percent in 1960 to over 13 percent of GDP more recently. Specifically, the demand for medical care increased because of rising income, an aging population, and a falling out-of-pocket price since 1960. In terms of the supply and demand model, all of these factors simultaneously created a shift in the demand curve to the right, causing a higher price and quantity of medical care over time. Expenditures on medical care, the product of price and quantity, also increased as a result.

On the supply side, Baumol (1967) points out that wages in service industries, like medical care, tend to increase with higher wages in the manufacturing sector. Higher wages in the manufacturing sector result from increased worker productivity caused by technological advances. Because wage increases in various medical care industries are tied to the growing manufacturing wage but are not necessarily matched with commensurate increases in productivity, per-unit costs of medical care are driven upward. In terms of supply and demand analysis, the supply curve for medical care has shifted to the left over time because of wages outpacing productivity. As a result, the price of medical care increased. And because the demand for medical care tends to be price inelastic, the increase in price caused health care expenditures to increase.

Cost-enhancing technologies provide another explanation for rising health care costs on both the supply and demand sides of the market. Over the years, a number of cost-enhancing technologies, such as computer tomography (CAT) scans, magnetic resonance imaging (MRI), and organ transplant technology, have raised the quality and costs of providing health care services. New technologies tend to supplement rather than supplant old technologies in the medical field. The widespread adoption of these cost-enhancing (rather than cost-saving) technologies shifted the supply curve to the left, causing health care expenditures to rise given the price-inelastic demand curve. In addition, since these technologies often simultaneously create a demand for new treatments because they can help to extend lives and are less risky, the demand curve also shifted to the right. Consequently, medical care expenditures increased due to the lower supply and greater demand caused by cost-enhancing technology.

In conclusion, rising income, an aging population, a declining out-of-pocket price, and the demand for new treatments helped fuel higher health care costs from the demand side of the market for medical care. From the supply side, the adoption of new technologies and higher wages also may have contributed to rising medical costs. Thus, supply and demand analysis can serve as a useful tool for explaining market changes even though the underlying assumptions may not closely conform to market realities.

equilibrium and firms have no incentive to either enter or exit the industry. **Normal profits** result when there are just enough revenues to cover the opportunity cost of each and every input, including a normal return to capital.

Long-run entry in response to excess profits can be treated as shifting the short-run market supply curve to the right. Similarly, long-run exit causes the short-run market supply curve to shift to the left. Given a stable demand curve, these adjustments in the short-run supply curve create a change in the price of the good and eventually restore a normal profit situation. In particular, long-run entry lowers price and eliminates excess profits, whereas exit leads to higher prices and eliminates the economic losses of the firms that remain in the industry. Because of entry and exit, we can expect that the typical perfectly competitive firm earns a normal profit in the long run.

The importance of long-run adjustments in a market is illustrated in the following example. In the mid-1980s, physicians, dentists, and other health care providers became concerned about contracting the AIDS and hepatitis B viruses in the work environment. This concern caused a considerable increase in the demand for form-fitting disposable latex gloves, which are preferred over vinyl gloves because they allow flexibility for detail work and are impermeable to blood and body fluids. From 1986 to 1990, annual sales of latex gloves increased by approximately 58 percent (Borzo, 1991). Initially, as the demand for latex gloves increased, a tremendous shortage of latex gloves developed. As the shortage gave way to higher prices in the short run, medical supply manufacturers operated their plants around the clock in an attempt to make higher profits. Consequently, the shortage declined as price increased and created an incentive for increased production. Greater profit opportunities in this market created incentives for medical suppliers to construct new manufacturing plants to produce more disposable latex gloves. According to the popular press, at one point in 1988, 116 permits were pending in Malaysia for the construction of disposable latex glove factories (Zikos, 1988). These new plants provided for new entry and an increased supply of latex gloves in the long run.

This example helps to highlight the importance of entry and exit in a marketplace. Entry of new firms leads to a greater allocation of resources in response to favorable profit opportunities. Likewise, exiting of firms helps to eliminate relatively inefficient resources and producers from a market. Profit, in both cases, serves as an important incentive mechanism and brings about an efficient allocation of resources in the long run. Of course, entry and exit of firms can take place only in perfectly competitive markets because entry and exit barriers are nonexistent. In the following discussion of monopoly, we will see that barriers prevent new firms from entering markets, resulting in an inefficient allocation of resources.

THE MONOPOLY MODEL OF MARKET BEHAVIOR AND PERFORMANCE

If a firm has some market power, the competitive model is an inappropriate tool of analysis and a noncompetitive model should be employed. The difference between the two models concerns how the individual firm treats market price. In a perfectly competitive market, the individual firm is a price taker. That is, price is beyond the control of a single firm so each time a perfectly competitive firm sells an additional unit of output, market price measures the additional revenues received. Economists refer to **marginal revenue**

(MR) as the additional revenues received from selling one more unit of a good. Thus $P = $ MR for a price taker. A noncompetitive firm with some degree of market power, in contrast, faces a downward-sloping demand curve and thereby has some ability to influence the market price. To illustrate how a noncompetitive model can be used to examine firm behavior, we will first consider a pure monopoly in which there is only one producer of a good or service in the entire market. A pure monopoly is the logical opposite of a perfectly competitive market. We will compare the equilibrium outcome for a monopoly to that of a perfectly competitive market.

Monopoly versus Perfect Competition

In precise terms, a monopoly is the sole provider of a product in a well-defined market with no close substitutes. Because it is the only firm in the market, a monopolist faces the market demand curve, which is always downward sloping because of the substitution and income effects associated with a price change. Given the downward-sloping demand, the only way the monopolist can increase quantity sold is to lower the price of the product. Assuming price is the same for all units sold at a point in time, price must be lowered not only for the additional unit but for the previous units as well. As a result, marginal revenue will be less than price at each level of output. In fact, it can be shown for a linear demand that marginal revenue has the same intercept but twice the slope.[2]

Figure 8–5 can be used to show how the equilibrium price and quantity for a monopolist compare to the market price and quantity in an otherwise equivalent perfectly competitive market. As before, our example is the market for generic aspirin. The market demand for aspirin is labeled AD. The supply curve is labeled GS and reflects the marginal private cost of producing aspirin. (Ignore the curve AMR for now.) Point C represents equilibrium in a perfectly competitive market where the supply and demand curves intersect. The market price and output of aspirin equal P_C and Q_C, respectively. Consumer surplus equals the triangular area $P_C AC$ and producer surplus equals the triangular area $P_C CG$. The entire triangular area ACG reflects the net gain from trade in a perfectly competitive market.

Now suppose only one firm produces and sells aspirin in that same market. Perhaps the award of a government franchise provides the aspirin manufacturer with the monopoly position. Further suppose that an entry barrier, such as the government franchise, prevents other firms from entering the market. Relevant to the monopolist's choice of price and quantity is the marginal revenue curve labeled AMR. Notice that marginal revenue shares the same intercept as the linear demand but has twice its slope. The monopolist chooses market price and quantity such that profits are maximized. Profit maximization occurs at the level of output, Q_M, where MR = MC because producing and selling additional tablets of aspirin always add more to revenues than costs up to that point. Beyond the Q_M level of output, production is unprofitable because marginal cost exceeds marginal revenue. Consequently, the monopoly outcome is represented by point M and the price charged equals P_M.

---

[2]Suppose the (inverse) demand is given by $P = a - bQ$. Total revenues equal P times Q or $(a - bQ) Q = aQ - bQ^2$. Taking the first derivative of this revenue funtion with respect to Q to get dTR/dQ gives MR = $a - 2bQ$. Notice the MR has the same intercept but twice the slope of the demand.

FIGURE 8–5
The Monopoly Outcome

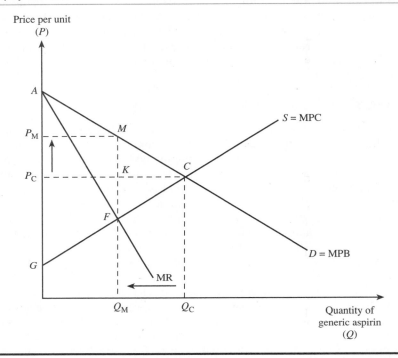

This illustration compares the perfectly competitive and monopoly outcomes. The perfectly competitive outcome is represented by point C. A monopoly produces at Q_M where MR = MC and charges price P_M. Because a monopoly exists in the market, consumer surplus shrinks to the triangle $P_M AM$ and the producer surplus increases to the area outlined by $P_M MFG$. Reflecting that society's scarce resources are misallocated, a deadweight loss of area MCF is created by the monopolist.

Notice that a monopoly charges a higher price and produces less aspirin than a perfectly competitive market. Also notice that the monopolist receives some of the surplus that consumers receive in a perfectly competitive market. More precisely, consumer surplus shrinks from triangular area $P_C AC$ in a perfectly competitive market to triangular area $P_M AM$ in a market dominated by a monopoly. Producer surplus increases from area $P_C CG$ to area $P_M MFG$. The rectangular area $P_M MKP_C$ reflects the surplus that is transferred from consumers to producers in a market controlled by a monopoly. In addition to this redistribution of income is the deadweight loss created by a monopoly. Notice that the net gain from trade is much smaller in a monopoly market than in a perfectly competitive market. The difference is the triangular area MCF that reflects the deadweight loss created by a monopoly. The deadweight loss shows that the value of the units no longer produced is greater than the opportunity costs of the resources used to produce them. It follows that a monopoly underproduces output and thereby misallocates society's scarce resources. The cost of monopoly shows up in the deadweight loss.

INSIGHT 8 – 2

Huge Market Share Today; Nearly Gone Tomorrow

A monopoly should not be confused with a dominant firm. Textbook economics tells us that a monopoly is a single seller of a well-defined product for which there are no close substitutes. Perfect entry barriers also allow a monopoly to maintain its market position. A dominant firm, in contrast, possesses a relatively large market share, and the stability of its market share is questionable because entry barriers are less perfect. For example, the U.S. government recently accused Microsoft of being a monopoly in the market for computer operating systems. However, according to textbook economics, Microsoft is a dominant firm rather than a monopoly because it faces competition from firms such as Lynx and Apple. Also, entry barriers are not insurmountable in the computer operating systems market.

Another example of the difference between a dominant firm and monopoly involves the medical supplier Johnson & Johnson (J&J). The relevant product in this case is a stent, which is used for treating patients suffering from blocked coronary arteries. A stent resembles a small metal mesh tube, no thicker than a pencil lead, which is squeezed on a tiny balloon and threaded into the heart's arteries. At the blockage site, the balloon is inflated to expand and deposit the stent, creating a scaffolding device resembling a ballpoint pen spring that remains in place to keep the vessel open after the balloon is withdrawn. Blood can then flow through the previously blocked artery.

At the beginning of 1997, J&J was a dominant firm, controlling 95 percent of the $600 million stent market through patent protection. By the middle of 1998, the stent market generated $1 billion annually, but J&J held a meager 8 percent market share! How could a company lose nearly 90 percent of its market share with a patented product over an 18-month span? It appears that J&J made a major blunder by failing to consider potential competitors. To be more specific, J&J angered key customers with rigid pricing for its $1,600 stent, refusing discounts even for hospitals that purchased more than $1 million of stents a year. With no comparable stent options, many doctors felt gouged.

The resentment caused cardiologists to pressure the Federal Drug Administration to approve new stents as quickly as possible. Physicians quickened the approval process by willingly testing the stent offered by new firms. Guidant Corporation, one new firm that entered the stent market, launched a competing stent that featured ease of implantation. Forty-five days after patent approval, Guidant Corporation controlled 70 percent of the stent market.

This insight clearly highlights the difference between the textbook definition of monopoly and dominant firms often observed in real-world markets. It also shows that patents do not always serve as perfect barriers to entry because patent approval can be received for products serving similar functions as an existing patented product but containing slightly different attributes. This insight also reveals that, without perfect barriers to entry, even the mighty Goliath may fall if price is set too high.

SOURCE: Ammon Adams developed most of the material for this insight from Winslow (1998).

Barriers to Entry

For a firm to maintain its market power for an extended period of time, some type of barrier to entry must exist to prevent other firms from entering the industry. Barriers to entry make it costly for new firms to enter markets and, by assumption, do not exist in perfect competition. Technical or legal reasons account for entry barriers. Exclusive control over a necessary input and scale economies represent two technical reasons to suspect entry barriers. If a firm has exclusive control over a necessary input, competitors are without the resources to produce substitute products. Exclusive control over bauxite, a necessary input in the production of aluminum, provided Alcoa with a monopoly position in the 1940s. After losing its antitrust suit, Alcoa was required to sell some of its bauxite to two new competitors, Reynolds and Kaiser Aluminum, created by the government. As a contemporary example, DeBeers supposedly owns 90 percent of the world's diamond mines.

Scale economies may also serve as an entry barrier. When production exhibits economies of scale, a firm operates on the downward-sloping portion of the long-run average cost curve, ATC, and the average cost of production decreases as output expands, as shown in figure 8–6. An existing firm in that situation has a cost advantage that results from the scale of production. Potential competitors could not effectively compete with the

FIGURE 8–6
Scale Economies as an Entry Barrier

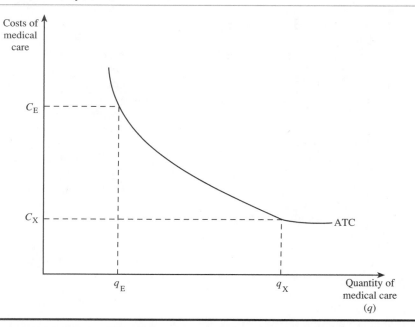

The declining average total cost curve, ATC, reflects scale economies in production. An existing firm producing a large volume of output at q_X produces at a cost of C_X. An entrant with a relatively small volume of output of q_E produces at a cost of C_E. Because of the scale economies, an existing firm can charge a price slightly below C_E and discourage the entry from actually entering the market. This practice is referred to as limit pricing.

established firm on a cost basis. In fact, the larger existing firm with average costs of C_X could set its price slightly below the average cost of the potential entrant, C_E, earn profits, and discourage the potential entry from actually entering the market. Pricing to deter entry is called **limit pricing**. Thus, economies of scale can serve as a barrier to entry that insulates an existing firm from potential competitors. Price regulations are often necessary when a firm holds a monopoly position of this kind (e.g., TV cable service).

Legal restrictions that prevent other firms from entering markets and providing services similar to existing firms can also serve as a barrier to entry. Legal patent protection provides a firm with a 20-year monopoly right to a product. As another example, prior to the late 1970s, the U.S. government purposely limited the number of firms in many industries, such as air transportation and long distance telephone services. However, deregulation took place in the late 1970s because many were dissatisfied with the performance of these industries. Patents on pharmaceutical products, occupational licensing, and certificate of need laws are examples of legal entry barriers in medical care markets. They are examined later in the book (and see Insight 8–3).

INSIGHT 8 – 3

CON Laws as an Entry Barrier into the Dialysis Industry

Many health economists hypothesize that certificate of need (CON) laws unduly restrict entry into various health care markets. A CON law requires health care providers to obtain government approval before constructing new buildings or purchasing a specified dollar amount of capital equipment. Until recently, however, they have been unable to point to any direct empirical evidence showing that CON laws reduce the entry of medical firms. Ford and Kaserman (1993) filled the void by analyzing the impact of certificate of need laws on entry of new firms into the dialysis industry.

Specifically, the authors used multiple regression analysis to explain entry into the dialysis industry in the 50 states from 1982 to 1989. As independent variables, they specified a 0/1 dummy variable indicating whether the state possessed CON regulations regarding dialysis clinics in a particular year, along with a number of control variables. The control variables essentially captured the potential profitability of firms entering the dialysis industry in the 50 states and included various cost and demand-side factors.

The authors found that the presence of CON laws significantly reduced the entry and expansion of dialysis firms. That finding, in conjunction with previous research on the dialysis industry, led Ford and Kaserman to conclude that

> by maintaining unnecessarily high levels of industry concentration and by restricting supply, CON regulation of the dialysis industry has sustained the monopoly power of incumbent clinics and, thereby, provided the wherewithal to increase profits by reducing service quality. Thus, CON regulation has promoted the interests of incumbent suppliers to the detriment of consumers (patients) (p. 790).

MONOPOLISTIC COMPETITION AND PRODUCT DIFFERENTIATION

Now that we have discussed the models of perfect competition and monopoly, we need to turn our attention to the other two models listed in table 8–1. In a monopolistically competitive market structure, there are many firms and low or no barriers to entry. The distinguishing characteristic of monopolistic competition is that firms within the same industry sell a slightly differentiated product. The product differentiation may result from a preferred location, different levels of quality (either real or perceived), or because of advertising and other promotional strategies. Because of product differentiation, each firm faces a downward-sloping demand curve that is highly but not perfectly elastic. Since the demand curve is downward sloping, the monopolistically competitive firm has some limited ability to raise price without losing all of its sales. Product differentiation leads to a certain degree of brand loyalty and that is why the individual firm can raise price and continue to sell output. Everything held equal, a more differentiated product translates into a less elastic demand curve facing the monopolistically competitive firm.

Figure 8–7 illustrates a model of a profit-maximizing, monopolistically competitive firm. Notice the highly elastic demand facing the individual firm reflecting the relatively large number but imperfect substitutes for its product. Bayer Aspirin may be a good example of a branded product that faces a downward-sloping demand. Bayer competes against many generic producers of aspirin but has a brand name that allows it to charge a higher price. Given the linear demand, the marginal revenue is drawn with the same intercept but has twice the slope. The long-run average total cost, ATC, and marginal cost, MC, curves allow economies and then diseconomies of scale.

Given the downward-sloping demand, the individual firm may earn an economic profit in the short run if the price charged is greater than average total cost at the level of output where marginal cost equals marginal revenue. However, the absence of any barriers to entry prevents excess profits from continuing in the long run in a monopolistically competitive industry. Over time other firms are attracted to the industry by the possibility of earning economic profits. As more firms enter the market, each firm sees its market share slowly diminish, which translates into a decrease in the demand for its product. The demand curve faced by each firm continues to shift to the left until the market price for the product is driven down to the point where economic profits are zero, or price equals average total cost. Demand becomes more elastic as well. At that point firms are no longer attracted to the industry and the market settles into a long-run equilibrium situation where economic profits are zero.

Figure 8–7 shows long-run equilibrium in a monopolistically competitive industry. Notice that the demand curve is tangent to the average total cost at the level of output where MR = MC. The monopolistically competitive firm earns zero profits in the long run because price equals average total costs. Notice that the monopolistically competitive firm does not produce at the point where price equals marginal cost as does a perfectly competitive firm. As a result, one might argue that this type of industry inefficiently allocates resources. But before that conclusion can be drawn, we must first consider the costs and benefits of production differentiation and whether such things as advertising and brand names impede or enhance competition among firms.

FIGURE 8-7
Long-Run Equilibrium for a Monopolistically Competitive Firm

A monopolistically competitive firm faces a downward-sloping demand curve because of product differentiation. Because there are no meaningful entry barriers, firms continue to enter the market until the representative firm earns only a normal profit. Hence, in the long run, the representative monopolistically competitive firm produces at Q_0 where MR = MC and charges a price equal to average total costs.

Procompetitive and Anticompetitive Aspects of Product Differentiation

In the perfectly competitive model, consumers are treated as being perfectly informed about the prices and quality of all goods and services in the marketplace. The assumption that all consumers possess perfect information about prices implies that all identical products sell at the same lowest possible price. Otherwise, high-priced businesses lose sales to low-priced businesses when consumers are perfectly informed.

But, just like other goods and services, there are both costs and benefits to acquiring information. In many situations, people choose to be less than perfectly informed, or **rationally ignorant**, because the marginal costs of additional information outweigh the additional benefits. Positive information and search costs mean that consumers may find it uneconomical to seek out all available suppliers. As a result, any one individual supplier faces a less than perfectly elastic demand and is able to restrict output and raise price to some degree. As a result, the price of a product in the real world is likely to be dispersed and higher, on average, than the competitive ideal (since theoretically prices cannot be lower than the competitive level). The average price and degree of price dispersion depend on the marginal benefits and costs of acquiring price information. Higher benefits and lower costs of acquiring information imply lower and less dispersed prices.

Imperfect consumer information may also affect the level of quality observed in a market, but the relation between information and product quality is more involved. It stands to reason that high-quality goods cost more to produce than low-quality goods. If consumers are perfectly informed, high-quality goods sell at a higher price than low-quality goods in a competitive market. In the real world with imperfect information, however, consumers are not fully knowledgeable about product quality. Consequently, if consumers base their willingness to pay on the average quality in the market and pay the average price, low-quality products drive out high-quality products, and the process continues until no products remain. The implication is that the level of product quality is higher when consumer information is more readily available.

Given imperfect information about various products in the real world, some economists argue that various features of production differentiation, like advertising, trademarks, and brand names, convey important information regarding the value of a good or service. For example, they argue that advertising provides relatively cheap information to consumers about the price and quality of a good and thereby promotes lower prices and higher quality. In fact, studies by Benham (1972), Cady (1976), and Kwoka (1984) found that the prices of eyeglasses and prescription drugs were higher, on average, in areas where price advertising was prohibited. Even when price and quality information is not directly conveyed, a large advertisement in the Yellow Pages or the local newspaper, for example, may signal consumers that the firm is willing to incur a sizeable expense because it is confident that it is offering a quality product at a reasonable price. Through repeat buying, the firm hopes to get a sufficient return on its advertising investment. In this case, the mere presence of an expensive advertising message generates information about the value of a product.

Other economists like Klein and Leffler (1981) argue that brand names and trademarks serve a similar purpose for promoting competition. Because the quality of many products cannot be properly evaluated until after purchase (or repeat purchase), brand names and trademarks help to identify businesses that have enough confidence in the quality of their products to invest in establishing a reputation. Given the sunk-cost nature of the investment, the argument is that a business will not sacrifice its established reputation by offering shoddy products on the market and take the chance of losing repeat buyers. A firm that expends considerable sums of money to polish its image and establish a brand name can lose a valuable investment by selling inferior products and tarnishing that image.

However, not all economists agree that advertising, trademarks, and brand names are always procompetitive. Some economists are concerned that promotional activities are used to establish brand loyalty, mislead consumers, and thereby cause "habit buying" rather than "informed buying." In this view, promotional activities are anticompetitive and advertising is treated as persuasive rather than informative. Persuasive advertising attempts to convince consumers that the attributes of product A are better than those of product B. Sometimes the advertising message points out real differences, but often the advertising is used to create imaginary or perceived differences across goods or services. For example, both Bayer and generic brands contain the same aspirin ingredient, yet many people are willing to pay a higher price for the Bayer product. Some argue that people pay a premium for branded products because past advertising successfully convinced people that Bayer aspirin, for example, is a superior product. Instead of creating a new market demand, persuasive advertising attempts to attract consumers from competitor firms. Considering advertising, trademarks, and brand names as quality signals, Robinson (1988) points out "a signal can be heard as long as it stands out over and against the background level of noise. As each seller amplifies his or her signal, the background noise level rises, necessitating further amplification on the part of individual sellers. This is clearly undesirable from a social perspective because the signaling mechanism imposes costs" (p. 469).

According to the anticompetitive view, product differentiation manipulates the demand for a product. For example, a successful advertising campaign can influence consumer tastes and preferences and thereby affect the position of the demand curve for the product. Advertising may affect the position of the demand curve in two ways. First, the demand curve may shift upward as a result of successful advertising because consumers are now willing to pay a higher price for the firm's product. Second, advertising may cause the demand curve to become less elastic with respect to price and, as a result, give the firm some ability to reduce output and raise the price of the good or service.

As an example, many public health officials claim that the purpose behind cigarette advertising is to manipulate the demand for cigarettes. Of major concern is advertising aimed at influencing teenager demand for cigarettes. A report by the Centers for Disease Control found that among smokers aged 12 to 18, preferences were greater for Marlboro, Newport, and Camel, three brands that are heavily advertised (Ruffenach, 1992). RJR Nabisco's Old Joe advertising campaign for Camel cigarettes was of particular concern to health officials. As George Will (1992) writes:

> *A study of children aged 3 to 6 showed that Old Joe was not quite as familiar as the McDonald's and Coca-Cola emblems but was more familiar than the Cheerio's emblem. An astonishing 91 percent of 6-year-olds recognized Old Joe, about as many as recognized Mickey Mouse.*

Existing firms may also use advertising or other types of product differentiation to create barriers to entry. If existing firms can control consumers through advertising, for example, new firms have a difficult time entering a market because they are unable to sell a sufficient amount of output to break even financially. It follows that product differentiation directed toward creating artificial wants, habit buying, or barriers to entry results in a misallocation of society's scarce resources. Resources are misused if they are employed to create illusory rather than real value.

When evaluating the social desirability of product differentiation, it is useful to remember that all products are homogeneous within the abstract model of the competitive industry and that most people agree that variety is the spice of life. People like diversity and enjoy choosing among a wide assortment of services selling at different money and time prices. People also receive utility when buying goods of different colors, shapes, and sizes. In this vein, the higher-than-competitive price that is paid for product differentiation may simply reflect the premium consumers place on variety. Nevertheless, economic theory suggests that firms may use product differentiation as a way to increase demand in some situations. If supply creates demand in this manner, some of society's scarce resources may be wasted.

INSIGHT 8-4

The Effect of Increased Competition on Dental Prices in New Zealand

Supply and demand theory leads us to believe that more sellers in a market results in increased competition and lower prices for goods and services. But the degree of competition is also dependent upon factors other than the number of sellers. Among other factors, the intensity of competition depends on the amount of information held by consumers regarding quality and prices, the degree of product differentiation, and whether entry barriers exist. With this notion in mind, the following illustrates the multifaceted nature of competition.

Before 1988, only dentists were legally permitted to supply and fit patients with complete or partial dentures in New Zealand. With the passage of the New Zealand Dental Act of 1988, clinical dental technicians (denturists) also were permitted to deal directly with the public and perform comparable denture services. Because the act essentially increased the total dental workforce by around 10 percent, one would expect that the greater supply should have led to a decline in the price of denture services.

Contrary to supply and demand theory, however, Devlin (1994) found that the increased legal supply had no statistically significant impact on the price of denture services. Devlin offers a number of explanations for why denture prices did not decline in response to increased competition. First, many dental technicians illegally supplied denture services before the act. Second, consumers may not have known about the legal availability of dental technicians given that little debate existed over the legislation, and advertising, though legal, is of minor importance in New Zealand dental markets. Third, consumers may believe that dental technicians offer an inferior quality of care relative to dentists.

Finally, Devlin notes that "the act itself also imposes some barriers to consumer search; for example, denturists may fit partial dentures only for persons whose oral health is certified by a dentist" (p. 1677). Although no evidence is offered to show that competition promotes lower prices, this insight is particularly appealing because it shows how the degree of competition is dependent on market conditions, such as consumer information, perceptions of quality, and barriers to exchange.

OLIGOPOLY

Oligopoly involves a market structure with a few large or dominant firms and relatively high barriers to entry. While there may be a large number of firms in the industry, those other than the few dominant firms have relatively small market shares and act as price takers. The important aspect of oligopoly is that the dominant firms must be sufficiently sized and limited so the behavior of any one firm influences the pricing and output decisions of the other major firms in the market. It is this **mutual interdependence** among firms that distinguishes oligopoly from the other market structures. Because the nature of the interdependence varies, economists have been unable to develop a single model of oligopoly behavior. As a result, many formal and informal models of oligopoly have been developed that depict firm behavior under a variety of different scenarios. It is beyond the scope of this text to delve into all of these models so we have limited the discussion to two broad models of firm behavior: the collusive and competitive models of oligopoly.

Collusive Oligopoly

According to the **collusive oligopoly** model, all the firms in the industry cooperate rather than compete on price and output and jointly maximize profits by collectively acting as a monopolist. To illustrate, assume that there are only three identical firms in a given market with similar demand curves and that these firms have decided to collude and jointly maximize profits. Under these circumstances, the firms collectively act like a monopolist and jointly set the price and output indicated by point M on the market demand curve in figure 8–5. It follows that a deadweight loss and a misallocation of society's scarce resources results from the collusive oligopoly.

The collusion among the oligopolistic firms may be of an overt or a tacit nature. Overt collusion refers to a situation where representatives of the firms formally meet, perhaps in a clandestine location such as a smoke-filled room, and coordinate prices and divide up markets. Tacit collusion occurs when firms informally coordinate their prices. The price leadership model represents an example of tacit collusion where the firms in an industry agree that one firm will serve as a price leader. The rest of the firms in the industry simply match or parallel the price of the leader. The resulting conscious parallelism can theoretically produce the same monopoly outcome as overt collusion and deadweight losses result (i.e., point M in figure 8–5).

While it appears that firms in an oligopoly have a strong incentive to collude and form a cartel, there are a number of factors that make collusion difficult. First and foremost are legal and practical considerations. The Sherman Antitrust Act prohibits overt collusion. Firms found in violation of overt price fixing can be subjected to severe financial penalties and the CEOs of these companies can be imprisoned.

However, antitrust officials, largely because of the difficulty of establishing proof, do not pursue cases involving tacit collusion. Firms in an industry may parallel their actions simply because they react to the same swings of demand and costs in the marketplace. But a tacit collusive arrangement has its practical difficulties. The informality of a tacit price-fixing arrangement can lead to problems because other firms in the industry may have a difficult time interpreting why the industry leader adjusts price. For example, suppose that the price leader decreases its price. Other firms in the industry can interpret this either as a simple reaction to an overall decrease in market demand or as an aggressive attempt on the part of the price leader to improve market share. In the first case, the other firms would simply lower prices and go on about their business. In the second case, however, they may aggressively counteract this move by decreasing their prices even further in an attempt to initiate a price war.

Second, cost differences make it more difficult for firms to cooperate and agree on a common price. High-cost firms will desire a higher price than low-cost firms. But the success of a cartel depends on all of the firms adhering to a common price. Third, collusion is less successful when entry barriers are low. New firms offering lower prices will seize market share away from the cartel members when entry barriers are low. Fourth, for several reasons, collusion is more likely when few firms exist in an industry. One reason is that the ability to collude becomes more difficult as more firms enter into collusive agreement. Low negotiation costs make it much easier for two firms to collude than it does a dozen. Another reason is that more firms increase the probability that any one firm will act as a maverick and act independently by charging a lower price than others. Finally, more firms increase the probability that one firm may cheat or chisel on the agreement. For example, one firm may grant a secret price concession to a large buyer to improve sales. Naturally, when the other firms in the industry learn of this behavior they will abandon the collusive agreement and strike out on their own. The potential for cheating behavior is greater when more firms exist in the industry because of high monitoring and detection costs. For these four reasons, collusive agreements are more difficult to negotiate and maintain than most people imagine.

Competitive or Collusive Oligopoly?

Competitive oligopoly lies at the opposite extreme of collusive oligopoly. **Competitive oligopoly** considers that rivals in an oligopolistic industry may not coordinate their behavior but instead aggressively seek to individually maximize their own profits. If the firms in an oligopolistic market sell relatively homogeneous products, and thus one firm's product is a strong substitute for the others, each firm may realize that consumers will choose to buy the product offering the lowest price. If so, each firm faces an incentive to lower its price to marginal cost because at that level it will at least share part of the market with the others and not be undersold. If oligopolistic firms act in a competitive manner like this, market output is produced at the point where price equals marginal cost and resources are efficiently allocated (point C in figure 8–5) even though a few dominant firms exit in the industry.

Whether firms act as a collusive or competitive oligopoly, or somewhere in between, depends on how each firm forms its beliefs or **conjectural variations** about how its rivals will react to its own price and output decision. Conjectural variations consider how, say, firm A believes its rivals will react to its output decision. For example, firm A might believe that rivals will offset its behavior by producing more if it reduces output. Firm A has no incentive to restrict output given that market output and price remain the same because of offsetting behavior. On the other hand, Firm A might believe that its rivals will react by matching its behavior and producing less. The matching behavior results in less market output and a higher price for the product. Thus, if firms form similar conjectural variations and each expects matching behavior, a point closer to point M in figure 8–5 and the associated deadweight losses result. In contrast, if firms form similar conjectural variations and each expects offsetting behavior, a point closer to C in figure 8–5 and the related efficiency gains occur.

Economic theory indicates that firm characteristics and market conditions influence the conjectural variations held by oligopolistic rivals. Many involve the same characteristics and conditions mentioned earlier that affect the success of a collusive oligopoly. First, firms are more likely to expect matching behavior when fewer exist and entry barriers are high because each firm realizes the greater profit potential from engaging in matching behavior. For example, each firm receives 50 percent of the monopoly profits when only two firms exist in the industry, so greater expectations can be attached to matching behavior.

Rivals are more likely to expect matching behavior when they share social and historical ties. Social and historical ties consider such things as industry trade associations, maturity and growth of an industry, and the proximity of firms in an industry. Specifically, rivals are more likely to anticipate matching behavior in industries where trade associations play an important role. Trade associations foster cooperative behavior by establishing common bonds and the sharing of information among firms. Anticipation of matching behavior is greater among rivals in older industries that are growing slowly. Less entry takes place and fewer new owners exist in older, slow-growing industries. New owners are more likely to act as independent mavericks and reduce the likelihood of matching behavior.

The proximity of firms in an industry considers how close firms are on a number of dimensions including location, products, technologies, and sources of capital. Rivals in closer proximity more likely share similar expectations. The organizational structure of the firms in an industry may also affect conjectural variations. More centralized firms respond slowly to market changes and thus may be biased toward cooperation and expecting matching behavior. Also, prices tend to be determined at the top of the hierarchy while output decisions are made at the lower levels in more centralized organizations. If firms within an industry possess similar centralized organizational structures, the hierarchical arrangement may lead to price rigidity but output flexibility. Lastly, bounded rationality may favor expectations of matching behavior among rivals. **Bounded rationality** refers to the limited ability of human behavior to solve complex problems. Bounded rationality may lead to rules of thumb for pricing in an industry and act as facilitating device for firms to match or coordinate their behavior.

INSIGHT 8–5

Price War in the Blood Banking Industry

Across the nation in 1998, American Red Cross held a 46 percent market share while America's Blood Centers (ABC), an affiliation of local independent blood banks, controlled another 47 percent of the market for blood. Individual hospital blood banks possessed the remaining 7 percent. Evidence suggests that the $2 billion blood banking industry resembles a monopoly in many regions of the United States but an oligopolistic market structure in others. According to Hensley (1998), either the American Red Cross or a local member of ABC holds a monopoly position in many regional markets because federal policy developed during the 1970s sanctioned local blood monopolies.

In 1998, however, American Red Cross made a bold move to increase its national market share to 65 percent. As a result, American Red Cross entered various markets, such as Kansas City, Dallas, and Phoenix, originally monopolized by one of the local members of ABC. Based on the outcome, it appears that a competitive oligopoly model does a better job of predicting the behavior of these two dominant firms than does a collusive oligopoly model. Recall that oligopolistic firms behave collusively or competitively depending upon market conditions such as entry barriers and how conjectural variations are formed. Evidence indicates a lower price of blood in markets where a local member of ABC interacts with American Red Cross than one where an independent operates alone. For example, the price of a unit of the same red blood cells was about $60 in Florida, one of the nation's most

(continued)

cutthroat markets, to $105 in upstate New York, where competition is minimal (Hensley, 1998).

These figures provide clear evidence concerning the impact of market structure on prices, even in the case of two dominant not-for-profit companies procuring and distributing blood. Probably the most telling commentary on market structure comes from Ken Wiebeck, who was interviewed for the Hensley article. Wiebeck states: "Competition can spur you on to better things. If you have a monopoly, it can cause you to get lazy and fail to see opportunities and take them" (p. 28).

SUMMARY

In this chapter, the structure, conduct, and performance (SCP) paradigm was offered as a way of conceptualizing how market structure affects both industry conduct and market performance. We saw that markets range from being perfectly competitive to pure monopoly depending on factors such as the number and size distribution of firms, height of any barriers to entry, and the type of product offered for sale by firms in an industry. In general, a greater degree of both actual and potential competition leads to greater efficiency because individual firms have less market power.

Perfect competition was the first market structure that we analyzed in some detail. Perfect competition means that individual firms are price takers and maximize profits, consumers maximize utility, no barriers to entry exist, and consumers possess perfect information. Based on these characteristics, it was shown that perfectly competitive markets allocate resources efficiently when all social benefits and costs are internalized by those engaged in the market exchange. Perfect competition also results in the maximum sum of consumer and producer surplus, another sign of allocative efficiency.

The model of pure monopoly was then offered as a logical extreme to the perfectly competitive model. One seller of a good or service and perfect barriers to entry characterize monopoly. Because a monopoly has market power and faces a downward-sloping demand, it was shown theoretically that a monopoly results in a restriction of output and a misallocation of society's resources. A deadweight loss and redistribution of income also occur when a monopolist exists in a market.

Monopolistic competition was introduced as an intermediate market structure. The distinguishing feature of monopolistic competition is a differentiated product. A differentiated product means that the individual firm possesses some slight market power because it can raise price without losing all sales. Because entry barriers are nonexistent in the long run, the typical monopolistically competitive firm makes normal profits in the long run. Given that variety is highly valued by consumers, the only legitimate criticism against a monopolistically competitive firm may be its use of product differentiation. While elements of product differentiation such as advertising, trademarks, and brand names may provide cheap information and promote competition, it was also argued that these same features might impede competition through habit buying and creating entry barriers.

Oligopoly, another intermediate market structure, was examined next. A few large dominant firms and, thus, mutual interdependence among firms distinguish oligopoly from the other market structures. The efficiency of an oligopolistic industry depends on whether the individual firms in the industry compete or cooperate with one another. Cooperation or collusion lead to monopoly-like behavior and a restriction of output and a misallocation of society's scarce resources. It was pointed out that the conjectural variations formed by firms influence their behavior if they expect offsetting or matching behavior by rivals in the industry. Expecting offsetting (matching) behavior leads to the competitive (monopoly) outcome. It was further discussed that matching behavior is more likely to be expected when the number of firms is fewer, entry barriers are higher, trade associations exist, the industry is mature and slow growing, organizational structures are more centralized, and firm decision makers possess bounded rationality.

Before concluding this chapter, it should be pointed out that the SCP analysis might become muddled when applied to medical markets for two reasons. First, conventional microeconomic theory is based on a profit maximization assumption, whereas many medical organizations are organized on a not-for-profit basis. Second, the industrial organization triad may not be appropriate for the medical care industry because quality usually matters more than price to consumers and government takes a more active role in the production, regulation, and distribution of output. These considerations diminish the role profits and price play in the allocation of health resources and rationing of medical goods and services.

Despite these considerations, we believe the SCP paradigm remains a useful tool for analyzing health care markets. Even the conduct of nonprofit organizations is influenced by market structure to some degree. For example, market structure places a restraint on the maximum price not-for-profit firms can charge, and even not-for-profit organizations are subject to a financial solvency constraint. Also, for-profit firms are strongly represented in the health care sector. Many community hospitals, home health and hospice care agencies, mental health facilities, and nursing homes are organized on a for-profit basis. All pharmaceutical and commercial health insurance companies and nearly all physician, dental, and optometric clinics are also organized on a for-profit basis. Thus, while the quest for profits may have a smaller impact on the behavior of firms in the health care sector than on that of firms in other industries, profits still play an important role. Certainly, the investigator should conduct the industry analysis very carefully and be cognizant of the peculiarities of health care industries when drawing any inferences from the SCP paradigm.

REVIEW QUESTIONS AND PROBLEMS

1. Suppose the supply curve of medical services is perfectly inelastic. Analyze the impact of an increase in consumer income on the market price and quantity of medical services. Next, assume the demand for medical services is perfectly inelastic while the supply curve is upward sloping. Explain the impact of an increase in input prices on the market price and quantity of medical services.
2. In the country of Drazah Larom (moral hazard spelled backwards), health insurance is nonexistent and all medical markets are perfectly competitive. Use supply and demand

analysis to explain the impact of the following changes on the price and output of physician services.

A. A decrease in the wage of clinic-based nurses.

B. The adoption of cost-enhancing medical technologies.

C. An aging population and a correspondingly more severe patient case-mix.

D. Declining consumer income.

E. A lower market price for physician services (be careful here!).

3. In the 1980s, a shortage of registered nurses in the United States led to an increase of almost 21 percent in the real average hourly earnings of RNs from 1981 to 1989 (Pope and Menke, 1990). This increase was the highest of any occupational group. Use supply and demand theory to show the shortage and explain why a dramatic rise in the wage rate occurred. Was there still a shortage of registered nurses by 1994?

4. Using supply and demand analysis, show graphically and explain verbally some of the factors that may have led to rising health care costs in the United States from 1960 to 2000.

5. In the mid-1980s, female nurses became increasingly aware that a relatively large number of attractive job opportunities existed outside the medical services industry. In fact, a large number of colleges offered life and transfer credits for nurses so that they could change careers at less cost. Using an equilibrium model of the market for nurses, show what impact this market change had on the wage rate and employment of nurses. Work through the comparative statics and explain whether a temporary shortage or surplus occurred and the various market adjustments that took place as a result of the temporary imbalance.

6. Assume the sale of human organs is legalized and a free market develops. Furthermore, assume the market is in equilibrium. Trace through the price and output effects of

A. An increase in the incomes of potential buyers of human kidneys.

B. A decrease in the price of kidney dialysis.

C. The development of a new drug that leaves the immune system intact while preventing transplant rejection (Waldholz, 1992).

D. A greater willingness by individuals to supply human kidneys.

7. A June 10, 1996, *Wall Street Journal* article titled "Americans Eat Up Vitamin E Supplies" discusses the shortage that existed for vitamin E at that time. According to the article, the shortage was created by two changes in the marketplace. First, the supply of soybeans, from which vitamin E is extracted, declined sharply. Second, a stream of scientific research from mainstream institutions shows that vitamin E helps to ward off such ailments as heart disease and cancer and some symptoms of aging.

A. Using two separate supply and demand graphs, graphically show and verbally explain how a shortage is created by each of the two changes.

B. Explain what eventually happens to price because of a shortage in a free market.

C. Explain how suppliers and buyers adjust their behavior as the shortage is eliminated in each of the two cases.

D. Explain what adjustment may take in the long run because of these changes.

8. Show graphically and explain verbally how a monopoly results in a deadweight loss. Also point out the redistribution that takes place in society because of monopoly.

9. Explain why economic profits are zero under monopolistic competition in the long run.

10. Explain the difference between the collusive and competitive oligopoly models and explain the role that the number of firms and barriers to entry play in determining how real-world oligopolistic industries behave.

11. Use the four market structures provided in the chapter to explain the critical role played by barriers to entry in determining the level of competition in any given market.

12. Critically evaluate the following statement made by a marketing executive: "Advertising is good because it always promotes competition."

13. Use economic theory to explain why consumer apathy may be efficient.

14. What beneficial role do trademarks and brand names serve when information imperfections otherwise exist?

15. Explain the economic reasoning underlying the following statement: "People often fail to acquire information about the price they pay for medical services because of health insurance."

16. Discuss the two ways product differentiation affects the demand for a product.

17. Explain how lack of information affects the price and quality of a medical good relative to a perfectly competitive situation.

ONLINE RESOURCES

To access Internet links related to the topics in this chapter, please visit our web site at http://santerre.swcollege.com.

REFERENCES

Baumol, William J. "Macroeconomics of Unbalanced Growth: The Anatomy of Urban Crisis." *American Economic Review* 57 (June 1967), pp. 415–26.

Benham, Lee. "The Effect of Advertising on the Price of Eyeglasses." *Journal of Law and Economics* 15 (October 1972), pp. 337–52.

Borzo, Greg. "Glove Shortage Creates Anxiety." *Health Industry Today* 54 (November 1991), p. 1.

Cady, John F. "An Estimate of the Price Effects of Restrictions on Drug Price Advertising." *Economic Inquiry* 14 (December 1976), pp. 493–510.

Devlin, Nancy Joy. "The Effects of Denturism: New Zealand Dentists Response to Competition." *American Journal of Public Health* 84 (October 1994), pp. 1675–77.

Ford, Jon M., and David L. Kaserman. "Certificate-of-Need Regulation and Entry: Evidence from the Dialysis Industry." *Southern Economics Journal* 59 (April 1993), pp. 783–91.

Hensely, Scott. "Out for Blood." *Modern Healthcare*, June 22, 1998, pp. 26–32.

Klein, Benjamin, and Keith B. Leffler. "The Role of Market Forces in Assuring Contractual Performance." *Journal of Political Economy* 89 (August 1981), pp. 615–41.

Kwoka, John E. "Advertising and the Price and Quality of Optometric Services." *American Economic Review* (March 1984), pp. 211–16.

Pope, Gregory C., and Terri Menke. "DataWatch: Hospital Labor Markets in the 1980s." *Health Affairs* 9 (winter 1990), pp. 127–37.

Robinson, James C. "Hospital Quality Competition and the Economics of Imperfect Information." *Milbank Memorial Quarterly* 66 (1988), pp. 465–81.

Ruffenach, Glenn. "Study Says Teen-Agers' Smoking Habits Seem to Be Linked to Heavy Advertising." *The Wall Street Journal*, March 13, 1992, p. B8.

Waldholz, Michael. "New Drug Leaves Immune System Intact While Preventing Transplant Rejection." *The Wall Street Journal*, August 7, 1992, p. B8.

Will, George. "Where There's Smoke There's Cancer and Death, Too." *Norwich Bulletin*, February 16, 1992.

Winslow, Ron. "Missing a Beat." *The Wall Street Journal*, September 18, 1998, p. A1.

Zikos, Joanna. "It's Tough to Get Grip on Rubber Gloves." *The Worcester Evening Gazette*, August 10, 1988, p. 1.

CEBS QUESTIONS

CEBS Sample Question on Subject Matter from CEBS Course 9 Study Manual

1. Explain the concept of rationally ignorant. (page 209)

CEBS Sample Exam Questions

1. A monopolist will maximize profits if it produces an output where:
   A. Average total costs are minimized
   B. Marginal costs equal marginal revenue
   C. Marginal costs equal demand
   D. Marginal revenue is zero
   E. Marginal revenue exceeds demand

2. Which of the following statements regarding a collusive oligopoly market is (are) correct?
   I.   Production costs differences make it difficult for firms to cooperate
   II. The beliefs each firm forms about its rivals affects market output and price
   III. The presence of trade associations in the market reduces the likelihood of collusive behavior
      A. I only
      B. II only
      C. I and II only
      D. I and III only
      E. I, II, and III only

3. All the following are correct statements regarding the types of economic markets EXCEPT:
   A. The major difference between perfect competition and monopolistic competition is that the latter has differentiated products.
   B. Imperfect consumer information is the dominant characteristic of an oligopoly.
   C. The exiting of firms in the long run in a perfectly competitive industry eliminates the economic losses of firms that remain in the industry.

D. Oligopolistic markets often have substantial barriers to entry.

E. The demand curve for a pure monopolist is downward sloping.

Answer to Sample Question from Study Manual

Acquiring information, just like purchasing any good or service, comes at a cost. A consumer may have to expend much effort and time in selecting a physician or a hospital that possesses certain desired characteristics. This is the case not just for medical services but also for nonmedical goods and services that are technically complicated, such as legal services, computers, and automobiles. Since becoming an educated consumer entails a cost, most people find it efficient to possess less than perfect information about goods and services. They choose to be less than perfectly informed, or rationally ignorant.

Answers to Sample Exam Questions

1. The correct answer is B. See page 203 of the text.

2. C is the correct answer. Statements I and II are correct. Statement III is incorrect because trade associations facilitate collusion. See pages 213–215 of the text.

3. B is the correct answer. It is a few dominant firms and substantial barriers to entry that characterized an oligopoly. Either perfect or imperfect consumer information may exist in an oligopolistic market. See pages 192–195 and 212–213 of the text.

PART 2

THE ROLE OF GOVERNMENT

GOVERNMENT, HEALTH, AND MEDICAL CARE

"Needham, Mass., Biotech Company Executive Criticizes FDA" (*Knight Ridder Tribune Business News*, June 12, 2002, p. 1).

"FTC Soon to Clear $6 B Bayer-Aventis Merger" (*The Daily Deal*, April 26, 2002).

"State Looks at Tax on Hospitals" (*Crain's Detroit Business*, January 14, 2002, p. 1).

"Doctors Resolve Antitrust Charges" (*USA Today*, May 14, 2002, p. B2).

"Unwanted HMOs, Hundreds of Massachusetts Doctors, Citing Low Fees, Refuse Medicare Plans" (*Boston Globe*, June 12, 2002, p. D1).

Up to this point, we have given little attention to the role and effects of government intervention in the U.S. health care system. Yet, as the above headlines suggest,[1] government plays an important role in the various medical markets and either directly or indirectly influences the health of the population in a number of ways. For example, regulatory and taxing policies affect the production or consumption of certain products (e.g., prescription drugs, narcotics, alcohol, and tobacco) and thereby beneficially or adversely affect the population's health. Regulations also have the potential to alter the price, quantity, or quality of medical services and can inhibit or promote efficiency in the allocation of resources. The degree of government intervention varies considerably across the country. Some state governments choose to actively regulate the production and reimbursement of nursing home, hospital, and psychotherapy services. Other state governments take more of a laissez-faire attitude toward the health care industry.

We have already seen several examples of government intervention in the health care sector. For example, earlier chapters pointed out that government-created legal barriers to entry, such as professional licensure requirements and CON laws, often confer monopoly status on

---

[1]FDA and FTC stand for the Food and Drug Administration and the Federal Trade Commission, respectively.

the established health care providers in a market. In addition, we know that the Medicare and Medicaid programs provide public health insurance to elderly persons, people with disabilities, and selected economically disadvantaged groups. These are just a few of an immeasurable number of government policies that affect the conduct and performance of medical care markets and the health status of American consumers.

This chapter provides an overview of the impact of public sector policies on the allocation of medical resources and the distribution of medical output. Although the design, complexity, and nature of health care policies differ across states, and federal health care policies are multidimensional in scope, a common body of economic theory is drawn upon to analyze such policies.

This chapter:

> Examines the reasons for government intervention in a market-based health care system.

> Discusses the implications of various types of public sector involvement, such as price and quality regulations and antitrust laws.

> Explores the methods used by government to redistribute income in society and the reason for such redistribution.

REASONS FOR GOVERNMENT INTERVENTION

Two general alternative views or models describe why government intervenes in a market-based health care system. These are the public interest and special interest group theories of government behavior. According to the **public interest theory**, government serves to promote the general interests of society as a whole and chooses policies that enhance efficiency and equity. Recall from Chapter 3 that an efficient allocation of resources is achieved when, for a given distribution of income, each good and service is produced at the point where marginal social benefit equals marginal social cost. In the presence of market imperfections, such as imperfect consumer information or monopoly, markets fail to allocate resources efficiently. We will see shortly that market failure also occurs when public goods such as national defense or externalities like air pollution are involved, or when distributive justice is a concern.

The public interest is served when government corrects instances where the market fails to allocate resources efficiently or to distribute income equitably. When the market fails, government attempts to restore efficiency and promote equity by encouraging competition, providing consumer information, reducing harmful externalities, or redistributing income in society. Consequently, the public interest model of government behavior predicts that the laws, regulations, and other actions of government enhance efficiency and equity.

According to the **special interest group theory** (Stigler, 1971; Peltzman, 1976; and Becker, 1983), the political forum can be treated like any private market for goods and services; that is, the amounts and types of legislation are determined by the forces of supply and demand. Vote-maximizing politicians represent the suppliers of legislation, while wealth-maximizing special interest groups are the buyers of legislation. In this model, incumbent politicians attempt to increase their probability of being reelected by supplying legislation that promises to redistribute wealth away from the general public and toward various special interest groups. In return, politicians expect votes, political support, and campaign contributions. Professional lobbies representing the special interest groups negotiate with politicians and arrive at the market-clearing prices and quantities of different kinds of legislation. Special interest group legislation changes over time when relative power shifts among different interest groups. Power or political pressure is determined by the amount of resources the group controls, the size of the group, and the efficiency with which the group transforms resources into pressure.

The successful politician stays in office by combining the legislative programs of various special interest groups into an overall fiscal package to be advanced in the political arena. The beneficiaries are the special interest groups, while the costs fall disproportionately on the general public. For example, individual pieces of legislation that provide protection from imported automobiles, milk price supports, and a larger education budget individually benefit those associated with the Automobile Workers Union, the American Dairy Association, and the National Education Association, respectively. The same politician can offer wealth transfers to each of these three groups and in return receive their combined votes, political support, and contributions. Naturally, special interest groups and politicians are made better off by the political exchanges; otherwise, these exchanges would not occur. Politicians retain or acquire elected positions, while the special interest groups receive wealth-enhancing legislation.

The general public, however, is unknowingly made worse off by the political exchanges. Individuals are typically rationally ignorant about the wealth implications of government activities because the personal cost of acquiring information about the true effect of legislation is high, whereas the corresponding private benefit is low. For example, suppose a certain piece of legislation redistributes $250 million a year away from the general public to a special interest group. Although this wealth transfer is a large amount of money in absolute terms, it is insignificant when expressed in per capita terms. In the United States, the cost of this wealth transfer is only about $1 per person. Raising the per capita cost of special interest group legislation to $100 increases the total wealth transfer to $25 billion. Yet even at a potential per-person savings of $100, few people are likely to become involved due to the money and time costs associated with political activity. To challenge special interest group legislation, a group or an individual must organize a legitimate counter political movement, inform others, circulate a petition, and engage in lobbying. All these activities entail sizable personal time and money costs.

Ross Perot's grassroots bid for the presidency in 1992 exemplifies this point on a grandiose scale. Perot attempted to challenge the political establishment by running for president as a third-party candidate. After spending millions of his own money, he garnered a respectable 19 percent of the overall vote, but not enough to win the presidential election. Imagine all the other potential "Perots" who never get involved in the political process at even the local or state level because of the staggering costs involved.

The special interest group model of government behavior implies that the typical individual consumer is "nickeled and dimed" by wealth-transferring legislation. Even worse, the wealth transfer is not simply a dollar-for-dollar transfer from the general public to the special interest groups. The political negotiations leading to the wealth transfer involve scarce resources such as the politicians' time and professional lobbies. As more resources are diverted to political negotiations, fewer are available for productive purposes. Consequently, inefficiencies are normally associated with special interest group legislation.

Therefore, according to the special interest group theory of government behavior, public regulations and laws exist because some special interest group benefits at the expense of the general public. Individuals in a special interest group are collectively powerful

INSIGHT 9-1

Special Interest Group Antilegislation

The preceding discussion examined how special interest groups purchase legislation offering wealth transfers. Another implication of the model is that a special interest group might pay politicians to refrain from supplying new legislation as a way to maintain the status quo and preserve their profits. While dated, the following newspaper article vividly highlights this point and richly illustrates the competitive nature of the political marketplace and the influence of political action committees (PACs) during the 1992 election year. The interested reader may also see Makinson (1992) for more information about special interest groups' lobbying efforts during this period.

Washington—Bracing for a fight over national health insurance, political action committees representing the medical and insurance industries have increased their congressional campaign contributions by 22 percent in the most recent election cycle, according to a study released yesterday. The PACs—representing individual companies and trade coalitions—donated a total of about $10 million to candidates during the first fifteen months of the 1992 election cycle. Most of the PACs oppose a "single payer" national health care system that would eliminate the need for the hundreds of insurance companies that now provide coverage.

"Health and insurance PACs are increasing the amount of money they spend on congressional campaigns because they want to blunt and undermine the groundswell of support for a 'single payer' national health care insurance system," said Robert Brandon, political director of Citizen Action, a Washington-based consumer advocacy group, which issued the report. The increase in health PACs' donations far outpaced the contributions of other PACs. Spending by other PACs increased by an average of only 14.5 percent.

PACs targeted members of committees likely to be most involved with health care legislation—the Senate Finance, and House Ways and Means, and the House Energy and Commerce committees. About 45 percent of the money contributed to members of the House went to members of the Ways and Means and Energy and Commerce, according to the study. The insurance industry is most worried about legislation sponsored by Marty Russo, D-Ill., which has attracted 74 co-sponsors in the House. It would create a "single-payer" system.

Brandon said industry opposition to the legislation and increased PAC contributions are "a clear statement that the health care industry and insurance companies are more interested in maintaining their enormous profits at the expense of the nation's economy and the health of the American people."

SOURCE: Blum, Justin. "Insurance PACs Increase Giving." *Norwich Bulletin*, July 23, 1992. Copyright 1992. Gannett Company, Inc. Reprinted with permission.

because they share a common concentrated interest. Consumers as a group, however, are generally diverse, fragmented, and powerless. Organization costs typically prohibit general consumers from taking action even when wealth transfers are known.

As an example, Ohsfeldt and Gohmann (1992) analyzed whether various state regulations concerning AIDS-related health insurance underwriting practices are influenced by the pressure of special interest groups. They focused on state regulations prohibiting (1) questions during the insurance application process about past HIV testing, (2) insurers from requiring insurance applicants to submit to HIV antibody tests, (3) questions on the application regarding sexual orientation, and (4) the exclusion of any AIDS-related costs from the services covered by the health insurance contract.

The authors argued that the losers from these insurance regulations are private health insurance companies (due to lower profits) and private insurance holders with a low average risk for AIDs (higher premium costs). Individuals who gain include those at high risk for AIDS (lower premium costs) and private providers of health care services (higher profits from more generous private insurance coverage). In general, the empirical findings of their regression analysis support the hypothesis that the presence of state regulations restricting AIDS-related health insurance underwriting practices is related to special interest group pressure. Specifically, Ohsfeldt and Gohmann found that underwriting regulations are more likely in states where the AIDS prevalence rate (as a proxy for the AIDS group) is high and insurance industry strength is low.

The public interest and special interest group models are two contrasting theories regarding the reasons government intervenes in a market-based system. In the real world, government most likely intervenes for both reasons. In some instances, government actions correct for market failure and thereby promote efficiency and equity. In other situations, government policies enhance the well-being of specific groups at an overall cost to society and thereby cause an inefficient allocation of resources and an inequitable distribution of income. Indeed, a careful cost-benefit analysis would have to be conducted before the winners and losers could be identified and the efficiency and equity implications determined for each piece of legislation. It is important to remember that both the government and the marketplace are imperfect institutions and, as a result, both fail to some extent; that is, government failure and market failure can coexist. Our job as policymakers or informed consumers is to determine which institution can accomplish which objective in the more efficient and equitable manner.

TYPES OF GOVERNMENT INTERVENTION

Government can alter the performance of markets in terms of efficiency and equity by providing public goods, levying taxes, correcting for externalities, imposing regulations, enforcing antitrust laws, operating public enterprises, and sponsoring redistribution programs. As an example of a public good, a government health officer inspects the sanitary conditions at local restaurants to protect the public's health. To correct for an externality, the government taxes the emissions of firms to reduce the level of air or water pollution in an area. A certificate of need (CON) law is essentially a health care regulation that restricts entry into hospital and nursing home markets, whereas the Sherman Antitrust Act of 1890 prohibits independent physicians from discussing their pricing policies to prevent monopolistic practices, such as price fixing. A hospital operated by the Veterans Administration provides an example of a government medical enterprise. Finally, the Medicare and Medicaid programs are examples of public medical care redistribution programs. Each of these government policies either directly or indirectly influences the allocation of medical resources and the distribution of medical output in the U.S. health economy. The following sections discuss the effects of these types of government intervention in more detail.

Public Goods

One legitimate function of government is to provide public goods. A public good must satisfy two criteria. First, unlike a private good, more than one individual can simultaneously receive benefits from a public good. That is, a public good exhibits no rivalry in consumption, thus allowing one person to increase his or her consumption of the good without diminishing the quantity available for others. Second, it is costly to exclude nonpaying individuals from receiving the benefits of a public good.

National defense is a good example of a public good. Everyone simultaneously benefits, and it is impossible to exclude nonpayers from receiving the benefits of national defense.

The preservation of water quality in public swimming areas by the local public health department is another example of a public good. A large number of people can simultaneously enjoy the benefits of improved water quality (at least until the beaches become overcrowded). In addition, it is costly to exclude nonpayers from receiving the benefits of improved water quality at the local pond (unless the entire pond can be fenced off).

Because of the high cost of excluding nonpaying individuals, private firms are unwilling to produce and sell public goods; thus, the private sector fails to provide public goods, and government intervention is necessary. Government ensures that public goods are produced in either the private or public sector and collects the necessary funding through taxation.[2]

Some people incorrectly consider medical services to be public goods because they are so essential for life. From a theoretical standpoint, however, the benefits of medical services are almost completely internalized by the individual buyer, and the cost of excluding nonpayers from receiving medical care is very low. Simply put, prospective patients can be required to pay the necessary fee at the door of the medical facility or be denied access to medical services. Thus, medical services are not public goods.[3]

Externalities

Ordinarily, all costs and benefits are fully internalized by the parties directly involved in a market transaction, and others not involved in the exchange are unaffected. For example,

---

[2]The aggregate demand for a public good is derived through a vertical summation of individual demands. See Chapter 6 in Rosen (1995).

[3]Closely related to a public good is the notion of a *merit good*. Musgrave and Musgrave (1989) point out that people are often bound by similar historical experiences or cultural traditions. The common bond gives rise to common interests, values, and wants, "wants which individuals feel obliged to support as members of the community" (p. 57). For example, people in the community may believe that everyone needs at least some minimal amount of food, housing, or medical services and therefore may be willing to support the provision of those merit goods through redistribution of income.

consider an individual who wakes up one morning with a bad toothache and decides to visit the dentist. After some probing, the dentist informs the patient that a wisdom tooth is causing the problem and recommends that the tooth be extracted immediately. The (uninsured) patient consents, the task is expertly performed, and the $100 fee is paid at the desk. In a competitive market, the $100 fee reflects the marginal benefit the individual receives from being relieved of pain and the dentist's marginal cost of providing the service. Notice that in this example, only the individual consumer and dentist internalize the benefits and costs of the market transaction. This transaction is efficient because both parties are made better off; otherwise the transaction would not have taken place.

Sometimes, however, a market transaction affects parties other than the individual consumer and producer. In this situation, an externality occurs. An **externality** is an unpriced byproduct of production or consumption that adversely or beneficially affects another party not directly involved in the market transaction. When an externality occurs, either the individual buyer or the individual producer does not fully internalize all the costs and benefits of the transaction. As a result, external costs or benefits are generated, and the product is usually under- or overproduced from a societal perspective. In the following discussion, we examine the impact and implications of demand-side and supply-side externalities.

Demand-Side Externalities   A demand-side externality occurs when the marginal social benefit diverges from the marginal private benefit associated with a good or service. A **positive demand-side externality** means that marginal social benefit is greater than marginal private benefit; a **negative demand-side externality** implies that marginal social benefit is less than marginal private benefit. Cigarette smoking provides a contemporary example of a negative demand-side externality.

According to Manning et al. (1989), external costs are associated with cigarette smoking, meaning smokers impose costs on nonsmokers. The external costs are generated in three ways. First, collectively financed programs, such as health insurance, pensions, sick leave, disability insurance, and group life insurance, are financed by taxes or group premiums and do not differentiate between smokers and nonsmokers. Because smokers have shorter life expectancies, they pay less taxes and premiums into the system. Second, smokers usually incur higher health care costs than nonsmokers.[4] Third, external costs arise when nonsmokers die prematurely from both passive smoking and smoking-related fires. The implication is that nonsmokers subsidize smokers and incur costs for which they are not compensated in the private marketplace.

Figure 9–1 shows the effect of cigarette smoking on resource allocation. The supply curve, S, corresponds to both marginal private and social costs and represents the marginal costs of using various inputs to produce cigarettes. Thus, it is assumed that all resource costs of production are internalized by the individual cigarette producers. On the demand side of the market, we must allow for the fact that the marginal private benefit, MPB, is likely to be greater than the marginal social benefit, MSB, of cigarette consumption. The MPB curve in the figure represents the marginal private benefit received from smoking, or the private demand curve for cigarettes. The MSB curve considers the additional costs in-

---

[4]Since smokers may die earlier and fail to live to the more medically intensive years of life, it is unclear theoretically whether smokers always incur higher overall health costs than nonsmokers.

FIGURE 9–1
External Costs of Cigarette Smoking

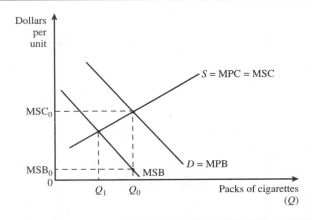

The graph captures the market for cigarettes. In the process of consumers maximizing utility and producers maximizing profits, market equilibrium results in the outcome at Q_0 where marginal private benefit, MPB, equals marginal private cost, MPC. However, the market outcome is inefficient because at that point, marginal social cost, MSC, exceeds marginal social benefit, MSB, because of the external damages caused by cigarette smoking. An efficient allocation of resouces occurs at Q_1 because MSB = MSC. Left alone, the market tends to overproduce goods that generate negative externalities in consumption.

flicted on society and therefore lies to the left of the MPB curve. The external costs underlie the difference between the two benefit curves.

For discussion purposes, we assume external costs per pack are the same at each level of cigarette consumption so that the two benefit curves are parallel to each other. We also assume the marginal social benefit is positive at every level, although it might be negative if the external costs exceed the marginal private benefits of cigarette consumption. As an illustration, Manning et al. (1989) estimated the external costs of cigarette smoking at approximately 15 cents per pack, exclusive of the costs due to passive smoking (2,400 deaths annually) and smoking-related fires (1,600 deaths annually). If we consider the value of lives lost from passive smoking and smoking-related fires, the total external costs increase to approximately 38 cents per pack.[5]

Consumers compare their marginal private benefit only to price (i.e., their internal costs) when deciding how many packs of cigarettes to purchase. Thus, in the process of maximizing personal utilities, consumers purchase Q_0 packs of cigarettes. This amount of cigarette consumption is inefficient from a societal perspective because at Q_0 the marginal social cost, MSC_0, exceeds the marginal social benefit, MSB_0, of cigarettes; that is, some nonsmokers are adversely affected by the consumption of cigarettes, and these external costs are not considered by smokers in the private marketplace. Since the individual consumers and producers do not fully internalize all the costs and benefits of their actions,

---

[5]The authors used a $1.66 million estimate of the willingness to pay for mortality reductions.

the quantity of cigarettes is overproduced and overconsumed. An efficient quantity of cigarettes exists at Q_1, where marginal social benefit equals marginal social cost. Because individual consumers and producers are unlikely to voluntarily alter their consumption and production behavior, some type of government intervention, such as a tax on cigarettes, may be necessary to curb this harmful type of consumption activity.[6]

This example represents a negative consumption externality because others not directly involved are made worse off by the exchange. A positive consumption externality can also occur when a consumption activity generates external benefits. A vaccination to prevent an infectious disease, such as rabies, is an example of a positive consumption externality. Figure 9–2 illustrates the logic underlying this example.

In the figure, the number of dogs receiving a rabies vaccine is shown on the horizontal axis. The marginal private benefit curve, MPB, reflects the value dog owners place on the rabies vaccination. The marginal social benefit curve, MSB, reflects the MPB plus all external benefits. The external benefits include the dollar benefit others receive when a dog gets the rabies vaccine and prevents the spread of the infection to humans or other animals. The supply curve, S, reflects the resource cost of providing the rabies vaccine.

In a free market, consumers compare their marginal private benefit to price when deciding whether to get the rabies vaccine for their dogs. As a result, Q_0 represents the total

---

FIGURE 9 – 2
External Benefits of Rabies Vaccines

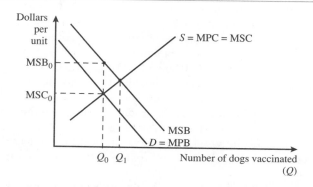

The graph captures the market for rabies vaccinations. In the process of consumers maximizing utility and producers maximizing profits, market equilibrium results in the outcome at Q_0 where marginal private benefit, MPB, equals marginal private cost, MPC. However, the market outcome is inefficient because at that point, marginal social benefit, MSB, exceeds marginal social cost, MSC, because of the external benefits caused by rabies vaccinations. An efficient allocation of resouces occurs at Q_1 because MSB = MSC. Left alone, the market tends to underproduce goods that generate positive externalities in consumption.

---

[6]To continue our illustration, Manning et al. (1989) point out that the average cigarette tax of 37 cents per pack nearly pays for the 38 cents of external costs from smoking in the United States. Their estimate of the external costs of alcohol, 48 cents per ounce, is well above the current excise and sales tax average of 23 cents per ounce. They conclude that smokers compensate for their external costs, but drinkers do not.

number of vaccinations in a free market where demand and supply intersect. But notice that at Q_0 the marginal social benefit, MSB_0, is greater than the marginal social cost, MSC_0, of providing the rabies vaccine. An inefficient outcome occurs because some individuals place very little value on the rabies vaccination (when maximizing personal utility) since they do not consider its external benefits. From a societal perspective, therefore, there are too few rabies vaccinations in a free market. An efficient number of vaccinations occurs at Q_1. This implies that government intervention of some kind, such as a mandatory requirement and a fine, may be needed to ensure the efficient number of rabies vaccinations. (For example, many states require a rabies vaccination to obtain a dog license, and failure to get a dog license results in a fine.)

In sum, externalities can arise on the demand side of a market if the social costs and benefits of a consumption activity are not fully internalized by the participants directly involved in the exchange. If the consumption activity generates either external benefits or costs, the good or service is likely to be under- or overproduced from a societal perspective. Consequently, government intervention may be necessary to correct the market's failure to allocate society's resources efficiently.

Supply-Side Externalities   As you now know, an externality creates an inefficient allocation of resources when the actions of one market participant affect another and no compensation is forthcoming. As in the case of a demand-side externality, the presence of an externality on the supply side usually distorts the allocation of resources in a market economy. A **negative supply-side externality** exists if a firm inflicts an uncompensated cost on another party in the process of production. In this case, a deviation arises between the marginal social cost and the marginal private cost of production. Because the firm bases its output decision on the private cost of production and not on the social cost, the good is usually overproduced. Figure 9–3 depicts this situation for a competitive market.

The demand curve, or marginal social benefit curve, is labeled $D = MSB$; the supply curve, or marginal private cost curve, is labeled $S = MPC$. The latter curve represents the amount it costs private industry to produce each additional unit of output. The MSC curve stands for the marginal social cost of production, and it lies above the MPC curve because it equals not only the marginal private cost of production but also the additional per-unit cost the firm inflicts on others. The distance between the two cost curves represents the per-unit dollar value of the cost imposed on society. The cost may reflect the greater health hazards from such factors as air pollution and toxic waste or higher time costs resulting from congested highways.

Profit maximization dictates that the good be produced up to point Q_0, where the marginal private cost equals the marginal social benefit, or the price. At Q_0, however, the marginal social cost of production exceeds the marginal social benefit of the product. From a societal perspective, resources are efficiently allocated if the Q_1 level of output is produced because the marginal social cost of production equals the marginal social benefit and the total social surplus is maximized. Because the market fails to assign the total social cost of production to the firm, the good is overproduced and resources are inefficiently allocated.

A classic example of a negative supply-side externality is acid rain. When fossil fuels are burned, they release sulfur and nitrogen oxides into the atmosphere; these substances combine with water to raise the acidic level of the water supply. Acid rain has caused extensive damage to marine and wildlife in certain regions of the country, such as New England. Because sulfur and nitrogen oxides can be carried hundreds of miles by wind

F I G U R E   9 – 3

Negative Supply-Side Externality

The graph captures a market where firms emit pollution as a by-product of production. Because of the external costs from pollution, marginal social cost, MSC, exceeds the marginal private cost, MPC, of production. In the process of consumers maximizing utility and producers maximizing profits, market equilibrium results in the outcome at Q_0 where marginal private benefit, MPB, equals marginal private cost, MPC. However, the market outcome is inefficient because at the point, marginal social cost, MSC, exceeds marginal social benefit, MSB, because of the external damages caused by the pollution. An efficient allocation of resources occurs at Q_1 because MSB = MSC. Left alone, the market tends to overproduce goods that generate negative externalities in production.

currents, it is extremely difficult to assign costs to them. As a result, many of the producers of these emissions do not bear the full cost of production.

In the health care sector, the problem of hazardous waste disposal by hospitals can be analyzed in the context of a negative externality. This became a national issue in the summer of 1988, when vials of blood, used syringes, and other hospital waste washed up onshore at a public beach in New Jersey (Baker, 1988). When five of the vials of blood tested positive for AIDS antibodies, many people became concerned that hospitals were attempting to pass the high cost of waste disposal on to the public by not properly disposing of infectious waste. From the public's perspective, the cost of inappropriate disposal of medical waste was in terms of an increased risk of accidentally acquiring AIDS. Rutala, Odette, and Samsa (1989) estimated that U.S. hospitals produce approximately 15 pounds of waste per patient per day and that infectious waste makes up 15 percent of that total. As a result, the Environmental Protection Agency (EPA), along with many states regulate the hazardous waste disposal of hospitals in an attempt to properly assign costs.

A **positive supply-side externality** occurs if firms in one market (say, A) provide uncompensated benefits for firms in another market (say, B). In that case, the marginal social cost is less than the marginal private cost of production; that is, the MSC curve lies below the MPC curve in market A (see figure 9–4). The distance between the two curves reflects the benefits received by the firms in market B. Since no compensation is paid to the firms in market A, they lack the incentive to produce the efficient amount of output. The profit-maximizing level of output equals Q_0, but at this amount the MSB exceeds the MSC. If total social surplus is to be maximized, output should expand to Q_1. Since the firms

FIGURE 9-4
Positive Supply-Side Externality

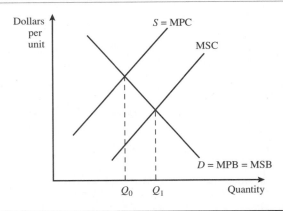

The graph captures a market where one firm generates external benefits for other firms in the market as a by-product of production. For example, suppose one firm discovers a more efficient production process and freely shares the idea with others. Because of the external benefits from the discovery, marginal social cost, MSC, is less than the marginal private cost, MPC, of production. In the process of consumers maximizing utility and producers maximizing profits, market equilibrium results in the outcome at Q_0 where marginal private benefits, MPB, equals marginal private cost, MPC (i.e., the firm does not freely share the idea). However, the market outcome is inefficient because at that point, marginal social cost, MSC, is less than marginal social benefit, MSB, because of the external benefits that can potentially be generated by the firm. An efficient allocation of resources occurs at Q_1 because MSB = MSC. Left alone, the market tends to underproduce goods that generate positive externalities in production.

in market A are not financially rewarded for the benefits other firms receive, they do not produce up to the point where total social surplus is maximized.

The transfer of medical knowledge across international borders is a good illustration of a positive supply-side externality. For example, assume the research funded by one country leads to a major breakthrough in the treatment of cancer that significantly lowers medical costs. This advance in medical knowledge is likely to be written up in a medical journal and, in the absence of intellectual property rights, quickly adopted by other countries at little or no cost. The firm in the country that developed the treatment and incurred the cost of research is not compensated for the full benefit of the breakthrough. Consequently, private medical researchers in any one country may face an incentive to underproduce medical knowledge in the absence of government subsidies because they would fail to receive a suitable return on their research investment.

In conclusion, economic theory suggests that the presence of an externality on the supply side impedes the market's ability to allocate resources efficiently. This occurs because production decisions are based solely on the private cost of production incurred by the firm rather than on the social cost.

Taxes and Subsidies as Corrective Instruments   By using taxes and subsidies, government can alter economic incentives and correct the unconstrained tendency of the market to misallocate society's resources when externalities are present. Specifically, taxes and subsidies can be used to alter the price of a good and discourage either overconsumption or underconsumption. Market participants are forced to consider the true net social benefit of their actions. For example, government can encourage an efficient amount of cigarettes by imposing a per-unit tax, T, on cigarette manufacturers equal to the vertical distance between MPB and MSB at Q_1 in figure 9–5. The per-unit tax raises the marginal private costs of producing cigarettes by the amount of the tax. As a result, the market price of cigarettes increases to P_1 and cigarette consumption falls to the socially efficient level (MSB = MSC). Cigarette producers receive P_2, the difference between the market price of P_1 and the per-unit tax (or vertical distance between the MPB and MSB) as after-tax revenues per unit.

Notice in this example that both sellers and consumers share the burden from the cigarette tax. The consumers pay the portion $P_1 - P_0$, and the sellers pay the portion $P_0 - P_2$. The sellers' portion of the tax burden typically results in a smaller profit margin or is shifted backward on to input suppliers. In our example, the cigarette tax may force producers to pay lower wages to their employees or lower the prices they pay to tobacco farmers. Whether consumers or producers pay a greater share of the cigarette tax depends on the relative magnitudes of the price elasticities of supply and demand. In general, when the price elasticity of demand (in absolute terms) exceeds the price elasticity of supply, the producer pays a greater fraction of the tax burden. The consumer incurs a relatively greater portion of the tax burden when the price elasticity of supply exceeds the price elasticity of demand.[7]

FIGURE 9 – 5

A Tax as a Corrective Instrument

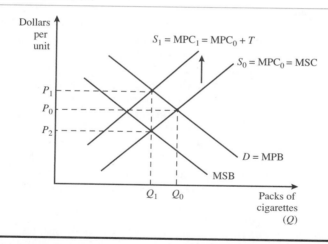

The graph captures the market for cigarettes. Like before, an unfettered market results in the outcome where MPB = MPC at Q_0. Efficiency, however, exists at the point where MSB = MSC at Q_1. Government, in this case, can bring about a more efficient allocation of resources by setting a tax equal to the external damages caused by cigarette smoking at the efficient level. The supply of cigarettes effectively shifts to the left from S_0 to S_1. In this example, both consumers and producers share the tax burden. Consumers pay the portion $P_1 - P_0$ and producers pay $P_0 - P_2$. In general, the incidence of a tax depends on the relative demand and supply elasticities.

---

[7]The answers to several questions at the end of the chapter provide the logic behind this statement.

Governments face an incentive to tax goods for which demand is price inelastic. That is because the quantity demanded declines by a smaller percentage than the percentage increase in taxes when demand is price inelastic. Thus, the total tax revenue to government, the product of the per-unit tax and quantity, increases when demand is price inelastic. In fact, one reason "sin taxes" on cigarettes and alcohol products are so politically popular is that the demand for these two products is price inelastic, thus providing a fruitful source of revenues for government.

The point is that taxes or a threat of fines can be used to discourage socially harmful activities. In contrast, subsidies can be used to encourage socially beneficial activities that are otherwise undervalued in the marketplace. Recall that underproduction and underconsumption occur when marginal social benefit exceeds marginal private benefit. A subsidy that reduces price creates an incentive for more buyers to engage in a socially beneficial activity.

A Market Solution for Externalities?   In the preceding section, we treated an externality as a situation where the market fails to allocate resources efficiently because a portion of the costs and benefits is not internalized by those participating in the exchange. Government is usually needed to tax a harmful activity or subsidize a beneficial one. In some situations, however, the market can automatically correct for any externalities because individuals— those who are harmed and those who benefit from the activity—bargain and come to agree on a mutually satisfying solution. As a result, the presence of an externality does not always require government intervention.

For this to happen, three conditions must hold (Coase, 1960). First, clearly specified property rights must be assigned to either the benefiting party or the harmed party. (Property rights are laws that describe what people can do with their property.) Second, the involved parties must have an equal amount of bargaining power; otherwise, one party in the ensuing negotiation may have an unfair advantage. Third, the transaction costs of negotiation, or bargaining costs, must be low to ensure that the bargaining actually takes place.

Figure 9–6 represents a situation where the bargaining between parties provides a solution to an externality problem. The horizontal axis measures the quantity of cigarettes, and the vertical axis reflects the associated dollar costs and benefits. The downward-sloping $NMPB_A$ curve shows the net marginal private benefit (MPB less the constant market price or, equivalently, the consumer surplus per cigarette) that person A receives from smoking cigarettes in a two-person dormitory room. MPC_B stands for the marginal private cost, or damages, that cigarette smoke imposes on person B. The curve is upward sloping to reflect the assumption that marginal private costs are likely to increase with a greater amount of cigarette smoking.

Suppose smoking is allowed in the dormitory rooms and person A is totally inconsiderate of person B's welfare. In this situation, person A is essentially granted property rights to the air in the room and faces a zero price for her actions (because the price per cigarette has been subtracted out from MPB). To maximize her utility, she smokes q_1 number of cigarettes, where NMPB equals zero. This amount of smoking, however, causes considerable harm to person B as indicated by point H on the MPC_B curve.

Given this scenario, person B faces an incentive to bribe person A into smoking fewer cigarettes in the room, or at least smoking them when B is not around. As long as person A receives a sum of money (or some in-kind compensation of equal monetary value) greater than the NMPB for a given quantity of cigarettes, she is made better off by smok-

FIGURE 9–6

A Market Solution to an Externality

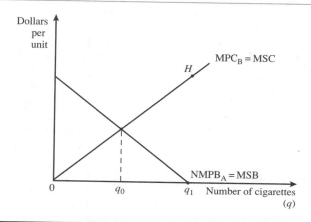

The graph shows the potential gains from two parties agreeing to some amount of cigarette smoking in a two-person dormitory room. The two curves represent the net marginal private benefit, NMPB, to one person and the marginal private cost, MPC, to another from different amount of cigarettes smoked. Person B, the harmed party, may bribe person A, the smoker to refrain from smoking the amount of cigarettes represented by the horizontal distance $q_1 - q_0$ because the cost to person B outweighs the benefit to person A. Or, person A might pay person B to allow the amount of cigarette smoking represented by the horizontal distance represented by $q_0 - 0$ because the benefit to person A exceeds the cost to person B. The idea is that voluntary exchange can sometimes correct for an externality. The assignment of property rights to the air in the room determines who bears the externality costs.

ing less in the room and taking the bribe. According to figure 9–6, person B is willing to pay a price, as indicated by the MPC, that is higher than the NMPB for all levels of cigarette smoking greater than q_0. For points to the left of q_0, NMPB exceeds MPC and person B is not willing to compensate person A enough for further reductions in smoking. As a result, bargaining ceases given the assignment of property rights. At q_0, the amount of smoking is optimal for both persons A and B.[8]

Now suppose college policy changes such that smoking is not allowed in the dormitory room unless all roommates consent. The nonsmoker, person B, is essentially assigned the property rights, and the origin in figure 9–6 represents the initial position before bargaining takes place. At zero cigarettes, however, the marginal benefit to person A greatly exceeds the marginal cost to person B. Therefore, person A faces an incentive to bribe or compensate person B to accept some positive amount of smoking in the room. Person B might leave the room while person A smokes or install a smoke-eater mechanism in the room with some of the money received from person A. In any case, bargaining results in q_0 cigarettes, where $NMPB_A$ equals MPC_B. As Coase pointed out, the final outcome is invariant as to who is assigned the property rights. Both assignments lead to q_0 for an efficient outcome. The assignment determines who incurs the externality costs.

---

[8]If MPC_B exceeds $NMPB_A$ at all levels of cigarette consumption, no smoking takes place in the room.

The "private market" reaches an efficient outcome in this case due to equal bargaining power. For example, if person A is physically larger than person B, the threat or actual use of violence might influence the relative bargaining power of the two parties. If so, physical violence rations the scarce air in the room, and the outcome is likely to be unsatisfactory to person B. Also, high transaction costs can prevent the exchange from taking place. If the group affected by the externality is large, free-rider effects will make cooperation on an efficient bribe difficult to achieve. For example, suppose three smokers and three non-smokers share a suite of rooms in the dormitory. If the members of each group are heterogeneous, they may disagree on the appropriate payment, and the externality will remain uncorrected. Moreover, some individuals in the group may attempt to free-ride the bribes of others. In fact, some restaurants voluntarily designate smoking and nonsmoking areas due to the high transaction costs of negotiation among restaurant customers, among other reasons. Because the model does not apply to a large-group setting, the Coase theorem is limited in scope.

In any event, one lesson of the Coase theorem is that government is not *always* needed to correct for an externality. The assignment of property rights can produce an efficient outcome to an externality problem as long as bargaining costs are low. Government is needed only to assign and enforce property rights. Note that in the process of assigning property rights, government determines who "should" incur the externality costs.

INSIGHT 9-2

Alcohol Commercial Bans and Alcohol Abuse: An International Perspective

Some products, like cocaine and marijuana, are banned, whereas the consumption of other medically harmful products, such as cigarettes and alcoholic beverages, is presently legal in the United States (although alcoholic beverages were banned during the Prohibition era from 1920 to 1933). Instead of directly banning legal but potentially harmful products, the government can try to influence adverse consumption practices indirectly through such policies as "sin" taxes, bans on commercial advertising, educational programs, and minimum age requirements. Saffer (1991) examined the effect on alcohol abuse of banning broadcast advertising of alcoholic beverages on television and radio. Given the controversy regarding whether advertising creates a demand for a product by manipulating consumer tastes, this study is especially interesting.

In his empirical investigation, Saffer used a panel data set that included 17 OECD countries for the years 1970 through 1983. Three measures of alcohol abuse—the per capita consumption of pure alcohol from beer, wine, and spirits; liver cirrhosis mortality rate; and motor vehicle mortality rate—were specified as the dependent variables in separate regression equations. Two dummy variables were employed to control for the banning of alcohol advertising broadcasts. One dummy variable took on the value of 1 if the country banned broadcast advertising of all types of alcoholic beverages (i.e., beer, wine, and spirits) and zero otherwise. The other equaled 1 if only spirits advertising was disallowed and zero otherwise. Saffer controlled for other explanatory variables, including the real price of a liter of pure alcohol and real income in each country.

Among the findings, the multiple regression results indicated that countries with a ban only on advertising spirits had about a 16 percent lower alcohol consumption rate than countries with no ban. Countries with bans on the advertising of all types of alcoholic products had about an 11 percent lower alcohol consumption rate than those that banned only spirits advertising. Some persuasive evidence was also found linking alcohol advertising bans to lower motor vehicle and liver cirrhosis mortality rates.

Apparently an advertising ban has the potential to reduce the consumption of alcoholic beverages and, more important, the harmful impact of excessive alcohol consumption on good health. If alcohol advertisements contain little useful information, the benefits of a ban may outweigh the cost. The same argument has been used to continue the ban on cigarette advertisements on radio and television in the United States.

Regulations

A government regulation that attempts to control either the price, quantity, or quality of a product or the entry of new firms into the marketplace represents another kind of government intervention. According to the public interest theory, the regulation is justified because a market imperfection exists that would otherwise cause a misallocation of society's resources. For example, insufficient consumer information often justifies government-imposed quality requirements. As another example, government might grant monopoly status to a firm and regulate its price because one large firm can produce output more cheaply than a large number of small firms (i.e., a natural monopoly, such as an electric utility or a short-distance telephone company). The effect of government regulations in medical markets is hard to predict. Whether government impedes or promotes efficiency and equity depends on a host of factors, such as the competitiveness of the market, the cost structure faced by the individual medical firm, objectives motivating medical decision makers, and whether the exclusion principle holds (i.e., externalities, third-party payer, or public good considerations). In the next section, we examine the impact of a per-unit price ceiling within a supply and demand model assuming that consumers possess health insurance coverage—the most common situation in medical markets.

The Effects of a Per-Unit Price Ceiling The price paid for a good or service is one item a third-party payer, like the government, might regulate. Government might regulate the price by establishing a maximum price or reimbursement level. In that case, the government sets a **price ceiling** for a product, and producers are prohibited by law from charging a higher price to consumers covered under the ceiling. Figure 9–7 shows the effect of a price ceiling within a supply and demand model of a market for physician services.

As you know, the equilibrium price and quantity are determined at the intersection point of supply and demand in a typical nonmedical market. But because the model represents a medical market, we must also consider the impact of health insurance coverage. To simplify the discussion, let's suppose consumers have complete rather than partial insurance coverage. Given the demand, consumers wish to purchase Q_D units of physician

FIGURE 9-7
Effect of a Per-Unit Price Ceiling in a Supply and Demand Model

The graph represents the market for physician services. At a zero out-of-pocket price, consumers desire Q_D amount of physician services. If a third-party reimburses physicians at the price P_D, consumer demand is satisfied and no shortage occurs. If for cost containment reasons the government implements a price ceiling and lowers the price to P_C, physicians supply only Q_S amount of services and a shortage results in the market.

services (say, office visits) because they have full health insurance coverage and effectively pay a zero out-of-pocket price. Assuming a third party initially reimburses physicians a price of P_D, which is sufficient to elicit the amount of physician services demanded by consumers, expenditures on physician services amount to area P_DAQ_D0, the product of the reimbursement price of P_D and Q_D, the quantity demanded by consumers. In this case, no shortage of physician services exists because quantity supplied equals quantity demanded. Notice that expenditures on physician services exceed the level that results when consumers face the full market price for physician care at the intersection of supply and demand, as discussed earlier in the text.

Now suppose that for cost containment reasons the government sets a cap or reimbursement ceiling at P_C. Because of the positively sloped supply curve, the lower reimbursement rate creates an incentive for physicians to reduce the quantity supplied to Q_S and, as a result, expenditures on physician services fall to area P_CBQ_S0. Notice because the reimbursement ceiling of P_C is set below P_D, quantity demanded exceeds quantity supplied and the price ceiling results in a shortage of physician services.

In a price ceiling situation where a shortage ensues and the price mechanism is not employed as a rationing device, some unintended outcomes may occur. For one, physicians may treat patients on a first-come, first-served basis even if some patients require more

INSIGHT 9-3

The Cost of Waiting for Hospital Services in Canada

We discussed some of the features associated with the Canadian health care system in Chapter 4. Among those features, consumers pay a zero out-of-pocket price for receiving most types of medical care services, and physicians and hospitals are directly reimbursed by the government. No balance billing is allowed, meaning physicians and hospitals are prohibited from charging patients for services beyond the payments they receive from the government. Given that consumers pay and health care providers receive a different price in Canada, excess demand results if quantity demanded at the zero consumer price exceeds quantity supplied at the reimbursement price as discussed in the text.

Because price does not perform a rationing function in Canada, the scarce medical services must be rationed by some nonprice method. Queues are the nonprice method used to ration hospital services, and waiting lists are the inevitable outcome. In fact, some articles in the popular press and professional journals have suggested that the waiting lists are excessive and socially costly. Prolonged pain, anxiety, inconvenience, and loss of productive time are some of the social costs associated with long waiting lists for hospital services.

In an interesting study, Globerman (1991) estimated the cost of waiting for various types of hospital services in British Columbia. To assess the social cost of waiting Globerman multiplied the loss of productive weeks for those experiencing significant disabilities by average weekly industrial earnings for British Columbia in 1989. The assumption is that the average industrial wage serves as a suitable measure of the opportunity cost of waiting for hospital services. Of course, some elderly people in the queue may be retired from the workforce so the industrial wage overestimates their opportunity cost.

The cost of waiting was calculated to be approximately .2 percent of the provincial gross domestic product in 1989. Although that percent may seem low, two points concerning the magnitude of the waiting costs should be made. First, the costs of pain and anxiety, for example, are not included in the calculation. Second, as Globerman noted, the estimated cost of waiting for hospital services is comparable to the total forgone wages and salaries associated with strikes and lockouts in British Columbia in 1989. Strike and lockout costs have long been a concern of economic policymakers in Canada. Because excess demand for hospital admissions may impose even greater societal costs than work stoppages, this seemingly low estimate may be cause for much alarm. Consequently, efficiency improvements may be in order.

The reader should be reminded, however, that the figures are purely estimates and the calculations rely on a host of assumptions. More studies are needed before any sweeping generalizations can be made. Nonetheless, Globerman's study focuses on an important policy question in addition to providing a useful application of several economic concepts, including shortages, nonprice rationing, and opportunity costs.

urgent attention than others. Physicians may also reduce the quality of visits in an attempt to lower costs. The quality reduction may mean a longer waiting time for a visit or shorter time spent with physicians during the actual visit. In addition, some unethical physicians may accept illegal side payments from wealthy people who want to jump to the front of the waiting line.

Political concerns may also dictate how a scarce medical service is rationed when a shortage exists. Perhaps politicians decide that medical services should be rationed on the basis of age, illness, or the amount of campaign contributions the individual donates. For example, in Great Britain, where price has virtually no rationing role, less rationing of medical care occurs for children than for adults. According to Aaron and Schwartz (1984), "Health expenditures per child in Britain are 119 percent of expenditures per prime age adult, whereas in the United States they are only 37 percent as much" (p. 97).

The point is that medical cost containment is typically not a free lunch. According to the above model, cost containment under plausible circumstances can result in shortages, longer waiting lines, nonprice rationing, and reductions in the quality of care. Society has to seriously consider the likely trade-offs before adopting cost containment strategies.

Two important caveats are in order at this point. First, if physicians are not subjected to an "all payer" price regulation, they may react by increasing the price of physician services to the consumers in an unregulated market to offset the lower, regulated price. This practice is referred to as **cost shifting**. For example, suppose figure 9–7 represents only the Medicare physician services submarket. Physicians might attempt to remain at point A and cover the losses on the Medicare submarket by increasing the price of physician services to non-Medicare patients. The ability to shift costs, however, depends on the price elasticity of demand for the non-Medicare physician services.

Second, the exact behavioral response of the medical firm is more multidimensional than presented thus far and depends largely on the base to which the price ceiling is applied (Cromwell, 1976). Specifically, health care providers, in general, may react to a lower charge by adjusting the length of stay, number of patients, or quality of services. For example, if hospitals are paid according to a per diem price ceiling (i.e., average revenue per patient-day), they may respond to a lower per diem charge by increasing the number of patient-days to obtain additional revenues and also by lowering quality. The number of patient-days can be increased by increasing the number of new admissions and/or increasing the average length of stay. By increasing the patient's length of stay, hospitals can use the profits received from the later days to subsidize the more costly, service-intensive earlier days and make greater profits.

As another example, hospitals (or nursing homes) that are reimbursed on a per-case or per-patient basis are likely to respond to a lower per-case charge by admitting more patients to obtain additional revenues and lowering quality and length of stay. In this regard, some observers have argued that harmfully low DRG payments, which are per-case reimbursements, have caused hospitals to release their Medicare patients "quicker and sicker."

In addition, some critics have argued that the DRG per-patient payment has created an incentive for patient dumping by hospitals. Although illegal in certain cases under the Federal Emergency Medical Treatment and Active Labor Act, **patient dumping** refers to the practice whereby private hospitals fail to admit severely sick patients and instead dump them on public hospitals. In practice, this may happen because the DRG payment is based on the historical cost of providing services to patients with an average level of sickness and does not necessarily cover the cost of providing hospital services to those patients with severe illnesses.

In sum, the impact of a price ceiling is difficult to predict before the fact. It depends on the base to which the price ceiling is applied and the degree of cost shifting that takes place. The degree of cost shifting, in turn, is a function of the price elasticity of demand in the unregulated market.

INSIGHT 9–4

The Regulated Market for Human Organs[1]

In the United States, the sale of human organs for transplantation is prohibited by the National Organ Transplant Act of 1984, and human organs, such as kidneys, hearts, and livers, can only be donated. In effect, the suppliers of human organs receive a zero price for each organ donated. As a result, relatively few human organs are supplied because a market incentive is nonexistent.

Figure 1 provides a graphical illustration of the market for human kidneys. The market demand for human kidneys, D, is drawn with its typical downward-sloping shape. Two

FIGURE 1
The Market for Human Kidneys

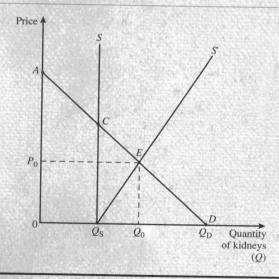

[1]Much of this analysis is borrowed from Barney and Reynolds (1989), Kaserman and Barnett (1991), and Pindyck and Rubinfeld (1995). The interested student should also read Barnett, Blair, and Kaserman (1992).

(continued)

supply curves are drawn. The inelastic or fixed supply curve, S, reflects the fact that human kidneys cannot be sold; thus, price is unimportant and the quantity of kidneys donated depends solely on other, nonprice factors. The positively sloped supply curve, S', allows for the possibility that human organs can be sold and suppliers are responsive to a price incentive.

Notice that Q_S kidneys are donated or supplied at a zero price in this example. At this zero price, however, Q_D kidneys are demanded. Because quantity demanded exceeds quantity supplied at a zero price, a shortage of $Q_S Q_D$ kidneys results. Thus, this analysis suggests that a shortage of human organs will exist as a result of the law banning the sale of human organs for transplantation.

Assuming the recipients pay a zero price under the present law banning the sale of human organs, consumer surplus equals the total area under the demand curve, or area ACQ_S0 in figure 1.[2] Kidney donors receive no producer surplus under the present law.

On the other hand, Q_0 kidneys are supplied and demanded if human kidneys can be sold at a market-clearing price of P_0. The shortage under the present law is eliminated. At the higher price of P_0, more individuals are willing to supply human organs due to the profit incentive. Fewer kidneys are demanded as some potential buyers turn to kidney dialysis, a substitute for transplantation, or choose to forgo transplantation. In this case, consumer surplus equals the area AEP_0 and producer surplus is represented by area P_0EQ_S0. A net gain to society of area CEQ_S results from an exchange of human organs for money. (This same area reflects the deadweight loss associated with the current law prohibiting the sale of human organs.)

Of course, society may be opposed to the sale of human organs for ethical reasons. Although many lives could be saved, the idea of reimbursing individuals for giving up parts of their bodies may repulse some people. In addition, legal considerations may impede the efficient and equitable operation of the market. Before the sale of human organs for transplantation is legalized, all the economic, legal, and ethical ramifications must be carefully weighed.

---

[2]Pindyck and Rubinfeld (1995) point out that hospitals and intermediaries may capture the consumer surplus if the fixed number of kidneys is rationed based on willingness to pay.

The Effects of Quality Regulations   Government may also attempt to regulate the quality of medical services when consumers are rationally ignorant. As mentioned earlier, quality differences show up in the structure, process, and outcomes of production. Because procedural and outcome guidelines are more difficult to set and enforce, quality regulations are typically directed at the structure of operation. For example, a public agency may require that medical workers be professionally licensed or may mandate a minimum staff-to-patient ratio. In both cases, the assumption is that a higher level of structural quality promotes increased quality at the process and outcome stages.

Regulations aimed at the quality of the employees typically mean higher costs of production and thereby reduce the supply of medical services in the medical marketplace.

The reduction of supply occurs because the acquisition of a professional license requires a greater human capital investment by the medical employee and raises the cost of providing the medical service. Figure 9–8 shows the implications of a quality regulation, such as professional licensing. The original supply and demand curves for medical employees are S_0 and D_0 and the corresponding market wage and employment levels are W_0 and N_0, respectively. Professional licensing, which raises the cost of entering an occupation due to the increased human capital investment, reduces supply to S_1 and thereby raises the wage rate to W_1. The difference between W_1 and W_0 captures the **compensating wage differential** necessary to attract the marginal worker with the appropriate professional license to the labor market.

FIGURE 9 – 8

Effect of Professional Licensure

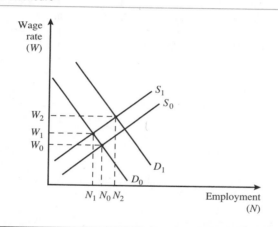

The graph represents a market for professional labor. Without occupational licensing, market equilibrium occurs at employment N_0 where D_0 intersects S_0. Occupational licensing potentially has two effects. First, the licensing requirement increases the human capital investment necessary to enter the occupation and thereby reduces supply from S_0 to S_1. Second, the higher wage of W_1 brought on by the supply reduction creates an incentive for professionals to improve their job performance. The quality assurance of occupational licensing, brought on by the improved job performance, leads to a greater demand for the output of the professional labor. As a result, demand increases from D_0 to D_1. If the demand shift exceeds the supply shift such that N_2 exceeds N_0, the occupational licensing reflects an efficient policy serving the public interest.

Two questions follow from the analysis. First, is professional licensing truly associated with increased procedural and outcomes quality? If not, the result may not justify the method of controlling quality. Second, was a professional group behind the implementation of the professional licensing requirement? This question follows because those inframarginal individuals in the labor group (particularly those who lack the required license but are grandfathered in) obviously gain from the higher wage rate.

Svorny (1987) provides an interesting way to analyze the second question by comparing a professional license to a trademark or brand name. All three of these devices may signal quality assurance to consumers. Specifically, Svorny argues that the higher wage resulting from the professional license creates a financial incentive for the typical medical worker to perform efficiently, satisfy patient wants, and provide a desirable amount and quality of output. This is because opportunistic behavior, when discovered, results in job termination and causes the medical worker to receive a low or negative return on the original human capital investment. The quality assurance generated by the higher wage, in turn, raises the marginal value of the employee's services to the consumer. The higher quality assurance can be represented by a shift to the right of the demand curve from D_0 to D_1 in figure 9–8.

Due to the greater demand arising from the increased quality assurance, the wage rate increases further to W_2 and employment rises from N_1 to N_2. Svorny goes on to note that the model provides a useful test of whether professional licensure requirements (and other quality regulations) serve the public interest or some special interest group, such as the entrenched medical employees. If the quality regulation provides benefits (quality assurance) that exceed its cost (human capital investment), the shift of the demand curve to the right should be greater in magnitude than the shift of the supply curve to the left. Thus, employment should increase overall if society is made better off and the public interest is served by the quality regulation (i.e., N_2 should exceed N_0). However, if the opposite occurs—the supply curve shifts to the left by more than the demand curve shifts to the right—the quality regulation favors special interests.

Svorny used the analysis to test whether basic science certification and citizen requirements for medical licensure made any difference in the number of physicians per capita across the 48 contiguous states of the United States in 1965. She noted that both requirements potentially involve some degree of human capital investment that increases wages and establishes a future return to discourage opportunistic behavior. Using multiple regression analysis, Svorny found an inverse relation between the presence of both requirements and the number of physicians. The theory suggests an inverse relation is evidence for the special interest model of the regulatory process.

The implication is that these quality regulations result in lower rather than higher consumption of physician services. A lower consumption of physician services results because the licensure restrictions increased entry costs by more than they increased the consumer benefits from quality assurance. Overall, the study found evidence supporting the special interest group theory of the regulatory process.

Two interesting and recent studies on the relationship between regulatory barriers and health care outcomes deserve mentioning. Anderson, Halcoussis, Johnston, and Lowenberg (2000) find empirically that physician income is higher in states with regulations restricting the practice of homeopathy, a type of alternative medicine. Kleiner and Kudrle (2000) find that tougher dental licensing does not improve dental health but does raise the price for consumers and the earnings of dental practitioners. Consequently, these studies also provide support for the special interest theory of regulation.

Antitrust Laws

Government also intervenes in a market economy by enacting and enforcing antitrust laws. Antitrust laws are concerned primarily with promoting competition among the firms within an industry and prohibiting firms from engaging in certain types of market practices that may inhibit efficiency. The Sherman Antitrust Act, passed in 1890, is the cornerstone of all antitrust laws. Other antitrust laws, such as the Clayton Act of 1914, the Federal Trade Commission Act of 1914, and the Cellar-Kefauver Amendment of 1950, either clarify, reinforce, or extend the Sherman Act. The Sherman Act stipulates two important provisions:

> *Section 1:* Every contract, combination in the form of trust or otherwise, or conspiracy, in restraint of trade or commerce among the several states or with foreign nations, is hereby declared illegal.
>
> *Section 2:* Every person who shall monopolize, or conspire with any other person or persons to monopolize any part of the trade or commerce among the several states, or with foreign nations, shall be guilty of a misdemeanor.

The Sherman Antitrust Act has been interpreted as prohibiting anticompetitive business practices, such as price fixing, boycotting, market allocations, and mergers, that promote inefficiencies and inequities in the marketplace. **Price fixing** occurs when business rivals in an industry abide to a collusive agreement, refrain from price competition, and fix the price of a good or service. Essentially, the firms collectively act as a monopolist, maximize joint profits, and, according to monopoly theory, create a higher price and a lower level of output. An agreement among a number of large hospitals to establish the price of various hospital services is an example of price fixing. Physicians who have been denied staff privileges frequently allege that the existing hospital physicians violated Section 1 of the Sherman Act by unlawfully conspiring to exclude them from the hospital (Jacobsen and Wiggins, 1992).[9]

A **boycott** is an agreement among competitors not to deal with a supplier or a customer. For example, suppose that in response to a Blue Shield ban on balance billing, the physicians in an area collectively agree not to offer services to Blue Shield patients.[10] While it is legal for any one physician to unilaterally refrain from dealing with Blue Shield, the combination is in violation of the Sherman Antitrust Act. In this case, the rival physicians are essentially trying to fix the price of medical services charged to Blue Shield subscribers.

Market allocation occurs when competitors agree not to compete with one another in specific market areas. This business practice can ultimately produce the same undesirable outcome that price fixing does, since each firm within the area is free to set a monopoly price and restrict output with no concern about competitive entry.

Price fixing, boycotting, and market allocations are *illegal per se*; that is, they are unreasonable by their very nature and therefore illegal. To be found in violation of the Sherman Act, the plaintiff must only prove that those practices took place.

The Sherman Act (in conjunction with Section 7 of the Clayton Act) has also been cited as a basis for preventing horizontal mergers among firms. A **horizontal merger** takes place when two or more firms in the same industry combine together. The economic concern is that a merger may harm consumers by making it easier for the remaining firms in the market to collude, expressly or tacitly (e.g., by following the leader), and thereby force price above the competitive level.

---

[9]See Felsenthal (1992) for an insightful discussion of how physicians and hospitals have attempted to fend off low-cost competitors, such as nurse-midwives, chiropractors, and optometrists.
[10]A physician boycott of this kind occurred in *Kartell v. Blue Shield of Massachusetts*, 749 F.2d 922 (1984). See Frech (1988) for an economic assessment of this antitrust suit.

Although a combination of two or more competitor firms can result in higher prices to the consumer, the merger may also benefit the consumer if economies exist with respect to large-scale production. Larger firms may not only produce with economies of scale and organizational economies but also have better access to technological innovations. Any cost or resource savings mean society can produce more output from a given amount of inputs. For example, according to hospital officials, a proposed merger of the 710-bed Iowa Methodist Medical Center and the 319-bed Iowa Lutheran Hospital in Des Moines "could save as much as $12 million annually during the first three years of the merger" (Burda, 1993, p. 24). Similarly, officials at St. Joseph Mercy and North Iowa Medical in Mason City claimed their proposed merger "would reduce their operating expenses by $2 million to $3 million per year." Thus, potential anticompetitive and procompetitive effects must be properly weighed when determining the social desirability of a merger. Assessing the net social benefits of a business practice such as a merger is referred to as the **rule of reason** doctrine.

The Williamson (1969) merger trade-off model in figure 9–9 provides an insightful way to conceptualize the net social benefit of a horizontal merger. Suppose the market in some geographical area is competitive before the merger and the industry is characterized by constant costs. As a result, the market price and quantity of hospital services are P_0 and Q_0, respectively, where the demand curve intersects the original supply curve S_0. Now suppose a merger of two hospitals in the area makes it easier for the remaining firms to collude and reduce output to Q_1 and raise price to P_1. Relative to the original competitive

---

FIGURE 9–9
Williamson's Merger Trade-Off

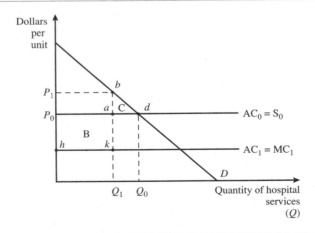

The graph represents the market for hospital services supposing a constant cost industry. Suppose the hospital market is initially in equilibrium at Q_0 where D intersects S_0. Now suppose two relatively large firms merge and the resulting collusion among the firms in the market causes output to fall to Q_1 and price to rise to P_1. The deadweight loss of *bad* represents the cost, C, of the merger. But suppose the merger also results in cost savings such that average costs falls to AC_1. The cost savings, represented by the area P_0akh, reflect the benefits of the merger. To determine if the merger provides net social benefits, the benefits of the merger must be compared to the costs of the merger.

equilibrium, a deadweight loss of area *bad* occurs. The deadweight loss reflects the social cost, C, associated with the merger.

Suppose that due to the horizontal merger and the associated greater production efficiency, the per-unit cost of producing hospital services declines from AC_0 to AC_1. Cost savings might accrue from economies of scale at the firm level, improved access to capital markets, purchasing discounts, or managerial economies. This reflects some important resource cost savings to society. Resources are saved and can be used for other purposes if a larger firm is more efficient in production. Compared to the costs in a competitive market, the total resource cost savings is measured by area P_0akh. The area reflects the social benefit, B, that arises from the merger. The net benefit of the merger is found by subtracting the deadweight loss of area C from the resource cost savings of area B. As drawn, the merger provides positive net benefits to society. Of course, actual mergers may cause net benefits or losses depending on the relative magnitudes of the cost savings and deadweight losses. The bottom line is that a proposed horizontal merger should be given careful scrutiny using cost-benefit analysis.

Although the Sherman Act was enacted in 1890, the health care field escaped its purview until the mid-1970s.[11] Up to that time, it was believed that members of the medical profession, like other professionals, such as lawyers and engineers, were exempted from antitrust laws. In the *Goldfarb v. Virginia State Bar* case of 1975, the Supreme Court unanimously rejected any claim to a professional exemption and stated

> *The nature of an occupation, standing alone, does not provide sanctuary from the Sherman Act . . . nor is the public service aspect of professional practice controlling in determining whether section 1 includes professions.*

Some early signs appeared to indicate that the courts may aggressively enforce antitrust laws in health care markets. For example, in *Arizona v. Maricopa County Medical Society* in 1982, the Supreme Court condemned as price fixing the attempt by a professionally sponsored foundation to set a maximum price on the fees charged to member physicians for services underwritten by insurers that had agreed to abide by the foundation's fee schedule. Typically, when firms collude and pursue their joint interests, they agree to a price floor rather than a price ceiling. The foundation claimed the maximum price was fixed for the benefit of the consumer. In this particular case, the Supreme Court invoked the *per se* illegality of price fixing, but opened the door to a possible rule of reason ruling in the future. The Court explained that the public service aspect and other features of the medical profession may require that a particular practice that could be properly viewed as a violation of the Sherman Act in another context be treated differently. The Court went on to explain that in *Maricopa*, the price-fixing arrangement was premised on neither public service nor ethical norms nor quality of care considerations.

Two merger cases prior to the mid-1990s, *Hospital Corporation of America v. FTC* (807 F.2d 1381 [7th Cir. 1986]) and *U.S. v. Rockford Memorial Corporation* (898 F.2d 1278 [7th Cir. 1990]) also demonstrated the Court's willingness to enforce antitrust laws aggressively and disallow horizontal mergers in the hospital services industry if they substantially lessen competition or tend to create a monopoly. In the *Rockford* case, for

---

[11]See Havighurst (1983) and Kopit (1983) for a thorough discussion of the application of antitrust laws to the health care industry.

example, the U.S. government brought suit to prevent the horizontal merger of Rockford Memorial Corporation and Swedish American Corporation, both of which are nonprofit institutions. Citing a high postmerger market share and, consequently, the potential for monopoly pricing, the Court ruled against the merger.[12]

However, not all health policy analysts believe antitrust laws should be stringently enforced in the health services industries. Some argue that various institutions, such as third-party payments, nonprofit organizations, and excessive government regulations, mean that antitrust laws are less applicable and necessary in health care markets than in other markets. With health care costs continually increasing, many analysts claim that the enforcement of antitrust laws could actually worsen the situation as cost-minimizing joint ventures and mergers are discouraged. Indeed, legislation in Maine, Minnesota, Ohio, Wisconsin, and Washington allows hospitals to cooperate if the benefits of the proposed venture substantially outweigh the disadvantages of any reduction in competition (Felsenthal, 1993). In 1993, the Department of Justice and the Federal Trade Commission issued a joint statement of antitrust enforcement in health care markets, basically echoing the notion that the procompetitive and anticompetitive effects of various business activities, such as mergers, joint ventures, joint purchasing, and provider networks, will be weighed when making an antitrust determination.

Greaney (2002) argues that anti-managed care sentiment has reduced the enthusiasm for applying competitive principles in health care markets since the mid-1990s. With respect to the hospital industry, for example, Greaney points out that the Federal Trade Commission and Department of Justice won five of six cases challenging hospital mergers between 1984 and 1994. Many other mergers were settled or abandoned after government investigation spotlighted potential antitrust concerns. In contrast, federal and state antitrust enforcement agencies have lost all seven cases brought before the federal court since 1995. It remains to be seen how stringently and consistently antitrust laws are enforced in various health care markets once the backlash against managed care subsides.

Public Enterprise

Instead of indirectly influencing the structure, conduct, or performance of private industry, government may take a more direct role in health care provision by producing and distributing a specific health care service. For example, many local governments are responsible for providing county and city hospital services to local residents. In addition, some nursing homes and mental health facilities are operated by local or state government agencies. Moreover, the federal government runs and operates Veteran Administration and military hospitals. Despite the fact that the government may operate health care facilities, economic analysis is still useful for analyzing the many production decisions that take place. Valuable resources are used in production, and some type of economizing behavior occurs.

The primary difference between public enterprise and private, for-profit enterprise is the lack of a profit motive. Like not-for-profit entities, public health care providers may pursue goals other than profit maximization. The upshot is that public health care providers may not minimize the cost of producing a given quantity of medical care services or attempt to satisfy consumer wants. Of course, even public agencies are subject to

[12]More discussion of merger policy in the hospital industry is provided in Chapter 13.

INSIGHT 9–5

Antitrust Shows Its Teeth

In January of 1999, the Department of Justice (DOJ) filed an antitrust lawsuit against Dentsply International Inc., a dental supply company in York, Pennsylvania. The lawsuit alleges that Dentsply, who controlled more than 70 percent of the U.S. market for prefabricated artificial teeth over the last ten years, illegally entered into exclusive-dealing arrangements with its dealers. The DOJ claims that the exclusive-dealing contract prevented independent dealers from selling other brands of false teeth, resulting in reduced competition and higher prices for false teeth. The Clayton Act of 1914 declares illegal various business activities that substantially lessen competition or tend to create a monopoly.

Antitrust analysts consider an exclusive-dealing arrangement as one of several types of vertical restrictions that often take place between manufacturers and distributors. Other types of vertical restrictions include exclusive territories, resale price agreements, and franchise arrangements. In general, vertical restrictions can have either anticompetitive or procompetitive impacts and thereby potentially harm or benefit consumers. In terms of exclusive dealings, consumers may be harmed if rival manufacturers are foreclosed from offering their products to distributors. The foreclosure limits competition and raises prices. However, exclusive-dealing contracts can also reduce the free-rider problem that sometimes accompanies exchanges between manufacturers and distributors.

For example, suppose that Dentsply spends a considerable sum of money training the staff of its distributors about the intricate details behind false teeth. Or, suppose that Dentsply advertises the general availability of false teeth and provides a list of potential consumers to its distributors. Obviously, consumers gain from the advertising message and when they purchase quality products from informed suppliers. It also follows that Dentsply may have to charge a higher price for its false teeth to cover the training and advertising costs and the establishment of the customer list. However a rival manufacturer may free-ride the efforts of Dentsply by selling its artificial teeth to the same distributors at a lower price and receiving the benefits of a well-trained staff and the advertising at the distribution outlets. In fact, if there was no exclusive-dealing contract and all manufacturers faced an incentive to free-ride the effort of the others, much less training and advertising would take place and consumers would be potentially harmed. Exclusive dealings represent a solution to the free-rider problem.

The Courts have generally embraced a rule of reason approach to cases involving exclusive-dealing arrangements. First, the manufacturer involved in the exclusive-dealing arrangement must be shown to possess a critical degree of market power in the relevant market. Second, the exclusive-dealing arrangement must be shown to inhibit competition and harm consumers. The ultimate proof of inhibited competition is to show that consumers both pay higher prices and receive fewer services because of the exclusive-dealing contract. With that in mind, the DOJ (1999, p. 14) argues, "Dentply's exclusion of its rivals has resulted in higher prices, loss of choice, less market information, and lower quality of artificial teeth." At the writing of this edition of the text, the case has yet to be resolved.

SOURCE: Based on Ridge (2002) and Department of Justice (1999).

least-cost constraints of various kinds. For example, bureaucrats and politicians are either directly or indirectly influenced by the consumer/voters' response to excessive taxation. The potential loss of job tenure may create a sufficient incentive for cost minimization even in public facilities.

Many analysts argue that public medical facilities are more likely to provide services to the more severely ill patients. Unlike their for-profit (and even not-for-profit) counterparts, public medical facilities do not have to worry about the profit consequence of servicing high-cost patients. Therefore, public provision of medical services is often argued to be more equitable because all individuals, rich and poor, are provided with equal access to public facilities.

Lindsay (1976) developed a useful model of government enterprise that may explain why public hospitals tend to operate with lower per-unit costs of production than proprietary hospitals. The author assumed that politicians tie managerial compensation to the level of net social income that public organizations generate. Net social income, an analogue to profits in the private sector, is the difference between the social value of the output and the total cost of production. Higher managerial pay results from a higher level of net social income.

To estimate the value of the output provided by the public agency, politicians monitor the levels of various attributes associated with the product. Some attributes are observable and measurable; others are not. Bureau managers, in pursuit of higher pay, face an incentive to divert resources away from the production of attributes that are not easily measurable to those that are to increase the perceived social value of their output. Therefore, a financial incentive exists to make the output of public institutions contain too few "invisible" attributes, such as quality (as reflected in the number of staff visits to a hospital ward, words of encouragement, number of smiles, etc.), and too many visible attributes, such as quantity (e.g., number of patients). In contrast, managers of private organizations are disciplined to a greater degree by the marketplace and forced by consumer demand to provide the desired level of quality. Price fails if private firms fail to satisfy the quality demands of customers, unlike in a public agency, where price is essentially fixed by politicians.

Lindsay's model of government enterprise predicts that the average cost of government enterprise—that is, total cost divided by visible output—will be lower than the comparable average cost of proprietary enterprise. The author offers some empirical evidence to support his view of government enterprise.

The Redistribution Function of Government

In addition to providing public goods, correcting for externalities, enforcing regulations and antitrust laws, and operating public enterprises, another function of government is to redistribute income more equitably because a pure market system cannot guarantee that everyone receives an adequate level of income. Some people own very little labor, capital, and land resources, and hence are often unable to generate a subsistence level of income in the marketplace. Redistribution involves taxing one group and using the resulting tax revenues to provide subsidies to another group. One may question why people in a free democratic society, such as that of the United States, support redistribution and rely on government to administer various programs. One justification for redistribution advanced by economists is the existence of interdependent utility functions such that donors get utility from increasing the welfare of recipients. More formally, when utility functions are interdependent, person A derives utility when person B is made better off. Person B might be made better off by receiving some income or benefits in kind, such as housing or food, from person A.

Consequently, redistribution takes place in a free society because it provides utility to both recipient and donor groups. Government must administer and require people by law to contribute to the redistribution scheme through taxation because some people in the donor group might otherwise attempt to free-ride the voluntary contributions of others. For example, person C may also derive utility if person B is made better off, but may attempt to free-ride by relying on the sole contributions of person A to finance the redistribution program. Person A, in turn, may decide not to voluntarily contribute to the redistribution scheme given that others, such as person C, will indirectly benefit but will not share in the overall costs. Given the likelihood of a free-rider problem on a large scale, redistribution tends to be underprovided in a free market. So, in effect, government acts as an intermediary or fiscal agent by legally stipulating and collecting the necessary taxes from the donor group and redistributing the income to the recipient group.

For a redistribution scheme to be considered equitable, the two principles of *vertical* and *horizontal equity* must be satisfied. **Vertical equity** means that "unequals are treated unequally." To determine whether this principle has been satisfied in practice, a standard of comparison must first be selected. In terms of financial equity, the usual standard of comparison is income. As a result, the principle of vertical equity is satisfied when people with higher incomes are treated differently than those with lower incomes. This principle by itself, however, does not establish whether the net taxes (i.e., taxes less subsidies) of higher-income people should be higher or lower than those of people with lower incomes. Therefore, notions of fairness dictate that net taxes be based on "ability to pay"; that is, those with more ability to pay should incur a greater net tax liability.

Even this additional principle is ambiguous, because it is unclear how much more net taxes higher-income people should pay or whether taxes, when assessing burden, should be expressed in absolute terms or as a fraction of income. For example, suppose a household with $10,000 of income pays $2,000 in net taxes and another household with $100,000 pays $4,000 in net taxes. In absolute terms, the richer household pays more taxes. When taxes are expressed as a fraction of income, however, taxes comprise only 4 percent of the rich household's income compared to 20 percent of the poor household's income.

In practice, many consider that vertical equity is achieved when the net tax system is sufficiently progressive. A redistribution scheme is considered to be **progressive** if net taxes as a fraction of income increase with income. Ignoring the subsidy side of the redistribution issue, the federal income tax system comes closest to being a progressive tax scheme. The underlying belief is that higher-income individuals should pay more taxes in both absolute and relative terms.

In a **proportional** redistribution scheme, net taxes as a fraction of income remain constant with respect to income. The Medicare tax is a proportional tax because all payroll income is subject to a fixed percentage rate.

Finally, net taxes as a fraction of income fall with income if the redistribution scheme is **regressive**. A sales tax is generally considered to be a regressive tax because although everyone pays the same tax rate, consumption expenditures as a fraction of income tend to decrease with income.

Horizontal equity means that "equals should be treated equally." Using income as the standard of comparison, horizontal equity implies that individuals with the same income should pay the same amount of net taxes. If not, the resulting outcome is not fair according to the principle of horizontal equity.

With these principles of horizontal and vertical equity in mind, let's examine supply-side and demand-side subsidies as different ways to redistribute medical services.

Supply-Side Subsidies   A **supply-side subsidy** is essentially a grant of money from a third party that is aimed at reducing the internal costs of producing some consumer-oriented good or service. As an example, the subsidy may be awarded to an institution like a public hospital or used to finance the education of an important labor input, such as a nurse or physician. A supply-side subsidy typically expands the production of a good in the marketplace by lowering the marginal private cost of production. Given a downward-sloping market demand curve, the price of the good to the consumer declines and quantity demanded increases.

In the absence of any positive externalities, economists generally argue that a supply-side subsidy leads to a misallocation of resources in a market economy. The subsidy distorts market prices and provides a false signal that production is cheaper than it really is. Output in the subsidized sector expands and resources are drawn from nonsubsidized sectors. Hence, too much output is produced in the subsidized sector and not enough resources are allocated to the nonsubsidized sectors. Some economists also argue that supply-side subsidies are an inequitable way of redistributing income. Because the subsidies are directed at the supply side of the market, individuals with different levels of income similarly benefit from the lower prices at the subsidized firms. Rich and poor alike end up paying the same price when redistribution takes place with a supply-side subsidy. Therefore, the principle of vertical equity is sometimes compromised with a supply-side subsidy.

Demand-Side Subsidies   Because a supply-side subsidy is often viewed as inefficient because it distorts resource allocation and as inequitable because it benefits all rather than only poor consumers, many economists favor **demand-side subsidies**. Often (but not always, as in the case of Medicare or the tax exemption on health care benefits) people must qualify for demand-side aid by passing a means test. A means test requires that a household of a certain size has a combined income below some stipulated level to be eligible for the aid. Tying eligibility to household income is one way to satisfy the principles of vertical and horizontal equity. In practice, however, the principle of horizontal equity is violated for Medicaid services because the 50 states specify different guidelines for income eligibility.

One type of demand-side aid is an **in-kind** subsidy that provides needy individuals with specific goods or vouchers for such items as food, housing, medical services, or transportation. The food stamp program, Medicare, and Medicaid are examples of in-kind subsidies. A second type of demand-side aid is a cash subsidy. People are granted a certain amount of income that they can use to purchase various goods and services of their own choice. Temporary Assistance for Needy Families (TANF) and the Supplemental Security Income (SSI) programs provide recipients with cash subsidies. The in-kind subsidy attempts to increase the quantity demanded of a specific good, whereas the cash subsidy is designed to increase the demand for various goods based on the recipient's preferences. Both programs are typically funded by taxes and do not directly affect the prices of the

INSIGHT 9–6

Who Pays for Medical Services in the United States?

As discussed in the text, vertical equity holds when the net tax burden, expressed as a fraction of income, increases with income. With equity analysis in mind, Holahan and Zedlewski (1992) analyzed the distribution of the health care financing burden associated with the current U.S. health care system. Specifically, the authors determined the financing burden on the nonelderly population in 1989 and took into account employer and employee contributions to health insurance premiums, private nongroup insurance premiums, out-of-pocket expenses, tax savings resulting from the exemption on employer-paid health benefits, and the taxes paid to finance Medicaid, Medicare, and the health benefit tax exclusion.

A microsimulation model employing demographic, economic, and health insurance data from the 1990 *Current Population Survey* was used to assign the various types of health care expenses and tax payments to nonelderly families in different income brackets. Data were also used from a variety of other sources that detail health care spending in the United States. For the families in each income decile, the assignment considered the type of insurance (e.g., private versus public and employer-based versus nongroup insurance), the extent of insurance coverage based on premiums, if any, and the amount of income and payroll taxes paid into the system.

The results showed that the distribution of the health care financing burden is regressive. People in the lowest income decile devoted nearly 20 percent of their cash income to finance health care compared with about 8 percent for people in the highest income decile. However, the authors failed to deduct the value of the Medicaid benefits and uncompensated care typically received by the families in each income decile from their financing burden to determine the "net" tax burden. After correcting for the receipt of medical subsidies, the net financial burden of people in the lowest income decile was about –27 percent.[1] As we might expect, people in the lowest income decile were more likely to receive Medicaid benefits and uncompensated care, and the value of the benefits, on average, exceeded the amount paid into the system. The equivalent fraction for people in the highest income decile remained at approximately 8 percent because Medicaid benefits and uncompensated care constituted such a small amount. In addition, the adjusted results imply that the net financial burden initially rose from the first to the fourth income decile (to about 12 percent), remained roughly constant over the fourth to seventh income decile, and declined thereafter. Consequently, the net financial burden of the health care system appears to fall disproportionately on the middle-income classes.

---

[1]Authors' estimates based on figures provided in the study by John Holahan and Sheila Zedlewski. "Who Pays for Health Care in the United States? Implications for Health System Reform." *Inquiry* 29 (summer 1992), pp. 231–48.

goods and services in the marketplace as long as the subsidized individuals are relatively few in number. A cash subsidy is preferred over in-kind aid if the goal of the donor group is to raise the utility of the recipients to the highest possible level for a given amount of transfer payments. The cash subsidy provides more utility per dollar because recipients are free to choose how they spend the money. If the donor group's goal is to ensure that the recipients consume at least a minimal amount of some specific goods, it can more easily target specific purchases with in-kind aid given the difficulty associated with enforcing spending restrictions on cash subsidies.

SUMMARY

Government intervention is often necessary to correct situations where the market fails to allocate resources efficiently or distribute income fairly. In this context, government has been assigned the task of providing public goods, correcting externalities, redistributing income, and regulating the marketplace. We should keep in mind, however, that market failure is a necessary but not a sufficient condition for government intervention. Although markets may fail and impose costs on society, the costs of government intervention may be much greater. For example, it may cost the government $10 million in labor and capital costs to correct a problem in the marketplace that is imposing $8 million of damages on society. If so, it is efficient to leave the problem uncorrected. Also, both markets and governments fail in certain circumstances. One objective of economics is to determine which institution can provide which particular services in the most efficient and equitable manner.

REVIEW QUESTIONS AND PROBLEMS

1. Discuss the two views of government intervention in a market-based health care system. What role does the politician play in both of these views?
2. Health officials have suggested that the spread of AIDS can be partly contained if more males use condoms while engaging in sexual intercourse. Use the concept of a demand-side externality to explain why the number of condoms sold in the United States is likely to be lower than the optimal number. Explain some ways the government might promote a more optimal use of condoms.
3. Draw a perfectly competitive market model for nursing home services. Discuss the effect of an all-payer price ceiling on allocative efficiency, transfer of surplus between producer and consumer, and the quality of nursing home care. Also, examine the effect of an all-payer price ceiling on a profit-maximizing, monopolistic nursing home. How might the results change in both cases if the price ceiling pertained only to some and not all buyers? Explain.
4. The discussion on price ceilings supposed that the medical firm faces increasing marginal costs of production. Suppose a for-profit, monopolistic hospital is experiencing

economies of scale (i.e., downward-sloping average and marginal cost curves) in the relevant range. Show graphically and discuss in writing the problems associated with a price ceiling set where the demand curve intersects the marginal cost curve and a price ceiling set where the demand curve intersects the average cost curve. Think in terms of allocative efficiency and financial solvency.

5. Allied health professionals (e.g., social workers) are required by law to possess a professional certificate in some states; in others, they are not. Assuming sufficient data exist, discuss how you might test empirically whether this law exists to protect the public interest or to provide benefits to special interests.

6. Minnesota and Tennessee, among other states, have recently begun to tax the sales of health care providers, such as hospitals and physicians. Analyze the incidence of this sales tax for three different scenarios: (a) The demand for medical services is completely inelastic, while the supply curve is positively sloped to the right; (b) the demand curve is downward sloping and supply is completely inelastic (for this case, it is best to shift the demand curve downward by the amount of the per-unit tax); and (c) the demand curve is downward sloping and the supply curve is positively sloped. When does the consumer or the health care provider pay a larger portion of the tax? Why?

7. Do you think subsidies should be provided to lower the cost of a medical education? Why or why not? Use a graphical model in your explanation, if possible.

8. Answer the following questions regarding redistribution.
   A. Why must the government perform the redistribution function?
   B. What are horizontal and vertical equity?
   C. What are the differences among proportional, progressive, and regressive taxation?
   D. What are the three ways subsidies can be provided in practice?
   E. Comment on the relative efficiency and equity of these three methods.

9. Define *price fixing*, *boycotting*, *exclusive-dealings conracts*, and *market allocations*. How have these business practices been viewed by the courts? Explain.

10. Discuss why the courts use a rule of reason when determining whether to allow a horizontal merger.

11. According to Lindsay (1976), why are the average costs of production likely to be lower for a public hospital than for an otherwise identical private hospital?

ONLINE RESOURCES

To access Internet links related to the topics in this chapter, please visit our web site at http://santerre.swcollege.com.

REFERENCES

Aaron, Henry J., and William B. Schwartz. *The Painful Prescription: Rationing Hospital Care.* Washington, D.C.: Brookings Institution, 1984.

Anderson, Gary M., Dennis Halcoussis, Linda Johnston, and Anton D. Lowenberg. "Regulatory Barriers to Entry in the Healthcare Industry; the Case of Alternative Medicine." *The Quarterly Review of Economics and Business* 40 (2000), pp. 485–502.

Baker, James N. "Blood in the Water." *Newsweek*, July 18, 1988, p. 35.

Barnett, Andrew H., Roger D. Blair, and David L. Kaserman. "Improving Organ Donation: Compensation versus Markets." *Inquiry* 29 (fall 1992), pp. 372–78.

Barney, Dwayne L., Jr., and R. Larry Reynolds. "An Economic Analysis of Transplant Organs." *Atlantic Economic Journal* 17 (September 1989), pp. 12–20.

Becker, Gary S. "A Theory of Competition among Pressure Groups for Political Influence." *Quarterly Journal of Economics* 93 (August 1983), pp. 371–400.

Blum, Justin. "Insurance PACs Increase Giving." *Norwich Bulletin*, July 23, 1992.

Burda, David. "Flurry of Merger Plans Has Eyes Focused on Iowa." *Modern Healthcare*, April 12, 1993.

Coase, Ronald. "The Problem of Social Cost." *Journal of Law and Economics* 3 (October 1960), pp. 1–44.

Cromwell, Jerry. "Hospital Productivity Trends in Short-Term General Nonteaching Hospitals." *Inquiry* 11, no. 2 (1976), pp. 181–87.

Department of Justice. "United States of America vs. Dentsply International" Civil Action No. 99-005, 1999, http://www.usdoj.gov/atr/cases/f2100/2164.htm (accessed June 18, 2002).

Felsenthal, Edward. "New Rules Let Hospitals Start Joint Ventures." *The Wall Street Journal*, May 14, 1993, p. B1.

———. "Antitrust Suits Are on the Rise in Health Field." *The Wall Street Journal*, October 29, 1992, p. B1.

Frech, H.E. "Monopoly in Health Insurance: The Economics of *Kartell v. Blue Shield of Massachusetts*." In *Health Care in America*, ed. H.E. Frech. San Francisco: Pacific Research Institute for Public Policy, 1988, pp. 293–322.

Globerman, Steven. "A Policy Analysis of Hospital Waiting Lists." *Journal of Policy Analysis and Management* 10 (spring 1991), pp. 247–62.

Greaney, Thomas L. "Whither Antitrust? The Uncertain Future of Competition Law in Health Care." *Health Affairs* 21 (March/April 2002), pp. 185–96.

Havighurst, Clark C. "The Contributions of Antitrust Law to a Procompetitive Health Policy." In *Market Reforms in Health Care*, ed. Jack A. Meyer. Washington, D.C.: American Enterprise Institute, 1983, pp. 295–322.

Holahan, John, and Sheila Zedlewski. "Who Pays for Health Care in the United States? Implications for Health System Reform." *Inquiry* 29 (summer 1992), pp. 231–48.

Jacobsen, Raymond A., Jr., and Robert B. Wiggins. "Denials of Staff Privileges Face Increased Antitrust Scrutiny." *Health Care Management Review* 17 (fall 1992), pp. 7–15.

Kaserman, David L., and A.H. Barnett. "An Economic Analysis of Transplant Organs: A Comment and Extension." *Atlantic Economic Journal* 19 (June 1991), pp. 57–63.

Kleiner, Morris M., and Robert T. Kudrle. "Does Regulation Affect Economic Outcomes? The Case of Dentistry." *Journal of Law and Economics* 43 (October 2000), pp. 547–82.

Kopit, William G. "Health and Antitrust: The Case for Legislative Relief." In *Market Reforms in Health Care*, ed. Jack A. Meyer. Washington, D.C.: American Enterprise Institute, 1983, pp. 323–31.

Lindsay, Cotton M. "A Theory of Government Enterprise." *Journal of Political Economy* 84 (October 1976), pp. 1061–77.

Makinson, Larry. "Political Contributions from the Health and Insurance Industries." *Health Affairs* 11 (winter 1992), pp. 119–34.

Manning, Willard G., et al. "The Taxes of Sin: Do Smokers and Drinkers Pay Their Way?" *Journal of the American Medical Association* (March 17, 1989), pp. 1604–9.

Musgrave, Richard A., and Peggy B. Musgrave. *Public Finance in Theory and Practice*. New York: McGraw-Hill, 1989.

Ohsfeldt, Robert L., and Stephan F. Gohmann. "The Economics of AIDS-Related Health Insurance Regulations: Interest Group Influence and Ideology." *Public Choice* 74 (July 1992), pp. 105–26.

Peltzman, Sam. "Toward a More General Theory of Regulation." *Journal of Law and Economics* 19 (August 1976), pp. 211–40.

Pindyck, Robert S., and Daniel L. Rubinfeld. *Microeconomics*. Englewood Cliffs, NJ: Prentice Hall, 1995.

Ridge, Pamela S. "Big Tooth? Suit Says Dentply has a Monopoly?" *The Wall Street Journal*, April 12, 2002, p. A13.

Rosen, Harvey S. *Public Finance*. Homewood, IL: Richard D. Irwin, Inc., 1995.

Rutala, William A., Robert L. Odette, and Gregory P. Samsa. "Management of Infectious Waste by U.S. Hospitals." *Journal of the American Medical Association* 262 (September 22–29, 1989), pp. 1635–40.

Saffer, Henry. "Alcohol Advertising Bans and Alcohol Abuse: An International Perspective." *Journal of Health Economics* 10 (1991), pp. 65–79.

Stigler, George J. "The Theory of Economic Regulation." *Bell Journal of Economics and Management Sciences* 2 (1971), pp. 137–46.

Svorny, Shirley V. "Physician Licensure: A New Approach to Examining the Role of Professional Interests." *Economic Inquiry* 25 (July 1987), pp. 497–509.

Williamson, Oliver E. "Economies as an Antitrust Defense: Reply." *American Economic Review* 59 (December 1969), pp. 954–59.

CEBS QUESTIONS

CEBS Sample Question on Subject Matter from CEBS Course 9 Study Manual

1. Using the special interest group theory, identify the likely winners and losers from a favorable tax treatment policy for long-term care premiums. (pages 226–229)

CEBS Sample Exam Questions

1. In a supply and demand model, what is the effect of a fee-for-service third-party price ceiling on physician services? (Assume consumers have full health insurance.)
   A. The quantity demanded will exceed the quantity supplied and a shortage of physician services will be created
   B. The price of physician services will increase
   C. Supply and demand will not apply after the price ceiling is imposed
   D. The demand curve for physician services will become kinked
   E. Prices for physician services will become more volatile

2. The Sherman Antitrust Act has been interpreted as prohibiting anticompetitive business practices in health care that include which of the following?
   I. Boycotting
   II. Profit maximization
   III. Price fixing
      A. I only
      B. III only
      C. I and II only
      D. I and III only
      E. I, II, and III
3. All the following are reasons for government intervention in a market-based health care system EXCEPT:
      A. Provision of public goods
      B. Correction for externalities
      C. Enforcement of regulations and anti-trust laws
      D. Redistribution of income
      E. Improvement in managerial quality

Answer to Sample Question from Study Manual

Owners of nursing homes, providers of services to such facilities, individuals suffering from debilitating diseases such as Alzheimer's and strokes and their family members would be the winners. The loss of revenues resulting from such a policy would produce losers in the section of the population that relies heavily on public welfare programs and public funding.

Answers to Sample Exam Questions

1. A is the answer. The lower price creates an incentive for physicians to reduce the quantity supplied and for expenditures on physician services to decline. See pages 241–245 of the text.
2. D is the answer. Statements I and III are correct. Statement II is false, the Act doesn't prohibit businesses from maximizing profits. See pages 248–252 of the text.
3. E is the answer. The government doesn't exercise its instruments of taxation and subsidies in the market to alter the performance of managers. See pages 229–230 of the text.

GOVERNMENT AS HEALTH INSURER

"No longer will older Americans be denied the healing miracle of modern medicine. No longer will illness crush and destroy the savings they have so carefully put away over a lifetime so they might enjoy dignity in their later years. No longer will young families see their own income, and their own hopes eaten away simply because they are carrying out their deep moral obligations to their parents, and to their uncles, and to their aunts. . . . No longer will this Nation refuse the hand of justice to those who have given a lifetime of service and wisdom and labor to the progress of this progressive country." (Speech by President Lyndon Johnson on July 30, 1965 at the Truman Library in Independence, Missouri upon signing into law the Medicare and Medicaid programs, as quoted in DeParle (2002).

And thus begun the Medicare and Medicaid programs, the most important domestic legislation of the post-World War II era. The legislation was the political brainchild of Congressman Wilbur Mills and was referred to as a "three layer cake." The first layer was the Johnson administration's proposed Medicare plan; a mandatory program to cover the hospital costs of the elderly and referred to as Part A. The second layer, called Medicare Part B, which was initially proposed by the AMA and Republican's who were opposed to the mandatory program, was designed to provide voluntary coverage to the elderly for physician costs while the third layer, Medicaid, expanded federal assistance to states for public insurance coverage of the poor elderly, disabled, and parents and their dependent children (DeParle, 2002).

These two public health insurance programs have continued to evolve and change over the years. The total costs of the Medicare and Medicaid programs, when combined, totaled over $427 billion in 2000, or approximately one-third of all national health expenditures. All indications are that these figures are going to increase in the future. Recent estimates have the total price tag for the Medicaid and Medicare programs increasing to $972 billion by 2011 (Heffler et al., 2002). This represents an increase of over 128 percent in a little more than a decade! Needless to say, elected officials are going to have their hands full over the next few years as they try to balance the desire to provide high-quality health care against competing needs and the want to hold the line on any major tax increases.

Given the importance of the Medicaid and Medicare programs, this chapter:

> Describes the structure and operation of the Medicaid and Medicare programs.

> Discusses recent reforms that have taken place in the Medicaid and Medicare programs.

The information presented should be useful to you in your role as a concerned citizen, health care policymaker, or future recipient of Medicare services.

WHY DOES THE GOVERNMENT PRODUCE HEALTH INSURANCE?

In the case of the Medicare and Medicaid programs, which are the focus of this chapter, government acts as a *producer* of health insurance for certain segments of U.S. society (elderly persons, some disadvantaged groups, and people with certain disabilities). As a producer, government collects the tax and/or premium revenues, bears some residual risk, and establishes the reimbursement paid to health care providers.[1] Economists normally argue that government should intervene when a market fails to allocate resources efficiently or distribute income equitably. As we saw in earlier chapters, an inefficient allocation of resources occurs when a small number of powerful sellers dominate the industry, barriers to entry are substantial, consumers lack perfect information, or the exclusion principle does not hold (i.e., externality or public good considerations). An inequitable distribution of income results when some people lack the production characteristics needed to generate a sufficient level of income in the private marketplace.

Usually, when markets fail, government intervenes by either subsidizing the prices of goods and services when inequities are present (e.g., food stamps and housing allowances) or regulating the production of goods and services when inefficiencies otherwise exist in an unregulated environment (e.g., electric utilities). That is, government typically subsidizes or regulates private production instead of directly producing the good or service. Consequently, the current system of public production of health insurance for certain population segments raises the following two related questions:

1. What is the source of market failure in the private health insurance industry that necessitates government intervention?
2. Why does the government act as a producer of health insurance for certain population segments?

Since individual buyers tend to internalize the benefit (i.e., financial security; see Chapter 6) health insurance provides, it appears that externality or public goods considerations can be ruled out. Also, as Chapter 11 confirms, the private health insurance industry appears to be reasonably competitive because of the large number of competitive fringe insurers and because self-insurance represents an alternative for large employers. In addition, barriers to entry are low, so a monopoly market structure cannot substantiate government intervention. Ruling out the exclusion principle and monopoly structure leaves imperfect information as the primary economic rationale for government intervention in the health insurance industry.

---

[1]The government often pays private health insurance companies to "administer" public health insurance. Private health insurers process the claims and pay the stipulated amounts to health care providers.

In particular, consider that public health insurance presently coexists with private for-profit and private not-for-profit health insurance in the United States. As we saw in Chapter 4, different forms of ownership may coexist in markets where imperfect information exists and demands for services are heterogeneous. The imperfect information exists because some consumers lack the information they need to understand the technical terms and conditions contained in health insurance policies. Think about it. The description and explanation of health insurance nomenclature, such as deductibles, copayments, benefit coverage, and maximum liability can be mind-boggling for even the most educated individuals (Garnick et al., 1993).

Individual consumers who are uninformed may feel vulnerable to noncompetitive behavior on the part of for-profit insurers and therefore may prefer to deal with not-for-profit insurance providers that they perceive as being less likely to profit from consumer ignorance. However, not all people are uninformed. Some people are fairly knowledgeable or belong to group policies represented by informed individuals. Informed consumers may be willing to deal with for-profit health insurance providers, especially when offered quality coverage at a low price.

As a result, it is likely that government acts as a producer of health insurance in the United States as a result of informational problems and an associated demand for government-produced health insurance by certain population segments. It should be noted that the Medicare and Medicaid programs were originally structured to provide health insurance to the "medically needy"—elderly, disabled, and poor individuals—a unique group in society. As a producer, the government not only subsidizes the health insurance to promote equity but also helps to avoid the inefficiencies normally associated with information imperfections in the private health insurance market.[2]

THE MEDICAID PROGRAM

The Medicaid program is designed to provide medical coverage to certain individuals with low incomes. Federal and state governments jointly share the cost of the program, but states administer the program and have wide latitude in determining eligibility and the medical benefits provided. As a result, it is difficult to describe the program except in the broadest of terms.

Eligibility under the Medicaid program is determined at the state level and varies extensively across states. At a minimum, states must provide medical coverage to most individuals covered under other federal income maintenance programs, such as the temporary aid for needy families and Supplemental Security Income programs, to receive matching federal funds. Among other additional requirements, states must provide coverage to children under the age of six and to pregnant women whose family incomes are below 133 percent of the federal poverty level, and to all children born after September 1983 who are under 19 years of age and are in families with incomes at or below the federal poverty level. The federal government also requires that certain basic medical benefits be provided, such as (but not limited to) inpatient and outpatient hospital services, physician services, prenatal care, and vaccines for children.

---

[2]Due to imperfect information, adverse selection problems are also associated with the private provision of health insurance. See Chapter 11.

As you can see from table 10–1, the total number of Medicaid recipients hovered between 21 and 23 million throughout most of the 1970s and 1980s. At the close of the 1980s, however, things changed dramatically as economic growth stagnated throughout the country and changes in the Medicaid program expanded eligibility. From 1990 to 1998, the number of Medicaid recipients increased by over 60 percent to more than 40 million individuals. A breakdown of recipients in 1998 shows that the single largest group was dependent children under age 21, accounting for 46.6 percent of the recipients. The next largest group, with 19.5 percent of the recipients, was adults in families with dependent children. Individuals with permanent and total disabilities (16.3 percent) and individuals 65 years of age and older (9.8 percent) constituted the next two largest groups of Medicaid recipients.

TABLE   10 – 1

Total Number of Medicaid Recipients and Total Vendor Payments for Medicaid, Selected Years 1972–1998

Year	Total Number of Recipients (millions)	Total Vendor Payments (millions)
1972	17.6	$6,300
1975	22.0	12,242
1980	21.6	23,311
1985	21.8	37,508
1990	25.3	64,859
1995	36.3	120,141
1998	40.6	142,318

SOURCE: U.S. Department of Health and Human Services, Social Security Administration. *Annual Statistical Supplement*, 2001, table 8.E.

A look at total vendor payments by group tells a slightly different story. The lion's share of vendor payments went to individuals with permanent and total disabilities (42.4 percent). The next largest group was elderly persons, with 31 percent of total payments, followed by dependent children with 16.0 percent. Finally, adults in families with dependent children accounted for 10.4 percent of the medical payments. The change in order between the two groupings based on total recipients and total costs reflects the high cost of caring for elderly and disabled individuals. For example, in 1998 the average Medicaid payment for elderly and disabled persons was $10,242 and $9,095, respectively. For dependent children the average payment was only $1,203; for adults it was $1,876. Much of the difference is explained by the high cost of nursing home care for elderly and disabled Medicaid recipients.

The Financing and Cost of Medicaid

Medicaid is financed jointly by the federal and state governments, with the federal portion varying between a low of 50 percent and a potential high of 83 percent. States with the lowest per capita income receive the largest federal subsidy. In 2001, a total of 11 states were reimbursed at the minimum level. Mississippi received the largest subsidy (76.06 percent), followed by West Virginia (75.27 percent). The average share subsidized by the federal government in 2001 was 57 percent.

The cost of the Medicaid program has increased substantially over time. As table 10–1 indicates, the Medicaid program cost a little more than $6 billion in 1972 and that figure ballooned to over $142 billion by 1998. A number of reasons account for this large increase in cost. First and foremost was a significant rise in the number of enrollees, especially between 1988 and 1993 when overall enrollments went from 22.9 million to over 33 million. The increase was primarily due to a number of changes in the Medicaid program that extended coverage to children and pregnant women. For example, federal mandates dictated that by 1990 Medicaid coverage was to be extended to children under the age of six and pregnant women in families with incomes below 133 percent of the federal poverty line.

Another reason for the increase in cost was a significant increase in medical prices, which forced states to increase reimbursement rates to medical care providers. High rates of medical price inflation and technological advances largely account for the increase in medical prices. Another factor was the increase in the number of elderly and disabled individuals in need of long-term medical care.

Efforts on the part of states to increase federal funding of Medicaid also contributed to rising Medicaid costs. As you can imagine, these efforts were met with some resistance from the federal government, which has had its own budgetary difficulties. Some of these efforts have been dubbed "Medicaid maximization" and involve shifting state-run health programs into the Medicaid program so that they will qualify for matching federal funds. Mental health and mental retardation services were the most common services shifted into state Medicaid programs (Coughlin et al., 1994).

Finally, **disproportionate share hospital payments** contributed to the rise in Medicaid expenditures. This was a way for states to acquire federal funds and help defer the expenses of hospitals that cared for a disproportionately high number of low-income individuals. Coughlin et al. describe these programs as follows:

> Providers, usually hospitals, donated funds or paid a tax to the state. The states would then use the donations or tax revenue to make Medicaid payments and, in the transaction, receive federal matching dollars. Generally the programs operated so that providers were held harmless; that is, providers were refunded their full donations or tax contribution. Most often they received a bonus.

The State Children's Health Insurance Program

In 1996 approximately 42 million people in the United States were without health insurance coverage and almost a quarter of that group were children under the age of 18. Feeling the political pressure to address what some felt was a national disgrace, Congress enacted the State Children's Health Insurance Program (SCHIP) as part of the Balanced Budget Act of 1997. The ultimate objective of SCHIP is to decrease the number of uninsured children by providing federal funds to states that initiate plans to expand insurance coverage to low-income, uninsured children. The federal government has committed approximately $40 billion to the program over a 10-year period from 1998 through 2007. For the fiscal years 1998–2000, state allotments were based on the percentage of low-income,

INSIGHT 10–1

Interstate Differences in Medicaid Fees

Most analysts agree that the fees paid for Medicaid services tend to be notoriously low, especially when compared to the prices paid by other payers (e.g., Medicare and private insurance) for equivalent services. Price differentials are important because the decision to participate in the Medicaid program may in part be dictated by how Medicaid fees compare to non-Medicaid prices. Generally, higher Medicaid fees tend to increase access to physician care for Medicaid enrollees. Thus, unreasonably low Medicaid fees can lead to access problems for Medicaid recipients.

Curious about the precise extent to which Medicaid fees vary across states, Norton and Zuckerman (2000) report on Medicaid physician fees for 1998. The results of the study indicate that the mean physician fee for a 30-minute office visit with a new patient was $39.29, while the fee for a 15-minute visit with an established patient was $21.25. More important, the authors found that the average Medicaid fee varied widely across the country. Developing an index that equaled 1.00 for the national average, Norton and Zuckerman found fees ranged from a low of .51 for New Jersey to a high of 2.34 for Alaska. Nine states had Medicaid fees that were at least 25 percent greater than the national weighted average fee while three states had fees that were at least 25 percent lower than the national weighted average. The survey also uncovered that Medicaid fees lag behind comparable Medicare fees, as the average Medicaid-to-Medicare fee ratio for the entire country equaled .64 in 1998. In only two states, Alaska and Texas, was the Medicaid-to-Medicare fee ratio above one. Finally, the authors found that Medicaid fees have all but stagnated in recent years, increasing a paltry 4.3 percent from 1993 through 1998. As a result, the Medicaid-to-Medicare fee ratio fell from .75 in 1993 to .64 in 1998.

The results from this study are interesting and point to the need for further research concerning the impact of Medicaid fees on access to care. If Medicaid fees continue to lag behind non-Medicaid fees, then the ability of those individuals in Medicaid to acquire quality health care may be seriously impaired because health care providers have little financial incentive to participate in the Medicaid program.

uninsured children in the state adjusted by a geographic cost factor. After that point a blended rate based on the number of insured and uninsured low-income children in the state is used.

SCHIP is designed to give states considerable latitude when addressing the problem of uninsured children. Each state that elects to participate in the program must submit a plan for approval that articulates how it intends to utilize the funds. States have the option of expanding insurance coverage through their existing Medicaid programs, developing separate child health insurance programs, or using a combination of the two. As of 2002, 56 states and territories have approved plans; they are about evenly divided among the three options. According to data supplied by the Center for Medicare and Medicaid Services,

INSIGHT 10–2

Are the Recent Expansions in Medicaid Crowding Out Private Insurance?

Beginning with the mid-1980s and throughout the 1990s, the Medicaid program expanded eligibility for vulnerable populations to improve health outcomes. Specifically targeted were children and pregnant women. For example, the State Children's Health Insurance Program was designed to provide publicly funded health insurance to cover targeted individuals without private health care coverage. Based on sheer numbers, these policy changes appear to have succeeded in providing health insurance to a large segment of the population who might otherwise have been denied access to health care. From 1985 through 1998 the number of Medicaid recipients increased over 60 percent to over 40 million people. However, do these numbers overstate the impact of Medicaid expansion? Might it be that those who became eligible for Medicaid would have otherwise opted for private health insurance? That is, has the recent Medicaid expansion simply "crowded out" private insurance? Blumberg, Dubay, and Norton (2000) point out that crowding out can occur if some people elect to drop private insurance coverage and become eligible for Medicaid, or if others who are uninsured opt for Medicaid as opposed to private insurance.

A study by Cutler and Gruber (1996) found significant levels of crowding out. In particular, the authors found that about 50 percent of the Medicaid enrollment from 1987 to 1992 resulted in a decrease in private insurance coverage. More recent studies have estimated more modest levels of crowding out. For example, Dubay and Kenney (1997) found that 14 percent of the increase in Medicaid coverage for pregnant woman caused crowding out, while Yazici and Kaestner (2000) estimated that almost 19 percent of the increase in Medicaid enrollment resulted in crowdiing-out of private insurance. Finally, Blumberg, Dubay, and Norton (2000) estimate the displacement impact to be a very modest 4 percent. Collectively, these studies suggest that while there appears to be certain amount of crowding out, the bulk of the increase in Medicaid enrollment in recent years came from the ranks of the uninsured.

there were 3.7 million children enrolled in SCHIP in the first quarter of 2002. This represents a 25 percent increase from the previous year. The income level for eligibility varies widely across states, from a high of 300 percent of the federal level in states such as Connecticut and Maryland to a low of 133 percent in Wyoming.[3]

Do Differences in the Medicaid Program Make a Difference?

To receive federal funds to support the Medicaid program, the federal government mandates that certain populations receive medical coverage and that certain basic medical

---

[3]The web address is http://www.cms.hhs.gov.

services be included in the coverage. After these minimum requirements are met, states are free to change the program to meet their individual needs. As a result, Medicaid programs vary widely across the country in terms of eligibility requirements, medical services covered, and payments to providers. In addition, the program has gone through a number of changes at the federal level that have involved relaxing eligibility requirements to provide health care coverage to needy populations, specifically children and pregnant mothers. The basic question arises as to whether differences in the program over time and across states have any impact on the Medicaid-eligible populations. For the sake of consistency, we focus on studies looking at poor children and their mothers.

In two related studies, Currie and Thomas (1995) and Currie and Gruber (1996) found that expanded Medicaid eligibility for low-income children improved access to health care. Specifically, Currie and Thomas found that Medicaid coverage decreased the probability that a child failed to have a routine checkup within the past year by 15 percent. Looking at the Medicaid program of 13 states, Long and Coughlin (2001/2002) found that significant differences existed across states in terms of access to and use of health care by children with Medicaid coverage even after controlling for demographic, socioeconomic, and health factors. Completing the circle, Kronebush (2001) examined the impact of policy changes across states from 1979 to 1998. He found that recent federal policy changes have increased Medicaid enrollment of children nationwide and at the same time have decreased state-level variations in enrollment patterns over time. However, significant state-level policy differences still existed.

The evidence also indicates that Medicaid fees vary widely across the country and are generally lower than comparable private or Medicare rates (consult Insight 10–1 for a detailed discussion of the evidence). If the rates are set too low by state authorities, access problems are created for those individuals covered under Medicaid. If rates are too low, profit-maximizing health care providers may find it in their best interest not to participate in the Medicaid program at all. Their time may be better spent servicing the medical needs of more lucrative private pay or Medicare patients. Low Medicaid fees may also impact the quality of the care provided to Medicaid patients. Take the case of the physician who finds the Medicaid fee for a well-child office to be below some acceptable level. To make up the difference, the physician may spend less time with the child than otherwise would be the case and at the same time minimize the level of beneficial services provided.[4] In either case, the overall quality of care provided to children on Medicaid is adversely impacted because the physician is being compensated at a level below the comparable private pay or Medicare rate.

The evidence appears to suggest that Medicaid fees have a direct impact on the level of medical care provided to Medicaid recipients. Utilizing a data set on physician practices from the late 1980s and early 1990s, Baker and Royalty (2000) found that a 10 percent increase in Medicaid fees resulted in a 2.4 percent increase in office-based physician visits for poor patients. Taking the discussion one step further, Currie, Gruber, and Fischer (1995) and Gray (2001) established a connection between Medicaid fees and health care outcomes. The first study found that a 10 percent increase in the Medicaid-to-private fee

---

[4]The economics of price differentials resulting from the Medicaid program are discussed in more detail in Chapter 15. The interested reader is urged to jump to the section on the dual-market model and apply the model to the current pricing problem.

ratio for obstetricians/gynecologists lowered the infant mortality rate by between .5 and .9 percent. In the second study, Gray (2001) found a relationship between Medicaid physician fees and birth outcomes. According to his estimates, a 10 percent increase in the average relative Medicaid fee decreased the risk of low birth rate by a newborn by .074 percent and the risk of a very low birth weight by .035 percent.[5]

This body of literature is extremely helpful to policy analysts because it suggests that any meaningful policy initiative aimed at improving health outcomes among needy populations by expanding Medicaid coverage must involve not only a careful look at eligibility requirements but also Medicaid fees. Naturally, this information is not likely to be greeted kindly by politicians and taxpayers because it implies and increase in both the number of enrollees in the Medicaid program as well as the cost per enrollee.

THE MEDICARE PROGRAM

The primary objective of the Medicare program is to improve access to medical care for elderly people by underwriting a portion of their medical expenditures. Anyone of age 65 or older is eligible for the program.[6] It is made up of two distinct components: Part A, the Hospital Insurance program, which is compulsory, and Part B, the Supplementary Medical Insurance program, which is voluntary. The Hospital Insurance portion of the program primarily covers (1) inpatient hospital services, (2) some types of posthospital care, and (3) hospice care.

The number of people age 65 or older covered under Part A has increased rapidly over the years and reflects the growing elderly population. In 1966, when the program first began, slightly more than 19 million elderly individuals were enrolled, and by 1999 the number had grown to more than 33 million. The Supplementary Medical Insurance program provides benefits for (1) physician services, (2) outpatient medical services, (3) emergency room services, and (4) a variety of other medical services.

Although Part B of Medicare is voluntary and requires a monthly premium to participate, a large number of elderly people have elected to purchase the insurance. During the initial year of the program, slightly more than 17 million elderly people participated, and by 1999 the number had increased to 33 million, almost matching the number of enrollees in the compulsory portion of Medicare. This trend reflects the fact that the federal government heavily subsidizes the cost of the supplementary insurance program.

The Financing and Cost of Medicare

Since its inception, total expenditures on the Medicare program have increased at a brisk pace. In 1966 the federal government spent $7.7 billion on the Medicare program; by 1980, this figure had increased almost fivefold to $37.8 billion. As of 2000, total expenditures exceeded $224.4 billion, with an annual rate of growth between 1980 and 1990 topping 11 percent. In more recent times the rate of growth has slowed considerably, with an average rate of increase of about 2.6 percent from 1998 through 2000. The rise in Medicare

---

[5]A low birth weight is less than 2.5 kg., a very low birth weight is less than 1.5 kg.
[6]In addition, the Medicare program covers some individuals younger than 65 who are severely disabled or suffer from kidney disease.

expenses through the years is explained by increases in both the number of enrollees and reimbursement per enrollee, with the latter accounting for a majority of the increase.

Figure 10–1 displays the major funding sources for the Hospital Insurance program. The main source of funding has been a payroll tax of 2.9 percent, which employees and employers share equally. The payroll tax accounted for approximately 87 percent of total revenues in 2000. The second largest revenue source has been interest income emanating from the Federal Hospital Insurance Trust Fund, which was established at the inception of the program and which has built up over the years. Interest income topped $11.7 billion in 2000 and accounted for 7 percent of total receipts. Income for the taxation of benefits accounted for another 5 percent of total receipts. The remaining receipts, "other" in figure 10–1, made up 1 percent of total receipts and included transfers from the railroad retirement account, reimbursements from general revenues for uninsured persons and military wage credits, and premiums of voluntary enrollees.

FIGURE 10–1
Receipts for the Hospital Insurance Program, 2000

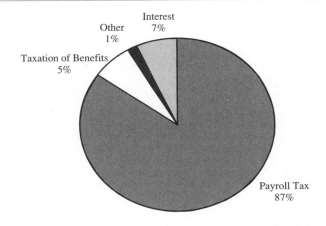

SOURCE: U.S. Department of Health and Human Services, Social Security Administration. *Annual Statistical Supplement, 2001.*

The enrollee is also responsible for a portion of inpatient expenses through a deductible and coinsurance payment. The first three columns in table 10–2 supply deductible and coinsurance information. In 1966 the deductible was $40. It increased steadily through the years, and by 2001 it was $792. Once the deductible is met, Medicare covers all inpatient hospital expenses for the first 60 days. For days 61–90, the enrollee is required to pay a daily coinsurance payment equal to 25 percent of the inpatient hospital deductible. After day 90, Medicare no longer covers hospital inpatient expenses. However, each enrollee is provided with additional 60-day lifetime reserve. The reserve can be used only once and has a daily coinsurance rate of 50 percent of the inpatient hospital deductible, which equaled $396 in 2001.

TABLE 1 0 – 2

The Cost Sharing for Medicare, Selected Years 1966–2001

	HOSPITAL INSURANCE			SUPPLEMENTARY MEDICAL INSURANCE		
	Deductible	Daily Coinsurance		Payment		
	1–60 days	61–90 days	After 90 days	Annual Deductible	Coinsurance Rate	Monthly Premium
1966	$ 40	$ 10	—	$ 50	20%	$ 3.00
1970	52	13	26	50	20%	5.30
1980	180	45	90	60	20%	9.60
1990	592	148	296	75	20%	28.60
2001	792	198	396	100	20%	50.00

SOURCE: U.S. Department of Health and Human Services, Social Security Administration. *Annual Statistical Supplement, 2001.*

The supplementary Medical Insurance program, or Part B of Medicare, is financed partly through premium payments for enrollees. In 2000, total revenues exceeded $89.9 billion, with premium payments contributing 23 percent of the total. According to figure 10–2, the largest source of revenues has been contributions by the government and represents the extent to which the federal government subsidies premiums. Over the years, the

FIGURE 1 0 – 2

Receipts for the Supplementary Medical Insurance Program, 2000

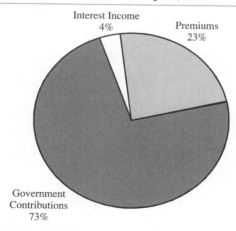

SOURCE: U.S. Department of Health and Human Services, Social Security Administration. *Annual Statistical Supplement, 2001.*

government has consistently provided approximately 75 percent of total revenues. The final source has been interest income from a trust fund, which has provided only a small fraction of revenues over the years (4 percent in 2000).

Despite the rapid growth in enrollees over the years, Supplementary Medical Insurance premiums had to increase to provide the necessary revenues. As noted earlier, this is largely because expenditures per enrollees grew at a much faster pace than the number of new enrollees. According to table 10–2, the monthly premium was $50 in 2001, up from $3 a month in 1966. In addition, the enrollee is obligated to pay an annual deductible equal to $100 and a coinsurance rate equal to 20 percent on most charges.

Medicare Program Reforms

Facing a growing federal deficit and an elderly population frustrated by ever-rising deductibles, copayments, and premiums, Congress was forced to alter the Medicare program over the years. The objective has always been to contain costs while at the same time improving access to medical care for elderly people. Instead of going through the tedious process of examining each policy change, we focus on three of the most significant reforms to the Medicare program. The first major reform took place in 1983, when a new payment system for hospitals was implemented based on diagnosis-related groups (DRGs). The second was the passage of the Omnibus Budget Reconciliation Act of 1989, which significantly altered the method of payment to physicians. Finally, the Balanced Budget Act of 1997 radically expanded plans available to beneficiaries and the rate of managed care.

Diagnosis-Related Groups   In just five years (1975 to 1980), Medicare expenditures on inpatient hospital services grew by over 120 percent from $8.8 billion to $19.5 billion (U.S. Department of Health and Human Services, 1993). In reaction to the expenditure increase. Congress instituted a prospective payment system (PPS) to compensate hospitals for medical services provided to Medicare patients.

Under the PPS, every Medicare patient is classified based on his or her principal diagnosis into one of approximately 500 or so diagnosis-related groups (DRGs) upon entering a hospital. The prospective payment received by the hospital is a fixed dollar amount per discharge and largely depends upon the DRG classification with adjustments made for factors that contribute to cost differences across hospitals.

In particular, Medicare sets a separate operating and capital payment rate for every discharge. These rates "are intended to cover the operating and capital costs that efficient facilities would be expected to incur in furnishing covered inpatient services" (MedPAC, 2002, p. 12). In most cases, the payment is established by multiplying a base payment by the relative weight for each DRG. The payment rate is then modified to account for variations in input prices across the country and a number of hospital and case-specific attributes. In 2000, the average Medicare payment per case was approximately $6,900.

Each DRG weight reflects the average cost of medical care for that particular medical problem relative to the average Medicare case. The DRG weight is an index number, based on the total medical charges, that reflects the relative costs across all hospitals of providing care to the average patient in a particular DRG. The higher the DRG weight, the greater the prospective payment. In 2001, the relative weight ranged from a low of .0975 for DRG 448 (an allergic reaction for someone under the age of 18) to a high of 7.52 for DRG 106 (a coronary bypass with a cardiac catheter). The five most common DRGs, accounting for 19 percent of all short-term hospital discharges in 2000, are shown in table 10–3.

TABLE 10-3
Five Most Common DRGs for 2000

DRG #	DRG Description	Total Discharges
127	Heart failure and shock	685,626
089	Simple pneumonia and pleurisy, with age greater than 17 and with complications and/or comorbidities	531,770
088	Chronic obstructive pulmonary disease	397,690
209	Major joint and limb reattachment procedures of lower extremities	346,360
116	Other permanent cardiac pacemaker implants	334,384
Total Top 5 DRGs		2,295,830
Total DRGs		11,778,705

SOURCE: http://www.cms.hhs.gov/statistics/medpar/default.asp

Prior to 1983, hospitals were paid on a retrospective basis for the actual medical services provided. As discussed in Chapter 4, under a retrospective payment system, health care providers bill for actual costs incurred. Economists have long argued that a retrospective payment system has the potential to drive up medical costs for two reasons. First, a retrospective system provides little incentive for cost efficiency, because hospitals are not penalized for any excess costs of production; higher costs can simply be passed on to the third-party payer. Second, when payment is based on the type and quantity of medical services actually provided, an incentive likely exists for hospitals to provide unnecessary medical services. For example, a patient may stay an additional day in the hospital to recuperate from surgery even if it is not medically necessary. The hospital earns additional profits due to the longer stay.

With a prospective system, fees are set in advance on a per-case basis. Hospitals essentially become price takers and face a perfectly elastic demand curve for Medicare patients. Inefficient behavior is no longer tolerated because hospitals are unable to pass higher costs on to the third payer, which in this case is the government. Under the PPS, hospitals that provide medical care at a cost below the preset fee retain the difference, whereas hospitals that incur costs in excess of the preset fee must sustain the loss. Naturally, inefficient hospitals have a difficult time operating in such an environment.

Finally, because compensation is now on a per-case basis, rather than a per-item basis, hospitals have the incentive to provide only necessary medical services. Any hospital that elects to provide additional medical services, such as allowing the patient to stay an additional day to recuperate after surgery, receives no additional compensation and thus has no economic incentive to provide those services (see the discussion surrounding figure 4–2).

Medicare's PPS appears to have successfully diminished the overall rate of growth in hospital expenditures. Over the eight years prior to the inception of the PPS (1977 to 1984), expenditures for the hospital insurance program grew at an average annual rate of over 15 percent. The rate dropped to 8.75 percent over the eight years immediately after the program was put in place (1985 to 1992). However, most of the decrease in the rate of growth took place when the program was first introduced. In particular, the average annual rate of growth in expenditures was only 5.1 percent from 1985 through 1988. The relative increase in Medicare hospital spending after 1988 may indicate that the ability of the PPS to control the costs may have waned over time as hospitals began to learn how to work the system. One way hospitals have learned to work the system is to place their patients into higher-weighted DRGs and raise their case-mix index to increase reimbursement. Artificial increases in the case-mix under the PPS are referred to as DRG creep.

Much has been written concerning the impact of the DRG program on the market for hospital services.[7] Foremost on the minds of many researchers is whether the Medicare prospective payment system has had a deleterious effect on the health status of Medicare patients. They fear that hospitals may react to the Medicare price controls by providing a lower quality of medical care. After reviewing the literature on the subject, however, Feinglass and Holloway (1991) concluded that there "is little direct, generalizable evidence that PPS has reduced the quality of care of Medicare patients" (p. 107).

Closely related to the issue of quality is the impact of the DRG system on admissions and length of stay. Economic theory suggests that hospitals may react to the fixed PPS price by attempting to increase admissions as a way to raise revenues. (See the discussion in Chapter 9.) In fact, just the opposite occurred after the PPS was implemented. The number of admissions under Medicare actually dropped by 11 percent during the first eight years of the PPS, and a large portion of the decrease took place within the first two years (Hodgkin and McGuire, 1994). The reason for the drop in admissions is difficult to explain. Feinglass and Holloway (1991) attribute the decline to the implementation of utilization review programs that screen the use of inpatient medical services and to the switch to outpatient facilities as a result of the PPS. The switch to outpatient treatment is substantiated by the fact that hospital outpatient surgery for Medicare patients doubled between 1983 and 1985 (Feinglass and Holloway, 1991). The new payment system also shortened the average length of stay for inpatient hospital visits. Estimates indicate that the average length of stay fell by 14.6 percent from 1982 to 1985 (Feinglass and Holloway, 1991).

The decline in admissions, coupled with the decrease in average length of stay, caused the overall number of inpatient days for Medicare clients to decrease by 20.7 percent from 1982 to 1988 (Schwartz and Mendelson, 1991). The decline in inpatient days during the mid-1980s largely explains the decrease in the overall rate of growth in Medicare hospital expenditures discussed earlier. The more recent increases in the overall rate of growth in Medicare expenditures may also indicate that the cost savings resulting from fewer inpatient days have largely been exhausted. The unsustained reduction of Medicare expenditures led Muller (1993) to report that the "effectiveness of the reforms began to diminish by 1986" (p. 298).

The prospective payment system has also had a significant negative impact on the overall financial condition of hospitals. Financial impacts are to be expected, since hospitals are no longer able to bill Medicare for medical services on essentially a cost-plus basis. Fisher (1992) examined the financial performance of over 4,600 hospitals that were continuously involved with the PPS from 1985 through 1990. Overall, the proportion of hos-

---

[7]For a review of the literature, consult Coulan and Gaumer (1991), Feinglass and Holloway (1991), or Chapter 13 in this text.

pitals that reported profits dropped marginally from 77.2 percent in 1985 to 72.4 percent in 1990. However, the proportion of hospitals that reported Medicare profits dropped more dramatically over the same period, from 84.5 percent in 1985 to 40.7 percent in 1990. Fisher also found a positive correlation between overall profitability and Medicare PPS inpatient net profits.

The Omnibus Budget Reconciliation Act of 1989   As the cost of Part B escalated over the years, Congress responded with various changes, including freezes on physician payments and annual limits on increases in fees. Despite these cost containment measures, Medicare expenditures for physician services continued to rise, placing an even greater financial burden on both the federal government and the elderly population. Forced into action, Congress passed the Omnibus Budget Reconciliation Act of 1989, or OBRA 1989, which was directed at restructuring the physician payment system. The act contained four major provisions:

1. A new payment system that bases compensation primarily on resources utilized.
2. A procedure was established for Congress to monitor the rate of growth in physician fees over time.
3. Limits were put on charges physicians may assess patients that are beyond the amount paid by Medicare.
4. The Agency for Health Policy Research was established to develop outcomes research and provide guidelines.

Each of these changes is discussed in turn next.

Resource-Based Relative Value Scale System   At the core of OBRA 1989 was a new fee schedule introduced in 1992. Prior to OBRA 1989, physicians were compensated based on the usual-customary-reasonable (UCR) or the customary-prevailing-and-reasonable (CPR) method. Under this method, physicians were paid the lowest of the bill submitted, the customary charge of the physician, or the prevailing rate in the area for services provided. The general consensus was that the UCR-CPR method of payment contributed to the increase in physician expenditures over the years. According to Yett, Der, Ernst, and Hay (1985), the UCR-CPR method of payment creates an incentive for physicians to increase their fees over time to raise what constitutes the reasonable rate in the future. The inflationary bias is especially acute when the overall rate of inflation is high.

In addition, the UCR-CPR method was criticized for creating distortions in relative prices of various types of physician services. Fees for technical procedures were overvalued, whereas fees for evaluations and management services were undervalued. As a result, primary care physicians, who generally provide more evaluation-type services such as physical exams, were being compensated less than specialists, who provide more technical services such as surgery. The price differential tended to distort physicians' income and potentially had an impact on the composition of physician services provided (Oliver, 1993).

The *resource-based relative value scale (RBRVS)* system of fees considers the time and effort of physician work, or physician resources, necessary to produce physician services. The relative work values are based on the research of William Hsiao and colleagues at Harvard University (Hsiao et al., 1988) and make up approximately half of the total value of physician services under the new fee schedule. The other half is accounted for by practice and malpractice expenses. A conversion factor that translates the scale into a fee schedule has also been developed. Yearly adjustments are made in the conversion factor to account for inflation and any other changes that take place.

Since the RBRVS fees are now based on relative work effort, the new fee schedule no longer provides a historical momentum for future fee increases. That is because past fee increases no longer provide the basis for future increases by inflating the "reasonable" rate. Also, a resource-based fee schedule no longer provides physicians with an incentive to supply more technical medical procedures, such as surgery, than evaluation and management services, such as office visits with established patients, which are more time consuming. As a result, physicians who provide primary care should see Medicare revenues increase, whereas those who provide more specialty types of care should see revenues decrease. This view is substantiated by the fact that in 1992, family practitioners saw fees increase by 10 percent while specialty surgeons endured an 8 percent decrease (Physician Payment Review Commission, 1993). Such changes are likely to have a major impact on the types and volume of physician services provided at the margin and the relative incomes of physicians in various specialties.

The RBRVS fee schedule is not without its critics, however. According to Hadley (1991), the entire approach is inconsistent with the theory of cost. A resource-based method determines the value of a service primarily by physician work effort and fails to consider input prices. Thus, contrary to the theory of costs presented earlier, input prices play no role in determining the marginal and average costs of production or the supply and prices of physician services. An example similar to the one developed by Hadley proves this point. In 1993, slightly more than 38,000 general surgeons were practicing in the United States. What would have happened had this number doubled by 1994, *ceteris paribus*? Supply and demand theory suggests that the average fee for surgical services would have dropped as the supply of general surgeons increased, or the supply curve would have shifted to the right. With a resource-based payment scheme, however, lower surgical fees do not result from a greater supply of surgeons because fees are based on work effort. Input prices play no role in determining market price.

Also, one might criticize the resource-based fee schedule on the grounds that it constitutes a price control. If relative fee schedules are set incorrectly, shortages or surpluses of different physician services may result. For example, more generous relative fees for primary care services may encourage an oversupply of those services and an undersupply of specialist services in the future. Consequently, considerable care must be taken when establishing the appropriate fees for the different services.

Medicare Volume Performance Standards   In an attempt to gain more control over the growth of Medicare expenditures, Congress adopted a Medicare volume performance standards (VPS) system that establishes expenditure limits. Each year Congress establishes a target rate of growth for physician expenditures under Medicare, or a VPS. The target considers such items as inflation, the number and ages of enrollees, barriers to access, the level of inappropriate care given, changes in technology, and any legislated changes in the program. Whether or not the target was met in a given year is used as a basis for determining the extent to which fees are updated the following year through the conversion factor. In other words, if the actual rate of growth in physician expenditures exceeds the VPS in a given year, the increase in physician fees for the following year may be set lower than planned through updates in the conversion factor. If, on the other hand, the actual rate of increase is below the target, the increase in fees may move upward (Physician Payment Review Commission, 1993).

The benefits from a VPS system are twofold. First, the VPS gives Congress a mechanism with which to control the rate of growth of physician expenditures. Second, the VPS gives physicians, as a group, the incentive to provide appropriate care. If excessive amounts of inappropriate care are provided, overall expenditures are driven upward, and this dampens the extent to which fees are increased in the future. Critics, however, point out that the system provides inappropriate incentives to physicians because it fails to take physician practice style into account. Given the wide variation in practice styles, a uniform payment system provides inequitable payments for medical services. In addition, a free-rider problem may exist because such a large number of physicians participate in the system. No one physician has the incentive to eliminate inappropriate care because there is no direct relationship between individual physician behavior and future fees increases (Holahan and Zuckerman, 1993; Miller and Welch, 1993). Ginsburg (1993) responds to the latter criticism by pointing out that the intent was to directly influence the behavior of physician organizations rather than that of individual physicians. The general idea is that the VPS will put pressure on physician organizations to monitor and control individual physician behavior.

Limits on Balance Billing and the Assignment Issue   Faced with the prospect that the new RBRVS fee schedule, along with the expenditures caps, could inhibit access to medical care by forcing up out-of-pocket payments for Medicare recipients, Congress put specific limits on the amount physicians can charge patients above the Medicare rate. When Part B was initially implemented, physicians were allowed to balance-bill patients for charges in excess of the established Medicare fee on a case-by-case basis. When this occurred, the physician was responsible for collecting the entire fee from the patient, and the patient received directly from Medicare a reimbursement check equal to the allowable fee less the 20 percent copayment. Under those circumstances, the physician bore the total risk of nonpayment.

To minimize the level of balance billing and therefore improve access to medical care, Medicare gave physicians the option to accept the assignment of benefits. Physicians who accept **assignment** give up the right to balance-bill, but in return receive a payment directly from Medicare equal to the preset fee minus any deductibles or copayments. The remainder of the bill had to be collected directly from the patient. The decision to accept assignment presents physicians with a classic risk-return trade-off. Physician who opt to balance-bill and not accept assignment receive higher fees but take on the added risk of nonpayment by patients.

The assignment rate, as measured by the percentage of total claims submitted that were assigned, hovered around 60 percent during the earlier years of the Medicare program. However, the rate fell thereafter and bottomed out at around 50 percent in the late 1970s. In response to the lower assignment rate, Congress passed the Medicare Participating Physicians program in 1984, which altered the method of assignment. Now physicians had to elect to either participate or not participate. Physicians who elected to participate had to accept assignment for all patients covered under Part B. Those who opted not to participate were still free to accept assignment on a case-by-case basis. To encourage participation, Congress provided a variety of incentives. For example, nonparticipating physicians had their fee schedule frozen under Medicare, while participating physicians saw a modest increase. These changes brought about the desired outcome, as the assignment rate increased from 53.9 percent in 1983 to 59 percent in 1984 and 68 percent in 1985. Later Congress made further changes in favor of participation. For example, the Omnibus Budget Reconciliation Act of 1986 placed maximum limits on the amount nonparticipating physicians could charge Medicare patients. As a result, the assignment rate reached 81 percent in 1990.

Fearing that the new fee schedule, along with voluntary performance standards, would cause the assignment rate to fall as physicians felt the pinch of more stringent price controls, OBRA 1989 placed even further constraints on the ability of physicians to practice balance billing. By 1991, physicians could not bill patients in excess of 125 percent of the Medicare rate. This rate fell to 120 percent in 1992 and to 115 percent in 1993 for most services. It should be noted that in 1993, the actual balance-billing rate was only 109.25 percent because nonparticipating physicians received only 95 percent of the Medicare fee for participating physicians (115 percent times 95 percent). As a result, the assignment rate increased to about 98 percent by 2000.

Health Outcomes Research   Finally, OBRA 89 calls for the government to take a more active role in outcomes research for the purpose of developing practice guidelines. The long-run objective is to contain the growth of physician and hospital expenditures in the future by minimizing the uncertainty surrounding alternative medical treatments. Outcomes research "involves not only the investigations of the link between medical care and outcomes, but also activities aimed at establishing which providers or systems of health care deliver a better quality of care than others" (Guadagnoli and McNeil, 1994, p. 14).

Payers are pressing for outcomes research so that medical guidelines can be developed to contain costs by eliminating ineffective medical care. Whether this will happen is open to question. For one thing, there is some debate concerning the level of inappropriate care. Some recent studies suggest that it is much lower than previously thought. For another, Guadagnoli and McNeil (1994) contend that outcomes research may force up costs because it may uncover some costly medical procedures that currently are underutilized. Physicians desire medical guidelines because they will aid them in treatment decisions and potentially diminish the possibility of malpractice suits. Another issue is whether guidelines can be effectively developed and implemented given the complexity of developing appropriate data sets and the difficulty in transferring this information into specific recommendations (Guadagnoli and McNeil, 1994). Many illnesses are patient specific, and consequently appropriate treatment cannot be standardized.

Balanced Budget Act of 1997   Despite the many changes in the Medicare program, many felt that rising Medicare costs throughout the 1990s could have jeopardized the financial viability of the program. One estimate indicated that if nothing were done, the trust fund for Part A of Medicare would be exhausted by 2001 (Physician Payment Review Commission, 1997). A glance at table 10–4 (page 282) indicates that the growth in expenditures has been rather uneven in recent years. For example, while expenditures for inpatient and physician services grew at annual rates of 9.2 and 6.0 percent from 1991 through 1995, expenditures for skilled nursing facilities, home health care, and hospice grew at annual rates in excess of 30 percent. Realizing that something needed to be done, Congress enacted the Balanced Budget Act of 1997 (BBA). According to MedPAC, BBA changes are expected to save $112 billion in Medicare expenditures from 1998 through 2002, of which $99 billion is to come from reduced provider payments and $13 billion from increased premiums.

INSIGHT 10-3

Advertising of MCOs—Information or Persuasion?

While everyone agrees that advertising is a fact of life in today's business environment, economists have long debated whether advertising enhances or diminishes society's overall well-being. As we learned in Chapter 8, proponents state that advertising provides consumers with additional information that can be used to make an informed decision, the result being a more efficient allocation of resources brought about through enhanced competition. Critics contend that advertising results in anticompetitive outcomes by creating artificial wants, habit buying, and barriers to entry. A recent study by Neuman et al. (1998) may rekindle that debate. Neuman et al. analyze newspaper and television ads placed by HMOs. They also review the presentations at marketing seminars to gain an understanding of the marketing strategies employed by HMOs to attract Medicare-eligible customers.

According to their findings, HMOs convey the message that they can provide more benefits at a lower cost than traditional Medicare plans. More importantly, the authors conclude that HMOs have developed and implemented marketing strategies based on attracting healthy seniors. To support their conclusion they cite the fact that "nearly half of all television ads include images of physically active seniors, in the midst of strenuous activities such as mountain biking, swimming and jogging up stairs" (p. 135). In addition, "none of the newspaper and television ad images includes beneficiaries in hospital beds or wheelchairs or with walkers, canes, or obvious handicaps or illnesses" (p. 135). They also report that in almost all cases the font size used in the fine print that appeared in TV and newspaper ads was smaller than the smallest print recommended for individuals 65 years old and older. What is even more astonishing is that one out of three seminars to prospective enrollees were held in facilities that were not wheelchair accessible.

Overall, the evidence supports the proposition that HMOs have been making a concerted effort to enroll healthy seniors and to avoid those with greater potential medical needs. Although it is difficult to determine the extent to which these advertising campaigns are impacting the decisions made by the elderly when choosing an insurance plan, there is no doubt that their intent is to play on the risk selection problem in order to improve the bottom line.

While some will debate these figures, all agree that this piece of legislation profoundly changed the Medicare program.

The centerpiece of the legislation was the **Medicare + Choice (M+C)** program, which significantly increased the types of insurance plans available to participants and altered the way in which Medicare pays for those plans. The M+C program changed Medicare in four important ways (Christensen, 1998):

- The number of capitation plans available to beneficiaries was greatly expanded.
- The conditions that participating plans must fulfill were relaxed.

TABLE 10-4
Average Annual Growth Rates in Medicare Expenditures, 1991–1995

Medical Service	Average Annual Rate of Growth, from 1991–1995
Part A	
Inpatient services	9.2%
Skilled nursing facility	37.7
Home health care	30.6
Hospice	37.4
Part B	
Physician services	6.0
Outpatient services	12.0
Home health care	29.4
Laboratory services	5.8

SOURCE: Physician Payment Review Commission. *Annual Report to Congress.* 1997, table 1–1.

- The method of calculated payment rates to plans was adjusted.
- The enrollment process for beneficiaries was changed.

To extend the range of options available to beneficiaries, the BBA allowed a number of alternative types of health insurance plans to participate in the program. Previous to this, only health maintenance organizations were allowed to offer risk-based insurance plans to Medicare participants. Now PPOs, PSOs, FFS plans, and MSAs will be allowed to participate, greatly expanding the range of options available to consumers.[8] To participate, plans must be licensed under state law and at a minimum cover the same medical services currently covered under the traditional Medicare fee-for-service plan. In an attempt to make it easier for plans to participate, the BBA made two changes. First, it dropped the fifty-fifty rule that required that at least half of the plan's enrollment come from the private sector. Second, it lowered the minimum enrollment requirements for PPOs to participate in the program (Christensen, 1998).

The BBA also significantly changes the method for calculating the monthly capitation payment received by private health plans who enter into contracts with Medicare. HMOs who contracted with Medicare prior to 1998 received a monthly capitation payment equal to 95 percent of the average expected costs of similar beneficiaries who were enrolled in the traditional Medicare plan (calculated at the county level).[9] In addition, capitated payments were further adjusted based on a number of factors, including age, gender, and Medicaid enrollment status prior to 1998.

---

[8]PPO stands for Preferred Provider Organization, while PSO stands for Provider-Sponsored Organizations, FFS stands for fee-for-service, and MSA for Medical Savings Accounts.

[9]The logic is that health maintenance organizations have a cost advantage over traditional fee-for-service organizations. Since they should be able to provide medical services at a reduced cost, Medicare reduces the payment by 5 percent.

However, analysts realized that this earlier M+C compensation scheme posed a number of methodological problems. First and foremost was the fact that the capitation payments did not consider the health status of the enrollees. To rectify this problem the BBA required that Medicare capitation payments be risk-adjusted beginning in the year 2000. In addition, the old method for setting the capitation payment had the problem of establishing payment rates that were highly variable from year to year within any given county. That variability tended to discourage companies from participating in the program because it was simply too difficult to project enrollment and profitability. To decrease the level of uncertainty and, therefore, encourage more plans to participate, the BBA mandated a new payment method. Currently, the payment is based on the beneficiary's relative expected health care costs plus county of residence. In determining relative expected medical costs, Medicare considers seven characteristics: age, sex, whether the beneficiary has end-stage renal disease, whether the beneficiary is on Medicaid, whether the beneficiary is institutionalized, whether the beneficiary is covered by an employer-sponsored plan, and a health risk factor based on diagnoses made during any Medicare-covered hospital stays in the past year. The county level payment is calculated as the highest of a blend of the local and national rate, a minimum payment amount (or floor) or a minimum increase from the previous year's county rates. In 2002 the monthly minimum rate was $553 for counties located in metropolitan areas and $500 for all other counties, while the minimum increase from the previous year was 2 percent (MedPAC, March 2002).

The general consensus is that the M+C choice program has not met expectations. First and foremost, the program has experienced a significant drop in participating plans. The number of contracts fell from a maximum of 348 in 1998 to 148 early in 2002. This drop in contracts was matched by a significant fall in M+C enrollees. Over the same four-year period, between 300,000 and one million individuals lost coverage through the M+C program annually (MedPAC, March 2002). In addition, many of the plans that elected to stay with the M+C program were forced to either curtail benefits or increase premiums because increases in Medicare payments did not keep up with the rising cost of health care. Needless to say, this created an additional incentive for enrollees to switch back to the traditional Medicare program. The program has also failed to generate any cost savings for Medicare. According to MedPAC (March 2002), the average spending per enrollee in the M+C program was about 4 percent higher than in the traditional Medicare plan in 2001 after controlling for the demographic attributes of the beneficiaries. While the estimates did not control for health status of recipients, they do provide preliminary evidence of a lack of cost savings.

Aside from the obvious problem that Medicare payments failed to keep pace with rising health care costs, Gold (2001) contends that there are five operational factors that contributed to the lack of growth of the M+C program. First, the M+C program was implemented following a rapid growth period in Medicare-managed enrollment. As a result, instead of experiencing an influx of new plans, just the opposite occurred as some plans began to withdraw from the market because of lower than expected returns. Second, the program was implemented at a time when Congress was wrestling with the very politically charged issue of containing Medicare costs. To keep the lid on costs, Congress established lower premium rates for the M+C program than otherwise would be the case, and that translated into reduced plan participation and limited benefits. Third, "bad time or bad luck also applies to the market environment in which the M+C choice program was born" (p. 133). The plan was inaugurated when the managed care backlash was in full swing and managed care organizations found it difficult to negotiate reduced prices from health care providers and build adequate provider networks. Fourth, the provisions established in the BBA for the development and implementation of the M+C choice plan were cumbersome and effectively hamstrung the ability of the Health Care Financing Administration to effectively administer the plan. Finally, the current payment system for the M+C plan is inadequate and has created geographic inequities. The payment rates are too low in some areas of the country and too high in others. As a result, beneficiaries in some counties have limited choice and benefits while others have benefited significantly from the plan.

Success with the price controls on inpatient hospital and physician services also prompted Congress to call for prospective payment schedules for skilled nursing facilities, hospital outpatient facilities, home health agencies, and rehabilitation facilities in the BBA legislation. These payment schedules were to be developed and put in place with the last implemented in October 2000 for rehabilitation facilities.

The BBA also addressed some issues with regard to Part B of the Medicare program. As we discussed previously, OBRA 1989 mandated a resource-based relative value scale system of payment for physician services. Practice and malpractice expenses were still based on historical charges. The BBA required that a resource-based method of payment be extended to practice expenses starting in 1999 and malpractice expenses in 2000.

In addition, the BBA replaces the volume performance standard with a new system that ties conversion factor updates to a sustainable growth target. This target is tied to the rate of medical inflation, changes in fee-for-service enrollment, growth in the overall economy, and any changes in spending resulting from any modifications in government policy. The old way of basing updates in the conversion factor on the volume performance standard system had come under criticism in recent years for a number of reasons. First, under the volume performance standard system, separate conversion factors were used for primary services, surgical services, and nonsurgical services, thus distorting relative payments across physician services over time. To remedy this problem a single conversion factor has been established (MedPAC, 1998).

Most important, however, was the fact that the volume performance standards were generating spending targets that were much too low. Previously, the target was based on the growth in the volume and intensity of physician services minus any legislated deduction to slow the rate of growth in spending. In recent years the growth in volume and intensity slowed down while at the same time the legislated deduction was increased. "As a result, performance standards, which originally were well above the gross domestic product growth are now projected to drop well below" (PPCS 1997, p. 252). Beginning in 1999 the updates in the conversion factor will be determined by a sustainable growth rate system that will be tied more closely to the overall economy. The idea is to link spending for physician services under Medicare more closely to what the economy can afford to finance over time.

Realizing that the drastic changes called for by BBA may cause undue hardship on health care providers, Congress passed the Balanced Budget Refinement Act, or BBRA, in 1999. Among other things, the BBRA increased Medicare spending by approximately $16 billion from 2000 through 2004 and delayed the implementation of several of the prospective payment systems called for by the BBA. In additions, the legislation decreased the reductions for managed care, disproportionate share payments, and indirect education payments. The overall objective of the legislation was to provide health care providers more time to transition into many of the changes called for in the BBA of 1997.

INSIGHT 10-4

A Synopsis of the Medicare Payment Schemes

Many have complained through the years that the Medicare Program imposes significant administrative costs on health care providers forced to navigate a highly complex payment system. Without a doubt, understanding Medicare's 15 payment systems currently in use is no easy matter. Following is a summary of the payment schemes currently in use.

Type of Medicare Service	Payment System
Acute hospital care	A prospective payment system based on over 500 distinct DRGs.
Psychiatric facilities	Payments based on incurred average operating costs per discharge subject to annual adjusted limits.
Physician services	A prospective payment system based on physician work, practice expenses, and expenses for liability insurance. The payment schedule contains payment rates for over 7,000 services.
Hospital Outpatient Services	A prospective payment system based on approximately 750 ambulatory payment classifications.
Ambulatory Surgical Centers	A prospective payment system based on eight payment groups with over 2,300 procedures.
Outpatient Laboratories	A prospective payment system based on 1,100 codes.
Skilled Nursing Home Facilities	A prospective payment system based on 44 resource-utilization groups (RUGS-III).
Home Health Agencies	A prospective payment system based on home health resource groups (HHRGs).
Inpatient Rehabilitation Facilities	A prospective payment system based on 385 intensive rehavilitation products, or case-mix groups (CMGs).
Long-Term Care Facilities	Payments are based on average costs per discharge, subject to annual adjustment limits.
Outpatient Dialysis Care	A prospective payment for dialysis treatment.
Hospice Health Care	A prospective payment system for four categories: routine home care, continuous home care, inpatient respite care, and general inpatient care.

(continued)

Type of Medicare Service	Payment System
Ambulance Services	Payments based on cost from previous year plus an annual update.
Durable Medical Equipment	A prospective payment system based on six basic categories.
Medicare + Choice Plans	A prospective payment system based on the individual's county of residence, and relative expected costs using a number of demographic and health factors.

SOURCE: Medicare Payment Commission. *Medicare Payment Policy Report to Congress.* Washington D.C., March 2002.

SUMMARY

This chapter focuses on Medicaid and Medicare, two public health insurance programs that account for a high and rising share of total health care costs in the United States. The Medicaid program has seen tremendous change in recent years and these changes have placed a number of states in rather precarious positions. States all across the country have been forced to control costs and at the same time meet federal mandates that call for the relaxation of eligibility requirements for certain segments of the poor. Most have turned to managed care as a way to contain Medicaid expenditures. Whether managed care offers the solution to Medicaid cost containment will most likely be a lively source of debate in the near future.

The Medicare program has also experienced significant change in the recent past. First and foremost the Medicare program over the last few decades has moved away from a fee-for-service method of payment as its major method of payment to a prospective payment system in an attempt to contain costs. This movement started with the implementation of the diagnosis-related group payment program in the 1980s and was followed by the resource-based payment program for physician services in the 1990s. More recently, prospective payment systems have been adopted for many other types of medical services covered by Medicare. The Medicare program has also turned to managed care with mixed results in the hopes of containing costs. What the future holds for the Medicare + Choice program remains to be seen as Congress continues to wrestle with the problem of balancing the federal budget and meeting the health care needs of the elderly.

REVIEW QUESTIONS AND PROBLEMS

1. Using economic theory, justify the need for the Medicaid and Medicare programs.
2. Discuss the methods states use to contain Medicaid costs.

3. Discuss the importance of Medicaid fees in determining the success of the Medicaid program in improving health outcomes of the poor.

4. What is the Medicaid crowding out problem and why is it important?

5. In 1983, Congress adopted the prospective payment system (PPS) to compensate hospitals for medical services. Prior to that point, hospitals were paid on a retrospective basis. Provide the economic justification for such a move.

6. Explain some of the advantages and disadvantages of the resource-based method of payment for physician services under Medicare.

7. The muffler on your car suddenly needs repair, and there are only two automobile repair shops in town. You drive to the first shop, and the mechanic tells you to leave the car and he will repair it. Payment will be due when you pick it up. A mechanic at the second shop looks at your car and guarantees that she will charge you only $99.95 to repair the muffler, as advertised. Which repair shop is likely to provide costly needless repairs to your car, and why? Which one may underprovide quality? In your answers, discuss the concepts of prospective and retrospective payment for services.

8. What is the assignment problem? How have recent changes in the Medicare program addressed the problem?

9. Discuss how health outcomes research is supposed to contain rising medical costs.

10. Explain how the Medicare + Choice program alters the role of private insurance in the Medicare program.

11. What factors explain the disappointing results from the Medicare + Choice program?

ONLINE RESOURCES

To access Internet links related to the topics in this chapter, please visit our web site at http://santerre.swcollege.com.

REFERENCES

Baker, Laurence, and Anne Beeson Royalty. "Medicaid Policy, Physician Behavior, and Health Care for the Low-Income Populations." *Journal of Human Resources* 35 (summer 2000), pp. 480–502.

Blumberg, Linda J., Lisa Dubay, and Stephen A. Norton. "Did the Medicaid Expansions for Children Displace Private Insurance? An Analysis Using the SIPP." *Journal of Health Economics* 19 (January 2000), pp. 33–66.

Christensen, Sandra. "Medicare+Choice Provisions in the Balanced Budget Act of 1997." *Health Affairs* 17 (July/August 1998), pp. 224–31.

Coughlin, Teresa A., et al. "State Responses to the Medicaid Spending Crisis: 1988 to 1992." *Journal of Health Politics, Policy and Law* 19 (winter 1994), pp. 837–64.

Coulan, R.F., and G.L. Gaumer. "Medicare's Prospective Payment System: A Critical Appraisal." *Health Care Financing Review* (Annual Supplement, 1991), pp. 45–77.

Currie, Janet, and Duncan Thomas. "Medical Care for Children: Public Insurance, Private Insurance and Racial Differences in Utilization." *Journal of Human Resources* 30 (1995), pp. 135–62.

Currie, Janet, Jonathon Gruber, and Michael Fischer. "Physician Payments and Infant Mortality: Evidence from Medicaid Fee Policy." *American Economic Review* 85 (1995), pp. 106–11.

Cutler, David M., and Jonathan Gruber. "Does Public Insurance Crowd Out Private Insurance?" *Quarterly Journal of Economics* 111 (May 1996), pp. 391–430.

DeParle, Nancy Min. "Celebrating 35 Years of Medicare and Medicaid." *Health Care Financing Review* 22 (fall 2000), pp. 1–7.

Dubay, Lisa, and Geneviere, Kenney. "Did Medicaid Expansion for Pregnant Women Crowd Out Private Insurance?" *Health Affairs* 16 (January/February 1997), pp. 185–93.

Feinglass, Joe, and James J. Holloway. "The Initial Impact of the Medicare Prospective Payment System on U.S. Health Care: A Review of the Literature." *Medical Care Review* 48 (spring 1991), pp. 91–115.

Fisher, Charles R. "Hospital and Medicare Financial Performance under PPS, 1985–1990." *Health Care Financing Review* 14 (fall 1992), pp. 171–83.

Garnick, Deborah W., et al. "How Well Do Americans Understand Their Health Coverage?" *Health Affairs* 12 (fall 1993), pp. 204–12.

Ginsburg, Paul B. "Refining Medicare Volume Performance Standards: Commentary." *Inquiry* 30 (fall 1993), pp. 260–64.

Gold, Marsha. "Medicare+Choice: An Interim Report Care." *Health Affairs* 20 (July/August 2001), pp. 120–38.

Gray, Bradley. "Do Medicaid Physician Fees for Prenatal Services Affect Birth Outcomes?" *Journal of Health Economics* 20 (July 2001), pp. 571–90.

Guadagnoli, Edward, and Barbara J. McNeil. "Outcomes Research: Hope for the Future the Latest Rage?" *Inquiry* 31 (spring 1994), pp. 14–24.

Hadley, Jack. "Theoretical and Empirical Foundations of the Resource-Based Relative Value Scale." In *Regulating Doctors' Fees: Competition, Benefits and Control under Medicare*, ed. H.E. Frech III. Washington, D.C.: AEI Press, 1991.

Heffler, Stephen, Sheila Smith, Greg Won, M. Ken Clemens, Sean Keenan, and Mark Zezza. "Health Spending Projections for 2001–2011: The Latest Outlook." *Health Affairs* 21 (March/April 2002), pp. 207–18.

Hodgkin, Dominic, and Thomas G. McGuire. "Payment Levels and Hospital Response to Prospective Payment." *Journal of Health Economics* 13 (1994), pp. 1–29.

Holahan, John, and Stephen Zuckerman. "The Future of Medicare Volume Performance Standards." *Inquiry* 30 (fall 1993), pp. 235–48.

Hsiao, William C., et al. "Results and Policy Implications of the Resource-Based Relative-Value Scale." *New England Journal of Medicine* 319 (September 29, 1988), pp. 881–88.

Kronebusch, Karl. "Children's Medicaid Enrollment: The Impact of Mandates, Welfare Reform, and Policy Delinking." *Journal of Health Politics, Policy and Law* 26 (December 2001), pp. 1217–22.

Long, Sharon, K., and Teresa A. Coughlin. "Access and Use by Children on Medicaid: Does State Matter." *Inquiry* 38 (winter 2001/2002), pp. 409–22.

Medicare Payment Advisory Commission (MedPAC). *Medicare Payment Policy Report to Congress*. Washington D.C., March 2002.

Medicare Payment Advisory Commission. *Report to the Congress: Medicare Payment Policy*. Vols. I and II. Washington, D.C., March 1998.

Miller, Mark E., and W. Pete Welch. "Growth in Medicare Inpatient Physician Charges per Admission, 1986–1989." *Inquiry* 30 (fall 1993), pp. 249–59.

Muller, Andreas. "Medicare Prospective Payment Reforms and Hospital Utilization." *Medical Care* 31 (1993), pp. 296–308.

Neuman, Patricia, et al. "Marketing HMOs to Medicare Beneficiaries." *Health Affairs* 17 (July/August 1998), pp. 132–39.

Norton, Stephen, and Stephen Zuckerman. "Trends in Medicaid Physician Fees, 1993–1998." *Health Affairs* 19 (July/August 2000), pp. 222–32.

Oliver, Thomas R. "Analysis, Advice, and Congressional Leadership: The Physician Payment Review Commission and the Politics of Medicare." *Journal of Health Politics, Policy and Law* 18 (spring 1993), pp. 113–74.

Physician Payment Review Commission. *Annual Report to Congress*. Washington, D.C., 1997.

Physician Payment Review Commission. *Annual Report to Congress*. Washington, D.C.: PPRC, 1993.

Schwartz, William B., and Daniel N. Mendelson. "Hospital Cost Containment in the 1980's." *New England Journal of Medicine* 324 (April 11, 1991), pp. 1037–42.

U.S. Department of Health and Human Services, Social Security Administration. *Annual Statistical Supplement, 2001*. Washington, D.C., 2001.

U.S. Department of Health and Human Services, Social Security Administration. *Annual Statistical Supplement, 1993*. Washington, D.C., 1993.

Yazici, Esel Y., and Robert Kaestner. "Medicaid Expansions and the Crowding Out of Private Health Insurance Among Children." *Inquiry* 37 (spring 2000), pp. 23–32.

Yett, Donald E., William Der, Richard L. Ernst, and Joel W. Hay. "Fee-for-Service Reimbursement and Physician Inflation." *Journal of Human Resources* 20 (spring 1985), pp. 278–91.

CEBS QUESTIONS

CEBS Sample Question on Subject Matter from CEBS Course 9 Study Manual

1. What are ways in which Congress over the years has encouraged physician participation in the Medicare program? (pages 279–280)

CEBS Sample Exam Questions

1. Not counting the 60-day lifetime reserve, Medicare covers hospital inpatient expenses for a maximum of:
   A. 30 days
   B. 60 days
   C. 90 days
   D. 120 days
   E. 360 days

2. The Balanced Budget Act of 1997 contained which of the following major changes in the Medicare program?
   I.   The Act limited reimbursement of Medicare expenditures to two-thirds the cost of comparable services in 1995, the base year of cost measurement
   II. The Act expanded the number of alternative types of risk-based health insurance plans eligible to participate in the plan.
   III. The Act changed the method of calculating the monthly capitation payment received by private health insurance plans that enter into risk contracts with Medicare.
   A. II only
   B. III only
   C. I and II only
   D. II and III only
   E. I, II, and III

3. All the following statements regarding the financing and cost of Medicaid are correct EXCEPT:
   A. The cost is financed jointly by the federal and state governments
   B. In the years 1992 through 1996 the rate of growth in Medicaid expenditures has increased dramatically
   C. Federal mandates, such as required coverage of children and pregnant women, have increased Medicaid expenditures
   D. The percent of Medicaid recipients enrolled in managed care plans varies widely across states
   E. Disproportionate share hospital payments have contributed to the rise in Medicaid expenditures

Answer to Sample Question from Study Manual

The ways in which Congress has encouraged physician participation has been by guaranteeing reimbursement minus any deductibles or copayments directly from Medicare, by placing limits on the amount nonparticipating physicians could charge Medicare patients, and by placing constraints on balance billing.

Answers to Sample Exam Questions

1. C is the answer. Except for the 60-day lifetime reserve, after the 90th day Medicare stops paying hospital inpatient expenses. See page 272 of the text.
2. D is the answer. The first statement is false but the other two are true. The Medicare + Choice program introduced by the Act increased the types of insurance available to the Medicare participants and required that Medicare capitation payments be made on a risk adjusted basis beginning in the year 2000. See pages 280–284 of the text.
3. B is the answer. In the years 1992 through the 1996 the rate of growth in expenditures dropped. All other statements are correct. See pages 266–267 of the text.

PART 3

INDUSTRY STUDIES

THE PRIVATE HEALTH INSURANCE INDUSTRY

Our pal Joe was sort of lucky. Sure he suffered a heart attack. That, in it-self, can be a medically frightening and painful experience. But as a fed-eral employee, Joe and his family were covered by a sound and generous health insurance policy so at least they did not have to bear the sharp psychological sting of the financial insecurity that can result from an un-expected medical occurrence.

However, Leo, Joe's brother, was not so fortunate. You see, Leo worked as a machinist in a specialty parts fabrication shop that employs five workers. Given the competitive nature of the market for specialty machined goods, Leo's employer was financially unable to sponsor any health insurance for the workers. But Leo and his wife, Sarah, really didn't care about the lack of health insurance anyway. They were both in their early fifties, which is relatively young by today's standards, and seemed to be in great health. They had built up a small nest egg of $100,000 and planned on using the money to support an early semi-retirement where Leo would quit his job and open a machine shop in his garage. At 65 years of age both Leo and Sarah would be eligible for Medicare and then they were all set—or so they thought.

Then all hell broke loose. Sarah found a lump in her breast! A visit to a local doctor confirmed her most feared suspicion. She was diagnosed with a cancerous tumor. Since Sarah had not received annual mammo-grams due to what she considered an unnecessary out-of-pocket expense, the cancer was at an advanced stage. Too late for a simple lumpectomy or chemotherapy, a radical mastectomy was deemed the necessary treatment. Not only were Leo and Sarah distraught over Sarah's physical and mental well-being, but also saddened that their hard-earned life savings would be completely wiped out.

This story helps to raise a number of important questions:

1. Who exactly are the uninsured? That is, are specific groups or indi-viduals, like employees of small businesses, at a greater risk of being uninsured than others?

2. Suppose that Leo had participated in a group health insurance pol-icy with his employer but decided to change jobs. Would he and Sarah be immediately eligible for health insurance with the new em-ployer, especially with Sarah's condition already diagnosed?

3. If Leo had a group health insurance policy with his employer, could the employer legally raise his health insurance premiums or exclude Sarah from the policy?

This chapter deals with these questions, among others, and raises a host of other problems and issues pertaining to the private health insurance industry. The examination is couched in terms of the structure, conduct, and performance paradigm discussed in Chapter 8. Specifically, this chapter:

>   Provides a brief history of the private health insurance industry.

>   Analyzes the structure of the private health insurance industry in terms of the number and types of sellers, buyer characteristics, barriers to entry, and other factors.

>   Describes the conduct of firms in the private health insurance industry with respect to pricing methods, managed care effects, and risk selection.

>   Assesses the performance of the private health insurance industry with regard to the number of insured and uninsured, pricing, and moral hazard.

A BRIEF HISTORY OF THE PRIVATE HEALTH INSURANCE INDUSTRY

The modern private health insurance industry started around 1929 when Baylor University in Dallas began accepting insurance premiums from local schoolteachers to cover any medical services provided at the university hospital (Temin, 1988).[1] The idea quickly spread during the Great Depression of the 1930s as a number of hospitals adopted similar financing methods. Shortly thereafter, the American Hospital Association created and organized several insurance plans, named Blue Cross, which allowed subscribers free choice among the hospitals within a given city. Corresponding to the alleged public service nature of Blue Cross plans, premiums were determined by community rating. The Blue Cross plans enjoyed a virtual monopoly position in the hospital insurance market throughout the 1930s.

The hospital insurance market expanded and the level of competition intensified during World War II, when the federal government imposed wage and price controls. Because wage increases were restricted, the only way employers could attract additional laborers was to offer fringe benefits, such as private health insurance. Initially, employers did not report the value of the fringe benefits to the Internal Revenue Service, but eventually regulations were passed requiring employers to include the value of medical care as part of reported wage income. By that time, however, workers had become accustomed to the tax-exempt status of medical insurance and expressed considerable alarm. Congress responded, and health insurance has remained tax exempt ever since (Friedman, 1992).

Commercial insurance companies were slow to branch off into the health insurance market because they were uncertain about its profitability (Sapolsky, 1991) and doubted whether medical care was an insurable risk due to the difficulty in predicting losses accurately (Iglehart, 1992). The Blue Cross experience demonstrated the viability of health in-

---

[1]According to Sapolsky (1991), a few paternalistic employers, including General Motors and Procter & Gamble, established welfare programs with medical benefits for their employees prior to 1926.

surance to commercial insurers. By the time the commercials entered the industry in the late 1940s, Blue Cross plans were viewed as pro-union, having established a strong union allegiance. As employers looked to alternative sources for private health insurance, commercial plans searched for clients. The commercial insurance segment later grew as the rate of union membership declined among workers and experience rating became more common among employer groups. According to Temin (1988), "Blue Cross accounted for only two-thirds of hospital insurance by the war's close, and it had less than half of the market in the 1950s and 1960s" (p. 89).

Today the private health insurance industry is the source of funds for 33 percent of all health care expenditures, providing coverage to roughly 70 percent of the population. The modern health insurance industry is very pluralistic, composed of many different types of health plan providers that include health maintenance organizations, preferred provider organizations, self-insurers, third-party administrators, and traditional insurers with and without utilization review. Some of these insurers are not-for-profit entities, whereas others are for-profit organizations. Moreover, many of them rely on different methods of reimbursing health care providers for medical services rendered to their subscribers. The rest of this chapter examines the structure, conduct, and performance of the private health insurance industry.

THE STRUCTURE OF THE PRIVATE HEALTH INSURANCE INDUSTRY

As noted in Chapter 8, structure is an important feature of an industry because it influences the conduct and performance of the member firms. In the following discussion, we take a closer look at some of the structural characteristics associated with the private health insurance industry.

Number, Types, and Size Distribution of Health Insurers

Private health insurance in the United States involves many different health insurers, including commercial carriers, Blue Cross/Blue Shield (BCBS) plans, HMOs, and other types of managed-care plans. Several practices of private health insurers are worth noting. First, it is normally the case that a private health insurer, like a commercial company or BCBS, offers its subscribers a choice among traditional plans and various types of managed-care plans. Second, insurers may specialize in either group or individual health insurance, or may choose to offer both. Lastly, private health insurers often are licensed to underwrite and sell health insurance in more than one state.

Data suggest that across the nation, a relatively large number of different insurers offer private health insurance. Chollet, Kirk, and Chow (2000) estimate that 2,450 insurers participated in the group health insurance market and another 690 insurers operated in the individual health insurance market in 1997. Also, Chollet, Kirk, and Chow report that (non-BCBS) HMOs, with a 45 percent market share of earned premiums, dominated the group health insurance market while BCBS plans, with nearly half of all earned premiums, dominated the individual health insurance market in 1997. Commercial insurers, while more numerous in both markets, held market shares of only 19 and 24 percent in the group and individual segments of the health insurance industry, respectively.

In terms of market concentration, Chollet, Kirk, and Chow point out that in most states, a few large insurers dominated the group health insurance market in 1997. For example, the largest three health insurers received at least 50 percent of earned premiums in the group market of 33 states. In 20 states the top three insurers received 60 percent or more of premiums earned, and in no state did the top three insurers receive less than 23 percent. Economists often consider four-firm concentration ratios of around 40 percent as reflecting mild oligopoly, so these relatively high three-firm concentration ratios may be cause for some alarm. Data from the study further revealed that a fairly large competitive fringe exists in the health insurance industry in each state. That is, in every state, the smallest 50 percent of insurers held less than 9 percent of the market in 1997.

Data for the individual health insurance market paints a picture of an even more concentrated marketplace. In every state, the top three insurers controlled at least 50 percent of the market for individual insurance, and in all but 7 states the top three insurers accounted for 60 percent or more of earned premiums. Like the group market, a large competitive fringe characterizes the individual market. For example, in states with four or more insurers in the individual market in 1997, the smallest half of insurers collectively held as little as 1 percent of the market in 7 states. As another example, the smallest half of insurers held more than 20 percent of the market in only 5 states.

The GAO (2002) finds similar evidence concerning the concentrated nature of the small group health insurance market. Small group health insurance is defined differently by the states but the definition typically allows for less than 50 employees in a plan. The study found that the median number of licensed carriers in the small group market was 28 per state. When combined, the five largest insurers represented more than 75 percent of the market in 19 of the 34 states providing information. In 7 states, the five top insurers covered 90 percent of more of those receiving health insurance in the small group insurance segment. Similar to the study by Chollet, Kirk, and Chow, another implication of the GAO study is the existence of a large competitive fringe of health insurers in the small group segment of the industry.

Consequently, the contemporary private health insurance industry appears relatively concentrated in most states. However, for some large employers, self-insurance offers an alternative to purchased health insurance. Large employers with self-insured plans assume the financial risk associated with paying medical claims, although third-party administrators may administer the plan for a fee. Alternatively, large employers may self-fund their plans but purchase stop-loss insurance to cover the risk of large losses or severe adverse claims experiences. According to the HIAA (1999/2000), about 62 million people, or 33 percent of all privately insured individuals, were covered by self-insured plans in 1996, rising from under 50 million members as recently as 1990. Self-insured plans expanded over time because they are exempt from paying premium taxes, which can run as high as 2 percent, and are subject to the Employee Retirement Income Security Act (ERISA) of 1974, which exempts self-insured plans from providing state-mandated benefits. According to Iglehart (1992), "there are now 900 such mandates nationwide, the most frequent among them being those for alcohol treatment (required in 42 states), mammography screening (41 states), mental health care (32 states), and drug abuse treatment (31 states)" (p. 1719).

Barriers to Entry

Although the data portray the private health insurance industry as being relatively concentrated, individual health insurers may continue to face an incentive to behave efficiently if they face a threat from potential competitors. Potential competition makes it more difficult for existing firms to collude and raise price because they encounter the like-lihood that new entrants may break into the market by offering a better deal to their cus-tomers. The degree of potential competition depends on the height of any barriers to entry. When high enough, barriers deter the entry of new firms.

In the private health insurance industry, scale economies in administering health in-surance may serve as a barrier to entry. Scale economies enable existing firms with large volumes of output to underprice new, low-volume competitors and discourage their entry. Pricing to deter entry is referred to as **limit pricing**. Blair, Jackson, and Vogel (1975) ex-amined the existence of economies of scale by using multiple regression analysis to inves-tigate the relationship between administration expenses and the size of insurance output for a sample of 307 insurance companies in 1968. If per-unit administrative costs declined with output, that would be evidence that scale economies exist in the administration of health insurance.

As a measure of average administrative costs, the authors used total operating costs di-vided by health insurance premiums. As a measure of the size of health insurance output, they selected the dollar value of premiums written. While premiums written captured both insurance output and price differences across firms, the use of premiums was legitimate if output was homogeneous and competitive pressure forced firms to charge the same price. Blair, Jackson, and Vogel found that per-unit administrative costs were inversely related to output, as measured by premiums, suggesting that long-run economies of scale exist in the administration of health insurance. The policy implication of the empirical findings is that the administration of health insurance should be centralized among a few insurance com-panies if the goal is to minimize administrative costs.

In a follow-up study, Blair and Vogel (1978) used survivor analysis (Stigler, 1958) to ex-amine the existence of economies of scale in the provision of health insurance. **Survivor theory** supposes that firm-size classes with expanding populations are more efficient than those with shrinking populations over time. Firms in expanding size classes have obviously met and survived the market test. The survivor test, unlike the econometric test discussed earlier, reflects overall economies in the provision of health insurance, not just scale economies associated with the administrative function. To conduct the survivor test, Blair and Vogel constructed seven firm-size classes for commercial health insurers based on real premium volume. They then analyzed the percentage of commercial health insurers falling into the various size classes over the period 1958 to 1973.

The authors found that the percentage of firms and total premium volume fell in the smallest firm-size category over time. The other six firm-size classes either grew or re-mained relatively constant as a percentage of either total premium volume or total firms. Thus, the results of their survivor test suggest that the optimal size extends over quite a large range of output, except for the smallest size category, providing support for constant returns to scale over a relatively vast range of output. According to Blair and Vogel (p. 528), the econometric and survivor tests, taken together, indicate that the administrative scale economies "must have been swamped by diseconomies elsewhere" in some other func-tion(s), such as risk bearing, marketing, and so on.

Wholey, Feldman, Christianson, and Engberg (1996) examined whether HMOs expe-rience scale economies by using a national sample of HMOs over the period 1988 to 1991. They recognized the multiproduct nature of HMO insurance by allowing for both non-Medicare and Medicare coverage. Like the previous studies on commercial health in-surers, Wholey et al. found that small HMOs face scale economies associated with both non-Medicare and Medicare beneficiaries but the scale economies are exhausted relatively quickly.

Finally, state price and quality regulations also exist and may deter entry of new insurance firms. But these barriers to entry do not appear to be overly restrictive, because about 50 insurance companies typically operate within a state (Chollet, Kirk, and Chow, 2000). All in all, barriers to entry are of minor importance in the health insurance industry.

Consumer Information

One of the likely noncompetitive features of the private health insurance industry concerns consumer knowledge. Recall that when individuals possess imperfect information they may pay higher prices and/or receive lower quality when compared to a situation with perfect information. For those people belonging to a group plan, this problem may not be as severe since specialists, like human resource managers or union representatives, often provide individuals with the information to make more educated choices. However, those people purchasing individual plans may lack the technical information needed to accurately assess the true value of a health insurance policy. For instance, an individual may be confronted with numerous plans, each offering slightly different benefits, exclusions, and out-of-pocket payments.

Prior to the Omnibus Budget Reconciliation Act (OBRA) of 1990, the market for medigap insurance provided a good example of the importance of consumer information when purchasing insurance. Medigap policies are purchased by individuals to cover any medical payments not reimbursed by Medicare, such as the monthly premium under Part B. Prior to the act, insurers were allowed to offer any number of medigap policies. Reinhardt (1992) pointed out that these policies have been so difficult to comprehend that "many of the elderly have been induced to buy multiple, duplicate policies—probably an intended byproduct of an intended confusion" (p. A5). Reinhardt goes on to note the low payout rate (percent of premiums paid out as benefits) and therefore higher price among commercial insurers for medigap policies (66 percent on average compared to 93.4 percent for traditional Blue Cross/Blue Shield policies) and on small business insurance plans (as low as 77 percent for firms with fewer than 20 employees).

Included as part of the Omnibus Budget Reconciliation Act of 1990 was a provision to reform the medigap market. The legislation attempted to provide more informed consumer choice and thereby promote competition in the medigap market. The law stipulated that after July 1992 only 10 standard insurance policies, based on increasing levels of comprehensiveness, could be sold as Medicare supplements to individuals. The basic belief was that 10 policies represented sufficient choice and that standardization would facilitate comparisons and promote informed buying of medigap policies.

According to McCormack, Fox, Rice, and Graham (1996), the legislation had the intended impact. After the law when into effect, consumer complaints declined considerably in various states because shopping for a policy became easier and more straightforward. Many of those interviewed believed that consumer confusion declined as a result of standardization and because consumers were able to make more informed decisions. In addition, the researchers found that the price of medigap insurance declined, as theory suggests when consumers make more informed decisions. Specifically, the price of an individual medigap policy fell from an average of $1.29 per benefit dollar during the period 1990–1992 to an average of $1.27 for the period 1993–1994.

However, other individual health insurance policies are not as standardized as medigap policies are now. Those not covered by Medicare and who purchase individual plans often face a choice among multitude plans with varying benefits, clauses, and exclusions. Although diversity of choices often provides utility, diversity can also be costly when it leads to confused choice. Consequently, informational imperfections may result in some noncompetitive behavior in the individual policy segment of the private health insurance industry.

THE CONDUCT OF THE PRIVATE HEALTH INSURANCE INDUSTRY

From a structural perspective, the private health insurance industry appears to resemble an oligopoly with a relatively large competitive fringe. While 50 health insurers sell group policies in the typical state, only a few insurers account for a relatively large proportion of earned premiums. Entry barriers do not seem to seriously impede mobility into the industry, which probably accounts for the relatively large competitive fringe. The low entry barriers and large competitive fringe most likely help to maintain a significant amount of price competition within the industry. Now we examine how a relatively competitive market structure affects the conduct of private health insurers as the structure, conduct, and performance paradigm suggests it should. Among the behavioral aspects discussed are pricing, managed-care effects, cherry-picking behavior, and adverse selection.

The Dominant Insurer Pricing Model

According to the data on the number and size distribution of health insurers in the United States, the health insurance industry in most market areas appears to resemble an oligopoly with a relatively large competitive fringe. For various reasons, some health insurers have become quite dominant over time while others have remained fairly small in terms of market share. Business organizations typically become dominant in their market for various reasons including sheer luck, technical and pecuniary economies, superior performance, or by merging with other organizations. Let us elaborate.

Like individuals, some organizations are just luckier than others. Mere chance may mean several successive years of tremendous growth such that a relatively small organization can be quickly transformed into a much larger one. Once relatively large, it becomes difficult for smaller competitors to catch up.

Organizations may also become dominant as they strive for survival in the marketplace by attempting to exploit any economies from larger size. Technical economies refer to any economies of scale or scope that may be conferred to a larger organization. Pecuniary economies occur when large organizations purchase inputs and supplies at a lower price than similar but smaller organizations. If a very large size is necessary to fully exploit technical and pecuniary economies in a particular industry, firms in that industry will seek a large size over time to survive in a competitive market. Thus, a few dominant firms may evolve and be observed in industries characterized by vast technical and pecuniary economies.

Some analysts refer to the existence of a few dominant firms that result from seeking the gains from large size as the Rule of Three. The Rule of Three states, "In competitive, mature markets, there is room for only three major players along with several (in some markets, many) niche players" (Sheth and Sisodia, 1998, p. 22). The large dominant firms are volume-driven generalists who compete across a wide range of differentiated, name brand products and services while the smaller organizations are either niche players or produce standardized versions of the name brand products. According to Sheth and Sisodia, the Rule of Three can be observed in the beer, cereals, tires, insurance, aluminum, oil, chemicals, and airline industries, among others.

A superior performance may also provide a business with a dominant market share. Superiority may result from an excellent product or a low-cost production process. Microsoft represents a good example of dominance resulting from a superior product. In fact, many analysts argue that a superior product tends to provide the best explanation for dominance although various business tactics and strategies such as limit pricing or persuasive advertising must be employed to prevent dominant market shares from eventually receding (see Insight 8-2).

Finally, organizations may become dominant in a particular market through horizontal or vertical integration. Recall that horizontal integration takes place when firms producing similar products merge together. As discussed in the context of the Williamson model in chapter 9, horizontal mergers benefit consumers if cost-savings and lower prices result from the larger size. However, monopoly pricing may occur if the larger size confers market power onto the firm. Vertical integration involves the combination of firms that produce at successive stages of production, or stated differently, among buyers and sellers. A merger between a hospital and a group physician practice or a hospital and a nursing home represent examples of vertical integration. Chapters 13 and 14 discuss vertical integrations in the context of the hospital and pharmaceutical industries, respectively. Let us just note here that vertical integration may also have procompetitive and anticompetitive impacts on consumers.

Now that we have some idea about how one or a few firms may dominate an industry, an interesting question emerges concerning how a dominant firm may influence the price of a good or service in a market with a competitive fringe. When a dominant firm exists in a market with a competitive fringe, economists often use the dominant firm-pricing model to analyze how market price and quantity are determined. The dominant firm-pricing model involves the following assumptions.

The first assumption is that only one dominant firm exists in the industry. While few markets, even health insurance markets, are characterized by a single dominant firm, this model still holds if the few dominant firms act in a concerted fashion by either overtly or tacitly coordinating their prices. Two, the dominant firm is assumed to be a low cost producer relative to the rest of the firms in the competitive fringe. In fact, the dominant firm gains its dominance in this model because of its favorable position as a low cost producer. Third, the model assumes a fixed number of firms in the competitive fringe and each firm is treated as being a price-taker. Fourth, the dominant firm is assumed to know industry demand and how much the competitive fringe firms will collectively supply at various prices. Finally, all firms, including the dominant firm and those in the competitive fringe, are assumed to produce a homogeneous product, which sells at an identical price.

Figure 11–1 provides a graphical depiction of the dominant firm-pricing model in the context of a market for health insurance. The quantity of health insurance (perhaps the number of policies written) is shown on the horizontal axis, and dollar values are shown on the vertical axis. Demand is represented by the downward-sloping demand curve labeled as D and the supply of the fringe firms is captured by the upward-sloping curve S_F.

FIGURE 11-1

Dominant Insurer Pricing Model

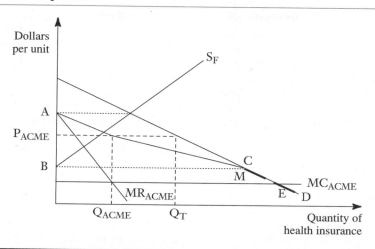

D represents the market demand curve for health insurance and the supply of the competitive fringe firms is labeled as S_F. ACME Insurance, the dominant firm in the market, derives its residual demand by subtracting the fringe supply from market demand at each and every price. At the price represented by point A, ACME offers no insurance on the market whereas ACME completely fills market orders for health insurance at a price indicated by point B. ACME's residual demand is thus found by the curve labeled as A-C-M-E. Following the usual procedure for a linear demand curve, ACME's marginal revenue curve, MR_{ACME}, is derived from its demand curve. ACME is assumed to be a lower cost producer than the competitive fringe and assumed to produce with constant marginal costs so the marginal cost curve is drawn as MC_{ACME}. To maximize profits where MR = MC, ACME sells Q_{ACME} amount of health insurance and charges P_{ACME}. The fringe firms take the price set by ACME and produce the rest of the market output indicated by the horizontal distance between Q_{ACME} and Q_T.

To maximize profits, the dominant firm must determine how much health insurance to sell and what price to charge given the market demand for health insurance and the competitive fringe supply.

Let's suppose that ACME Insurance Company represents the dominant health insurer in some market area. To maximize profits, ACME must first determine its residual demand. Residual demand equals the amount of health insurance left over for ACME in the market after deducting the amount of health insurance offered for sale by the competitive fringe insurers. Mathematically, ACME's residual demand is found by subtracting the quantity supplied of the competitive fringe insurers from market demand at each and every price. Figure 11–1 reflects the graphical derivation of the residual demand curve facing ACME. At a price represented by point A, ACME's residual demand equals zero because the fringe supply insurers completely satisfy market demand at that price. Oppositely, at a price indicated by point B, market demand equals ACME's residual demand because at that price, the competitive fringe insurers do not produce and sell any health insurance. In fact, at any price below point B, market demand also represents ACME's residual demand.

ACME's residual demand curve can be derived by drawing a line from point A to point C, opposite B on the market demand curve, and connecting it to the segment of the market demand curve labeled as ME. Thus, A-C-M-E represents ACME's kinked residual demand curve. Let's assume that section AC of ACME's demand curve represents the relevant range for price so the kink in its demand curve plays no role in the analysis. Given this assumption, ACME's marginal revenue curve can be derived from its demand curve. Recall from chapter 8 that the marginal revenue curve shares the same intercept as a linear demand curve but has twice its slope (in absolute terms). Following this procedure, ACME's marginal revenue curve is graphically depicted and labeled as MR_{ACME}.

One of the assumptions behind this model is that the dominant firm is a low cost producer. As a result, ACME's marginal cost curve is drawn below the fringe supply. Following the empirical studies previously discussed, it is further assumed that ACME produces health insurance with constant marginal costs, so a horizontal marginal cost curve is drawn.

To maximize profits, ACME sells the amount of health insurance indicated by Q_{ACME} because marginal revenue equals marginal costs at that point. ACME charges a price of P_{ACME} for its health insurance. As price-takers, the competitive fringe accepts the price set by ACME and produces the rest of the market demand as indicated by the horizontal distance between Q_{ACME} and Q_T. Conceptually that horizontal distance is the same as the one between the origin and the quantity read off the fringe supply curve at a price of P_{ACME}.

Several implications can be drawn from the dominant firm-pricing model. First, market price is lower because of the dominant firm. In our example, market price would be determined by the intersection of market demand and fringe supply at point A in figure 11–1 if ACME, with its lower costs, did not exist. However, if ACME acted competitively and charged a price corresponding to the marginal costs of production, market price would be even lower. In fact, if ACME set a price corresponding to its marginal costs, the competitive fringe would be driven from the market according to the graphical model in figure 11–1.

Second, the model implies that a larger competitive fringe causes the price set by the dominant firm to fall. In figure 11–1, a larger competitive fringe can be treated as a fringe supply located further to the right. If so, the residual demand facing ACME shifts downward to the left and thus market price falls. Third, a more elastic fringe supply also puts downward pressure on the market price set by the dominant firm according to the model. For example, if the fringe supply in figure 11–1 became flatter (more elastic) but pivoted off of the same vertical point, ACME's residual demand shifts downward to the left and price declines.

In sum, the dominant firm-pricing model is a useful conceptual device when considering the pricing behavior of a market characterized by a single dominant firm or a few dominant firms and containing a competitive fringe. The model suggests that even a dominant firm must consider the reaction of the smaller firms when setting prices. Moreover, the model predicts that the dominant firm faces more pressure to set a low price when the competitive fringe market share is greater and when the fringe supply is more responsive to price.

Other Issues Relating to the Pricing of Health Insurance

Health insurers determine premiums by using community or experience rating. When an insurance company uses **community rating**, the premium is based on the risk characteristics of its entire membership. However, pure community rates may differ by geographical location due to cost-of-living considerations, type of contract (individual or family), and benefit design (level of copayments, deductibles, and benefit coverage). Rates paid by individuals in the plan do not differ according to health history or status if premiums are community rated. As a result, some cross-subsidization among subscribers takes place as low-risk individuals subsidize high-risk individuals. That is, low-risk people pay more than their expected medical costs, and high-risk people pay less when the plan is community rated. For example, elderly and nonelderly subscribers pay the same community-rated premium even though elderly people use medical services more intensively.

In contrast, when premiums are determined using **experience rating**, insurers place individuals, or a group of individuals, into different risk categories based on various identifiable personal characteristics, such as age, gender, industrial occupation, and prior illnesses. Premiums are then based on geographical location, type of contract, and benefit design but also on the relation between risk category and expected health care costs as determined by using historical data. Under experience rating, individuals or groups of individuals pay a price closer to their expected medical costs.

In either case, a private health insurance company sets the premium equal to the expected benefits to be paid out (E[BEN]), plus any marketing and administrative expenses (ADMIN), federal, state, and local taxes (TAX), and profits (PROFIT), or

(11–1) $$\text{Premium} = \text{E[BEN]} + \text{ADMIN} + \text{TAX} + \text{PROFIT}.$$

The dollar benefits the insurance company expects to pay out are equal to the actual benefits, BEN, plus some forecast error, e; that is,

(11–2) $$\text{E[BEN]} = \text{BEN} + e.$$

Since people can expect to receive some of their premiums back in the form of reimbursed medical expenditures, health economists sometimes measure the price of insurance, or loading fee, using the ratio of premiums to actual benefits paid out, or Premium/BEN. The ratio can be obtained by substituting equation 11–2 into equation 11–1 and dividing by the actual dollar benefits paid out, or

(11–3) $$\text{Price} = 1 + \frac{\text{ADMIN} + \text{TAX} + \text{PROFIT} + e}{\text{BEN}}.$$

The price of health insurance reveals the average amount that must be spent in premiums to receive one dollar in benefits. For example, a price of $1.25 means the representative individual pays $1.25 to receive $1 in benefits, on average. The remaining 25 cents is the loading fee. The magnitude of the loading fee depends on a host of factors, including the administrative technology, tax laws, any forecast errors, and the competitive nature of the market for private health insurance (Sindelar, 1988).

In a competitive market, the loading fee is driven to a normal level, that is, a level that is sufficient to pay for necessary administrative and marketing costs, taxes, and a normal profit rate (if a for-profit insurer). Given that the health insurance industry seems reasonably competitive, at least in the group health insurance market, incentives most likely exist for some degree of price competition among health insurers.

However, many health insurers now compete not only on the basis of price (loading fee) but also on the ability to control health care costs—the actual health benefits paid out. Prior to the 1980s, the not-for-profit Blue Cross plans dominated many markets and were controlled by hospital interests. Lacking incentives, Blue Cross plans pursued a policy of

INSIGHT 11-1

Tracing the Profitability Cycle of Health Insurance

Over the past several decades, private health insurers have generally experienced three consecutive years of underwriting gains, followed by three consecutive years of underwriting losses, in the group health insurance market. This phenomenon is referred to as the **underwriting or profitability cycle.** The profitability cycle holds for both commercial insurers and not-for-profit Blue Cross and Blue Shield plans. Health insurance premium increases are shown to follow the profitability cycle with a lag of about two years (Gabel, Formisano, Lohr, and Di Carlo, 1991).

In seeking to explain the root cause of the cycle, Gabel, Formisano, Lohr, and Di Carlo point to three broad causes: supply and demand forces, industry pricing actions, and external factors. According to the authors, supply and demand forces can affect the profitability of health insurers in two ways.

First, because of free entry in health insurance markets, firms enter the market in times of excess profits. As a result, price falls and some firms experience losses and exit the market. Exit reduces supply, price increases, and profits return. The cycle begins once again.

Second, the "cobweb" model may explain the cycle. When the price of health insurance is relatively high in the present period, insurers act on the information by deciding to sell more insurance policies in the next period. The greater supply, in turn, leads to lower prices in the next period, especially because the demand for group health insurance is relatively price inelastic and modest supply changes lead to dramatic price changes. Hence, current prices affect future supply decisions, and this results in a continual cycling of prices and profits.

Industry pricing actions consider that insurers may reduce prices to increase market share and raise them later to compensate for past losses. In addition, actuarial pricing techniques often extrapolate the recent past to the future from recent claims experience. If decision makers form "adaptive expectations," they will systematically overestimate true premiums in periods of falling claims and underestimate true premiums in periods of rising claims. According to Gabel, Formisano, Lohr, and Di Carlo, this type of pricing behavior, although irrational, has been shown to result in a cyclical profitability pattern.

Another industry pricing explanation supposes that all insurers tacitly collude at first and follow the pricing pattern of the leader firm(s). At some point, however, individual firms are tempted to reduce prices to gain greater market share, and the informal cartel breaks down. Eventually, the pattern repeats itself.

Finally, external factors, including underlying claims events and general economic conditions, may cause the profitability cycle. That is, medical care costs and general factors ranging from the budget deficit, national unemployment, and interest rates may follow a business cycle pattern and generate the insurance profitability cycle.

No studies to date have tested the alternative explanations for the profitability cycle. A lack of suitable data most likely accounts for the void in the literature. In a more recent study, Gabel and Jensen (1992) point to industry pricing policies as the primary culprit behind the profitability cycle. Specifically, they write,

Because insurers forecast a continuation of the experience of the recent past in the future, they systematically understate and overstate trends. As sellers of a substitutable product in a competitive market, and based on erroneous projections of future costs, when earning underwriting profits, insurers attempt to increase market share by underpricing their competitors, only to face financial losses subsequently. This sets up the next phase of catch-up pricing, where premiums increase by excessive double digit amounts (p. 260).

One of the most important lessons of this insight is that premium increases must be properly interpreted in the context of the profitability cycle. To say that premium increases are low this year does not mean some trend of low premium increases has set in. Rather, the low premium increases of today may mean tomorrow's premium increases will be larger if the profitability cycle continues to hold.

encouraging complete health insurance coverage. The policy led to high hospital prices and medical costs and elevated health insurance premiums (Hay and Leahy, 1987). Now most insurers are forced by the cost consciousness of their payers to control health benefits paid out by adopting managed-care practices. Thus, competition has created an incentive for health insurers to hold down both the loading fee and actual medical benefits paid out.

In trying to contain both the loading fee and benefits paid, health insurers now face an interesting trade-off. Managed care contains health care costs (or benefits paid out) most effectively through various administrative functions such as utilization review. However, more spending on administrative functions leads to a higher loading fee (see equation 11–3). Economic principles suggest that an insurer chooses the optimal amount of an input by equating its marginal benefit and marginal cost. Hence, the optimal amount of administrative services occurs when the marginal medical cost savings (marginal benefit) equals the price (marginal cost) of an additional administrative input. Cost containment means that managed-care activities will continue to increase in scope and, consequently, larger loading fees are likely to result. The magnitude of the premium level, the sum of benefits paid out, and the loading fee will reflect the overall success or failure of managed-care activities. With that idea in mind, the following section discusses the role and effects of managed-care organizations.

Managed-Care Organizations and Insurance Premiums

Managed-care organizations (MCOs), which include HMOs and PPOs, integrate the delivery of health care with the insurance function. Advocates have claimed that MCOs are capable of reducing the level and growth of health insurance premiums. The reduction of health insurance premiums comes about in two ways. First, because MCOs are prepaid, they face a profit incentive to contain medical costs by adopting utilization controls and by negotiating discounted medical prices. In response to competition, MCOs lower health insurance premiums in line with the actual costs of servicing their own subscribers.

Second, the competition from MCOs motivates traditional insurers to make similar improvements in utilization and costs and to reduce their premiums or face the prospect of losing business.

As will be discussed in Chapter 13, a host of studies (e.g., Manning et al., 1984; Rapoport, 1992; Miller and Luft, 1994) have found that MCOs, especially HMOs, attain medical cost savings of about 15 to 20 percent through a reduced hospital-intensive practice style.[2] The question is whether the reduced medical costs brought on by managed care translate into lower premiums system-wide. According to Morrisey (2001), the answer to this question depends on the degree to which employers change plans in response to lower premiums, the extent to which competition among managed-care plans leads to lower managed-care premiums, and how lower managed-care premiums influence the premiums of traditional insurers. As discussed in Chapter 6, the few studies examining choice of plans from the perspective of the employer found relatively high premium elasticities ranging as high as –8 when multiple plans are offered and employees must pay more for expensive plans. Consequently, available studies, for the most part, suggest that employers do respond to lower premiums.

In terms of whether managed-care premiums decline, some economists point out that the greater administrative costs (loading fee) associated with MCOs may swamp any medical cost savings (benefits paid out) as previously pointed out. McLaughlin (1988) argues that the health insurance market initially responded to managed-care insurance with cost-increasing rivalry, not price competition, as both traditional and managed-care insurers have chosen to compete on service offering rather than on price.

Feldman, Dowd, and Gifford (1993) note that "many companies accuse HMOs of 'shadow-pricing,' that is, setting their premiums just below that of commercial carriers. HMOs can profit from shadow pricing if they tend to enroll a disproportionate share of young, healthy workers in the firm" (p. 781). The authors compared the weighted average HMO and fee-for-service (FFS) premiums in firms that offer both HMOs and FFS plans to the premium of FFS-only firms. They found that offering a HMO plan raises rather than lowers the average premium of an insurance policy for family and single coverage. Insurance premiums rise if HMOs skim the healthiest patients and thereby drive up FFS costs and premiums (Baker and Corts, 1995).

Studies using more recent data, however, support the notion that competition among managed-care companies has led to lower managed-care premiums. Wholey, Feldman, and Christianson (1995) used multiple regression analysis to examine the impact of HMO competition and penetration on the level of HMO premiums in various metropolitan areas of the United States for the years 1988 to 1991. The authors found that a greater number of HMOs in the market area resulted in lower HMO premiums. Higher penetration of HMOs was also found to be associated with reduced HMO premiums.

As a complementary study, Pauly, Hillman, Kim, and Brown (2002) analyzed the impact of competition among HMOs on their profitability using a sample of 262 U.S. metropolitan areas in 1994. Competition was measured by the number of HMOs and also by the relative size distribution of the various HMOs in each metropolitan area. The authors found that greater competition among HMOs tends to be associated with lower profit rates, as

---

[2]See the various health care industry studies in the following chapters for detailed information about the relation between managed care and medical cost savings.

measured by metropolitan areawide HMO profits divided by the comparable premium revenues. For example, their simulation showed that profits decline by about 12 to 30 percent if one new HMO enters the market with a 10 percent share. The authors also found that high profitability did not persist over the period 1994 to 1997, suggesting that entry and expansion forced HMOs to actively compete.

Empirical studies have also examined if lower managed-care premiums influence the premiums of traditional insurers and system-wide premiums levels. Wickizer and Feldstein (1995) used multiple regression analysis to isolate and examine the impact of the HMO market penetration rate on the growth of indemnity premiums for 95 insured groups over the period 1985 to 1992. They found empirically that the HMO penetration rate had an inverse impact on the growth of indemnity premiums. As an illustration, they estimate that the real rate of growth in premiums would be approximately 5.9 instead of 7 percent for the average group located in a market where the HMO penetration rate increased by 25 percent. The authors concluded by noting that their results "indicate that competitive strategies, relying on managed care, have significant potential to reduce health insurance premium growth rates, thereby resulting in substantial cost savings over time (p. 250)."

Baker, Cantor, Long, and Marquis (2000) investigated the impact of HMO market penetration on the costs of employer-sponsored health insurance. Using data for over 20,000 private employers in both 1993 and 1997, the authors found that costs for employer health plans were about 8 to 10 percent lower in metropolitan areas with an HMO market penetration rate above 45 percent than ones with HMO market penetration rates below 25 percent. The result reflects both lower HMO premiums as well as lower premiums for non-HMO plans in markets where the HMO penetration rate exceeds 25 percent. This latter result refutes the notion that HMOs achieve savings by only selecting the healthiest and least expensive patients because, if so, non-HMO premiums would increase with greater HMO penetration.

In sum, MCOs, particularly HMOs, have achieved sizeable medical cost savings from various utilization and cost-control techniques. Recent studies have tended to find that these cost savings have translated into lower premiums provided that a sufficient degree of competition exists among HMOs. In addition, recent evidence suggests that system-wide premiums savings result from increased penetration and competition of HMOs.

Do HMOs Possess Monopsony Power?

As we know, monopoly involves a single seller of a well-defined product for which there are no close substitutes. According to economic theory, a monopolist results in a restriction of output and thereby creates a deadweight loss reflecting an inefficient allocation of resources. A market may also be characterized by a **monopsony**, which involves a single buyer of a good or service. When a monopsony exists in an otherwise competitive marketplace, economic theory suggests that both the price and quantity of the product are lower than the competitive model predicts. Figure 11–2 clarifies the economic logic behind this point by examining the impact of a hypothetical monopsonist in the market for hospital services. The price and quantity of inpatient days are shown on the vertical and horizontal axes, respectively. Market demand and supply are labeled D and S, respectively (ignore the MFC curve for now).

In a competitive market consisting of a large number of buyers and sellers, each individual buyer and seller acts as a price taker. For example, suppose we view the market for

FIGURE 11–2

Monopsony Model of the Market for Hospital Services

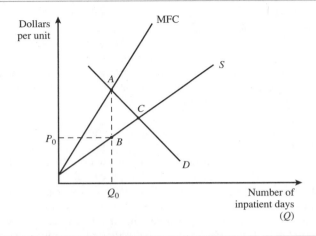

Point C in the graph indicates the competitive outcome when all market participants are price takers. The MFC curve represents the incremental cost of purchasing an additional patient day when the insurer has monopsony power. In this case, the monopsonist purchases hospital inpatient days up to the point where the demand curve crosses the marginal factor cost curve, Q_0, and pays P_0. Notice that when the buyer has monopsony power both price and quantity are lower than the competitive level.

hospital services as containing a relatively large number of hospitals supplying services and a large number of health insurance companies negotiating hospital prices on behalf of subscribers. If each health insurer and each hospital represents only a tiny fraction of the total market, all market participants can be treated as price takers. In effect, each health insurer faces a horizontal individual supply curve (rather than market supply) of hospital services and, given its inconsequential market share, can purchase hospital services without influencing its market price. Each hospital, also as a price taker, faces a horizontal or perfectly elastic demand for its product and cannot influence the market price of hospital services. As all of the hospitals and health insurers each act as price takers, competitive equilibrium occurs at point C in figure 11–2, as supply and demand theory suggests.

Now, instead of a large number of health insurers with tiny individual market shares, suppose only one health insurer, as a monopsonist, covers all of the people and represents the only purchaser of hospital services in an area. However, continue to suppose the existence of a large number of hospitals with relatively small market shares such that each hospital can be treated as a price taker. As a monopsonist, the health insurer faces the market supply curve for hospital services, which is positively sloped reflecting the higher costs for hospitals when supplying additional inpatient days. The positively sloped supply curve means that the monoponist must pay a higher price to negotiate a greater number of inpatient days at the beginning of the contract period. Assuming the health insurer practices uniform pricing, the monopsonistic health insurer must not only pay a higher price for any higher cost additional patient days but also for the other lower cost patient days. Since the monopsonist must pay a higher price for each and every day when purchasing an additional inpatient day, the total incremental cost to the insurer of purchasing an additional day exceeds the average cost per inpatient day as revealed by supply. As a result, the marginal factor cost (MFC) associated with an additional patient day lies above market supply, as depicted by the MFC curve in figure 11–2.

To determine the profit-maximizing amount of inpatient days to purchase from the hospitals, the monopsonistic health insurer equates demand to marginal factor cost. In the figure, the profit-maximizing number of inpatient days occurs at Q_0. The price necessary to attract this number of inpatient days from the various hospitals in this area can be read off the supply curve as P_0. Thus monopsony theory suggests that a single buyer pays a lower price and purchases a lower quantity than the competitive level typically indicates. Similar to a monopoly situation, a deadweight loss of the triangular area ACB results as a result of the monopsonistic distortion, reflecting an inefficient allocation of resources. Monopsony, like monopoly, is clearly undesirable from a societal point of view.

Feldman and Wholey (2001) investigated whether HMOs have monopsony power in the markets for ambulatory and inpatient hospital services. They used a data set containing all of the HMOs in the United States from 1985 through 1997. The authors used multiple regression analysis to investigate the importance of an HMO as a buyer on both the price paid and utilization. Feldman and Wholey rightfully argue that monopsony theory predicts that *both* price and quantity should decline with the importance of an HMO as a buyer. Finding that price declines is not enough to indicate monopsony power because HMOs, through their buying power, may simply "beat back" or countervail the monopoly power of medical suppliers rather than drive price below the competitive level.

In their study, HMO buying power for hospital services was measured by the percentage of community hospital days in the market area that was purchased by the HMO. HMO buying power for ambulatory services was measured by the number of ambulatory visits purchased by the HMO per 1,000 active physicians in the market area. The dependent variables in the various regression equations were the prices paid by individual HMOs for ambulatory care and inpatient hospital days and, as utilization measures, the annual number of ambulatory visits and hospital days per member. Feldman and Wholey also controlled for a host of other supply and demand factors that influence price and utilization in the regression analysis. Their empirical results showed that HMO buying power over hospitals had a negative and significant effect on hospital price per day but no impact on the price of ambulatory visits. They also found that HMO buying power led to increased hospital use but had no statistically significant effect on ambulatory visits. Feldman and Wholey note that their results support the "monopoly busting" and not the monopsony view of HMO buying power. They also suggest that HMO buying power has improved the efficiency of markets for hospital services.

Cherry-Picking Behavior and Benefit Denial

Many health care experts believe that competition among insurers in conjunction with experience rating provides an incentive for insurers, as a group, to offer health insurance to healthy individuals but deny coverage to people with poor health. The best cherries (the healthy) are picked off the tree, while the worst are left dangling. The reasoning behind the cherry-picking behavior is rather straightforward. Facing increased market competition, insurers are forced to lower premiums. One way to lower premiums is to insure only low-risk individuals. The end result is that health insurance companies tend to compete for low-risk individuals, that is, healthy people. Those in poor health are either denied access to health insurance or charged prohibitively high prices.

Individuals who belong to large, employment-based group policies, which are the predominant form of private health insurance in the United States, are relatively insulated from this problem. While premiums for experience-rated group policies are adjusted annually based on the actual claims experience of the group and changes in medical care prices, the total cost is distributed equally among all group members, thus minimizing the burden for any one individual.

In contrast, people who lack access to large-group coverage have difficulty obtaining health insurance at comparable premiums. People who apply for insurance, either individually, as a family, or through small businesses, are usually subject to stringent insurance underwriting procedures because providing insurance to these individuals is much riskier. A health status questionnaire or physical exam is normally required. Depending on the resulting risk status of the individual(s), insurance companies usually offer health insurance at an increased premium and/or exclude coverage for any preexisting conditions for a period of one year or more. Preexisting conditions are serious illnesses that were diagnosed before the policy took effect and might include cancer, heart disease, AIDS, or care for low-birthweight babies. Conditions that trigger higher rates vary widely across insurance companies but routinely include such common conditions as hypertension, allergies, arthritis, and asthma. Thus, for individual purchasers of health insurance, especially those with chronic health problems or high-risk conditions, high premiums may be an obstacle to obtaining coverage.

Health insurers may practice cherry-picking (or equivalently, cream-skimming) behavior in a number of subtler ways depending upon what information they possess (Van De Ven and Ellis, 2000). If unable to identify the health risks of individuals in the market and what the precise health risks are, insurers may structure their health insurance coverage so high-risk individuals reveal themselves. For example, the benefits package may not cover prescription drugs or may contain high out-of-pocket expenses. If insurers know the precise health risks such as AIDs but not the risk characteristics of specific individuals, they may not contract with physicians known to treat patients with high-cost illnesses. Finally, if insurers can predict unprofitable individuals, marketing strategies might be focused away from high-risk individuals and towards low-risk individuals.

While this view of cherry-picking behavior and access denial is generally accepted at face value, empirical studies on this topic have been relatively lacking. The only study to date, by Beauregard (1991), used data from the 1987 National Medical Expenditure Survey to estimate the number of uninsured people who were denied private health insurance or could purchase only limited coverage because of poor health.

Beauregard's study found that benefit denial is not as widespread as typically believed. In particular, only a very small proportion of the uninsured population, less than 1 percent, was found to have ever been denied private health insurance due to poor health. However, the author cautions that the figure does not include currently insured individuals whose policies exclude coverage for preexisting conditions. In 1995, about 60 percent of group health insurance plans excluded coverage for preexisting conditions. Moreover, 10 months was the average waiting period before a new employee receives coverage for a preexisting condition (Jensen et al., 1997). Finally, Beauregard's findings do not consider the number of individuals who do not apply for private health insurance because they fear denial.

Adverse Selection and Community versus Experience Rating

Adverse selection is a situation where an information asymmetry can lead to undesirable results in insurance markets (Rothschild and Stiglitz, 1976). Adverse selection occurs when high-risk consumers who know more about their own health status than insurers do subscribe to an insured group composed of lower-risk individuals. To secure low premiums, the high-risk consumers withhold information concerning their true health status. Once insured, the insurer has no alternative but to increase premiums on all plan subscribers in the next period due to the higher-utilization rates of high-risk consumers. As low-risk subscribers leave the high-priced plans, "musical insurance plans" result as high-risk individuals follow low-risk individuals in pursuit of lower premiums. In addition, some insurers may find it difficult to earn a normal profit. Alternatively, some low-risk individuals may eventually find it cheaper to self-insure. If so, high-risk individuals will end up in homogeneous pools paying high premiums or being excluded from health insurance coverage.

INSIGHT 11-2

Adoption of Health Insurance Reform in New York State

As of April 1, 1993, the state of New York requires that health insurers adopt community rating and guarantee issue for all individual and small-group policies. Insurers must accept all applicants and charge all policyholders the same premium regardless of health status, gender, occupation, or age (State Health Watch, 1994). The law intends to prevent insurance companies from taking all the good risks and leaving the bad ones, thereby providing individuals with greater access to health insurance. One concern was that community rating would lead to a reduction in the number of individuals covered because low-risk individuals would choose not to purchase health insurance. Another concern was that premiums would increase as insurers and low-risk individuals left the market because of community rating.

Hall (2000) found that the reform had a profound impact on the operation and performance of the market for individual health insurance coverage in New York State. Among the effects of the reforms, Hall analyzed enrollment patterns, pricing, rate shocks, adverse selection, and market structure. With respect to enrollment, Hall found that following the enactment of the health insurance reform, the percentage of the nonelderly population without insurance in New York worsened from 16.5 percent in 1992, which was below the national average, to 18.3 percent in 1994, which was above the national average. Enrollment in both the individual and small group markets declined after the reform but enrollment in the small group market rebounded in the following year whereas membership in individual plans continued to decline until 1997.

In terms of pricing, indemnity rates for individual policies rose by approximately 40 percent per year for the first two years following reform compared to rate increases of 10 to 14 percent for similar small group policies. HMO rates for individual coverage rose much less dramatically, but the increases were considerably greater than small group market

(continued)

HMO coverage. Evidence of rate shock was also found. About 20 percent of small group and 25 percent of individual subscribers received rate increases of 40 percent or more, while about 10 percent of small group and 20 percent of individual subscribers received rate decreases of 20 percent or more following the 1993 reform.

Hall also determined that adverse selection took place in the market for individual coverage. As Hall notes: "Community rating increases costs for healthier subscribers, thereby at the margin driving some from the market, and guarantee issue attracts higher risks into the market. The combined effect was expected by some to set into place an adverse selection spiral that would cause the market to collapse into a high-risk pool" (p. 86). Data suggest that significant adverse selection occurred in the individual market. For example, in the year prior to the reform, the average age of Mutual of Omaha's New York enrollees increased by .2 years each quarter but three years after reform the quarterly increase in average age jumped to .77 years.

Finally, Hall examined the impact of the reform on market structure. He found that there was a sizeable exodus of indemnity insurers from New York's individual market following reform. Nine withdrew immediately and two more withdrew within the first year or so, leaving Mutual of Omaha as the only significant commercial insurer and a number of smaller companies. Even those indemnity insurers that remained raised their deductibles on insurance policies to such a height that essentially they sold only catastrophic coverage. Hall concludes by noting: "it seems likely that New York's individual market will become essentially a widely dispersed high-risk pool funded by HMOs and Blue Cross plans in which enrollment will continue to shrink and rates will continue to rise faster than medical inflation" (p. 98).

An unstable environment of this kind is undesirable because it imposes substantial adjustment costs on society as people continually change insurers and insurers adjust employment levels to meet demand. In fact, the unstable environment may be one reason health insurers have been reluctant to pay for preventative types of care such as annual physical exams. Why should the insurer pay for the yearly exam when, in all likelihood, the benefits of reduced future medical costs cannot be appropriated because individuals have changed plans?

Insurers can prevent adverse selection to some degree by limiting people's ability to change plans or through prior screening and experience rating. However, experience rating, which charges different premiums to individuals based on risk status, is often viewed as being unfair and costly. Many argue that experience rating is inequitable because some people are charged a higher price for insurance simply because of their poor health status. The inequity of experience rating is particularly acute when the poor health status is uncontrollable rather than a function of a chosen adverse lifestyle. It is further claimed that experience rating encourages cherry-picking behavior and causes higher administrative expenses as insurers laboriously sift through applicants to find low-risk individuals. It has been pointed out that if insurers community-rated and accepted all applicants for coverage, they would be more interested in creating system-wide medical cost savings rather than choosing among individual low-risk subscribers.

Others, however, point to the inefficiency and inequity of community rating. Under a community rating scheme, low-risk individuals are discouraged from purchasing insurance because the premium is set higher than their expected medical costs. Consequently, low-risk individuals are made worse off by community rating. Also, it is claimed that experience rating creates an incentive for people to adopt favorable lifestyles. That is, if people are required to pay more for health insurance because they smoke cigarettes or drink excessively, they will be more inclined to practice good health behaviors. Advocates of experience rating also claim there is no good reason why high-risk people are likely to be less wealthy than low-risk people, and thus a community rating system can end up redistributing income from the poor to the rich. For example, young low-income individuals may subsidize wealthy elderly individuals under a community rating system.

THE PERFORMANCE OF THE PRIVATE HEALTH INSURANCE INDUSTRY

The structural characteristics of the private health insurance industry imply that individual insurers may be pressured to behave competitively. While a few large health insurers typically dominate the industry in most states, low barriers to entry and a large competitive fringe most likely create incentives for price competition. Health insurers in the group health insurance segment of the industry face additional pressure to behave competitively because large employers may self-insure.

According to some of the topics covered in the section on conduct, however, unfettered competition in the private health insurance industry may not be totally desirable. One reason is that unchecked price competition encourages cherry-picking behavior and denial of coverage for preexisting conditions by health insurers. Such behavior limits the ability of the private health insurance industry to provide universal health insurance coverage, which is a primary goal of many health policymakers. In addition, critics have claimed that the private health insurance industry has failed to contain health care costs.

In this section, we examine evidence on the performance of the private health insurance industry more thoroughly. We will consider measures capturing the price and output of health insurance and underinsurance and overinsurance.

Output of Private Health Insurers

Private Health Insurance Coverage One measure of the performance of an industry is the amount of output provided. Incentives should exist so suppliers produce the optimal amount of a product—neither too much nor too little. In the case of the private health insurance industry, optimal provision implies that the right number of people are covered by private health insurance and each person is neither overinsured nor underinsured. Theoretically, the right number of insured individuals occurs at the level where the marginal social benefit and marginal social cost of health insurance coverage are equal. Those pushing strongly for universal health insurance coverage in the United States apparently believe that marginal social benefit exceeds costs at all levels of the population.

Table 11–1 sheds some light on the first aspect of optimal insurance coverage by providing data on the number and percentage of people with private health insurance over time in the United States. A number of observations can be drawn from the data. First,

TABLE 11–1
Persons with Private Health Insurance Coverage, Selected Years, 1940–2000

Year	Number (millions)	Percentage of Population
1940	12.0	9.1%
1945	32.0	22.9
1950	76.6	50.3
1960	122.5	67.8
1970	158.8	77.4
1980	187.4	82.5
1990	182.1	73.0
1995	185.9	70.7
2000	200.2	71.0

SOURCE: *Source Book of Health Insurance Data 1999–2000.* Washington, D.C.: Health Insurance Association of America, Table 2.10, and U.S. Census Bureau, *Health Insurance Coverage 2000* at http://www.census.gov/hhes/www/hlthins.htm.

notice how the number of privately insured individuals skyrocketed from 12 to 200 million, or from 9 percent to 71 percent of the population from 1940 to 2000. The tremendous jump in private insurance coverage during the 1940s reflects the point made at the beginning of this chapter about how employers offered health insurance as a tax-exempt fringe benefit during the wage and price control period of World War II.

The 1950s and 1960s witnessed further huge increases in private insurance enrollments. Enrollments in private insurances expanded, in part, because of the declining health insurance prices during that time as a result of experience-rated premiums. According to Morrisey (2001) "commercial insurers identified employer groups that had lower than average claims experience and offered them premiums lower than those charged by the then dominant carrier, Blue Cross" (p. 209). Also notice that the percentage of people covered by private health insurance reached a peak of over 80 percent in 1980 but declined thereafter. Several factors account for the decline in the percentage of privately insured individuals after 1980.

One simple reason for the relative decline in private health insurance coverage is the increasing percentage of people 65 years of age and older who are eligible for Medicare coverage because of their age. Recall that Medicare took effect in the late 1960s. Rising health insurance premiums provide the second and probably most significant reason for the decline in private health insurance coverage. Specifically, health insurance premiums rose rapidly from the mid-1980s to early 1994, causing many employers, mostly small businesses, to either raise employee contributions or drop their health insurance coverage altogether (Acs, 1995).

A third explanation for declining coverage deals with occupational shifts from traditionally higher coverage manufacturing sector jobs to lower coverage service sector jobs. However, Long and Rodgers (1995) find employment shifts explain only about 15 percent of the decline in employer provided private health insurance coverage. The final reason for declining coverage is the growing fraction of people covered by Medicaid. For example, almost 22 million people were covered by Medicaid in 1980. This same figure mushroomed to nearly 41 million people by 1998 (See table 10–1). While many people became eligible for Medicaid coverage because they lost private health insurance coverage due to the reasons previously mentioned, a study by Cutler and Gruber (1995) found that liberalized government programs caused some families to drop their private health insurance coverage in favor of Medicaid. Hence, public coverage crowded out private coverage (see Insight 10–2).

Who Are the Uninsured?   Although the long-term growth of private health insurance coverage has been fairly impressive, about 38.7 million people, or 14 percent of the population, were uninsured during the entire year in 2000, even after allowing for public health insurance coverage. As we will mention later, the uninsured are particularly disadvantaged financially, physically, and psychologically, because they lack health insurance coverage. Policymakers generally wish to know which groups and individuals are more at risk so that policies might be properly designed to reduce the number of people who are uninsured. Let us examine which groups and individuals are more likely to be uninsured.

Mills (2001) reached a number of conclusions regarding who represent the uninsured in the United States. First, almost 30 percent of the poor had no health insurance of any kind during 2000 despite the existence of Medicaid. Second, about 27 percent of the individuals in the age group 19 to 24 were found to be uninsured. Typically, young adults who are not full-time students and who are excluded from parental insurance have jobs that offer no health insurance coverage.

Third, larger percentages of blacks and Hispanics than whites were uninsured. About 19 percent of blacks and 32 percent of Hispanics were uninsured in 2000, compared to 10 percent of whites not of Hispanic origin. Fourth, among adults, the likelihood of being uninsured declined with educational attainment. For example, 27 percent of the individuals without a high school diploma were uninsured whereas only 7.1 percent of those with a bachelor's degree or higher lacked health insurance coverage. (Curiously, among the poor, educational attainment had little if any impact on health insurance coverage.)

Fifth, part-time workers and those without a job were more likely to be uninsured compared to those who worked full-time during the year. Specifically, about 21 percent of part-time workers and 24 percent of the unemployed lack health insurance coverage compared to a figure of 15 percent for full-time workers. However, among the poor, nonworkers were more likely to be insured than workers. Sixth, noncoverage rates fall as household income rises. For example, slightly under 23 percent of households, with annual incomes of $25,000 or less, lacked health insurance coverage. The comparable figure for households with annual incomes of $75,000 or more was only 6.9 percent. Finally, health insurance coverage was found to rise with firm size. Only 31.6 percent of the workers in firms hiring less than 25 workers had health insurance coverage in 2000 compared to an overall average of 57 percent for all firms and a rate of 69.8 percent in firms hiring 500 or more persons.

Problems with Measuring the Uninsured   Some critics argue that the reported statistic for the uninsured is deceptive because it masks some other underlying problems. Some believe the true percentage is much higher because the reported rate fails to count underinsured people and ignores **job lock**, the idea that nonportable employer-provided health insurance limits job mobility. The 1990 report of the Pepper Commission defines **underinsurance** as

> *health insurance that leaves the person covered at risk of spending more than 10 percent of income on health care in the event of a costly illness. An estimated 13*

percent of the under-65 population were underinsured by this definition in 1981—about 20 million people in 1982. (Bodenheimer, 1992)

The nonportability of employer-sponsored health insurance means workers and their dependents face the possibility of being without health insurance while the former are between jobs. Long waiting periods, preexisting health conditions, and the potential for less extensive health insurance coverage at the new job all increase the financial risk associated with costly, unanticipated medical events. In addition, the resulting job lock disrupts the proper functioning of a macroeconomy because workers are discouraged from switching to more efficient jobs. The resulting immobility of labor resources leads to a lower level of labor productivity and national income. Whether job lock truly inhibits job mobility is a concern for many health care policymakers.

Cooper and Monheit (1993) used data from the 1987 National Medical Expenditure Survey to examine the severity of job lock. They empirically studied the factors influencing job mobility, including workers' insurance status at the initial job and the prospects of obtaining coverage at a new job, initial wages and expected wage offers at new employment, other fringe benefits, and workers' and dependents' health status. The authors found that those individuals most likely to change jobs are young workers with little experience, part-time workers, people with limited education, and workers earning low hourly wages.

More important for our concerns, Cooper and Monheit found that married men who expect to lose health insurance coverage are 23 percent less likely to change jobs. Madrian (1994) concurs with Cooper and Monheit's findings and estimates that job lock reduces the voluntary employment turnover rate of married men with employer-provided health insurance by 25 percent, from 16 percent to 12 percent per year.[3]

As a result, some people argue that the reported statistic underestimates the true extent of uninsured individuals due to underinsurance and job lock concerns. Others believe the reported uninsured rate provides an overestimate. As mentioned earlier, a large percentage of young individuals lack health insurance. Most of them are healthy and are without coverage only briefly. Because young, single adults may view the price of health insurance as too high and the risk of uninsurance as low, they may choose to be uninsured.

Another issue concerns how long individuals remain in an uninsured state. The reported rate measures the number of uninsured for the entire year, and does not consider the duration of the uninsured spell. Swartz (1994) explains that the median spell without health insurance is about six months. A median uninsured spell of six months means 50 percent of all spells without insurance are rather short and end before six months. However, another 50 percent of spells last longer than six months. At least 28 percent of uninsured spells last more than one year, and 15 to 18 percent last more than two years. Being uninsured, as Swartz notes,

frequently means receiving fewer services than insured patients and running a higher risk of dying when hospitalized. Even with fewer services, being hospitalized without health insurance is expensive. At a minimum, we can speculate that the nearly 3.5 million people hospitalized during an uninsured spell in 1992 had $7 billion worth of hospital expenses. For the 58 million people who had at least

---

[3]But compare these two studies to Kapur (1998).

1 month without insurance during 1992, the fear of being unlucky and drawing the "go to a hospital" card with its chancy care and high bills is real. (p. 65)

Some of the spells without private health insurance reflect the fact that people are between jobs. Seventy-three percent of employees covered by health insurance work for companies that require a waiting period averaging three months before extending medical insurance benefits to a new employee (Steinmetz, 1993). Swartz, Marcotte, and McBride (1993) found that monthly family income, educational attainment, and industry of employment in the month prior to losing health insurance are the characteristics that have the greatest impact on the duration of a spell without health insurance.

Health Insurance Portability and Accountability Act of 1996   Concern over the nonportability of health insurance, lengthy waiting periods for preexisting conditions, and insurance benefit denial led to the passage of the Health Insurance Portability and Accountability Act (HIPAA) in 1996. The basic idea behind HIPAA was to make it more difficult for health insurers to segment insurance risk pools and deny or revoke access to specific individuals or groups on the basis of health status. Considered by many as the most significant federal health care reform legislation since the passage of the Medicare and Medicaid programs in 1965, HIPAA created the first national standards for the availability and portability of group and individual health insurance coverage.

Prior to HIPAA (or Kassebaum/Kennedy Act) uniform standards were lacking in the health insurance industry for two reasons. First, states had been granted authority over health insurers within their jurisdictions by the McCarran-Ferguson Act of 1945 (Nichols and Blumberg, 1998). Some states chose to aggressively regulate and set standards in the health insurance industry; others did not. Second, the federal government has full responsibility for self-insured plans under the Employee Retirement Income Security Act (ERISA) of 1974. States are therefore unable to regulate the health insurance of a large percentage of U.S. workers. Furthermore, no federal regulations existed regarding the availability and portability of health insurance for self-insured plans.

HIPAA has wide-sweeping implications as the law generally applies to all health plans, including large and small group plans, state regulated plans, self-funded ERISA plans, indemnity and HMO plans, and individual plans. The major provisions as they relate to the health insurance industry are:[4]

Guaranteed Access and Renewability

1. With certain exceptions, insurers participating in the small group market (2 through 50 employees) cannot exclude a small employer or any of the employer's eligible employees from coverage on the basis of health status.
2. Eligibility or continued eligibility of any individual to enroll in a group plan, regardless of size, cannot be conditioned on the following health-related factors: health status, medical condition (physical or mental), claims experience, receipt of health care, medical history, genetic information, or evidence of insurability or disability.

---

[4]There are other provisions regarding such things as medical savings accounts, tax deductibility of health insurance costs for the self-employed, long-term care insurance, and life insurance.

3. Individuals within a group plan cannot be charged a higher premium based on their health status. This requirement does not restrict the amount an employer may be charged for coverage under a group plan.

4. Except for certain specific exceptions (e.g., fraud, nonpayment, discontinuance of market coverage), all group coverage in both the small and large group markets and individual coverage must be renewed.

5. Generally, individual insurers must provide coverage to individuals coming off of group insurance if the individual had previous coverage for 18 months, was not eligible for other group coverage, was not terminated from the previous plan due to nonpayment, and was not eligible or had exhausted COBRA-type coverage.[5]

6. Individual insurers must guarantee to provide at least two policies. These two policies may be the insurer's most popular plans, based on premium volume, or a package of lower-level and higher-level coverage plans based on actuarial averages. The latter plans must be covered under a risk-spreading mechanism. States may elect to institute an approved alternate mechanism to provide the transition from group to individual coverage.

Portability

1. Employees moving from one employer to another (and individuals coming off group coverage to individual coverage) are protected against a newly imposed preexisting condition limitation. In general, a plan may not impose a new preexisting condition if no more than 63 days have passed between covered jobs, not including any applicable employer waiting period for new hires. The plan must also give credit for the portion of the preexisting condition satisfied under a prior plan, which can include individual coverage, dependent coverage, etc.

2. There is a maximum exclusion period for preexisting conditions. The period is no more than 12 months, or 18 months for a late enrollee. The look-back period to determine a preexisting condition is no more than six months prior to the person's enrollment date.

3. Preexisting condition exclusions may not apply in the case of pregnancies, or for newborns and adopted children who are covered by insurance 30 days from the date of birth or adoption.

By setting national standards, proponents hope that HIPAA will encourage health insurers to compete more on the basis of efficiency and quality rather than risk selection. Moreover, by setting national standards for availability and portability, it is hoped that there will be greater opportunities for risk-pooling. Opponents fear that the reforms will raise the price of health insurance to individuals and thereby reduce the number of insured individuals. It should be pointed out that HIPAA does not change how health care is delivered or how it is financed. Moreover, HIPAA does not increase access to health insurance for the uninsured or regulate the rates that health plans can charge (Atchinson and Fox, 1997). While HIPAA represents a major step, advocates of health care reform believe there is much more work to be done in health insurance markets.

---

[5]The Consolidated Omnibus Reconciliation Act of 1985 (COBRA) requires employers to offer their former employees an option to purchase health insurance for a maximum of 18 months after termination of employment. The employee must pay the full premium plus a 2 percent administration fee.

INSIGHT 11–3

Who Pays for Employer-Mandated Health Insurance?

To reduce the number of uninsured, various policymakers over the years have pushed for an employer-mandated health insurance program in the United States. For example, Clinton's ill-fated National Health Security Act of 1993 required that employers provide health insurance to their full-time employees and finance at least 80 percent of the premiums. As a result, many believed, at the time, that employees would pay the remaining 20 percent of the mandated health insurance costs.

Economic principles suggest, however, that the actual economic incidence of a mandate (or tax) may differ from its statutory or legal incidence. For example, in the case of employer-mandated health insurance, it might be the case that employers simply pass on their legal share of the mandate to the employee in the form of lower wages. If so, the employee could actually pay the entire cost of the mandate.

Lee (1996) provides a conceptual model that can be used to examine who pays for an employer-mandated health insurance program. The model is presented graphically in figure 1. The figure depicts a competitive labor market in equilibrium where W stands for the

FIGURE 1

The Impact of an Employer Mandate on a Labor Market

(continued)

annual money wage and L represents the number of full-time workers. Assuming no health insurance benefits are initially provided, equilibrium is at point W_0, L_0, where the supply and demand curves intersect. We will now compare this initial equilibrium to one with a mandated health insurance program.

According to Lee's analysis, the mandate shifts both the supply and demand curves. The demand curve shifts downward by the amount of the per-employee cost of the insurance program, M. The shift of the demand curve from D_0 to D_1 reflects that any insurance costs must be potentially offset by wage reductions given that each worker generates a particular amount of revenues for a company. The interesting question then becomes: What happens to the supply of labor?

Just as the shift in demand reflects the per-employee cost of the health insurance, the shift in the supply curve captures the benefit of the mandated insurance to the typical employee. If the supply curve shifts downward by the dollar amount of the mandated benefit, it means that the typical employee values the health insurance by exactly the same amount that it costs. That is, the employee is willing to give up wage income equal to the cost of the mandated health insurance. A supply curve that shifts downward by less than the mandated cost suggests that the value of the health insurance is less than its cost.

For discussion purposes, let us suppose that the supply curve shifts downward by more than demand from S_0 to S_1. That would mean that the new equilibrium wage becomes W_1 and that the employee pays more than the full cost of the mandated benefit. The implication is that the mandated health insurance is efficient since its benefit exceeds its cost. That is, the mandate makes employees better off, and it shows in the form of a much lower wage.

If, on the other hand, the supply curve shifts downward by less than the mandated insurance costs, wages decline but by less than the mandated cost, reflecting that wage income is more important than health insurance at the margin. (You may want to work through this exercise.) Workers would be made worse off by the mandated benefit in this case. Consequently, the economic incidence is determined by the degree to which employees gain from the mandate. When they benefit more, employees pay a greater amount for mandated benefits in the form of lower wages.

Overinsurance, or the Moral Hazard Problem   Consumers normally pay the full cost of acquiring goods and services and internalize the full resource cost of their actions. Paying the full price creates a financial incentive for people to economize and use societal resources efficiently. **Moral hazard** refers to a situation where individuals, once they are covered by health insurance, change their behavior because they are no longer liable for the full cost of their actions (Pauly, 1968). In particular, people may choose to pursue activities that increase the probability and/or magnitude of the loss covered by health insurance. For example, some individuals may choose to overconsume medical services (e.g., visit the doctor more often than medically necessary), pay higher than necessary prices for medical care, or fail to produce a sufficient amount of home health care services (e.g., diet and exercise). All these activities increase either the magnitude of the medical expenses or the probability of an illness occurring. The moral hazard problem manifests itself because insurers are unable to monitor the actions of the insured and an asymmetry of information results. If sufficient information existed about the true behavior of the insured, insurers could simply charge a higher premium to discourage such individuals from pursuing costly medical activities.

To the individual consumer, the current health insurance premium represents a sunk cost and is unaffected by his or her spending on medical care services.[6] In addition, any one individual is likely to believe that his or her own medical spending in isolation does not affect the future premiums of the insured group. However, if a sufficient number of people act in a similar fashion and increase their spending on medical services due to the moral hazard situation, future insurance premiums increase to reflect the greater benefits paid out.

Seidman (1982) likens the moral hazard problem to restaurant bill splitting. If two people have lunch together and decide to split the bill, each person may realize that he or she is paying only one-half of the cost of an additional dollar spent on the meal. Therefore, each individual might purchase the higher-priced imported beer rather than the lower-priced domestic beer or order the restaurant specialty rather than the less expensive special of the day. Of course, if both people behave similarly and overspend, the restaurant bill is higher than it would be if they paid separately for their own meals. Also, each person's share of the bill falls as the size of the sharing group increases (say, from two to six). As a result, the incentive to overspend increases with the size of the group, *ceteris paribus*, when the bill is split.

In terms of the market for medical services, moral hazard results from five different types of actions.[7] First, at any point in time when an insured event takes place, the quantity demanded of medical services may exceed the amount the consumer would buy if he or she paid the full cost. Quantity demanded may be greater because the insured consumer faces a price that lies below the marginal cost of the medical service. Figure 11–3 helps to

FIGURE 11-3
The Effect of Moral Hazard on Medical Services Utilization

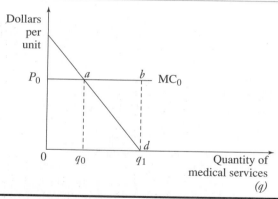

A consumer without health insurance pays P_0 per unit and purchases q_0 units of medical care. Consumer expenditures are identified by the area P_0aq_00. With complete health insurance coverage, consumption and expenditures increase to q_1 and area P_0bq_10, respectively.

---

[6]Sunk costs are irretrievable costs and therefore have no bearing on marginal decisions.
[7]Coyte (1990) is credited with categorizing the first two and the fourth moral hazard effects.

explain the reasoning behind this moral hazard effect. The curve MC_0 represents the true marginal cost or market price, P_0, of producing units of medical services, q. An individual's willingness-to-pay or uninsured demand curve for medical services is represented by curve d. If the consumer has to pay the full cost, she or he consumes q_0 units of medical services. Medical expenditures equal the area $P_0 a q_0 0$.

If the consumer pays a zero coinsurance with no deductible, however, q_1 units of medical services are demanded. At this quantity, medical expenditures increase to area $P_0 b q_1 0$. The implication is that insurance lowers the consumer's out-of-pocket price and creates an incentive to overconsume medical services. For example, the consumer may visit the local physician more often than is medically necessary. The degree to which insurance leads to overconsumption depends on the price elasticity of demand for medical services. Less overconsumption results when the uninsured demand is more price inelastic. For example, if the uninsured demand curve in figure 11–3 is perfectly inelastic (completely vertical), no overconsumption results from a lower price because of insurance coverage.

Second, the moral hazard problem may show up over time as consumers have less incentive to guard against the insured event. Reductions in preventative activities such as exercise or dieting may raise the probability of an illness occurring. As consumers compensate for a poorer health status with more medical services, the demand curve in figure 11–3 effectively shifts to the right and a higher quantity demanded is associated with a zero price. The greater demand leads to increased medical expenditures.

Moral hazard may arise from a third type of behavior that deals with technological advances in medical care. Third-party payments may encourage the development and adoption of new technologies offering low-benefit, high-cost care (Weisbrod, 1991). The adoption and diffusion of these high-priced technologies, in turn, cause the demand for health insurance and the range of services covered by health insurance to increase. A vicious cycle encompassing health insurance, technology, and rising medical costs is set in place. In terms of figure 11–3, the rapidly developing technologies offering high-cost, low-benefit medicine are responsible for shifting the demand curve to the right and thereby raising medical expenditures.

Moral hazard results in a fourth behavioral change as insurance lowers the consumer's incentive to monitor the behavior of health care providers. Less monitoring gives the health care provider the incentive to prescribe unnecessary tests or surgery. Since the consumer's out-of-pocket costs are largely unaffected by the unnecessary services, the consumer has little incentive to seek a second opinion. As a result, the demand curve in figure 11–3 shifts to the right and results in greater medical expenditures.[8]

Finally, a moral hazard effect occurs when insurance lowers the consumer's incentive to shop around and find the lowest price for medical services. In terms of figure 11–3 less comparison shopping means the price and the marginal cost curve are at an artificially higher level than MC_0; thus, medical expenditures increase.

Insurers can reduce the extent of the moral hazard problem by increasing the coinsurance and making the consumer pay a larger share of the full cost. The higher coinsurance creates an incentive for the consumer to purchase fewer medical services, shop around and

---

[8]This action is referred to as supplier-induced demand in Chapter 12.

pay the lowest possible price, produce medical services in the home when doing so is cost effective, and acquire more medical information to prevent opportunistic behavior by health care providers. Of course, the higher coinsurance also increases the consumer's financial insecurity, because a greater proportion of his or her income is subject to uncertainty. The optimal coinsurance considers risk and balances the cost of the moral hazard problem with the benefit of financial security (less financial risk). Therefore, it is very likely that the optimal coinsurance is not zero except for purely catastrophic medical events.

Since health insurance enables the consumer to avoid risk, the net social costs of excess insurance are found by subtracting the social benefit of risk avoidance from the social cost due to excess medical spending. Feldstein (1973) showed that the net social costs of overinsurance depend on values for the price elasticity of demand for medical services and the degree of risk aversion. Specifically, net social costs increase with a greater price elasticity of demand and a lower degree of risk aversion.

Manning and Marquis (1996) examine empirically the trade-off between the gains from risk reduction and the deadweight loss from moral hazard by estimating the demand for health insurance to measure the degree of risk aversion and the demand for health services to measure the price elasticity of demand. They use data from the Rand health insurance study of the 1970s that was discussed in Chapter 5. The authors find that a coinsurance rate of 40 to 50 percent is optimal and point out that it is not far from the present average coinsurance rate of 30 percent. However, they note that focusing on the average coinsurance rate may be misleading. The 14 percent of the population without health insurance face sizeable net losses from high out-of-pocket expenses. Also, those who have more generous coverage and face out-of-pocket prices less than 30 percent generate losses. Manning and Marquis write: "Thus, the losses in the current mix of uninsured and insured are substantially larger than would occur if every family faced the same coinsurance rate of 30 percent. Instead, the current loss is probably of the order of $480 per family in 1995 dollars—an average loss of some $690 per uninsured family and $400 per insured family relative to our estimated optimal pure coinsurance plan" (p. 632).

The Price of Private Health Insurance

Another measure of the performance of an industry is the price of the product relative to cost. A high price/cost margin normally denotes the presence of some monopoly power. As noted earlier, the price of health insurance is the loading fee, which covers administrative costs, marketing expenses, profits, and taxes. Recall that economists often express the price of health insurance as the premium to benefit ratio. A premium to benefit ratio greater than 1 reflects the loading fee. In a competitive market, administrative cost, marketing expenses, and profits will be kept to a normal level such that the price of insurance, net of taxes, reflects a reasonable or normal amount.

Table 11–2 shows the price of health insurance, defined as the ratio of premiums to benefits paid out, for various health insurers for selected years from 1950 to 1996. The data suggest that the price of health insurance fell over the 46-year span. For example, the price of a typical individual commercial policy declined from $2.01 to $1.41 per benefit dollar over the period. The price of the typical group commercial policy and BCBS policy also fell by 27 cents and 4 cents, respectively. It is interesting to note that the 1996 price

TABLE 11–2

Price of Private Insurance in the United States, Selected Years, 1950–1996

	COMMERCIAL INSURANCE COMPANIES			Combined Self-Insured and HMOs	Blue Cross and Blue Shield
Year	Total	Group	Individual		
1950	$1.62	$1.44	$2.01	—	$1.17
1960	1.57	1.23	2.47	—	1.08
1970	1.26	1.09	2.11	—	1.04
1980	1.18	1.12	1.73	$1.07	1.03
1990	1.22	1.19	1.55	1.11	1.12
1991	1.19	1.16	1.51	1.10	1.12
1992	1.19	1.16	1.52	1.09	1.12
1993	1.20	1.17	1.56	1.09	1.15
1994	1.22	1.19	1.46	1.09	1.14
1995	1.22	1.19	1.46	1.08	1.13
1996	1.20	1.17	1.41	1.08	1.13

Note: Price is measured by dividing premium income by medical benefits paid out.

SOURCE: Health Insurance Association of America, *Source Book of Health Insurance Data*, various editions.

of a group commercial plan per benefit dollar was appreciably lower than the price of an individual plan. The higher risk associated with individual plans and the individual consumer's higher costs of acquiring information most likely account for the observed price differential. The price of health insurance for the industry as a whole was $1.14 per benefit dollar in 1996 compared to $1.54 in 1950 (not shown).

Some health policy analysts (e.g., Woolhandler and Himmelstein, 1991) argue that the 14 cents per benefit dollar for administrative costs, marketing expenses, profits, and taxes is much too high compared to either the publicly provided health insurance in the United States (about 3 cents) or the provincial health plans in Canada (almost 1 cent) and reflects the wastefulness of a private health insurance program. However, Danzon (1992) points out that in a world of imperfect information and costly transactions the overhead expenditures of private insurers do not represent pure waste. The overhead provides benefits by helping to avoid even larger costs to policyholders. Benefits accrue from controlling incentives to overuse medical care due to the moral hazard problem.

According to Danzon, "private insurers compete by devising ways to control moral hazard more cost effectively, including structured copayments, utilization review, case management, selective contracting with preferred providers, and provider-targeted financial incentives such as capitation and other risk-sharing forms of prospective reimbursement. The costs of implementing these strategies appear as claims administration costs to insurers, providers and patients" (p. 26). She goes on to note that the total overhead costs from society's perspective are measured by overhead plus the net social loss associated with moral hazard. In the absence of the tax subsidy on employer-provided health benefits, competition creates incentives for insurers to minimize the total overhead costs.

Danzon also comments that the 1980s was a time of intense innovation in strategies to control moral hazard. Indeed, some signs of the competition to control moral hazard are apparent in table 11–2. Notice that the prices of the various plans, other than the individual commercial insurance plans, have tended to increase from 1980 to 1990 but leveled off thereafter. For example, the price of commercial group insurance increased from $1.12 to $1.17 and the price of the Blues plans rose from $1.03 to $1.13 during the period 1980 to 1996. The higher price of BCBS insurance may also reflect that many not-for-profit plans converted to for-profit plans and now must earn profits for investors and pay taxes. Even the price of the combined self-insured and HMO plans increased slightly since 1980. The higher price per benefit dollar reflects the greater administrative costs necessary to control the moral hazard problem.

INSIGHT 11–4

News of Adverse Selection and Cherry-Picking Behavior in Australia

As discussed in Insight 6–3, the major provider of health insurance in Australia is the Medicare program, which provides universal, tax-financed public insurance to its citizens. Beginning with the National Health Act of 1953, the government allowed individuals in Australia to purchase private health insurance to gain access to private hospitals. Recently, the Australian government implemented various policies to stimulate the demand for private health insurance in order to relieve pressure on the much larger public hospital system. As a result of policies such as the Lifetime Health Cover that allowed people to join at one-time low lifetime rates and a 30 percent subsidy, enrollment in the private system eventually increased.

Apparently the policy changes initially brought 3 million new, mostly young members into the program because they did not want to miss out on the low one-time lifetime insurance rates. Beginning in September 2000, when membership in private plans hit its peak, enrollment slipped but by only 30,000 out of 9 million members. One might think this slight decline would not matter. But Mcauley (2002) points out that these aggregate numbers may mask an important trend. According to Mcauley, the private funds lost 140,000 healthy 25 to 54 year-olds and gained 120,000 older members since September 2000. Young members left, he points out, because of the opportunity cost of private insurance premiums relative to the low benefits they can expect to receive over a sustained period of time. He goes on to note that if the young members provided the private companies with pure profits of $700 (Australian) per member, their departure would mean $100 million less dollars to subsidize the costs of the older, less healthy members. Mcauley questions whether this situation reflects the beginning of a cycle of adverse selection, rising prices, and membership loss.

Another issue relating to the recent private health insurance policy changes concerns cherry picking. According to Australian health minister, John Thwaites, private hospitals

(continued)

have been cherry-picking patients and turning away sick elderly people. Figures show that private hospitals refused ambulance patients more often in 2001 than public hospitals and public hospitals were forced to cope with an 8 percent increase in emergency patients as a result. Mr. Thwaites said the Federal government might not be getting value from its 30 percent private health insurance subsidy.

SOURCE: Based on Ian Mcauley. "Lies and Statistics." *Australian Financial Review*, February 23, 2002 and Tom Noble. "Make Private Hospitals Do Their Share: Thwaites." *The Age*, April 2, 2002.

SUMMARY

Recent data suggest that the private health insurance industry is relatively concentrated but with a large competitive fringe in most states. However, health insurance is fairly homogeneous, at least within a particular product line, such as traditional or managed-care health insurance. While state regulations and administrative economies exist, barriers to entry do not appear to be very binding on the entry of new health insurance companies, perhaps because existing insurance companies can easily switch among alternative insurance product lines (health, casualty, life, etc.). Group plans also face the prospect that large employers may self-insure.

Individual buyers may possess imperfect information regarding the quality of health insurance. However, the information problem is much less severe in the group insurance submarket. Thus, overall the market for private health insurance appears to be reasonably competitive. While the market demand for health insurance is found to be inelastic, an individual insurer is likely to face a highly elastic demand curve given the relative ease of entry and available substitutes.

Competitive insurance markets in conjunction with experience rating can give rise to cherry-picking behavior, the notion that only healthy individuals are offered adequate health insurance coverage. Less healthy people are denied access to health insurance, are not covered for preexisting conditions, or are charged prohibitively high prices. This problem is also more pronounced in the individual health insurance market.

In terms of performance, the price of private health insurance (premium to benefits) has tended to decline over the long run. In the recent short run, the price has increased moderately in response to cost containment efforts. Some output problems continue to prevail in the market for private health insurance. First, moral hazard results as overinsured individuals change their behavior and increase the probability and magnitude of a health loss. Indeed, many health economists have pointed to the moral hazard problem as the prime reason underlying rising medical care expenditures in the United States. Second, adverse selection, which occurs when high-risk individuals join a low-risk group, can impose substantial adjustment costs on society as high-risk people pursue low-risk individuals from plan to plan. Appropriate pricing and utilization review can reduce the extent of the moral hazard and adverse selection problems.

Third, a significant percentage of Americans lack health insurance coverage. Some argue that this figure is biased downward because it fails to consider underinsurance and job lock. Others believe it is biased upward because many uninsured people choose to be without health insurance and because the spell without insurance coverage is relatively short.

REVIEW QUESTIONS AND PROBLEMS

1. Many economists point to moral hazard as the primary reason underlying rising health care costs in the United States.
   A. Explain the general argument behind moral hazard.
   B. Explain the five ways by which moral hazard takes place (explain with a graph when possible).
   C. How does price elasticity of demand influence the moral hazard problem?
   D. Explain how an insurer could reduce the scope of the moral hazard problem by introducing a consumer copayment.
   E. What two considerations determine the optimal copayment rate?

2. Many economists argue that the group health insurance industry is reasonably competitive. Based on various determinants of industry structure, explain the reasoning underlying this view.

3. Fully explain the two reasons the individual health insurance market may be less competitive than the group health insurance market.

4. Blair, Jackson, and Vogel (1975) found that substantial economies of scale exist in the administration of health insurance, yet survivor analysis finds no scale economies in the provision of health insurance. How can this inconsistency be explained?

5. Verbally and graphically explain how a profit-maximizing dominant health insurer determines the premium to charge for its policies.

6. Explain how the competitive fringe influences the premiums charged by a dominant health insurer.

7. Explain why someone may make the following seemingly contradictory statement: "High administrative costs are good because they sometimes lead to lower costs of providing health insurance."

8. Private insurers tend to experience three consecutive years of profits followed by three consecutive years of losses. What are the various explanations offered for this profit cycle?

9. Managed-care plans tend to lower health care costs, yet the level and growth of managed-care premiums are similar to those of traditional fee-for-service insurance plans. How can that be explained?

10. What does *cherry-picking behavior* mean? What does the evidence suggest about this type of behavior? Why is it less troublesome in the group health insurance market?

11. What does *adverse selection* mean? How does this type of behavior impose costs on society?

12. Explain why experience rating may be more efficient and equitable than community rating. Explain why community rating may be more efficient and equitable than experience rating.

13. Why is it so difficult to measure the number of people who lack health insurance? Explain fully.
14. How can overinsurance coexist with underinsurance and uninsurance?
15. How is the price of health insurance measured? What happened to the price of health insurance in the United States from 1950 to 1980? What has happened since 1980? Why?
16. Explain how a monopsonist determines the price paid for and the quantity purchased of a good or service. According to Feldman and Wholey (2001), do HMOs have monopsony power? Why or why not?
17. Would a theory X'er favor community or experience rating? Why?
18. Provide a description of the typical uninsured person.
19. What were the main reasons behind the Health Insurance Portability and Accountability Act? What are the main features of the act?
20. Suppose the government imposes an employer-mandated pet insurance program. All employers must sponsor and finance an insurance policy for the pets (dogs and cats) of their employees. Use the appropriate graphical model of a labor market to illustrate and explain who will pay for the mandate.

ONLINE RESOURCES

To access Internet links related to the topics in this chapter, please visit our web site at http://santerre.swcollege.com.

REFERENCES

Acs, Gregory. "Explaining Trends in Health Insurance Coverage between 1988 and 1991." *Inquiry* 32 (spring 1995), pp. 102–10.

Atchinson, Brian K., and Daniel M. Fox. "From the Field: The Politics of the Health Insurance Portability and Accountability Act." *Health Affairs* 16 (May/June 1997), pp. 146–50.

Baker, Laurence C., Joel C. Cantor, Stephen H. Long, and M. Susan Marquis. "HMO Market Penetration and Costs of Employer-Sponsored Health Plans." *Health Affairs* 19 (September/October 2000), pp. 121–28.

Baker, Laurence C., and Kenneth S. Corts. "The Effects of HMOs on Conventional Insurance Premiums: Theory and Evidence." National Bureau of Economic Research, Working Paper no. 5356, November 1995, pp. 1–33.

Beauregard, Karen M. *Persons Denied Private Health Insurance Due to Poor Health.* AHCPR Pub. No. 92–0016, 1991.

Blair, Roger D., and Ronald J. Vogel. "A Survivor Analysis of Commercial Health Insurers." *Journal of Business* 51 (July 1978), pp. 521–29.

Blair, Roger D., Jerry R. Jackson, and Ronald J. Vogel. "Economies of Scale in the Administration of Health Insurance." *Review of Economics and Statistics* 57 (May 1975), pp. 185–89.

Bodenheimer, Thomas. "Underinsurance in America." *New England Journal of Medicine* (July 23, 1992), pp. 274–78.

Chollet, Deborah J., Adele M. Kirk, and Marc E. Chow. "Mapping State Health Insurance Markets: Structure and Change in the States' Group and Individual Health Insurance Markets, 1995–1997." Academy for Health Services Research and Health Policy, Washington, D.C., December 2000.

Cooper, Philip F., and Alan C. Monheit. "Does Employment-Related Health Insurance Inhibit Job Mobility?" *Inquiry* 30 (winter 1993), pp. 400–16.

Coyte, Peter C. "Canada." In *Advances in Health Economics and Health Services Research, Comparative Health, Systems*, eds. Richard M. Scheffler and Louis F. Rossiter. Greenwich, CT: JAI Press, 1990, pp. 103–43.

Cutler, David M., and Jonathan Gruber. "Does Public Insurance Crowd Out Private Insurance?" National Bureau of Economic Research, Working Paper no. 5082 (Cambridge, MA: 1995).

Danzon, Patricia M. "Hidden Overhead Costs: Is Canada's System Really Less Expensive?" *Health Affairs* 11 (spring 1992), pp. 21–43.

Feldman, Roger, Bryan Dowd, and Gregory Gifford. "The Effect of HMOs on Premiums in Employment-Based Health Plans." *Health Services Research* 27 (February 1993), pp. 779–811.

Feldman, Roger, and Douglas Wholey. "Do HMOs Have Monopsony Power?" *International Journal of Health Care Finance and Economics* 1 (2001), pp. 7–22.

Feldstein, Martin S. "The Welfare Loss of Excess Health Insurance." *Journal of Political Economy* (March–April 1973), pp. 251–80.

Friedman, Milton. "The Folly of Buying Health Care at the Company Store." *The Wall Street Journal*, February 3, 1992, p. A14.

Gabel, Jon R., and Gail A. Jensen, "Can a Universal Coverage System Temper the Underwriting Cycle?" *Inquiry* (summer 1992), pp. 249–62.

Gabel, Jon, Roger Formisano, Barbara Lohr, and Steven Di Carlo. "Tracing the Cycle of Health Insurance." *Health Affairs* (winter 1991), pp. 49–61.

General Accounting Office. "State Small Group Health Insurance Market." GAO-02-536R, U.S. General Accounting Office, Washington D.C., March 25, 2002.

Hall, Mark A. "An Evaluation of New York's Reform Law." *Journal of Health Politics, Policy and Law* 25 (February 2000), pp. 71–98.

Hay, Joel W., and Michael J. Leahy. "Competition among Health Plans: Some Preliminary Evidence." *Southern Economic Journal* 50 (January 1987), pp. 831–46.

Health Insurance Association of America (HIAA). *Source Book of Health Insurance Data 1999/2000*, Washington, D.C., 2001.

Iglehart, John K. "The American Health Care System—Private Insurance." *New England Journal of Medicine* 326 (June 18, 1992), pp. 1715–20.

Jensen, Gail A., Michael A. Morrisey, Shannon Gaffney, and Derek K. Liston. "The New Dominance of Managed Care: Insurance Trends in the 1990s." *Health Affairs* 16 (January/February 1997), pp. 125–36.

Kapur, Kanika. "The Impact of Health on Job Mobility: A Measure of Job Lock." *Industrial and Labor Relations Review* 51 (January 1998), pp. 282–98.

Lee, Dwight. "Why Workers Should Want Mandated Benefits to Lower Their Wages." *Economic Inquiry* 34 (April 1996), pp. 401–7.

Long, Stephen H., and Jack Rodgers. "Do Shifts Toward Service Industries, Part-time Work, and Self-Employment Explain the Rising Uninsured Rate?" *Inquiry* 32 (spring 1995), pp. 111–6.

Madrian, Brigitte. "Employment-Based Health Insurance and Job Mobility: Is There Evidence of Job-Lock?" *Quarterly Journal of Economics* (February 1994), pp. 27–54.

Manning, Willard, et al. "A Controlled Trial of the Effect of a Prepaid Group Practice on Use of Services." *New England Journal of Medicine* 310 (June 7, 1984), pp. 1505–10.

Manning, Willard, and M. Susan Marquis. "Health Insurance: The Tradeoff Between Risk Pooling and Moral Hazard." *Journal of Health Economics* 15 (1996), pp. 609–39.

Mcauley, Ian. "Lies and Statistics." *Australian Financial Review*, February 23, 2002.

McCormack, Lauren A., Peter D. Fox, Thomas Rice, and Marcia L. Graham. "Medigap Reform Legislation of 1990: Have the Objectives Been Met?" *Health Care Financing Review* 18 (fall 1996), pp. 157–74.

McLaughlin, Catherine G. "Market Responses to HMOs. Price Competition or Rivalry?" *Inquiry* (summer 1988), pp. 207–18.

Miller, Robert H., and Harold S. Luft. "Managed Care Plan Performance since 1980." *Journal of the American Medical Association* 271 (May 18, 1994), pp. 1512–19.

Mills, Robert J. "Health Insurance Coverage: 2000." *Current Population Reports*, P60–215, U.S. Department of Commerce, Washington D.C., September 2001.

Morrisey, Michael A. "Competition in Hospital and Health Insurance Markets: A Review and Research Agenda." *Health Services Research* 36 (April 2001), pp. 191–222.

Nichols, Len M., and Linda Blumberg. "A Different Kind of 'New Federalism'? The Health Insurance Portability and Accountability Act of 1996." *Health Affairs* 17 (May/June 1998), pp. 25–42.

Noble, Tom. "Make Private Hospitals Do Their Share: Thwaites." *The Age*, April 2, 2002.

Pauly, Mark V. "The Economics of Moral Hazard: Comment?" *American Economic Review* 58 (June 1968), pp. 531–37.

Pauly, Mark V., Alan L. Hillman, Myoung S. Kim, and Darryl R. Brown. "Competitive Behavior in the HMO Marketplace." *Health Affairs* 21 (January/February 2002), pp. 194–202.

Rapoport, John, et al. "Resource Utilization among Intensive Care Patients." *Archives of Internal Medicine* 152 (November 1992), pp. 2207–12.

Reinhardt, Uwe. "The Market Won't Make Health Insurers Efficient." *Norwich Bulletin*, April 12, 1992, p. A5.

Rothschild, Michael, and Joseph Stiglitz. "Equilibrium in Competitive Insurance Markets: An Essay on the Economics of Imperfect Information." *Quarterly Journal of Economics* 90 (November 1976), pp. 630–49.

Sapolsky, Harvey M. "Empire and the Business of Health Insurance." *Journal of Health Politics, Policy and Law* 16 (winter 1991), pp. 747–60.

Seidman, Laurence S. "Health Care: Getting the Right Amount at the Right Price." *Business Review*, March–April 1982.

Sheth, Jagdish, and Rajendra Sisodia. "Only the Big Three Will Thrive." *The Wall Street Journal*, May 11, 1998, p. A22.

Sindelar, Jody L. "The Declining Price of Health Insurance." In *Health Care in America,* eds. H.E. Frech III. San Francisco: Pacific Institute for Public Policy, 1988, pp. 259–91.

State Health Watch. "Community Rating Law Hikes Premiums in NY." (January 1994), p. 2.

Steinmetz, Greg. "Number of Uninsured Stirs Much Confusion in Health-Care Debate." *The Wall Street Journal,* June 9, 1993, p. A1.

Stigler, George J. "The Economies of Scale." *Journal of Law and Economics* 1 (October 1958), pp. 54–71.

Swartz, Katherine. "Dynamics of People without Health Insurance." *Journal of the American Medical Association* 271 (January 5, 1994), pp. 64–66.

Swartz, Katherine, John Marcotte, and Timothy D. McBride. "Personal Characteristics and Spells without Health Insurance." *Inquiry* 30 (spring 1993), pp. 64–76.

Temin, Peter. "An Economic History of American Hospitals." In *Health Care in America,* eds. H.E. Frech III. San Francisco: Pacific Research Institute for Public Policy, 1988, pp. 75–102.

Van De Ven, Wynand P.M.M., and Randall P. Ellis. "Risk Adjustment in Competitive Health Plan Markets." In *Handbook of Health Economics, Volume 1,* eds. A.J. Culyer and J.P. Newhouse, Amsterdam: Elsevier Science, 2000.

Weisbrod, Burton A. "The Health Care Quadrilemma: An Essay on Technological Change, Insurance, Quality of Care, and Cost Containment." *Journal of Economic Literature* 29 (June 1991), pp. 523–52.

Wholey, Douglas, Roger Feldman, and Jon B. Christianson. "The Effect of Market Structure on HMO Premiums." *Journal of Health Economics* 14 (1995), pp. 81–105.

Wholey, Douglas, Roger Feldman, Jon B. Christianson, and John Engberg. "Scale and Scope Economies among Health Maintenance Organizations." *Journal of Health Economics* 15 (1996), pp. 657–84.

Wickizer, Thomas M., and Paul J. Feldstein. "The Impact of HMO Competition on Private Health Insurance Premiums." *Inquiry* 32 (fall 1995), pp. 241–51.

Woolhandler, Steffie, and David U. Himmelstein. "The Deteriorating Administrative Efficiency of the U.S. Health Care System." *New England Journal of Medicine* 324 (May 2, 1991), pp. 1253–58.

CEBS QUESTIONS

CEBS Sample Question on Subject Matter from CEBS Course 9 Study Manual

1. Describe how the Omnibus Budget Reconciliation Act (OBRA) of 1990 addressed the problem of Medicare consumers lacking the necessary technical information to purchase medigap insurance policies. (page 298)

CEBS Sample Exam Questions

1. When the price of health insurance is expressed as the premium to benefit ratio, which of the following statements is correct?

   A. The cost of commercial insurance companies, self-insured and HMOs, and Blue Cross-Blue Shield plans has increased over the last 50 years

   B. Self-insured and Health Maintenance Organizations (HMOs) have a lower cost than insurance companies

   C. The cost of Blue Cross-Blue Shield is lower than the cost for commercial insurance companies

   D. Individual insurance costs less than group insurance

   E. The ratio is about .80 for most insurance companies

2. Which of the following is (are) correct statements regarding barriers to entry to the health insurance industry?

   I.   Scale economies in administering health insurance may serve as a barrier to entry

   II. Lack of managerial expertise has been shown to be a significant barrier to entry

   III. Barriers to entry are of minor importance in the health insurance industry

     A. I only

     B. III only

     C. I and II only

     D. I and III only

     E. I, II, and III

3. The Health Insurance Portability and Accountability Act of 1996 contains all the following features EXCEPT:

   A. Health insurers that meet specified quality and quantity standards qualify for partial reimbursement of increased costs created by the new legislation

   B. Insurers in the small group market cannot exclude any of the employer's eligible employees from coverage on the basis of health status

   C. Individuals with a group plan cannot be charged a higher premium based on their health

   D. With some exceptions, all group coverage must be renewable

   E. There is a maximum exclusion period for preexisting conditions

Answer to Sample Question from Study Manual

Prior to OBRA of 1990, Medicare beneficiaries who wanted to purchase medigap insurance found it difficult to differentiate among the provisions and limitations of a myriad of policies being sold. It was not unusual for individuals to purchase policies that duplicated other policies or, worse, that failed to provide supplemental Medicare coverage. OBRA of 1990 reformed the medigap market. It mandated that only 10 standard policies based on increasing levels of coverage could be sold. The standardization enabled the consumer to assess the value and incremental cost of each of the 10 policies.

Answers to Sample Exam Questions

1. B is the answer. Table 11–2 on page 324 shows that the price of self-insured and HMO plans has been consistently lower than that of other types of insurance.

2. D is the answer. Statements I and III are correct. Scale economies enable existing insurers to underprice new, low-volume competitors and discourage new entrants. However, despite the scale economies barrier, there appears to be no overly restrictive barriers that deter new entrants. See pages 296–298 of the text.

3. A is the answer. All statements are true except A. The Act makes no provisions for subsidizing high-performing insurers. See pages 317–318 of the text.

CHAPTER 12

THE PHYSICIAN SERVICES INDUSTRY

Throughout the 19th century, the physician services industry was largely unregulated. Many physicians were practicing without proper medical training, primarily because the country was dotted with numerous medical schools of questionable quality. In reaction to this state of affairs, the American Medical Association (AMA) was founded in 1847. At its inception, the organization adopted the improvement of medical education in the United States as its major goal. Although improvements were made over the years, significant changes did not take place until the turn of the 20th century. The impetus for change was the Flexner Report published in 1910 by the Carnegie Foundation.

Concerned that not enough was being done to improve medical education, the Carnegie Foundation, with the blessing of the AMA, asked Abraham Flexner to conduct a study of the medical schools in Canada and the United States. The final report, commonly referred to as the Flexner Report, was highly critical of the medical training provided by an overwhelming majority of the schools in North America. The report was so controversial that Flexner received threats on his life. As a result of the report, many low-quality medical schools were forced to improve or close their doors. In addition, states began to take the role of licensing physicians more seriously (Raffel and Raffel, 1989). Thus, the formation of the AMA, coupled with the Flexner Report, ushered in the modern regulated physician services industry, which requires an individual to fulfill strict educational and licensing requirements before being allowed to practice medicine.

Over the past quarter-century, the scope and complexity of physician services have increased dramatically, and this has had a profound impact on the structure and performance of the industry. Increases in demand for medical services and the introduction of many new, costly technologies have increased expenditures on physician services almost fortyfold since 1960. Nearly gone are the days when an appointment with the doctor meant a visit to a self-employed male physician who owned a solo fee-for-service practice. Today, almost one out of four physicians is female and only about one-quarter of all physicians are self-employed and operating a solo practice. Multiphysician practices are the norm, and physicians who wish to survive are now forced to negotiate with MCOs for additional patients, adjust to many new and different fee schedules, and subject themselves to utilization reviews.

In keeping with the methodology laid out in the previous chapter, this chapter employs the structure-conduct-performance paradigm to analyze the ever-changing physician services industry. The first part of the chapter describes the current structure of the industry. In particular, it looks at the number and specialty distribution of physicians, examines the mode of practice, analyzes methods of payment, reviews the reimbursement practices of managed-care buyers, and concludes with a discussion of the production and cost of physician services. The conduct section of the chapter discusses the impact of compensation schemes on physician behavior and examines geographic variations in the use of physician services. In addition, it looks at the supplier-induced demand hypothesis, reviews the physician practice hypothesis, and explores the implication of a quantity setting model on physician behavior. The conduct section finishes with an analysis of the impact of managed care on physician behavior. The performance section traces expenditures on physician services over time, reviews the utilization of physician services, and discusses the growth of physician income over time.

THE STRUCTURE OF THE PHYSICIAN SERVICES INDUSTRY

Because the conduct of buyers and sellers depends directly on the structure of the market, we begin with an analysis of the structure of the physician services market. Among the structural elements, we look at the number and specialty distribution of physicians, along with the organization arrangements adopted by physicians to produce medical services. Next we review the sources of physician revenues and examine the impact of managed care on the physician services market. Finally, we analyze barriers to entry and the production of physician services.

The Number of Physicians in the United States

It seems only logical to begin our analysis of the market for physician services with a look at the supply of physician labor, the primary input in the production of physician services.[1] According to figure 12–1, the United States experienced a substantial increase in the number of physicians from 1970 to 2000. In 1970, a total of 334,028 physicians were in the United States; by 2000 that number had increased by almost 150 percent to 813,770.

To get a clearer picture of the impact of this increase in physician labor on the delivery of patient care, we need to look at a breakdown of physicians by major professional activities. According to figure 12–1, almost 80 percent of all physicians, 647,430, were involved in direct patient care in 2000. That percentage has remained remarkably stable over time. The remaining 20 percent of the physicians were engaged in other activities such as medical teaching, administration, or research.

Although the absolute supply of physicians in the United States increased in recent years, it is impossible to make inferences regarding the relative supply of physicians without comparing the increase in physician labor to the overall increase in population. One crude measure of the relative supply of physician labor is the physician-to-population ratio. Data supplied by the AMA[2] indicate that the number of total nonfederal patient care

---

[1] As we will see later in the chapter, physician services are produced with a combination of various inputs, including physician labor, nurse labor, clerical staff, physician assistants, lab technicians, and so on.
[2] *Physician Characteristics and Distribution in the US 2002-2003 edition* (Chicago: American Medical Association, 2002), table 5.17.

FIGURE 12–1
Number of Physicians in the United States, 1970–2000

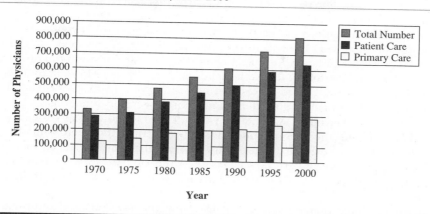

SOURCE: *Physician Characteristics and Distribution in the US 2002-2003 edition.* Chicago: American Medical Association, 2002, table 4.1.

physicians per 100,000 civilians increased substantially from 124 in 1970 to 230 in 2000, an increase of about 85 percent. Put in other terms, in 1970 there was one patient care physician for every 807 people in the civilian population in the United States and by 2000 that number had dropped to 435 individuals.

It is apparent that the United States experienced a significant increase in physician labor over the last three decades. The increase outpaced the overall increase in the population and has led to a greater relative supply of labor, as measured by the physician-to-population ratio.

Distribution of Primary Care and Specialty Care Physicians in the United States

Figure 12–1 provides additional information on the number of physicians providing primary care in the United States as defined by the AMA to include family practice, general practice, internal medicine, obstetrics and gynecology, and pediatrics, but excluding subspecialties within each of these general specialties. While the overall number of primary care physicians in the United States increased from 134,354 in 1970 to 274,699 in 2000, the proportion of primary care physicians decreased from approximately 40 percent in 1970 to 34 percent in 2000. The implication is that the number of specialty physicians in the United States over the last three decades increased at a faster pace than the number of primary care physicians. AMA data (not shown) also suggests the number and distribution of physicians by major specialties indicates the single largest category is internal medicine, with 134,539 physicians in 2000. Other specialties of note include general surgery, 36,650, psychiatry, 39,457, and anesthesiology, 35,715.

Many analysts believe the United States has too many specialists and too few primary care physicians and that the problem has worsened over time. According to Schroeder

(1992), the growth in the number of specialists relative to primary care physicians is one reason health costs are so high in the United States. Specialists are more prone to overutilize costly new, high-technology medical procedures that drive up medical costs. Higher surgery rates and a greater availability of medical technology in the United States relative to other industrialized nations are used as evidence to support this hypothesis. To prove his point, Schroeder (1984, 1992) compared the proportion of specialists in the United States to that of various Western European countries in 1980. He found the proportion of specialists in Belgium, Germany, the Netherlands, and the United Kingdom to lie between 25 and 50 percent. In the United States, the proportion of specialists was slightly more than 60 percent, substantially higher than in most other developed nations.

Another study (Government Accounting Office, 1994) found basically the same thing for 1990. For example, the report found that 58 percent of the doctors in the United Kingdom are in primary care. It is interesting to note that one developed nation has a lower percentage of primary care physicians than the United States. According to the GAO report, only 18 percent of the physicians in Sweden are considered primary care doctors.

Whether the United States has more or less than the efficient level of primary care physicians is difficult to determine objectively. One way researchers have attempted to answer this question is by first establishing the medical *need* for primary care physicians— that is, how many primary care physicians are needed to deliver adequate care to the population. However, from an economic perspective, demand rather than need is really at issue. Next, the most cost-effective way to deliver physician services must be determined. Only after this has been established can one determine the total number of primary and nonprimary care physicians clinically needed to provide medical services to the entire population. These estimates must then be compared to the actual number of primary and nonprimary care physicians practicing in the United States to determine whether a surplus or a shortage of specialists exists. Obviously, the process of calculating the optimal number of many specialists is complicated and laced with value judgments.

Politzer et al. (1996) look to the future to estimate whether the United States will have an adequate supply of physicians in the year 2020. To establish need, the authors conducted a statistical technique called meta-analysis on five alternative projection methods already developed in the literature. Meta-analysis allows them to establish bands of physician requirements for primary and specialty care physicians. Physician supply projections were based on a number of factors, including the number of first-year residency positions likely to exist in the future. The authors conclude that the "future physician supply does not appear well-matched with requirements" (p. 181). For example, assuming a 30/70 ratio of generalists to specialists and an increase in U.S. medical graduates equal to 110 percent of their 1998 levels, the authors project a shortage of approximately 33,000 primary care physicians by the year 2020. The same set of assumptions also generates a surplus of specialists.

Another study with many of the same authors (Gamliel et al., 1995) reaches the same conclusion. According to the results from this study, in all likelihood there will be an overall surplus of physicians of between 56,000 and 71,000 doctors by the year 2020, which will be due primarily to an oversupply of specialists. The problem of an oversupply of physicians is further complicated by the fact that the authors forecast a shortage of primary care physicians in the future.

The Relative Supply of Physicians for Select OECD Countries

A cursory look at the number of practicing physicians around the world as shown in figure 1 indicates that the relative supply of physicians varies substantially from country to country. According to data supplied by the Organization for Economic Cooperation and Development, the number of practicing physicians per 100,000 population in 1998 ranged from a low of 120 in Turkey to a high of 590 in Italy. Other countries on the low end of the scale include Korea at 130 and the United Kingdom at 170 physicians per 100,000 population. Joining Italy at the opposite end of the spectrum is Spain at 440 and Germany at 350 physicians per 100,000 population. Although not shown in figure 1, the United States appears to be in the center of the distribution at approximately 230 physicians per 100,000 population.

FIGURE 1

Number of Practicing Physicians per 100,000 Population for Select OECD Countries, 1998

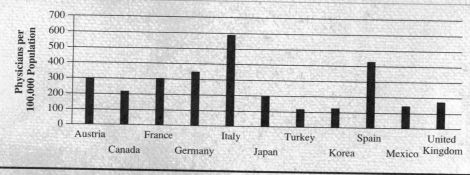

SOURCE: *OECD Health Data 2000 Comparative Analysis of 29 Countries.*

While it is impossible to infer from these data whether any one country has too many or too few physicians without a detailed examination of the market for physician services, some evidence suggests the market for physician services is in flux in some countries. According to Bosch (1999), 22 percent of the physicians in Spain were unemployed in the late 1990s. What is most troubling is that a high proportion of the physicians in Spain are in their mid-40s and are not likely to retire from practice soon. As a result, the oversupply of physicians in Spain is likely to worsen in the future. Bosch argues that the government of Spain must take a more active role in correcting the imbalance between the supply of and demand for physicians.

Cooper, Getzen, McKee, and Laud (2002) take a very different approach to projecting the adequacy of physician supply and develop a macroeconomic forecast based on four trends that greatly impact the supply of and use of physician services. First and foremost, they consider the strong relationship between the growth of physician supply and economic growth over time. Next, they factor in the impact of population trends, physician work efforts, and the capacity of nonphysician health care professions to provide medical care. Their results are thought provoking because they contradict conventional wisdom that the United States has too many physicians. According to their results, a substantial shortfall of approximately 200,000 physicians is likely to exist in the United States by the year 2020.

Clearly, these results point to a need for a better understanding of factors that are likely to impact the demand for and supply of physician services in the coming years. The strong likelihood that there is going to be a mismatch between physician supply and demand also raises some interesting policy questions. For example, what role should the government play in correcting any imbalances that may exist in our health workforce given the fact that it has traditionally subsidized the education of many health professionals, including physicians? Also, what role should the market play in correcting any labor market imbalances?

Mode of Practice

Economists view the provision of physician services as a production process that involves a multitude of inputs aside from physician labor. It includes other labor inputs, such as nurses, nurse practitioners, physician assistants, medical technicians, and receptionists, along with various nonlabor inputs, such as office space, medical supplies, and diagnostic equipment. In light of this view, it is extremely important to distinguish between physician labor as a strategic input in the production of medical services and the firm, or production arrangement, adopted by physicians to produce medical care. Self-employed profit-maximizing physicians act as entrepreneurs when they combine various inputs, including their own labor, to produce medical care for their patients.

Data from the AMA (1997/1998, 2000) provide a glimpse of the modes of practice utilized by physicians from 1989 to 1999. The figures indicate that the majority of physicians are self-employed. In 1989 slightly more than 70 percent of all physicians were self-employed, and by 1999 this number had dropped to just under 59 percent. This drop appears to have resulted primarily from a decrease in the proportion of physicians operating solo practices. By 1999, fewer than 44 percent of all self-employed physicians were engaged in a solo practice. There was also a decrease in the percentage of self-employed physicians involved in practices with two or three physicians. A greater percentage of self-employed physicians are now involved in larger practices with four or more physicians.

Based on this information there appears to be a trend away from smaller practices toward larger, multidoctor modes of production. This trend might reflect the economies of scope offered by large multidoctor, multispecialty practices or economies of scale in the production of physician services. We review some empirical evidence concerning economies of scale later in the chapter.

By far the greatest change in recent years has been an increase in the proportion of physicians who are not self-employed but are paid on a salary basis. By 1999, 38.2 percent

INSIGHT 12-2

The Geographical Distribution of Physicians

Concern that many rural communities are without physician services has sparked a renewed interest in the physician location decision. The issue was popularized in a movie starring Michael J. Fox entitled *Doc Hollywood* and in the television show *Northern Exposure*. In both instances, the main story line dealt with how a small rural community of modest means wrestled with the problem of attracting and retaining a primary care physician.

Using county-based data, Carpenter and Neun (1999) examined the factors that influence the location decisions of young primary care physicians. Their results call into question the widely held belief that physicians prefer to set up practice in large metropolitan areas. It appears that young physicians have a preference for small- to medium-sized cities as opposed to either sparsely populated communities or major metropolitan areas. Young physicians also favor counties where the crime and poverty rates are low and taxes are not excessive and prefer to locate in counties where there is a strong academic presence and the cost of living is moderate.

Escarce, Polsky, Wozniak, and Kletke (2000), and Polsky, Kletke, Wozniak, and Escarce (2000) studied the impact of HMO growth on physician location. The first study found that greater HMO penetration results in smaller increases in total physicians and medical/specialists than otherwise would be the case. In particular, a 10 percent increase in HMO penetration reduces the rate of increase in total physician supply by 7.2 percent and by 10.2 percent for medical/specialists supply. The second study found that increases in HMO penetration decrease the probability that young market/surgical specialists stay in a given market, but had no impact on other categories of physicians.

Collectively, these studies indicate that the decision to practice medicine in a given location depends upon a complex set of health industry characteristics, economic factors, and demographic attributes. Any policy aimed at attracting young physicians to an area must offer the economic opportunities and amenities compatible with launching a career in medicine.

of all physicians were paid on a salary basis, an increase of approximately 15 percentage points from 1989.

Buyers of Physician Services and Methods of Remuneration

A review of the methods of remuneration provides insight into the number and types of buyers of physician services and the extent to which any one buyer, or group of buyers, may exhibit some degree of monopsony power. In 1999, 41 percent of all physician revenues emanated from the government sector, with Medicare making up 70 percent of that total. This is in sharp contrast to the market for hospital services, where the government sector accounted for nearly 60 percent of total revenues (see Chapter 13). This suggests that although the government sector is clearly a major player in the physician services market, its ability to exercise monopsony power may not be as great as in the market for hospital services.

Rising health care costs have forced politicians to reevaluate the Medicare and Medicaid programs. For example, after much debate Congress passed the Omnibus Budget Reconciliation Act (OBRA) in 1989, which, among other things, called for major changes in Part B of the Medicare payment system, which provides compensation to physicians for medical services rendered to elderly patients. As of 1992, physicians are now compensated based on resources utilized rather than on the "usual customary and reasonable" rate. This Medicare reimbursement scheme for physician services, referred to as the *resource-based relative value scale* system, is reviewed in Chapter 10. OBRA 1989 was followed by the Balanced Budget Act of 1997, which extended the resource-based method of payment to include practice and malpractice expenses.

The private sector accounted for about 59 percent of physician revenues in 1999, with 45 percent coming from private insurance companies. The remaining 14 percent was the result of out-of-pocket payments. This is somewhat different from the hospital services market, where out-of-pocket payments accounted for only 3.2 percent of total revenues. The relatively higher out-of-pocket expenses for physician services are not too surprising, because insurance theory suggests that coverage is lower for more predictable and lower-magnitude losses.

Overall, the private sector accounts for a much greater share of revenues in the physician services market than it does in the hospital services market. This is largely because out-of-pocket payments are a more important source of funds for physicians than for hospitals. This is not to say, however, that the government plays only a minor role in the physician services market. On the contrary, the recent Medicare reforms indicate that the federal government intends to play a more active role in this market for years to come.

Reimbursement Practices of Managed-Care Buyers of Physician Services

Managed care, which embodies a broad set of policies designed by third-party payers to control the utilization and cost of medical care, has had a profound impact on the physician services market. Through the use of alternative compensation schemes, utilization reviews, quality controls, and the like, MCOs hope to modify the behavior of physicians to contain costs. These control mechanisms diminish the autonomy physicians traditionally enjoyed in practicing medicine, and, as a result, many physicians have resisted the movement toward managed care. Despite these reservations, managed care presently has a major impact on the allocation of resources in the physician services market.

The strong presence of managed care in the physician services market is reflected in the fact that 92 percent of all physicians practicing medicine in 1997 had at least one managed-care contract. A more detailed look at the data confirms the significant role of managed care in the physician services market. The proportion of physicians with a minimum of one managed-care contract varied little across regions of the country, practice size, or specialty in 1997. For example, the rate of contract involvement for physicians ranged from a high of 95 percent in New England to a low of 91 percent in the Middle Atlantic region. In relation to practice arrangement, there appears to be a weak but positive connection between practice size and managed-care involvement. Almost 88 percent of those physicians in a solo practice had at least one managed-care contract, while 96 percent of all physicians in a practice with eight or more doctors had at least one contract. Finally, for almost all specialties the percent of physicians with one or more managed-care contract topped 90 percent. The lowest was psychiatry with slightly more than 80 percent having signed at least one contract (American Medical Association, 1998).

Managed care also appears to account for a significant proportion of revenue generated by physicians. In 1997, 44 cents out of every dollar generated by practicing physicians was the result of some type of contractual arrangement with an MCO.

Barriers to Entry

It is generally accepted that substantial barriers to entry in the market for physician services impede competition primarily by legally limiting the supply of physicians. Before being allowed to practice medicine, a person must meet a minimum educational requirement (usually a degree from an accredited medical school), participate in an internship or a residency program at a recognized institution, and pass a medical exam. These various requirements entail substantial time and money costs and raise the opportunity cost of becoming a medical doctor. Advocates for these legal restrictions base their argument on the public interest theory. Market failure brought about by an asymmetry of information between patient and physician concerning the appropriateness and quality of medical care justifies the need for government intervention. Because consumers generally have imperfect information concerning the medical care received given its technical sophistication, they are sometimes unsure about the appropriateness and quality of physician services. As a result, the market cannot be relied on to weed out incompetent doctors or those who would take advantage of their position and prescribe needless and costly medical care.

The necessity of government intervention has also been justified based on the possibility that a negative supply-side externality will occur if incompetent physicians are allowed to practice medicine. For example, if an incompetent physician misdiagnoses a patient infected with the AIDS virus due to a faulty test, others may contract the virus. As a result, government intervention is necessary to ensure that consumers will not become innocent victims of medical malfeasance.

Over the years, proponents of the special interest theory, including Kessel (1958), Moore (1961), Friedman (1962, 1980), and Leffler (1978), have argued that barriers exist primarily to protect the economic interests of physicians. By restricting supply through the creation of educational and training barriers to entry, physicians have succeeded in generating economic profits. As evidence, these analysts point to high physician salaries. Control of medical licensure is the primary mechanism physicians use to restrict their numbers. In the United States, the licensure of physicians is under the control of the states, and most states have medical boards composed of physicians that establish, review, and maintain the criteria for obtaining a license to practice medicine. The fact that these requirements control the process of becoming a physician rather than encourage the maintenance of medical knowledge has been used as evidence to support the special interest interpretation of these restrictions.[3]

Control over medical licensure is not the only method physicians use to maintain their monopoly power. Physicians as a group play a critical role in the accreditation of medical

---

[3]The same argument can be made for lawyers and certified public accountants, who are required to pass the bar exam and CPA exam, respectively.

schools. For example, the Liaison Committee on Medical Education, the main accrediting body of medical schools, is composed of 17 people, 6 of whom are representatives of the American Medical Association (Wilson and Neuhauser, 1985). By maintaining control over the number of medical schools, physicians are in a position to indirectly restrain the supply of their services.

The establishment of limits on the use of physician extenders is yet another method physicians employ to protect their economic interests. Physician extenders, such as physician assistants and nurse practitioners, have the medical training necessary to perform a number of medical tasks traditionally carried out by the physician.[4] Production theory indicates that when more than one variable input is utilized in the production of physician services, a cost-conscious firm combines these inputs to produce in the most cost-efficient manner. For example, let's suppose a staff-model HMO faces an increase in wages for physicians. To counteract this increase, the HMO may attempt to substitute physician extenders for physicians in the production of certain medical services. To limit the possibility of this occurrence, physicians may flex their political muscle to legally limit the duties of physician extenders. The goal would be to legally constrain the marginal rate of technical substitution between physicians and physician extenders to near zero.

Given many of the recent changes in medical care, Svorny (1992) questions the need for medical licensure in the physician market. She believes market incentives can now be relied on to ensure an efficient level of quality. In particular, Svorny points to changes in medical liability, the rapid growth in for-profit medical care providers, the increased use of brand names, and the growth in employed rather than self-employed physicians as lessening the need for the licensure of physicians.

For example, recent legal decisions have shifted some of the liability for medical malpractice away from physicians and toward institutions, such as hospitals and HMOs. As a result, hospitals and HMOs now have a greater incentive to monitor the behavior of physicians who practice medicine on their premises by assessing the quality of care provided. Institutional liability decreases the need for licensing because it is now in the self-interests of hospitals to weed out incompetent physicians.

The growth in for-profit medical care providers may have the same effect. Because at least one owner has a financial stake in a for-profit medical institution, there may be a greater incentive to oversee the performance of physicians than in a not-for-profit institution, which is run by a board of directors who have no financial commitment to the institution. The expanded use of brand names by hospitals, group practices, and HMOs also increases the incentive for these institutions to more closely monitor the performance of physicians. An incompetent physician can financially hurt the institution by damaging its reputation and tarnishing its image, which took a substantial amount of time and money to establish. Much goodwill is at stake, and hence there is an increased incentive to dismiss incompetent physicians.

---

[4] A physician assistant must study for two years in an accredited physician assistant program and pass a certification exam before being allowed to practice. A nurse practitioner is a licensed registered nurse who has received an additional one or two years' training and passed a certification exam. In terms of duties, the difference between the two labor inputs is one of emphasis. Physician assistants concern themselves primarily with the direct application of medical care, whereas nurse practitioners deal mostly in education and wellness.

The growing use of employed as opposed to self-employed physicians also provides medical institutions with an increased incentive to monitor the activities of physicians. Naturally, it is in the interests of these institutions to eliminate those physicians providing low-quality or unnecessary medical care. In addition, because the physician is a salaried employee, the incentive to provide unnecessary care has been diminished. According to Svorny, all these changes have lessened the need for the licensure of physicians because market forces can now be relied on to force doctors to provide quality medical care at least cost.

These institutional and structural changes imply a weakening of barriers to entry into the physician services market. If this is indeed the case, the level of competition should have intensified over time. To test for this phenomenon, Noether (1986) developed a system of stock and income equations to depict behavior in the physician services market. According to her results, competition in the physician services markets has increased since 1965, and this increase has caused the supply of physician labor to increase by 6 to 20 percent and physician incomes to fall by 19 to 45 percent. All this indicates that the degree of monopoly power in the hands of physicians may have waned in recent years.

Production, Costs, and Economies of Scale

Thus far, we have focused primarily on the supply of physicians. In this section, the perspective changes from the physician as an input in the production of medical services to the physician as an entrepreneur: one who makes allocation decisions concerning the most cost-effective way to produce medical services. Unfortunately, the literature on the production and cost of physician services is rather thin compared to the multitude of studies on the hospital services market.

The most comprehensive studies on the production of physician services were carried out by Reinhardt (1972, 1973, 1975). In these studies, the author estimated a production function for physician services using data from a survey of doctors in 1965 and 1967. Given the controversy surrounding the most appropriate means to measure output in the physician services market, the author employed three measures of physician output: total weekly patient visits at the office, home, or hospital; weekly office visits; and annual gross billings to patients. Inputs included physician labor, as measured by total practice hours per week; number of auxiliary personnel; medical supplies; and capital equipment. In addition, a host of control variables were included in the estimate equations.

The regression results with total patient visits as a measure of output are particularly interesting. To no one's surprise, Reinhardt found physician labor to be highly correlated with output, with an elasticity of output to physician time equal to .70.[5] Capital inputs appeared to have a far smaller impact on output. The capital elasticity of output was estimated at .05. The effect of auxiliary personnel appeared to be somewhat greater than that of capital, with an elasticity of approximately .32. Finally, Reinhardt found that physicians in group practices were about 5 percent more productive in terms of patient visits than physicians in a solo practice.

---

[5]This output elasticity means the output of physician services increased by 7 percent for each 10 percent increase in physician hours, assuming all other factors remain constant.

In a more contemporary study, Brown (1988) also examined the factors that influence physician output. He found, among other things, that group practice physicians were 22 percent more productive than their counterparts in solo practices. These estimates are substantially greater than Reinhardt's and justify the organizational movement in the physician services market away from solo practices that we discussed earlier in the chapter. Solo practices face some difficulty in competing with group practices with such a significant productivity disadvantage.[6]

Brown's study also uncovers some interesting results concerning the efficient use of auxiliary personnel. According to Brown, the estimated marginal products for various labor inputs clearly show that physicians, registered nurses, and practical nurses are the most productive inputs, whereas secretaries, technicians, and physician assistants are the least productive inputs in the production of physician services. To determine whether physicians are utilizing inputs efficiently, we must compare the marginal product per dollar spent on each input. Recall from Chapter 7 that the firm is optimally utilizing all inputs if the marginal product of the last dollar spent on each input is equal across all inputs. Brown shows that the marginal product per dollar spent for physicians' time equals .114 and is higher than the marginal product to price ratio for all other inputs except licensed practical nurses. Thus we can conclude that physicians overutilize auxiliary personnel. For licensed practical nurses, the evidence suggests that they are underutilized, with a marginal product per dollar spent of .129.

Estimating a more general production function than Reinhardt, Thurston and Libby (2002) found that the marginal product of an additional hour of physician labor equals .55 office visits per week. Like Brown, Thurston and Libby also found the marginal productivity to be highest for nurses among nonphysician personnel such as administrative and clerical workers and technicians and aides. In particular, they found that the employment of one additional nurse increases physician office visits by between seven and eight visits per week. They also found the marginal productivity of capital, as measured in thousands of dollars, to equal .19, suggesting that the average physician practice would have to invest approximately $5,000 in capital equipment to generate an additional office visit per week.

The literature also suggests that moderate economies of scale exist in the production of physician services. A recent study by Pope and Burge (1996), which estimated the gross revenue production function for self-employed physicians, found the lowest-cost practice size to be 5.2 physicians. The lowest-cost practice size is somewhat higher than the average practice size of 2.4 physicians in their sample. The authors also found that group physicians have the ability to handle 17 percent more office visits than physicians in a solo practice. Escarce and Pauly (1998) also found the presence of economies of scale in the production of physician services. In particular, they found that a 10 percent increase in physician services causes total costs, as measured by the sum of nonphysician input costs and the opportunity cost of physician labor, to increase by 6 percent. Contradicting these results, Defelice and Bradford (1997) found no statistical difference in efficiency between solo practice and group practice physicians.

---

[6]The cost differential may reflect the value, or utility, that a proprietor/physician places on working independently and being his or her own boss. Otherwise, why would the proprietor/physician remain in the less profitable solo practice?

The literature on survivor analysis also indicates the existence of economies of scale in the production of physician services. As it pertains to the market for physician services, survivor analysis examines the distribution of practice sizes over time to determine which practice size produces medical services most efficiently. Studies by Frech and Ginsburg (1974) and Marder and Zuckerman (1985) indicate that solo and two-physician practices are inefficient at the margin relative to group practices. Relying on more recent data, Marder and Zuckerman also found medium-sized groups to be less efficient than large practices (100 or more physicians). Taken together, these studies suggest that multiphysician practices have a cost advantage over solo practices and that economies of scale exist in the production of physician services at least up to the three-to-seven practice size. Marder and Zuckerman's results go one step further and suggest that economies of scale may exist for practices as large as 100 physicians. Referring to our earlier discussion on the mode of practice, these results explain why the proportion of solo and two- and three-person practices decreased from 1989 to 1997 relative to physician practices with four-to-eight and over-eight persons.

Summary of the Structure of the Market for Physician Services

Whether the physician services market is measured based on real expenditures or the number of physicians practicing medicine, it has increased dramatically in size over the past three decades. Since 1970, the number of physicians and real expenditures on physician services in the United States have more than doubled. The increase has outpaced the overall growth in the economy and the general population, as illustrated by the significant increase in the physician-to-population ratio from 148 in 1970 to 288 in 2000 per 100,000 total population.

The increase in physician labor in the United States has not been without controversy. Some people believe the United States has too many specialists and too few generalists. This issue is likely to play an integral role in the health care reform debate over the coming years.

The mode of practice in the physician services market has also changed significantly in recent years. There appears to be a movement away from single- and two-physician practices and toward multiphysician practices with four or more physicians. In addition, significant growth appears to be occurring in the number of employed physicians. In all probability, this trend reflects changing economic conditions in the health care field. For example, productivity studies and survivor analysis studies indicate the existence of economies of scale that confer a distinct cost advantage on large multiphysician practices.

MCOs also appear to play a key role in the physician services market. Over 90 percent of all physicians have at least one contract with an MCO. The growing presence of MCOs in the physician services market may also partly explain the growth of multiphysician practices relative to smaller ones. Since larger practices have a cost advantage over smaller practices, they are in a better position to negotiate price discounts with MCOs.

Despite the presence of barriers to entry, such as medical licensure, the physician services market has become even more competitive over time as large, institutional buyers challenge the authority of independent physicians. This has caused some policymakers to call for the elimination of these barriers. As the market for physician services becomes more competitive, perhaps market forces can be relied on more heavily to dispose of incompetent or unprofessional doctors.

THE CONDUCT OF THE PHYSICIAN SERVICES INDUSTRY

Now that we have established the market determinants of behavior, or the structure of the physician services industry, we are in a position to discuss the conduct of that market. As you know, market structure interacts with economic objectives to establish conduct. We will look at the supplier-induced demand hypothesis, McGuire's quantity setting model, the effects of various compensation schemes on physician behavior, geographical variations in the utilization of physician's services, and the impact of managed-care practices.

The Supplier-Induced Demand Hypothesis

Without a doubt, one of the most controversial issues in health economics over the years is whether the **supplier-induced demand (SID) hypothesis** can be used to explain physician behavior. The basic premise of the SID hypothesis is that physicians abuse their role as medical advisors to advance their own economic self-interests. This involves prescribing medical care beyond what is clinically necessary and can include such items as additional follow-up visits, an excessive number of medical tests, or even unnecessary surgery. According to the model, consumers are relatively ill-informed concerning the proper amount of medical care to consume because there exists an asymmetry of information regarding the various health care options available. The asymmetry forces consumers to rely heavily on the advice of their physicians for guidance. This implies that physicians are not only the suppliers of physician services but also play a major part in determining the level of demand for those services. For example, physicians advise patients about how frequently they should have office visits, medical tests, and appropriate treatments. This rather unique situation places physicians in a potentially exploitative situation. It may be possible for physicians to manipulate the demand curves of patients to advance their own economic interests.

For example, assume the market for physician services is initially in equilibrium in figure 12–2, where equilibrium occurs at point (Q_0, P_0) and Q represents the quantity of physician services. Now assume for some reason an increase occurs in the number of practicing physicians. An increased number of physicians causes the supply curve to shift to the right from S_0 to S_1, which in turn forces the average price of physician services to fall from P_0 to P_1. Faced with an increase in competition along with a loss in income, physicians may exercise their ability to influence patients' behavior by inducing them to demand more services. The increased demand may involve more office visits, additional tests, or even unnecessary surgery. As a result, the demand for physician services increases from D_0 to D_1. In the end, the price of physician services could actually increase, as shown in figure 12–2, where the new equilibrium price and quantity equal P_2 and Q_2, respectively.

The SID model can also be described in the context of the principal–agent theory. The principal–agent theory is traditionally used to explain the interaction between the managers of a major corporation, who are the agents, and its stockholders, who are the principals. The fiduciary responsibility of the agent is to manage the firm in the best interest of the principal, and that means maximizing profits. Due to an asymmetry of information between the principal and the agent, the manager is likely to have more information than the stockholders concerning the true operation and performance of the firm. In this situation, the manager has the opportunity to shirk his or her responsibilities to the stockholders by

FIGURE 12–2

The Supplier-Induced Demand Model

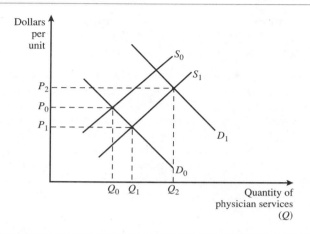

Assume initially that the market for physician services is in equilibrium at point (Q_0, P_0) off of the D_0 demand curve and the S_0 supply curve. Now assume that there is an increase in the number of physicians practicing medicine and the supply curve for physician services shifts outward from S_0 to S_1. Under ordinary circumstances, the equilibrium price for physician services would fall to P_1 while the equilibrium quantity would increase to Q_1. In reaction to the decrease in the price of medical services, however, physicians induce the demand for their services and cause the demand curve to shift outward to D_1. The end result is that the equilibrium price and quantity for physician services increases to P_2, Q_2.

not seeking to maximize profits. Instead, the manager may use company funds to advance her or his self-interests. Advancing self-interests may involve such things as higher pay, a large support staff, or a more luxurious office.[7]

Concerning the doctor–patient relation, the physician is hired to address the health concerns of the patient, the principal. Specifically, the physician, as agent, is given the responsibility of demanding medical services on behalf of the patient, who possesses much less information concerning the appropriateness of medical care. Given that patients are typically covered by health insurance and the physician's personal financial interests are at stake, the physician has the opportunity to exploit the situation by convincing the patient to consume more medical care than is clinically necessary. The increased medical services most likely do no harm, but they do mean increased income for the physician-agent.

The task of reviewing the empirical evidence on the SID hypothesis is daunting given the extensive work on the subject. In one of the earlier studies, Fuchs (1978) uncovered substantial support for the supplier-induced demand hypothesis. In particular, he estimated that a 10 percent increase in the supply of surgeons, as measured by the surgeon-to-population ratio, leads to a 3 percent increase in the per capita surgery rate. Cromwell

---

[7]In the case of corporate managers, incentive contracts (e.g., bonus pay) might be designed to align the manager's personal interests with the actions desired by stockholders.

INSIGHT 12–3

Physician Behavior and the Supplier-Induced Demand Theory: Evidence from Japan and the United States

Some recent international evidence appears to substantiate the supplier-induced demand theory. Japanese consumers spend much more on prescription drugs than Americans on a per capita basis. Many reasons may account for the difference, but one explanation is that Japanese physicians prescribe more drugs than American doctors because doing so is financially rewarding. Physicians in Japan not only prescribe drugs, as their American counterparts do, but also sell them to their patients. They purchase the drugs directly from the pharmaceutical companies and sell them to patients at a profit. This unique situation gives Japanese doctors an incentive to prescribe medicine whenever possible. The prescribing behavior may explain the disparity in the level of prescription medicine consumed in the two countries.

In the United States, there is concern that physicians who own diagnostic equipment require that their patients undergo more medical tests to generate additional income. For example, one study revealed that physicians who operate their own imaging equipment are approximately four times more likely to require imaging examinations than physicians without such equipment (Hillman et al., 1990). Those doctors who not do not possess their own imaging equipment must refer patients who need an examination to a radiologist. In addition, physicians who own diagnostic equipment are likely to charge a higher price for each examination. Although it is impossible to determine from the study which group of physicians employs imaging equipment more appropriately from a medical standpoint, the results bring into question whether physicians with an ownership interest use diagnostic equipment more frequently because it generates financial returns.

Both of these articles tend to verify the supplier-induced demand theory. In each case, physicians appear to manipulate the demand for their services to advance their own financial self-interests.

and Mitchell (1986) also found evidence that surgeons induce demand. However, their estimates were substantially smaller than Fuchs's. They estimated that a 10 percent increase in surgeon density leads to only a .9 percent increase in surgeries and a 1.3 percent increase in elective surgeries per capita. Rossiter and Wilensky (1984) and McCarthy (1985) also uncovered evidence that substantiates the inducement hypothesis, although the magnitude of the inducement was estimated to be marginal. Looking at the issue of physician ownership of ancillary services, Mitchell and Sass (1995) also found evidence of induced demand. According to their findings, physical therapy clinics in Florida owned by physicians required 50 percent more visits from patients than those clinics that received no referrals from owners, with no discernible difference in the quality of care across ownership structures. A partial list of additional studies that corroborate the inducement hypothesis includes Grytten and Holst (1990), Hemenway and Fallon (1985), Tussing (1983), and Tussing and Wojtowyzc (1986).

A number of the more recent studies do not support the supplier-induced demand hypothesis. For example, Escarce (1992) employed Medicare enrollment and physician claims data to test the inducement hypothesis. The results indicate the increases in the supply of surgeons are associated with increases in the demand for initial contacts with surgeons but have no impact on the demand for services among surgery patients in terms of intensity of use. Thus, the author attributes the greater demand for surgeries to improvements in access, lower time costs, and better quality. These conclusions do not support the inducement hypothesis. Recent studies by Carlsen and Grytten (1998) and Grytten and Sorensen (2001) also do not support the SID hypothesis. Using data collected in 1998 from Norway, Grytten and Sorensen test how two different groups of physicians in Norway have reacted to increased competition. The first group comprised contract physicians who were compensated on a fee-for-service basis. Presumably, they had an incentive to induce the demand for medical services when faced with increased competition. The second group included salaried physicians who had little incentive to induce demand. According to their empirical results there is no evidence that either group of physicians induced the demand for medical services when faced with increased competition. They conclude from their results that there is little evidence to support the SID hypothesis in the delivery of medical services by primary care physicians in Norway.

There are three reasons why empirical support for the SID hypothesis has been waning in recent years. First, older studies tended to rely on aggregate data that made it difficult to discern the extent to which variations in the consumption of physician services can be attributed to induced demand. For example, increased consumption in physician services attributed to induced demand may have resulted from decreased waiting times or travel costs. More recent studies generally employ physician-based practice data. Second, more recent studies rely on more sophisticated models and estimating techniques that allow researchers to more accurately control for other market conditions such as time costs and price effects. Finally, more recent studies utilize contemporary data sets and all agree that the ability of physicians to manipulate demand has diminished in recent years with the growth of managed care.

It is obvious from this brief overview of the literature that the issue of whether physicians possess the ability to induce demand is unlikely to be resolved in the near future. Overall, the evidence suggests that although physicians may possess the ability to induce demand, the extent to which they can do so is mush less now then initially thought.

McGuire's Quantity Setting Model

McGuire (2000) develops an interesting model of physician decision making that is based on monopolistic competition. Recall that many sellers exist in a monopolistically competitive industry, but each seller faces a downward-sloping demand curve because of imperfect substitutability among the products offered by the various sellers. In the case of physicians, imperfect substitutability may simply result from location if consumers value convenience. McGuire's model treats physicians as being quantity setters and shows that physicians respond to a lower administered price by increasing quantity supplied. Interestingly, the inverse relation between price and quantity is obtained in McGuire's model without resorting to supplier inducement of demand.

Figure 12–3 provides a graphical illustration of McGuire's quantity setting model. The horizontal axis represents the quantity of physician services and the vertical axis measures

INSIGHT 12–4

Price Discrimination and Physician Pricing Behavior Prior to the Mid-1950s

Prior to the mid-1950s few people purchased health insurance to cover physician services and, as a result, physicians collected fees directly from consumers. In his seminal article Kessel (1958) noted that under these circumstances physicians commonly scaled their fees to their patients' incomes in order to maximize profits. In economics this practice is known as **price discrimination**. It occurs when the physician charges patients different prices for the same product.

For price discrimination to take place, three conditions must be satisfied. First, the physician must be able to segment the market into at least two distinct submarkets based on the price elasticity of demand or willingness to pay. Second, the physician must face a downward-sloping demand curve because of a distinguishing feature such as convenience. Finally, something must prevent arbitrage from taking place. In other words, consumers cannot purchase medical services from one physician and sell them in another market.

Figure 1 depicts the situation of a physician who has segmented the market into two submarkets: patients from affluent families (panel a) and patients from the general population (panel b). Note that the demand for physician services is less elastic in panel a than in panel b. Presumably patients from more affluent families have the economic means to purchase medical care and are, therefore, less concerned about the price of physician services. To keep matters simple, we assume the marginal cost is constant so that the MC curve is horizontal and equal for two submarkets. A profit-maximizing physician in this situation charges more-affluent patients a higher price (P_a) for the medical services and those of more modest means a lower price (P_b).

In summary, the physician practices price discrimination to take advantage of the fact that some patients are less sensitive to price than others. In our example, the physician charges patients of more affluent means a higher price for medical services because they have a less elastic demand for medical services. Notice in this case that the practice of price discrimination, although negative in connotation, results in more medical care provided to less-affluent individuals.

FIGURE 1 The Price Discrimination Model

F I G U R E   1 2 – 3
McGuire's Basic Quantity Setting Model

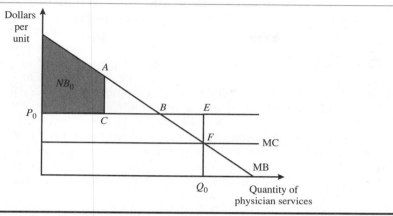

The MB curve represents the marginal benefits the consumer receives from consuming each additional unit of medical care and the MC curve equals the marginal cost of producing physician services. NB_0 represents the net benefit the consumer receives if she visits an alternative physician. Dr. Maxwell chooses P and Q such that profits are maximized and the consumer receives at least NB_0 amount of net benefits. Thus, Dr. Maxwell will require the average consumer to consume no more than Q_0 amount of medical care at price P_0. At this combination of price and quantity the patient is indifferent between having all or none of the care provided by Dr. Maxwell.

the dollar value of cost and benefits. To make the model easier to explain, let's pretend that the analysis represents how Dr. Maxwell determines price and quantity. The downward-sloping curve, MB, identifies the marginal benefit of the physician services provided by Dr. Maxwell to a typical patient. The horizontal curve, MC, represents Dr. Maxwell's constant marginal cost of producing physician services.

To make this basic model even easier, suppose for now that the patient has no insurance and pays the full price for the physician care. According to McGuire's model, Dr. Maxwell retains a patient by providing at least the amount of net benefits that the patient would receive from an alternative physician. Suppose NB_0, the shaded area, represents the net benefit that the patient would receive from an alternative physician. Dr. Maxwell has to select the price and quantity that maximizes her profits and also provides the patient with at least NB_0 amount of net benefits. In graphical terms, Dr. Maxwell attempts to raise price up vertically above MC and slide quantity over horizontally as much as possible to maximize profits yet provide at least NB_0 amount of net benefits.

Following this logic, Dr. Maxwell chooses a price no greater than P_0 and a quantity not to exceed Q_0. Notice at this combination of price and quantity the consumer is indifferent between having all or none of the care provided by Dr. Maxwell. That is, the patient's net benefits lost by having Dr. Maxwell provide Q_0 amount of care, area BEF, is exactly equal to the net benefits not received by the patient if Dr. Maxwell does not provide any care at all, area ABC. Any further increase in quantity causes the patient to visit an alternative physician where net benefits are greater.

The model predicts that greater competition causes profits to decline. Notice that Dr. Maxwell's profits equal the rectangular area formed by the difference between price and marginal cost over the range of quantity provided or Q_0. Both price and quantity are influenced by the level of competition in the industry as indicated by NB_0. If the market for physician services becomes more competitive, NB_0 increases. If NB_0 increases, price, quantity, and profits all decline, otherwise Dr. Maxwell loses the patient to a competitor. In a perfectly competitive situation, NB_0 equals the area below MB but above MC and Dr. Maxwell is forced by competition to price and produce the quantity of services at the point where MB equals MC. At the opposite extreme, If NB_0 equals zero, Dr. Maxwell faces no competition and can act like a monopolist and extract all of the patient's net benefits.

An interesting aspect of the McGuire quantity-setting model concerns how Dr. Maxwell responds to a regulator or third-party administrator with the power to lower price. In McGuire's model, Dr. Maxwell reacts to a lower administered price by increasing quantity supplied because the doctor need only provide a fixed level of net benefits to the patient. Hence, the model predicts that quantity increases in response to a lower regulated price. It is interesting to note that an inverse relationship exists between price and quantity supplied in McGuire's basic model much like the supplier-induced demand theory also predicts. In this case, however, the inverse relationship occurs without requiring demand inducement.

McGuire extends this basic model to include a third-party administered price and insurance coverage. A graphical illustration of the extended model is provided in figure 12–4. We suppose that the consumer pays coinsurance equal to $c \times P$, where c represents the coinsurance rate and P equals the fixed price set by the third party. Notice that the third-party payer sets price above marginal cost to encourage Dr. Maxwell to participate in the health plan. The shaded area NB_0 once again represents the net benefit provided to the patient from an alternative physician. Dr. Maxwell no longer chooses price because it is set

---

F I G U R E   1 2 – 4
McGuire's Quantity Setting Model with Administered Pricing and Insurance

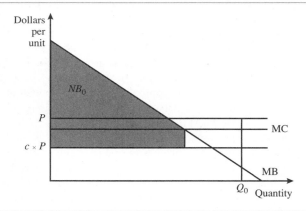

The MB and MC curves represent the marginal benefit and marginal cost curves, respectively. The price ceiling, *P*, which is established by a third party, lies above the MC curve to ensure physician participation in the plan. The $c \times P$ line represents the out-of-pocket price for physician services. Dr. Maxwell chooses the quantity of services, Q_0, such that the patient is indifferent between receiving all or no care from the doctor and profits are maximized.

by the third-party payer but she does select the quantity of services that maximizes her profits and provides at least NB_0 amount of net benefits to the patient.

The amount Q_0 gives Dr. Maxwell the best choice of quantity. At that quantity of services the patient is indifferent between all or no care provided by Dr. Maxwell and profits are maximized. Like the basic model, the extended analysis predicts that Dr. Maxwell responds to a lower administered price by increasing quantity supplied as long as price remains above marginal cost.

The Impact of Alternative Compensation Schemes on Physician Behavior

Concern for growing health care costs has caused third-party payers, both private and public, to seek new ways to reimburse physicians. The traditional fee-for-service method of payment has fallen out of favor because it creates an incentive for overutilization of medical care as the SID and McGuire models suggest. The problem becomes particularly acute when the fee-for-service method of reimbursement is combined with a nominal, or zero, consumer copayment, because under these circumstances consumers have little incentive to monitor the behavior of their physicians. To rectify this problem, many managed-care providers and private insurance companies have adopted alternative physician reimbursement schemes.

Based on a survey of over 100 managed care plans in 1994, Gold et al. (1995) uncovered some interesting information concerning the methods presently used to recruit and compensate physicians. Over 70 percent of the managed care plans in the sample said they utilized a careful selection process when recruiting new physicians. Over 60 percent of all plans considered qualitative information, such as professional reputation or patterns of care, during the selection process. However, only 37 percent of the plans reviewed any quantitative data from indemnity claims and/or hospital-discharge data when selecting a new doctor.

As we might expect, staff-model HMOs rely more heavily on a salary-based method of payment, whereas IPA HMOs tend to rely on other methods of payment. According to the study, 28 percent of staff-HMOs used a salary-based method, while only 2 percent of the IPA HMOs used this method of compensation. Fee-for-service was the main form of compensation for PPOs, with 90 percent of the PPOs in the sample stating that it was the predominant form of payment for physician services.

Sixty percent of all plans in the survey used some type of risk-sharing mechanism when compensating physicians, which included some form of capitation payment, or withholdings or bonuses. Withholdings generally involve more sophisticated reimbursement schemes in an attempt to control costs. According to Hillman (1987), MCOs may direct premiums into a series of special-purpose funds after deducting administrative costs. These funds pay for such items as physician services, hospital services, and outpatient laboratory tests. Sometimes, a specific portion of the payment directed to physicians is withheld until the end of the fiscal year, when it can be established whether there is a surplus or a deficit in the remaining funds. If a surplus exists, the MCO generally returns the withheld portion to the physicians. If a deficit exists, the MCO applies all or part of the withheld funds against the loss. By establishing such a compensation system, the MCO creates a direct financial relationship between its own economic viability and the clinical behavior of its physicians. Those physicians who overutilize medical resources and drive up costs receive less compensation.

With a system of bonuses, the plan gives a portion of any surplus remaining at the end of the year to physicians to elicit cost-effective behavior. Hellinger (1996) states that some MCOs also set up special-purpose referral accounts to pay for the cost of specialists. Primary care physicians may receive some portion of any unused funds in these accounts at the end of the accounting period. The objective is to control the high cost of specialty care by providing primary care physicians with a financial incentive to limit referrals.

A recent study by Rosenthal, Frank, Buchanan, and Epstein (2002) provides additional information concerning the many compensation schemes currently in use. Based on a survey of physician organizations in California that included medical groups, independent practice associations, and other types of physician organizations, the authors found that fee-for-service contracts play only a minor role in revenue generation. The overwhelming majority of the revenue (84 percent) generated by physician organizations resulted from capitation contracts. They also found that bonuses and withholds were a common form of compensation. About one out of six physician organizations used bonuses and withholds based on the cost of care, while one-quarter of the physician organizations based bonuses and withholds on the quality of care provided. In addition, about one-half of the physician organizations used some form of profit sharing, while 13 percent employed productivity bonuses.

A study by Grumbach et al. (1998) also points to the importance of financial incentives in physician compensation. According to a survey of primary care physicians involved in managed care, almost 40 percent of the doctors received at least some income based on incentives. Among the incentive factors considered were use of referrals, use of hospital services, quality of care provided, patient satisfaction, and productivity. The study also reported that over half of the physicians felt some pressure from managed-care organizations to limit referrals while three-quarters felt pressure to increase the number of patient visits.

Hillman, Pauly, and Kerstein (1989) used samples of over 300 MCOs to examine the impact of alternative physician compensation schemes on the utilization of medical services and firm profitability. The authors regressed a host of explanatory variables on three measures of MCO performance: the rate of hospitalization, visits per enrollee, and the break-even status of the MCO. The first two variables gauged the utilization of medical resources, and the last measured profitability. The independent variables fell into three categories: physician compensation variables, MCO descriptors, and market characteristics. A total of 11 variables controlled for the various types of compensation schemes used.

Overall, the results indicate that financial incentives affect the medical decisions of physicians and therefore the utilization of medical resources. In terms of utilization of medical services, hospitalization rates were found to be inversely related to whether physicians are paid on a salary or capitation basis. MCOs that used a salary-based method of compensation had 13.1 percent fewer hospitalization days per 1,000 enrollees per year than those using the more traditional fee-for-service methods. Likewise, the capitation method of payment was associated with 7.5 percent fewer hospitalization days. Visits per enrollee were also found to be inversely related to the use of financial penalties. For example, MCOs that established a referral fund whereby the individual physicians were at risk for any deficits had 10.5 percent fewer visits per enrollee, on average. The relationship between type of compensation scheme and profitability, as measured by the break-even status of the HMO, was far from clear. Hillman, Pauly, and Kerstein attributed these findings to the fact that profitability depends on many factors other than the utilization of medical resources. Be that as it may, this work is important because it establishes that clinical decisions are based at least in part on the financial incentives physicians face. This is not to suggest that physicians necessarily jeopardize the welfare of their patients; rather, in some circumstances, physicians consider their own self-interests when making marginal clinical decisions.

Geographical Variations in the Utilization of Physician Services

The phenomenon of **small area variations** in the delivery and consumption of physician services across geographic regions has been documented by an almost limitless number of studies worldwide. For example, wide physician utilization variations exist in countries such as Norway, England, and Canada, where government plays a major role in the delivery or financing of health care services. Physician utilization variations also occur among the counties within a single state and among states. For example, Miller and Holahan (1995) found substantial variation in the utilization of physician services across states, with Florida utilizing physician services at a rate 38 percent above the U.S. mean while Montana was 29 percent below the mean. They also found significant variation among urban and rural areas.

In addition, an extensive body of literature has suggested that selected medical services are overutilized. The estimates regarding the proportion of inappropriate medical care given range from 15 to 30 percent, with a number of more recent studies putting it at about 4 percent.[8] As a result, the public has become fond of blaming high medical costs on physicians who prescribe needless medical tests or perform unnecessary surgery.

The **physician practice hypothesis** has been used to explain variations in utilization rates across regions. This hypothesis, which is most closely associated with the work of Wennberg (1984, 1985), contends that per capita variations in the use of medical care, particularly surgery, reflect systematic differences in clinical opinions regarding the appropriate amount and type of medical care.

These subjective differences are collectively referred to as "practice style" and exist primarily because of the uncertainty surrounding the practice of medicine. As Eddy (1984) so aptly wrote, "Uncertainty creeps into medical practice through every pore. Whether a physician is defining a disease, making a diagnosis, selecting a procedure, observing outcomes, assessing probabilities, assigning preferences or putting it all together, he is walking on very slippery terrain" (p. 75). Physician uncertainty is likely to be greatest when the diagnosis is complicated and the medical procedure is relatively new. As Phelps (1992) writes,

When the disease is very easy to diagnose, the consequences of not intervening are well understood, and few alternative interventions exist to treat the disease, then

---

[8]Greenspan et al. (1988) estimated that 20 percent of the permanent pacemakers implanted in Philadelphia County in 1983 were unwarranted, while Chassin et al. (1986) notes that 17 percent of coronary angiographies for elderly patients had been unnecessary. However, a more recent group of studies found the level of unnecessary care to be much lower. Leape et al. (1993) found that 2 percent of coronary artery bypass surgeries were inappropriate, while Hilborne et al. (1993) found that 4 percent of percutaneous transluminal coronary angioplasties were inappropriate.

observed variability is quite low. . . . Hernia repair and removal of an inflamed appendix (appendectomy) provide two good examples. Alternatively, when the "indications" for surgery are less clear, or when alternative treatments exist (such as surgery or bed rest plus therapy for low back injuries) variations increase. (p. 25)

The rate at which medical technology and knowledge are diffused plays a critical role in determining the level of physician uncertainty and degree of practice variations. Other factors also come into play, such as the background and set of beliefs of the individual physician.

Phelps (1992) believes different local "schools of thought" evolve regarding appropriate practice style. The schools of thought develop as a physician invents a new medical treatment strategy and other doctors in the immediate local community learn and adopt the practice style. Since no property rights are assigned to treatment strategies, the individual physician faces little financial incentive to test and market the new idea on a broader basis. Consequently, the treatment strategy or practice style remains confined to the local area. Phelps claims that "allowing doctors to patent treatment strategies offers a tantalizing step into a market economy where 'professionalism' has previously remained. This would be a two-edged sword, however; doctors who produced and patented a strategy for treatment would reap potential profits, but they would also incur liability for subsequent use of that strategy throughout the country" (p. 41).

Addressing the issue of geographic variations from a slightly different but related angle, Chassin (1993) offers the enthusiasm hypothesis. According to him, geographic differences result primarily because certain physicians, for one reason or another, become "enthusiastic" about a particular medical procedure and therefore use it more frequently than other procedures. When the number of enthusiasts in an area becomes sufficiently large, geographic variations occur. Why the number of enthusiasts differs from area to area is open to conjecture. One explanation offered by the author is that a noteworthy teacher from, say, a teaching hospital in an area becomes enamored with a medical technique and persuades residents and other local practicing physicians of its merits. If she or he convinces enough physicians in the immediate area, geographic variations occur. This is especially true because, as Phelps notes, the new idea is not patentable.

The most interesting element of the enthusiasm hypothesis is the manner in which it differs from the more conventional physician practice hypothesis. Recall that under the physician practice hypothesis, the uncertainty surrounding the efficacy of a particular medical procedure is a primary reason for geographic variations. This is not the case with the enthusiasm hypothesis. Enthusiasts are anything but uncertain because they are thoroughly convinced of the benefits their patients receive from their medical procedure.

Despite the large number of studies on the physician practice hypothesis, it is difficult to determine the extent to which physician practice style explains geographic variations in the utilization of medical services. This is largely because it is very difficult to quantify practice style. One way to get around this problem is to look at those studies that use regression analysis to analyze the consumption of medical care and assume the unexplained variation, or residual, is partly the result of practice style. Because not all the residual can be explained by any one factor, we can assume the unexplained variation represents an upper bound estimate of the impact of practice style on the consumption of medical services.

Utilizing the residual approach, Folland and Stano (1990) and Stano (1991) reviewed numerous studies and concluded that a significant portion of the variation in the consumption of medical services can be explained by traditional supply and demand factors. Although the authors do not dismiss the role of physician practice style, they suggest it may not play a large role in explaining differences in the aggregate consumption of medical care across geographic regions.

Other studies have attempted to test directly the impact of practice style on the quantity and type of medical care consumed on a micro level. For example, Roos (1989) developed an index that measures physician hospitalization practice style and tested whether it affected the probability that elderly patients would be hospitalized. The results indicate that practice style cannot be ignored when examining the decision to hospitalize elderly patients.

Because physician practice style is difficult to measure, especially at the aggregate level, its impact on the amount and type of medical care consumed is difficult to judge. There is no doubt, however, that the presence of uncertainty means individual physicians will follow different courses of action when treating patients. Insofar as clinical decisions are based on subjective factors, physician practice style is likely to influence medical care.

The Impact of Utilization Review on the Physician Services Market

Various programs under the heading of managed care have been implemented in recent years to contain the costs of medical care. Most of these programs are directed at altering physician behavior primarily because physicians make most of the clinical decisions. As noted earlier, utilization review (UR) is one of the most frequently used methods to contain costs. Programs such as prospective, concurrent, and retrospective reviews evaluate the medical decisions of hospitals and physicians in an attempt to minimize medical costs by eliminating unnecessary medical care and educating patients and physicians concerning proper medical treatments.

Overall, the cost savings from UR programs have been modest in recent years. For example, Feldstein, Wickizer, and Wheeler (1988) found that UR programs decreased hospital inpatient days by 8.0 percent and total medical expenditures by 8.3 percent, while Scheffler, Sullivan, and Ko (1991) discovered that Blue Cross and Blue Shield utilization review programs decreased hospital patient days by 4.8 per-cent and inpatient payments by 4.2 percent. Equally important, Feldstein, Wickizer, and Wheeler found that UR programs have a one-time effect on decreasing utilization and costs. The implication is that UR programs may not significantly decrease the growth of medical expenditures over time. In fact, one can argue that any cost savings from UR programs may erode over time as physicians learn to practice in this new environment. Put another way, as physicians eventually learn to "game the system" and present their diagnoses and treatment plans in a manner that will make them more likely to be approved, UR programs may become increasingly unable to control costs by influencing physician behavior over time.

The tremendous growth in UR programs has led some to question who is reviewing the reviewers. Since the clinical bases for medical appropriateness and level of claim reviewers' skills vary widely across the insurance industry, there is some concern that consumers may be receiving inferior medical treatment. For example, an insurer may reject legitimate medical claims because the clinical information is dated or because the reviewer misinterpreted a diagnosis. In addition, physicians argue that they are forced to spend too much

INSIGHT 12–5

Does It Pay Physicians to Advertise?

Since the early 1980s, when the last restrictions on physician advertising were lifted, more and more physicians have advertised their services. A case in point is television station KESQ-TV of Palm Springs, California, which developed an advertising segment called the *Health Minute*, featuring local doctors who answer medical questions concerning their specialty practices. To appear on a segment that airs at least three times a week, doctors pay approximately $1,500 (Cooper, 1993). All indications are that the number of advertisements is likely to grow in the future, leading economists to wonder about the market implications. Theory tells us that advertising can either enhance or impede competition (what else did you expect?).

The procompetitive camp argues that advertising leads to a more competitive outcome because it decreases information costs regarding the price and quality of physician services. With more information regarding physician behavior at their disposal, consumers are in a better position to do some comparison shopping. This should cause the market for physician services to approach the competitive outcome in terms of price and quality. The anticompetitive camp argues just the opposite: Since product differentiation is so extensive in the physician services market, advertising arms physicians with the means to enhance their monopoly power. Through advertising, physicians attempt to differentiate themselves from others, thereby causing the demand for their services to not only increase but also become less elastic.

Using data from a sample of over 1,600 self-employed primary care physicians, Rizzo and Zeckhauser (1992) assessed the impact of advertising on the elasticity of demand for physician services. If advertising was found to cause the demand for primary care physician services to become more price elastic, it could be inferred that advertising enhances competition. Naturally, the opposite would be true if advertising were found to cause the demand for primary care services to become less price elastic. The authors found that advertising directly affects price and inversely affects output. From this finding, they inferred that advertising impedes competition by causing the demand for primary care services to become less price elastic. However, they also found a strong direct relation between advertising and quality as measured by the average time spent per office visit or with patients in all practice settings. It appears that those physicians who advertised charged a higher price for their services but also spent more time with each patient. In fact, advertising tended to increase quality by a greater percentage than price. Thus, Rizzo and Zeckhauser showed that advertising lowers the *quality-adjusted* price for physician services and reduces the total quantity of physician services. The overall impact of advertising on the level of competition is unclear from their analysis.

time trying to understand the nuances of each review process. This involves determining the basis for medical decisions and understanding the appeal process for protesting the rejection of a medical claim. Hence, it has been argued that the government needs to take a more active role in regulating UR programs to ensure consistent application of acceptable medical standards (Field and Gray, 1989).

Second surgical opinion programs comprise another type of UR aimed directly at altering the behavior of physicians, particularly surgeons. These programs, which can be either voluntary or mandatory in nature, have two major objectives. The first is to increase patient knowledge and thereby reduce the asymmetry of information problem. The second is to establish a procedure whereby physicians' decisions are routinely scrutinized by their peers. The ultimate goal is to reduce the number of unnecessary or avoidable operations and thereby reduce medical costs.

Empirical evidence suggests that second opinion programs have failed to significantly reduce medical costs. For one thing, studies have found that voluntary programs have little or no impact on medical cost savings. The evidence on mandatory programs is not much better. For example, Scheffler, Sullivan, and Ko (1991) found that mandatory second opinions have no impact on hospital utilization or payments. After reviewing the literature on the subject, Lindsey and Newhouse (1990) concluded that because of design flaws, studies fail to provide any conclusive evidence of cost savings from second opinions. The implication is that cost savings from second surgery opinions are likely to be small.

Several studies have examined the impact of prepaid health plans on the utilization of physician services. The question is whether prepaid health plans lead to fewer or more physician office visits than fee-for-service practices. According to the exhaustive review made by Miller and Luft (1994), "Most recent data showed either higher rates or little difference in HMO plan office visits per enrollee" compared to fee-for-service plans (p. 1514). Not enough studies were available to enable Miller and Luft to draw a definitive conclusion about the relation between PPOs and the utilization of physician services, however.

Other efforts to control medical costs have involved the development of clinical practice guidelines for physicians. Numerous medical societies and the Agency for Health Care Policy and Research (AHCPR) are in the process of developing and disseminating guidelines that provide physicians and patients with the preferred methods of treating different types of medical conditions. The hope is that guidelines will improve the quality of medical care and at the same time lower costs by providing timely information to physicians concerning the efficacy of various medical procedures. Rice (1993) argues that practice guidelines may backfire and result in higher medical costs. Any cost savings reaped by preventing a few physicians from using an unacceptable medical procedure may be offset by an increase in costs brought about by the adoption of a new, accepted medical procedure by many physicians. Despite the fact that some medical care providers have begun to implement medical guidelines, it is too early to ascertain their overall effect.

Medical Malpractice and Defensive Medicine

When properly designed, malpractice liability law serves two important functions. First, the malpractice legal system, as a type of tort liability law, compensates victims for any damages caused by the negligence of health care providers. Tort law refers to rules and practices governing wrongful injuries to persons or property. Damages include economic losses and pain and suffering costs. Second, the malpractice system helps to deter health care providers from engaging in future acts of negligence. Indeed, the deterrence effect of malpractice liability, by creating incentives for health care providers to offer appropriate medical care, may play a more important role than the compensation function because compensation might be provided more efficiently through other forms of social or private insurance (Danzon 2000). Because of imperfect information and the associated difficulty of establishing properly designed medical liability rules, many are dissatisfied with the current malpractice system and have called for various kinds of reforms.

Medical malpractice reform has been one of the most contentious health care issues in recent years and the issue is complicated by the lack of data measuring the number and severity of medical injuries. One of the most comprehensive studies, commonly referred to as the Harvard study (Weiler et al., 1993, and Brennan et al., 1991), reviewed over 30,000 patient records from 51 randomly selected acute care hospitals in New York in 1984. The study found that 3.7 percent of the patients in the study experienced a medical injury, and of that number a little more than 25 percent were the result of medical negligence. Most of the injuries were relatively minor with complete recovery occurring within one month. However, 2.6 percent of the negligent injuries resulted in total disability and another 13.6 percent in death. Extrapolating these results, the researchers estimated that in 1984 medical negligence was responsible for 6,895 deaths and 877 cases of permanent and total disability in the state of New York. The study also found that only 2 percent of those identified as having had sustained a medical injury through negligence filed a malpractice claim, with the ratio of claims to negligent injury increasing for more severe injuries. Evidence also indicates that a large number of claims were filed with little evidence of negligence.

In a nutshell, these figures reflect the general frustration with the malpractice system. Patient advocates are concerned because so few cases of medical negligence translate into malpractice claims and even fewer result in some type of financial settlement. In addition, there is the frustration that health care providers, particularly physicians, are not held accountable for providing inferior medical care. Health care providers are upset because of the large number of frivolous malpractice claims they must contend with along with the excessive jury awards that appear to have little relationship to damages incurred. The end result is higher liability premiums and higher practice costs. Physicians are also frustrated because they are encouraged by the current malpractice system to overutilize medical services in an attempt to stave off potential malpractice suits. This phenomenon is known as **defensive medicine**.[9]

Any discussion on medical malpractice must begin with a discussion of the cost of medical malpractice. Physician liability costs generally fall into two categories: medical malpractice insurance costs and defensive medical costs. Figure 12–5 traces out the average liability premiums for self-employed physicians from 1990 to 1998. The graph illustrates that liability premiums have increased only modestly throughout the 1990s and far below the overall rate of growth in medical expenditures. In 1990 the average premium equaled $14.5 thousand and increased to $16.8 thousand by 1998. Figure 12–5 also indicates that

---

[9]This discussion is based on a presentation entitled *The Malpractice Problem* developed by Professor Vivian Ho at the University of Alabama at Birmingham. The authors thank her for providing us an electronic copy of her PowerPoint presentation.

FIGURE 12-5

Mean Professional Liability for Self-Employed Physicians, 1990–1998

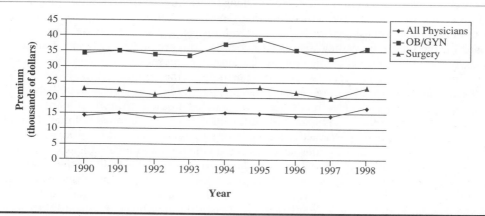

SOURCE: *Physician Socioeconomic Statistics 2000-2002 edition.* Chicago: American Medical Association, 2000, table 187.

liability premiums varied widely across specialties with specialists generally paying more for liability insurance than generalists. For example, in 1998, OB/GYNs paid nearly $36 thousand for liability insurance while family practice physicians paid less than $12 thousand. In the aggregate, most studies estimate physician malpractice premiums to account for only 1 percent of total health care spending (Carlstrom, 1993).

A number of studies have attempted to estimate the extent to which physicians overutilize medical care to reduce the risk of medical malpractice claims. Estimating the cost of defensive medicine poses a unique challenge to researchers because aside from having to precisely define the phenomenon of defensive medicine, they must also distinguish it from the amount of clinically justified medical care provided (GAO, 1995). Several studies on the subject have found that physicians are encouraged to practice defensive medicine and provide more medical care than is justified. For example, Kessler and McClellan (1996) utilized Medicare data for serious heart disease to estimate whether recent malpractice reforms have reduced medical costs. They found that malpractice reforms have reduced medical expenditures from between 5 to 9 percent without adversely impacting the quality of medical care. Based on their estimates they conclude that defensive medical practices contribute to rising medical costs. After reviewing the evidence a GAO report (1995) estimated the cost of defensive medicine to be approximately $10 billion a year. While this figure is large in absolute terms, it represents only a small fraction of overall health care expenditures.

Finally, the practice of defensive medicine may encourage physicians to cut back on certain medical services to avoid the possibility of lawsuit. For example, physicians may avoid treating high-risk patients or providing high-risk procedures where the medical outcome is more in doubt and the likelihood of a lawsuit is greater. This behavior is commonly referred to in the literature as negative defensive medicine because it reduces the availability of medical care.[10] Dubay, Kaestner, and Waidmann (2001) studied the impact of malpractice liability on the utilization of prenatal care and infant health and their results are consistent with the notion of negative defensive medicine. In particular, they found that higher malpractice premiums resulted in an increase in the incidence of late prenatal care among women. Thus, faced with higher premiums some obstetricians reacted by holding back on the high-risk medical services to decrease the probability of being involved in a costly malpractice suit. They also found the impact of increases in malpractice premiums to differ across income groups and other pertinent demographic factors. For example, they found that unmarried women of lower socioeconomic status were more likely to be impacted by negative defensive medicine than married women of more affluent means. Clearly, future work in this area needs to examine more closely the impact of medical malpractice on access to care, particularly among more vulnerable economic groups.

This rather brief review of issues surrounding medical malpractice indicates that malpractice reform is likely to be on the public agenda for years to come. While the economic costs of malpractice as measured by malpractice premiums and defensive medical costs are not as high as some would believe, they are significant and have prompted a call for serious medical liability reform. The mismatch between the number of medical injuries resulting from negligence and the number of medical claims has also encouraged many to call for reform.

Kinney (1995) argues that there have been two generations of malpractice reform thus far. The first generation took place throughout the 1970s and early 1980s and was directed primarily toward tort and insurance reform. The primary goal was to decrease the number and magnitude of claims. For example, caps on awards aimed to limit the monetary size of settlements, while pretrial screening panels and limits on attorney's fees attempted to limit the number of suits. Other reform measures aimed at making it more difficult for claimants to win by establishing expert witness requirements. Reforms of the insurance industry centered around making it easier and less expensive for physicians to acquire malpractice insurance. Based on her research, Kinney concluded that these reforms have had little impact even though most states adopted one or more of them.

As a result, a second generation of reforms has been evolving since the late 1980s. These reforms aim at streamlining "the adjudication and compensating system from the perspective of the claimants and providers" (Kinney, 1995, p. 99). One major element has been the development and use of practice guidelines to define a standard of care. Such guidelines make it easier to establish in a court of law whether or not a physician has provided inappropriate care to a patient. Another major component of the second-generation reforms is the establishment of a schedule for damages. A preset schedule of damages for various injuries makes compensation "more predictable and fair" (p. 105).

Enterprise liability, which involves shifting the legal liability away from physicians and onto the hospital or HMO of the affiliated physician, is another reform.[11] With enterprise liability, physicians are relieved from medical liability and therefore are less likely to practice costly defensive medicine. Additional cost savings result due to a reduction in the number of claimants. Instead of having to sue their doctors, the hospitals, and anyone else

---

[10]At the other extreme is positive defensive medicine of the type discussed earlier that leads to an increase in the utilization of medical care.

[11]Another alternative is to transfer the liability to the patient's insurance company.

involved in the case, patients need only sue the health care organization under enterprise liability (Carlstrom, 1993). The number of overall claims also decreases because health care organizations, such as hospitals and insurance companies, have a much greater financial incentive to monitor the behavior of physicians and weed out those who are incompetent. Other changes involve the mandatory use of alternative dispute resolution mechanisms, such as arbitration instead of a trial.

THE PERFORMANCE OF THE PHYSICIAN SERVICES INDUSTRY

Now that we have reviewed structure and conduct, we are in a position to examine the overall performance of the physician services market. Although the physician services industry appears to be structurally competitive in terms of the actual number of physicians, some evidence concerning practice variations and supplier-induced demand suggests that behaviorally physicians may act with some market power. An analysis of performance in this industry sheds some light on the net effect of these two contradictory perspectives. This section examines measures of physician price, output, and income over time in the United States.

Expenditures on Physician Services

Expenditures on physician and clinical services increased dramatically over the previous decade. According to table 12–1, expenditures on physician and clinical services equaled $157.5 billion in 1990 and by 2000 grew to $286.4 billion. This represents an overall increase of almost 82 percent. The annual rate of growth topped 10 percent in the early 1990s and it was not until the mid-1990s that the rate of increase in physician and clinical expenditures began to slow down. From 1994 through 1996 the rate of growth hovered at between 4 and 5 percent. By 1997 the rate of growth in physician and clinical expenditures was again on the rise and in 2000 it equaled 6 percent.

The Physician Services Price Inflation Rate

The most commonly used instrument to measure movements in the average price of physician services is the consumer price index (CPI) for physician services, which is provided for selected years from 1990 to 2001 in figure 12–6. The data reveal that the average price of physician services increased at an annual rate higher than the general rate of inflation but slightly less than the overall rate of inflation for medical services. From 1990 to 2001 the CPI for physician services increased from 160.8 to 253.6, and increase of almost 58 percent, while the CPI less medical care increased by a little more than 33 percent. Thus it appears the average rate of inflation for physician services was almost twice that of the overall rate of inflation less medical care from 1990 through 2001. Figure 12–6 also indicates that the rate of inflation for physician services was slightly less than the rate of inflation for health care in general and the disparity appears to have grown in recent years.

Another way to gauge the rate of increase in the price of physician services is to examine data collected by the AMA concerning the average fee for an office visit with established and new patients. In 1986, the average fee for a physician office visit equaled $30.10

T A B L E   1 2 – 1
Total Expenditures on Physician and Clinical Services for Selected Years (in billions of dollars)

Year	Total Expenditures	Annual Rate of Increase*	Total Real Expenditures
1990	157.5	11.2%	97.9
1995	220.5	4.8	105.6
1997	241.0	5.1	108.1
1998	256.8	6.6	111.9
1999	270.2	5.2	114.5
2000	286.4	6.0	117.0

*Physician expenditures are deflated by the physician services index of the CPI, where 1982–1984 is the base year.

SOURCE: Centers for Medicare and Medicaid Services. http://cms.hhs.gov/statistics.

F I G U R E   1 2 – 6
Consumer Price Index for Physician Services*

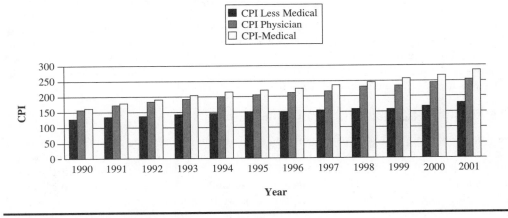

*The base period is 1982–1984.

SOURCE: Bureau of Labor Statistics http://www.bls.gov.

for an established patient and $55.57 for a new patient, and these rates increased to $60.63 and $102.46, respectively, by 1997. The average rate of increase from 1990 to 1997 was 6.4 percent for regular patients and 5.3 percent for new patients. It is interesting to note that according to the AMA, the mean fee for both established and new patients actually fell in 1996 by 1.4 percent and 5.3 percent, respectively.

INSIGHT 12–6

The Economics of Hospital Admitting Privileges

Traditionally, physicians must be granted admitting privileges at a hospital before being allowed to admit patients and utilize the hospital's medical facilities. In return for these privileges, a physician accepts certain duties and responsibilities, which can vary substantially across hospitals. For example, a small hospital may require only that the physician serve on a committee or two at the hospital, while a larger teaching hospital may require the physician to hold a staff appointment and share in some of the teaching responsibilities.

Regardless of the duties specified, it is clear that admitting privileges place the hospital and physician in a symbiotic relationship. From the physician's perspective, admitting privileges positively impact earnings by enhancing productivity. Among other things, admitting privileges give the physician the opportunity to provide a broader scope of medical services along with having access to more expensive inpatient services (Rizzo and Goddeeris, 1998).

To gain a better understanding of the relationship between hospitals and physicians, Rizzo and Goddeeris estimated the effects of hospital admitting privileges on physician earnings for a sample of self-employed physicians in 1992. In particular, they utilized regression analysis to estimate the effect on earnings of an exogenous change in admitting privileges after holding constant a host of control variables. For primary care physicians they found that admitting privileges have no impact on earnings. The authors argue that these findings were not surprising given that primary care physicians derive a relatively small portion of their income in a hospital setting.

The same cannot be said for specialists, however. The authors found a strong positive relation between earnings and the number of admitting privileges held by a specialist. As economic theory would suggest, the authors also found the relation to be nonlinear. According to their estimates, the marginal impact on earnings for a specialist having admitting privileges at one hospital is over $65,000 and increases to over $103,000 when a specialist acquires admitting privileges at a second hospital. At three hospitals, the marginal impact reaches its peak at over $106,000 and from that point begins to decrease. The marginal impact on earnings actually becomes negative when the representative specialist acquires admitting privileges at a fifth hospital.

Overall, the evidence indicates that most specialists cannot generate enough patients from one hospital and that it is in their financial interests to have admitting privileges at more than one hospital. Maximum income appears to be reached when a specialist has admitting privileges at four different hospitals. Beyond that point, however, the added time costs of having admitting privileges at one more hospital appear to outweigh any additional revenue that might be generated.

The CPI and AMA data both indicate that although the rate of growth in the average fee for physician services decreased in the 1990s, it still exceeded the general rate of inflation. During the 1990s, physician fees grew at an annual rate of between 4.9 and 6 percent, whereas the overall price level, excluding medical care, grew in the neighborhood of 2 to 3 percent. These figures overstate the inflation of physician fees for two reasons. First, the fees reported may not adequately reflect any discounts given to patients because they are covered by Medicare or belong to an HMO. Given the expanding role of MCOs, it is safe to assume the volume and extent of discounts negotiated with physicians increased over time. This means that there may be a significant disparity between the fee reported and the transaction fee. Second, the figures fail to consider any improvements in the quality of physician services that have taken place over time.

The Utilization of Physician Services

Expenditures on physician services increased significantly in the past decade, with much of that increase occurring early in the 1990s. From 1990 to 2000, physician expenditures increased roughly by 6.6 percent per year. Over the same period the CPI for physician services increased by slightly more than 4.5 percent. Combined, these figures suggest that almost two-thirds of the average annual increase in physician expenditures was the result of price increases, while the remaining one-third was due to increased utilization. The last column in table 12–1 provides data for real expenditures on physician and clinical services, which is found by dividing nominal values by the relevant CPI. Real expenditures grew less than 2 percent per year on average from 1990 to 2000.

Physician Income

The last item we examine is changes in physician income over time. Data for nominal and real (i.e., total physician income deflated by the CPI and in 1990 dollars) income from 1990 to 1999 appear in figure 12–7. Over the period in question nominal income increased

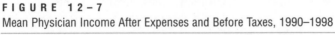

FIGURE 12–7

Mean Physician Income After Expenses and Before Taxes, 1990–1998

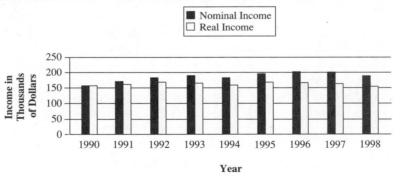

SOURCE: *Socioeconomic Characteristics of Medical Practice 2000-2002.* Chicago: American Medical Association, 2000, table 190.

from $164.3 thousand to $194.4 thousand, for an increase of slightly more than 18 percent. The data on real income tell a slightly different story. It appears that while nominal income increased modestly during the 1990s, real income actually decreased. From 1990 to 1998 real income shrank from $164 thousand to $154 thousand, with the largest decreases taking place between 1993 and 1994, and 1997 and 1998. No doubt these changes can be attributed to the growth in managed care (Simon and Born, 1996) along with the implementation of tighter fee controls for the Medicare and Medicaid programs.

To gauge the relative standing of physician income, we need to compare compensation to the growth in real income sustained by other professionals with extensive graduate training. In particular, consider the ratio of total physician income to total compensation of college faculty at doctoral granting institutions. The ratio remained rather stable throughout the early 1990s at around 2.7, indicating that the average physician earned 2.7 times the earnings of the average college professor. By the mid-1990s, however, that ratio began to fall slightly and by 1998 it equaled 2.4. These relative income figures suggest that not only did physicians in general experience a slight decrease in real income throughout the 1990s, they also lost ground relative to other professionals with substantial graduate training.

This conclusion is substantiated by a study that looked at the relative income of physicians from an investment perspective. If expenditures on higher education are treated as an investment in human capital and the increment to earnings received in the job market as a return on that investment, the rate of return received on investments in higher education can be calculated. Utilizing that approach, Weeks, Wallace, Wallace, and Welch (1994) compared the rates of return on educational investments for various professionals, including physicians. According to their results, primary care physicians receive an annual rate of return of 15.9 percent on educational investments over a working life, while specialists receive a 20.9 percent return. As a point of comparison, the authors found that businesspeople and attorneys receive a 29.0 and 25.4 percent rate of return, respectively. These findings imply that physicians receive a rate of return on investments in educational expenditures that is comparable to, if not less than, that of other professionals.

SUMMARY

The physician services market has experienced profound changes in recent years, with both the size and scope of the market increasing substantially. Since 1990 the size of the market has increased, whether measured on the basis of real physician expenditures or the number of practicing physicians. The mode of production has also changed considerably, with economies of scale forcing physicians into large-group practices as opposed to small-group or solo practices. All these changes, coupled with an erosion of barriers to entry, have intensified the level of structural competition in the physician services market. Most of the market power physicians currently possess appears to result primarily from the asymmetry of information that exists between doctor and patient. Although the level of competition varies across regions, overall the market can be classified as being monopolistically competitive. The physician services industry contains a large number of sellers, moderate barriers to entry, a certain amount of product differentiation, and some information imperfections.

The well-publicized geographic variations in physician utilization rates have been the source of much concern for policy analysts and politicians alike. The evidence indicates that much of this concern is uncalled for, since most of the variation can be explained by traditional supply and demand factors.

Without a doubt, the single greatest change in the physician services market has been the growing presence of managed care. Over 90 percent of all physicians are involved with at least one MCO. All indications suggest that these numbers will increase in the future. Managed care has ushered in a new set of compensation schemes, along with a host of utilization review programs. The evidence on compensation schemes suggests that clinical decisions are sensitive to the method of payment. For example, the utilization of medical resources is inversely related to whether the physician is compensated on a salary or capitation basis rather than the more traditional fee-for-service system. Findings concerning the impact of utilization review programs on utilization and costs have been mixed, however. For example, second opinion programs appear to have little impact on the level of medical care. There does appear to be a movement toward the development and use of clinical guidelines for physicians. It remains to be seen whether such efforts will affect the amount and cost of physician care.

REVIEW QUESTIONS AND PROBLEMS

1. Physician assistants have long argued that they have the ability to provide as much as 70 percent of the medical services provided by primary care physicians at a much lower cost. Yet government regulations limit their ability to work independently of physicians. Explain what would happen to the level of competition in the physician services market if all the statutes limiting the activities of physician assistants were eliminated.

2. Discuss how enhanced competition in the physician services market has affected the ability of physicians to induce the demand for medical services.

3. Analyze the alternative compensation schemes discussed in this chapter that private insurers use to pay physicians. Think in terms of the incentive to provide an excessive amount of medical services.

4. As you know, various medical groups are in the process of developing medical guidelines. Assuming guidelines are developed and widely adopted by physicians, how will this affect the physician services market?

5. Some argue that practice variations exist because information on practice style is disseminated slowly. Phelps (1992) argues that physicians should be allowed to patent and sell their practice strategies. Explain how this policy might affect practice variations.

6. Discuss the theoretical and empirical issues surrounding the supplier-induced demand theory.

7. Discuss the factors that have contributed to the increase in expenditures on physician services over the past decade.

8. Explain the many institutional and structural changes that might make physician licensing obsolete.

9. Why may the physician inflation rate be exaggerated?

10. According to McGuire (2000) the problem of defensive medicine can be analyzed in the context of the supplier-induced demand model because physicians induced the demand for their services to decrease the chances of a medical malpractice suit. Use the supplier-induced demand to illustrate McGuire's point.
11. Use each of McGuire's quantity setting models to explain how a physician is likely to react to price controls. In particular, explain how the physician continues to earn economic profits despite the implementation of price controls.

ONLINE RESOURCES

To access Internet links related to the topics in this chapter, please visit our web site at http://santerre.swcollege.com.

REFERENCES

American Medical Association. *Physician Characteristics and Distribution in the U.S., 1997/98*. Chicago: AMA Center for Health Policy Research, 1998a.

————. *Physician Marketplace Statistics, 1997/98*. Chicago: AMA Center for Health Policy Research, 1998b.

————. *Socioeconomic Characteristics of Medical Practice, 1997/98*. Chicago: AMA Center for Health Policy Research, 1998c.

————. *Physician Characteristics and Distribution in the US 2002-2003 edition*. Chicago: AMA Center for Health Policy Research, 2002.

————. *Physician Socioeconomic Statistics 2000-2002 edition*. Chicago: AMA Center for Health Policy Research, 2002.

Bosch, Xavier. "Too Many Physicians Training in Spain." *Journal of the American Medical Association* 282 (September 15, 1999), pp. 1025–26.

Brennan, Troyen, et al. "Incidence of Adverse Events and Negligence in Hospitalized Patients." *New England Journal of Medicine* 324 (February 7, 1991), pp. 370–76.

Brown, Douglas M. "Do Physicians Underutilize Aides?" *Journal of Human Resources* 23 (summer 1988), pp. 342–55.

Bureau of Labor Statistics. http://stats.bls.gov.

Carlsen, Fredrick, and Jostein Grytten. "More Physicians: Improved Availability or Induced Demand?" *Health Economics* 7 (1998), pp. 495–508.

Carlstrom, Charles T. "Enterprise Liability: A Prescription for Health Care Reform." *Economic Commentary, Federal Reserve Bank of Cleveland*, July 1, 1993.

Carpenter, Bruce, and Stephen Neun. "An Analysis of the Location Decision of Young Primary Care Physicians." *Atlantic Economic Journal* 27 (June 1999), pp. 135–49.

Centers for Medicare & Medicaid Services. http://cms.hhs.gov/statistics.

Chassin, Mark R. "Explaining Geographic Variations: The Enthusiasm Hypothesis." *Medical Care* 31 (supplement 1993), pp. YS37–YS44.

Chassin, Mark R., et al. "Variations in the Use of Medical and Surgical Services by the Medicare Population." *New England Journal of Medicine* 314 (January 30, 1987), pp. 285–90.

Cooper, Jim. "Doctors Try Dose of TV." *Broadcasting and Cable*, October 25, 1993, p. 47.

Cooper, Richard A., Thomas E. Getzen, Heather J. McKee, and Prakash Laud. "Economic and Demographic Trends Signal an Impeding Physician Shortage." *Health Affairs* 21 (January/February 2002), pp. 140–54.

Cromwell, Jerry, and Janet B. Mitchell. "Physician-Induced Demand for Surgery." *Journal of Health Economics* 5 (1986), pp. 293–313.

Danzon, Patricia M. "Liability for Medical Malpractice." In *Handbook of Health Economics*, Volume I, eds. A.J. Culyer and J.P. Newhouse. Amsterdam: Elsevier Science, 2000.

Defelice, Lisa C., and W. David Bradford. "Relative Inefficiencies in Production Between Solo and Group Practice Physicians." *Health Economics* 6 (1997), pp. 455–65.

Dubay, Lisa, Robert Kaestner, and Timothy Waidmann. "Medical Malpractice Liability and its Effect on Prenatal Care Utilization and Infant Health." *Journal of Health Economics* 20 (July 2001), pp. 591–611.

Eddy, David M. "Variations in Physician Practice: The Role of Uncertainty." *Health Affairs* 3 (summer 1984), pp. 74–89.

Escarce, Jose J. "Explaining the Association between Surgeon Supply and Utilization." *Inquiry* 29 (winter 1992), pp. 403–15.

Escarce, Jose J., and Mark V. Pauly. "Physician Opportunity Costs in Physician Practice Cost Functions." *Journal of Health Economics* 17 (April 1998), pp. 129–51.

Escarce, Jose J., Daniel Polsky, Gregory D. Wozniak, and Phillip R. Kletke. "HMO Growth and the Geographical Redistribution of Generalist and Specialists Physicians, 1987–1997." *Health Services Research* 35 (October 2000), pp. 825–44.

Feldstein, Paul J., Thomas M. Wickizer, and John R.C. Wheeler. "Private Cost Containment: The Effects of Utilization Review Programs on Health Care Use and Expenditures." *New England Journal of Medicine* 318 (May 19, 1988), pp. 1310–14.

Field, Marilyn J., and Bradford H. Gray. "Should We Regulate Utilization Management?" *Health Affairs* 8 (winter 1989), pp. 103–12.

Folland, Sherman T., and Miron Stano. "Small Area Variations: A Critical Review of Propositions, Methods and Evidence." *Medical Care Review* 47 (winter 1990), pp. 419–65.

Frech, H.E., and Paul B. Ginsburg. "Optimal Scale in Medical Practice: A Survivor Analysis." *Journal of Business* 47 (1974), pp. 23–36.

Friedman, Milton. *Capitalism and Freedom*. Chicago: University of Chicago Press, 1962.
———. *Free to Choose*. New York: Harcourt Brace Jovanovich, 1980.

Fuchs, Victor R. "The Supply of Surgeons and the Demand for Operations." *Journal of Human Resources* 13 (supplement 1978), pp. 35–56.

Gamliel, Sandy, et al. "Will Physicians Meet the Managed Care Challenge?" *Health Affairs* 14 (summer 1995), pp. 131–42.

Gold, Marsha R., et al. "A National Survey of the Arrangements Managed-Care Plans Make with Physicians." *New England Journal of Medicine* 333 (December 21, 1995), pp. 1678–83.

Government Accounting Office. *Medical Liability Impact on Hospital and Physician Costs Extends Beyond Insurance*. Washington D.C., September 1995.

Government Accounting Office. *Primary Care Physicians Managing Supply in Canada, Germany, Sweden, and the United Kingdom*. Washington, D.C., May 1994.

Greenspan, Allan M., et al. "Incidence of Unwarranted Implantation of Permanent Cardiac Pacemakers in a Large Medical Population." *New England Journal of Medicine* 318 (January 21, 1988), pp. 158–63.

Grumbach, Kevin, Dennis Osmond, Karen Vranizan, Deborah Jaffe, and Andrew B. Bindman. "Primary Care Physicians' Experience of Financial Incentives in Managed-Care Systems." *New England Journal of Medicine* 339 (November 19, 1998), pp. 1516–21.

Grytten, Jostein, and Dorthe Holst. "Supplier Inducement: Its Effect on Dental Services in Norway." *Journal of Health Economics* 9 (1990), pp. 483–91.

Grytten, Jostein, and Rune Sorensen. "Type Contract and Supplier-Induced Demand for Primary Physicians in Norway." *Journal of Health Economics* 20 (2001), pp. 379–93.

Hellinger, Fred J. "The Impact of Financial Incentives on Physician Behavior in Managed Care Plans: A Review of the Evidence." *Medical Care Research and Review* 53 (September 1996), pp. 294–314.

Hemenway, David, and Deborah Fallon. "Testing for Physician-Induced Demand with Hypothetical Cases." *Medical Care* 23 (April 1985), pp. 344–49.

Hilborne, Lee H., et al. "The Appropriateness of the Use of Percutaneous Transluminal Coronary Angioplasty in New York State." *Journal of American Medicine* 269 (February 10, 1993), pp. 761–65.

Hillman, Alan L. "Financial Incentives for Physicians in HMOs." *New England Journal of Medicine* 317 (December 31, 1987), pp. 1743–48.

Hillman, Alan L., Mark V. Pauly, and Joseph J. Kerstein. "How Do Financial Incentives Affect Physicians' Clinical Decisions and the Financial Performance of Health Maintenance Organizations?" *New England Journal of Medicine* 321 (July 13, 1989), pp. 86–92.

Hillman, Bruce J., et al. "Frequency and Costs of Diagnostic Imaging in Office Practice—A Comparison of Self-Referring and Radiologist-Referring Physicians." *New England Journal of Medicine* 323 (December 6, 1990), pp. 1604–8.

Kessel, Reuben. "Price Discrimination in Medicine." *Journal of Law and Economics* 1 (1958), pp. 20–53.

Kessler, Daniel, and Mark McClellan. "Do Doctors Practice Defensive Medicine?" *Quarterly Journal of Economics* 111 (May 1996), pp. 353–90.

Kinney, Eleanor D. "Malpractice Reform in the 1990s: Past Disappointments, Future Success?" *Journal of Health Politics, Policy and Law* 20 (spring 1995), pp. 90–135.

Leape, Lucian L., et al. "The Appropriateness of Use of Coronary Artery Bypass Graft Surgery in New York State." *Journal of the American Medical Association* 269 (February 10, 1993), pp. 753–60.

Leffler, Keith B. "Physician Licensure: Competition and Monopoly in American Medicine." *Journal of Law and Economics* 21 (1978), pp. 165–86.

Lindsey, Phoebe A., and Joseph P. Newhouse. "The Cost and Value of Second Surgical Opinion Programs: A Critical Review of the Literature." *Journal of Health Policy, Politics and Law* 15 (fall 1990), pp. 543–70.

Marder, William D., and Stephen Zuckerman. "Competition and Medical Groups." *Journal of Health Economics* 4 (1985), pp. 167–76.

McCarthy, Thomas R. "The Competitive Nature of the Primary-Care Physician Services Market." *Journal of Health Economics* 4 (1985), pp. 93–117.

McGuire, Thomas. "Physician Agency." In *Handbook of Health Economics*, Volume I, eds. A.J. Culyer and J.P. Newhouse. Amsterdam: Elsevier Science, 2000.

Miller, Mark E., and John Holahan. "Geographic Variations in Physician Utilization." *Medical Care Research and Review* 52 (June 1995), pp. 252–78.

Miller, Robert H., and Harold S. Luft. "Managed Care Plan Performance Since 1980." *Journal of the American Medical Association* 271 (May 18, 1994), pp. 1512–19.

Mitchell, Jean M., and Tim R. Sass. "Physician Ownership of Ancillary Services: Indirect Demand Inducement or Quality Assurance." *Journal of Health Economics* 14 (1995), pp. 263–89.

Moore, Thomas. "The Purpose of Licensing." *Journal of Law and Economics* 4 (1961), pp. 93–117.

Noether, Monica. "The Growing Supply of Physicians: Has the Market Become More Competitive?" *Journal of Labor Economics* 4 (1986), pp. 503–37.

Organization for Economic Cooperation and Development. *OECD Health Data 2002*, Paris, 2002.

Phelps, Charles E. "Diffusion of Information in Medical Care." *Journal of Economic Perspectives* 6 (summer 1992), pp. 23–42.

Politzer, Robert M., et al. "Matching Physician Supply and Requirements: Testing Policy Recommendations." *Inquiry* 33 (summer 1996), pp. 181–94.

Polsky, Daniel, Phillip R. Kletke, Gregory D. Wozniak, and Jose J. Escarce. "HMO Penetration and the Geographic Mobility of Practicing Physicians." *Journal of Health Economics* 19 (2000), pp. 793–809.

Pope, Gregory C., and Russel T. Burge. "Economies of Scale in Physician Practice." *Medical Care Research and Review* 53 (December 1996), pp. 417–40.

Raffel, Marshall W., and Norma K. Raffel. *The U.S. Health System: Origins and Functions*. 3rd ed. New York: John Wiley and Sons, 1989.

Reinhardt, Uwe E. "A Production Function for Physician Services." *Review of Economics and Statistics* 54 (February 1972), pp. 55–66.

———. "Manpower Substitution and Productivity in Medical Practices: Review of Research." *Health Services Research* 8 (1973), pp. 200–27.

———. *Physician Productivity and Demand for Health Manpower*. Cambridge, MA: Ballinger Publishing Company, 1975.

Rice, Thomas H. "An Evaluation of Alternative Policies for Controlling Health Care Costs." In *Building Blocks for Change: How Health Care Reform Affects Our Future*, eds. Jack A. Meyer and Sharon Silow-Carrol. Washington, D.C.: The Economic and Social Research Institute, 1993.

Rizzo, John A., and John H. Goddeeris. "The Economic Returns to Hospital Admitting Privileges." *Journal of Health Politics, Policy and Law* 23 (June 1998), pp. 483–515.

Rizzo, John A., and Richard J. Zeckhauser. "Advertising and the Price, Quantity, and Quality of Primary Care Physician Services." *Journal of Human Resources* 27 (summer 1992), pp. 381–421.

Roos, Noralou P. "Predicting Hospital Utilization by the Elderly: The Importance of Patient, Physician, and Hospital Characteristics." *Medical Care* 27 (October 1989), pp. 905–17.

Rosenthal, Meredith B., Richard G. Frank, Joan L. Buchanan, and Arnold M. Epstein. "Transmission of Financial Incentives to Physicians By Intermediary Organizations in California." *Health Affairs* 21 (July/August 2002), pp. 197–205.

Rossiter, Louis F., and Gail R. Wilensky. "Identification of Physician Induced Demand." *Journal of Human Resources* 19 (spring 1984), pp. 232–44.

Scheffler, Richard M., Sean D. Sullivan, and Timothy Hoachung Ko. "The Impact of Blue Cross and Blue Shield Plan Utilization Management Programs, 1980–88." *Inquiry* 28 (fall 1991), pp. 263–75.

Schroeder, Steven A. "Western European Responses to Physician Oversupply." *Journal of the American Medical Association* 252 (July 20, 1984), pp. 373–84.

———. "Physician Supply and the U.S. Medical Marketplace." *Health Affairs* 11 (spring 1992), pp. 235–54.

Simon, Carol J., and Patricia H. Born. "Physician Earnings in a Changing Managed Care Environment." *Health Affairs* 15 (fall 1996), pp. 124–33.

Stano, Miron. "Further Issues in Small Area Variations Analysis." *Journal of Health Politics, Policy and Law* 16 (fall 1991), pp. 573–88.

Svorny, Shirley. "Should We Reconsider Licensing Physicians?" *Contemporary Policy Issues* 10 (January 1992), pp. 31–38.

Thurston, Norman K., and Anne M. Libby. "A Production Function for Physician Services Revisited." *Review of Economics and Statistics* 84 (February 2002), pp. 184–91.

Tussing, A. Dale. "Physician-Induced Demand for Medical Care: Irish General Practitioners." *Economic and Social Review* 14 (1983), pp. 225–47.

Tussing, A. Dale, and Martha Wojtowyzc. "Physician-Induced Demand by Irish GPs." *Social Science and Medicine* 23 (1986), pp. 851–60.

Weeks, William B., Amy E. Wallace, Myron M. Wallace, and H. Gilbert Welch. "A Comparison of the Educational Costs and Incomes of Physicians and Other Professionals." *New England Journal of Medicine* 330 (May 5, 1994), pp. 1280–86.

Weiler, Paul C., et al. *A Measure of Malpractice: Medical Injury, Malpractice Litigation and Patient Compensation*. Cambridge: Harvard University Press, 1993.

Wennberg, John E. "Dealing with Medical Practice Variations: A Proposal for Action." *Health Affairs* 3 (summer 1984), pp. 6–32.

———. "On Patient Need, Equity, Supplier-Induced Demand, and the Need to Assess the Outcome of Common Medical Practices." *Medical Care* 23 (May 1985), pp. 512–20.

Wilson, Florence A., and Duncan Neuhauser. *Health Services in the United States*. 2nd ed. Cambridge, MA: Ballinger Publishing Company, 1985.

CEBS QUESTIONS

CEBS Sample Question on Subject Matter from CEBS Course 9 Study Manual

1. Advocates for the elimination of medical licensure requirements point to which recent changes to advance their position? (pages 341–343)

CEBS Sample Exam Questions

1. Which statement describes average physician income in recent years?
    A. Gains have been far greater than those of other professionals
    B. Slight decreases in real income have made physicians lose ground relative to other professionals with graduate training
    C. Decreases have been substantial

   D. Specialty physicians have experienced substantial increases while general practitioners have experienced substantial decreases
   E. Only research physicians have experienced an increase in real income
2. Which of the following statements regarding the supplier-induced demand (SID) hypothesis regarding physician behavior is (are) correct?
   I.   An important element of the hypothesis is the asymmetry of information that exists regarding the various health care options available
   II. The SID hypothesis suggests that physicians are not motivated by increases in personal income
   III. Empirical support for the SID hypothesis has been waning in recent years
       A. III only
       B. I and II only
       C. II and III only
       D. I and III only
       E. I, II, and III
3. All the following statements regarding the structure of the market for physician services are correct EXCEPT:
       A. There has been a significant increase in the physician-to-population ratio in the past two decades
       B. Over 90 percent of all physicians have at least one contract with a managed care organization
       C. Many experts believe there are too many general practitioners and not enough specialists
       D. The physician services market has become more competitive over time
       E. There appears to be a movement away from single and two-physician practices toward multi-physician practices

Answer to Sample Question from Study Manual

Proponents question the need for medical licensure given: (1) the recent shifts in medical liability from physicians to institution; (2) the growth in for-profit medical care providers; and (3) the growing use of employed rather than self-employed physicians. The growth in for-profit providers and employed physicians has created a greater incentive for institutions to monitor the performance of physicians and, if necessary, to terminate incompetent physicians.

Answers to Sample Exam Questions

1. B is the answer. See figure 12–7 and text on pages 366–367.
2. D is the answer. The basic premise of the SID hypothesis is that physicians abuse their role as health care providers to augment their personal income. Therefore, Statement II is false. Statements I and III are correct. See pages 346–349 of the text.
3. C is the answer. It is believed that there are too many specialists in the United States and not enough primary care physicians. The other statements are all true. See pages 335–336 of the text.

CHAPTER 13

THE HOSPITAL SERVICES INDUSTRY

Just about everyone, either as a patient, a visitor, or an employee, has had some experience at a hospital. Some people conceive of hospitals as cold, lifeless facilities that spell gloom and doom. Others imagine hospitals as wondrous places where miraculous life-saving feats, such as human organ transplants, are performed. Regardless of one's view, it is safe to say that the hospital of today bears little resemblance to its early-nineteenth-century predecessor. According to Peter Temin (1988), a noted economic historian,

> *Hospitals were primarily nonmedical institutions throughout most of the nineteenth century. They existed for the care of marginal members of society, whether old, poor, or medically or psychologically deviant. Medicine was practiced outside the hospital, and the medical staffs of hospitals were small. Hospitals were charitable institutions, and they looked for moral rather than physical improvement in their patients. . . . In short, the nineteenth century hospital was closer to an almshouse than to a modern hospital. (pp. 78–80)*

With the development of the germ theory of disease, the advent of new technologies, and increased urbanization, the "modern" hospital replaced the old-style version in the years following 1880. Hospitals have subsequently evolved into vibrant centers of medical and business activities.

Today's hospital is a technological marvel. The once simple hospital bed can now cost up to $10,000 when it includes customized accessories, such as automatically inflating air mattresses for patients with bed sores, voice-activated adjustments for paraplegics, and in-bed weight scales for bedridden patients (Anders, 1993a). Aided by advances in computer and pharmaceutical technologies, the modern hospital has proven capable of offering numerous therapeutic and diagnostic services that extend and improve the quantity and quality of lives. Indeed, one may point to the success of modern medicine as the culprit behind the ever-rising cost of delivering hospital services. Accounting for expenditures of $412.1 billion and 36 percent of all personal health care expenditures in 2000, the hospital services industry is the largest of the medical care industries.

This chapter explores the structure, conduct, and performance of the hospital services industry. Specifically, the chapter:

> Describes the number, types, and size distribution of U.S. hospitals.

> Defines the relevant product and geographical markets for hospitals.

> Examines sources of barriers to entry in the hospital services industry.

> Discusses the relation between managed care and hospital structure and behavior.

> Focuses on hospital competition, regulation, and pricing behavior.

> Assesses the output and pricing performance of the hospital services industry.

THE STRUCTURE OF THE HOSPITAL SERVICES INDUSTRY

According to the industrial organization triad, as discussed in Chapter 8, the structural competitiveness of an industry can be evaluated to some extent by focusing on a number of characteristics affecting the degree of actual and potential competition. *Actual competition* refers to the intensity of the competition that currently coexists among the firms in an industry. Among the more important factors influencing the degree of actual competition are the number and size distribution of the existing firms, the type of product offered for sale, and the amount of information consumers possess. *Potential competition* depends on how easy it is for new firms to enter an industry. The degree of potential competition can be measured by the magnitude of any barriers to entry resulting from economies of scale or legal impediments, such as patents and government restrictions. These and other structural characteristics of the hospital industry are discussed in more detail next.

Number, Types, and Size Distribution of U.S. Hospitals

The last 20 years have witnessed a dramatic and continual decline in the number of hospitals in the United States. Only about 5,800 of the nearly 7,000 hospitals that existed in 1980 still remained in 2000 (Health Forum LLC, 2002). The number of hospital beds also fell by nearly 30 percent over the 20-year span. Increased competitive and regulatory forces brought on by managed-care health plans and federal cost-containment measures have been cited as part of the explanation for the decline in the number of hospitals and hospital beds.

Hospitals are categorized based on ownership, types of services, and length of stay. In terms of ownership, hospitals can be separated into those operated by the federal government and those that are nonfederal hospitals. Federal hospitals are usually based at military institutions or run by the Veterans Administration. Based on service offerings and average length of stay, nonfederal hospitals can be grouped into community, long-term general and special, psychiatric, and tuberculosis hospitals. Community hospitals, the largest category at roughly 85 percent of all hospitals, provide general medical and surgical services and specialty services, such as ear, nose, and throat care; obstetrics and gynecology; or orthopedic services; and offer short-term stays (i.e., an average length of stay of less than 30 days).

Community hospitals can be further differentiated based on type of ownership. The dominant ownership type is the nonprofit hospital, representing about 61 percent of the community hospitals and controlling nearly 71 percent of all community hospital beds as of 2000. The nonprofit market share in terms of total beds remained fairly stable since

1980. For-profit hospitals currently account for almost 15 percent of all community hospitals. The market share (in beds) of for-profit hospitals rose from 9 percent in 1980 to 13 percent in 2000, with the increase corresponding to a decline in the state and local government market share from 21 to 16 percent.

The typical community hospital operates with 168 beds; almost one-half of all community hospitals have between 50 and 200 beds. Only 6 percent of community hospitals have less than 25 beds and only 9 percent have more than 400 beds. The same relative size pattern holds for both not-for-profit and for-profit hospitals, except that for-profit hospitals are smaller than not-for-profit hospitals, on average. Specifically, the average not-for-profit hospital holds 194 beds whereas the typical for-profit hospital contains 147 beds. Public hospitals are smaller yet, a typical one possessing only 113 beds. The relatively small size most likely reflects that a large fraction of public hospitals provide county hospital services in sparsely populated rural areas.

Although these data provide some insight into the ownership structure and size distribution of the different types of hospitals, they offer little information about the market power held by individual hospitals in the United States. The geographical market for hospital services is primarily local in scope, whereas the data are summarized at the national level. In addition, although hospitals compete among themselves, they might also be viewed as competing against other types of health care providers, such as freestanding surgical centers. Before we can draw any behavioral or performance implications from market structure statistics, we must properly define the product and geographical markets.

Defining the Relevant Product and Geographical Markets for Hospital Services

Although some hospitals produce specialized services, such as psychiatric or nose, throat, and eye care services, most hospitals can be treated as multiproduct firms that simultaneously offer a multitude of diagnostic and therapeutic services. The large number and variety of services make it difficult to define and measure the relevant product market (RPM). Some health economists, such as Wilder and Jacobs (1987), have proposed that the RPM should be based on specific diagnoses, such as obstetrics, nervous system, tonsillectomy, or hernia repair services. However, Frech (1987) notes that hospitals are potential suppliers of most medical services even if they do not presently produce them, since they are capable of shifting resources from producing one service to producing another. Furthermore, some hospital services, such as X rays, blood tests, and surgery, are complements to one another, reflecting the joint nature of the hospital production process. The implication is that the hospital RPM should be treated as a cluster of hospital services. As Frech (1987) notes, "The hundreds or thousands of individual procedures or services should not be viewed as individual markets" (p. 266).

One problem associated with a cluster of hospital services approach to defining the relevant product market is that some hospital facilities provide different levels of care in terms of the degree of technical sophistication and quality of services rendered or the seriousness and complexity of illnesses treated. Thus, some hospitals may not be in the same relevant product market because the level of care differs. Professionals in the hospital industry generally distinguish among four types of care.

Primary care services involve the prevention, early detection, and treatment of disease. Services of this nature include obstetrics, gynecology, internal medicine, and general surgery. A hospital that limits itself to providing primary care typically has some diagnostic equipment to perform X ray and laboratory analysis. *Secondary* care involves more sophisticated treatment and may include cardiology, respiratory care, and physical therapy. Equipment and laboratory capabilities are more sophisticated in secondary care hospitals. *Tertiary* care is designed to arrest disease in process, including heart surgery and such cancer treatments as chemotherapy, and requires still more sophisticated equipment than do primary or secondary services. Community hospitals normally provide both primary and secondary care, and some offer tertiary care. Research hospitals associated with university medical schools are argued to provide state-of-the-art *quaternary*-level care.[1]

Another potential problem with the cluster of services approach is that hospital and nonhospital providers offering partial product lines are excluded from the relevant product market. Those excluded include specialized hospitals, physician clinics, and freestanding outpatient surgery centers. The cluster of services approach to the RPM typically excludes outpatient services when determining a hospital's relevant product market, largely because it is so difficult or costly to account for the relatively numerous and small market shares of providers delivering outpatient services. In effect, the cluster of hospital services approach treats hospital outpatient services as belonging to a separate market: the market for outpatient or ambulatory care services. Consequently, the size of the hospital market is measured in inpatient terms by either beds, admissions, inpatient days, or inpatient revenues.

Once the RPM is defined as a **cluster of inpatient hospital services**, the next step is to determine the relevant geographical market (RGM). The proper geographical area reflects the ability of the patients to switch to alternative suppliers when price is raised or quality is reduced by a nontrivial amount. Due to data availability and practical concerns, many researchers have based the RGM on geopolitical boundaries, such as counties, metropolitan areas, or cities. Some have used health service areas to define the RGM; others, such as Luft et al. (1986), have used a fixed 5- or 15-mile radius around each hospital as the appropriate RGM. The problem with RGM definitions of these kinds, however, is that they are based on convenience rather than on sound economic principles.

According to Elzinga and Hogarty (1978), patient flow data should be analyzed when determining the RGM. Patient flow data reflect both the consumer's willingness to travel and the ability to substitute among hospital providers. An appropriately defined RGM has small percentages of patients flowing into and out of it. This means geographic markets are defined such that only a small percentage of people leave to purchase hospital services elsewhere and a small fraction of individuals enter from outside the area to buy hospital services. Based on such a definition of the RGM, geographical market areas tend to be small or local in nature. For example, in *U.S. v. Rockford Memorial*, the court ruled that Rockford, Illinois, and the immediate hinterland was the RGM because 87 percent of Rockford Memorial's patients came from the area immediately surrounding Rockford and 90 percent of Rockford residents were hospitalized in Rockford itself. A relatively small geographical market area for hospital services should not be surprising. As Judge Posner noted in this antitrust case, "For highly exotic or highly elective hospital treatment, patients will sometimes travel long distances, of course. But for the most part hospital services are local.

---

[1]See *U.S. v. Carilion*, 707 F. Supp. 840 (W.D. Va. 1989); 843.

People want to be hospitalized near their families and homes, in hospitals in which their own—local—doctors have hospital privileges."[2]

Measuring Market Concentration

After the relevant product and geographical markets are defined, market share data are used to gauge how output is concentrated among the hospitals within a market area.[3] The Herfindahl-Hirschman index (HHI) is the most commonly used method of measuring the degree of concentration in the market. The HHI is derived by summing the squared market shares, expressed as percentages, of all the hospitals in the relevant market, or

(13–1)
$$\text{HHI} = \sum_{i=1}^{N} S_i^2,$$

where $0 < \text{HHI} \leq 10{,}000$ and S_i stands for the percentage market share or percentage of industry output produced by the ith hospital. For the hospital services industry, market share can be calculated by using the number of inpatient days, beds, admissions, or net inpatient revenues (gross revenues less charity care, bad debt, and contractual allowances or discounts), which serve as measures of output.

When a market area is dominated by one hospital (a monopolist), the HHI takes on the maximum value of 10,000. The HHI takes on a value closer to zero when a greater number of hospitals, N, exists in the market area and/or when a given number of hospitals are more similarly sized. As the value of the HHI approaches zero, an industry is considered to be less structurally concentrated (or more competitive).

For example, suppose there are five hospitals within a geographical area with market shares of 35, 30, 20, 10, and 5 percent. Applying equation 13–1, the HHI is computed as 2,650. Now suppose the two smallest hospitals merge. The postmerger HHI is now ($35^2 + 30^2 + 20^2 + 15^2$), or 2,750. Notice that a smaller number of hospitals leads to a higher value for the HHI and reflects the greater concentration of output among a smaller number of hospitals in the marketplace. Finally, suppose the market shares of the four remaining hospitals become equal over time. If so, the HHI becomes 2,500. Hence, the HHI has a lower value and output in the market is less concentrated when a larger number of equally sized hospitals exist.

Although microeconomic theory predicts that firms are more likely to form a cartel and behave in a monopolistic manner by restricting output and raising price (and reducing quality) when firms are fewer in number, it is unable to predict the precise value of the HHI at which collusion among firms takes place. The HHI reflects only the structural competitiveness of the market; it reveals nothing explicit about the behavioral intensity of competition among the hospitals. Consequently, economic theory is unable to identify a specific competition—monopoly cutoff level for the HHI.

However, by consulting the Department of Justice (DOJ) Merger Guidelines, we can get a rough approximation of what HHI value constitutes a near monopoly (at least according

---

[2]*U.S. v. Rockford Memorial*, 898 F.2d 1278; 1284 (1990).
[3]See Baker (1988) for a thorough discussion of the many assumptions and difficulties associated with defining the RGM and RPM.

to DOJ policymakers). The DOJ generally challenges a merger when the postmerger HHI would be above 1,800 and the merger would increase the premerger HHI by more than 50 points, or a merger that would lead to a postmerger HHI above 1,000 and raise the premerger HHI by more than 100 points. A merger that has a postmerger HHI of less than 1,000 is seldom challenged by the DOJ. Obviously, DOJ officials believe monopolylike market conditions arise when the HHI is at least above 1,000.

Schramm and Renn (1984) point out that many hospital markets already exceed the threshold concentration figure set by the Justice Department. For example, only two hospitals of equal size are necessary in a market area with a population of 100,000. Two hospitals of equal size result in an HHI of 5,000, well above the DOJ threshold of 1,800. When assessing the competitiveness of a market, however, the DOJ also considers the degree of potential competition as reflected by any barriers to entry into the market.[4] Barriers to entry into the hospital services market are the topic of the next section.

Barriers to Entry

According to Schramm and Renn (1984), "an entry barrier is a condition that imposes higher long-run costs of production on a new entrant than those borne by firms already in the market" (p. 880). Entry barriers make it difficult for new firms to enter markets and, during periods of excess demand, allow existing firms to make supranormal economic profits. State certificate of need (CON) laws are often cited as a type of entry barrier into the hospital services industry. Schramm and Renn take issue with this view of CON laws, however. They point out that the hospital industry is usually characterized by excess capacity rather than excess demand. According to them, it would be irrational for new hospitals to enter in the presence of excess capacity because hospitals already in the industry can satisfy any expansion in demand. Therefore, according to their view, excess capacity rather than CON laws deters entry into the industry.

Noether (1987), however, found that hospital prices were 4.0 to 4.9 percent higher, on average, in areas where CON laws exist. Furthermore, she noted, "In at least two states, a surge in notices of intent to build has been noted since abolition of the entry review program" (p. 37). Both of these findings suggest that CON laws deter entry and allow entrenched firms to raise prices. Thus, it is not surprising that, in 1987, the federal government ended its policy, which began in 1975, of encouraging the development of CON programs. According to Baker (1988), nearly one-quarter of the states abolished their CON laws by the end of 1987.[5]

Baker (1988) argues that even in the absence of CON laws, entry into the hospital industry may be difficult. The technological specifications for modern hospital buildings, including wide corridors and doorways, large elevators, strongly supported flooring, and extensive plumbing, require about four to nine years of planning and construction time. The relatively hugh investment in the hospital infrastructure represents a **sunk cost** that

---

[4]The DOJ Merger Guidelines also allow for "efficiency" and "failing firm" defenses. See Scherer and Ross (1990, p. 186) or http://www.ftc.gov/bc/docs/horizmer.htm, which contains the 1992 Horizontal Merger Guidelines.

[5]For a comprehensive review of the empirical literature on the CON program and some additional empirical findings, see Conover and Sloan (1998).

may discourage new hospitals from entering a market. Sunk costs are irretrievable costs that cannot be recovered if the venture does not prove as profitable as originally thought. Hence, high sunk costs may serve as an entry barrier when sufficiently sizeable. A question not yet answered empirically concerns whether sunk costs in the hospital industry are sufficiently high to significantly deter or slow entry.

In addition to sunk costs, other cost conditions may serve as barriers to entry. In particular, economies of scale, learning curve effects, and system affiliation can all make it costlier for new firms to enter markets. Specifically, long-run economies of scale provide high-volume entrenched firms with a relative cost advantage over new firms entering the market with low volumes of output. Facing economies of scale, the entrenched firms can discourage new entry by pricing the product just below the break-even price of potential entrants. This limit-pricing strategy keeps out potential competitors and allows the entrenched firms to make excess economic profits.

The econometric evidence in support of economies of scale in the hospital services industry is mixed, however. For example, hospital cost studies in the 1960s, which simply related hospital costs to measures of output and capacity, generally concluded that "there was evidence of significant economies of scale, at least up to moderately sized hospitals of around 500 beds" (Cowing, Holtmann, and Powers, 1983, p. 264). However, post-1970 hospital cost studies, controlling for other determinants of hospital costs, including case-mix, input prices, and the number of admitting physicians, reveal that "economies of scale may exist for small hospitals but . . . moderate- and large-size hospitals can generally be characterized by constant returns to scale" (Cowing, Holtmann, and Powers, 1983, p. 276). Unfortunately, the econometric evidence for the post-1970 studies is suspect because the cost functions employed are generally not well grounded in neoclassical cost theory, as presented in Chapter 7. In addition, like the hospital cost studies of the 1960s, the 1970 research fails to treat hospitals as multiproduct firms and assumes rather than tests for long-run cost minimization (see Chapter 7).

To overcome the limitations associated with the hospital cost studies of the 1960s and 1970s, econometric analyses by Cowing and Holtmann (1983), Grannemann, Brown, and Pauly (1986), Eakin and Kniesner (1988), Vita (1990), and Fournier and Mitchell (1992) rely to a much greater degree on neoclassical cost theory and treat hospitals as multiproduct firms. Generally, these studies fail to provide any strong and consistent econometric evidence for the presence of long-run economies of scale in the production of inpatient services. In fact, the evidence suggests that the production process for inpatient hospital services exhibits long-run diseconomies of scale, at least for the average-size hospital in the various studies (in particular, see Vita [1990], Eakin and Kniesner [1988], and Grannemann, Brown, and Pauly [1986]). The implication of the recent econometric studies is that long-run economies of scale are not a serious deterrent to potential entrants.

Given the problems associated with econometric studies, some researchers have relied on the **survivor test** developed by Stigler (1958) to determine whether economies of scale exist (Bays, 1986). According to the survivor technique, firm or plant sizes that account for an increasing fraction of industry output over time are considered to be efficient because they have apparently met and survived the market test. Correspondingly, those that provide a declining share are viewed as inefficient. The survivor test provides a broad measure of efficiency, capturing the ability of firms to both produce with least-cost methods and satisfy consumer wants in the long run.

Table 13–1 shows the percentage of community hospitals in various bed size categories for each decennial year since 1970. According to the data, the percentage of hospitals in the four largest bed size categories increased until the 1980s or 1990s but decreased there-after while the two smallest bed size categories followed the opposite pattern. Santerre and Pepper (2000) found that increased price sensitivity since the early 1980s had a negative effect on the very largest hospitals and a positive impact on the percentage of hospitals in the 100–199 bed size category. The authors also found that the removal of CON laws and rate regulations in various states favored the very smallest hospitals at the expense of the very largest. They argue that increased competition in the hospital services indus-try should favor hospitals with less than 200 beds. The data in table 13–1 further suggest that the 100–199 bed size category was the only one to experience a continual increase in the share of hospitals throughout the entire 30-year period. Thus, survivor analysis indi-cates that hospitals within the 100–199 bed size category may represent the most efficient sized organizations in the long-run.

TABLE 13–1

A Comparison of the Size Distribution of Community Hospitals, Selected Years 1970–2000

Bed Size Category	PERCENTAGE OF HOSPITALS IN EACH BED SIZE CATEGORY			
	1970	1980	1990	2000
0–24	6.8%	4.4%	4.2%	5.9%
25–49	22.6	17.7	17.4	18.5
50–99	25.4	25.1	23.5	21.5
100–199	21.8	23.5	24.3	25.1
200–299	10.1	12.3	13.7	13.3
300–399	6.1	7.1	7.6	6.9
400–499	3.2	4.6	4.1	3.7
500 and over	4.0	5.4	5.3	5.0

SOURCE: American Hospital Association. *Hospital Statistics*, various years, table 4.A.

Considering both the econometric evidence and the survivor test, a best guesstimate is that the long-run average cost of a short-term community hospital reaches its lowest point at a size of around 200 beds, give or take 100 beds. The long-run average cost curve is probably shallow, with costs rising only modestly to the left and right of the minimum point(s). It is important to remember, however, that economies of scale are limited by the size of the market; that is, demand conditions and transportation costs limit the economies of scale that can be realized. Thus, hospitals in rural areas operate with fewer beds than the number dictated by economies of scale considerations simply because the market is smaller. Also, some small hospitals may satisfy niche or specialized demands and continue to operate profitably despite their relative size. All in all, it does not appear that economies of scale are a significant deterrent to potential entrants into the hospital services industry.

Learning-by-doing is another characteristic associated with the cost structure the individual hospital faces. Learning-by-doing results when a hospital produces more cumulative output over time and gains greater experience. The greater cumulative output and experience translate into lower average costs of production for a given level of quality or a higher level of quality for a given level of costs. Studies focusing on learning economies in the hospital industry usually investigate the latter of the two relations: how the volume of output affects the quality of patient outcomes.

For example, Farley and Ozminkowski (1992) analyzed whether patient outcomes improve in hospitals as the volume of admissions increases for specific diagnoses and procedures. They found that over time, greater volume at a hospital leads to significantly lower risk-adjusted in-hospital mortality rates for three types of admissions: acute myocardial infarction, hernia repair, and respiratory distress syndrome in neonates. Providing further evidence for learning economies in hospital care, Stone, Seage, Hertz, and Epstein (1992) found that the relative risk of death for AIDS patients is more than twice as great in low-experience hospitals. Their results further indicate that the better outcome at high-AIDS-experienced hospitals is not associated with greater use of medical services. For example, AIDS patients in low-experience hospitals are more likely to be placed in an ICU, have longer ICU stays, and tend to have longer overall lengths of stay and higher costs.[6]

If "practice makes perfect," as the studies suggest, hospitals with greater volume may tend to attract an even larger market share over time. The learning economies, combined with limit-pricing techniques, may discourage new firms from entering the industry. Thus, most evidence suggests that learning-by-doing may act as a barrier to entry into hospital markets and provide existing firms with some market power to raise price.

Membership in a **multihospital system** or chain may also provide an existing hospital with a cost advantage relative to a potential freestanding hospital that is contemplating whether to enter the market. The American Hospital Association defines a multihospital system as two or more hospitals that are owned, leased, sponsored, or managed by a single corporate entity. According to Morrisey and Alexander (1987), a member of a multihospital system may possess four general advantages over an independent hospital, which may result in lower average costs at any given level of output:

(1) economic benefits *such as economies of scale and access to capital;*

(2) improved personnel and management benefits *such as ability to recruit, train and retain high-quality medical and administrative staffs, expand patient referral networks, and provide access to specialists to assist in coping with increasingly complex environments;*

(3) organizational benefits *due to expansion of the service area, increased market penetration, and organizational survival through reduced financial deficits, manpower shortages, and facilities problems; and*

(4) community benefits *such as improved access and quality of care through enhanced resources, lower costs, and improved regional planning. (p. 61)*

---

[6]However, unlike Farley and Ozminkowski (1992), Stone, Seage, Hertz, and Epstein (1992) did not correct for the likelihood of reverse causation—the so-called selective referral bias. It is entirely possible that AIDS patients flock to those hospitals that provide higher-quality care; that is, higher quality leads to higher admissions rather than the reverse.

With these four potential advantages in mind, several empirical studies have examined whether system affiliation actually confers any significant performance differential. While some minor differences have been found, statistical studies have generally established that system affiliation does not lead to lower costs of production. For example, the 18 studies reviewed by Ermann and Gabel (1984) reveal contradictory evidence regarding cost differences between multihospital and independent hospitals. In addition, Renn, Schramm, Watt, and Derzon (1985) found no significant differences in costs between investor-owned chains and freestanding for-profit hospitals or between system-affiliated and freestanding nonprofit hospitals. Finally, Wilcox-Gok (2002) found that system affiliation had no isolated impact on hospital costs when proper controls are made for other hospital characteristics. Thus, available studies suggest empirically that system affiliation offers no major cost advantage to established hospitals.[7]

In sum, learning-by-doing appears to be the only significant cost structure basis for barriers to entry. Evidence suggests that more experience is associated with lower costs and higher quality, implying that potential entrants may be deterred from entering markets when the existing hospitals possess considerable expertise. Thus, learning economies may give existing firms the potential to raise price above the competitive level and earn excess economic profits. In contrast, economies of scale and multiplant economies seem to have little impact on the relative long-run costs of existing and new hospitals.

Number, Types, and Size Distribution of the Buyers of Hospital Services

Another important aspect of the market structure of an industry is the number, types, and size distribution of the buyers. For example, an influential buyer who purchases a sizeable amount of a product from several different sellers may be able to negotiate significant price discounts by playing one seller against the others. Table 13–2 shows the main sources of hospital funds in 2000. Of the $412.1 billion spent on hospital services, governments at all levels are collectively responsible for 59 percent, with the federal government being the main purchaser at 48 percent. The relatively high percentage implies that the federal government may wield considerable power concerning how resources are allocated in the hospital services sector given its large share of spending in both national and local markets. In particular, the DRG system for Medicare reimbursement places many hospitals "at risk" for a sizeable proportion of their operating costs. Similarly, some state governments may be able to influence resource allocation in local markets, where they purchase a large fraction of hospital services under the Medicaid program.

About 41 percent of hospital care spending originates in the private sector. Individual consumers, accounting for only 3.2 percent of all hospital payments, are most often price insensitive and therefore have little impact on the market price of hospital care. The private insurance category, representing commercial insurance companies, Blue Cross plans, and independent managed-care organizations, directly account for slightly over 32 percent of all spending on hospital services. Whether these buyers have the willingness and ability to bargain successfully for low prices and thereby affect the allocation of resources to hospital services depends on a host of considerations, including their goals (profit or nonprofit objectives), the competitiveness of the health insurance market, and their individual

---

[7]But compare Menke (1997) who found that system-affiliated hospitals have lower costs.

TABLE 13-2
Sources of Hospital Funds, 2000

	Dollars (billions)	Percent
Total hospital care expenses	$412.1	100.0%
All private funds	168.9	41.0
Out-of-pocket	13.0	3.2
Private insurance	133.9	32.5
Other	22.0	5.3
Government	243.2	59.0
Federal	199.2	48.3
State and local	50.3	12.2

SOURCE: Centers for Medicare & Medicaid Services, http://www.hcfa.gov/stats/nhe–oact/.

INSIGHT 13-1

The Difficulty of Balancing the Benefits and Costs of Hospital Mergers

In October 1993, Mease Health Care, a 358-bed not-for-profit hospital in Dunnedin, Florida, announced its intention to merge with Morton Plant Hospital, a 672-bed not-for-profit hospital in nearby Clearwater, Florida. Executives at the two hospitals claimed the proposed merger had the potential to save as much as $80 million over five years (Anders 1993c).

However, the U.S. Department of Justice and the state of Florida argued that the proposed combination violated Section 7, the antimerger clause, of the Clayton Act. Government officials claimed that the merging hospitals constituted the two largest general acute care hospital systems in the area and that the combination might substantially lessen competition in the provision of acute inpatient hospital services in North Pinellas County and would likely increase the prices for those services to health care consumers. In their claim, government officials pointed out that the relevant product market should be considered as the market for acute care inpatient services because patients whose treatment requires overnight hospital stays cannot be treated safely and effectively on an outpatient basis.

Government officials also alleged that the relevant geographical market should be treated as North Pinellas County. In 1992, over 85 percent of North Pinellas County residents who were hospitalized were admitted to general acute care hospitals in North Pinellas. In addition, few physicians who practiced at hospitals in North Pinellas admitted patients to hospitals outside the area, and major hospital care purchasers such as managed-care companies did not consider hospitals outside the area to be good substitutes for North Pinellas hospitals. Given the government's definitions of the relevant product and geographical markets, the proposed merger would mean that Morton Plant and Mease would dominate the market for acute inpatient hospital services with a combined share of 58 percent. It was explained that Morton Plant and Mease had vigorously competed for the

(continued)

business of MCOs in the past and a full-fledged merger would eliminate the competitive rivalry between the two hospitals.

The U.S. District Court for the Middle District of Florida ruled against the merger but allowed the two hospitals to enter a partnership or joint venture (or as later referred to, a virtual merger) in the provision, but not pricing and marketing, of outpatient care, specific types of tertiary care such as open-heart surgery, and certain administrative services (e.g., accounting, housekeeping, and laundry). The hospitals would continue to compete in more routine areas such as general surgery, emergency care, and obstetrics and gynecology. The final consent judgment was designed to achieve substantial efficiencies while preserving maximum competition between the two hospitals. The partnership, composed of appointed members from each hospital's board, was to sell all services back to the two hospitals at cost and the hospitals would compete in the sale of those services.

The final consent judgment also directed the two hospitals to not share competitively sensitive information concerning pricing, managed-care contracts, and marketing and planning functions. The court justified the joint venture for the various functions by stressing that outpatient care markets are very competitive. The court also noted that the specified tertiary services are not currently provided by both hospitals, and geographical markets for tertiary services are more broadly defined. It was also explained by the court that administrative services constitute only a small fraction of inpatient costs.

The "partial merger" was heralded by many as a clever way of balancing the potential costs and benefits of consolidation among hospitals. However in June 2000, it was discovered that the partnership violated the final consent judgment by selling outpatient services directly to managed-care plans and other purchasers. Recall that the two hospitals were allowed to jointly produce outpatient services but were required to separately price and market them. It was learned that partnership executives discussed managed-care contracts and gave directives about managed-care contracts to representatives of both hospitals. Partnership personnel also transmitted information and recommendations on managed-care contracts and pricing to both hospitals and coordinated the sale of services to managed-care plans. In fact, on various occasions the two hospitals simultaneously negotiated similar contracts with the same managed-care companies using the partnership to coordinate identical provisions and rates.

Because they failed to follow the final consent judgment, the two hospitals were allowed to continue their partnership but were subjected to minor civil penalties and various enforcement and compliance provisions. Most importantly, the two hospitals were required to cease the joint contracting and marketing of their services.

This insight is particularly valuable because it shows how the potential benefits and costs of a horizontal merger must be considered, as the Williamson model argues. It also demonstrates the importance of properly identifying the relevant product and geographical markets. It also shows how even the best intentions can sometimes go astray and how regulatory micromanagement may be necessary when normal market forces are circumvented.

SOURCE: Based on Davidson (1994), *United States of America and State of Florida v. Morton Plant Health System, Inc. and Trustees of Mease Hospital, Inc.* (1994), *United States of America v. Morton Plant Health System Inc. and Trustees of Mease Hospital, Inc.,* (Undated), and *United States of America v. Morton Plant Health System Inc. and Trustees of Mease Hospital, Inc.* (2000).

market penetration rates. For example, an individual private health insurance plan is more able to negotiate favorable hospital prices when it represents a relatively large market share of subscribers in a local hospital market and thereby possesses some bargaining power.

How buyers reimburse hospitals may also affect the way in which resources are allocated to hospital care. Third-party payers contracting with hospital providers choose among a variety of hospital reimbursement plans, including usual and customary charges, discounted usual and customary charges, per diem payments, DRG payments, and capitation payments. Some of these reimbursement schemes shift a greater amount of financial risk onto hospital care providers. For example, DRG payments and capitation fees shift much more risk onto hospital care providers than do usual and customary charges. "At-risk" charges generally create more incentives for cost-effective practices because the health care providers are responsible for absorbing any cost overruns.

Comparative data are unavailable for the different hospital reimbursement practices adopted by various third-party payers. Hoy, Curtis, and Rice (1991), however, provide some information regarding the hospital reimbursement practices of HMO and PPO plans sponsored by commercial insurance companies. Although the data on hospital reimbursement methods are limited to the managed-care plans owned by commercial insurers, they are nonetheless interesting, fairly representative, and deserving of discussion.

Hoy et al. found that fewer than 20 percent of the PPOs and HMOs owned by commercial insurers reimburse hospital providers on the basis of usual and customary charges, with the most popular reimbursement method being the discounted charge. They also found that PPO plans are much more likely to use per diem payments than HMOs. Specifically, nearly 25 percent of insurer-owned PPOs reimburse by per diem payments, whereas the comparable figure for insurer-owned HMOs is only 5.3 percent.

Data also suggested that the reimbursement schemes of insurer-owned HMOs are generally less oriented toward hospital risk sharing than are those of PPOs. Almost 22 percent of the insurer-owned PPOs reimburse hospitals with either DRG or capitation payments, whereas only 11.5 percent of insurer-owned HMOs reimburse with these at-risk charges. Hoy, Curtis, and Rice provide a rationale for this finding by noting that physician gate-keepers and the strong orientation toward avoiding hospitalization make hospital risk sharing less critical to HMOs.

Due to the large variety of reimbursement practices suggested by their study, it is evident that not all HMOs or PPOs should be treated or expected to behave similarly with respect to the buying of hospital services. Indeed, Feldman et al. (1990) found that IPA/HMOs are less likely than the more tightly organized staff-network (S/N) HMOs to switch hospitals and concentrate patients at specific hospitals on the basis of price. They argue that a strong and ongoing physician affiliation is more important to IPA physicians than is price. This view is substantiated by the fact that the elasticity of demand for hospital admissions was found to be more elastic for S/N HMOs (–3.044) than IPAs (–1.024). Moreover, Feldman, Kralewski, Shapiro, and Chan (1990) show that S/N HMOs secure larger discounts for inpatient services than IPAs. They found that the average discount is 26 percent for general medical and surgery care services at S/N HMOs but only 4 percent at IPAs. The authors also determined that S/N HMOs are more likely to use per diem charges than IPAs, which tend to employ discounted charges.

In sum, the number, size distribution, and types of buyers are important structural features of local hospital markets. Government is responsible for a majority of all hospital purchases and, with the associated purchasing power, has some ability to influence hospital prices and costs through the Medicare and Medicaid programs at the national or state level. The private sector, composed of a large number of different types of insurer/buyers, may be able to influence hospital prices at the local level. The ultimate success of private insurers in negotiating low prices and controlling costs in local hospital markets depends on a host of factors, including the chosen hospital reimbursement strategy, the competitiveness of the hospital and insurance markets, and the goals of the insurer.

Type of Product

Whether the hospitals in a market offer a differentiated or standardized product is another determinant of market structure. According to the anticompetitive view, product differentiation causes the demand curve to become less price elastic and enables the firm to restrict output below and raise price above the competitive level. Hospital choice studies have confirmed that product differences matter in the hospital services industry. For example, from their review of the literature, Lane and Lindquist (1988) cited seven categories of factors—care, staff, physical facilities, clientele, experience, convenience, and institutional—that strongly affect the choice of hospital. Of these factors, quality of care and staff, equipment and technology, and convenient location were found to be among the more important determinants of choice of hospital. Cost or price appears to play a secondary role in hospital choice, most likely due to the patient's low out-of-pocket price for hospital services.

Marketing and advertising also play important roles in the hospital services industry. The typical hospital engaging in promotion activities spends nearly $500,000 annually on marketing (Japsen, 1997), amounting to approximately .8 percent of sales. While that percentage figure pales in comparison to the advertising-to-sales ratios of 10 percent or more observed in the pharmaceutical, cosmetics, soft drink, cereal, and other industries, Gray (1986) notes that hospitals devote as much as 5 percent of gross sales to advertising in some highly competitive areas of the country. Gray notes, "Hospitals plug such things as Saturday surgery (a convenience for patients), referral services, gourmet food, depression clinics—even free transportation" (p. 183).

Of the total marketing budget at hospitals, about 50 percent is spent on advertising. About 43 percent of the advertising budget is devoted to print advertisements in newspapers and magazines. The rest of the advertising budget is directed to radio (14 percent), direct mail (12 percent), yellow pages (11 percent), television (11 percent), bus/billboards (4 percent), and other media (5 percent).

Reflecting the significance of advertising competition in the hospital services industry, five of the six hospitals in Des Moines, Iowa, were accused of agreeing to limit their advertising, an action in violation of antitrust laws. The hospitals involved in the suit eventually settled with the Justice Department (Burda, 1993).

Consumer (Mis)Information

The final factor affecting the market structure of the hospital services industry is the amount of information consumers possess. Due to low out-of-pocket costs, one suspects that consumers are rationally ignorant about the prices of most hospital services. For example, when asked to estimate the cost of open-heart surgery, consumer estimates ranged from $10 to $99,000 (Ruffenach, 1993). The average figure of $12,804 was almost twice

INSIGHT 13–2

Informed Choices and Financial Incentives

Informed choices are crucial for competition to work in health care markets. Buyers must be informed about prices and quality so that they can make efficient choices. As a result, the government and a number of state organizations have begun to chart hospital performance by collecting and assessing hospital-specific data on the charges, utilization, and outcomes of various medical procedures. Similar to the way *Consumer Reports* rates refrigerators, cars, and stereo equipment, these organizations assess hospitals according to several criteria. For example, the Pennsylvania Health Care Cost Containment Council released 1988 data comparing 33 Pittsburgh-area hospitals on 55 common hospital procedures. The number of patients, average length of stay, average charge, and risk-adjusted mortality rates and complication rates were compared (Winslow, 1990). The risk-adjusted outcome figures attempted to adjust for the severity of patients' illnesses so that results would be standardized across hospitals.

Similarly, four major Cincinnati employers and the Cleveland Health Quality Choice Initiative recently tried to reduce health care costs with new systems for rating hospitals on the basis of cost and quality of care (Winslow, 1993a, 1993b). If collected properly, the data should help employers, insurers, and consumers make informed choices and exert pressure on hospitals to improve services. High-quality, low-cost hospitals will be rewarded, while low-quality, high-cost hospitals will be disciplined by the informed buying. The inefficient hospitals will be forced to change their practice patterns and adopt more cost-effective ways to treat patients. Some observers expect the process to promote hospital mergers and cause unprofitable product lines to be cut as hospitals pursue cost-saving strategies.

Many employers are beginning to use financial incentives to induce employees to comparison shop for medical services just as they do for housing, cars, and refrigerators. For example, at International Paper Company (IP), employees are provided with information about the prices and quality of many different medical services offered by various health care providers in the local area (Ruffenach, 1993). In addition, the ceiling on out-of-pocket costs was increased to $6,500 a year so that employee/consumers will be more price conscious. An employee in Greenville, South Carolina, facing gallbladder surgery can use IP's database to find out that the company pays maximums of $1,219 to the surgeon, $257 a day for a semiprivate hospital room, and $178 a day for nursing care. The employee is responsible for any balance billing. IP also provides a listing identifying the numbers, backgrounds, and prices of surgeons in the area.

At the NCR Corporation division of AT&T, employees are given information about the prices the company pays for 11,000 different procedures. These prices provide a benchmark for employees when discussing terms with health care providers. Employees who do not use the company's managed-care network are responsible for paying a higher percentage of some medical bills. This acts as an incentive for employees to stay within the network. Some companies, such as Quaker Oats Company, provide profiles of local hospitals, including average charges, average length of stay, and how often a given hospital handles a particular surgery.

the actual cost of $7,280. Similarly, consumer estimates for a normal delivery of a baby ranged from $45 to $80,000. The average estimate of $2,595 was much closer to the actual cost of $1,999 in this case, but still over 25 percent too high.

In a traditional fee-for-service environment with first-dollar health insurance coverage, consumers most likely do too little comparison shopping. Lacking adequate information, consumers are at a serious disadvantage when purchasing hospital services, and this places hospital decision makers in the enviable position of being able to practice opportunistic behavior. One rationale for MCOs is that these third-party payers, acting essentially as information brokers, perform the comparison shopping task for the consumer/patient. Unlike the general consumer, decision makers in managed-care systems are sufficiently informed about hospital prices and quality, helping to overcome the usual asymmetry of information existing directly between the patient and hospital services provider. In addition, the financial success of MCOs partly hinges on the ability to either employ or contract with high-quality providers at reasonable prices. In the conduct section of this chapter, we examine whether managed-care programs have succeeded in containing hospital care costs.

Summary of the Structure of the Hospital Services Industry

For all practical purposes, the market for hospital services is best defined as those hospitals offering a similar cluster of inpatient services within the same geographical area. The geographical market area of most primary and secondary care hospitals tends to be local in nature, whereas the market area of tertiary care hospitals may be regional or national in scope. In fact, it is becoming common for large employers and health insurers to negotiate price discounts with hospitals outside local markets for major types of tertiary care services, including organ transplants and major heart surgery.

The structural competitiveness of the hospital services market is determined by the number, types, and size distribution of hospitals; number, types, and size distribution of buyers/insurers; barriers to entry; type of product; and the extent of any asymmetry of information between patients and hospitals. In terms of the supply side, most local hospital markets are characterized by a relatively few competing hospitals except in major metropolitan areas, where hospitals are more numerous. For example, cities with populations of 100,000 can generally support only two or three hospitals. In addition to the degree of actual competition, the behavior of hospitals depends on the ease of potential entry or the magnitude of any barriers to entry. Learning-by-doing rather than long-run economies of scale or multihospital systems appears to be the major reason for barriers to entry into the hospital services industry. More experienced hospitals tend to have lower costs and higher quality than newer ones. Hence, based on the number of competitors and barriers to entry in most areas, the supply side of the hospital services industry can be characterized as oligopolistic.

Another important structural factor affecting hospital behavior from the demand side of the market is buyer concentration. Simply put, buyer concentration has the ability to negate seller concentration. The federal government, state governments, and some private insurers may possess the appropriate size on the demand side of the market necessary to influence hospital pricing and output behavior. Also, reimbursement policies that place hospitals at risk for high costs have the potential to promote cost-effective medicine.

Finally, hospitals currently compete for patients through nonprice means. For example, many hospitals rely on advertising and hospital amenities to attract patients. Because patients are typically uninformed about and unresponsive to prices, hospitals may be able to raise price or lower quality below the competitive level. Financial incentives and public information are beginning to take on a much greater role in raising consumer consciousness with regard to hospital prices and quality of hospital services.

THE CONDUCT OF THE HOSPITAL SERVICES INDUSTRY

The industrial organization triad predicts that market structure influences the conduct of the hospitals within a given market area. According to traditional microeconomic theory, a large number of sellers and low barriers to entry promote competition. More intense competition usually shows up in increased output, higher quality, and lower prices. The general conduct of real-world hospitals is difficult to predict on a market or an aggregate basis, however. Hospitals pursue different objectives, operate in various market settings, face alternative types of reimbursement methods from third-party payers, and are subject to a variety of government regulations. Ideally, from a societal point of view, we hope that incentives exist such that hospitals act independently and strive to minimize costs and satisfy consumer wants. However, some structural features of the hospital services industry, such as barriers to entry, product complexity, and asymmetry of information, suggest that such incentives may be lacking in many local markets across the nation. Also, a substantial body of empirical evidence indicates that hospitals compete on the basis of cost-enhancing quality instead of price in many markets. In this section, we focus on the pricing behavior of hospitals, particularly not-for-profit hospitals. We also discuss what is known empirically about the relation between hospital market structure and various measures of conduct, such as price, costs, and quality. We also examine the effects of ownership structure, managed care, and government regulations on the conduct of hospitals. The section closes with a discussion of integrated delivery systems.

Pricing Behavior of Not-for-Profit Hospitals

In Chapter 8, we developed several market models, including perfect competition and monopoly, to analyze the pricing behavior of for-profit organizations. However, we just learned that for-profit hospitals make up only 15 percent of all community hospitals. Therefore, the previously discussed market models may be inappropriate for analyzing the conduct of not-for-profit hospitals, which because of their nondistribution constraint may pursue goals other than profit maximization.

Over the years, a number of utility maximization models have been developed to explain the behavior of not-for-profit organizations. In general, utility maximization models assume that the manager of a not-for-profit hospital attempts to maximize his or her own personal utility. Although debate exists over what variables belong in the manager's utility function, most analysts have assumed that the manager derives utility either directly or indirectly from things such as organizational size, quality of services, and discretionary profits. We next discuss the managerial utility maximization models most commonly discussed in the literature about the pricing behavior of not-for-profit hospitals.

Quantity Maximization   Baumol (1967) has argued that rather than pursuing profit maximization, large firms with a substantial amount of monopoly power tend to maximize output subject to a break-even level of profits. Because executive salaries and prestige are more strongly correlated with firm size than with profits, managers try to expand sales at the expense of profits. Figure 13–1 depicts the situation for a hospital where Q stands for the number of patient-days. An output- or quantity-maximizing hospital produces output up to the point where the average cost of production equals average revenue, or at Q_0 patient-days in the figure. At that point, the hospital is servicing the maximum number of patient-days without incurring an economic loss. If it expanded services beyond Q_0, the hospital would operate with an economic loss, since AC exceeds AR. A profit-maximizing hospital with the same cost curves produces up to the point where MR = MC and provides Q_1 patient-days and charges P_1. It follows that an output-maximizing hospital produces more output and charges a lower price than a profit-maximizing hospital, *ceteris paribus*.

FIGURE 13–1
The Output Maximization Model

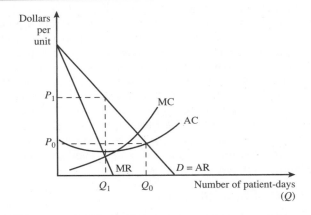

Suppose the typical not-for-profit hospital faces a downward-sloping demand curve and the usually shaped average and marginal cost curves and attempts to maximize the quantity of hospital services subject to a break-even constraint ($P =$ AC). If so, the not-for-profit firm produces more services (Q_0) but charges a lower price (P_0) than an otherwise comparable for-profit hospital (P_1, Q_1).

Davis (1972) points out that most hospitals offer a wide array of services, each with its own price, and it is logical to assume that an output-maximizing hospital follows a pricing strategy that increases the number of patients admitted. The chosen pricing strategy involves a certain degree of *cross-subsidization*. Specifically, the hospital may charge a price below cost on those services for which demand is more elastic to generate more admissions and then make up for the loss by charging a much higher price for those services for which demand is more inelastic. For example, the hospital may charge a price below cost for basic room services to attract more patients and cover the loss by charging a higher price for ancillary services. The net effect is that the hospital breaks even. In the process, however, the hospital services more patients through cross-subsidization.

The long-run implications of the model are interesting. In the long run, an output-maximizing hospital may generate some profits to acquire the funds it needs for expansion. It obtains the profits by charging a price that is slightly above the average cost of production. As a result, an output-maximizing hospital should not only provide more output than a profit-maximizing hospital at any point in time but should also have a higher rate of expansion over time.

The quantity maximization model can be used to explain the behavior of a not-for-profit organization. Since such a firm is restricted by law from earning a profit, managers may opt to maximize quantity to increase the firm's market share and enhance its prestige in the community. Economists have pointed out that the assumption of output maximization is consistent with the public's perception concerning how a not-for-profit hospital should operate (Newhouse, 1970). From the public's point of view, hospitals are given nonprofit status because they are expected to provide care to some people in the community who otherwise might not receive care due to profit considerations. If the managers of a not-for-profit hospital maximize quantity, they validate the public's view that their firm plays an important role in the provision of health care to the community at large. That may make it much easier for the hospital to gather community support for such activities as fund-raising.

In the case of a quantity-maximizing not-for-profit hospital, the interests of the managers may also be aligned with the board of trustees, or board of directors, which oversees the general operation of the hospital. Board members, who generally are leading citizens, may also want to maximize quantity to increase their presence in the community. They may wish to be perceived as taking a leading role in the provision of health care to the community.

The quantity maximization model can also explain why in a given community there might be a certain degree of excess capacity in hospital services. A quantity-maximizing hospital may acquire an additional piece of medical equipment even if it does not generate a profit, provided it may attract a sufficient number of additional admittances. Such buying behavior may lead to a duplication of resources and overcapacity as each hospital expands its facility beyond the profit-maximizing point. The quantity maximization model, however, cannot explain why the cost of hospital services has been rising so rapidly over time in recent decades, because it offers only a static rather than a dynamic view of hospital behavior.[8] The other models, discussed next, set quality of services as an attainable goal. Because quality of services is heavily dependent on technology and medical technology has changed dramatically over time, these models may provide a partial explanation for rising health care costs.

Quality Maximization   It has been argued that managers derive utility from the quality of hospital care provided. As you know, quality is immeasurable and is associated with the spectrum of services the hospital offers. Thus, the quality of care is enhanced every time the hospital widens the spectrum of services to patients or retains more specialists on staff. Any increase in the quality of care is also likely to drive up the cost of producing medical services.

---

[8]A static view analyzes behavior or performance at a point in time. Dynamic analysis considers behavior or performance over time.

Lee's (1971) model of hospital behavior is consistent with the quality maximization argument. The basic premise of the model is that managers of not-for-profit hospitals maximize utility by attempting to enhance the status, or prestige, of their institutions. Since status is defined to be positively related to the "range of services available and the extent to which expensive and highly specialized equipment and personnel (including M.D.'s) are available" (p. 49), the only way managers can achieve their goal is to maximize quality. This quest for status is the force driving the behavior of managers.

According to Lee's theory, the hospital has a desired level of status that it will attempt to achieve. The desired status depends on the mission of the hospital and the hospital's relative standing in the medical community. Because the actual level of status tends to be below the desired level, managers are constantly attempting to improve on status by increasing the quality of care. The hospital must provide that level of quality of care that is consistent with the desired level of status the managers are trying to achieve. For example, a large teaching hospital with a prestigious reputation is obligated to possess the most technologically sophisticated equipment and have a large number of specialists on staff because the managers view their organization as being on the forefront of medical development. In other words, the reputation and status of the hospital demand that it offers the highest-quality care. A small nonteaching hospital, on the other hand, will try to achieve a much more modest status level. The small nonteaching hospital will offer a quality of care below that of a larger hospital but on a par with hospitals of similar status.

Given a relatively inelastic demand for hospital services, managers can pursue a policy of quality maximization with little concern for costs. Any increase in the cost of hospital services associated with an enhancement in quality can be passed on to the payer through a higher price with minimal impact on output. The quest for status through quality maximization may provide one explanation for rising hospital costs in recent years.

Because the physicians on staff at the hospital are also likely to receive utility from any increase in the quality of care, the interests of the managers and medical staff are likely to be aligned in this instance. As the hospital acquires more advanced medical inputs, physicians are given the opportunity to provide more varied and sophisticated medical treatment to their patients. The more sophisticated medical inputs may allow physicians on staff to expand their practices. In addition, the hospital is likely to find it easier to recruit and retain medical personnel if it improves the quality of care. The same argument may apply to the board of trustees. Board members may also receive utility from enhanced hospital status.

The quality maximization model suggests that new technology is diffused in a tiered fashion. Any new piece of equipment or medical technology is likely to be adopted first by the most status-conscious institutions, such as research and teaching hospitals. Their lofty status requires that research and teaching hospitals be on the cutting edge of medical technology. Hospitals of lesser status acquire the technology only after it has become a more accepted part of medical treatment and some of the hospitals in that status group have begun to acquire it. The implication is that most hospitals acquire new technology not because it is a prudent investment but because managers do not want to jeopardize the institution's status or relative standing in the medical community. Thus, new technology is acquired primarily for defensive purposes. The quality maximization model may explain why there is a tendency in the hospital sector toward duplication of resources and overspecialization. Hospitals are constantly attempting to expand services to enhance their status, not because profit maximization or efficiency calls for the expansion of services.

Quality and Quantity Maximization   Feldstein (1971) and Newhouse (1970) extended the quality maximization model by combining it with the quantity maximization model. According to Newhouse, management jointly determines the quantity and quality of output and produces the levels that maximize utility. Since any increase in quality comes at the expense of quantity, and vice versa, managers face an important trade-off and must jointly determine the optimal levels of quality and quantity to produce. Figure 13–2 illustrates this trade-off.

Given that quality can be enhanced only by increasing the cost of production (see Chapter 7), every time a hospital attempts to increase quality, its cost curves shift upward. This situation is depicted in figure 13–2, where initially an output-maximizing hospital produces at point A. If management decides to increase quality, that decision causes the average cost curve to shift upward from AC_0 to AC_1. With no change in demand, the output-maximizing level of output equals Q_1 (point B), and the increase in quality is associated with a decrease in output. If quality is adjusted further, a trade-off curve between quality and quantity can be derived.[9] The trade-off curve appears in figure 13–3. Points A and B on the graph correspond to points A and B in figure 13–2. The curve is downward sloping, indicating the trade-off between the quality and quantity of medical care produced.

FIGURE 13–2
The Impact of Changes in Quality on Costs

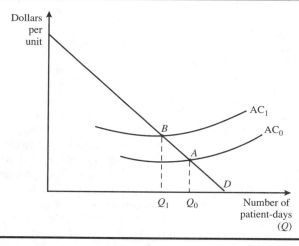

A not-for-profit hospital that chooses to produce with higher quality faces increased costs of AC_1. As a result, the hospital must produce fewer services (Q_1) if it faces a break-even constraint.

---

[9]In all likelihood, any increase in quality will lead to an increase in the demand for hospital services. Consumers may be more willing to purchase medical services of higher quality at a higher price. This does not change the analysis, however, provided the increase in demand is relatively small. In terms of figure 13–2, a trade-off between quantity and quality still exists if the AC curve shifts upward by more than the demand curve shifts to the right with any increase in quality.

FIGURE 13-3
The Quality/Quantity Maximization Model

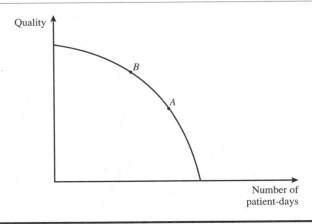

This figure shows the various combinations of quality and quantity of hospital services that can be produced given a fixed budget constraint. To maximize their utility and given the trade-off, decision makers at a not-for-profit hospital must choose a specific point like *A* or *B*, given their preference weights for the two goods.

The quality/quantity maximization model indicates that the managers of not-for-profit hospitals face the dilemma of trying to maximize the level of services provided to the public while at the same time increasing the quality of care to improve the status of the hospital. Because a trade-off exists between the two, managers must choose that mixture of quantity and quality that maximizes their personal utility.

The Managerial Expense Preference Model   The final model discussed in this section is the managerial expense preference model (Williamson, 1963). The model was developed to explain the behavior of large firms that are not directly managed by major stockholders. The basic tenet of the model is that managers use their authority to divert funds away from profits to serve their own self-interests—that is, to enhance their own utility. Among other things, the funds are used to pursue the five Ps of increased pay, perquisites, power, prestige, and patronage. In a sense, managers absorb profits in the process of increasing their own utility by maximizing the amount of discretionary expenditures.

The ability of managers to provide stockholders with less than the maximum amount of profits stems from the existence of an asymmetry of information between the stockholders and the managers regarding firm performance. Stockholders do not always have the means to fully monitor activities of managers and ensure that they are providing the maximum amount of profits. Managers are afforded a certain amount of freedom to run the firm, provided stockholders receive what they consider an acceptable level of profits.

In the context of the model we have been working with, managerial expense preference behavior suggests that managers maximize discretionary expenditures by choosing the profit-maximizing level of output and price and then absorbing the profits through discretionary expenditures. The pursuit of discretionary expenditures can be treated as a kind of rent-seeking behavior because the manager is attempting to obtain a bigger slice of the pie for him or herself rather than trying to enlarge the size of the pie. Figure 13–4 illustrates this rent-seeking process. For simplicity's sake, assume marginal cost is constant and equals average cost. As such, the marginal and average cost curves are equal and horizontal and represented by MC_{true} in figure 13–4. The MC_{true} curve reflects the true costs that exhibit production efficiency.

FIGURE 13–4
The Managerial Expense Preference Model

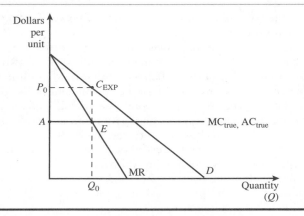

A not-for-profit hospital that maximizes discretionary profits will choose to produce at Q_0 where MR = MC just like an otherwise comparable for-profit hospital. The difference is that the not-for-profit hospital uses the discretionary profits to finance unnecessary expenditures and thereby raises the costs of production to C_{EXP}, a point above the true costs of production. The not-for-profit hospital reports the same price and quantity of services as the for-profit hospital but shows no economic profit.

To maximize discretionary expenditures, the difference between revenue and the true cost of production, the firm follows the typical profit maximization rule, producing at the Q_0 level of output and charging P_0. However, instead of reflecting excess profits, the rectangle $P_0 AEC_{EXP}$ represents the amount of profits managers absorb as discretionary expenditures or income. In the process of enhancing their own utility, managers drive up the cost of production in the form of discretionary expenditures. The point C_{EXP} represents the average cost of production after the expense preference behavior of managers has been taken into account. The vertical distance between points E and C_{EXP} (or that between A and P_0) represents the inefficiencies brought about by expense preference behavior.[10] The firm reports a normal profit rather than excess profits.

---

[10]In a different context, the inefficiency has been referred to as *X*-inefficiency. The inefficiency exists because managers of firms with some market power do not have the incentive to employ inputs efficiently. Inputs are either overemployed or are not used to their fullest potential. In addition, managers may pay input prices beyond the necessary amount.

The managerial expense preference model has some interesting implications. The model suggests that managers consciously drive up the cost of production in an attempt to further their own self-interests. The model can also help explain the behavior of not-for-profit firms. Surprisingly, the expense preference model suggests that managers of not-for-profit firms act much like their counterparts at for-profit firms; that is, they maximize profits. The difference lies in the extent to which managers absorb profits as discretionary income. Since not-for-profit providers are prohibited by law from distributing profits to external parties, all the profits can be diverted by managers. As a result, we should observe not-for-profit firms having higher costs than for-profit firms that are closely controlled by profit-conscious owners, *ceteris paribus*. The cost differential reflects the wider latitude that not-for-profit managers are given to absorb profits. The fact that some of these profits are spent on additional personnel and equipment may help explain the duplication of resources in the health care sector.

In conclusion, utility maximization models have many positive attributes. First, they explain how firm behavior is affected when managers address their own utility functions rather than attempting to maximize profits. Behavior other than profit maximization is especially important to address when we consider that a significant proportion of health care providers function in not-for-profit settings. Second, the models explain why there may be a tendency in the health care sector toward duplication of resources and overspecialization, as in the case of the market for hospital services. Third, utility maximization models help explain why health care costs have increased over the years. Managers who are seeking to advance their personal goals, such as maximizing the quality of output at the expense of profits, are not likely to be overly concerned with the impact any policy change may have on the financial "bottom line." A lack of concern for the bottom line naturally causes the cost of medical care to increase.

Market Concentration and Hospital Behavior

Another conduct issue of interest to economists concerns the impact of market concentration on the price, cost, and quality of hospital care. The issue is whether lower prices and higher levels of quality result in a market where output is concentrated among a few large firms or dispersed among a relatively large number of smaller-sized firms. In hospital services markets characterized by insured consumers, not-for-profit entities, government-regulated prices, managed-care organizations, and informational asymmetries, economic theory alone cannot predict the impact of increased concentration on societal welfare, so we must turn our attention to empirical studies on the relationship.

Economists investigating the impact of market concentration on hospital behavior tend to examine the periods before and after the mid-1980s. The mid-1980s acts as the cut-off because after that period prospective payment systems like the DRG system began to replace cost-based systems, the market share of for-profit hospital increased in many areas, and enrollments in MCOs started to explode. In simple terms, health care payers became more price conscious, and hospital competition changed from being patient driven to being payer driven (Dranove, Shanley, and White, 1993).

Studies using data prior to the mid-1980s found evidence to support a "medical arms race" among hospitals in more competitive areas (Robinson and Luft, 1985). The argument is that in more competitive areas, hospitals provide physicians with high levels of hospital quality in the form of advanced medical technologies, excess bed capacity, and amenities

INSIGHT 13-3

Inside the Black Box of the Hospital

We have introduced a number of economic models describing how the price and quantity of hospital services are determined in a not-for-profit setting based upon various assumptions about the objectives of the ultimate decision maker. Harris (1977), however, criticizes these models for failing to capture the internal organization and institutional details of real-world hospitals and offers an alternative model. The reader may find it interesting to know that Professor Harris of MIT is a practicing M.D. who also holds a Ph.D. in economics. While his model is not designed to predict the price and quantity of hospital services, it does provide a rich and insightful description of the internal workings of actual hospitals with respect to economic decision making and resource allocation. To give you a flavor of his paper, we provide a brief synopsis. However, we strongly encourage you to read the entire article.

Harris treats the hospital as a firm designed to solve a complicated decision problem—the diagnosis and treatment of illness, which typically involves a "complicated sequence of adaptive responses in the face of uncertainty" (p. 469). He notes that when people become hospitalized they do not really buy the various inputs used during the hospitalization period but, instead, purchase a general guarantee to be given appropriate medical care. And because of the guarantee purchased, it becomes impossible to cease the delivery of care once some cost limit is achieved, especially because medical problems often have numerous idiosyncrasies and therefore each patient receives customized attention. Consequently, any hospital organization must have a certain amount of standby capacity.

Harris goes on to treat the hospital as a split organization resulting from an internal market composed of demanders and suppliers. On the supply side, administrators offer various ancillary services, such as pharmaceuticals, operating rooms, and blood banks, standing ready to deliver a particular medical input. On the demand side, various physicians decide which patients need which ancillary inputs and when.

An important consideration, as Harris notes, is that administration does not make patient care decisions and physicians do not hire the medical inputs. The separation is intended, however, because it eliminates the necessity of the physician to perform repeated cost calculations during an episode of care. The physician is supposed to do everything scientifically indicated for the welfare of his or her patient without reference to costs. The role of the administrator, however, is to manage the costs of the hospital but at the same time provide necessary inputs for the physician.

Harris relates his split organization theory of the hospital firm to the capacity problem hospitals often face. He recognizes that the medical staff and administration each have their own objectives and constraints. When excess capacity exists and resources are relatively abundant, the system seems to allocate resources reasonably well. However, when capacity limits are neared, physicians, "fearing they will lose access to necessary inputs, grab their own exclusive shares to keep themselves protected" (p. 476). Each physician engages in rent-seeking behavior vying for his or her own separate empire.

Another aspect of the capacity problem relates to the conflict between physicians and administrators. For the most part administrators want to keep the hospital full because

(continued)

revenues are greater. Physicians, however, desire excess capacity because it assures a continuous supply of resources and reflects higher levels of quality. Internal conflict emerges between physicians and administrators about the hospital's short-run policies regarding capacity. Because price does not serve as an allocation device within the hospital, nonprice methods must be used to allocate resources when capacity constraints exist, such as "loosely enforced standards, rules of thumb, side bargains, cajoling, negotiations, special contingency plans, and in some cases literally shouting and screaming" (p. 478). Physicians may also hedge against shortages by ordering inputs well in advance or various groups of physicians may form exclusive clubs along clinical lines to better control their share of the hospital inputs. For example, orthopedic beds may become differentiated from general surgical beds and operating rooms may be held for specific uses.

Because conflict ensues when capacity constraints set in, physicians will want to expand capacity in the long run. Administration, on the other hand, will expand capacity only if the resulting beds are full. Physicians are faced with an incentive to expand utilization and increase quality to obtain their share. Administration, as a result, tolerates the creation and perpetuation of the separate clubs or empires even though it negates the risk reduction advantages of sharing resources within the hospital. Interestingly, this model, like the ones developed earlier, can be used to predict the widespread adoption and dispersion of new technologies in the past. Physicians embrace new technologies to expand capacity instead of replacing the existing capacity as a way of at least preserving their share of hospital resources and to improve quality. Indeed, the innovations may have little to do with reducing the intensity of resources used per illness episode and thereby raise the costs of providing medical care.

in return for admitting their patients. The high quality shows up as increased costs of producing hospital services. In support of the medical arms race hypothesis, many studies using data prior to the mid-1980s found empirical evidence linking increased competition (a lower value for the HHI) with increased hospital costs (Hersch, 1984; Robinson and Luft, 1985; White, 1987; Noether, 1988; Fournier and Mitchell, 1992), lower levels of technical efficiency (Wilson and Jadlow, 1982), greater excess bed capacity (Joskow, 1980; Farley, 1985), and a larger number of duplicate specialized services in local markets (Dranove, Shanley, and Simon, 1992; Farley, 1985).

Beginning after the mid-1980s with heightened payer-driven competition, empirical studies no longer found support for the medical arms race. The earliest studies found that after the mid-1980s increased competition had no impact on hospital costs (Zwanziger and Melnick, 1988), lowered the hospital inflation rate (Robinson and Phibbs, 1990), or increased costs of not-for-profit hospitals but not the costs of public and for-profit hospitals (Santerre and Bennett, 1992). Studies using more recent data uncover even stronger evidence in support of payer-driven competition. For example, using data for 1987, Melnick, Zwanziger, Bamezai, and Pattison (1992) determined that more hospital competition resulted in a lower Blue Cross PPO negotiated price for hospital services in California. Further studies using data after 1990 have found that increased hospital competition improves technical efficiency (Rosko, 2001), reduces excess capacity (Santerre and Adams, 2002), lowers hospital prices (Town and Vistnes, 2001) and hospital costs, and results in lower rates of adverse outcomes (Kessler and McClellan, 2000).

By analyzing the impact of horizontal mergers in the hospital services sector during the 1990s, we can obtain further information about the effects of market structure on hospital prices, costs, and quality of care. Using the estimated parameters from their empirical model determining HMO negotiated prices with hospitals during the period 1990 to 1993, Town and Vistnes (2001) simulated hospital mergers in the Los Angeles region, where competition is relatively fierce, and found that a significant number of the simulated mergers led to predicted price increases in excess of 5 percent. Spang, Bazzoli, and Arnould (2001) analyzed changes in cost and prices from 1989 to 1997 for merging and nonmerging rival hospitals in various metropolitan statistical areas of the United States. The authors found that merging hospitals generally had lower growth in costs and prices compared with their rivals but found the cost savings to be very modest and nearly identical price growth in markets with high HMO penetration rates. Ho and Hamilton (2000) compared the quality of health care before and after hospital mergers and acquisitions in California between 1992 and 1995. They determined empirically that consolidation had no measurable impact on the inpatient mortality of heart attack and stroke patients but found some evidence linking consolidation to higher readmission rates and early discharges.

Without a doubt, the hospital services industry has undergone a tremendous economic transformation over the last 20 years. Most important, payer-driven competition has replaced patient-driven competition and, as a result, the degree of price competition among hospitals has greatly intensified. From this brief review of the literature it appears that hospitals are now forced to consider the cost implications of many of their decisions in competitive areas. If society values low hospital prices and better quality, available evidence for the most part suggests that competition among hospitals has the ability to improve societal welfare.

Hospital Ownership and Hospital Behavior

Recall that property rights theory argues that for-profit hospitals may behave differently than not-for-profit hospitals because the latter face a nondistribution constraint. That is, it is illegal for a not-for-profit hospital to distribute any residual of revenues over costs, which represent profits to a for-profit hospital, to outside parties. The residual must be retained and used to support the purpose for which the not-for-profit hospital was formed. For example, the residual might be used to expand the facilities of the hospital, purchase new equipment, or pay for the hospital care of indigent individuals.

It is sometimes argued that not-for-profit and government hospitals face less of an incentive than for-profit hospitals to behave efficiently because of the absence of outside owners or residual claimants who face a strong, direct financial incentive to monitor activities and who are able to discipline management when deviations from cost minimization occur. Thus the property rights theory suggests that not-for-profit hospitals may operate with higher costs than otherwise similar for-profit hospitals, as the previously discussed expense preference model predicts.

Also, public choice theorists point out that public hospitals lack a further incentive to minimize the cost of production. Unlike private hospitals, public hospitals can rely to some extent on direct funding from the government in addition to patient-driven revenues. As a result, public hospitals are not at the complete mercy of the marketplace to minimize costs, unlike not-for-profit and especially for-profit hospitals. Keep in mind, however, that public hospitals are typically monitored directly by elected or appointed committees and those participating on the committees may wish to be reelected or reappointed to their positions. The threat of losing their position on the committee may give them a stakeholder (rather than stockholder) interest in the efficient operation of the organization. If so, one type of incentive system and disciplining mechanism simply replaces the other.

Property rights theory also suggests that the quality of care might be lower in for-profit hospitals than otherwise similar not-for-profit and public hospitals. To make greater profits, for-profit hospitals may face an incentive to skimp or cut corners on quality, especially quality of care that cannot be easily monitored by outside individuals. In contrast, not-for-profit hospitals, because of the attenuation of property rights, face less of an incentive to sacrifice quality for the sake of profits. This would be particularly true for situations where quality of care enters the utility function of the managers running the not-for-profit hospitals.

Given the theoretical discussion, it should not be too surprising that a relatively large amount of research has examined whether ownership status affects price, costs, and quality of care. Studies tend not to find any systematically large efficiency differences across hospitals with different ownership types. The cost differences that are sometimes observed can usually be explained by unmeasurable variations in quality. Although for-profit hospitals do tend to charge higher prices, the price differences can often be explained by the fact that not-for-profit hospitals do not pay most taxes, borrow at lower interest rates because interest on their bonds is tax exempt, and receive donations from outside parties.[11]

There are other explanations for the cost and price similarity. Sloan (1988) argues that physicians on the medical staff may act as residual claimants in not-for-profit hospitals and thus "have a financial stake in keeping such hospitals efficient. Inefficient hospitals are candidates for acquisition by for-profit hospitals" (p. 138). Pauly (1987) claims there is little theoretical justification to assert that not-for-profit hospitals do not minimize production costs. Consider a not-for-profit hospital that maximizes output. Although the managers are not maximizing profits, they still face an incentive to produce output as cheaply as possible. An incentive to minimize costs exists because more output can be produced from a given budget if managers keep per-unit costs to a minimum. Finally, various analysts note that market competition forces hospitals of all ownership forms to produce as cheaply as possible and charge reasonable prices. High-cost, high priced hospitals do not survive in competitive markets.

Economists have conducted much less research on quality of care differences across hospitals of different ownership types.[12] Representative of the few conducted, in terms of the empirical results, Sloan, Picone, Taylor, and Chou (2001) compare probability of death at one month, six months, and one year following admission into public, for-profit, and not-for-profit hospitals. The authors use patient data drawn from the National Long Term Care Survey for various years from 1982 to 1994. Persons selected for analysis were admitted to

---

[11]But see Sloan, Picone, Taylor, and Chou (2001) who find that payments on behalf of Medicare patients admitted to for-profit hospitals during the first six months following a health shock were higher than those admitted to not-for-profit and public hospitals. They argue that the higher payment to for-profits "plausibly reflects their greater incentive to maximize reimbursements from payers by various means including formal and informal contractual relationships with other suppliers of health care services. (p. 18).

[12]See Sloan (2000) for a review of the other studies.

the hospital with primary diagnoses of hip fracture, stroke, coronary heart disease, or congestive heart failure. After holding constant other determinants of mortality, they find no discernible difference in mortality rates between hospitals with different ownership forms.

While costs, prices, and quality of care tend to be reasonably similar across differently owned hospitals, most studies have found that public hospitals are much more likely to provide greater amounts of uncompensated care. Uncompensated care is usually defined as bad debts and charity and is measured as a percent of total hospital expenses. As evidence, Mann, Melnick, Bamezai, and Zwanziger (1997) estimate that uncompensated care as a percentage of expenses was 15.4 and 6.3 percent for urban public and rural public hospitals, respectively, in 1994. The comparable figures for not-for-profit and for-profit were 5.0 and 4.2 percent, respectively. Not surprisingly, public hospitals have been dubbed the "hospital provider of last resort" because of their charitable nature. In fact, one study found that private hospitals provide less uncompensated care when a public general hospital exists in the area (Thorpe and Brecher, 1987).

These figures on uncompensated care help to motivate two other interesting questions. First, why do for-profit hospitals provide any uncompensated care? Supposedly, the business of for-profit hospitals is business and therefore the maximization of profits or stockholder wealth. Providing care to the indigent subtracts from maximum profits and reduces the return to owners. However, Herzlinger and Krasker (1987) point out that for-profit hospitals may not deny poor individuals access to care because "hospital costs are mostly fixed and the marginal costs of an additional patient day, generally low. Even an indigent patient contributes somewhat to covering the hospital's fixed costs" (p. 103).

The second question deals with not-for-profit hospitals. One reason not-for-profit hospitals are granted tax-exempt status is because they are supposed to apply any unused revenues (or profits) toward the express purpose for which they were formed. Not-for-profit hospitals are formed to provide medical care to the sick and needy and are responsible to the community at large. Therefore, not-for-profit hospitals are expected to provide charitable care. The fact that their uncompensated care is only 5 percent of expenses and quite close to that of for-profit hospitals raises the question whether the tax-exempt status of not-for-profit hospitals should be revoked. In fact, state and local governments in Texas, Pennsylvania, and Utah, among others, have introduced legislation intended to pressure not-for-profit hospitals into providing more charity care. Not-for-profit hospitals would be required to prove that they benefit their areas or lose their tax exemption (Lutz, 1993). Morrisey, Wedig, and Hassan (1996) demonstrate that the concern about the tax-exempt status of not-for-profit hospitals may be warranted. Using 1988 and 1991 data for 189 not-for-profit hospitals in California, they compare the amount of uncompensated care to the estimated tax subsidy that each not-for-profit hospital receives. While not as widespread as commonly believed, the researchers find that nearly 20 percent of all not-for-profit hospitals do not provide uncompensated care sufficient to compensate for the tax subsidies they receive.

Taking the analysis a step further, Nicholson, Pauly, Burns, Baumritter, and Asch (2000) argue that the dollar value of the tax exemption to not-for-profit hospitals should be compared to total community benefits rather than to the value of uncompensated care. Since not-for-profit hospitals do not have to return profits to residual claimants like for-profits do, the authors note that not-for-profits should be expected to provide community benefits equal to those provided by for-profit hospitals plus the profits these hospitals earn. Based upon data for the three largest for-profit hospital systems over the period 1996 to

1998, they find that community benefits (taxes plus estimated cost of uncompensated care) and profits as a percent of equity and assets equaled 30 and 10 percent, respectively. When applied to the equity and assets of an average not-for-profit hospital, these percentages imply that a not-for-profit would be expected to spend $9.1 to $13.2 million on community benefits per year, yet uncompensated care accounts for only about $3.3 million. Even after accounting for a host of other public benefits the typical not-for-profit might provide, such as subsidized medical research and price discounts, the authors write "nonprofit hospitals appear to fall far short of providing the expected level of community benefit that would justify current levels of investment" (p. 176).

Managed-Care Buyers and Hospital Behavior

Another interesting aspect of hospital conduct is the relation between managed-care institutions, such as HMOs, PPOs, and utilization review organizations, and hospital behavior. The question is whether managed care provides the proper incentives for efficiency without seriously sacrificing quality. Most of the research on the relation between MCOs and hospital behavior has examined the effect of HMOs on hospital costs, utilization rates, or the quality of health outcomes. In general, studies suggest that HMO hospitalization rates are about 15 to 20 percent lower than those of fee-for-service insurance plans after controlling for a host of health-related factors, including ages of the patients, case-mix, severity of illnesses, and hospital-specific influences (Luft, 1981; Manning et al., 1984; Dowd, Feldman, Cassou, and Finch, 1991; Miller and Luft, 1994). Moreover, studies imply that the lower hospitalization rates tend to hold for both staff and IPA/HMOs (Dowd, Feldman, Cassou, and Finch, 1991; Bradbury, Golec, and Stearns, 1991). Even among intensive care patients, a setting that appears to allow very little room for discretion in treatment decisions, some evidence indicates that managed care results in cost savings when compared to traditional insurance (Rapoport, Gehlbach, Lemeshow, and Teres, 1992).

Research has also indicated that inpatient outcomes are not systematically worse (Retchin et al., 1992; Retchin and Brown, 1991; Carlisle et al., 1992; Miller and Luft, 1994; Miller and Luft, 2002) for HMOs compared to fee-for-service medicine, although some disagreement remains about the care of low-income patients in HMOs (compare Ware et al. [1986] and Greenwald and Henke [1992]). Most studies do report worse results on many measures of access to care and lower levels of satisfaction for HMO enrollees (Miller and Luft, 2002). The relatively comparable level of quality has surprised some critics of HMOs because they suspected that the prepaid nature of these institutions creates an incentive for an underproduction of care. A number of empirical and theoretical factors may account for the quality of care similarity in MCO and non-MCO plans. First, empirically it is very difficult to distinguish among health plans in practice, especially when health insurers have multiple plans and health care providers treat patients belonging to a number of alternative plans. Quality of care may appear similar because the observations are wrongly assigned into MCO and non-MCO plans.

Second, some MCOs are structured as not-for-profit institutions. For example, 42 percent of all HMO enrollees received their care from organizations that were structured as not-for-profit in 1994 (Corrigan et al., 1997). Many researchers argue that not-for-profit institutions pursue goals other than profit maximization, as we discussed earlier in this chapter. If not-for-profit MCOs attempt to maximize some other objective rather than the "bottom line," it is not theoretically apparent why the quality of care in those MCOs should differ from that of traditional indemnity insurers.

Third, like traditional indemnity plans, MCOs often invest huge sums of money establishing brand names that can be tarnished by offering inferior care. The prospect of losing repeat buyers and not receiving a proper return on investment can place a considerable amount of pressure on MCOs to provide the proper level of care. Of course, well-informed consumers are necessary for that kind of pressure to materialize. In this regard, it would be interesting to know if the constant attention given MCOs in the popular press and political arena has had any effect on the behavior and performance of MCOs.

Fourth, physicians that contract with MCOs most likely subscribe to the same basic ethical code of conduct (like the Hippocratic Oath) as the doctors that deal with indemnity insurers. In fact, many physicians simultaneously contract with both types of insurers. Although doctors may find themselves pressured by the financial incentives and management strategies of MCOs at the margin, it is not clear theoretically if these pressures dominate over ethical concerns, on average.

In contrast to HMOs, there have been only a few published assessments of PPO effects on hospital utilization rates and expenditures. The few existing studies fail to reach a consensus on the *overall* cost-containment effectiveness of PPOs. While Zwanziger and Auerbach (1991) report that PPOs lead to a reduction in inpatient expenditures, the increased expenditures stemming from expansions in outpatient benefits tend to swamp these cost savings (Hester, Wouters, and Wright, 1987; Garnick et al., 1990; Diehr et al., 1990).[13] According to Fielding and Rice (1993), PPOs are ineffective in controlling overall costs because the typical participating physician has only 11 enrollees from a particular PPO. Consequently, an individual PPO has limited ability to exert any monopsony power over the prices and utilization practices of physicians.

Another aspect of managed care is **utilization review (UR)**.[14] According to Ermann (1988), UR "programs seek to determine whether specific services are medically necessary and whether they are delivered at an appropriate level of intensity and cost" (p. 683). Utilization management began in 1972 in the public sector when the federal government established professional standards review organizations (PSROs) to provide UR services for Medicare and Medicaid patients as a result of the concern over unnecessary and low-quality care. However, the PSROs proved to be ineffective. For example, the Congressional Budget Office (1981) reported that "for every dollar spent on PSRO review of Medicare patients, only $.40 in resources were recouped, for a net loss of $.60" (p. xiii). As a result, PSROs were terminated in 1982 and, in the following year, replaced by peer review organizations (PROs). PROs are regionally based organizations that compete for government contracts and are responsible for ensuring the quality of services and eliminating unnecessary care through UR.

The first privately sponsored UR programs began in the mid-1960s and focused on hospital utilization. Private UR programs covered very few employees until the middle to late 1980s, but over the last 10 years the UR industry has developed rapidly, covering about 90 percent of individuals with private medical insurance. In addition to large national commercial health insurers, such as Aetna, and HMO companies that provide a full spectrum of managed-care services, about 200 companies offer only UR services. Some of these

---

[13]But see Smith (1997/98) who finds that, on average, PPOs were associated with cost savings of 12 percent per covered life as compared to traditional plans with utilization review. The cost savings were primarily through lower rates of physician visits and hospital admissions.

[14]The following discussion borrows heavily from Bailit and Sennett (1991).

companies are national in scope, but most are regionally or locally based. These companies usually specialize in one area of UR (e.g., medical and surgical or psychiatric and substance abuse); thus, it is not unusual for an employer to contract simultaneously with several UR companies.

There are three types of UR services, based on time of review. **Prospective** UR addresses the necessity of hospital care while it is still being planned and consequently has the capacity to change or avert planned treatments. Prior authorization and second opin-

INSIGHT 13-4

Drive-Through Deliveries

Managed-care organizations developed, in large part, to curb the rising tide of health care costs that arose from traditional fee-for-service insurance. They were initially championed as the providers of cost-effective, high-quality medicine. Times have changed. Critics of managed care now contend that MCOs have gone overboard in their pursuit of cost savings by unnecessarily denying medical care to patients. As evidence, critics have pointed to the unduly short hospital stays of new moms and babies enrolled in managed-care plans. Indeed, numerous articles have appeared in the popular press citing the drive-through maternity care practices of MCOs. As concern over drive-through deliveries escalated, many state governments and the federal government legislated "motherhood mandates," which established minimum postdelivery hospital stays for new moms and their babies (usually 48 hours following a vaginal birth and 96 hours following a cesarean section).

But is it true that hospital stays are significantly shorter for mothers and newborns enrolled in managed-care plans? Also, is it true that patient well-being is compromised by short hospital stays? Gazmararian and Koplan (1996) attempted to answer these questions.

Specifically, the authors examined national data from the Prudential Healthcare claims system on 13,945 enrollees who had normal vaginal deliveries in 1994. Of those, 4,547 were enrolled in HMOs, 5,342 belonged to point-of-service plans, and 4,056 were members of indemnity plans. The authors obtained data on hospital length of stay and readmission rates for the mothers and newborns by type of plan, among other variables. Readmission rates were used to determine the quality of care during the initial stay.

The authors found that the length of stay for both new mothers and newborns differed across health plan types. For example, 81.7 percent of the mothers enrolled in HMOs were discharged within one day. The comparable figures for point-of-service and indemnity enrollees were only 61.4 and 48.1 percent, respectively. Only in the Northeast was there no significant difference in the length of stay by type of plan.

No difference was found for newborn readmission rates by plan type. However, among women discharged within one day, those enrolled in HMOs had a readmission rate more than 50 percent higher (0.56) than that of women enrolled in either point-of-service (0.27) or indemnity (0.20) plans. Because most of the maternal readmissions occurred more than three days after delivery, however, the authors note that an additional day in the hospital after delivery would most likely not have prevented most readmissions.

ions are examples of prospective UR. **Concurrent** review programs focus on the necessity of continual care for patients and thus intervenes to change planned treatments. For hospitalized patients, review organizations monitor by telephone or through onsite nurses to determine whether patients need certain types of hospital-level care. Finally, **retrospective** programs review care after the fact from records and claims that have little potential to directly affect care provided to patients, except by altering the practice patterns of providers that face retrospective denial of reimbursement.

Although studies on the effectiveness of private UR services in containing hospital costs are relatively limited, the available literature indicates that hospital admissions and length-of-stay prospective review programs have led to a significant reduction in beds per 1,000 employees. In addition, a few studies of hospital review programs report net total health care savings of 4.5 to 8 percent at the individual plan level (e.g., Feldstein, Wickizer, and Wheeler, 1988). Likewise, at the system level, Schwartz and Mendelson (1991) claim that UR programs were associated with a significant reduction in the rate of hospital costs during the 1980s. No evidence yet exists on the relation between UR services and the quality of patient care.

In sum, research has shown that HMOs, PPOs, and UR can contain inpatient hospital costs to some degree. Research further indicates that HMOs contain inpatient care costs without seriously sacrificing health care quality but timely access and consumer satisfaction remain concerns. Evidence on the quality implications of PPOs and UR programs is unavailable. The ability of PPOs to contain *overall* health care costs appears to be limited due to the small number of PPO patients assigned to the typical physician.

Price Regulations and Hospital Behavior[15]

Public policies may also affect the conduct of hospitals. In 1972, Congress passed Section 222 of the Social Security Amendments giving states the authority to establish rate-setting programs. By the late 1970s, more than 30 states had adopted some form of hospital rate-setting program (Coelen and Sullivan, 1981). However, only three of the states had a mandatory "all-payer" program that controlled rates for all patient groups, including private payers, commercially insured patients, patients with public insurance, and Blue Cross plans. By 1996 only one state, Maryland, still had an all-payer rate-setting program.

Proponents of rate-setting programs have argued that these programs can contain health care costs with no concomitant reduction in the quality of care because they view hospitals as operating with organizational slack. The organizational slack, taking form in such factors as higher than necessary hospital salaries, duplication of facilities, and unnecessary hospital amenities, results from imperfect markets or hospital objectives other than cost minimization. When slack is present, price regulations or ceilings may promote lower expenditures without an associated reduction in patient care.

Empirical studies have almost unanimously supported the view that state regulation of hospital fees can lower health care costs. For example, Lanning, Morrisey, and Ohsfeldt (1991), whose study correctly controlled for the endogenous nature of state programs, found that states with mature rate-setting programs have 14.6 percent lower per capita

---

[15]The following discussion is based largely on Anderson (1991).

health care expenditures than otherwise comparable states without such policies.[16] The reduction in medical costs includes both hospital and nonhospital expenditures, which tends to refute the hypothesis of Morrisey et al. (1984) that rate setting results in an unbundling of services. *Unbundling* refers to the practice whereby decision makers shift the production of services from the regulated (hospital) to the unregulated (physician) sector in response to rate setting.

The findings of empirical studies focusing on the relation between rate setting and quality of care have been mixed, however. For example, Shortell and Hughes (1988) found a strong association between the stringency of state rate review programs and higher mortality rates among inpatients after holding other determinants of health status constant. Gaumer et al. (1989) report a small adverse impact of the presence of rate-setting policies on mortality at the national level but inconsistent effects at the individual state level and no effect of program stringency on mortality. Conversely, a study by Smith, McFall, and Pine (1993) indicates that regulated states had lower mortality rates among Medicare beneficiaries than unregulated states. Finally, a Rand study (e.g., Kahn et al., 1990; Draper et al., 1990) concluded that the Medicare PPS, which can be considered a federal rate-setting program, has contained hospital costs without generally lowering the quality of care for Medicare patients. However, a comparable study by Fitzgerald, Moore, and Dittus (1988) found that the overall care for Medicare patients with hip fracture worsened since the implementation of PPS. Clearly, more studies are needed before we can make any generalizations about the relation between government rate-setting programs and the quality of care.

Integrated Delivery Systems

As mentioned in Chapter 12, the autonomous, solo-physician clinic, once the mainstay organization in the physician industry, is being gradually replaced by the multiphysician group practice. Interestingly, the hospital industry is undergoing a similar transformation as many formerly independent hospitals are now becoming part of multihospital chains or systems. These horizontal mergers among individual physician practices and among individual hospitals take place largely because increased market power is sought after or because of economies of scale, economies of scope, and the other cost advantages associated with health care systems, as previously discussed.

Another organizational transformation currently taking place in the health care sector that involves both the hospital and physician industries is the integration of physician practices with hospitals. According to Robinson (1997, p. 6), "The **integrated delivery system (IDS)** combines physicians and hospitals into a vertically integrated organization with a single ownership and structure, a single chain of authority, and a single bottom line." There are basically four types of IDSs: the physician-hospital organization, the management service organization, the foundation model, and the integrated health organization, although other hybrid organizational forms also exist. These alternative physician-hospital arrangements differ in the degree to which risk, governance, revenue and capital, planning,

---

[16]But see Antel, Ohsfeldt, and Becker (1995). Earlier studies that did not control for the endogeneity of rate setting suggest that the percentage effect is much smaller, at about 2.0 to 4.1 percentage points (see Morrisey, Conrad, Shortell, and Cook, 1984). Some empirical evidence (e.g., Romeo, Wagner, and Lee, 1984) has also linked states' prospective payment systems to a slower diffusion of new medical technologies, although the results are too limited to generalize.

and management are shared (Burns and Thorpe, 1993). An IDS may include nursing homes, home health care units, and an insurance component in addition to physicians and hospitals.

IDSs have developed in large part due to the financial pressure from MCOs, which in recent years have exercised their growing power to control costs. A movement by the government toward fixed payment systems, such as the prospective payment system for hospitals and the resource-based relative value scale system for physicians, also served as an impetus for change (Burns and Thorpe, 1993; Morrisey, Alexander, Burns, and Johnson, 1996).

Why vertically integrated systems are formed is a question that interests economists, among others. Economists generally analyze organizational arrangements through the "conceptual lens" of agency theory and transaction cost economics (Robinson, 1997; Shortell, 1997). **Agency theory** considers the contractual relationships among parties. According to agency theory, the principal, or owner(s), of the firm enters into a multitude of contracts, either implicitly or formally, with other firms or agents who are the suppliers of inputs. Each contract stipulates the input or product that will be provided, the price that will be paid, and other terms of the agreement, such as product quality and time of delivery. Consequently, agency theory regards the firm as a nexus of many contracts. Within the agency model, the firm essentially serves as a facilitator and coordinator of the many contracts and is responsible for transforming the resulting inputs into an output or multiple outputs. The contractual relationships provide the firm with considerable flexibility to switch among input suppliers when better terms of exchange, such as a lower price or better product quality, become available.

But if agency theory perfectly describes the firm, why do we observe some firms producing inputs internally rather than contracting out for them? For example, why do some hospitals possess their own maintenance staffs, MRI facilities, or nursing home units while others contract out for these same services?

Transaction costs economics provides a reason why firms choose to produce inputs or services internally rather than contracting out. Transaction costs refer to the costs associated with the negotiating, writing, and enforcing of contracts and includes the costs of searching out the best price and quality. Transaction cost theory considers that many contracts are incomplete because not all possible contingencies can be written into a contract. **Bounded rationality**, especially in the face of uncertainty, is one reason for incomplete contracts. Bounded rationality refers to the limited capacity of the human mind to formulate and solve problems (Williamson, 1985). When contracts are incomplete, some stipulations will require renegotiation. During the renegotiation process, one of the parties may have an advantage and the advantage can lead to **opportunistic behavior**. Opportunistic behavior involves self-interest seeking with guile and allows for strategic behavior or deception. The potential for opportunistic behavior increases the cost of contractual relationships.

As an example, suppose a hospital contracts with a company to repair the masonry around the bricks on the exterior of its buildings for $17,000. The company rents and installs the necessary scaffolding and begins the repairs. Upon closer inspection, however, the repair crew realizes that a good proportion of the repair is unnecessary and informs the hospital administrator. Naturally, the hospital administrator asks how much of the $17,000 will be returned. The contractor relates that the scaffolding must be rented for a minimum of one month. The contractor also mentions that transporting, installing, and disassembling the scaffolding is very costly. As you can see, the contractor is in a good position to practice opportunistic behavior by inflating the cost figures. Who would have thought to stipulate a contingency of that kind in the contract?

Transaction cost theory suggests that firms may sometimes find internal production more efficient than outsourcing due to the relatively high cost of contracting. The theory by itself, however, suggests that firms should continually find it optimal to vertically integrate through greater internal production or by merging with suppliers. Obviously there must be some limiting factors; otherwise, most firms would be immense.

The same agency relationship discussed above places a limiting factor on the size of firms. Like outside contractors, employees and management are bound to the firm through implicit or formal contracts. For example, employees are expected to show up for work on time and perform well; otherwise, their jobs may be in jeopardy. While ownership of the nonhuman assets gives the firm more control over internal negotiations than external ones (Hart, 1995), greater firm size may lead to higher production costs at some point. As a firm grows physically larger, it becomes increasingly more complex and costly for the owners to monitor the behavior of management and employees. Inefficient behavior may arise as a result of the high monitoring costs.

For example, consider the large corporation where the principal is represented by the stockholders, and the chief executive officer (CEO) serves as the primary agent. Stockholders, wishing high dividends and stock value appreciation, want the CEO to maximize profits. The CEO, however, may attempt to pursue goals other than maximum profits, especially when he or she is paid a fixed salary. For example, the CEO may use some of the firm's profit to pay for plush office accommodations, a limousine, or various other expensive perquisites. Alternatively, the CEO may be more interested in empire building and, therefore, may acquire several other unprofitable companies rather than maximize profits. As a result, the corporation may perform poorly because of the CEO actions. The CEO, however, may blame general economic conditions, and, therefore, the unknowing stockholders may not punish the CEO for the unprofitable behavior.[17]

As another example, salaried employees, particularly when they work as a team, may shirk their responsibilities, engage in on-the-job leisure time, and free-ride on the productive efforts of others. If a sufficient number of those on the team behave similarly, team output suffers and profits decline. The larger the organization, the greater the cost of monitoring the efforts of management and employees because of the proportionately greater interactions among workers (Carlton and Perloff, 1994).

To prevent internal agents, such as CEOs or employees, from operating in an unproductive manner, agency theory suggests that compensation might be tied to performance or profits so as to align the interests of the principal and agents. For example, the CEO's pay may be linked to the profits or stock value of the company. CEOs often receive bonus pay and stock options as part of their total compensation for that reason. The contracts help to align the interests of the principal and agents so the interests of the principal are better served. It is important to note, however, that employment contracts are not always complete, so inefficient behavior may result as the firm continues to produce increasingly more services internally rather than purchasing them in the marketplace. Organizational

---

[17]This possibility was alluded to when we discussed the implications of the utility maximization models. When the ownership constraint is weak, managers may maximize their own personal utilities, which are partly derived from the five Ps of increased pay, perquisites, power, prestige, and patronage.

independence, in contrast to internal production, preserves the risk and rewards for efficient performance (Robinson, 1997).

As another limit on firm size, managerial diseconomies may set in as the firm gets too large because of bounded rationality. Managers at the top may lose sight of the production process taking place at the floor level. Communication flows from top to bottom may break down. Bureaucratic inertia may also set in as regimentation replaces innovation and risk-taking is not properly rewarded. The loss of control, breakdowns in communication, and loss of innovativeness may all place limits on the size of the firm.

As long as decision makers act rationally, each firm can be expected to choose that size where marginal benefit equals marginal cost. A greater amount of internal production creates benefits because of reduced transaction costs but also may come at a cost as larger firms become more costly and complex to monitor and innovation suffers. The costs of contracting and monitoring differ from firm to firm and from industry to industry. Some firms find market exchange more efficient than internal production at the margin. Transaction costs depend on various factors, such as the degree of market uncertainty, the number of suppliers in the market, and how often the service or input must be obtained. In general, when market conditions are more uncertain, the number of suppliers is fewer and frequency of use is greater, transaction costs are greater, and internal production becomes more efficient.

You are probably asking yourself how the discussion on agency theory and transaction cost economics relates to physician-hospital integration. Hospitals and physician practices vertically integrate or fail to vertically integrate for the same reasons as other organizations do. Vertical integration leads to lower transaction costs but can impose incentive problems in large organizations. Robinson (1997) expands upon this theme by noting that a contractual relationship between a hospital and physicians can be thought of as **virtual integration**. The term *virtual integration* is just a convenient way of stating that a combination of two or more organizations takes place through contractual relationships rather than through unified ownership. Robinson goes on to compare the relative advantages of vertical and virtual integration with regard to coordination, governance, and clinical innovation, three key activities in a hospital-physician relationship.

Coordination deals with how the individual parts are woven into an overall productive unit. For example, are the various services that combine to form medical care, such as lab tests, imaging, physician care and inpatient hospital services, all coordinated through one large, unified structure or through two or perhaps more contractual relationships? At the extreme, authority and induced loyalty and commitment might be used to coordinate care in a unified model, while negotiation may be relied upon in a purely contractual network (Robinson, 1997; Shortell, 1997). For example, a hospital may offer to process the bills of a physician or purchase and then rent a medical facility to a physician as a way of achieving better coordination through contracting. As another example, hospital and physician services might be better coordinated by allowing more physicians to serve on the hospital's board of trustees.

Governance considers who controls the firm's policies and how much flexibility the firm has to adapt and modify its policies when confronted with changing external events. An important aspect of governance is whether the decision-making process is centralized or decentralized and whether it is dependent on for-profit or not-for-profit objectives. Decentralized governance tends to provide more flexibility, but vertical arrangements between decentralized for-profit and not-for-profit organizations may not last because of a

clash of missions (e.g., the virtual integration of a Catholic hospital with a physician practice providing abortion services).

Clinical innovation is a function of the entrepreneurial, risk-taking spirit. At the
one extreme, virtual integration involves arm's length agreements with little sharing of
financial risks. At the other extreme, vertical integration, hospitals and physician groups
might jointly share in the financial risks of the organization through an ownership stake.
One issue here is how the resulting organizational arrangement affects the incentive of
the firm to minimize costs and undertake innovative activities. For example, Robinson
(1997) notes when "physicians sell their practices and merge into larger systems, they risk
losing the entrepreneurial, risk-taking spirit and developing the civil service mentality
of the hospital employee" (p. 17). The incentive attenuation might be overcome, however,
by providing the physician with an ownership stake in the larger system or by paying
performance-based compensation.

Shortell (1997) points out that vertical and virtual arrangements can be thought of as
a continuum with respect to the essential activities of coordination, governance, and clinical innovation. In the real world integration is rarely at either extreme but instead is
somewhere along the virtual-vertical continuum. Along the coordination continuum, for
example, a corporate joint venture falls somewhere in the middle of contracts and unified
ownership. Under a joint venture, a hospital and physician group might remain legally separated but agree to jointly coordinate some single type of patient care, for example. A joint
task force or committee represents an intermediate governance structure. A Physician
Hospital Organization, where a hospital and physicians jointly own and operate ambulatory care projects or jointly act as an agent for managed-care contracts, provides an example of an organizational structure that falls halfway along the clinical innovation
continuum.

Shortell further notes that organizations position themselves along the various contin-
uums depending on the demands of the local marketplace for a coordinated health care
system, the organization's own capabilities, and the historical context of the organization.
For example, if the local market demands a perfectly seamless, coordinated health care
system, the unified ownership of vertical integration will be favored over the contractual
relationship.

Many analysts initially anticipated that IDSs would lead to improved financial performance for hospitals as well as encourage greater quality of care through coordinated delivery systems. But only about 23 percent of all hospitals participated in some kind of
physician-hospital arrangement in 1993 and much vertical disintegration has occurred
since that date (Morrisey, Alexander, Burns, and Johnson, 1996; Burns and Pauly, 2002).
Vertical disintegration most likely occurred because studies failed to find any systematic
evidence linking IDSs with greater financial performance (Goes and Zhan, 1995). Burns
and Pauly (2002) argue that hospitals and physicians entered into vertical arrangements
for reasons that conflict with economic logic.

Summary of the Conduct of the Hospital Services Market

A number of structural and related factors simultaneously influence the conduct of hospitals in the marketplace. The degree of actual competition, barriers to entry, reimbursement practices of third-party payers, and hospital objectives jointly affect how an
individual hospital behaves, and therefore only carefully conceived studies can sort out

how any one individual factor in isolation influences hospital conduct. Most empirical studies using data prior to 1983 have found that hospitals competed on the basis of quality rather than price, but recent evidence suggests that the growing price consciousness among health care payers may be causing increased price competition among hospitals.

Empirical evidence also suggests that efficiency differences are quite small among not-for-profit, public, and for-profit hospitals after controlling for quality and case-mix differences. The reason cited for the similarity is that physicians act as residual claimants in not-for-profit hospitals and thus ensure that the hospitals behave as efficiently as possible. The provision of indigent care has been found to be considerably higher in public hospitals than in otherwise identical not-for-profit and for-profit hospitals. In addition, the amount of indigent care has been found to be quite similar for not-for-profit and for-profit hospitals, raising doubt about the desirability of the tax-exempt status generally conferred on not-for-profit hospitals.

MCOs appear to offer modest hospital cost savings without reducing the quality of patient outcomes compared to traditional fee-for-service medicine. HMOs and UR appear to provide more consistent cost savings than PPOs, however. As consumers become more price conscious and the hospital market becomes more competitive, increased cost savings may result from a managed-care environment. State rate review programs have also proven effective in containing hospital care costs. However, studies investigating the effect of state rate review policies on the quality of hospital outcomes have failed to reach a definitive conclusion.

Finally, MCOs and fixed reimbursement methods have motivated some hospitals and physician practices to form integrated delivery systems. IDSs involve either vertical or virtual (contractual) integration. Vertical integration may offer cost-savings by reducing the transaction costs associated with external market exchanges. Vertical integration can lead to higher operating costs as monitoring costs rise, communication flows break down, or innovation suffers in large corporations. To date, empirical studies have uncovered mixed results regarding improved financial performance in IDSs.

THE PERFORMANCE OF THE HOSPITAL SERVICES INDUSTRY

This final section focuses on the overall performance of the hospital services industry by assessing the growth of hospital expenditures, the hospital inflation rate, and hospital input utilization in the aggregate. While it might be best to analyze the performance of the hospital industry in each state or, perhaps, in each metropolitan area in the United States given the structural diversity of hospital markets, the analysis would be unwieldy and the necessary data are less widely available at a disaggregated level. As a result, we examine and discuss various hospital pricing and utilization trends over time to get some idea about the overall or aggregate performance of the hospital services industry in the United States.

The Growth in Hospital Expenditures

Over the years, expenditures on hospital services, which include spending on both inpatient and outpatient services, have tended to comprise about 30 to 40 percent of all health care spending, making it the dominant expense of most health care payers. The big-ticket aspect of hospital spending should not be surprising given that it is the severely ill that typically receive hospital care and also the technologically intensive method of delivering most types of hospital care. As table 13–3 reveals, hospital expenditures were $9.2 billion in 1960, increasing by nearly 400 percent in nominal terms to $412.1 billion in 2000. On an annual basis, hospital expenditures grew about 10 percent from 1960 to 1990. In addition, as a percentage of gross domestic product, hospital spending increased from 1.7 to 4.4 percent over that same period. These figures imply that a continually rising share of the nation's income had to be siphoned off to pay for hospital care in the United States and that hospital spending grew considerably in both absolute and relative terms over those three decades.

TABLE 13–3

Hospital Expenditures in the United States, Selected Years, 1960–2000

Year	Total Hospital Expenditures (billions of dollars)	Average Annual Change from Previous Period	Spending as a Percentage of Gross Domestic Product
1960	$ 9.2	—	1.7%
1970	27.6	11.0%	2.7
1980	101.5	13.0	3.6
1990	253.9	9.2	4.4
1995	343.6	6.1	4.6
2000	412.1	3.6	4.2

SOURCE: Center for Medicare & Medicaid Services at http://www.hcfa.gov and Bureau of Economic Analysis at http://www.bea.gov.

The encouraging news is that hospital expenditure growth has slowed in more recent times and hospital spending has stabilized as a percentage of gross domestic product. Specifically, hospital expenditure growth has declined since 1990, falling to an annual rate of 6.1 percent over the period 1990 to 1995 and 3.6 percent over the period 1995 to 2000. Many analysts cite increased enrollments in MCOs as the reason behind the slower growth of hospital expenditures, pointing to lower rates of adoption and diffusion of new technologies by hospitals when confronted by managed-care incentives. For example, Baker (2001) finds that increases in HMO market share are associated with slower diffusion of magnetic resonance imaging (MRI) equipment into hospitals and substantially lower MRI availability and procedures use.[18] If so, the interesting question is whether hospital expenditures will continue to grow slowly or, at some point, begin to rise rapidly, as the one-time impact of managed care tapers off.

---

[18]But see Chernew, Hirth, Sonnad, Ermann, and Fendrick (1998), who, from their review of the relevant literature, conclude that "the evidence that managed care will control technology diffusion is mixed at best" (p. 282).

As you are well aware, hospital expenditures equal the product of the price and quantity of hospital services. As yet, we do not know whether the change in hospital expenditures over time is attributable to higher price changes, an increased quantity of services, or a combination of the two factors. This is an important consideration because, first, a greater quantity of hospital services makes people better off, whereas price increases have the opposite effect of reducing real incomes and consumer welfare. Second, as mentioned earlier, various structural elements of health care markets, such as extensive third-party coverage, may give rise to the overproduction of hospital services at the expense of all other goods and services and thereby result in allocative inefficiency. Thus, to get a better understanding of hospital expenditure growth, we next examine trends in various measures of hospital price and output.

The Hospital Services Price Inflation Rate

The intangible nature of hospital services makes it difficult to decompose hospital expenditures into price and quantity components. The Bureau of Labor Statistics (BLS) collects data from hospitals to construct a hospital and related services price index. Effective January 1997, the BLS regards the entire hospital visit as the relevant output of hospitals and therefore includes all the individual components, such as the number of days in a hospital room, inpatient treatment, and outpatient procedures, that make up a hospital visit. BLS also now uses the reimbursed or transaction price rather than the list price when calculating the hospital and related services price index.

Figure 13–5 shows the general price inflation rate as measured by the percentage change in the urban consumer price index and the hospital services inflation rate over the period 1980 to 2001. The data have several implications. First, the data suggest that the

FIGURE 13–5
General and Hospital Services Price Inflation

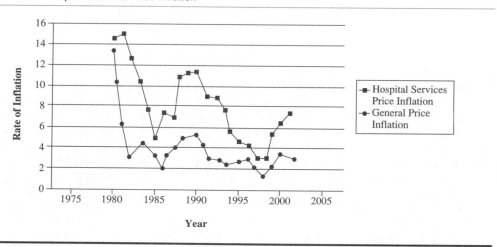

SOURCE: U.S. Department of Labor, Bureau of Labor Statistics, at http://www.bls.gov.

hospital services inflation rate exceeded the general price inflation rate in every year over the 22-year span. Second, the hospital sector experienced double-digit inflation rates seven times throughout the time span, unlike the entire economy, which faced double-digit inflation only twice. The recession of the early 1980s helped to bring inflationary pressures down in both the health sector and the macroeconomy. Third, despite the introduction of the Medicare PPS system and other public and private cost containment practices after 1983, hospital prices continued to rise more quickly than the prices of other goods. Finally the data indicate that increased managed-care enrollments may have had a disinflationary impact on hospital service prices during the early to late 1990s. Specifically, the rate of growth of hospital prices slowed from a high of 11.4 percent in 1990 to a low of 3.2 percent in 1998. However the data also suggest that the effects of managed care may be weakening as the hospital services inflation rate has continued to increase since 1998 to 7.1 percent in 2001.

The time-series data for the hospital services inflation rate suggest that hospital prices have risen more quickly than most other prices in the U.S. economy over the last decade. Unfortunately, the data cannot identify the source of the relative price increase in the hospital sector. Lack of a profit motive, fee-for-service medicine, first-dollar insurance coverage, quality competition, and unbridled hospital pricing power could all conceivably contribute to the relatively high and rising hospital inflation rate in the United States.

However, the normal functioning of a market economy can also provide an explanation for rising hospital prices. That is, relative prices normally rise for goods and services that become more highly valued or more costly to produce than others. Information on marginal social benefit and cost is needed before one can determine whether hospital services are efficiently produced. Unfortunately, the marginal benefit and cost of hospital services are difficult to estimate. Therefore, we must resort to analyzing information about input usage and hospital utilization to indirectly identify trends in the output performance of hospitals. We do so in the next section.

Hospital Input Usage and Utilization

Some of the more commonly discussed hospital performance indicators include the hospital staffing ratio (number of full-time equivalent personnel per weighted sum of outpatients and inpatients), occupancy rate (average daily inpatients per bed), admission rate per 100 population, average length of stay (average days per patient), and outpatient visits per 100 population. The first two indicators are intended to represent input usage, and the last three are proxy measures for the quantity or utilization of hospital services.

Data for these variables are drawn from Health Care Forum LLC (2002) and show a number of systematic trends. For one, the hospital staffing ratio increased throughout the period 1975 to 2000, rising from approximately 3 to nearly 5 full-time equivalent employees per patient. The higher staffing ratio may reflect the more severely ill patients resulting from the Medicare PPS, since less-sickly patients are now unlikely to be admitted to hospitals. On the other hand, the greater staffing ratio may represent the expense preferences of hospital administrators. Alternatively, the higher staffing ratio may signify the continuing ability of hospitals to generate revenues to support their not-for-profit, human service orientation toward providing more services to patients (Pope and Menke, 1990).

Figures for the hospital occupancy rate point to a similar conclusion regarding rising input usage. While fluctuating around 75 percent in the late 1970s and early 1980s, the average occupancy rate at U.S. hospitals declined from its highest level of around 76 percent in 1981 to slightly under 62 percent in 1996. The decline in the occupancy rate began one year before the Medicare PPS in 1983. The implication is one of excess beds at the typical American hospital. According to Anders (1993b), these beds are not cheap; each costs about $30,000 to $40,000 a year in maintenance, staffing, and depreciation charges.[19] With about 200,000 unnecessary beds in the nation, the aggregate cost of excess bed capacity runs about $6 billion to $8 billion a year. While too early to draw any meaningful conclusions, the encouraging news is that the occupancy rate has risen slightly to roughly 64 percent in 2000. The recent rise in the occupancy rate might reflect the increased pressure from competitive forces and MCOs to better manage their excess capacity (Santerre and Adams, 2002).

Data for the hospital admission rate show an interesting trend. The hospital admission rate hovered near 16 per 100 population from 1975 to 1982. Thereafter the rate fell and equaled 11.8 admissions per 100 population in 2000. The decline in the admission rate has surprised some health policy analysts who expected an increase in the admission rate with the advent of the Medicare PPS because reimbursement under this system is based on a per-case charge. Others argue that the reduced hospital admission rate was inevitable as health care providers substituted for inpatient care with less regulated outpatient and nursing home care.

Figures for the average length of stay (ALOS) show a pattern similar to that for the admission rate, roughly constant at 7.6 days in the years preceding the Medicare PPS. After that point, the ALOS fell precipitously to 7.1 days in 1985 and then leveled off through 1990. From 1991 to 2000, the ALOS fell further from 7.2 to 5.8 days. The reduction in length of stay was predicted as hospitals responded to the per-case charge of the Medicare PPS. A portion of the reduction in the hospital admission rate and length of stay shows up in the higher outpatient visit rate over time in the United States. The outpatient visit rate continually increased since 1985 from nearly 66 to 140 outpatient visits per 100 population in 2000, a growth of about 5 percent per year.

In sum, since the mid-1980s, a smaller percentage of people have been admitted into hospitals, and those admitted typically stay for a shorter duration. Also, hospital occupancy rates have fallen but staffing ratios continue to climb, in part to provide more services to more severely ill inpatients and to provide increased outpatient services. Health policy analysts have questioned whether the increased services provided to inpatients and outpatients are inappropriately supplied. Let us examine that question in more detail.

Do Hospitals Provide Inappropriate Care?   The supplier-induced demand theory and McGuire's model, as discussed in Chapter 12, predicts that health care providers may unnecessarily provide various diagnostic and therapeutic services to patients due to the associated financial gain. With this theory and rising health care costs in mind, a number of studies

---

[19]However, see Friedman and Pauly (1981), who estimated that the excess bed cost is about one-tenth of those figures. Gaynor and Anderson (1995) find evidence supporting the figures above, whereas Keeler and Ying (1996) indicate that the cost of excess bed capacity is much greater, at about $25 billion in 1993. Also see Carey (1998), who estimates the implied benefit of an empty bed in the range of $25 to $35 thousand for the period 1987 to 1992; again suggesting a high cost associated with unoccupied beds in the United States.

have attempted to determine whether various types of medical services are inappropriately provided to patients. One of the first studies, by Chassin et al. (1987), measured how appropriately physicians performed coronary angiography, carotid endarterectomy, and upper gastrointestinal (GI) tract endoscopy for the Medicare population in 1981 in several areas of the United States.[20] A panel of physicians was selected to rate a number of indications or clinical settings, each consisting of a unique combination of clinical information and other factors considered in recommending treatment, with respect to the appropriateness of each procedure.[21] *Appropriateness* was defined to mean that the expected health benefits (prolonged life, relief of pain, and cure of disease) of a procedure exceed its expected negative consequences (operative mortality, complications, pain, and anxiety) by a sufficiently wide margin. Only medical appropriateness was considered; the monetary costs of the procedure were ignored.

The authors found significant levels of inappropriate use: 17 percent of the cases for coronary angiography, 32 percent for carotid endarterectomy, and 17 percent for upper GI tract endoscopy. Uncertain use rates for these three services were 9, 32, and 11 percent, respectively. Similarly, Winslow et al. (1988), using data for 1979, 1980, and 1982, found an inappropriate rate of 14 percent and an uncertain rate of 30 percent for coronary artery bypass graft surgery. These two studies have been widely cited as offering concrete evidence that a large number of medical services are provided unnecessarily in U.S. hospitals.

Three studies using data for 1990 have raised serious doubt about whether medical services are inappropriately provided. Specifically, Leape et al. (1993), Hilborne et al. (1993), and Bernstein et al. (1993) found very low inappropriate rates for coronary bypass graft surgery (2.4 percent), coronary angioplasty (4 percent), and coronary angiography (4 percent) in a sample of New York hospitals. While the uncertain rate was also low for coronary artery bypass surgery (7 percent), the authors expressed some concern that the uncertain rates for coronary angioplasty and angiography were quite high at 38 and 20 percent, respectively. The authors of these three studies point to changing practice patterns and the regulatory environment in New York as possible reasons for the large differences in the two sets of studies.

The Concentration of Health Care Expenditures   Related to the concern over the provision of unnecessary medical care is the concentration of health care spending among a small minority of the U.S. population. According to data provided by Berk and Monheit (2001), 1 percent of the U.S. population accounted for 27 percent of all health care spending in 1996. The top 5 percent was responsible for more than one-half of all health care spending in the United States in that same year. The authors also found that the distribution of health care spending remained remarkably stable over the period from 1970 to 1996 despite the in-

---

[20]The areas studied were Arkansas, Colorado, Iowa, Massachusetts, Montana, Pennsylvania, South Carolina, and northern California. Coronary angiography is an X-ray study of the inside of the heart. Carotid endarterectomy is the removal of the core of the carotid artery, a blood vessel beginning at the large artery of the heart (aorta) and running straight up through the neck, that has become thickened by fatty deposits. Upper gastrointestinal tract endoscopy is an examination of the inside of the body from the mouth to the stomach with a lighting device.

[21]An *indication* is a reason to prescribe a medication or perform a treatment.

creased presence of MCOs in more recent times. The fact that the distribution of health care expenditures is concentrated among a small fraction of people should not be surprising given that the major users of health care services are severely ill patients receiving high-cost critical care in hospitals. In fact, it has been estimated that one in every seven health care dollars is spent during the last six months of someone's life (Clark, 1992). Data also suggest that 18.8 percent of Medicare patients accounted for 81 percent of all Medicare expenditures in 1991 (Iglehart, 1992). The dilemma, as Aaron (1991) notes, is that successful cost containment may "require rationing of services to the very ill"[22] (p. 53).

INSIGHT 13 – 5

The Relative Performance of Hospitals in the United States and Canada

Because per capita health care expenditures are lower in Canada than in the United States, a number of studies have examined whether variations in hospital performance account for some of the cost differential between the two countries. Using data from 1987, Redelmeier and Fuchs (1993) discovered that costs per hospital admission were 39 percent higher in the United States than in Canada. Moreover, when hospitals in California and Ontario were compared, costs were found to be 63 percent higher in the state than in the province.

These investigators then examined the factors responsible for the higher costs per hospital admission in the United States. While the United States had proportionately fewer hospital beds, fewer admissions, and a shorter mean length of stay than Canada, higher hospital costs were explained partly by a more complex case-mix and slightly higher input prices. However, the real reason for the cost disparity appeared to be a greater amount of resources used per hospital admission in the United States. Higher administrative costs (Woolhandler and Himmelstein, 1991) and the greater decentralization of equipment and personnel in the United States account for the greater use of hospital resources. Specifically, Redelmeier and Fuchs note that U.S. care is scattered among many small community hospitals that often operate far below capacity, unlike in Canada, where care is centralized at large, heavily used hospitals. For example, they point out that the lithotripsy machine at Canada's Wellesley hospital is used nearly 50 times per week, whereas the average use of a

(continued)

---

[22]However, Emanuel and Emanuel (1994) estimate that greater use of advanced directives (e.g., living wills), hospice care, and less aggressive interventions at the end of life will save only 3.3 percent of health care costs. Among the reasons they cite: even less aggressive humane care at the end of life is labor intensive and costly to produce.

similar lithotripsy machine is less than one-tenth that amount at the Stanford University Medical Center.[1]

Interestingly, the greater use of resources in American hospitals does not appear to lead to more favorable health outcomes. For example, Rouleau et al. (1993) found that patients' mortality rates and likelihood of a second heart attack were virtually identical in the two countries, even though U.S. doctors are twice as likely to do heart bypasses and angioplasties as their Canadian counterparts. Echoing these findings, Roos et al. (1992) determined that postsurgical mortality was lower in Manitoba, Canada, than in New England for most of the medical procedures they studied.

Hamilton, Ho, and Goldman (2000) investigate another potential performance differential by examining the difference between the United States and Canada in terms of queuing for surgery. Specifically, they compare surgical queues and outcomes between hospitals in Quebec and Massachusetts after a patient has fractured his or her hip. Inpatient mortality and post-surgical length of stay served as their outcome measures; the data covered the period 1990 to 1992. The authors found that while surgical wait times were longer in Canada, the predicted hazard of inpatient mortality was virtually the same in both countries. Although post-surgical length of stay was found sensitive to wait times for surgery and wait times were longer in Canada, its effect was shown to be small relative to other patient- and hospital-specific factors.

Consequently, the various studies, taken together, tend to provide convincing evidence that some valuable resource savings might accrue if the United States were to adopt a more centralized hospital system, such as Canada's, without a serious sacrifice of health outcomes.

---

[1]Haber et al. (1992) reached a similar conclusion that the quantity of inputs and nature of output account for the relatively higher hospital costs in the United States.

SUMMARY

Hospital expenditures represent the largest component of health care spending, accounting for slightly over 4 percent of U.S. gross domestic product. Without a doubt, any realistic cost-containment policies must be directed at the hospital sector of the health economy. The hospital services industry is best characterized as oligopolistic in nature. In most markets there are a few competing hospitals, with existing hospitals generally having a cost advantage over new ones due to learning curve economies. Combined with sophisticated product offerings and patient price inelasticity, hospitals have some ability to raise price above the competitive level and produce with inefficient methods.

Countervailing the ability of hospitals to raise price is the dominance of some third-party payers in the market for hospital services. Government and large insurers, along with managed-care organizations, are beginning to flex their market clout to negotiate price discounts and influence production practices with utilization review and various "at-risk" reimbursement methods. By and large, studies have found that both managed care and government price regulations are able to contain hospital costs at the micro level. In addition, recent studies have found evidence suggesting a decline in the inappropriate use of hospital services.

Despite these changes, hospital care prices and costs continue to rise in the aggregate. Whether the aggregate hospital price and expenditure increase is due to imperfect hospital markets or normal market forces remains to be determined. We must keep in mind, however, that a noncompetitive market structure predicts only higher prices and not continual increases in prices. The only way inflation can be associated with market structure is if the market were to become increasingly monopolistic over time, but that does not appear to be the case (Baumol, 1988). Some health policy analysts want the federal government to encourage increased competition in the entire health sector so that macro-level cost savings are realizable. Others look to government to adopt blanket regulations, such as an "all-payer" Medicare PPS, as a way to contain aggregate hospital care costs. The merits of market-based and government-based solutions continue to be debated.

REVIEW QUESTIONS AND PROBLEMS

1. Answer the following questions on the number, size distribution, and ownership of American community hospitals.
   A. What has happened to the number of community hospitals and beds since the 1980s? Using the demand theory developed in Chapter 5, what reasons can you think of for that change?
   B. Which is the dominant form of hospital ownership? What percentage of community beds were owned by for-profit, not-for-profit, and public hospitals in 2000? Rank the average for-profit, not-for-profit, and public hospital in terms of bed size.
   C. Within which particular bed size category do most hospitals operate?
2. Explain how the relevant product market is typically defined for community hospitals. Why? How is the relevant geographical market defined? Why?
3. Assume there are 10 equally sized hospitals in a market area. Calculate the Herfindahl-Hirschman index. Two hospitals in the market area inform the Department of Justice that they wish to merge. According to the current DOJ Merger Guidelines, will the merger be contested? Explain.
4. What are some possible sources of barriers to entry into the hospital industry? What has the literature concluded about the severity of these barriers?
5. Compare and contrast the technique and results associated with the econometric and survivor techniques of determining long-run economies of scale in the hospital services industry.

6. Answer the following questions on the buyers of hospital services.
   A. Who is the largest buyer of hospital services?
   B. What percentage of hospital costs are paid directly by the consumer?
   C. What factors affect the willingness of private third-party payers to negotiate for low hospital prices?
7. What are some of the different ways third-party payers have reimbursed hospitals? Which methods are considered to constitute "at-risk" payments?
8. Compare and contrast the various managerial objectives in the quantity maximization, quality maximization, quality/quantity maximization, and managerial expense preference models.
9. In your words, discuss the fundamental difference between the profit maximization and utility maximization models. Also, identify what factors are likely to enter into a manager's utility function.
10. Use the quality maximization model to describe the role not-for-profit hospitals play in the diffusion of new medical technologies.
11. A study by Mark (1996) found that not-for-profit psychiatric hospitals were no more efficient than their for-profit counterparts after controlling for quality. At the same time, the study found that not-for-profit psychiatric hospitals provided a higher quality of care as measured by the number of violations and complaints received. Use the quality/quantity maximization model to explain these results.
12. Executives of not-for-profit hospitals have been criticized for being overcompensated (but see Santerre and Thomas, 1993). Use the managerial expense preference model to illustrate the theory behind these accusations.
13. According to Schlesinger et al. (1996), the not-for-profit firm "must engage in activities that generate prestige or otherwise enhance the reputation of those affiliated with the agency" (p. 712). For example, a not-for-profit hospital may conduct medical research in a particular area in order to develop a national reputation and gain what Schlesinger refers to as "prestige from exclusivity" (p. 712). Use the quality maximization model to explain this behavior.
14. Some economists have suggested that the best way to control medical costs is to remove the profit incentive for health care providers, particularly hospitals. This would involve making all hospitals not-for-profit institutions. Use the utility maximization model to explain the likely impact such a policy would have on the cost of producing hospital services. What would happen if instead a policy was instituted that reduced barriers to entry in the hospital sector and therefore made the market more competitive?
15. According to Lutz (1993), the attorney general of Texas recently challenged the tax-exempt status of the Methodist Hospital of Houston. At the heart of the controversy was a disagreement over the amount of charitable care the hospital had been providing in recent years. The attorney general claimed that the hospital provided only $25.9 million in charity care from 1986 through 1990. Using a much broader definition of charity care that included items that were not reimbursed, such as the costs of community service programs and education, the hospital claimed it had provided $191.9 million of charity care from 1986 through 1990. In addition, the hospital was criticized for adding in 1989 an extravagant, nine-story building called the John S. Dunn Tower that in-

cluded a spacious, two-story lobby, a health club, and a gourmet restaurant. Use the economic theory developed in this chapter to put the debate between the attorney general of Texas and Methodist Hospital in a broader context.

16. Studies using data prior to 1983 found that increased hospital competition led to higher hospital prices. How do researchers explain that result? What have more recent studies concluded about the relation between competition and prices in the hospital industry? Why has this change occurred?

17. Explain the property rights and public choice theories concerning how differences in ownership affect the costs of producing hospital services. Why do empirical studies tend to find few cost differences among the various hospital ownership types?

18. According to empirical studies, what effect do managed-care programs have on the costs of producing hospital services? How has managed care affected the quality of care according to studies?

19. According to empirical studies, what effect do state rate review regulations have on the costs of producing hospital services? How have state rate review regulations affected the quality of care?

20. Why may vertically integrated delivery systems lead to lower production costs? Why may these systems lead to higher costs? Use agency theory and transaction cost economics in your explanations.

21. Answer the following questions on the aggregate performance of the hospital sector by filling in the blanks.

   A. Hospital expenditures as a fraction of GDP were _____ in 1960 and increased to _____ by 2000.

   B. Since 1980, the hospital inflation rate has _____ the general inflation rate in every year.

   C. Since 1982, the hospital occupancy rate, admission rate, and average length of stay have tended to _____. The hospital staffing ratio has tended to _____. (Why?)

22. Discuss the general conclusions researchers have reached concerning the provision of inappropriate hospital services.

23. Explain what studies have found concerning the concentration of health care expenditures. What may that finding mean in terms of serious cost-containment efforts?

ONLINE RESOURCES

To access Internet links related to the topics in this chapter, please visit our web site at http://santerre.swcollege.com.

REFERENCES

Aaron, Henry J. *Serious and Unstable Condition: Financing America's Health Care.* Washington, D.C.: The Brookings Institution, 1991.

American Hospital Association. *Hospital Statistics.* Chicago: AHA, 1998.

Anders, George. "Medical Luxury: Hospital Beds Go High-Tech, and Some Cost As Much As a Car." *The Wall Street Journal*, May 6, 1993a, p. A1.

———. "As Outpatient Care Gains, Communities Need to Trim Their Excess Hospital Beds." *The Wall Street Journal*, February 22, 1993b, p. B1.

Anderson, Gerard F. "All-Payer Ratesetting: Down but Not Out." *Health Care Financing Review* (annual supplement, 1991), pp. 35–41.

Antel, John J., Robert L. Ohsfeldt, and Edmund R. Becker. "State Regulation and Hospital Costs." *Review of Economics and Statistics* 77 (August 1995), pp. 416–22.

Bailit, Howard L., and Cary Sennett. "Utilization Management as a Cost-Containment Strategy." *Health Care Financing Review* (annual supplement, 1991), pp. 87–93.

Baker, Jonathan B. "The Antitrust Analysis of Hospital Mergers and the Transformation of the Hospital Industry." *Law and Contemporary Problems* 51 (spring 1988), pp. 93–164.

Baker, Laurence C. "Managed Care and Technology Adoption in Health Care: Evidence from Magnetic Resonance Imaging." *Journal of Health Economics* 20 (2001), pp. 395–421.

Baumol, William. *Business Behavior, Value and Growth*. Englewood Cliffs, NJ: Prentice Hall, 1967.

Baumol, William J. "Containing Medical Costs: Why Price Controls Won't Work." *Public Interest* 93 (fall 1988), pp. 37–53.

Bays, Carson W. "The Determinants of Hospital Size: A Survivor Analysis." *Applied Economics* 18 (1986), pp. 359–77.

Berk, Marc L., and Alan C. Monheit. "The Concentration of Health Expenditures: Revisited." *Health Affairs* 20 (March/April 2001), pp. 9–18.

Bernstein, Steven J., et al. "The Appropriateness of Use of Coronary Angiography in New York State." *Journal of the American Medical Association* 269 (February 10, 1993), pp. 766–69.

Bradbury, R.C., Joseph H. Golec, and Frank E. Stearns. "Comparing Hospital Length of Stay in Independent Practice Association HMOs and Traditional Insurance Programs." *Inquiry* 28 (spring 1991), pp. 87–93.

Burda, David. "Flurry of Merger Plans Has Eyes Focused on Iowa." *Modern Healthcare* (April 12, 1993), p. 24.

Burns, Lawton R., and Mark V. Pauly. "Integrated Delivery Networks: A Detour on the Road to Integrated Health Care?" *Health Affairs* 21 (July/August 2002), pp. 128–43.

Burns, Lawton R., and Darrell P. Thorpe. "Trends and Models in Physician-Hospital Organization." *Health Care Management Review* 18 (fall 1993), pp. 7–20.

Carlisle, David M., et al. "HMO vs. Fee-for-Service Care of Older Persons with Acute Myocardial Infarction." *American Journal of Public Health* 82 (December 1992), pp. 1626–30.

Carlton, Dennis W., and Jeffrey M. Perloff. *Modern Industrial Organization*. Addison-Wesley, 1994.

Carey, Kathleen. "Stochastic Demand for Hospitals and Optimizing 'Excess' Bed Capacity." *Journal of Regulatory Economics* 14 (1998), pp. 165–87.

Chassin, Mark R., et al. "Does Inappropriate Use Explain Geographic Variations in the Use of Health Care Services?" *Journal of the American Medical Association* 258 (November 13, 1987), pp. 2533–37.

Chernew, Michael E., Richard A. Hirth, Seema S. Sonnad, Rachel Ermann, and A. Mark Fendrick. "Managed Care, Medical Technology, and Health Care Cost Growth: A Review of the Evidence." *Medical Care Research and Review* 55 (September 1998), pp. 259–88.

Clark, Nicola. "The High Costs of Dying." *The Wall Street Journal*, February 22, 1992, p. A16.

Coelen, C., and D. Sullivan. "An Analysis of the Effects of Prospective Reimbursement Programs on Hospital Expenditures." *Health Care Financing Review* 2, no. 3 (1981), pp. 1–40.

Congressional Budget Office. *Impact of PSROs on Health-Care Costs: Update of CBO's 1979 Evaluation*. Washington, D.C.: U.S. Government Printing Office, 1981.

Conover, Christopher J., and Frank A. Sloan. "Does Removing Certificate of Need Regulations Lead to a Surge in Health Care Spending?" *Journal of Health Politics, Policy, and Law* 23 (June 1998), pp. 456–81.

Corrigan, Janet M., Jill S. Eden, Marsha R. Gold, and Jeremy D. Pickreign. "Trends Toward a National Health Care Marketplace." *Inquiry* 34 (spring 1997), pp. 11–28.

Cowing, Thomas G., Alphonse G. Holtmann, and S. Powers. "Hospital Cost Analysis: A Survey and Evaluation of Recent Studies." In *Advances in Health Economics and Health Services Research*, vol. 4, eds. Richard M. Scheffler and Louis F. Rossiter, Greenwich, CT: JAI Press, 1983, pp. 257–303.

Cowing, Thomas G., and Alphonse G. Holtmann. "Multiproduct Short-Run Hospital Cost Functions: Empirical Evidence and Policy Implications from Cross-Section Data." *Southern Economic Journal* (January 1983), pp. 637–53.

Davidson, Joe. "Partial Merger of 2 Hospitals Approved, Allowing for Efficiencies, Competition." *The Wall Street Journal*, June 20, 1994, p. B6.

Davis, Karen. "Economic Theories of Behavior in Nonprofit, Private Hospitals." *Economic and Business Bulletin* (winter 1972), pp. 1–13.

Diehr, Paula, et al. "Use of a Preferred Provider Plan by Employees of the City of Seattle." *Medical Care* 28 (November 1990), pp. 1073–88.

Dowd, B.R., Roger Feldman, Stephen Cassou, and Michael Finch. "Health Plan Choice and the Utilization of Health Care Services." *Review of Economics and Statistics* 73 (February 1991), pp. 85–93.

Dranove, David, Mark Shanley, and Carol Simon. "Is Hospital Competition Wasteful?" *Rand Journal of Economics* 23 (summer 1992), pp. 247–62.

Dranove, David, Mark Shanley, and William D. White. "Price and Concentration in Hospital Markets: The Switch from Patient-Driven to Payer-Driven Competition." *Journal of Law and Economics* 36 (April 1993), pp. 179–204.

———. "How Fast Are Hospital Prices Really Rising?" *Medical Care* 29 (August 1991), pp. 690–96.

Draper, D., et al. "Studying the Effects of the DRG-based Prospective Payment System on the Quality of Care: Design, Sampling, and Fieldwork." *Journal of the American Medical Association* 264 (October 17, 1990), pp. 1956–61.

Eakin, B. Kelly, and Thomas J. Kniesner. "Estimating a Non-minimum Cost Function for Hospitals." *Southern Economic Journal* (January 1988), pp. 583–97.

Elzinga, K.G., and T.F. Hogarty. "The Problem of Geographic Market Definition Revisited: The Case of Coal." *Antitrust Bulletin* 23 (1978), pp. 1–18.

Emanuel, Ezekiel J., and Linda L. Emanuel. "The Economics of Dying: The Illusion of Cost Savings at the End of Life." *New England Journal of Medicine* 330 (February 24, 1994), pp. 540–44.

Ermann, Dan. "Hospital Utilization Review: Past Experience, Future Directions." *Journal of Health Politics, Policy and Law* 13 (winter 1988), pp. 683–704.

Ermann, Dan, and Jon Gabel. "Multihospital Systems: Issues and Empirical Findings." *Health Affairs* 3 (spring 1984), pp. 50–64.

Farley, Dean E. *Competition among Hospitals: Market Structure and Its Relation to Utilization, Costs and Financial Position.* Research note 7, Hospital Studies Program, National Center for Health Services Research and Health Care Technology Assessment, 1985.

Farley, Dean E., and Ronald J. Ozminkowski. "Volume-Outcome Relationships and Inhospital Mortality: The Effect of Changes in Volume over Time." *Medical Care* 30 (January 1992), pp. 77–94.

Feldman, R., et al. "Effects of HMOs on the Creation of Competitive Markets for Hospital Services." *Journal of Health Economics* 9 (September 1990), pp. 207–22.

Feldman, Roger, John Kralewski, Janet Shapiro, and Hung-Ching Chan. "Contracts between Hospitals and Health Maintenance Organizations." *Health Care Management Review* 15, no. 1 (winter 1990), pp. 47–60.

Feldstein, Martin S. "Hospital Cost Inflation: A Study of Nonprofit Price Dynamics." *American Economic Review* 61 (December 1971), pp. 853–72.

Feldstein, Paul J., T.M. Wickizer, and J.R. Wheeler. "Private Cost Containment: The Effects of Utilization Review Programs on Health Care Use and Expenditures." *New England Journal of Medicine* 318 (May 19, 1988), pp. 1310–14.

Fielding, Jonathan E., and Thomas Rice. "Can Managed Competition Solve the Problems of Market Failure?" *Health Affairs* 12 (supplement, 1993), pp. 216–28.

Fisher, Charles R. "Trends in Total Hospital Financial Performance under the Prospective Payment System." *Health Care Financing Review* 13 (spring 1992), pp. 1–16.

Fitzgerald, John F., Patricia S. Moore, and Robert S. Dittus. "The Care of Elderly Patients with Hip Fracture: Changes Since Implementation of the Prospective Payment System." *New England Journal of Medicine* (November 24, 1988), pp. 1392–97.

Fournier, Gary M., and Jean M. Mitchell. "Hospital Costs and Competition for Services: A Multiproduct Analysis." *Review of Economics and Statistics* (November 1992), pp. 627–34.

Frech, H.E., III. "Comments on Antitrust Issues." In *Advances in Health Economics and Health Services Research,* vol. 7, eds. Richard M. Scheffler and Louis F. Rossiter. Greenwich, CT: JAI Press, 1987, pp. 263–67.

Friedman, Bernard, and Mark Pauly. "Cost Functions for a Service Firm with Variable Quality and Stochastic Demand: The Case of Hospitals." *Review of Economics and Statistics* 63 (November 1981), pp. 620–24.

Garnick, Deborah W., et al. "Services and Charges by PPO Physicians for PPO and Indemnity Patients: An Episode of Care Comparison." *Medical Care* 28 (October 1990), pp. 894–906.

Gaumer, Gary L., et al. "Effects of State Prospective Reimbursement Programs on Hospital Mortality." *Medical Care* 27 (July 1989), pp. 724–36.

Gaynor, Martin, and Gerard F. Anderson. "Uncertain Demand, the Structure of Hospital Costs, and the Cost of Empty Hospital Beds." *Journal of Health Economics* 14 (1995), pp. 291–317.

Gazmararian, Julie A., and Jeffrey P. Koplan. "Length of Stay After Delivery: Managed Care versus Fee-for-Service." *Health Affairs* 15 (winter 1996), pp. 74–80.

General Accounting Office. *Hospital Costs: Cost Control Efforts at 17 Texas Hospitals.* GAO/AIMD-95–21. Washington, D.C., December 1994.

Goes, James B., and Chun Liu Zhan. "The Effects of Hospital-Physician Integration Strategies on Hospital Financial Performance." *Health Services Research* 30 (October 1995), pp. 507–30.

Grannemann, Thomas W., Randall S. Brown, and Mark V. Pauly. "Estimating Hospital Costs: A Multiple-Output Analysis." *Journal of Health Economics* 5 (1986), pp. 107–27.

Gray, James. "The Selling of Medicine, 1986." *Medical Economics* (January 20, 1986), pp. 180–94.

Greenwald, Howard P., and Curtis J. Henke. "HMO Membership, Treatment, and Mortality Risk among Prostatic Cancer Patients." *American Journal of Public Health* 82 (August 1992), pp. 1099–1104.

Haber, Susan G., et al. "Hospital Expenditures in the United States and Canada: Do Hospital Worker Wages Explain the Difference?" *Journal of Health Economics* 11 (December 1992), pp. 453–65.

Hamilton, Barton H., Vivian Ho, and Dana P. Goldman. "Queuing for Surgery: Is the U.S. or Canada Worse Off?" *The Review of Economics and Statistics* 82 (May 2000), pp. 297–308.

Harris, Jeffrey E. "The Internal Organization of Hospitals: Some Economic Implications." *The Bell Journal of Economics* 8 (1977), pp. 467–82.

Hart, Oliver. *Firms, Contracts, and Financial Structure*. Oxford: Clarendon Press, 1995.

Health Care Forum LLC. *Hospital Statistics*. Chicago: American Hospital Association, 2002.

Hersch, Philip L. "Competition and the Performance of Hospital Markets." *Review of Industrial Organization* 1 (winter 1984), pp. 324–40.

Herzlinger, Regina E., and William S. Krasker. "Who Profits from Nonprofits?" *Harvard Business Review* (January–February 1987), pp. 93–106.

Hester, James A., AnneMarie Wouters, and Norman Wright. "Evaluation of a Preferred Provider Organization." *The Milbank Quarterly* 65 (1987), pp. 575–613.

Hilborne, Lee H., et al. "The Appropriateness of Use of Percutaneous Transluminal Coronary Angioplasty in New York State." *Journal of the American Medical Association* 269 (February 10, 1993), pp. 761–65.

Ho, Vivian, and Barton H. Hamilton. "Hospital Mergers and Acquisitions: Does Market Consolidation Harm Patients?" *Journal of Health Economics* 19 (2000), pp. 767–91.

Hoy, Elizabeth W., Richard E. Curtis, and Thomas Rice. "Change and Growth in Managed Care." *Health Affairs* 10 (winter 1991), pp. 18–36.

Iglehart, John. "The American Health Care System—Medicare Program." *New England Journal of Medicine* 327 (November 12, 1992), pp. 1467–72.

Japsen, Bruce. "Ad Budget Drop." *Modern Healthcare* 27 (February 17, 1997), pp. 70–71.

Joskow, Paul L. "The Effects of Competition and Regulation on Hospital Bed Supply and the Reservation Quality of Hospitals." *Bell Journal of Economics* (autumn 1980), pp. 421–47.

Kahn, K.L., et al. "Comparing Outcomes of Care Before and After Implementation of the DRG-based Prospective Payment System." *Journal of the American Medical Association* 264 (October 17, 1990), pp. 1984–88.

Keeler, Theodore E., and John S. Ying. "Hospital Costs and Excess Bed Capacity: A Statistical Analysis." *Review of Economics and Statistics* 78 (August 1996), pp. 470–81.

Kessler, Daniel P., and Mark B. McClellan. "Is Hospital Competition Socially Wasteful?" *The Quarterly Journal of Economics* (May 2000), pp. 577–615.

Lane, Paul M., and Jay D. Lindquist. "Hospital Choice: A Summary of the Key Empirical and Hypothetical Findings of the 1980s." *Journal of Health Care Marketing* 8 (December 1988), pp. 5–20.

Lanning, Joyce A., Michael A. Morrisey, and Robert L. Ohsfeldt. "Endogenous Hospital Regulation and Its Effects on Hospital and Non-hospital Expenditures." *Journal of Regulatory Economics* 3 (1991), pp. 137–54.

Leape, Lucian L., et al. "The Appropriateness of Use of Coronary Artery Bypass Graft Surgery in New York State." *Journal of the American Medical Association* 269 (February 10, 1993), pp. 753–60.

Lee, Maw Lin. "A Conspicuous Production Theory of Hospital Behavior." *Southern Economic Journal* 38 (July 1971), pp. 48–58.

Luft, Harold S. *Health Maintenance Organizations: Dimensions of Performance.* New York: Wiley-Interscience, 1981.

Luft, Harold S., et al. "The Role of Specialized Clinical Services in Competition among Hospitals." *Inquiry* 23 (spring 1986), pp. 83–94.

Lutz, Sandy. "Charity Care and the Law: Case Is Far from Closed." *Modern Healthcare* (March 8, 1993), pp. 26–28.

Mann, Joyce M., Glenn A. Melnick, Anil Bamezai, and Jack Zwanziger. "A Profile of Uncompensated Hospital Care, 1983–1995." *Health Affairs* 16 (July/August 1997), pp. 223–32.

Manning, Willard G., et al. "A Controlled Trial of the Effect of a Prepaid Group Practice on Use of Services." *New England Journal of Medicine* 310 (June 7, 1984), pp. 1505–10.

Mark, Tami L. "Psychiatric Hospital Ownership and Performance." *Journal of Human Resources* 31 (summer 1996), pp. 631–49.

Melnick, Glenn A., Jack Zwanziger, Anil Bamezai, and Robert Pattison. "The Effects of Market Structure and Bargaining Position on Hospital Prices." Journal of Health Economics 11 (1992), pp. 217–33.

Menke, Terri J. "The Effect of Chain Membership on Hospital Costs." Health Services Research 32 (June 1997), pp. 177–96.

Miller, Robert H., and Harold S. Luft. "Managed Care Performance Since 1980: A Literature Analysis." *Journal of the American Medical Association* 271 (May 18, 1994), pp. 1512–19.

Miller Robert H., and Harold S. Luft. "HMO Plan Performance Update: An Analysis of the Literature, 1997–2000." *Health Affairs* 21 (July/August 2002), pp. 63–86.

Morrisey, Michael A., and Jeffrey A. Alexander. "Hospital Participation in Multihospital Systems." In *Advances in Health Economics and Health Services Research*, vol. 7, eds. Richard M. Scheffler and Louis F. Rossiter. Greenwich, CT: JAI Press, 1987, pp. 59–82.

Morrisey, Michael A., Jeffrey Alexander, Lawton R. Burns, and Victoria Johnson. "Managed Care and Physician/Hospital Integration." *Health Affairs* 15 (winter 1996), pp. 62–73.

Morrisey, Michael A., Douglas A. Conrad, Stephen M. Shortell, and Karen S. Cook. "Hospital Rate Review: A Theory and an Empirical Review." *Journal of Health Economics* 3 (September 1984), pp. 25–47.

Morrisey, Michael A., Gerald J. Wedig, and Mahmud Hassan. "Do Nonprofit Hospitals Pay Their Way?" *Health Affairs* 15 (winter 1996), pp. 132–44.

Newhouse, Joseph. "Toward a Theory of Nonprofit Institutions: An Economic Model of a Hospital." *American Economic Review* 60 (March 1970), pp. 64–74.

Nicholson, Sean, Mark V. Pauly, Lawton R. Burns, Agnieska Baumritter, and David A. Asch. "Measuring Community Benefits Provided by For-Profit and Nonprofit Hospitals." *Health Affairs* 19 (November/December 2000), pp. 168–77.

Noether, Monica. "Competition among Hospitals." *Journal of Health Economics* 7 (1988), pp. 259–84.

———. *Competition among Hospitals*. Washington, D.C.: Federal Trade Commission, 1987.

Pauly, Mark V. "Nonprofit Firms in Medical Markets." *American Economic Review Proceedings* 77 (May 1987), pp. 257–62.

Pope, Gregory C., and Terri Menke. "Hospital Labor Markets in the 1980s." *Health Affairs* 9 (winter 1990), pp. 127–37.

Rapoport, John, Stephen Gehlbach, Stanley Lemeshow, and Daniel Teres. "Resource Utilization among Intensive Care Patients: Managed Care vs. Traditional Insurance." *Archives of Internal Medicine* 152 (November 1992), pp. 2207–12.

Redelmeier, Donald A., and Victor R. Fuchs. "Hospital Expenditures in the United States and Canada." *New England Journal of Medicine* 328 (March 18, 1993), pp. 772–78.

Renn, Steven C., Carl J. Schramm, J. Michael Watt, and Robert A. Derzon. "The Effects of Ownership and System Affiliation on the Economic Performance of Hospitals." *Inquiry* 22 (fall 1985), pp. 219–36.

Retchin, Sheldon M., and Barbara Brown. "Elderly Patients with Congestive Heart Failure under Prepaid Care." *American Journal of Medicine* 90 (February 1991), pp. 236–42.

Retchin, Sheldon M., et al. "How the Elderly Fare in HMOs: Outcomes from the Medicare Competition Demonstrations." *Health Services Research* 27 (December 1992), pp. 651–69.

Robinson, James C. "Physician-Hospital Integration and the Economic Theory of the Firm." *Medical Care Research and Review* 54 (March 1997), pp. 3–24.

Robinson, James C., and Harold S. Luft. "The Impact of Hospital Market Structure on Patient Volume, Average Length of Stay, and the Cost of Care." *Journal of Health Economics* 4 (December 1985), pp. 333–56.

Robinson, James C., and Ciaran S. Phibbs. "An Evaluation of Medicaid Selective Contracting in California." *Journal of Health Economics* 8 (February 1990), pp. 437–55.

Romeo, Anthony A., Judith L. Wagner, and Robert H. Lee. "Prospective Reimbursement and the Diffusion of New Technologies in Hospitals." *Journal of Health Economics* 3 (1984), pp. 1–24.

Roos, Leslie L., et al. "Health and Surgical Outcomes in Canada and the U.S." *Health Affairs* 11 (summer 1992), pp. 56–72.

Rosko, Michael D. "Impact of HMO Penetration and Other Environmental Factors on Hospital X-Inefficiency." *Medical Care Research and Review* 58 (December 2001), pp. 430–54.

Rouleau, J.L., et al. "A Comparison of Management Patterns after Acute Myocardial Infarction in Canada and the United States." *New England Journal of Medicine* 328 (March 18, 1993), pp. 779–84.

Ruffenach, Glenn. "Firms Use Financial Incentives to Make Employees Seek Lower Health-Care Fees." *The Wall Street Journal*, February 9, 1993, p. B1.

Santerre, Rexford E., and Ammon S. Adams. "The Effect of Competition on Reserve Capacity: The Case of California Hospitals in the Late 1990s." *International Journal of Health Care Finance and Economics* (forthcoming 2002).

Santerre, Rexford E., and Dana C. Bennett. "Hospital Market Structure and Cost Performance: A Case Study." *Eastern Economic Journal* 18 (spring 1992), pp. 209–19.

Santerre, Rexford E., and Debra Pepper. "Survivorship in the US Hospital Services Industry." *Managerial and Decision Economics* 21 (2000), pp. 181–89.

Santerre, Rexford E., and Janet M. Thomas. "The Determinants of Hospital CEO Compensation," *Health Care Management Review* 18 (summer 1993), pp. 31–40.

Scherer, F.M., and David Ross. *Industrial Market Structure and Economic Performance*. Boston: Houghton Mifflin, 1990.

Schlesinger, Mark, Bradford Gary, and Elizabeth Bradley. "Charity and Community: The Role of Nonprofit Ownership in a Managed Card System." *Journal of Health Politics, Policy and Law* 21 (winter 1996), pp. 697–752.

Schramm, Carl J., and Steven C. Renn. "Hospital Mergers, Market Concentration and the Herfindahl-Hirschman Index." *Emory Law Journal* 33 (fall 1984), pp. 869–88.

Schwartz, William B., and D.N. Mendelson. "Hospital Cost Containment in the 1980s—Hard Lessons Learned and Prospects for the 1990s." *New England Journal of Medicine* 324 (April 11, 1991), pp. 1037–41.

Shortell, Stephen M. "Physician-Hospital Integration and the Economic Theory of the Firm: Comment." *Medical Care Research and Review* 54 (March 1997), pp. 25–31.

Shortell, Stephen M., and Edward F.X. Hughes. "The Effects of Regulation, Competition, and Ownership on Mortality Rates among Hospital Inpatients." *New England Journal of Medicine* 318 (April 28, 1988), pp. 1100–07.

Sloan, Frank A., Gabriel a. Picone, Donald H. Taylor, Jr., and Shin-Yi Chou. "Hospital Ownership and Cost and Quality of Care: Is There a Dime's Worth of Difference?" *Journal of Health Economics* 20 (2001), pp. 1–21.

Sloan, Frank A. "Property Rights in the Hospital Industry." In *Health Care in America*, ed. H.E. Frech III, San Francisco: Pacific Research Institute for Public Policy, 1988, pp. 103–41.

Sloan, Frank A. "Not-For-Profit Ownership and Hospital Behavior." In *Handbook of Health Economics, Vol. 1B,* eds. A.J. Culyer and J.P. Newhouse. Amsterdam: Elsevier Science, 2000, pp. 1141–74.

Smith, David W., Stephanie L. McFall, and Michael B. Pine. "State Rate Regulation and Inpatient Mortality Rates." Inquiry 30 (spring 1993), pp. 23–33.

Smith, Dean. "The Effects of Preferred Provider Organizations on Health Care Use and Costs." *Inquiry* 34 (winter 1997/98), pp. 278–87.

Spang, Heather R., Gloria J. Bazzoli, and Richard J. Arnould. "Hospital Mergers and Savings for Consumers: Exploring New Evidence." *Health Affairs* 20 (July/August 2001), pp. 150–58.

Stigler, George J. "The Economies of Scale." *Journal of Law and Economics* 1 (October 1958), pp. 54–71.

Stone, Valerie E., George R. Seage, Thomas Hertz, and Arnold M. Epstein. "The Relation between Hospital Experience and Mortality for Patients with AIDS." *Journal of the American Medical Association* 268 (November 18, 1992), pp. 2655–61.

Temin, Peter. "An Economic History of American Hospitals." In *Health Care in America*, ed. H.E. Frech III. San Francisco: Pacific Research Institute for Public Policy, 1988, pp. 75–102.

Thorpe, Kenneth E., and Charles E. Brecher. "Improved Access for the Uninsured Poor in Large Cities: Do Public Hospitals Make a Difference?" *Journal of Health Politics, Policy and Law* (summer 1987), pp. 313–24.

Town, Robert, and Gregory Vistnes. "Hospital Competition in HMO Networks." *Journal of Health Economics* 20 (2001), pp. 733–53.

United States of America and State of Florida v. Morton Plant System Inc. and Trustees of Mease Hospital, Inc. *Competitive Impact Statement*, United States District Court for the Middle District of Florida, Tampa Division, Civ. No. 94-748-CIV-T-23E, June 30, 1994.

United States of America v. Morton Plant Health System Inc. and Trustees of Mease Hospital, Inc. *Motion and Stipulation for Entry of an Enforcement Order*, United States District Court for the Middle District of Florida, Tampa Division, Civ. No. 94-748-CIV-T-23E, June 28, 2000, at http://www.usdoj.gov/atr/cases/f5100/5157.htm (accessed July 9, 2001).

United States of America v. Morton Plant Health System Inc. and Trustees of Mease Hospital, Inc. *Enforcement Order*, United States District Court for the Middle District of Florida, Tampa Division, Civ. No. 94-748-CIV-T-23E, Undated, at http://www.usdoj.gov/atr/cases/f5100/5155.htm (accessed July 9, 2001).

Vita, Michael G. "Exploring Hospital Production Relationships with Flexible Functional Forms." *Journal of Health Economics* 9 (June 1990), pp. 1–21.

Ware, John E., et al. "Comparison of Health Outcomes at a Health Maintenance Organization with Those of Fee-for-Service Care." *The Lancet* (May 3, 1986), pp. 1017–22.

White, Stephen L. "The Effects of Competition on Hospital Costs in Florida." *Policy Studies Journal* 15 (March 1987), pp. 375–93.

Wilcox-Gok, Virginia. "The Effects of For-Profit Status and System Membership on the Financial Performance of Hospitals." *Applied Economics* 34 (2002), pp. 479–89.

Wilder, R.P., and P. Jacobs. "Antitrust Considerations for Hospital Mergers: Market Definition and Market Concentration." In *Advances in Health Economics and Health Services Research*, eds. Richard M. Scheffler and Louis F. Rossiter, Greenwich, CT: JAI Press, 1987, pp. 245–62.

Williamson, Oliver E. "Managerial Discretion and Business Behavior." *American Economic Review* 53 (December 1963), pp. 1032–57.

Williamson, Oliver E. *The Economic Institutions of Capitalism*. New York: Free Press, 1985.

Wilson, George W., and Joseph M. Jadlow. "Competition, Profit Incentives, and Technical Efficiency in the Provision of Nuclear Medicine Services." *Bell Journal of Economics* (autumn 1982), pp. 472–82.

Winslow, Constance Monroe, et al. "The Appropriateness of Performing Coronary Artery Bypass Surgery." *Journal of the American Medical Association* 260 (July 22–29, 1988), pp. 505–9.

Winslow, Ron. "Data Spur Debate on Hospital Quality." *The Wall Street Journal*, May 24, 1990, p. B1.

————. "Cincinnati Firms Cutting Costs with Hospital-Ranking System." *The Wall Street Journal*, April 2, 1993a, p. B1.

————. "Pioneer Project Publishes First Rankings of Cleveland Hospitals." *The Wall Street Journal*, April 29, 1993b, p. B6.

Woolhandler, Steffie, and David U. Himmelstein. "The Deteriorating Administrative Efficiency of the U.S. Health Care System." *New England Journal of Medicine* 324 (May 2, 1991), pp. 1253–58.

Zwanziger, Jack, and Rebecca R. Auerbach. "Evaluating PPO Performance Using Prior Expenditure Data." *Medical Care* 29 (February 1991), pp. 142–51.

Zwanziger, Jack, and Glenn A. Melnick. "The Effects of Hospital Competition and the Medicare PPS Program on Hospital Cost Behavior in California." *Journal of Health Economics* 7 (1988), pp. 301–20.

CEBS QUESTIONS

CEBS Sample Question on Subject Matter from CEBS Course 9 Study Manual

1. Discuss the property rights theory as it applies to not-for-profit hospitals. (pages 401–402)

CEBS Sample Exam Questions

1. The supply side of the hospital services industry can be characterized as:
   A. Perfect competition
   B. Oligopoly
   C. Monopolistic competition
   D. Static dynamism
   E. Pure monopoly
2. The Herfindahl-Hirschman index (HHI)
   I. Is a measure of the degree of concentration (monopoly power) in a market
   II. Is used by the Department of Justice in the evaluation of mergers
   III. Has a maximum value of 100 percent
      A. I only
      B. II only
      C. I and II only
      D. II and III only
      E. I, II, and III

3. All the following statements regarding the utilization of hospital services in recent years are correct EXCEPT:

   A. A smaller percentage of the population has been admitted to hospitals

   B. Hospital admissions typically are for a shorter duration

   C. Hospital occupancy rates have fallen

   D. Outpatient visits (per 100 population) have decreased

   E. Staffing ratios in hospitals have increased

Answer to Sample Question from Study Manual

The property right theory suggests that not-for-profit hospitals may operate with higher costs than otherwise similar for-profit hospitals because of the absence of outside owners or residual claimants. The theory also suggests that not-for-profit hospitals, because of the attenuation of property rights, face less of an incentive to sacrifice quality for the sake of profits. This is particularly true for situations where quality of care enters the utility function of the managers running the not-for-profit hospitals.

Answers to Sample Exam Questions

1. B is the answer. Oligopoly is the market term that best describes the hospital services industry. See pages 390–391 of the text.

2. C is the answer. Both Statements I and II are correct; however, the HHI index has a maximum value of 10,000, which is a market area dominated by one organization See pages 379–380 of the text.

3. D is the answer. With the decrease in inpatient admissions and shorter length of hospital stays, outpatient visits have increased. See pages 416–418.

CHAPTER 14

THE PHARMACEUTICAL INDUSTRY

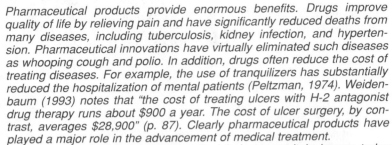

Pharmaceutical products provide enormous benefits. Drugs improve quality of life by relieving pain and have significantly reduced deaths from many diseases, including tuberculosis, kidney infection, and hypertension. Pharmaceutical innovations have virtually eliminated such diseases as whooping cough and polio. In addition, drugs often reduce the cost of treating diseases. For example, the use of tranquilizers has substantially reduced the hospitalization of mental patients (Peltzman, 1974). Weidenbaum (1993) notes that "the cost of treating ulcers with H-2 antagonist drug therapy runs about $900 a year. The cost of ulcer surgery, by contrast, averages $28,900" (p. 87). Clearly pharmaceutical products have played a major role in the advancement of medical treatment.

The research-based pharmaceutical industry as it is known today began with the development of sulfanilamide in the mid-1930s and penicillin in 1938.[1] With World War II came an increased demand for sulfa drugs and penicillin to protect soldiers from infection. The pharmaceutical industry quickly responded by replacing handicraft methods of preparing drugs, traditionally required for individual prescriptions, with mass production techniques (Egan, Higinbotham, and Weston, 1982). Chemical firms, such as Lederle and Merck, found ways to produce drugs in bulk form, which were then transformed into dosage form (e.g., powders and tablets) by drug companies, such as Upjohn. Pfizer developed a fermentation process to allow penicillin to be produced in large quantities. Penicillin was soon followed by other antibiotics, and research was stimulated in other therapeutic fields as well (Statman, 1983).

Following the war, high potential profits generated further innovation and drew other companies into the pharmaceutical industry. Many drug firms expanded and acquired sales forces to market their drugs in finished form. Research and development efforts in the pharmaceutical industry continually expanded during the postwar period.

This chapter provides a contemporary analysis of the pharmaceutical industry. Although the pharmaceutical industry of today closely resembles its postwar antecedent in terms of many supply-side characteristics, we will see that several institutional changes on the demand side of the market have had wide-sweeping effects on the conduct of the industry. The chapter studies the structure, conduct, and performance of the pharmaceutical industry. Specifically, it:

---

[1]Statman (1983) points out that the drug trade is very old. The Ebers Papyrus lists 811 prescriptions used in Egypt in 550 BC.

> Discusses seller concentration, buyer concentration, barriers to entry, and product differentiation to see whether existing drug firms are endowed with some market power.

> Examines some topics pertaining to the conduct of the pharmaceutical industry, including price competition, promotional strategies, and product innovation. The important question concerns the actual degree of price and product competition that presently takes place in this industry.

> Assesses the performance of the contemporary pharmaceutical industry in terms of aggregate prices, output, and profits. The main query here is whether firms in the pharmaceutical industry have tended to charge high prices and earn excess profits.

THE STRUCTURE OF THE PHARMACEUTICAL INDUSTRY

Number and Size Distribution of Sellers

When one thinks of the pharmaceutical industry, only a few large firms, such as Merck, Pfizer, and Eli Lilly, normally come to mind because they are research-based firms known for producing and selling brand-name pharmaceutical products. Interacting with these and other brand-name pharmaceutical companies, however, are a multitude of lesser known, smaller firms that primarily manufacture and retail generic drugs and place little, if any, emphasis on new-drug research and discovery. Based on the overall number and relative sizes of drug firms, the pharmaceutical industry appears to be fairly competitive. Table 14–1 displays some information on the number and size distribution of pharmaceutical companies in 1997. To put the pharmaceutical industry in proper perspective, it also gives comparative information on some other industries. Based on the six-digit North American Industry Classification System (NAICS) of 325412 for pharmaceutical preparations, 707 firms exist in the U.S. pharmaceutical industry. The largest four firms account for 36 percent of industry output, and the largest eight are responsible for 50 percent. The Herfindahl-Hirschman index of market concentration (HHI) is very low at 462, implying that the pharmaceutical industry contains a considerable number of equally sized firms, especially when compared to many of the other industries in the table.

Data from earlier editions of the *Census of Manufacturers* suggest that the degree of seller concentration in the pharmaceutical industry, while relatively stable in past years, may have started to increase in more recent years.[2] For example, the four-firm concentration ratio was approximately 28 percent in 1947, 22 percent in 1963, and 22 percent in 1992. The upward spike in the aggregate level of concentration since 1992 may have resulted from the many mergers involving relatively large drug companies. The ten largest pharmaceutical companies and their market shares in 2002 were Pfizer (10%), GlaxoSmithKline (8.8%), Merck (7.1%), Johnson & Johnson (6.2%), Bristol-Meyers-Squibb (6%), AstraZenaca (5.7%), Lilly (4.3%), Wyeth (4%), Novartis (3.9%), and Pharmacia (3.7%).[3]

---

[2]Earlier industry statistics were based on the Standard Industrial Classification (SIC) system so the comparison may not be perfectly consistent.

[3]IMS Health, Retail and Provider perspective, 2002, www.imshealth.com.

TABLE 14–1

Concentration Ratios for Selected Industries, 1997

NAICS Code	Industry Description	Four-Firm Ratio	Eight-Firm Ratio	Number of Firms	HHI Index
325412	Pharmaceutical Preparations	36	50	707	462
311511	Fluid Milk	21	31	402	205
311230	Cereal Breakfast Foods	83	94	48	2446
312111	Soft Drinks	47	56	388	800
325611	Soap and Detergents	66	78	738	1619
324110	Petroleum Refining	29	49	122	422
326211	Tires	72	91	110	1690
327213	Glass Containers	91	98	11	2960
327320	Ready-Mixed Concrete	7	11	2888	29
331312	Primary Aluminum	59	82	13	1231
332431	Metal Cans	58	87	107	1180
333292	Textile Machinery	24	36	454	269
336111	Automobile	80	96	173	2350

SOURCE: U.S. Bureau of the Census, "Concentration Ratios in Manufacturing," *1997 Census of Manufacturers*, table 4. Issued June 2001, http://www.census.gov/prod/ec97/M31S-cr.pdf.

Many of the companies listed obtained their large size through merger and acquisitions with other companies.

Pharmaceutical market analysts claim that the classification scheme used by the Census of Manufacturers defines industries much too broadly to draw any meaningful conclusions about the level of competition from the concentration ratios or HHI. The industry classification scheme contains all firms producing drug products of any kind despite their intended use. Most drugs, however, are not substitutes in consumption because they treat different illnesses and therefore do not belong in the same relevant product market. For example, a physician looking to relieve a patient's ulcer condition does not choose among various brands of antidepressants and antiulcer drugs. So instead, many point to therapeutic markets as a better way to narrowly define the relevant product market for pharmaceutical goods. Therapeutic markets are designed to include only those drugs that treat common diseases or illnesses. In our example, all antiulcer drugs, such as Tagamet, Zantac, and Pepcid, are included in the same therapeutic or relevant product market.

Data for concentration ratios based on therapeutic markets suggest a more concentrated market environment. For example, Statman (1981) shows four firm concentration ratios ranging from 46 percent (sedatives) to 86 percent (the antacids and oral contraceptives markets) in 1972. Welsch (1995) and Tanouye (1995) report four-firm concentration ratios of 55 and 66 percent for the analgesics (pain killers) and antacid markets, respectively, in 1995. Express Scripts identifies four-firm concentration ratios ranging from 18 percent for antivirals to 90 percent for antihistamines in 1997. These figures imply that a few major drug companies normally interact within most therapeutic markets. Thus, seller concentration ratios based on therapeutic markets paint a more monopolistic view of the structure of the pharmaceutical industry.

The Buyer Side of the Pharmaceutical Market

In contrast to the concentrated nature of the seller side of many therapeutic markets, the buyer side appears to be very fragmented. To see why this is so, consider table 14–2, which lists the main purchasers of prescription drugs in 2000. Unlike spending on hospital and physician services, a large percentage of drug expenditures is paid directly by consumers. Out-of-pocket expenses amount to $39 billion and represent nearly one-third of all prescription drug expenditures. Private insurance is the largest buyer of ethical drugs, accounting for roughly 46 percent of all pharmaceutical spending. Government purchases explain the remaining 22 percent of the $121 billion spent on pharmaceutical products in 2000. It is worth noting that pharmaceutical expenditures represented 9.4 percent of all health care spending in 2000.

T A B L E   1 4 – 2
Buyers of Prescription Drugs, 2000

Source	Expenditures (billions of dollars)	Percentage of Total
Total	$121.8	100.0%
All private	95.3	78.2
Out-of-pocket	39.0	32.0
Private insurance	56.3	46.2
All government	26.5	21.8
Federal	15.2	12.5
State	11.3	9.3

Note: Includes spending on drugs and other medical nondurables. Percentages do not sum to 100 percent due to rounding.

SOURCE: National Health Expenditures—Historical and Current Years. http://www.hcfa.gov/stats (accessed June 24, 2002).

The Realized Demand for Pharmaceutical Products   Although consumers are responsible for footing much of the drug bill, they generally are not responsible for making the choice concerning which specific drug to buy. Since the passage of the Federal Food, Drug and Cosmetic Act of 1938, consumer access to powerful drugs has been severely restricted (Temin, 1992). The 1938 act gave drug manufacturers the responsibility to assign new drugs to either of two classes: over-the-counter (OTC) or prescription (Rx).[4] Directions for

---

[4]According to the *Henry Holt Encyclopedia of Word and Phrase Origins*, "Rx. The Latin 'recipere,' 'take this,' provides the R in the symbol Rx used by pharmacists for centuries, while the slant across the R's leg is a sign of the Roman god Jupiter, patron of medicine. The symbol looks like Rx and is pronounced that way."

use on the label make a drug available for self-medication. A prescription-only warning makes a drug available only by a physician's prescription. The Food and Drug Administration has to approve the manufacturer's proposed label.

Because prescription drugs remain the dominant type sold today, the "realized demands for pharmaceuticals depend not only on ultimate consumer tastes but also on the behavior of physicians who prescribe these drugs and the retail and hospital pharmacists who dispense the prescriptions" (Caves, Whinston, and Hurwitz, 1991, p. 4). Physicians are not always in a position to serve the best financial interests of consumers, primarily because they are unaffected financially by the choice of prescription and often lack suitable information about the price, effectiveness, and risk of substitute drug products (Temin, 1980). Moreover, customary prescribing behavior minimizes effort and also provides a legal defense if a malpractice suit arises. Custom tends to favor high-priced, brandname pharmaceutical products, especially because the "trademarked *brandname* attached to a pioneering product by the innovator is short, and easier to remember than its *generic name*, which in turn is a shorter, simpler version of the *chemical name* that describes the molecular structure of the active chemical entity to scientists" (Caves, Whinston, and Hurwitz, 1991, p. 5).

INSIGHT 14–1

Orphan Drugs and the Salami-Slicing Problem

In 1983, Congress passed the Orphan Drug Act to stimulate the development of "orphan drugs." Orphan drugs treat rare diseases, and pharmaceutical companies have little incentive to produce them because development costs are too high and/or potential markets are too small to make such ventures profitable.

If the Food and Drug Administration (FDA) determines that a particular drug should be considered an orphan, the company that holds the patent receives two major incentives from the government. First, the company may be awarded tax credits for up to 50 percent of the drug development costs. Second, the firm is awarded the exclusive right to market the drug for seven years. The intent is to stimulate the development of drugs necessary to treat rare diseases. According to PhRMA (2002), more than 200 orphan drugs have been approved under the Orphan Drug Act.

The orphan drug policy has come under criticism because some believe pharmaceutical companies are undermining the program by earning excess profits. For example, in the mid-1980s, the FDA designated AZT (azidothymedine) an orphan drug. AZT is used in the treatment of AIDS (acquired immunodeficiency syndrome), and Burroughs Wellcome, a British pharmaceutical company, holds the exclusive patent on it in the United States. In 1986, patients were paying approximately $10,000 a year for the drug and Burroughs was earning a substantial economic profit. The firm came under fire from various activist groups and the U.S. government for taking advantage of its monopoly position and charging too much for AZT. This pressure led Burroughs to reduce the price of AZT to $6,400 in 1989.

Others claim that drug companies misuse the program by misrepresenting their data so that a drug is granted orphan status by the FDA. To be designated as an orphan, a drug must be used to treat a rare disease that afflicts fewer than 200,000 people. Many drugs treating more than 200,000 people in total, however, have been granted orphan status. By presenting evidence to the FDA regarding only one of the many possible uses for a particular drug, a company can set its target market for that particular "use" of a drug at fewer than 200,000 people. In fact, an imaginative company could simultaneously develop several orphan-type uses for a given drug. Thus, a designated orphan drug may treat a number of diseases with a total combined market well in excess of 200,000 people. This practice is commonly referred to as "salami slicing." Instead of presenting the whole salami, the drug company presents only a small slice at a time to receive the incentives provided under the orphan drug program.

Tregarthen (1992) claims that Biogen Incorporated has been very successful at salami slicing. The company received orphan status for a drug called f-IFN-beta to treat metastatic renal cell carcinoma. Two months later, the same drug was granted orphan designation in the treatment of cutaneous malignant melanoma. Approximately two weeks after that, the drug was again given orphan status for the treatment of cutaneous T-cell lymphoma. Still later, this drug was given orphan status for the treatment of two more rare diseases.[1] As you might imagine, the total number of prospective patients for this drug exceeds the 200,000 maximum limit set by the FDA.

The extent to which drug companies presently abuse the orphan drug program is unknown. Obviously the success of the program depends on how well the FDA scrutinizes drugs applying for orphan status. The objective is to stimulate the discovery of drugs for rare diseases but at the same time limit the monopoly power firms receive from orphan protection for those drugs that turn out to be big money makers.

---

[1] According to the *Mosby Medical Encyclopedia* (1992), a carcinoma is a cancerous tumor that starts with the cells covering inner and outer body surfaces. Melanoma is skin cancer of which there are various types. Lymphoma is a tumor of the lymphoid tissue. Lymphoid tissue is netlike and holds lymphocytes, a type of white blood cell, in its spaces.

SOURCE: Based on Suzanne Tregarthen, "Prescription to Stop Drug Companies' Profiteering," *The Wall Street Journal,* March 5, 1992, p. A15.

The point is that physicians are responsible for prescribing medicines, yet lack a financial incentive to make cost-effective choices. The result is often the selection of a high-priced, brand-name drug when an equally effective lower-priced generic is available. Back in the 1950s, cost-effective buying was even less common than it is today because states had enacted antisubstitution laws that prevented pharmacists from substituting lower-priced but therapeutically equivalent generics for brand-name drugs. Antisubstitution laws required pharmacists to fill prescriptions as written, precluding the dispensing of a lower-priced substitute when the physician had specified a brand-name product.

By 1984, the last of the antisubstitution laws was repealed (Caves, Whinston, and Hurwitz, 1991). Pharmacists are now permitted to substitute generic products on prescriptions written for brand-name drugs. According to Carroll and Wolfgang (1991), "while consumers and prescribers have the legal right to request or deny substitution, for the great majority of prescriptions they leave choice to the pharmacists. Thus, for the most part, pharmacists determine the extent to which generic substitution will occur"(p. 110). Grabowski and Vernon (1986) point out that generic products generally provide higher profit margins to pharmacists, suggesting that pharmacists face a financial incentive to substitute bioequivalent generic drugs for brand-name drugs. According to Caves, Whinston, and Hurwitz (1991), generic substitution increased remarkably from 5 to 29 percent of brand-written, multisource prescriptions over the period 1980 to 1989.[5] Estimates indicate that the generics' share of the U.S. pharmaceutical market is now about 47 percent (PhRMA, 2002). Temin reports that when explicitly choosing between brand names and generics, pharmacists divide their choices 60 to 40 in favor of brand-name drugs (Caves, Whinston, and Hurwitz, 1991). Some of the reasons for pharmacists' slanted preferences toward brand-name products become apparent in Insight 14–2.

Third-Party Influences on the Demand for Pharmaceutical Products   Many third-party payers have turned to formularies, drug utilization review, and required generic substitution as ways to control the decisions of prescription-writing physicians or pharmacists and rein in pharmaceutical costs. A **formulary** is a list of selected pharmaceutical products that physicians are required to prescribe. The listed drugs are thought to be medically effective and reasonably priced. Virtually all hospitals use formularies. A majority of MCOs and many state Medicaid programs employ formularies.

Like hospital utilization review, **drug utilization review** is designed to monitor the actions of physicians. By monitoring, third-party payers can ensure that physicians follow the formulary and can single out physicians who inappropriately prescribe medicines. Third-party payers also sometimes require that pharmacists substitute lower-priced generic products for higher-priced brand-name products whenever medically possible. Many MCOs have adopted drug utilization review programs and generic substitution requirements.

The federal Maximum Allowable Cost (MAC) program, which began in 1974, also mandates drug substitution in government health programs, such as Medicare and Medicaid. The MAC program limits reimbursement for multiple-source drugs to the lowest cost at which chemically equivalent drugs are generally available, plus a reasonable fee for dispensing a drug (Schwartzman, 1976). If a doctor prescribes a specified drug whose price exceeds the MAC price, the pharmacist can obtain reimbursement only for the MAC price unless the doctor certifies in writing that the drug is medically necessary. Such certification entitles the pharmacist to full reimbursement. Otherwise, the pharmacist must bill the patient for the difference between the price of the drug and MAC reimbursement (Schwartzman, 1976).

Two laws enacted during the 1990s by the federal government effectively impose price controls on drugs sold to Medicaid patients and federal agencies (Price Waterhouse, 1993). First, under the Omnibus Budget Reconciliation Act of 1990, federal matching subsidies are granted to state Medicaid programs only for drugs covered by a manufacturer rebate

---

[5]A **single-source drug** is normally covered by a patent. A **multisource drug** is available from a number of suppliers.

INSIGHT 14-2

What Factors Influence the Drug Substitution Practices of Pharmacists?

Obviously consumers pay lower prescription prices when pharmacists dispense low-priced generic drugs instead of high-priced brand-name drugs. Economic theory suggests that the substitution practices of pharmacists depend on relative costs and benefits. As we saw in Chapter 1, an activity, X, takes place when its expected benefit, $B^e(X)$, exceeds its expected cost, $C^e(X)$. Expected benefit (cost) takes into account both the probability of occurrence and the magnitude of the gain (loss).

Carroll and Wolfgang (1991) point out that the dispensing of generic drugs may provide pharmacists with time, financial, psychological, and social benefits. In terms of time benefits, the lower prices associated with generic drugs may mean less time spent dealing with consumer complaints about prescription prices. Pharmacists might derive financial benefits from substituting generic drugs, since they yield larger profit margins. Additional financial benefits may arise if lower generic prices promote greater consumer loyalty. Psychological benefits reflect the satisfaction pharmacists may receive when saving customers money. Finally, the dispensing of a product other than the one prescribed by the physician may provide pharmacists with the social benefit of an enhanced professional status.

Pharmacists may also incur certain costs when they dispense generic substitutes. In particular, Carroll and Wolfgang note that there exists the potential for financial, time, psychological, performance, and social costs associated with the dispensing of generic drugs. The financial costs reflect the likelihood that a lawsuit will result from substituting a generic drug. Time costs arise if generic drugs involve more time spent communicating with the patient. Psychological costs accrue from any worries about generic drug quality, while performance costs emanate from the increased use of generic drugs that are not bioequivalent. Social costs reflect the possibility of a diminished role for pharmacists if they continually dispense generic substitutes and physicians react by specifying "dispense as written" more frequently.

To assess the relative importance of these various costs and benefits associated with generic substitution, Carroll and Wolfgang collected data via a mail questionnaire from 401 pharmacists. The questionnaire contained a list of 24 multiple-source, frequently prescribed brand-name drugs. Pharmacists were asked about their willingness to substitute with generic drugs, including items to assess the probability and importance (or magnitude) of the various types of costs and benefits associated with generic substitution.

The authors found that pharmacists' perceptions of costs and benefits of generic substitution significantly influenced their substitution decisions. Pharmacists perceived that the greatest benefit of generic substitution comes from dimensions relating to cost savings (financial and psychological benefits). Pharmacists expected highly probable and important benefits from increased profits and from feeling good about saving customers money. Pharmacists who faced greater expected benefits were more likely to engage in generic substitution.

Pharmacists anticipated the most losses from dimensions relating to product quality (performance and psychological costs). Those pharmacists who expected higher costs were

(continued)

less likely to substitute. Pharmacists believed that financial losses from legal liability were important but improbable. Social losses were also considered unlikely.

Carroll and Wolfgang concluded that efforts to increase the incidence of generic substitution should focus on the quality and monetary savings of generic drugs, since these two factors tend to influence pharmacists' willingness to substitute. The authors argued that better information about the comparability of generic drugs, higher dispensing fees for generic products, and elimination of laws requiring pharmacists to pass on cost savings to consumers should all create a greater incentive for generic substitution.

agreement. The rebate agreement normally contains both a basic and an additional component. The basic rebate per unit dispensed is the difference between the average manufacturer price and the "best price" for a drug, the latter being the lowest price charged to any other private or government buyer. There is also a minimum basic rebate equaling about 15 percent of the average manufacturer price. The additional rebate per unit dispensed equals the excess of the increase in the average manufacturer price over the increase in the urban consumer price index since September 1990.

The second federal law affecting pharmaceutical prices is the Veterans Health Care Act of 1992, which influences the price federal agencies, such as the Veterans Administration and the Department of Defense, pay for pharmaceutical goods. The act mandates that drug manufacturers enter into pricing agreements with the Federal Supply Schedule, the Veterans Administration depot, and the Department of Defense depot as a condition for conducting business with the federal government. The price of a branded drug purchased under these agreements must be no higher than 76 percent of the nonfederal average manufacturer's price during the most recent year. In addition, any increase in the price of a prescription drug is limited to the increase in the urban consumer price index.

The intent behind both the Medicaid rebate scheme and the Veterans Health Care Act is to reduce the prices the federal government pays for pharmaceutical goods as a way to control drug costs. One unintended consequence of these laws is that drug manufacturers may be forced to raise their prices to nonfederal buyers to maintain profits. If so, the federal government is merely shifting the drug cost burden to other buyers.

In sum, consumers pay relatively high out-of-pocket costs for pharmaceutical products, yet exert only a very small influence over the choice and prices of prescription products. Physicians, pharmacists, and third-party payers have more control over the ultimate choice and price paid. Changes, such as required substitution, formulary restrictions, and drug utilization review, suggest that the buyer side of the market has become more cost conscious for those drugs paid for by a third-party payer. Changes such as these most likely increase the elasticity of demand for any one company's pharmaceutical product and make the seller side of the market more price competitive, especially as more individuals enroll in MCOs.

Pharmacy Benefit Management Companies Another influential player in pharmaceutical markets, in addition to the consumer, third-party payer/health plan, physician, manufacturer, and pharmacist, is the pharmacy benefit management company (PBM). In fact, over 200 million Americans currently obtain their drugs through a PBM (PricewaterhouseCooper, 2001). PBMs never physically handle prescription drugs, only serving as intermediaries between health plans and both drug manufacturers and pharmacies. Health plans pay a fee to PBMs. The fee paid to the PBM may be based on the number of covered lives or on a fee-for-service basis whereby the health plan pays the PBM the (reduced) cost of the prescription plus an administration fee. In return, the PBM negotiates rebates from drug manufacturers by offering to include their products on a formulary. PBMs also arrange price discounts from pharmacies by channeling a relatively large volume of consumers/patients to them.

PBMs promote generic substitution through their formularies and also through their interactions with pharmacies. Many PBMs use lower copayments as a financial inducement for consumers to purchase generic as opposed to brand-name drugs and formulary versus non-formulary drugs. In addition to focusing on cost containment, some PBMs have turned their attention to disease management. Disease management involves the assembly of comprehensive databases on current prescribing practices and health outcomes to determine cost-effective methods of treating various diseases. As Cohen (2000) writes:

> *Diabetes is a prime candidate for PBM-led disease management, as it is a chronic high-cost illness with multiple symptoms covering a wide range of therapeutic classes, and whose treatment relies heavily on the extended delivery of pharmacotherapy. With the current claims databases at their disposal, PBMs already can identify a number of factors leading to above-average treatment costs and lower-than-average quality of care (for example, inappropriate drug treatment and/or poor patient compliance) (p. 317).*

In the early 1990s, several drug manufacturers acquired large PBMs. For example, Eli Lilly purchased PCS in 1994, Merck purchased Medco in 1993, and Smithkline Beecham bought Diversified Pharmaceutical Services in 1994.[6] If a drug company acquires a PBM, the antitrust concern is that the newly created vertically integrated pharmaceutical organization may give unwarranted favorable treatment to its own drugs and may not include competitor drugs, perhaps some that are even more cost-effective, on its formulary. The foreclosure of competitors from the market might thereby lessen competition and lead to higher prices and lower quality. Another antitrust concern is that the PBM may share information on drug prices with rival manufacturers and the PBM could be used as a facilitating devise in a collusive arrangement among drug manufacturers. These concerns may be valid. According to PricewaterhouseCoopers (2001), the market for pharmacy benefit management is relatively concentrated with four PBMs accounting for more than 80 percent of the market in 2001.

But recall that economic theory also offers an efficiency justification for vertically integrated organization like PBMs. In the chapter on the hospital services industry, we learned that a supplier might merge with a buyer to minimize the transaction costs associated with market transactions. By producing internally, the combined firm avoids the transaction costs of negotiating, writing, and enforcing contracts. In addition, the combined firm can avoid the opportunistic behavior that results from incomplete contracts. If

---

[6]Both Eli Lilly and Smithkline Beecham later divested their PBMs.

a vertical arrangement like a PBM results in efficiencies and adequate market competition exists, consumers benefit from the resulting lower prices.

It follows that both the potential benefits and costs must be considered when determining the economic desirability of PBMs. It is interesting to note that the Federal Trade Commission imposed conditions on both of the Medco and Eli Lilly acquisitions of PBMs. Among the conditions, the FTC required that companies maintain "open formularies" that include drugs selected and approved by an independent Pharmacy and Therapeutics committee. Also, the vertically integrated organizations were not allowed to share proprietary and nonproprietary information they received from competitors such as prices (FTC 1998).

Barriers to Entry

Economic theory suggests that barriers to entry may prevent potential competition and confer monopoly status on pharmaceutical companies. Three types of barriers to entry into the pharmaceutical industry are typically cited. The first and most effective source is a *government patent* that gives the innovating firm the right to be the sole producer of a drug product for a legal maximum of 20 years.[7] The argument is that a patent is necessary to protect the economic profits of the innovating firm over some time period. Otherwise, easy imitation, lower prices, and smaller profits reduce the financial incentive for firms to undertake risky and costly, but socially valuable, research and development activities. The economic rationale underlying the patent system is that even though the patent confers monopoly power on the innovator, the monopoly restriction of output is better than having no product at all. That is, the new drug might not be introduced on the market if not for the patent protection; thus, some of the drug is better than none.

Patent protection does not guarantee that the company will remain perfectly insulated from competition. Lu and Comanor (1994) observe that a pharmaceutical patent is granted for a new drug's *chemical composition*, not its *therapeutic novelty*. This means a new drug may receive patent protection because of a different chemical composition even though it treats the same disease that an established, already patented drug does. For example, SmithKline held a patent on its antiulcer drug, Tagamet, until May 1994. Prior to patent expiration, SmithKline faced competition from Glaxo's Zantac and Merck's Pepcid, which are also antiulcer drugs but have different chemical compositions. In fact, while Tagamet was first to market and was the world's biggest-selling drug at one point, Glaxo's Zantac took over as drug leader for more than six years. While Zantac was considered less of a scientific breakthrough, it was marketed more aggressively (Moore, 1993). Thus, a legal patent does not guarantee a monopoly position. The entry of new brand-name drugs expands the choices of physicians and provides competition for an established drug with a similar indication.[8]

Another point concerning a legal patent is that its effective duration is often less than 20 years because the FDA takes a number of years to approve a product for commercial introduction. With the passage of the Drug Price Competition and Patent Term Restoration

---

[7]The legal patient period was changed from 17 to 20 years in 1996.
[8]According to the *Mosby Medical Encyclopedia* (1992), "an indication is a reason to prescribe a medication or perform a treatment, as a bacterial infection may be an indication for prescribing a specific antibiotic or as appendicitis is an indication for appendectomy" (p. 411).

Act of 1984 (Hatch-Waxman Act), the effective life of a new drug patent is extended by a maximum of 5 years, but not beyond 14 years of effective life, if it can be shown that the FDA delayed its introduction into the market by at least that amount of time.

The Hatch-Waxman Act not only increased the effective patent life of new drugs but also quickened the approval process for generic drugs. No longer must producers of generic drugs prove safety and effectiveness; they need only show that the generic is bioequivalent to a brand-name drug (i.e., contains the same active ingredient[s]). Consequently, the act has made it easier for generics to enter pharmaceutical product markets once the patent period expires. Partly in response to this act and to third-party pressure for drug cost control, the generic share of prescriptions increased sharply from 19 percent in 1984 to 47 percent by 2000 (PhRMA, 2002). Overall, the impact of the Hatch-Waxman Act is interesting. On the one hand, it increased the monopoly power of the drug innovator by extending the effective patent life. On the other hand, the Act enhanced postpatent competition by reducing the cost of generic entry.

The second type of barrier to entry into the pharmaceutical industry is a **first-mover** or **brand loyalty advantage** (Schmalensee, 1982). A drug innovator can usually acquire and maintain a first-mover advantage because the quality of a substitute generic product is generally unknown and requires one to experience it. Generic drugs can be considered experience goods because consumers normally lack the knowledge they need to judge or experience the drugs' quality. Physicians have little time or financial incentive to seek out information about the efficacy and risk of new generic products. Furthermore, the cost of a bad consumption experience can be particularly harmful in terms of a prolonged illness, adverse side effect, or malpractice suit when switching from a known brand name to an unknown generic drug (Scherer and Ross, 1990). Therefore, unless a generic drug offers different and important therapeutic advantages or a very large discount, physicians and consumers, when faced with the choice, are reluctant to choose generic over brand-name drugs after the patents expire.

Many industrial organization economists believe that a first-mover advantage confers monopoly power on the innovator of a new product. A first-mover advantage allows pioneer firms to charge high prices and maintain a dominant market share even after the expiration of a patent. McRae and Tapon (1985) write,

> Being first on the market with a new product or process enhances a firm's image; in many industries, this enhanced image may be further exploited after patent expiry through the continued promotion of brand names. To the extent that consumer preference schemes give a market advantage to pioneering brands, it appears that the trademark protection of brand names effectively replaces patent protection after 17 years. De facto, the combination of patent and trademark protection may produce a composite entry barrier which extends indefinitely into the future (p. 44).

It is because of a first-mover advantage that McRae and Tapon found that compulsory licensing of patented pharmaceuticals was not sufficient to induce more competition in the Canadian pharmaceutical industry. **Compulsory licensing** means that a firm is given legal permission to import or manufacture a patented drug if it pays a stipulated royalty rate (of 4 percent in Canada) to the patent holder. Despite the effective elimination of the patent barrier through the compulsory licensing program, the market power of first entrants, in terms of high prices and market shares, declined only modestly over a six-year period in Quebec. The authors attribute that finding to the high postpatent barrier associated with first-mover brand loyalty.

Finally, *control over a key input*, such as a specific chemical or active ingredient, can also make it difficult for new firms to enter a drug market (Ballance, Pogany, and Forstner, 1992). New competitors require access to the input, and the originating firm may sell it to the new entrants only if it is profitable to do so. If it is not, and replication is difficult or costly, new firms may find it unprofitable to enter the industry.

In sum, significant barriers to entry exist in the pharmaceutical industry. Legal patents and brand names may give entrenched firms an advantage over potential entrants. Theoretically, the advantage translates into monopoly power and the ability to maintain market share despite high prices. FDA approval lags reduce the effective patent life, but brand-name recognition typically increases the effective monopoly period for a drug product.[9]

Consumer Information and the Role of the FDA

As with most medical goods and services, a substantial amount of technical knowledge is necessary to judge a pharmaceutical product. Because pharmaceutical products are experience goods, or in some cases credence goods, that require repeated use, they are difficult to evaluate on an a priori basis. Consumers therefore face some risk when directly purchasing pharmaceutical products. Temin (1980) points to three types of risk. First, there is the risk associated with overpaying or receiving a pharmaceutical product of inferior quality. Second, an adverse reaction to a drug may lead to sickness or death. Third, a consumer may purchase the wrong drug or take the wrong dosage and therefore fail to recover from an illness or injury.

In the early 1930s, before prescription-only pharmaceuticals became the norm, drug products were less complex and were limited mainly to anti-infection drugs. Thus, self-medication was more feasible during that time period. Today, however, many substitute drugs are available to treat any given disease, and some are associated with adverse side effects for certain patients. Others cannot be used in conjunction with other drugs or alcoholic beverages. It is not surprising that physicians, as experts, are assigned the role of prescribing most medicines to consumers as a way to reduce consumer risks.

The FDA also plays an important role in protecting consumers from the risks associated with drug purchases. In addition to determining whether drugs should be assigned over-the-counter or prescription status, the FDA must approve a new drug before it can be sold in the marketplace. Government approval is necessary, it is argued, because drug firms may otherwise perform insufficient testing in an attempt to gain a first-mover advantage or to avoid high costs. The elixir sulfanilamide and thalidomide tragedies in the

---

[9]Schwartzman (1976) also examined economies of scale in pharmaceutical manufacturing, promotion, and research and development as barriers to entry. While Schwartzman found no evidence supporting manufacturing economies, he noted that larger firms tend to be associated with promotion and R&D economies. These two economies make it harder for small potential competitors, but not large ones, to compete with entrenched pharmaceutical companies. This and other studies on research economies are taken up in the conduct section.

1930s and 1960s are two examples where people have either died or become harmed by unsafe drug products.[10]

Because the market may fail in the absence of government intervention and provide either unsafe or ineffective drugs, the FDA has been assigned the role of approving new drugs. Many critics (e.g., Grabowski and Vernon, 1983) argue that the stringent regulations of the FDA since 1962 have led to higher R&D costs and a lower number of new chemical entities introduced into the marketplace. We explicitly address this notion later in the chapter. Grabowski and Vernon point out that the FDA tends to err on the side of conservatism, resulting in long FDA approval times and a slower rate of pharmaceutical innovations. The economic argument goes like the following.

Suppose the safety and effectiveness of a new drug submitted to the FDA for approval are associated with some uncertainty. An all-knowing FDA approves the drug application when the therapeutic benefits of the drug outweigh its risk. Thus, a correct decision means the FDA approves a safe and effective product or rejects an unsafe or ineffective one. Due to uncertainty, however, the FDA may make two types of errors.

The first error, called *type 1* error, occurs when the FDA rejects the application for a new drug that is truly safe and effective. In contrast, a *type 2* error occurs when the FDA approves a drug that is unsafe or ineffective. As Grabowski and Vernon (1983) write, "Both types of error influence patients' health and well-being since consuming a 'bad' drug or not having access to a 'good' drug can have deleterious effects on health" (p. 10). One would think either type of error is random and therefore equally likely to occur in an uncertain world. However, that is not the case. An FDA member who unknowingly approves an unsafe drug faces personal losses: job loss and political indignation. Moreover, the outcome from approving an unsafe drug is eventually known and highly visible.

The cost associated with rejecting a safe and effective drug, a type 1 error, on the other hand, is borne by a third party (the drug manufacturer or a sick patient) rather than by an FDA member and therefore is less visible. The rejection of a good drug may never be known. Thus, according to this view, the FDA faces an incentive to reject rather than accept, or at least delay the approval of, a drug more often than is necessary in a perfect world.

Interestingly, an unconstrained market faces incentives to accept "bad" drugs and commit a type 2 error. Profit-seeking drug firms wishing to be the first to market with a new drug may skimp on necessary testing. The FDA faces an incentive to reject or delay "good" drugs and commit a type 1 error. Longer approval periods translate into further testing, higher R&D costs, lower expected profitability, and fewer drug innovations. Thus, both the market and the government potentially make mistakes. The gnawing question is which institution, the market or the government, makes fewer and less costly ones.[11]

---

[10]The elixir sulfanilamide disaster occurred when Massengill Company used diethylene glycol as a solvent to formulate a liquid form of sulfanilamide without testing it for toxicity. More than 100 children died from the poisonous chemical. The other tragedy happened in Germany and other European countries when thalidomide, a sleeping pill, caused babies to be born without hands or feet (phocomelia).

[11]The Prescription Drug User Fee Act of 1992 and the Food and Drug Administration Modernization Act of 1997 included provisions designed to improve the efficiency of FDA review procedures and the clinical development process. See Reichert, Chee, and Kotzampaltiris (2001) for more information on these laws and their effectiveness in achieving their goals.

INSIGHT 14–3

The Switch from Rx to OTC

Due to high medical care costs, the FDA adopted a policy in the mid-1970s, which continues today, of switching selected drugs from Rx to OTC status if pharmaceutical companies can prove that any misuse of the drugs will not endanger a consumer's health. Since consumers can self-medicate and avoid a visit to a physician, they often gain from the switch.[1]

Pharmaceutical companies value the switch from Rx to OTC because they can avoid the intense generic and brand-name competition that results after their patents expire, especially given that big brand-name drugs generally gain three years' exclusivity after receiving OTC status. The exclusivity, which resulted from the Hatch-Waxman Act of 1984, means no other companies can make a similar OTC version until the three-year period expires (Tanouye and Burton, 1993). In addition, drug companies value the switch because Rx drugs are more heavily regulated by the government than OTC drugs. Well-known examples of recent switches include Advil, a pain killer; Monistat 7, a vaginal yeast infection treatment; and Benadryl, an allergy medication.

To get a sense of the magnitude of the net benefit of switching drugs from Rx to OTC status, Temin (1992) focused on the benefits and costs associated with the OTC switch of cough and cold medicines. The benefit of switching to OTC cough and cold medicines is the consumer surplus associated with a lower price and the medical savings, in terms of both time and money, resulting from fewer physician visits. The cost includes any resource costs the FDA incurs for reviewing the switch and the expected costs of any adverse reactions from misusing the drugs.

First, Temin measured the consumer surplus from OTC cough and cold medicines. Consumer surplus is the triangle below the demand curve and above the actual market price (assuming a linear demand curve). Since the area of a triangle equals one-half the base times the height, consumer surplus equals one-half of the quantity sold times the price differential between the maximum willingness to pay for the first unit and the actual price paid.

To estimate the maximum willingness to pay for the first unit, Temin estimated a demand for cough and cold medicines. As economic theory suggests, the demand for cough and cold medicines was found to be negatively related to price, with an own-price elasticity of about –.5 to –.74. Demand was also found to be positively related to advertising expenditures on cough and cold medicines. Using the estimated demand equation, Temin solved for the maximum willingness to pay for the first unit and determined the price differential. Multiplying the price differential by one-half of the annual sales revealed that the consumer surplus from switching cough and cold medicines amounted to $700 million in 1989.

Adding the consumer surplus to the resource saving from the reduced use of medical services (monetary and time costs of visiting a physician) gave a total gain of $770 million. Temin notes that there was virtually no cost to the cough and cold medicine switch because

---

[1]Insurance policies, however, frequently cover the cost of prescription drugs but not OTC drugs.

the FDA devoted very few resources to it and because cough and cold medicines present no dangerous adverse side effects. Thus, the implication is that consumers are clearly better off with the switch to OTC cough and cold medicines to the tune of $770 million per year. However, Temin cautions that the costs of some switches may be greater than their benefits and thus should be given careful scrutiny.

The Structure of the Pharmaceutical Industry: A Summary

From an aggregate market perspective, the seller side of the pharmaceutical industry appears to be highly competitive with a large number of equal-size companies. Closer examination, however, reveals that a small number of drugs generally compete within a given therapeutic market. Legal patents and brand loyalty can make it difficult for new firms to enter various therapeutic markets by establishing a barrier to entry.

On the buyer side of the market, consumers are found to pay relatively high out-of-pocket costs for pharmaceutical goods. This by itself suggests that the demand for pharmaceutical goods may be elastic with respect to price. However, physicians have historically been the decision makers responsible for choosing among prescription drugs. One suspects that, given no financial incentives, physicians are not very sensitive to drug price differentials, especially if patients have medical insurance.

The demand for pharmaceutical products covered by third-party payments may have become more sensitive to price differentials. Third-party payers have shown signs of price responsiveness, as evidenced by drug formularies, mandated generic substitution, and drug utilization review programs. Managed-care institutions are increasingly relying on these kinds of drug programs. Finally, the government plays a major role in the pharmaceutical industry, by approving new drugs for commercial introduction and the switch from Rx to OTC and the direct financing of 22 percent of pharmaceutical expenditures.

THE CONDUCT OF THE PHARMACEUTICAL INDUSTRY

In this section, we analyze evidence regarding the behavior of pharmaceutical companies in recent years. Three practices of drug firms are examined: pricing, promotion, and product innovation. The basic question is whether evidence exists for competitive or monopoly behavior in the pharmaceutical industry. For example, we ask the following four questions, among others:

1. Are drug prices lower when drug firms face more intense competition?
2. Are newcomers more likely to enter pharmaceutical markets when existing firms' profits are high during the postpatent period, or do postpatent barriers prevent entry?
3. Is drug promotion informative or persuasive? Do the promotion expenditures of established firms impede the entry of new firms?
4. Is a large firm size necessary for product innovation in the pharmaceutical industry?

Pricing Behavior

The relatively high concentration of sales among a few firms and substantial barriers to entry in many therapeutic markets imply that pharmaceutical companies possess the ability to price their drug products above the marginal costs of production and generate economic profits. In addition, first-mover advantages may mean that leading firms have the power to maintain brand-name prices above costs and still dominate the market over generic companies even after patent expiration. Promotion expenditures by the leading pharmaceutical firms may help to reinforce the habit-buying practices of many buyers, especially physicians.

The potential for monopoly pricing has motivated several researchers to examine the pricing practices of pharmaceutical companies. One of the first studies on pharmaceutical competition, by Hurwitz and Caves (1988), analyzed how generic competition affected the postpatent pricing practices of 56 leading brand-name pharmaceuticals during 1978 and 1983. In particular, they developed a sample of 56 observations by drawing from a list of drug products that had eventually become available as generics but were originally subject to patents held by the pharmaceutical firms that developed them.

Next, the authors estimated a multiple regression equation relating the leading firm's market share (in terms of pills sold) during 1978 and 1983 to the relative drug prices of the leader and follower firms, sales promotion spending by the leader and follower firms, and several variables reflecting the degree of brand loyalty to the leading firm's product. The relative difference in the prices of drugs offered by the leading firm and follower firms was calculated as $(P_L - P_F)/P_F$, where P_L and P_F reflect the weighted average drug prices of the leading firm and those of the follower firms, respectively. The expectation was that the relative drug price ratio inversely affects the market share of the leading firm, as the law of demand suggests.

The logarithm of the leading firm's and follower firms' sales promotion expenditures were also specified to capture own- and cross-promotion effects. Sales promotion outlays were calculated to include spending on detailing (i.e., personal promotion by pharmaceutical salespersons), medical journal advertising, and direct-mail advertising. The expectation was that own-promotion causes the market share of the leading firm to increase, whereas cross-promotion causes the leader's market share to decline.

Several variables were also included to capture the brand loyalty built up by the leader during the patent period. One such variable was the number of years the leader's brand was marketed exclusively under a patent (i.e., the effective patent life). The market share of the leading firm was expected to increase with the effective patent life given the greater opportunity to establish goodwill and entrench buying habits. However, because goodwill and buying habits might also erode as health professionals gain some experience with generic substitutes, Hurwitz and Caves also specified the number of years since the entry of the first generic competitor and the total number of generic suppliers. The hypothesis was that the market share of the leading firm decreases with respect to both of these variables as health professionals and consumers gain more information about the availability of generic brands.

Hurwitz and Caves obtained some interesting results and were able to explain about 66 percent of the variation in the leading firm's market share. The results generally supported the various hypotheses. First, as expected, a higher positive price differential between the leader and follower firms was associated with a reduction in the leading firm's market share, *ceteris paribus*. Specifically, the authors calculated that a 10 percent increase in the average leader's price differential resulted in a market share loss of less than one-half of 1 percent. This result suggests that the leader's market share declined by very little when price was raised above the followers' average prices—not too surprising, the authors argue, when one considers that the average price differential was 127 percent, yet the average leader commanded a 63.4 percent market share.

The regression results associated with the other variables proved interesting, as well. First, the own- and cross-promotion effects were found to positively and inversely affect the leader's share, as expected. Thus, one implication of the analysis is that producers of generic brands are able to penetrate the leader's market share through their promotional outlays and pricing policies. Second, the results indicated that a longer "monopoly" marketing period helps to build brand loyalty and to prevent generic entry from chipping away at the leader's share. Third, the regression analysis showed that the leader's market share falls with a greater number of generic firms as health care professionals become more experienced with generic brands. The arrival of an additional supplier was estimated to reduce the leader's market share by about 1.25 percentage points, on average.

In sum, Hurwitz and Caves found that price differentials affect the choice between brand-name and generic products, but buyers are relatively insensitive to relative price changes. Goodwill established during the patent period extends the effective patent life of a pharmaceutical product as buyers continue to pay a substantial premium after the patent has expired. Finally, promotion by the leader firms helps to protect market share from eroding, but promotion by followers tends to reduce the leader's market share.

In another study, Caves, Whinston, and Hurwitz (1991) examined the effect of generic entry on both brand-name and generic pricing practices. The study covered the postpatent competition between 30 brand-name and a number of generic drugs over the period 1976 to 1987 and reached a number of interesting conclusions. First, the authors found that the innovator's (the leading brand-name firm's) price initially rises after patent expiration up until the point where a generic competitor enters the market. That finding implies that leading pharmaceutical firms do not engage in **limit pricing** because they would otherwise set a low price to discourage or limit entry.[12] Second, the authors discovered that the innovator's price declines with a greater number of generic entrants, but by only 4.5 percent, on average. Third, they found some evidence indicating that innovators' prices were more sensitive to entry during the 1980s compared to past periods, most likely reflecting the growing price consciousness of pharmaceutical buyers. Fourth, Caves, Whinston, and Hurwitz found that generic producers enter markets offering prices much lower than the brand-name price. Generic prices also fall with further generic competitor entry, potentially declining to 17 percent of the brand-name producer's preentry price. Despite the huge discount, generic producers were found to gain a relatively small market share.

Grabowski and Vernon (1992) examined the pricing patterns associated with 17 major pharmaceutical products that were first exposed to generic competition from 1983 to 1987. The 1980s are a particularly interesting period, because barriers to entry by generic companies had been lowered by the Hatch-Waxman Act. Among their results, Grabowski

---

[12]Recall that limit pricing occurs when the dominant or innovator firm prices its product just below the break-even price of a potential entrant as a way to discourage entry. The price of a dominant firm tends to decline over time if limit pricing is practiced.

and Vernon found that a 10 percent increase in the brand-name profit margin at time of entry resulted in a 6 percent increase in the number of entrants by the end of the first year. Thus, the entry of new generic products is sensitive to expected profits in the product market, as economic theory suggests, when barriers to entry are low.

In addition, the authors found that price accounts for most of the variation in a generic company's market share but noted that other factors, such as first- (or second-) mover advantages and perceptions of quality differences among generic suppliers, may also be important in specific circumstances. As far as pricing patterns are concerned, their evidence, like that of Caves, Whinston, and Hurwitz (1991), suggests that generics offer significant discounts and that their prices decline substantially over time.

One seemingly inconsistent finding of Grabowski and Vernon's study was that branded drugs' prices increase in nominal terms by 11 percent after two years of entry. One suspects that innovator firms react to competition by lowering price. But Grabowski and Vernon note that the higher branded drug price occurs in response to the dynamics of a segmented market. That is, as generics enter the market and satisfy price-sensitive buyers with lower prices, brand-name firms are left with buyers who are relatively price insensitive. As a result, brand-name companies are able to raise price, at least in the short run, because they now effectively face a less elastic demand for their pharmaceutical products. Although the innovator's price increases, the average market price of a drug is found to decline to 79 percent of the preentry price after two years as generics attain a greater share of the market. On average, brand-name drugs lose one-half of the market to generics after two years, according to Grabowski and Vernon.

A study by Lu and Comanor (1994) is particularly interesting because it examined price competition among the brand-name producers of 148 new molecular entities between 1978 and 1987. Prior studies have not examined price competition among rival patented products.

Lu and Comanor argue that an innovator's pricing decision is influenced by several factors, including the drug's therapeutic properties, physician brand loyalty, adoption rate by demanders, and the reactions of rivals. As a result, their empirical model links a measure reflecting a drug's relative price to its FDA rating as an indicator of therapeutic novelty, a dummy variable indicating whether the drug treats an acute or a chronic illness as a measure of frequency of buying, and the number of branded substitute suppliers as an indicator of rivalry. According to the authors, therapeutic novelty should lead to a higher relative price, while the number of substitute suppliers should result in a lower relative price.

Lu and Comanor discovered that a greater number of substitute branded products results in lower prices, as expected. In addition, they found that the therapeutic novelty of a drug influences pricing strategy over time. In particular, the authors noted that therapeutically innovative drugs are generally introduced under a modified price-skimming strategy. A modified price-skimming strategy means that therapeutically innovative drug prices are initially set high and then held relatively constant over time. Imitative drugs, on the other hand, are introduced under a market penetration strategy. The prices of imitative drugs are low at first to enlarge market share, but are then increased over time as information about their availability spreads.

Finally, Wiggins and Maness (1994) examined price competition among 98 anti-infective products (e.g., penicillins, tetracyclines, erythromycins, and cephalosporins) over the 1984 to 1990 period. Their analysis provides two major conclusions. First, in contrast to the studies previously cited, they found that prices fall sharply with initial entry. Second, they found that subsequent entry continued to reduce prices although at a much smaller rate even when there were a relatively large number of competitors. The authors argue that the increased price sensitivity may result from the easier entry of generics brought on by the Hatch-Waxman Act of 1984 and/or because anti-infectives may be more price sensitive than other segments of the pharmaceutical industry.[13]

Taken together, these five studies suggest that both prepatent and post-patent price competition often exist in pharmaceutical markets. The prices of both brand-name and generic products are found to be lower when a greater number of substitute products are available. Pioneer firms sometimes raise the prices of their branded products upon entry in response to a less elastic demand. The goodwill established during the patent period plays an important role, allowing established firms to maintain a large market share despite the huge discounts offered by generic companies.

Promotion of Pharmaceutical Products

Medicines are cited as one of the first products advertised in printed form (Leffler 1981). Timely product information is especially valuable in the pharmaceutical industry due to the continual introduction of new life-saving drugs. With about 22,000 different drugs on the market, doctors have a great deal to learn and remember (Schwartzman, 1976). Before prescribing, doctors must know the appropriate drug, the correct dosage, and the properties of the drug for different patients, classified by various characteristics, such as age, weight, and general health status. Thus, it is not surprising that promotion expenditures can run as high as 20 to 30 percent of sales for many research-based pharmaceutical companies. Nearly 70 percent of the promotional budget is spent on personal promotion by detailers (pharmaceutical salespersons), and another 27 percent is spent on journal advertising. Direct-mail advertising accounts for the rest of the promotional budget (Hurwitz and Caves, 1988).

It is unclear to economists whether pharmaceutical promotion strategies enhance or reduce societal welfare. As we saw in Chapter 8, advertising may promote or impede competition depending on whether informed or habit-buying behavior results. Studies on this topic by Leffler (1981), Hurwitz and Caves (1988), and Caves, Whinston, and Hurwitz (1991) found evidence supporting both the informational and persuasion effects of pharmaceutical promotion.

Specifically, Leffler found that advertising intensity is greater for newer and more important pharmaceutical products, which, he argues, reflects the informational content of the promotion message. Leffler, as well as Hurwitz and Caves, found that the new entrants' promotion expenditures helped them to expand their market shares. Caves, Whinston, and Hurwitz concluded that increased generic competition results in less advertising by the innovator, which, they argue, must reflect the informational rather than persuasive content of the innovator's pharmaceutical advertising during the preentry period.

The evidence for persuasive advertising is equally strong. In particular, Leffler found that less detailing of younger physicians occurs for older products. That is, advertisers tend

---

[13]Also see Ellison, Cockburn, Griliches, and Hausman (1997), who find relatively high elasticities between generic substitute and also significant elasticities between therapeutic substitutes at both the prescribing and dispensing stages.

INSIGHT 14–4

Can Physician Drug Recommendations Be Bought?

According to the text discussion, it is unclear whether the promotion practices of drug companies encourage or impede competition. Essentially it depends on whether drug promotion practices encourage informed or habit buying. Because the effect of drug promotion is uncertain, many managed-care organizations and hospitals have turned to drug formularies as a way to control physician prescribing behavior. The intent is to include only effective and reasonably priced drugs on the formulary as a means of controlling overall drug costs.

A study by Chren and Landefeld (1994), however, found that the prescription drug recommendations of physicians are influenced by the marketing practices of drug companies even in the face of managed-care drug controls, such as drug formularies. Specifically, the authors compared the interactions with drug companies of 40 physicians who had recommended that certain drugs be added to a hospital's formulary with 80 other physicians who had not made such requests.

Chren and Landefeld discovered that those physicians who recommended drug adoptions were more likely to have received monetary support from drug companies for travel, lodging, speaking, engagements, or research expenses. Yet the two groups of physicians had not differed in the frequency of their exposure to drug companies' other promotional activities, such as visits from detailers. According to the study, all but 6 of the 52 requested drugs were added to the hospital formulary, including 20 drugs classified as having little or no advantage over drugs already on the formulary. Another 13 drugs added to the formulary were classified as having only a modest advantage over existing drugs.

The study raises some doubt about whether managed care can restrain drug costs through formulary restrictions, unless, of course, tighter scrutiny is placed on the formulary approval process. The authors contend that stricter guidelines may be necessary to minimize or eliminate physician relationships with pharmaceutical companies.

to direct their advertisements to the physician age group that was in medical school when the drug product was originally introduced. Thus, the creation of brand loyalty and reinforcement of habit buying must be the real purpose behind advertising. Hurwitz and Caves found that the leading firms' promotion expenditures preserved their market share from new generic entrants. Finally, the study by Caves, Whinston, and Hurwitz notes that generic firms gain relatively small shares despite their huge discounts, perhaps reflecting the goodwill built up by the innovator's promotion expenditures during the patent period.

Given the inconsistent findings in the literature, Rizzo (1999) investigated the informative versus persuasive aspects of promotional activities in an entirely different manner by examining the impact of promotional expenditures on price elasticity of demand. According to economic theory, demand becomes more elastic and price declines when buyers are more fully informed because of promotional activities. In contrast, persuasive promotional activities cause habit buying, less elastic demand, and higher prices according to economic theory. Therefore, we can infer if promotional activities are persuasive or informative by empirically studying how such activities influence price elasticity of demand.

In his empirical study, Rizzo considered how detailing expenditures influenced the price elasticity of demand for antihypertensive drug products. There are several major classes within the group of drugs used to treat hypertension, including ACE inhibitors, calcium channel blockers, beta-blockers, diuretics, and other types. These broad classes of antihypertensive drugs, as well as the drugs within each class, can be considered differentiated competitors. Rizzo estimated the yearly demand for 46 different antihypertensive drugs over the period 1988 to 1993. The demand for each drug was estimated as a function of its price, detailing expenses, average competitor price within the same drug class, average detailing expenditures within the same drug class, and other factors.

Of interest to us, Rizzo allowed the detailing expenses of each drug to interact with its price in the estimation equation so the impact of detailing on price elasticity could be isolated. Both stock and flow measures of detailing expenses were included in the empirical model. The stock measure captured past detailing efforts to allow the effects of promotional activities to accumulate over time. The flow measure represented detailing expenditures in the current period so the short-run impact of promotional activities on price elasticity could also be studied.

In support of the persuasive view of promotional activities, Rizzo found that greater detailing efforts led to a lower price elasticity of demand for antihypertensive drugs. As an example of his findings, Rizzo reported that price elasticity with no detailing equaled –1.98 for one of his models. For that same model, price elasticity of demand equaled –1.46 when the stock of detailing was considered. Notice that the accumulated effects of past promotional activities caused price elasticity to decline as the persuasive view of advertising suggests. Finally, price elasticity of demand equaled –.48 in the short run as a result of increased current detailing activities. Thus, Rizzo provided direct empirical evidence "that product promotion inhibits price competition in the pharmaceutical industry, lowering price elasticities and leading to higher equilibrium prices" (pp. 112–113). It will be interesting to learn if future studies find similar results about the relation between promotional activities and price elasticity of demand for other types of drugs.

Product Innovation

The most important contribution associated with the pharmaceutical industry is the timely introduction of new drug products that can extend or improve lives. New drug discoveries require research and development activities. In this section, we look at several issues relating to the R&D process, including the various stages of the R&D process, determinants of R&D, and the relation between firm size and innovative activity.

Stages of the R&D Process   Product innovation in the pharmaceutical industry is argued to be both very risky and time consuming. The research and development (R&D) process for new chemical entities is normally spread over many years, and only a small fraction of new drug discoveries are eventually approved for marketing. Research and development costs constitute a sizable proportion of sales revenues. For example, Figure 14–1 shows that R&D expenditures for research-based pharmaceutical companies ranged from a low of 10.9 in 1974 and 1978 to a high of 20.4 percent of sales in 1994.

FIGURE 14–1

R&D Expenditures as a Percent of Total Sales

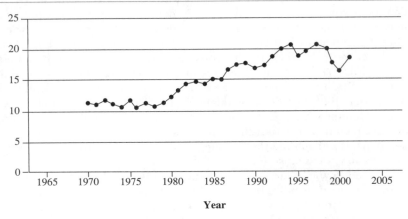

SOURCE: Phrma, *Industry Profile 2002*, http://www.phrma.org (accessed June 25, 2002).

Due to the high cost and risk associated with R&D, the decision-making process underlying new-drug development tends to unfold sequentially. At several points in the R&D process, a company reviews the development status of a drug and makes a decision about whether to continue or abandon the project. The decision rests on the expected net profitability of the proposed drug and thus takes both expected revenues and costs into consideration. Expected revenues depend in part on the therapeutic properties of the drug, the size of the target market, and the number of substitute drugs. Anticipated costs depend on the frequency and severity of adverse reactions to the drug and the projected additional development, marketing, distribution, and production costs (DiMasi, Hansen, Grabowski, and Lasagna, 1991).

Researchers generally identify eight stages in the R&D process; these stages are summarized in table 14–3, including the duration of each stage, in months. DiMasi, Hansen, Grabowski, and Lasagna (1991) estimate that the preclinical period of discovery, animal testing, and IND filing lasts about 42.6 months. Almost 58 percent of the (uncapitalized) expected costs per marketed new chemical entity (NCE) are incurred during this period, most likely reflecting the huge number of misses before a pharmaceutical company discovers a drug that warrants further testing at the clinical stage.

DiMasi, Hansen, Grabowski, and Lasagna estimated that the clinical period from the initiation of Phase I testing to drug approval lasts about 98.9 months, with the FDA approval process taking about $2\frac{1}{2}$ years, on average. The average time needed to complete the entire process from synthesis to marketing approval is estimated at 12 years.[14] About 75 percent of the NCEs in Phase I testing enter Phase II testing, and about 36 percent

---

[14]Some overlap occurs across the various stages.

TABLE 14-3

Stages of the Drug Development Process

1. *Discovery stage.* Basic research synthesis of new chemicals and early studies of chemical properties. Identification of a specific new chemical entity worthy of further testing.
2. *Preclinical animal testing.* Short-term animal toxicity testing for evidence of safety in the short run in preparation for human testing.
3. *IND filing.* A request is made for authorization to begin human testing by filing a notice of claimed investigational exemption for new drug (IND). If there is no hold on the application, the firm begins clinical testing 30 days after filing. (42.6 months for the first three stages)
4. *Phase I of clinical testing.* Dosage administered to a small number of healthy volunteers for information on toxicity and safe dose ranges in humans. Data are gathered on the drug's absorption and distribution in the body, its metabolic effects, and the rate and manner in which the drug is eliminated from the body. (15.5 months)
5. *Phase II of clinical testing.* Drug is used on a larger number of people whom the drug is intended to benefit. Evidence of therapeutic effectiveness and additional safety data are obtained. (24.3 months)
6. *Phase III of clinical testing.* Large-scale tests on humans over a longer period to uncover unanticipated side effects and additional evidence of effectiveness. (36.0 months)
7. *Long-term animal studies.* The effects of prolonged exposures and the effects on subsequent generations are determined. Such studies are typically conducted concurrently with other studies. (33.6 months)
8. *New-drug approval.* Application for commercial marketing of the new drug. Review of evidence by the FDA. Marketing for approved uses may begin upon notification by the FDA. (30.3 months)

SOURCES: Adapted from Joseph A. DiMasi, Ronald W. Hansen, Henry G. Grabowski, and Louis Lasagna, "Cost of Innovation in the Pharmaceutical Industry," *Journal of Health Economics* 10, (1991), pp. 107–42, and John R. Virts and J. Fred Weston, "Expectations and the Allocation of Research and Development Resources," in *Drugs and Health*, ed. Robert Helms (Washington, DC: American Enterprise Institute, 1981), pp. 21–45.

eventually enter Phase III testing. Only 18.3 percent of the drugs that entered clinical trials during 1980–1984 are now marketed (DiMasi, 1995).

Determinants of R&D Spending[15]   As with any investment, the optimal amount of R&D spending depends on the expected future streams of revenues less costs or economic profits. Expected marginal revenues, MR, decline with respect to R&D expenditures due to the law of diminishing marginal productivity.[16] The marginal or opportunity cost, MC, is likely to rise or remain constant with respect to R&D spending. The expected net profits from R&D are

---

[15]This section is based on Grabowski and Vernon (1981).

[16]R&D can be considered as an input in the discovery of new drugs. Thus, the marginal revenue—or, more correctly, the marginal revenue product of R&D—is equal to the market price of the resulting new drug, P, times the marginal productivity of R&D, MP, in the innovation process.

maximized when MR is set equal to MC. In mathematical terms, the firm finds the optimal amount of R&D spending, R^*, by solving the following equation:

(14–1) $MR(R, X) = MC(R, Z)$,

where R equals investment expenditures on R&D, X stands for a vector of exogenous factors influencing the rate of return from new-drug R&D, and Z represents a vector of exogenous variables influencing the marginal cost associated with new-drug R&D.

Solving equation 14–1 for R yields a reduced-form equation for the optimal level of R&D spending in terms of X and Z:

(14–2) $R^* = f(X, Z)$.

Variables that increase the rate of return, X, lead to increased spending on R&D. Similarly, variables that raise the opportunity cost, Z, lead to lower R&D expenditures.

Grabowski and Vernon (1981) were among the first to estimate an R&D regression equation based on equation 14–2 for a pooled sample of 10 pharmaceutical companies taken over the entire 14-year period from 1962 to 1975. For a factor influencing the firm's expected rate of return in each time period, they used an indicator of past R&D success, measured by the number of NCEs per dollar of R&D spending in the previous five years. The expectation was that R&D spending increases with greater past success. They also specified an index of firm diversification as a revenue-influencing factor. The argument was that a more diversified firm is better able to exploit R&D spending on a number of different drugs and thus is more inclined to undertake R&D.

To control for factors influencing the opportunity cost of R&D, Z, the authors specified a variable measuring each firm's cash flow margin in each year. The opportunity cost of internal funds is less than that of external funds. That is, because of transaction costs, the cost of borrowing external funds (i.e., loans from banks or sales of stocks and bonds), is generally higher than that of using internal funds. Thus R&D spending was expected to increase with the cash flow margin. Following convention, R&D spending was deflated by sales to get a measure of R&D intensity.

Their regression results provide important insights. As expected, R&D investment spending was found to be influenced by variables affecting marginal benefit and cost. In particular, R&D spending was observed to increase with a greater degree of past R&D success and, more importantly, with a larger cash flow margin. This is a critical finding, because, as we will learn later, the decline in R&D spending during the 1970s was due in large part to falling real drug prices and the associated reduction in cash flows. Conversely, the upturn in R&D spending during the 1980s (see figure 14–1) was due to the reversal in the real drug price trend.

Firm Size and Innovation   Another important issue regarding the conduct of pharmaceutical firms is the relation between firm size and innovative activities. The question is whether large pharmaceutical firms are more likely than small firms to engage in successful innovative ventures. Given the importance of product innovation in this industry, antitrust laws concerning mergers may not be enforced so strictly if larger firms are found to be more innovative than smaller ones.

Economic theory by itself offers only limited insight on the relation between firm size and innovation. Schumpeter (1950) is among the first economists to propose that larger firms may be more successful at innovation than smaller firms because they have the resources necessary to engage in modern large-scale R&D activities. Modern and commercially successful innovations are very expensive to undertake, and therefore small firms may lack the necessary physical and financial resources. In addition, larger firms diversify their R&D efforts among various projects and thus can better absorb the risks associated with innovative activities. Finally, many analysts believe that economies of scale exist in research such that per-unit costs fall with a greater production of R&D activities because more efficient, specialized research inputs are used.

These three factors—resource capability, risk absorption, and research economies— suggest that larger firms tend to face a greater incentive to undertake successful R&D activities than smaller firms. Opposing this tendency, however, is the argument that greater bureaucratic red tape in larger organizations stifles creativity. Since important decisions are normally made at a centralized level in a large, bureaucratic firm, communication flows ultimately break down and decisions take longer to execute. The resulting time lags delay or discourage new product ideas from being pursued or continued.

Because theory cannot offer a definitive answer, a number of researchers have empirically questioned whether larger drug firms are more innovative than smaller ones. Schwartzman (1976) summarizes the pre-1960s empirical research on firm size and innovation as follows:

> *According to Edwin Mansfield and Henry Grabowski, large drug companies do not spend proportionately more money on research than smaller ones. W. S. Comanor observes diseconomies of scale in research. Jerome Schnee concludes that leading companies do not produce proportionately more innovations than other firms[17] (p. 83).*

Thus, the pre-1960s research suggests that larger drug firms are not more innovative than smaller ones. Close examination of these studies by Schwartzman, however, revealed poor data for the measurement of firm size or faulty analysis of the data.

Schwartzman's own empirical work, using data for the late 1960s, reached three separate conclusions supporting the premise that large firm size encourages greater innovation in the pharmaceutical industry. First, he found that research effort, as measured by laboratory employment, increases more than proportionately with the size of the drug firm. Second, his study reveals that research output, as measured by either the number of new chemical entities or the number of patents, increases more than proportionately with research effort, indicating economies of scale in research. Third, Schwartzman shows that larger firms discover relatively more new drugs per employee than do smaller firms.

The general conclusions reached by Schwartzman have recently come under attack. Using data for 1982, Acs and Audretsch (1988) analyzed the innovative contributions of small and large firms, defined as firms having fewer or more than 500 employees, respectively. The Small Business Administration constructed the innovation database by examining over 100 technology, engineering, and trade journals covering a number of different manufacturing industries for evidence of new-product innovations. For the pharmaceutical industry, the authors found that larger firms had 9.23 times the innovations of smaller firms in 1982. However, larger pharmaceutical firms also had 19.41 times the employment

---

[17]See Mansfield (1968), Grabowski (1968), Comanor (1965), and Schnee (1971).

of smaller drug firms. Together these results indicate that larger firms generate only half the number of pharmaceutical innovations that smaller firms do on a per-employee basis. Thus, according to their empirical results, large firm size may not be necessary for pharmaceutical innovation. Taking all the manufacturing industries in their entire sample into consideration, Acs and Audretsch concluded that small firms are about 43 percent more innovative than their larger counterparts.

In a related study, Acs and Audretsch (1987) analyzed the specific characteristics affecting the differential innovation rates of large and small firms across different industries. The authors determined that large firms tend to have an innovative advantage in industries that are capital intensive, advertising intensive, and relatively concentrated at the aggregate level. In contrast, small firms are more innovative in industries in which total innovation and the use of skilled labor play a large role and some, but not many, large firms exist.

We mentioned earlier that the pharmaceutical industry is characterized by high advertising intensity. This industry characteristic tends to favor the innovation of large pharmaceutical firms. However, most of the characteristics described above suggest that small pharmaceutical companies may be more innovative. First, total innovation plays a very important role in the pharmaceutical industry. In fact, Acs and Audretsch (1988) cite the pharmaceutical industry as the fourth most innovative out of 247 four-digit SIC industries in 1982. Second, the skilled labor of pharmacologists, biochemists, and immunologists, among others, is necessary in the drug industry given the high technical sophistication of pharmaceutical R&D. Third, casual empiricism suggests that a number of large, highly visible firms coexist with a much larger number of smaller firms in the pharmaceutical industry. Fourth, Schwartzman (1976) notes that capital requirements for manufacturing are relatively low in the pharmaceutical industry. Finally, we saw that the pharmaceutical industry is characterized by relatively low aggregate seller concentration.

Thus, the safest conclusion to draw is that a mixture of firm sizes is most favorable for fostering pharmaceutical innovation.[18] While smaller drug firms seem to hold a decisive advantage, the preceding results suggest that the innovativeness of smaller firms is greatest when large firms dominate in an industry. Encouraging innovation through a diversity of firm sizes should not be too surprising. Many researchers note that new ideas are relatively cheap to conceive, but the commercial development and successful marketing of new products are costly and risky. Small firms might have the edge at the discovery stage, but large firms possess development and marketing advantages. Greer (1992) contrasts the innovativeness of large and small firms as follows:

> *The foot-dragging behavior of leading firms is so common that theorists have dubbed it "the fast-second strategy." Briefly the idea is that, for a large firm, innovation is often costlier, riskier, and less profitable than imitation. A large firm can lie back, let others gamble, then respond quickly with a "fast second" if anything started by their smaller rivals catches fire (p. 669).*

---

[18]Like studies in the past, recent empirical analyses uncover mixed evidence concerning the relation between firm size and innovation. On the one hand, studies by DiMasi, Grabowski, and Vernon (1995) and Henderson and Cockburn (1996) find that research efforts are proportionately more productive in larger firms. Langowitz and Graves (1992), on the other hand, find that research output is subject to diminishing returns with respect to both R&D expenditures and firm size.

Greer notes that Genentech, an infant firm in the late 1970s, founded biotechnology. Larger pharmaceutical firms, such as Eli Lilly, followed Genentech's lead into biotechnology in the mid-1980s.

The Conduct of the Pharmaceutical Industry: A Summary

The studies discussed in this section show that a considerable amount of competition takes place in the pharmaceutical industry. Drug firms sometimes face price competition during the patent period from other branded products, and prices are lower when more branded competition exists. Branded drugs also compete with generics on the basis of price during the postpatent period. Generics offer huge discounts relative to branded products. Also, product competition is particularly important in the pharmaceutical industry. Incentives for new-product development exist because a new drug product, especially a therapeutically important one, can easily supplant others in the market.

However, the degree of competition in the pharmaceutical industry is not perfect. Firms offering single-source drugs are able to raise price above the marginal cost of production because substitutes are unavailable. Furthermore, evidence shows that pharmaceutical marketing is used partly to reinforce the habit-buying practices of physicians. Hence, some drug buyers still remain price insensitive due to brand loyalty.

THE PERFORMANCE OF THE PHARMACEUTICAL INDUSTRY

In this section, we appraise the performance of the contemporary pharmaceutical industry. Competitive market impediments, such as patents, trademarks, and high promotion expenditures, characterize the pharmaceutical industry and suggest that entrenched companies may possess sufficient monopoly power to raise price, restrict output, and earn excessive profits. Direct aggregate measures of pharmaceutical prices and output are unavailable, but some suitable proxy indicators exist.

First, we compare the prescription drug price inflation rate to the general inflation rate in the United States and identify trends and measurement problems. Second, since product innovation is the true output of the pharmaceutical industry, we examine and evaluate historical data on the number of new chemical entities. Finally, we look at some comparative data on the aggregate profitability of pharmaceutical companies.

The Relative Price Inflation Rate of Pharmaceutical Products

To gauge performance, policy-makers often examine how the price of a product changes over time. While the price of a good or service most likely changes over time because of imbalances in supply and demand, policy-makers feel that continually rising prices harm consumers by reducing consumer surplus, especially if their incomes are relatively fixed. With that in mind, let's study how drug prices have tended to change over time.

Figure 14–2 compares the prescription drug price and general price inflation rates in the United States for the period 1970 to 2001. The figure indicates that throughout most of the 1970s, the general price inflation rate outpaced the prescription drug inflation rate. Specifically, prices in general increased at an average annual rate of 7.4 percent–almost

FIGURE 14-2
Urban Consumer Price Inflation Rates, All Items and Prescription Drugs

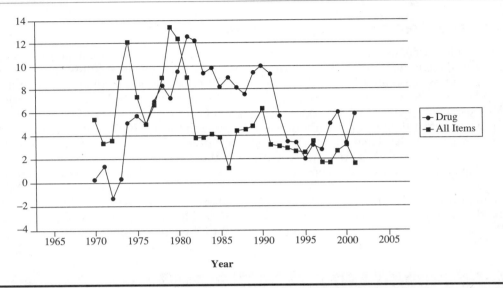

SOURCE: Bureau of Labor Statistics, http://www.bls.gov (accessed June 29, 2002).

twice the rate of 3.9 percent at which drug prices grew. Thus, real or relative drug prices declined throughout most of the 1970s.

During the 1980s there was a reversal in the relative price trend. According to figure 14–2, real drug prices continuously surged as the drug price inflation rate outstripped the general price inflation rate. In particular, drug prices grew at an average annual rate of 9.6 percent compared to an average annual increase of 5.1 percent for prices in general during the 1980s. The figure further suggests that drug price increases have moderated somewhat since 1990, growing at an average annual rate of 5 percent. Given the average annual increase of 2.9 percent for prices in general, real drug prices have tended to increase since 1990.

Before moving on to the next section, it should be noted that the price indices used to calculate inflation rates are not flawless measures. Hence, reported rates may be under or overstated. Of relevance to pharmaceutical products, the Bureau of Labor Statistics (BLS), the government agency responsible for determining price indices, faces a difficult task when measuring changes in the quality of products over time. Yet as Scherer (1993) has noted, "some new drugs, by improving the quality of life or making expensive surgery unnecessary, plainly yield enormous increments of consumer surplus" (p. 103). Because new pharmaceutical products are introduced and utilized at such a rapid rate, quality-adjusted price inflation rates may be lower than the BLS reported rates. If pharmaceutical manufacturers adjust new drug prices to compensate for the higher quality, however, no overstating of the true drug price inflation rate occurs.

INSIGHT 14–5

Pharmaceutical Price Differences in the United States and Canada

The relatively rapid growth of drug prices during the 1980s and early 1990s has led many analysts to wonder whether individual drug prices are higher in the United States than in Canada. In Canada, introductory prices for new patented drugs and price increases on existing drugs are reviewed and controlled by the Patented Medicine Prices Review Board, a quasijudicial price-monitoring board. In addition, provincial drug benefit plans in Canada possess a significant amount of purchasing power and are able to negotiate substantial price discounts. Formularies that list approved drugs and maximum prices are also used to control drug costs in Canadian provinces. Finally, the Canadian patent law has traditionally promoted the sale of relatively low-cost generic alternatives through the compulsory licensing of patented drugs.

This concern prompted the General Accounting Office (GAO) to examine the factory price differential associated with 121 drugs matched in the two countries by brand name, manufacturer, dosage strength, and dosage form. The 121 matched drugs included 39 of the 50 most commonly prescribed drugs in U.S. drugstores in 1990. The prices reflected, as closely as possible, what wholesalers and retailers would pay if they purchased the drugs directly from manufacturers on May 1, 1991. Table 1 on the following page, shows some price differences for selected top-selling drugs.

The GAO (1992) study found that factory price differentials ranged from 44 percent lower to 967 percent higher in the United States than in Canada. The median price per package (of a common dosage size in the United States) was found to be 43 percent higher in the United States than in Canada. Of the 121 drugs studied, 98 were priced higher and 23 priced lower in the United States. Nearly half of the drugs were priced 50 percent or above higher in the United States than in Canada.

Danson and Chao (2000) reexamined the GAO study. They argue that the cross-national drug price comparison in the GAO study may have been biased because of the "use of inappropriate index methods applied to small, non-random samples of branded products, omitting all generics" (p. 160). Using comprehensive data for manufacturer prices of all outpatient drugs sales in 1992, Danzon and Chao found that the differences in drug prices in Canada and the United States are much smaller than the GAO study suggested. According to the authors, three reasons accounted for the different findings in the two studies. First, the selection of leading branded products in the GAO study created an upward bias in U.S. drug prices. Second, the use of unweighted mean prices added a second source of bias in the GAO study. If consumption patterns are different across countries, the idea is that various drug prices should be weighted based on use to determine overall drug price differences across countries. Third, use of a single price instead of a weighted average price per unit of all forms, strengths, and packsizes created an additional, smaller bias. The authors concluded by noting that "any generalizations about relative prices for drugs in different countries are tentative at best, because of the diversity of products, prices, and volumes, which makes conclusions very sensitive to the sample and methods" (p. 192).

(continued)

TABLE 1
Differences in Drug Prices in the United States and Canada
(Wholesale Price for 100 Tablets in 1991 U.S. Dollars)

Drug	Use	Company	United States	Canada
Amoxil	Antibiotic	Beecham	$ 17.27	$ 16.46
Premarin	Postmenopause	Ayerst	26.47	10.10
Ceclor	Antibiotic	Lily	134.18	84.14
Naprosyn	Arthritis	Syntex	72.36	42.64
Tagamet	Antiulcer	SmithKline	57.16	34.27
Pepcid	Antiulcer	Merck	103.74	76.72
Prozac	Depression	Dista	139.85	129.12
Lopressor	Hypertension	Geigy	35.71	15.80
Dilantin	Epilepsy	Parke-Davis	15.03	4.67
Halcion	Tranquilizer	Upjohn	47.69	16.09
Valium	Tranquilizer	Roche	40.41	7.57
Feldene	Arthritis	Pfizer	167.54	123.61
Ativan	Tranquilizer	Wyeth	49.43	6.16
Coumadin	Heart disease	Du Pont	36.70	19.59

SOURCE: General Accounting Office, *Prescription Drugs: Companies Charge More in the United States than in Canada*, GAO/HRD-92–110 (Washington, DC: U.S. Government Printing Office, 1992), Appendix II.

Output of New Pharmaceutical Products

Another measure of an industry's performance is output. According to theory, societal welfare is enhanced when goods are produced up to the point where marginal social benefit equals marginal social cost (see Chapter 3). Empirically, costs and benefits are hard to measure, so we must often rely on information regarding industrial structure and conduct, as well as sound judgment, to determine whether the right incentives exist for efficient output levels. Because of some monopolistic structural conditions (i.e., patents, trademarks, promotion) existing in the pharmaceutical industry, one might expect some restrictions on output. The question is whether evidence supports this expectation.

The most important measure of pharmaceutical output is the number of new chemical entities (NCEs) introduced into the market. As you know, new drug products extend and/or improve the quality of life and often substitute for expensive types of invasive surgery. Data on the number of NCEs introduced into the United States appear in figure 14–3. Until 1960, new drug introductions showed a clear pattern. According to Statman (1983).

> Sixty-seven new drugs were introduced into the U.S. market during the first half of the 1940s. The drug innovation rate doubled during the second half of the 1940s. It increased to 125 during the late 1940s, then nearly doubled again to 205 in the first half of the 1950s. It increased further to 248 during the second half of the 1950s. (p. 6)

FIGURE 14-3
Annual Number of New Drug Entities

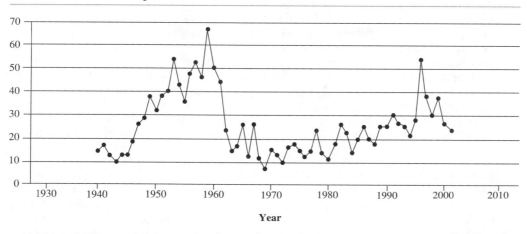

SOURCE: *Statistical Fact Book.* (Washington D.C.: Pharmaceutical Manufacturers Association, various years), as cited by William S. Comanor and Stuart O. Schweitzer, "Pharmaceuticals," in *The Structure of American Industry*, ed. Walter Adams and James Brock (Englewood Cliffs, NJ: Prentice Hall, 1995), Table 7–2. Since 1990 the figures represent approvals rather than introductions and are from PhRMA, *Industry Profit* (Washington, D.C.: 2002), Figure 3.2 and the Federal Drug Administration, http://www.FDA.gov..

However, the 1960s witnessed a decline in the number of NCEs. Although 453 drugs were introduced in the 1950s, only 236 new drugs were introduced during the 1960s. The 1970s saw no reversal in the downward trend since the 1960s, with only 158 NCEs introduced in the marketplace by pharmaceutical companies.

Two reasons have been cited for the decline in drug innovations after the early 1960s. First, the decline may have been caused by a "depletion of research opportunities," as early evidence suggests that the innovation slowdown continued worldwide in the 1970s and 1980s (Grabowski, 1989). Second, the decline may have been the result of the 1962 amendment to the Food, Drug and Cosmetic Act, which significantly increased the costs of pharmaceutical innovations due to safety and efficacy concerns. The so-called Kefauver-Harris Act prompted the FDA to adopt more stringent rules concerning new-drug testing and approval. The greater amount of testing and approval time raised drug manufacturers' costs and reduced the effective patent life of a new drug, thereby discouraging new drug discoveries.

Regardless of the reason, there have been some encouraging signs concerning the innovative activities of pharmaceutical companies since the early 1980s. First, as figure 14–3 reflects, the number of NCEs increased from 158 in the 1970s to 202 in the 1980s and then increased even farther to 312 during the 1990s. Second, figure 14–1 shows that while R&D intensity was relatively stable over the 1970s, an upward trend in R&D intensity emerged during the 1980s and continued through most of the 1990s. Several explanations for the improvement in innovative activities have been offered.

First, the Hatch-Waxman Act of 1984 was designed in part to correct for the regulatory lag created by the 1962 act. As mentioned previously, the life of a new-drug patent can be extended for up to five years (but no more than 14 years in total) to compensate for any approval delay by the FDA. The longer expected effective patent life for new drugs creates a better opportunity for profits and encourages more innovation.

Second, the faster pace of new drug discoveries has been attributed to the recent revolution in methods of drug discovery and development. Previously, pharmaceutical R&D largely involved **molecule manipulation**, the trial-and-error examination of the therapeutic properties of a large number of chemical entities, especially closely related derivatives of known entities (Duetsch, 1993). Today, technologies, such as genetic engineering, monoclonal antibodies, cellular biology, and immunology—all contributing to the creation of biotechnology—enable researchers to better understand the sources of diseases and how the human body potentially reacts to drug treatment. This more scientific approach to R&D is referred to as **discovery by design**. According to the Boston Consulting Group (1993),

> With knowledge about the relation between the structure and function of the molecule targeted for the drug action, small molecules can be designed that interact very specifically with the target. The target molecule is commonly a receptor on a cell surface—for example, the H_2 receptors that help to regulate acid production in the stomach. Rational drug design promises to supplement the traditional random search for activity and to provide specific guidance to researchers seeking useful drugs for diseases that have largely resisted treatment in the past (p. 31).

In fact, as a result of genetic engineering, scientists have recently discovered the gene responsible for Huntington's disease, among others (Boston Consulting Group, 1993).

Third, unlike the 1970s, during which real drug prices were declining, real drugs prices were high during the 1980s and for most of the 1990s (review figure 14–2). The high real drug prices and the resulting sizable cash flow margins helped to fund R&D expenditures, a necessary ingredient for innovation. Recall that Grabowski and Vernon (1981) found empirically that cash flow is a major determinant of R&D expenditures. Thus, the large number of NCEs in both the 1980s and 1990s may be an indirect function of the relatively high drug prices observed during those periods.

Profits in the Pharmaceutical Industry

Most complaints aimed at the pharmaceutical industry have concerned excessive profits. Patents, brand loyalty, and an inelastic demand for drugs written by physicians are cited as the causes of high pharmaceutical profits. Some comparative data for the after-tax return on equity (ROE) and return on assets (ROA) are shown in table 14–4 for all manufacturing firms and drug firms for selected years from 1986 to 2001. ROE and ROA are determined by dividing net income (net sales less operating costs and expenses) after taxes by the value of stockholder equity and the firm's assets, respectively. The data clearly show that the profitability of drug firms, as measured by either ROE or ROA, was consistently much higher than that of the manufacturing industry average. Specifically, the ROE and ROA for drug firms, on average, were more than twice the manufacturing industry average for the six periods.

Researchers point out that pharmaceutical accounting rates of return may be biased upward due to unusually high R&D and marketing outlays (e.g., see Scherer, 1993). Expenditures on these "intangible assets" are expensed, but should be capitalized and then

TABLE 14-4

Return on Assets and Stockholder Equity for Drug and All Manufacturing Companies, Various Years

	AFTER-TAX RETURN ON EQUITY					
	1986	**1989**	**1992**	**1995**	**1997**	**2001**
All manufacturing	9.6%	13.5%	2.6%	16.2%	16.6%	2.0%
Drugs (SIC 283)	24.1	25.3	22.3	27.0	23.2	32.1
	AFTER-TAX RETURN ON ASSETS					
	1986	**1989**	**1992**	**1995**	**1997**	**2001**
All manufacturing	4.2%	5.5%	0.9%	6.2%	6.6%	.8%
Drugs (SIC 283)	11.8	12.5	10.5	10.4	9.5	12.2

SOURCE: U.S. Bureau of the Census, *Quarterly Financial Report* (various issues) at http://www.census.gov/prod/2002pubs/qfr-01q4.pdf.

depreciated over an appropriate time period because they ordinarily yield a long-term flow of benefits to drug manufacturers. Studies have found that pharmaceutical returns are 20 to 25 percent lower when R&D and marketing outlays are treated as intangible assets (Office of Technology Assessment, 1993).

Even after accounting biases have been eliminated, pharmaceutical returns generally remain higher than the manufacturing average (Comanor, 1986). Pharmaceutical industry spokespersons point out that research and development is a risky venture. High R&D risks translate into high pharmaceutical returns, because otherwise risk-averse individuals would be unwilling to invest in drug firms. They note that the successful introduction of a pharmaceutical product costs about $200 million or more because a drug firm encounters a large number of misses before finding a commercial hit (DiMasi, Hansen, Grabowski, and Lasagna, 1991).[19]

So is it true that pharmaceutical R&D is a risky undertaking? According to the evidence provided in table 14-4, rates of return in the pharmaceutical industry seem to be more stable than the average return in the manufacturing sector, at least for the six years reported.

Perhaps focusing on aggregate industry returns masks the variability of returns at the individual firm or product level. Indeed, some evidence suggests that may be the case. A study by Grabowski and Vernon (1990), which analyzed the returns associated with 100 new-drug introductions during the 1970s, uncovered evidence indicating that pharmaceutical R&D is very risky and costly. Based on a number of assumptions concerning product duration, cash flow margins, R&D costs, and worldwide sales, the authors found that the variation in returns for new-drug introductions is highly skewed, with only the top 30 drugs

---

[19]A new estimate puts the cost of developing a new drug at $802 million (DiMasi, 2001).

INSIGHT 14-6

Has the United States Remained the World Leader in Pharmaceutical Innovation?

Competition in the pharmaceutical industry largely involves the development and commercial introduction of new drug products. Market positions in the pharmaceutical industry can shift dramatically and swiftly when companies develop new breakthrough drugs. Until the mid-1970s, the United States was acknowledged as the world leader in pharmaceutical innovation. Evidence after that point initially suggested that the U.S. share of world pharmaceutical R&D spending fell from 60 percent in the 1950s to less than 30 percent by the end of the 1970s. The main explanation was that the declining U.S. position was a natural consequence of the depleted conditions in Europe and Japan after World War II. That is, the United States had an advantage immediately after the war that eroded as the European countries and Japan eventually recovered (Grabowski, 1989).

Further evidence, however, suggests that the United States did not lose its leadership position in the world pharmaceutical industry during the 1980s. Specifically, Grabowski (1989) points out that the R&D expenditures of U.S. drug firms grew at an annual rate of 14.3 percent over the period 1980 to 1985, which far surpassed the rate of 1.1 percent from 1973 to 1979. Moreover, the R&D spending of U.S. firms grew at a much faster rate than those of British (8.7 percent), West German (9.8 percent), and Japanese (11.5 percent) drug firms in the first half of the 1980s.

Further evidence presented by Grabowski indicates that NCEs originating in the United States were more commercially important than those originating from other countries. According to the evidence, U.S. drug firms accounted for 41.7 percent of the 170 consensus NCEs introduced from 1970 to 1983. (Consensus NCEs are defined as new drugs introduced in at least 6 of 11 major markets during a particular period.) Switzerland, the next largest provider, accounted for a comparatively small 12.9 percent of all consensus NCEs during the period. Because Japanese drug firms concentrated on imitative rather than innovative research, they were responsible for only 4.1 percent of all consensus drugs.

Additional evidence suggests that U.S. firms continued to develop new drugs on a much larger scale than their foreign competitors during the later half of the 1980s. According to Ballance, Pogany, and Forstner (1992), U.S. firms accounted for 40 percent of all self-originating drugs under development in 1989. Japanese drug firms, the closest rivals to U.S. companies in this innovation category, were responsible for 20.9 percent of the self-originating drugs under development in the same year.

Evidence also appears to indicate that U.S. drug firms have not relinquished their leadership position in the worldwide pharmaceutical industry during the 1990s. Data show that U.S. pharmaceutical companies increased spending on R&D at almost twice the rate of all European pharmaceutical companies combined. In addition, eight of the top ten worldwide prescription drugs based on sales originated in the United States compared to only two from Europe. Furthermore, U.S. pharmaceutical companies are also expected to produce 34 of the 55 breakthrough medicines entering the market in 2002 (PhRMA, 2002). All in all, the evidence suggests that the United States has not lost its position as the world leader in pharmaceutical research.

covering average R&D costs. Moreover, the authors discovered that the present value of the cash flow associated with the 10 least profitable of the top 30 drugs just barely covered the present value of their R&D costs.

One implication of Grabowski and Vernon's study is that a successful drug company must have an occasional "blockbuster" to cover the large fixed costs that characterize the R&D process. Another implication is that the real drug price increases of the 1980s, as evidenced by figure 14–2, may have been necessary for the average new-drug innovation to recover its R&D costs. Overall, their study implies that the high rate of profit observed in the pharmaceutical industry may be justified by the significant risk and cost of new-product innovations. The authors found that the average return to R&D equaled the 9 percent industry cost of capital, implying a normal rate of return on pharmaceutical R&D investment.

However, another study on the returns to R&D by the Office of Technology Assessment (OTA, 1993) shows that Grabowski and Vernon's results do not hold for drugs introduced from 1981 to 1983. The OTA study found that each NCE, on average, can be expected to return a net present value of at least $36 million more than necessary to bring forth the investment in R&D. The implication is that drug prices could be reduced across the board by at least 4.3 percent without reducing returns below the amount necessary to repay R&D investors. One reason the OTA's results differ from those of Grabowski and Vernon is that the increasing real drug prices and associated greater pharmaceutical revenues during the 1980s were more than adequate to cover R&D costs. The OTA study claims,

> Together, the findings on returns on pharmaceutical R&D and to the industry as a whole explain why R&D expenditures have risen so dramatically in real terms throughout the 1980s. Investors have followed the promise of high returns on future innovations. Ultimately investment in research is determined by expected revenues. The dramatic increase in real revenues to new drugs throughout the 1980s has sent signals to the industry that more investment will be rewarded handsomely. The industry has responded as expected, by increasing its commitment to investment, including investment in R&D (p. 104).

The Performance of the Pharmaceutical Industry: A Summary

In this section, we reviewed data concerning the prescription drug price inflation rate and profits as measures of industry performance. Drug prices were shown to have increased more rapidly than general prices for all but a few years since 1981. The average profit rate in the pharmaceutical industry was also shown to be higher than the average profit rate in the manufacturing sector during the 1980s and 1990s. By themselves, these two performance measures suggest that society's scarce resources may be misallocated in the pharmaceutical industry.

Data regarding the introduction of NCEs paint a somewhat different picture of the pharmaceutical industry. After slowing during the 1960s and 1970s, the number of new chemical entities by U.S. drug firms actually increased during the 1980s and 1990s. The R&D spending of U.S. drug firms also increased during the 1980s, and this trend continued through the 1990s. Two reasons for the greater innovation of U.S. drug firms in recent years are rising real drug prices and consistent profits. As Grabowski and Vernon (1981) show, a major determinant of pharmaceutical innovation is cash flow.

This discussion implies that a tradeoff might exist between "static" and dynamic" efficiency. Static efficiency refers to the efficiency of firms at a point in time and reflects how successfully firms employ a given technology or produce a given product. In contrast, dynamic efficiency relates to the efficiency of firms over time and captures how successful they are at developing new products and processes. As Berndt (2002) writes:

> Although this conflict between static efficiency (price new drugs low, near short-run marginal cost) versus dynamic efficiency (price new drugs high, maintain incentives for innovation) is a deep and enduring one, as the costs of bringing new drugs to market have increased sharply in recent years, this tradeoff is becoming more severe. The resolution of this static versus dynamic efficiency conflict is likely the single most important issue facing the pharmaceutical industry over the next decade (p. 45).

SUMMARY

This chapter assessed the structure, conduct, and performance of the U.S. pharmaceutical industry. Based on the six-digit NAICS, the pharmaceutical industry was shown to contain a relatively large number of equally sized firms, but disaggregation of the pharmaceutical industry into therapeutic markets showed that only a few major drugs typically compete with one another. Legal patents and brand loyalty built up during the patent period are argued to cause substantial barriers to entry into therapeutic markets. Generic drug companies offering huge discounts are particularly ineffective in influencing the loyalty attached to brand-name drugs because physicians are often responsible for selecting drugs. Physicians are not normally price sensitive since they are effectively spending someone else's money.

Evidence shows that price competition takes place among multisource drugs. Price competition sometimes occurs among branded drugs during the patent period and between generic and brand-name drugs during the postpatent period. Drug prices are usually lower when there are more substitute products. Studies show that generic competition causes the brand-name firm's market share to fall by an average of 50 percent two years after entry. The innovator firm's advertising helps to preserve its market share, while the follower firms' advertising helps them to gain market share.

New-product innovation, the major benefit of the pharmaceutical industry, tends to be a risky endeavor and was shown to depend on past R&D success and cash flow. Debate still continues over the relation between firm size and innovation. The safest conclusion to draw from recent studies is that a mixture of firm sizes in the pharmaceutical industry best favors innovation.

Recent data suggest that real drug prices have risen and pharmaceutical firms have experienced relatively high rates of return since the beginning of the 1980s. The resulting cash flow has financed the increase in R&D spending as a percentage of sales and the resulting greater number of new chemical entity introductions during the 1980 and 1990s. All in all, the pharmaceutical industry seems to best fit the model of a "mild to tight differentiated oligopoly." That is, there is some evidence of a few competitors in therapeutic markets, substantial but not perfect barriers to entry based on patents and trademarks, product differentiation, evidence of price and product rivalry rather than cooperation, and evidence of relatively high profits.

The future should witness a continual evolution in the pharmaceutical industry. The demand side of the market will most likely adopt further cost-saving methods, such as formularies, drug review utilization, and generic substitution. Government may be prone to impose price controls if drug prices continue to soar. Seller concentration in many therapeutic markets should diminish as many drug patents soon expire and generic competition increases. It will be interesting to follow the effects of these demand- and supply-side changes on new-drug innovation.

REVIEW QUESTIONS AND PROBLEMS

1. Describe three benefits associated with pharmaceutical products. Cite one example of each.
2. How do the six-digit NAICS and the therapeutic market definition of the pharmaceutical industry differ in terms of seller concentration? Which is the better measure? Why? Think in terms of actual and potential competition.
3. Explain some of the methods adopted by third-party payers to control drug prices.
4. Cite three reasons unconstrained physicians tend to purchase brand-name instead of generic products.
5. What benefits and costs do pharmacists face when dispensing generic drugs?
6. Explain the purpose and functioning of a PBM company. What are the antitrust concerns about a drug manufacturer purchasing a PBM company? What is the efficiency justification for such an acquisition?
7. What is the economic rationale behind a patent? Why may the effective patent life of a drug be shorter than the legal life? Why may the effective patent life be longer than the legal life?
8. What two effects did the Hatch-Waxman Act of 1984 have on the supply side of the pharmaceutical market?
9. Why might the FDA tend to delay the drug approval process? Explain in terms of type 1 and type 2 errors.
10. What general conclusions have studies reached concerning drug price competition?
11. What general conclusion have studies reached concerning the promotion of pharmaceutical products? Cite some evidence.
12. What are the two main determinants of R&D spending according to Grabowski and Vernon? What is the relation between firm size and pharmaceutical innovation? Briefly summarize the theoretical considerations and empirical findings.
13. How has the pharmaceutical producer price index compared to the general producer price index since the 1970s?
14. Explain the trend in the number of NCE introductions from after WWII until 2000. What factors account for any changes?
15. What three reasons are claimed to account for the high reported profits of pharmaceutical companies? Do you think drug companies earn excessive profits? Why or why not?

ONLINE RESOURCES

To access Internet links related to the topics in this chapter, please visit our web site at http://santerre.swcollege.com.

REFERENCES

Acs, Zoltan J., and David B. Audretsch. "Innovation in Large and Small Firms: An Empirical Analysis." *American Economic Review* 78 (September 1988), pp. 678–90.

———. "Innovation, Market Structure, and Firm Size." *Review of Economics and Statistics* 69 (November 1987), pp. 567–74.

Anders, George. "Mergers of Hospitals Surge Amid Pressure to Cut Costs." *The Wall Street Journal*, December 1, 1993, p. B1.

Ballance, Robert, Jano Pogany, and Helmut Forstner. *The World's Pharmaceutical Industries*. Brookfield, VT: Edward Elgar, 1992.

Berndt, Ernst B. "Pharmaceuticals in U.S. Health Care: Determinants of Quantity and Price." *Journal of Economic Perspectives* 16 (fall 2002), pp. 45–66.

Boston Consulting Group. *The Changing Environment for U.S. Pharmaceuticals*. Boston: Boston Consulting Group, 1993.

Carroll, Norman V., and Alan P. Wolfgang. "Risks, Benefits, and Generic Substitution." *Journal of Consumer Affairs* 25 (summer 1991), pp. 110–21.

Caves, Richard E., Michael D. Whinston, and Mark A. Hurwitz. "Patent Expiration, Entry, and Competition in the U.S. Pharmaceutical Industry." *Brookings Papers: Microeconomics 1991*, 1991, pp. 1–66.

Chren, Mary-Margaret, and C. Seth Landefeld. "Physician Behavior and Their Interactions with Drug Companies." *Journal of the American Medical Association* 271 (March 2, 1994), pp. 684–89.

Cohen, Joshua P. "PBMs and a Medicare Prescription Drug Benefit." *Food and Drug Law Journal* 55 (2000), pp. 293–476.

Comanor, William S. "Research and Technical Change in the Pharmaceutical Industry." *Review of Economics and Statistics* (May 1965), pp. 182–90.

———. "The Political Economy of the Pharmaceutical Industry." *Journal of Economic Literature* (September 1986), pp. 1178–1217.

Comanor, William S., and Stuart O. Schweitzer. "Pharmaceuticals." In *The Structure of American Industry*, eds. Walter Adams and James Brock. Englewood Cliffs, NJ: Prentice Hall, 1995, pp. 177–96.

Danzon, Patricia M., and Li-Wei Chao. "Cross-national price differences for pharmaceuticals how large, and why?" *Journal of Health Economics* 19 (2000), pp. 159–95.

DiMasi, Joseph A. "Tufts Center for the Study of Drug Development Pegs Cost of New Prescription Medicine at $802 Million." press release, Tufts University, 30 November 2001.

DiMasi, Joseph A. "Success Rates for New Drugs Entering Clinical Testing in the United States." *Clinical and Pharmacology Therapeutics* 58 (July 1995), pp. 1–14.

DiMasi, Joseph A., Henry G. Grabowski, and John Vernon. "R&D Costs, Innovative Output and Firm Size in the Pharmaceutical Industry." *International Journal of the Economics of Business* 2 (1995), pp. 201–19.

DiMasi, Joseph A., Ronald W. Hansen, Henry G. Grabowski, and Louis Lasagna. "Cost of Innovation in the Pharmaceutical Industry." *Journal of Health Economics* 10 (1991), pp. 107–42.

Duetsch, Larry L. "Pharmaceuticals: The Critical Role of Innovation." In *Industry Studies*, ed. Larry L. Duetsch. Englewood Cliffs, NJ: Prentice Hall, 1993.

Egan, John W., Harlow N. Higinbotham, and J. Fred Weston. *Economics of the Pharmaceutical Industry*. New York: Praeger Publishers, 1982.

Ellison, Sara F., Ian Cockburn, Zvi Griliches, and Jerry Hausman. "Characteristics of Demand for Pharmaceutical Products: An Examination of Four Cephalosporins." *Rand Journal of Economics* 28 (Autumn 1997), pp. 426–46.

Federal Trade Commission. "Merck Settles FTC Charges that Its Acquisition of Medco Could Cause Higher Prices and Reduced Quality for Prescription Drugs." Press Release (August 27, 1998), http://www.ftc.gov/opa/1998/9808/merck.htm.

General Accounting Office. "Prescription Drugs: Companies Charge More in the United States than in Canada." GAO/HRD-92–110. Washington, D.C.: U.S. Government Printing Office, 1992.

Grabowski, Henry G. "An Analysis of U.S. International Competitiveness in Pharmaceuticals." *Managerial and Decision Economics* 10 (March 1989), pp. 27–33.

———. "The Determinants of Industrial Research and Development: A Study of the Chemical, Drug and Petroleum Industries." *Journal of Political Economy* (March-April 1968), pp. 292–305.

Grabowski, Henry G., and John M. Vernon. "Brand Loyalty, Entry, and Price Competition in Pharmaceuticals after the 1984 Drug Act." *Journal of Law and Economics* 35 (October 1992), pp. 331–50.

———. "A New Look at the Returns and Risks to Pharmaceutical R&D." *Management Science* 36 (July 1990), pp. 804–21.

———. "Longer Patents for Lower Imitation Barriers: The 1984 Drug Act." *American Economic Review Papers and Proceedings* 76 (May 1986), pp. 195–98.

———. *The Regulation of Pharmaceuticals: Balancing the Benefits and Risks*. Washington, D.C.: American Enterprise Institute, 1983.

———. "The Determinants of Research and Development Expenditures in the Pharmaceutical Industry." In *Drugs and Health*, ed. Robert Helms. Washington, D.C.: American Enterprise Institute, 1981, pp. 3–20.

Greer, Douglas F. *Industrial Organization and Public Policy*. New York: Macmillan, 1992.

Henderson, Rebecca, and Ian Cockburn. "Scale, Scope and Spillovers: The Determinants of Research Productivity in Drug Discovery." *Rand Journal* 27 (spring 1996), pp. 32–59.

Hurwitz, Mark A., and Richard E. Caves. "Persuasion or Information? Promotion and the Shares of Brand Name and Generic Pharmaceuticals." *Journal of Law and Economics* 31 (October 1988), pp. 299–320.

Langowitz, Nan S., and Samuel B. Graves. "Innovative Productivity in Pharmaceutical Firms." *Research Technology Management* 35 (March-April 1992), pp. 39–41.

Leffler, Keith B. "Persuasion or Information? The Economics of Prescription Drug Advertising." *Journal of Law and Economics* 24 (April 1981), pp. 45–74.

Lu, Z. John, and William S. Comanor. "Strategic Pricing and New Pharmaceuticals." Mimeo, University of California at Santa Barbara, 1994.

Mansfield, Edwin. *Industrial Research and Technological Innovation*. New York: W.W. Norton, 1968.

McRae, James J., and Francis Tapon. "Some Empirical Evidence on Post-Patent Barriers to Entry in the Canadian Pharmaceutical Industry." *Journal of Health Economics* 4 (1985), pp. 43–61.

Moore, Stephen D. "Glaxo, SmithKline Renew Their Rivalry in Medicines Used to Prevent Vomiting." *The Wall Street Journal*, November 19, 1993, p. B4D.

Mosby Medical Encyclopedia. New York City: C. V. Mosby, 1992.

Office of Technology Assessment. *Pharmaceutical R and D: Costs, Risks and Rewards*. OTA-H-522. Washington, D.C.: U.S. Government Printing Office, February 1993.

Peltzman, Sam. *Regulation of Pharmaceutical Innovation: The 1962 Amendments*. Washington, D.C.: American Enterprise Institute, 1974.

Pharmaceutical Research and Manufacturers of America (PhRMA). *Industry Profile*. Washington, D.C. (2002).

Price Waterhouse. *Financial Trends in the Pharmaceutical Industry and Projected Effects of Recent Federal Legislation*. Report prepared for the Pharmaceutical Manufacturers Association, October 21, 1993.

PricewaterhouseCooper. "Study of Pharmaceutical Benefit Management." HCFA Contract No. 500-97-0399/0097 (June 2001) http://www.hcfa.gov/research/PharmBM.pdf.

Reichert, Janice M., Jennifer Chee, and Claire S. Kotzampaltiris. "The Effects of the Prescription Drug User Fee Act and the Food and Drug Admisistration Modernization Act on the Development and Approval of Therapeutic Medicines." *Drug Information Journal* 32 (2001) pp. 85–94.

Rizzo, John A. "Advertising and Competition in the Ethical Pharmaceutical Industry: The Case of Antihypertensive Drugs." *Journal of Law and Economics* 42 (April 1999), pp. 89–116.

Scherer, F.M. "Pricing, Profits, and Technological Progress in the Pharmaceutical Industry." *Journal of Economic Perspectives* 7 (summer 1993), pp. 97–115.

Scherer, F.M., and David Ross. *Industrial Market Structure and Economic Performance*. Boston: Houghton Mifflin, 1990.

Schmalensee, Richard. "Product Differentiation Advantages of Pioneering Brands." *American Economic Review* 72 (June 1982), pp. 349–65.

Schnee, Jerome. "Innovation and Discovery in the Ethical Pharmaceutical Industry." Chapter 8 in *Research and Innovation in the Modern Corporation*, eds. Edwin Mansfield, John Rapaport, Jerome Schnee, Samuel Wagner, and Michael Hamburger. New York: W.W. Norton, 1971.

Schumpeter, Joseph. *Capitalism, Socialism and Democracy*. New York: Harper, 1950.

Schwartzman, David. *Innovation in the Pharmaceutical Industry*. Baltimore: Johns Hopkins University Press, 1976.

Statman, Meir. *Competition in the Pharmaceutical Industry: The Declining Profitability of Drug Innovation*. Washington, D.C.: American Enterprise Institute, 1983.

Tanouye, Elyse. "Heartburn Drug Makers Feel Judge's Heat." *The Wall Street Journal* (October 16, 1995), p. B8.

Tanouye, Elyse, and Thomas M. Burton. "More Firms 'Switch' Prescription Drugs to Give Them Over-the-Counter Status." *The Wall Street Journal*, July 29, 1993, p. B1.

Temin, Peter. "Realized Benefits from Switching Drugs." *Journal of Law and Economics* 35 (October 1992), pp. 351–69.

————. *Taking Your Medicine: Drug Regulation in the United States*. Cambridge, MA: Harvard University Press, 1980.

Tregarthen, Suzanne. "Prescription to Stop Drug Companies' Profiteering." *The Wall Street Journal*, March 5, 1992, p. A15.

Virts, John R., and J. Fred Weston. "Expectations and the Allocation of Research and Development Resources." In *Drugs and Health*, ed. Robert Helms. Washington, D.C.: American Enterprise Institute, 1981, pp. 21–45.

Weidenbaum, Murray. "Are Drug Prices Too High?" *The Public Interest* 112 (summer 1993), pp. 84–89.

Welsch, Jonathan. "American Home Used a Blitz for Orudis." *The Wall Street Journal* (December 4, 1995), p. B3.

Wiggins, Steven N., and Robert Maness. "Price Competition in Pharmaceutical Markets." Mimeo, Department of Economics, Texas A&M University (June 1994).

CEBS QUESTIONS

CEBS Sample Question on Subject Matter from CEBS Course 9 Study Manual

1. List and define the methods used by third-party payers to control pharmaceutical costs. (pages 440 and 442)

CEBS Sample Exam Questions

1. Which of the following statements is the safest conclusion regarding the relationship between firm size and the innovation process in the pharmaceutical industry?
   A. Large firms are the best innovators because they have the financial resources to conduct effective research and development
   B. Large firms are the best innovators because they can advertise more effectively
   C. Small firms are the best innovators because there is less bureaucratic red tape in smaller firms
   D. Small firms are the best innovators because they have more creative talent
   E. A mixture of firm sizes is most favorable for fostering pharmaceutical innovation
2. Which of the following is (are) correct statements regarding the economic performance of the pharmaceutical industry in recent years?
   I. Drug prices have increased more rapidly than general prices
   II. The average profit rate is higher than that in the manufacturing sector
   III. The risk of the pharmaceutical industry is less than of the manufacturing sector
      A. I only
      B. II only
      C. I and II only
      D. II and III only
      E. I and III only

3. All the following statements regarding a patent for a pharmaceutical drug are correct EXCEPT:
   A. The legal maximum number of years for a patent is 14 years
   B. The effective life of a patent is often less than the legal maximum because the FDA takes a number of years to approve a product for commercial introduction
   C. A pharmaceutical patent is granted for a drug's chemical composition, not its therapeutic novelty
   D. A legal patent does not guarantee a monopoly position
   E. The Hatch-Waxman Act quickened the approval process for generic drugs

Answer to Sample Question from Study Manual

The methods used are formularies, drug utilization review, and required generic substitution. A formulary is a required list of selected pharmaceutical products that physicians are required to prescribe for the third-party payers' patients. A drug utilization review monitors the actions of physicians and identifies physicians who inappropriately prescribe medicines. Generic substitution requires that pharmacists substitute lower-priced generic products for higher priced brand-names whenever possible.

Answers to Sample Exam Questions

1. E is the answer. See pages 458–460 of the text.
2. C is the answer. Statement III is incorrect. The pharmaceutical industry faces high risks in product innovations and product liability. Statements I and II are correct. See pages 467 and 469 of the text.
3. A is the answer. The legal patent period was changed from 17 years to 20 years in 1996. See pages 444–445 of the text.

CHAPTER 15

THE LONG-TERM CARE INDUSTRY

In a cult movie of the 1970s, "Wild in the Streets," Max Frost, a rock star and newly elected 21-year-old president, created an imaginative solution to what was perceived as an "elderly" problem in the United States. He placed all the elderly people into concentration camps and fed them hallucinogens like LSD. Far away in the concentration camps, elderly people were kept out of sight and out of mind (literally so because of the hallucinogens). You see, Max and his followers despised authority. To Max and friends, if you were 35 or older, you were elderly. Elderly people like parents, teachers, and policemen possessed authority. Hey! What do you expect from a movie that was designed to appeal to the rebellious young adults growing up during the 1960s?

Today, one could rightfully argue that we do have a problem concerning the elderly in the United States. The problem has nothing to do with authority, however. The problem pertains to the delivery and financing of long-term care for those individuals incapable of caring for themselves. Elderly people make up a majority of the individuals requiring long-term care, and the number of elderly persons has grown both in absolute and relative terms over time. In fact, while only one of ten people in the United States were 65 years of age or older in Max Frost's day (the 1960s), today that number is one in eight. And the population is expected to get even older on average in years to come. Projections suggest that by the year 2050 one out of every five people will be a senior citizen. Indeed, nearly 5 percent of the U.S. population is expected to be 85 years of age and older by 2050!

We learned earlier in the text that health capital depreciates more rapidly with age. Consequently, the graying of the United States will likely be associated with a more intensive use of medical services for a growing number of elderly, all of which will contribute to rising health care costs in the future. Of particular concern is the increasing cost of caring for the chronically ill elderly on a long-term basis. Finding ways of containing long-term care costs without compromising the quality of care or lives will be a tremendous challenge. Society will have to make hard choices and trade-offs are inevitable unless some truly imaginative solutions are found.

With these choices, trade-offs, and imaginative solutions in mind, this chapter investigates the market for long-term care services. Specifically, this chapter:

> Studies the structure of the long-term care industry by analyzing the number and size distribution of the various providers of long-term

care services such as nursing homes and home health care agencies. We also look at the buyer side and barriers to entry in the long-term care market, among other structural features.

> Discusses the conduct of long-term care providers. In particular, the behavior of long-term care providers, mainly nursing homes, in response to market competition, various pricing methods (e.g., prospective versus retrospective reimbursement), form of ownership, and regulations are extensively studied. Quality issues pertaining to long-term care are also highlighted.

> Examines the performance of the long-term care industry by observing and discussing various indicators such as aggregate price, input usage, output, insurance coverage, and expenditures.

The information obtained will help us better understand the structure, operation, and performance of the contemporary long-term care services industry. The resulting information will be vital in our roles as informed consumers and voters, health care providers, or public policy makers.

THE STRUCTURE OF THE LONG-TERM CARE SERVICES INDUSTRY

Before we begin our discussion of the industry, it would be useful to define **long-term care**. Long-term care is typically defined as:

> . . . *a set of health care, personal care, and social services delivered over a sustained period of time to persons who have lost, or never acquired, some degree of functional capacity, as measured by an index of functional ability.*

According to the definition, long-term care primarily enhances the quality of life rather than cures a particular medical problem. In many instances, patients in need of long-term care have one or more physical limitations that will be with them for the rest of their lives or, at the very least, for an extended period of time. For example, an elderly man may need help bathing and walking because of a recent stroke. Or a young woman may need continual assistance because of a car accident that left her permanently paralyzed from the neck down. In each instance the need for long-term care is likely to be permanent and the emphasis is on enhancing the quality of life and gaining some measure of independence for the patient. While it is certainly the case that hospitals and physicians offer some level of long-term care, it is safe to say that hospitals and physicians primarily provide short-term treatment aimed at curing rather than caring for or rehabilitating a patient.

Scanlon (1980) points out that, unlike the demand for medical services, the demand for nursing home care reflects a basic rather than a derived demand. He goes on to note that nursing homes are long-term substitutes for independent living and that the function of nursing homes is not to restore health, or "cure," but to provide "care" to those with permanent disabilities. Consequently, physicians play only a minor role in the choice process concerning nursing home care, unlike the choice concerning hospital services where they play a dominant role.

Other elements to keep in mind are that the continuum of care and the organizational settings in which care is provided varies widely. The continuum of care varies from the occasional need for assistance to perform various household chores, such as mowing the lawn or shopping for groceries, to the need for around-the-clock nursing care. Or the continuum of care may include a rehabilitation program that involves physical, occupational, and/or speech therapy. The spectrum of organizational settings that provide long-term care also varies extensively. For example, friends and family members may provide long-term care on an informal basis in the elderly person's own home, or long-term care can be provided in a formal, highly intensive setting such as a skilled nursing home. Intermediate care can be provided by a home health care agency or at an assisted living facility. We begin the analysis of the structure of the long-term care industry by examining the need for long-term care. This discussion is followed by a review of the major providers of long-term care services.

The Need for Long-Term Care

It is generally recognized that an individual needs long-term care when faced with a long-term physical or mental limitation severe enough to impede the ability to carry out the everyday activities of independent living. One of the most frequently used methods to determine if an individual requires long-term care is to assess whether that individual has the ability to carry out a predetermined list of activities of daily living (ADL), or instrumental activities of daily living (IADL) (see Insight 15–1). Using these criteria, the General Accounting Office (1995) estimated that 12.8 million Americans needed some type of long-term care in 1994. Of that number 7.3 million, or 57 percent, were elderly.[1] The remaining 43 percent was made up of 5.7 million working-age adults and 400 thousand children. Put in relative terms, while only 1 person in 20 required long-term care out of the general population in 1994, almost 1 in 4 elderly was in need of some type of long-term care. Clearly, the need for long-term care is greatest among the elderly population. The report also indicates that a vast proportion, almost 81 percent of those individuals needing long-term care in 1994, received the care at home or in a community setting. The remaining 19 percent, or 2.4 million people, lived in institutions such as nursing homes or chronic care hospitals.

Given the diversity of long-term care providers, it is no easy task to describe the structure of the long-term care services industry. The three major providers in the market for long-term care are informal providers, nursing homes, and home health care agencies, so attention will be paid to these three delivery systems.[2] A profile of informal caregivers follows and then a separate analysis of the structural characteristics of the nursing home care and home health care markets are considered, such as the number of firms, characteristics of the buyers, and barriers to entry.

Structure of Informal Care Providers

It is generally agreed that family members and friends provide a substantial amount of long-term care on an informal basis. By its very nature, however, the amount of care provided is difficult to accurately measure. Fortunately, two recent surveys shed some light on

---

[1]Throughout this chapter, the elderly population is defined as all individuals 65 years of age and older.
[2]Other providers of long-term care services include adult day care facilities, senior centers, and continuing care retirement communities.

INSIGHT 15–1

A Measurement of the Need for Long-Term Care

Activities of daily living, ADL, and instrumental activities of daily living, IADL, are sets of activities used by health care professionals to measure the ability of individuals to perform routine daily living activities. While the number of daily living activities included in rating scales varies across survey instruments, most include the basic functions listed below. These rating scales are of value because they provide policy analysts with an objective means of establishing the need for long-term health care, both in terms of the number of people who require long-term care and the intensity of care needed. For example, the GAO study cited in the text estimated that 4.3 million working-age adults and 5.7 million elderly required long-term care because they were in need of assistance with one or more ADLs or IADLs (GAO 1995, p. 19).

Measurement	Examples of Basic Functions
Activities of daily living (ADL)	Bathing
	Dressing
	Eating
	Getting in and out of a chair or bed
	Toileting
Instrumental activities of daily living (IADL)	Going outside the home
	Performing household chores
	Keeping track of household finances
	Cooking and preparing meals
	Using the telephone
	Taking medicine

SOURCES: "Long-Term Care, Current Issues and Future Directions." General Accounting Office, April 1995 (GAO/HEHS-95-109); "Long-Term Care–Baby Boom Generation Presents Financing Challenges." (Testimony 3/9/98) General Accounting Office (GAO/T-HEHS-98-107).

the number of people providing long-term care on an informal basis and the backgrounds of those individuals. According to McNeil (1999), approximately 9.3 million individuals provide 29 hours of informal care per week. That translates into slightly more than 14 billion hours of informal long-term care provided each year. The second study, sponsored by the National Alliance of Caregivers (NAC) and American Association of Retired Persons (AARP) in 1997, generated similar findings. Based on a sample of 1,509 English-speaking households, the study found that slightly more than 23 percent of all households in the United States provide an average of 17.9 hours of informal care of some form or another per week. Population estimates for the nation suggest that more than 22 million households provide some type of informal long-term care. The study also found that Asian and African-American households are somewhat more likely to provide informal care than Hispanic or White households.

The NAC and AARP study also found that the representative informal caregiver tends to be a married woman in her forties. She is most likely employed on a full-time basis, possesses at least a high school degree, and is of relatively modest means with a median household income of about $35,000 per year. Not surprisingly, most caregivers are related to the recipient with most entailing a relationship involving a daughter and her mother. Finally, in almost 80 percent of the cases the caregiver does not reside with the recipient of the long-term care.

Thus, the evidence appears to indicate that on a macro level a substantial amount of informal care is being provided on a routine basis throughout the U.S. economy. Whether the amount and intensity of informal care provided has increased or decreased over time, however, is difficult to determine given a lack of time series data. A comparison of the results of the NAC and AARP study for 1997 with a study by Wagner (1997) using 1987 data does provide some insights. The results indicate that while the demographic makeup of informal health care providers changed little over the period, the overall amount of care provided increased significantly. From 1987 to 1997 the number of households providing informal care increased from approximately 7 million to slightly more than 22 million. At the very least this rather substantial increase in the number of households providing some level of informal care indicates that "caregiving for an elder has become a 'normative' experience for US families" (Wagner, p. 2).

Structure of the Nursing Home Care Industry

The structure, conduct, and performance paradigm of industrial organization suggests that the structure of an industry matters. In conjunction with the firm's objectives and various government regulations, structure affects how intensely firms compete and ultimately their performance in the health and overall economy. Among the more critical factors influencing market structure are the number and size distribution of firms, the number and size distribution of buyers, and the height of any barriers to entry into the industry. We next assess each of these structural features with respect to the nursing home industry.

Number and Characteristics of Nursing Home Providers.   Table 15–1 provides estimates for the number, amount of beds, ownership status, size distribution, and occupancy rate of nursing homes in the United States. According to the data, roughly 15,000 nursing homes function in the United States with approximately 1.6 million beds.[3] These two figures suggest that the typical nursing home facility operates with about 100 beds, roughly one-half the bed-size of the typical hospital in the United States.

Most nursing homes are organized on a for-profit basis although the percentage has declined slightly over time. Data (not shown) also suggest that 80 percent of the nursing homes are Medicare and Medicaid certified and half of the nursing homes belong to a chain or group. About two-thirds of all for-profit nursing homes are members in a chain (Rhoades, Potter, and Kraus, 1996). The data in table 15–1 also indicate the percentage of

---

[3]For consistency, every attempt was made to include figures only for freestanding nursing homes with nursing home beds. Some nursing homes provide only independent living or personal care services and others are hospital based. A total of 16,840 nursing home units existed in 1996. About 77 percent were freestanding nursing homes with nursing home beds, 11 percent provided independent living services, and 11 percent were hospital based.

TABLE 15-1

Characteristics of the Nursing Home Industry

	1986	1991	1996
Nursing Homes	16,388	14,744	14,930
For-profit	75%	71%	66%
Not-for-profit	20	24	26
Government	5	5	8
Nursing Home Beds (1,000)	1,507	1,558	1,633
For-profit	72%	70%	67%
Not-for-profit	22	24	24
Government	7	6	9
Size Distribution			
3–74 beds	46%	35%	36%
75–199 beds	48	57	56
200+	7	8	8
Occupancy	92%	91%	89%

SOURCE: Data for 1986 and 1991 are from the 1993 and 1996 issues of the *Statistical Abstract of the United States*, respectively. Data for 1996 are obtained from Jeffrey Rhoades, D.E.B. Potter, and Nancy Krauss. "Nursing Homes—Structure and Selected Characteristics, 1996" at http://www.meps.ahcpr.gov.

nursing homes in the smallest bed-size category, 3–74 beds, has tended to decline over time while the percentage of nursing homes in the largest bed-size category, 200 or more beds, has remained fairly constant over time. As a result, the survivorship principle suggests that the 75–199 bed-size category may be the optimal size given that most nursing homes find it best to operate in this bed-size range over time. We will examine later what econometric studies tend to suggest about the existence of scale economies in nursing homes. Finally, the data in table 15–1 imply that the occupancy rate of the typical nursing home in the United States is approximately 90 percent and that occupancy has declined marginally over time. The 90 percent nursing home occupancy rate is dramatically higher than the 60 to 70 percent occupancy rate observed in the hospital services industry.

Taking all of the information together, we can get a clearer picture of the typical nursing home. The representative nursing home is organized on a for-profit basis and is most likely affiliated with a nursing home chain. It contains approximately 100 beds and 90 of those beds are occupied on a typical day. About 300 nursing homes operate in the typical state in the United States.

Buyers and Users of Nursing Home Services   Nursing home expenditures were slightly more than $92 billion in 2000. According to figure 15–1, four groups are primarily responsible for paying for nursing home services: the Medicaid program, the Medicare program, consumers, and private health insurers. The single largest payer of nursing home services is the Medicaid program, accounting for approximately 48 percent of nursing home expenditures. The next largest category of government funding is the Medicare program, accounting for about 10 percent of total funding.

FIGURE 15-1

Expenditures Shares for Nursing Home Services 2000

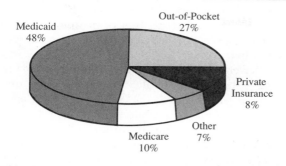

SOURCE: *Centers for Medicare and Medicaid Services.* National Health Expenditure Tables, table 7.

Individual consumers represent the second largest payer group for nursing home care services. Out-of-pocket costs account for 27 percent of nursing home expenditures and largely reflect the amount paid by the private payers for long-term care services. Roughly 40 percent of all nursing home residents are private-pay patients. Empirical studies find that the price elasticity of demand for private-pay nursing home care varies widely, ranging from –.16 to –2.30. Studies also find that the income elasticity of demand for nursing home care varies considerably with estimates ranging from –.38 to 2.27 (Reschosky, 1998). As one might expect, price and income tend to be more elastic for those elderly individuals who are either married or less chronically ill (Reschosky, 1998) because home care represents a viable alternative in these two cases. The availability of informal care is another determinant of the demand for long-term care by private-pay individuals.

Finally, private insurers represent the next largest payer for nursing home care at 8 percent of the cost. Most of the reimbursement pays for short-term post-acute nursing home services. Presently, only a small percentage of individuals have private insurance coverage for long-term care. We will take up the reasons for the low long-term care insurance coverage rate later.

In sum, data suggest that most nursing home care is paid for by federal and state governments, reflecting the large amount of short-term services provided to individuals under the Medicare program and long-term services provided to individuals under the Medicaid program. The government, because of its dominance in the market, may exert some influence on the operation and performance of short-term Medicare and long-term Medicaid nursing home services. Out-of-pocket costs remain sizable for nursing home care. Studies find that the demand for nursing home care by private payers is more elastic with respect to price and income compared to the demand for medical care. The elastic nature of the private demand for nursing home care services may also place a limit on the ability of an individual nursing home to raise price or reduce quality below the competitive level.

Barriers to Entry   As discussed throughout the text, barriers to entry play an important role in the structure, conduct, and performance of an industry. Simply put, barriers to entry reduce the degree of potential competition and thereby may provide existing firms with some market or monopoly power depending on the degree of actual competition. The monopoly power may show up in high prices and/or reduced quality of care. It was also pointed out in earlier chapters that barriers to entry may be government created (e.g., certificate of need programs, government franchises, or patents) or because of technical considerations (e.g., economies of scale, high sunk costs, learning curve effects, or exclusive control over a necessary input).

As mentioned in earlier chapters, econometric studies examine the existence of scale economies by estimating cost functions for goods or services. The estimated cost function shows the isolated empirical relationship between total operating costs and some measure of output or size after controlling for other determinants of costs such as input prices, quality of care, and patient case-mix. According to Rosko and Broyles (1988), "most research findings suggest that scale economies are minimal in the nursing home industry and that there are no pronounced scale effects beyond 40 beds" (p. 253). Therefore, it follows that scale economies do not represent a significant entry barrier into nursing home markets.

Sunk or irretrievable costs may cause a barrier to entry into an industry. Irretrievable costs may involve initial investments or assets that cannot be easily salvaged when a firm exits the industry. Contestability theory suggests that markets are more contestable or potentially competitive when sunk costs are low because new entrants realize they can leave an industry relatively costlessly if economic circumstances do not turn out as initially suspected. Conversely, if sunk costs are significant, firms will be reluctant to enter new markets, *ceteris paribus*. We saw in Chapter 13 that hospitals entail huge sunk costs because of the immense cost and time involved in hospital construction. Nursing homes, however, are much smaller on average than hospitals. In addition, unlike hospitals with numerous floors and wide elevators, nursing homes tend to have one or two floors to minimize access problems of chronically ill residents. Also, unlike hospitals, very little diagnostic and therapeutic equipment is necessary to provide nursing home care. The upshot is that much less sunk costs are involved in nursing home care than hospital care with the implication that sunk costs most likely do not seriously inhibit entry into the nursing home marketplace.

Certificate of need programs may represent a serious entry barrier in the nursing home industry. Recall that CON laws require that new and existing health care providers, like nursing homes, obtain approval before building new medical facilities or purchasing new capital items. CON laws are designed to control the amount of capital devoted to medical care as a way of controlling health care costs. However, if enforced too stringently, CON laws might result in inefficiency if too much capital is discouraged, competition is stymied as a result, and monopoly pricing ensues. Consequently, the effect of CON laws on the behavior and performance of nursing homes remains an empirical issue.

Unfortunately, only a few studies have examined empirically the impact of CON laws on the provision of nursing home care. After controlling for a host of factors such as income, age composition, and the state Medicaid reimbursement rate, Gulley and Santerre (2003) found that the existence of a state CON law program had no impact on the number of nursing homes or the number of nursing home beds per elderly persons across the 3,040 counties in the United States in 1991. As Harrington et al. (1997) note, the ineffectiveness of CON laws in reducing the number of homes and beds may result from the "lack of coordination with other regulatory programs, lack of significant compliance mechanisms, politicized review processes, and high approval rates for most requests" (p. 575).

Focusing on the growth rather than the level of nursing home beds, Harrington et al. (1997) found that the presence of a CON/moratorium program does matter. Specifically, Harrington et al. determined empirically that state regulations measurably slow the growth of nursing home beds. What remains to be determined is whether the reduction in the rate of growth is optimal from a societal perspective. While the reduced growth in nursing home beds may help to contain the rising costs from excessive capital creation, it may also provide existing nursing homes with some market power. If so, existing nursing homes may desire CON laws because of the resulting market power. But according to Harrington et al., "the nursing home industry in general has been strongly ideologically opposed to CON and moratorium regulatory controls" (p. 586).

In sum, the nursing home industry contains a relatively large number of nursing homes with low market shares. Barriers to entry are relatively low, especially in areas without binding growth regulations such as CON laws. While the typical nursing home most likely faces a downward-sloping demand curve because most residents prefer locations near friends and relatives, the individual nursing home probably has very little control over price since it faces the countervailing power of government and the highly price elastic demand of private buyers. From a structural perspective, the nursing home industry comes closest to resembling a monopolistically competitive industry.

Structure of the Home Health Care and Hospice Industry

Similar to the nursing home industry, we now conduct an analysis of the structure of the home health care and hospice industry. Once again, the characteristics of the seller and buyer side of the market are discussed to assess the structural competitiveness of the market. These structural features become important when evaluating the conduct and performance of the industry.

Number and Characteristics of Home Health Care and Hospice Care Providers   Because of its dynamic nature, agencies may provide either home health care services or hospice care, or both. Haupt (1998) differentiates between home health care and hospice care in the following manner:

> *Home health care is provided to individuals or families in their place of residence to promote, maintain, or restore health or to maximize the level of independence while minimizing the effects of disability and illness, including terminal illness. Hospice care is defined as a program of palliative care and supportive care services that provides physical, psychological, social, and spiritual care for dying persons, their families, and other loved ones.*

Given that home health care agencies can potentially provide both home health and hospice care, the following information on the number of providers refers to those institutions providing either type of care unless noted differently.

About 13,500 home health and hospice care agencies existed in 1996, increasing dramatically by 70 percent from just four years earlier. The sharp increase in the number of agencies occurred largely in response to the shift away from hospitals and nursing homes in an effort to contain health care costs. The 13,500 agencies provided services to approximately 2.5 million patients in 1996. While over 50 percent of the agencies were organized on a for-profit basis, for-profit agencies serviced slightly less than 41 percent of all patients.

Most of the care provided by for-profit agencies was directed toward home health care rather than hospice care.

Not-for-profit providers accounted for about one-third of all agencies but one-half of all patients; comparable government figures were 11 and 9 percent, respectively. In both absolute and relative terms, not-for-profit home care and hospice care agencies treated many more hospice patients than for-profit agencies. Most agencies, 92 percent, are Medicare and Medicaid certified. Nearly one-half of all agencies were affiliated with a group or chain and slightly over one-quarter were operated by a hospital. Thirty-seven percent of all agencies were freestanding institutions.

In sum, the typical home health care patient is cared for by a not-for-profit agency that is affiliated with either a chain of home care agencies or a hospital. Also, the typical home care agency is likely to be Medicare and Medicaid certified and services approximately 185 patients throughout the year. While not noted previously, there are 220 patients per agency located in a metropolitan area but only 111 patients per agency in non-metropolitan areas.

Buyers and Users of Home Health Care Services   Home health care costs amounted to approximately $32 billion in 2000. The largest payer for home health care services, amounting to 39 percent of all purchases, was the federal government, with the bulk of these funds coming from the Medicare program. Private insurers were responsible for 23 percent of total expenditures, while out-of-pocket expenses picked up an additional 20 percent. The remaining 18 percent came from other public and private sources. It should be pointed out that the Medicaid program does not currently reimburse for long-term care provided in the home. Generally, home health care is demanded because a person is receiving long-term custodial services, recovering from an illness or a surgical procedure, or receiving hospice care. The demand for home health care, both in the short and long term, depends on the out-of-pocket price for home health care, out-of-pocket price for institutional care, the wealth of the individual, the availability of informal care, and the demographic characteristics of the individual.

Barriers to Entry   Entry barriers are most likely minimal in the home care services industry. Since the provision of the services takes place in the home, very little capital is necessary. Hence sunk costs play virtually no role. While most home care agencies are Medicaid and Medicare certified, which could cause an entry barrier, some states, such as Ohio, have as many unlicensed home care agencies as certified.

Economic theory suggests that cost structure characteristics such as scale and scope economies or learning curve effects might prohibit the entry of new firms. Cost characteristics do not appear particularly binding on the entry of new firms, however. For example, Kass (1987), in a study of 1,704 home health agencies using 1982 data, finds that economies of scale and scope are not substantial. For another study on approximately 100 home health agencies in Connecticut over the period from 1987 to 1991, Gonzales (1997) finds similar results, showing that economies of scope are fully exhausted at nine services (e.g., skilled nursing care, physical therapy, occupational therapy, etc.). Given that most of the home health agencies in the sample normally provided between 7 to 11 services, scope economies do not seem to provide existing home health agencies with a cost advantage over new ones. While Gonzales does provide some evidence for scale economies, the relation between size and total costs does not appear to be particularly sizable. Specifically, Gonzales finds that a 10 percent increase in size, as measured by home visits, leads to a 7.6 percent increase in costs. Therefore, the average cost curve is relatively flat such that the per-unit cost of production is fairly close for both small- and large-sized home health care agencies, *ceteris paribus*.

The Structure of the Long-Term Care Industry: A Summary

It is difficult to judge the degree of structural competitiveness in the long-term care industry. Long-term care tends to take place in local markets because elderly people wish to remain fairly close to family and friends. Consequently, detailed micro-information on the number and size distribution of nursing home and health care agencies are necessary before conclusions can be drawn about the structural competitiveness of the long-term care industry in each local market area.

Having stated this limitation, long-term care most likely can be treated as a monopolistically competitive industry. There appears to be a sufficient number of actual competitors. For example, one nursing home competes against others and also with home health care agencies for patients. Also, for some recipients of long-term care, informal care remains an alternative to formal care. Moreover, most studies find that the demand for private-pay long-term care, particularly nursing home care, is highly elastic with respect to price. In addition, sources of technical barriers to entry such as economies of scale, sunk costs, and chain organizations do not seem to reduce the degree of potential competition. Only CON laws and other government-created barriers limit the entry of new firms. We next assess how the conduct of the long-term care industry is influenced by its monopolistically competitive nature.

THE CONDUCT OF THE LONG-TERM CARE INDUSTRY

In this section of the chapter we discuss how various external circumstances such as government regulations influence the behavior of long-term care providers. The price and quality of long-term care are two of the behavioral issues discussed. Virtually all of the discussion focuses on the nursing home industry because that is where most research has been directed. The monopolistically competitive nature of the nursing home industry, and the resulting downward-sloping demand curve, suggest that individual nursing homes may have some latitude in determining the price charged for private long-term care. Up against this framework, we examine the effect of Medicaid reimbursement, as a type of price regulation, on the behavior of nursing homes. We also examine if type of ownership matters and the impact of market competition on the behavior of nursing home care providers.

The Dual Market Model of Nursing Home Pricing

The nursing home industry provides an interesting but complex setting to examine the pricing behavior of individual firms. Complexities result because, on a routine basis, nursing home decision makers must question the financial consequences of admitting patients who seek care on either a short- or long-term basis and who may privately pay or receive insurance coverage from public programs like Medicare or Medicaid. Consequently, decision makers in nursing homes must recognize the trade-offs involved and simultaneously determine the price charged and number of patients for each type of service and payer category. In this chapter we ignore short-term nursing home care because our concern is solely with issues relating to the delivery of long-term nursing home care. Neglecting short-term care is not too problematic because, as we saw when we examined the market structure of long-term care providers, most individuals receive long-term rather than short-term care in nursing homes.

We also saw that the dominant payers for nursing home care are private individuals who pay out of pocket and the Medicaid program. These two purchasers add an interesting twist to the pricing issue. While each state government sets the price paid by its Medicaid program for long-term care, the individual nursing home must still determine how many private-pay and Medicaid patients to treat and the price charged to private payers. Luckily for us, Scanlon (1980) provides an insightful model to investigate this choice-making process of an individual nursing home. A graphical illustration of his dual market model is provided in figure 15–2.

Dollar values are shown on the vertical axis and the total number of private-pay and Medicaid patients are shown on the horizontal axis. The aggregated demand curve facing the individual health care provider has three distinct segments. The first segment, labeled AB, shows the private demand that lies above the Medicaid reimbursement rate of P_M. The second segment, BC, represents the Medicaid reimbursement rate of P_M for a particular number of Medicaid eligible individuals in the market area, as measured by the horizontal distance BC. The third segment, CD_P, reflects the remaining portion of the private-pay demand. The curve AMR_P indicates the marginal revenue associated with the first segment of the private-pay demand curve. Given that the Medicaid reimbursement rate is independ-

---

FIGURE 15–2
The Dual Market Model of Nursing Home Behavior

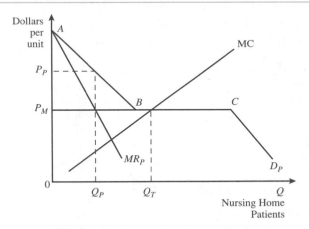

Lines AB and AMR_P represent the demand and marginal revenue curves for private-pay patients. Line segment BC represents the Medicaid reimbursement rate of P_M for the number of individuals eligible for Medicaid coverage in the market area. Line segment CD_P identifies the remainder of the private demand curve. The nursing home admits $0Q_T$ patients because the marginal revenue of $P_M = $ MC. Of the total patients, $0Q_P$ are private pay and the remaining portion Q_PQ_T, represents the number of Medicaid patients. Private-pay patients pay P_P for nursing home care. Because the horizontal distance Q_PQ_T, representing the number of Medicaid patients admitted, is less than the horizontal distance BC, showing the number eligible for Medicaid coverage, an excess demand for Medicaid nursing home care exists in the market area.

ent of the number of Medicaid patients, P_M also reflects the marginal revenue associated with treating each additional Medicaid patient.

The profit-maximizing nursing home continues to treat additional patients as long as the additional revenues compensate for the added costs, MC. Thus, in equilibrium, the nursing home treats a total of $0Q_T$ patients where P_M = MC. Of the $0Q_T$ patients, $0Q_P$ are private-pay patients because they add more to profits over that range (i.e., $MR_P > P_M$). The number of Medicaid patients lie between Q_P and Q_T. The theoretical model indicates that private-pay patients pay a higher price than Medicaid patients for the same services. According to the figure, each private-pay patient pays P_P, whereas the health care provider receives P_M for each Medicaid patient. In addition, the figure suggests that excess Medicaid demand exists at the government-established price of P_M because the horizontal distance between Q_P and Q_T, the number of admitted Medicaid patients, is less than the horizontal distance BC, reflecting the number of Medicaid eligible individuals in the market area.

An interesting policy question concerns what the government might do to reduce any excess demand for nursing home care. As one option, the government might raise the Medicaid reimbursement rate. As the Medicaid fee increases, the horizontal segment of the MR curve shifts upward along the MC curve and the nursing home expands its number of Medicaid patients relative to the number of private-pay patients. The exact number of additional Medicaid patients depends on the slopes of the private demand and marginal cost curves. Flatter curves imply that more Medicaid patients are admitted in response to a higher Medicaid reimbursement rate.

Notice, according to the analysis, that private-pay patients are required to pay a higher price if the Medicaid reimbursement rate is increased. Gertler (1989) points out another possible consequence of a higher Medicaid reimbursement rate when a capacity constraint exists such as a CON law. Recall from Chapter 5 that higher quality shifts demand upward to the right and lower quality shifts it to the left. In response to a higher Medicaid reimbursement rate, Gertler notes that nursing homes may react by lowering quality instead of, or in addition to, raising the private-pay price. Both actions reduce the quantity demanded of nursing home care by private-pay patients and provide additional rooms for the marginally more profitable Medicaid patients. Consequently, private-pay patients may pay a higher price and/or receive a lower quality of care as a result of the higher Medicaid reimbursement rate if a capacity constraint exists. It should be pointed out that Medicaid patients also face a lower quality of care because it is illegal and also may not be cost effective for nursing homes to provide different levels of care to private-pay and Medicaid patients. For one reason, complementarities exist with respect to providing various activities such as food and laundry services to both private-pay and Medicaid patients. Although reduced, as long as the resulting quality of care is beyond the level of care provided in private homes, both private-pay and Medicaid patients may find it preferable to remain in the nursing home. Thus, when a capacity constraint and excess Medicaid demand exist, higher Medicaid reimbursement may be associated with reduced quality. Gertler (1989), Nyman (1985), and Zinn (1994) all find that a higher Medicaid reimbursement lowers quality.[4]

---

[4]Using more recent data, Grabowski (2001) finds that higher Medicaid reimbursement has only a small negative impact on quality, pointing to a lessening of the capacity constraint over time because of the elimination of CON laws in many states and a decline in nursing home utilization.

Raising the Medicaid reimbursement rate is likely to be a costly public policy option. Taxes on the general public must be raised to support the increased subsidy, especially if the higher price causes more individuals to become financially eligible for Medicaid coverage. Also, the nursing home may earn excess economic profits if price increases relative to average cost and entry barriers exist. If entry barriers do not exist, however, the greater profitability may create an incentive for new firms to enter the nursing home industry in the long run. Entry will shift down the private demand curve facing each individual nursing home and could result in a lower price paid by private-pay patients.

Another policy option is for the government to directly subsidize the costs of providing nursing home care. The subsidy reduces the marginal costs of production and shifts the MC curve downward. The lower marginal cost, in turn, creates an incentive for the representative nursing home to admit more Medicaid eligible patients. Once again, however, this may be a costly alternative, as general taxes must be increased to cover the subsidy to nursing homes.

The Effect of Alternative Payment Methods

While useful for predicting the impact of changes in the Medicaid reimbursement rate or marginal costs on the behavior of nursing homes, the static analysis of figure 15–2 may ignore some dynamic aspects of the reimbursement issue. As discussed in previous chapters, third-party payers may pay health care providers in a number of different ways. For example, the payment from the state government to the nursing home may be based on the actual cost at each nursing facility or some fixed amount based independently on some industry-wide standard. Differences in payment methods matter because they influence how individual nursing homes behave over time in terms of costs, quality of care, and patient case-mix. Some examples may highlight the differences.

First, suppose a state government sets the reimbursement rate for the next period based on the nursing facility's actual costs of servicing Medicaid patients. In fact, many states paid for nursing home care using retrospective cost-based reimbursement systems before 1980 (Coburn, Fortinsky, McGuire, and McDonald, 1993). Because of the retrospective and facility-specific nature of the reimbursement method, the nursing home faces less incentive to control costs, realizing it can simply pass on any cost increases to the state government. The higher costs will impose a greater tax burden on the general public. There is a silver lining to this dark cloud, however. If the nursing home can easily pass on any cost increases to the state government, it may be less likely to compromise quality of care and more likely to admit patients in more severe case-mix categories.

Second, suppose a state government sets a flat rate independent of actual facility costs or prospectively sets the reimbursement rate at the industry average projected forward with an automatic annual adjustment for inflation. The important consideration is that no allowance is made for actual costs incurred by the nursing facility for either the flat rate or prospective payment method. Nursing homes are permitted to keep any profits but must also incur losses if actual costs exceed the Medicaid reimbursement, so they are at financial risk for any cost overruns. In this case the nursing facility faces an incentive to control the costs of servicing patients. Lower nursing home costs imply lower taxes for the general public but also mean that nursing homes may control costs by skimping on the quality of care or by practicing cherry-picking behavior. As a result, patients in the heavier case-mix categories may experience admission discrimination, and those that are admitted may not be provided with the proper quality of care.

As we can see, the government faces a policy dilemma not only when establishing the level of reimbursement but also with the method of reimbursement under Medicaid. Some hybrid forms of reimbursement exist that attempt to rectify some of the weaknesses of pure retrospective or prospective systems. One such method is case-mix adjusted reimbursement, which tries to compensate each nursing facility based on its particular patient case-mix and may include financial penalties and/or rewards to encourage efficient behavior. Price regulations like these, while well intended, can be difficult in practice to design correctly and typically involve substantial administrative costs (e.g., see Nyman and Connor, 1994).

Empirical studies tend to find that the reimbursement method influences the incentives of nursing homes with respect to costs, quality, and patient case-mix. In terms of costs, an early study by Frech and Ginsburg (1981) used national data for 1973 and 1974 with the number of inpatient days and input prices specified as typical arguments in a cost function and also controlled for the type of reimbursement, among other factors. The authors found that pure cost reimbursement without ceilings was associated with the highest costs. Specifically, compared to simple flat-rate systems, pure cost reimbursement led to costs that were 21 percent higher in the typical home. They also found that prospective reimbursement systems led to costs that were between pure cost and flat-rate reimbursement. The exact outcome depended on whether the prospective rates were established on the basis of the industry or the individual facility's experience in a previous year. When prospective rates are based on a facility's cost experience in the previous period, incentives are diluted and more resemble cost reimbursement. Using cost data for 1978 to 1980, Holahan and Cohen (1987) reached a similar conclusion that prospective and flat-rate systems generally reduced cost growth more than retrospective payment.

In terms of quality, Zinn (1994) found that both fixed rate and prospective systems led to fewer RNs per resident and worse process quality (a greater percentage of patients restrained and greater percentage not toileted, respectively) when compared to retrospective reimbursement. Case-mix reimbursement was found to increase the number of RNs per resident and improve process quality (lower percentage not toileted) relative to cost reimbursement. Using national data for 1987, Cohen and Spector (1996) found that in states with fixed reimbursement, nursing homes use more lower skilled and fewer higher skilled professional nurses than homes in states with cost-based approaches. Finally, for case-mix, based on national data for 1981, Cohen and Dubay (1990) determined that nursing homes respond to flat-rate systems by decreasing the severity of their case-mixes through admission discrimination and also decrease their staffing levels.

INSIGHT 15-2

The RUG III Classification System

Case-mix reimbursement has become a widely adopted method for the public financing of nursing care. For example, a case-mix approach forms the basis for the new prospective payment system for skilled nursing facilities under the Medicare program. Also, many state Medicaid programs now rely on some type of case-mix reimbursement for long-term care.

(continued)

Compared to flat-rate reimbursement, case-mix reimbursement provides less financial incentive for nursing homes to practice admission discrimination against individuals with severe mental, physical, or social limitations. If designed appropriately, case-mix reimbursement can also create an incentive for relatively independent individuals to receive community rather than more costly institutionalized care.

A way of sorting individuals into different case-mix categories is critical for the successful implementation of case-mix reimbursement. Since the early 1990s, many states adopting case-mix reimbursement have relied upon the Resource Utilization Group (RUG III) classification model (Arling and Daneman, 2002). RUG III is a model for classifying nursing home residents into homogeneous groups according to common health characteristics and the amount and type of resources used. The RUG III system was developed as part of the multi-state Nursing Home Case Mix and Quality demonstration project. The classification system was designed using characteristics from the Minimum Data Set (MDS) and wage-weighted staff time. The MDS is a federally mandated resident assessment instrument used to assess residents' physical, mental, emotional, cognitive, and functional limitations and strengths. The MDS must be administered to all residents, regardless of payer type, in Medicare and Medicaid certified facilities at time of admission, quarterly, annually, and when significant changes in residents' conditions occur.

Residents are classified into different RUG cells based on their clinical conditions, extent of services used, and functional status. First, the RUG III system hierarchically arranges patients into seven major groups based on certain clinical conditions. For example, rehabilitation, which includes residents with the most intensive need for services, is one category. It is divided into five levels of intensity based on the total minutes of therapy received per week, the days of therapy per week, and the number of different types of therapy received.

Next, the seven major groups are segmented based on an ADL index or other factors such as the presence of nursing rehabilitation. The ADL index is based on the amount of support required for the ADL activities of bed mobility, transferring, toilet use, and eating, and it ranges from 4 (fully independent) to 18 (totally dependent). Continuing with our example, 14 rehabilitation RUG cells result from the categorization process when combined with the breakdown of patients based on the ADL index.

Residents whose clinical conditions do not require skilled therapy are classified into six additional groups, which descend in order of severity, the number of services used, and the amount of time and resources required to care for the residents. The six groups are extensive services, special care, clinically complex, impaired cognition, behavioral problems only, and physical functioning reduced. Like rehabilitation services, patients are further disaggregated into different RUG cells for these six groups based on the ADL index and other factors.

In total, the classification system results in 44 different RUG cells to which a case-mix index is assigned. The dollar amount of the case-mix reimbursement is determined by multiplying the case-mix index by the monetary conversion factor established by the third-party payer. If case-mix reimbursement rates are set correctly, the health care provider faces less incentive to practice admission discrimination against patients with severe limitations.

Scale Economies with Respect to Quality

Notice in the previous discussion that nursing homes may respond to changing external circumstances by altering the quality of care. Generally a trade-off exists between costs and quality of care. The severity of the trade-off depends on whether scale economies hold with respect to quality. Figure 15–3, where total costs are shown on the vertical axis and the level of quality is depicted on the horizontal axis, helps to clarify this point. Notice that two curves, $0A$ and $0B$, are drawn in the figure. Both curves show how much it costs to provide varying levels of quality at a representative nursing home. Suppose we begin with costs of C_0 and, correspondingly, a quality level of X_0 in each case. Now suppose that policymakers wish to reduce nursing home costs to C_1. Notice the degree to which the level of quality must change to accommodate the reduction in costs in the two cases. In the case of curve $0A$, quality declines by a relatively small amount to X_1^A, but for curve $0B$ quality falls by a much larger amount to X_1^B. The difference in the reduction of quality can be explained by scale economies. Curve $0B$ reflects decreasing costs or increasing returns with respect to quality so costs increase proportionately slower than quality. Consequently, it takes a relatively large change in quality to achieve a given level of cost savings. Curve $0A$, in contrast, reflects increasing costs or decreasing returns so smaller reductions in quality can attain a given level of cost savings.

In an imaginative paper, Gertler and Waldman (1992) measured scale economies with respect to quality in nursing homes. Based upon some relatively sophisticated theoretical and empirical modeling techniques, they found that the nursing home cost function exhibits diseconomies of scale in quality. As a result the authors point out that policies aimed at improving quality will be very costly. Policies aimed at cost savings, however, can be

FIGURE 15–3
The Cost Savings from Quality Reductions

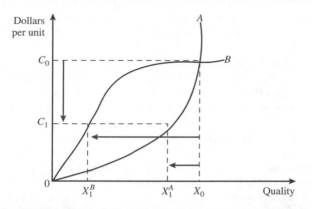

Curve $0B$ depicts scale economies with respect to quality whereas curve $0A$ shows diseconomies of scale with respect to quality. The graphical model suggests that quality must be sacrificed a great deal to achieve a given cost savings of C_0C_1 when scale economies hold. Conversely, the model indicates that quality improvements come at a much larger cost when the quality/cost relation exhibits diseconomies of scale.

achieved with very small reductions in quality. For example, the authors determined that an increase in the Medicaid reimbursement rate lowers quality as the Scanlon model with a capacity constraint predicts. However, the quality reduction was relatively small at two-hundreds of one percent whereas the cost savings were relatively larger at two-tenths of one percent given a one standard deviation increase in Medicaid reimbursement. As another example, the authors found that increased market competition improves quality. More specifically, an increase in competition, as measured by a one standard deviation reduction in the Herfindahl-Hirschmann Index, raised quality by only 2.5 percent but increased costs by a much larger 20 percent.

Ownership and Conduct

According to property rights theory, ownership status may also influence how institutions behave. In for-profit organizations, individuals claim private ownership to any residual profits. In contrast, public and not-for-profit institutions are subject to a nondistribution constraint, meaning that any residual earnings cannot be distributed to private individuals (Hansmann, 1996). As a result, some theorists believe that the lack of property rights to any residual profits provides less of an incentive for public and not-for-profit organizations to operate with least cost methods of production. However, other theorists point out that although not-for-profit organizations do not maximize profits, they do pursue goals such as quantity and quality maximization. Alternative goals can be more easily realized when costs are held to a minimum.

Although the theory may be suspect, a relatively large number of studies have supported the basic prediction of property rights theory in the case of nursing homes. One of the more cited studies, Nyman and Bricker (1989), compared the technical efficiency of not-for-profit and for-profit nursing homes. **Technical efficiency** exists when a given amount of output is produced with the fewest inputs. The authors employed a linear programming technique called **data envelopment analysis (DEA)** to determine the factors that influence the technical efficiency of a sample of nursing homes operating in Wisconsin. Briefly, this technique identifies those benchmark firms that produce a fixed level of output with the fewest inputs. The inputs used in the Nyman and Bricker study included total nursing hours, total social service worker hours, total therapist hours, and total all other hours in an average day.

The benchmark firms are then used as a reference set to calculate an efficiency score for the remaining firms in the sample. The benchmark or most efficient firms are assigned a score of 1, while the less efficient firms are given scores less than 1 depending on their level of technical inefficiency. The efficiency scores in Nyman and Bricker's sample ranged from .226 to 1.

The efficiency scores are then regressed on a series of independent variables to determine the factors that influence the extent to which nursing homes efficiently utilize inputs. In their study, the factors used in the regression equation included a dummy variable controlling for the ownership status of the nursing home. The dummy variable, profit, equaled 1 if the nursing home was a for-profit firm and zero if it was organized on a not-for-profit basis. The hypothesis was that for-profit homes have higher efficiency scores as the basic property rights theory indicates.

Nyman and Bricker's findings indicate that for-profit nursing homes employed 4.5 percent fewer inputs per patient day than otherwise comparable not-for-profit homes. The authors' findings are consistent with the predictions of the managerial expense preference model, as discussed earlier in the context of not-for-profit hospitals. Because managers of not-for-profit nursing homes are not pressured by owners to operate in an efficient manner, they increase costs by expanding discretionary expenditures and employing more than the minimum amount of inputs. The authors go on to state that if for-profit managers similarly acted in an inefficient manner, the owners would replace them. If the findings of this study are generally indicative of managerial behavior in the nursing home industry like other studies such as Nyman, Bricker, and Link (1990), Fizel and Nunnikhoven (1992), and Chattopadhyay and Heffley (1994) tend to confirm, ownership status does affect the performance of nursing homes. In the absence of an ownership constraint, managers of not-for-profit nursing homes act in an inefficient manner by overemploying labor inputs and operating at a point above the cost curve of otherwise similar for-profit nursing homes.

In their study, Nyman and Bricker attempted to control for quality differences among nursing homes by specifying the number of Medicaid certification code violations and other indirect measures of quality in the regression equation. Controlling for quality is particularly important when it comes to a service such as nursing home care because fewer labor inputs per patient may reflect a lower level of quality rather than greater efficiency. Their approach to holding quality constant is troublesome, however. Like the number and types of patients and inputs, the level of quality is also a variable decided by nursing home administrators. Stated in econometric terms, the level of quality is endogenous to the individual nursing home—a choice variable decided within the model—and not an exogenous variable, a parameter determined outside the model. The failure to properly specify quality as an endogenous variable could have led to improperly drawn conclusions.

In fact, theory suggests that not-for-profit organizations, because of the attenuation of property rights, may provide better quality of service than for-profits do when asymmetric information exists. Without sufficient consumer information, for-profit organizations may have more incentive to engage in opportunistic behavior in the process of maximizing profits. Not-for-profit institutions, in contrast, have less incentive to take advantage of consumers because of the nondistribution constraint. Consequently, not-for-profit status may signal an interest in quality over profits and serve as a guarantee of quality assurance, much like a trademark does.

Using a large sample of nursing facilities for 1998, Harrington, Woolhandler, Mullan, Carillo, and Himmelstein (2001) examined if the level of quality varied systematically across nursing homes with different ownership structures. As a measure of quality the authors used the number of deficiencies as revealed by state inspections at a total of nearly 14 thousand nursing homes. According to their results, investor-owned nursing facilities averaged 5.89 deficiencies per home compared to 4.02 at not-for-profit homes and 4.12 at public nursing homes. After controlling for other determinants of quality such as patient case-mix by an ADL index and the proportion of Medicaid patients, among other factors in a multiple regression model, the authors found that an investor-owned hospital was associated with .679 more deficiencies than an otherwise comparable not-for-profit nursing home. Moreover, a nursing home belonging to a chain was associated with .633 additional deficiencies than an otherwise comparable freestanding nursing facility, and for-profit nursing homes are more likely to be a member of a chain.

The authors also provide several cautionary comments, however. First they point out that the number of deficiencies may yield an incomplete measure of quality; other measures such as patient outcomes and satisfaction would be useful supplements. Second, the authors note inspectors' decisions may be somewhat subjective and biased against for-profit homes. Third, they mention that the ADL may not be a sufficient measure of patient case-mix severity. Despite these qualifications, the authors believe "the most obvious explanation for our findings is that profit seeking diverts funds and focus from clinical care" (p. 1454).

But showing empirically that not-for-profit nursing homes provide higher quality of care than do for-profits does not necessarily offer evidence supporting the theory that for-profits pursue profits over quality when asymmetric information exists. Quality is just one of the many attributes that make up a good and service. For a given price, more quality generally means less and lower amounts of other types of attributes. In this case, people who value quality highly will be drawn to those institutions offering high levels of quality. Decision makers of not-for-profit nursing homes may maximize quality or quality and quantity rather than profits as discussed in Chapter 13. As a result quality may be higher in not-for-profit nursing homes not because of asymmetric information but because of differences in the taste for quality and alternative goals of organizations. It is important to understand the theoretical reason for any disparity in quality. If ownership form by itself results in quality differences, public policy might be directed toward encouraging one type of ownership form over another if quality improvement is an issue. However, if asymmetric information is the cause for quality differences, public policy might be aimed at offering improved information to consumers.

Chou (2002) sorts out the differences by comparing the effect of ownership status on the quality of nursing home care in the presence and non-presence of asymmetric information. For the test, Chou measures quality of care by mortality and several adverse health outcome measures (decubitus ulcers, dehydration, and urinary tract infection). Asymmetric information is defined as existing when nursing residents have no spouse or no child visiting within a month after admission. Chou argues that nursing home residents are usually frail and disabled; therefore, family members often serve as representatives to monitor or evaluate the quality of care.

Chou's empirical findings prove to be very interesting. The results for two of the four quality indicators suggest that not-for-profit nursing homes provide better quality than for-profits when asymmetric information exists. That is, when the residents lack family members to monitor the service, for-profit nursing homes face less incentive to maintain the quality of care. Chou's empirical results support the theory that for-profit nursing homes practice opportunistic behavior and sacrifice quality of care for more profits when asymmetric information exists.

Grabowski and Hirth (2002) take the analysis a step further by analyzing if competitive spillovers from not-for-profits cause for-profits nursing homes to deliver higher quality of care. The authors argue theoretically that patients in for-profit nursing homes will be better informed because not-for-profits attract a greater proportion of uninformed consumers given the quality assurance signal generated by the nondistribution constraint. Grabowski and Hirth test their theory by empirically examining how the market share of not-for-profits affects nursing home quality while holding constant a host of demand and supply side factors. They find that a higher not-for-profit market share improves for-profit and market-wide nursing home quality as measured by several structural, procedural, and outcome indicators. Grabowski and Hirth conclude by noting that if not-for-profits "have a competitive advantage in "trustworthiness" while for-profits have greater incentives for efficiency, intersectoral competition can yield better outcomes than a market consisting exclusively of one type of firm." That is, competition from not-for-profits raises the quality of nursing home care while competition from for-profits places limits on inefficiency and the exercise of market power.

Market Concentration and Nursing Home Conduct

Conventional microeconomic theory predicts that more competition results in lower prices and greater quality. Costs of production are unaffected by competition according to conventional microeconomic theory because firms are assumed to be motivated by maximum profits. The drive for maximum profits ensures that firms operate on and not purposely above the cost curve.

We have been learning throughout this text that conventional microeconomic theory does not always relate perfectly well to medical markets. Motivations other than profit maximization, third-party reimbursement, low out-of-pocket prices, and rational consumer ignorance are some of the various features of medical markets that point to that conclusion. It is also important to realize that some of these features apply only to specific medical markets and not to all of them. For example, we learned in an earlier chapter that hospitals reacted to increased competition by raising quality, costs, and prices prior to the 1980s because of the so-called medical arms race. But the medical arms race does not apply to the caring rather than curing that primarily takes place in nursing homes. Furthermore, unlike the market for hospital services, the nursing home market may be characterized by excess demand. That is why it is so important to carefully consider the theoretical relation and review the empirical findings between conditions like market structure and the conduct of firms in each specific medical market such as the nursing home industry. To that we now turn our attention.

Market Concentration and the Price of Nursing Home Care Following in the footsteps of industrial organization theory, health economists have been interested in the relationship between the degree of competition, as measured by market concentration, and the pricing behavior of medical firms of various kinds of which nursing homes are no exception. Nyman (1994) was among the first to apply IO theory to an analysis of market behavior in the nursing home industry. Nyman begins by deriving and specifying the price markup function or Lerner (1934) index facing the individual nursing home in the following form.

(15–1) $$(P_i - C_i)/P_i = 1 / [\alpha|E_m| + (1 - \alpha)|E_i|]$$

In equation 15–1, P_i and C_i stand for the price charged by the individual nursing home and marginal cost, respectively, so the expression on the left-hand side of the equality symbol represents the firm's markup of price above marginal cost expressed as a percentage of price. The expressions $|E_m|$ and $|E_i|$ stand for market demand elasticity and the individual nursing home's price elasticity of demand stated in absolute terms. Because of fewer alternatives, market demand elasticity is less than the price elasticity of demand faced by the individual nursing home and depends on the availability of other substitutes for nursing home care like home health agencies and informal care provided in the home.

The α parameter reflects the conjectural variations held by nursing homes in the market and captures if the typical nursing facility expects the others to match or offset its output decision. If nursing homes expect matching or coordinated behavior, α equals 1 and the markup depends on market elasticity alone. The markup is the largest and equals that of a monopoly when firms in a market perfectly collude.[5] If firms compete rather than collude, α equals 0, and the individual nursing home's markup depends on the degree to which the firm can successfully differentiate its product from others in the same market. A less differentiated product means a higher price elasticity of demand facing the individual nursing home and hence a lower markup of price over the costs of production.

Based upon equation 15–1, Nyman uses multiple regression analysis to investigate the determinants of the markup percent across a sample of nursing homes in Wisconsin using 1988 data. Since Nyman examines the factors affecting the markup on private payers of nursing home care, he uses the Medicaid reimbursement rate instead of marginal cost in the Lerner index, as the analysis surrounding figure 15–2 suggests. That is, the opportunity cost of caring for a private-pay patient is the additional revenues that would be received from caring for a Medicaid patient. Nyman specifies a Herfindahl-Hirshman Index of market concentration with the county defined as the relevant geographical market in the multiple regression equation along with other variables affecting market elasticity and the price elasticity of demand facing the individual firm. Recall from the discussion in Chapter 8 that matching behavior and collusion are more likely to prevail in highly concentrated markets. Thus, one expects a direct relation between the HHI and the markup of private price relative to the Medicaid reimbursement rate.

For his sample, the average markup over the Medicaid fee for a skilled nursing facility was 18.2 percent and the average HHI was 2,240. Although Nyman estimated a positive coefficient on the HHI, the estimate was not statistically different from zero, suggesting that a marginal change in the level of market concentration had no appreciable impact on the price markup charged by the typical nursing home. An insignificant estimate on the HHI might reflect that nursing home markets were highly contestable in Wisconsin because of low entry barriers at that time. The threat of potential competition may have forced nursing homes to charge a price independent of the low degree of actual competition given that matching behavior was not expected because of low entry barriers.

More recently, Mukamel and Spector (2002) used 1991 data for a sample of for-profit nursing homes in New York to estimate the price elasticity of the private demand facing individual nursing homes to assess their degree of market power. They implicitly assumed that the representative nursing home expects offsetting behavior (i.e., α equals zero in equation 15–1) and thus $(P_i - MC_i)/P_i = 1/|E_i|$. As noted above, lower price elasticities of demand suggest more power to elevate price above the marginal costs of production. Mukamel and Spector consider that CON laws may or may not be binding, different degrees of patient case-mix severity, and that the Medicaid reimbursement rate may replace marginal cost in the Lerner index as noted earlier. The authors calculate that the average price elasticity facing the individual nursing home lies between 3.46 and 3.85, depending on whether estimated marginal costs or the Medicaid rate is used to calculate the Lerner index. The authors note that these elasticities are relatively low and result in compara-

---

[5]The expression on the right-hand side of the equality symbol can be referred to as a modified Lerner index of monopoly power. The Lerner index of monopoly power holds that the markup of price over marginal cost as a percentage of price equals one divided by the price elasticity of market demand, or $(P - MC)/P = 1/E_m$. For a price-taker facing a perfectly elastic demand curve, E_m equals infinity, so $(P - MC)/P$ equals zero as perfect competition suggests. The Lerner index suggests that a monopolist's power over price falls with a higher price elasticity of market demand.

tively high price markups to private payers. Mukamel and Spector go on to note that the "large price mark ups and the possibility that nursing homes behave as monopolists in the private pay market raise the question of whether this aspect of the market should be regulated" (p. 419).[6]

Market Competition and Quality   Another important issue concerns how the degree of market competition influences the quality of nursing home care. From a theoretical perspective, the impact of market concentration, one aspect of competition, on quality is theoretically ambiguous. On the one hand, when a few for-profit firms command a large share of market sales and competition is thereby diminished, traditional IO theory suggests that the few firms may face an incentive to restrict both output and quality in an attempt to earn greater profits. On the other hand, when few firms exist in the market, consumers may be able to gather better information on potential suppliers, which can promote better quality (Pauly and Satterthwaite, 1981).

Zinn (1994) attempted to clear up the theoretical ambiguity by empirically examining the relation between various measures of market competition and alternative structural and process measures of the quality of nursing home care. Process measures of quality included the proportion of residents not toileted, the prevalence of urethral catheterization, and the prevalence of physical restraint usage. The number of registered nurses per nursing home resident represented the structural measure of quality. The unit of analysis was the 2,713 counties in the 48 contiguous states of the United States. Among the measures of competition were market share concentration, measured by the HHI based on bed capacity in the county; the presence of an entry barrier, measured by a statewide moratorium on nursing home bed construction; and the availability of substitutes, measured by home health staff per capita and the percentage of women aged 15 through 64 not in the workforce (i.e., availability of informal care).

Control variables included education of the county population, excess bed capacity, proportion of for-profit facilities, and three variables measuring patient case-mix. Data were for 1987. Using multiple regression analysis, Zinn estimated the impact of each independent variable on each of the four quality measures and obtained some insightful results relating to the effects of market competition. First, she found that increased market concentration, as indicated by a higher HHI, tends to improve the quality of care, particularly process quality. Hence the empirical results suggest that better quality of care results when fewer nursing homes exist in a market, *ceteris paribus*, providing support for the Pauly and Satterthwaite (1981) argument that less providers means more-informed choices and greater competition.

While Zinn finds empirically that more actual competitors results in lower quality of nursing home care, she also finds that entry barriers are associated with reduced quality. That is, registered nurse staffing tends to be lower and the use of physical restraints higher in markets where a moratorium on nursing home bed construction erects barriers to new competitors. Consequently, her empirical results indicate that more actual competition lowers quality, but greater potential competition (i.e., no entry barriers) raises quality. The

---

[6]An elasticity of demand of 5.13 can be inferred from Nyman's (1994) study using his average measures for private price of $66.67 per patient day and the average Medicaid reimbursement rate of $53.76 per day.

reason for the inconsistent finding is not readily apparent unless it is the size and not the number of nursing homes that really matters. Recall that the HHI increases with fewer firms but also with more unequally distributed sizes. Perhaps quality of care is better when nursing homes produce a greater volume of services. That might be the case if practice makes perfect in the nursing home industry. Unfortunately, Zinn does not control for the average size of the typical nursing home in the market to test if this hypothesis is valid.

The empirical results regarding the availability of substitutes on the quality of nursing home care were also mixed. The availability of home health resources was found to be associated with higher levels of RN staffing but not with any of the process quality measures. The proportion of women aged 15 to 64 not in the workforce, representing an informal substitute for nursing home care, was found to lower the proportion of residents not toileted but is associated with the greater use of physical restraints and lower RN staffing. Zinn explains that it is possible that fewer women participating in the workforce translates into a smaller labor pool for nursing homes.

Conduct of the Long-Term Care Industry: A Summary

We have examined theoretically and empirically a large number of issues relating to how long-term care providers react to influences such as the level and type of Medicaid reimbursement, form of ownership, and market competition. Because few studies focus on the home health care industry, the analysis focused solely on how these various factors influence the private price of nursing home care, the quality of nursing home care, and patient case-mix. What follows is a brief summary of the findings.

Under normal conditions, the dual market model of nursing home behavior predicts that a greater Medicaid reimbursement rate increases the access of Medicaid recipients to nursing home beds. Interestingly, the dual market model also predicts that the quality of nursing home care suffers if the Medicaid reimbursement rate increases when a capacity constraint exists. According to the model, nursing homes lower quality to reduce the number of private-pay patients and thereby make additional room for the marginally more profitable Medicaid patients. While earlier empirical studies have found an inverse relation between Medicaid reimbursement and nursing home quality, some recent evidence suggests that the relation may no longer hold because an excess demand condition may no longer exist in the nursing home industry. Excess demand may no longer apply because of the elimination of CON laws in some states and a growing availability of alternatives to nursing home care such as home health care and assisted living arrangements.

The method of Medicaid reimbursement was also found to matter in terms of the incentives faced by nursing homes. Nursing homes face less financial risk when Medicaid payments are more flexible and facility specific. Thus, we can think of the degree of financial risk imposed on nursing homes as ascending from retrospective, facility-specific prospective, class prospective, to flat-rate reimbursement systems. Empirical studies clearly suggest that the reimbursement method matters because of financial incentives. Studies tend to suggest that more restrictive methods are associated with lower nursing home costs and reductions in quality and patient case-mix severity. Recently, Chen and Shea (2002) question if the cost reductions brought on by restrictive payments systems reflect efficiency or simply unwanted cuts in quality. Using a national sample of 4,635 nursing homes and 1994 data, the authors find that costs are unaffected by prospective reimbursement when quality differences among facilities are controlled for and the endogeneity of quality variables is addressed. As a result, like Zinn (1994) and some others, Chen and Shea argue that the level and method of Medicaid reimbursement should be linked to the quality of care.

Next we addressed the efficiency and quality implications of the type of ownership. Property rights theory suggests that for-profit nursing homes may behave more efficiently than not-for-profits although the precise objective of the latter ownership form is theoretically unclear. Empirical studies indicate that for-profit nursing homes are more technically efficient and produce at a lower cost than not-for-profits. However, many question if the cost savings associated with for-profit nursing homes reflect lower quality when compared to otherwise similar not-for-profits. Indeed, the theory implies that not-for-profit organizations may provide a higher quality of care than for-profits when an asymmetry of information exists. Chou's (2002) study empirically supports the theory.

We then examined the impact of market competition on the price and quality of nursing home care. The Lerner index of monopoly power tells us that the ability of firms to elevate price above the marginal costs of production depends on market elasticity of demand, the individual firm's elasticity of demand, and the conjectural variations formed by the firms in the industry. Using multiple regression analysis, Nyman was unable to empirically link the Lerner index to a Herfindahl-Hirschman Index of market concentration using a sample of nursing homes in Wisconsin in 1975. Directly calculating the Lerner index, Mukamel and Spector (2002) find empirically that the mean price elasticities calculated for nursing homes in New York State in 1991 ranged from 3.46 to 3.85, quite low for an industry professed to be monopolistically competitive. Further evidence is needed on this issue before wide-sweeping conclusions can be drawn about the relative profitability of nursing homes in the private pay segment of the industry.

Finally, we turned our attention to the impact of market competition on the quality of care and relied on Zinn's (1994) study for empirical insights. With respect to market competition, her study analyzes the impact of market concentration, entry barriers, and the availability of substitutes on various structural and process measures of quality. We discussed how the relation between market concentration and quality of care is theoretically unclear and depends on whether less firms in an industry lead to a restriction of quality or less firms means more informed choices. Zinn's results lend empirical support for the latter hypothesis as greater market concentration is found to improve the quality of nursing home care. Entry barriers were found to be associated with lower levels of quality and the empirical results concerning the availability of substitutes was mixed. It is unclear what policy implications arise for the proper structure of the nursing home industry given that greater market concentration improves whereas entry barriers lower the quality of care.

THE PERFORMANCE OF THE LONG-TERM CARE INDUSTRY

We conclude the chapter with an examination of the overall performance of the market for long-term care. This presents a number of interesting challenges because the long-term care industry is somewhat unique and differs in three important respects from the previous medical industries discussed. First, long-term care is generally associated with chronic care and care for those with disabilities rather than acute care. As a result, care is generally provided on a long-term basis and the cost may be spread out over a number of years, possibly even decades. Second, much of the long-term care provided is informal in nature and provided by family and friends. Since no direct payment is made for the care provided, the cost is indirect and involves foregone wages. Third, the number and type of formal health providers is diverse and runs the gamut from skilled nursing home facilities to

INSIGHT 15-3

Is There an Excess Demand for Nursing Home Care?

Policy analysts have long questioned whether an excess demand for Medicaid patients exists in the market for nursing home services. Excess demand occurs when, at some price, quantity demanded exceeds quantity supplied. Private prices typically adjust to eliminate market imbalances but government-set prices like Medicaid reimbursement may not because of bureaucratic delays, among other reasons. As we learned earlier, the dual market model theorizes that Medicaid patients may be unable to acquire needed nursing home services when the price for private-pay patients is higher than the Medicaid reimbursement rate. Under these circumstances, nursing homes prefer private-pay patients and only after all these patients are accommodated will beds become available for Medicaid patients.

Testing for the existence of excess demand in the nursing home market has proven to be a difficult task for researchers. Nyman (1993) approached the problem by developing a three-part empirical test and estimating a trio of utilization equations where the dependent variable equaled either the number of total, private-pay, or Medicaid patients. For the first part of the test, Nyman (1993) estimated the extent to which the total number of nursing home patients was positively related to total number of beds available, the idea being that if there exists an excess demand for nursing home services, beds would be highly correlated with utilization. Or, put in other terms, a bed built is a bed filled when excess demand exists.

The second part of the test involved examining the empirical relationship between beds and the number of private-pay and Medicaid patients. If an excess demand situation exists, the marginal bed would be filled by a Medicaid patient rather than a private-pay patient, the assumption being that the needs of private-pay patients have already been satisfied, making the additional bed available for a Medicaid patient. The third portion of the test examined if private patients crowd out Medicaid patients in areas with greater overall need for care.

Using 1988 county-level data, Nyman performed the three-part empirical test for three states: Wisconsin, Minnesota, and Oregon. The empirical results are interesting in that they do not support the proposition that the market for nursing home services is subject to excess demand. In particular, the empirical results find no evidence of excess demand in Wisconsin and Oregon and only limited evidence of excess demand in Minnesota. The implication is that Medicaid patients are not crowded out of the nursing home market by private-pay patients who are willing to pay a higher price for long-term care.

SOURCE: John Nyman. "Testing for Excess Demand in Nursing Home Care Markets." *Medical Care* 31 (1993), pp. 680–93.

assisted living centers with everything in between, such as meals on wheels programs and senior centers. To keep the discussion manageable, we focus primarily on nursing homes and home health care. The objective of this section is to assess the overall performance of the long-term care industry by examining such measures as expenditures on long-term care; private insurance for long-term care; the price of nursing home care; and the utilization of nursing home, home health care, and hospice services.

Expenditures on Long-Term Care

Informal Expenditures on Long-Term Care   Calculating the cost of informal care poses an interesting challenge to researchers because they must impute the economic cost of the caregiver's time. For example, what is the economic value of a caregiver's time when she spends all day Saturday helping her grandmother with some household chores and bringing her to the doctor? Or, what is the economic value of a semi-retired man's time who drives every afternoon to his father's house to help him prepare his meals?

A study sponsored by MetLife (1997) estimated the cost of informal caregivers on U.S. businesses and focused on the loss in productivity that results when full-time employees provide informal care. According to the report, overall productivity can be negatively impacted in six ways. First, the firm incurs recruitment and training costs when an employee leaves to provide care. Second, the firm experiences absenteeism costs when an employee fails to show for work because of caregiving responsibilities. Third, productivity diminishes when an employee cuts the workday short to provide care. For example, an employee may show up late for work, leave work early, or take an extended lunch break to attend to caregiving problems or issues. Fourth, the firm bears the cost of workday interruptions when employees address caregiving responsibilities while at work. A case in point would be an employee who spends the better part of the morning at work on the phone with a physician's office straightening out whether her mother received the proper medical treatment during her last visit with the doctor. Fifth, there are the costs associated with an eldercare crisis. Such costs occur when, for example, an employee is forced to take time off from work because his father fell down the stairs at home and fractured his hip. Finally, the authors consider the increase in administration costs that result when supervisors take time during work to accommodate the needs of those employees addressing caregiving issues.

The study estimates the total cost of lost productivity because of caregiving at approximately $11.4 billion a year, with the replacement and training cost being the largest single component equaling just under $5 billion a year. This estimate should be considered low because it focuses on only one segment of informal health care providers: full-time workers.

Taking a slightly different approach, White-Means and Chollet (1996) estimate the imputed average wage or value of time for caregivers to equal $6.23 per hour in 1989 dollars. The average imputed wage was estimated to be relatively higher for males, $11.84, and full-time workers, $9.26, and substantially lower for females, $6.01, and caregivers who did not work, $5.26. Overall, these value of time estimates are lower than you might expect because, in addition to estimating a wage equation based on a human capital model, the authors corrected the results to control for those individuals who were not employed.

Finally, Arno, Levine, and Memmott (1999) estimate the cost of informal caregiving using current market wage rates. According to the authors, their main focus is to estimate "the potential cost . . . of informal caregiving if informal caregivers had to be replaced by paid workers" (p. 184). Based on the results generated from the NAC and AARP study (1997) referred to earlier in the chapter, the authors estimate that approximately 24 billion hours of informal care are provided on an annual basis. Multiplying this figure by an hourly wage of $8.18, the authors calculate the market value of informal care to equal $196 billion in 1997.[7]

The astute reader will notice that the economic value of informal caregiving estimated by Arno, Levine, and Memmott (1999) is substantially higher than the previous two studies. Three reasons account for the difference. First, they consider the work effort of all informal caregivers and not just full-time workers, as was the case in the MetLife study. Second, Arno, Levine, and Memmott utilize the market wage rate rather than the imputed wage rate like White-Means and Chollet (1996). Third, the authors base their analysis on a more contemporary data set that considers slightly higher nominal wages and a greater prevalence of informal caregiving.

Overall, these three studies indicate that a substantial amount of informal care is provided at a significant cost to the U.S. economy. Unfortunately, differences in methodology across studies and changes in the amount and type of informal care provided over time make it difficult to trace the increased cost of informal care with any degree of accuracy. Most researchers would agree, however, that the economic value of informal care has increased in recent years because of increases in the amount of informal care provided and the opportunity cost of providing care to caregivers in terms of foregone wages.

Formal Expenditures on Long-Term Care

Data in table 15–2 examine the extent to which formal expenditures on long-term care have changed over time. The analysis focuses exclusively on expenditures for nursing home care provided by freestanding nursing homes and home health care delivered by freestanding home health facilities. We focus on these two types of facilities for two reasons. First, the data are available and consistent, which provide us with the opportunity to trace expenditures over time. Second, since expenditures on nursing home and home health care represent the bulk of the institutional expenditures on long-term care, they can serve as a proxy for total formal expenditures.

In 1970 expenditures on nursing home care and home health care equaled $4.2 billion and $200 million, respectively, and in total they accounted for only 6 percent of total national health expenditures. The next two and one-half decades saw a phenomenal growth in expenditures on nursing home and home health care. As a result, by 1995 nursing home expenditures and home health care represented 10.6 percent of national health care expenditures. The largest increase in percentage terms took place in home health care as expenditures on freestanding home health care facilities increased at an annual rate in excess of 20 percent from 1970 through 1995. This increase was the direct result of an increase in both the number of individuals receiving home health services and an increase in the number of visits per patient (MedPac, 1999).

---

[7]This wage rate was chosen because it equaled the average of the minimum wage of $5.15 and the average hourly wage for home health aides, $11.20. Since the skill level needed to provide informal care is likely to be somewhere between that of an unskilled worker and a skilled home health aide, the authors opted to average the two wage rates.

T A B L E   1 5 – 2

Nursing Home and Home Health Care Expenditures in the United States, Selected Years 1970–2000

	1970	1980	1990	1996	1997	1998	1999	2000
National Health Expenditures								
(billions of dollars)	$ 73.1	$ 245.8	$ 695.6	$ 1,040.0	$ 1,091.2	$ 1,149.8	$ 1,215.6	$ 1,299.5
Annual rate of increase*	10.6%	12.9%	11.7%	5.0%	4.9%	5.3%	5.7%	6.9%
Nursing Home Expenditures								
(billions of dollars)	$ 4.2	$ 17.7	$ 52.7	$ 79.9	$ 85.1	$ 89.1	$ 89.3	$ 92.2
Annual rate of increase	17.4%	15.4%	14.1%	7.1%	6.5%	4.7%	0.2%	3.3%
Home Health Care Expenditures								
(billions of dollars)	$ 0.2	$ 2.4	$ 2.6	$ 33.6	$ 34.5	$ 33.6	$ 32.3	$ 32.4
Annual rate of increase	14.5%	26.9%	22.1%	10.2%	2.6%	-2.6%	-3.7%	0.3%

*This is the average annual increase from the previous period. For 1970, it equals the average annual increase from 1960 and for 1996 it equals the average annual increase from 1995.

SOURCE: *Centers for Medicare and Medicaid Services*. National Health Expenditures Tables, table 4.

As was the case with national health care expenditures, the rate of increase in nursing home and home health care decelerated in the mid-1990s. For example, in 1997 the rate of increase in expenditures on nursing home care fell to 6.5 percent, which was slightly more than the 4.9 percent increase in overall national health expenditures. Much of the decrease in the rate of growth in nursing home care expenditures can be attributed to a more modest growth in medical prices and increased use of alternative forms of long-term care such as home health care and assisted living facilities (Levit at al., 2002). Changes in the rate of growth of home health care expenditures have been much more volatile. The volatility results because home health care is one of the smallest categories in the national health accounts and even modest changes in spending generate significant changes in rates of growth. In 1996 home health care expenditures increased by over 10 percent and by 1997 they increased by only 2.6 percent.

From 1998 through 2000 expenditures on nursing home and home health care continued to grow, but at a much lower rate. In fact, home health care expenditures actually fell by over 2 percent in 1998 and by almost 4 percent in 1999. Most of this decrease can be attributed to changes in public policy that brought about a decrease in the proportion of medical expenditures financed through public sources in 1998 for the first time in a decade. The most significant change took place in the Medicare program with the passage of the Balanced Budget Act (BBA) of 1997 that called for significant savings by restraining payments to providers. The slight increase in spending in 2000 resulted from the Balance Budget Refinement Act (BBRA) of 1999. Faced with the criticism that the BBA of 1997 reduced spending too much and too quickly, Congress passed the BBRA of 1999 that limited or delayed some of new payment provisions (MedPac, 2000).

Taken together, these figures indicate that the economic cost of long-term care is substantial, with informal caregivers paying for the bulk of the care measured in terms of foregone wages. Using 1997 as a benchmark, it appears that nearly two-thirds of all long-term care provided in the United States is on an informal basis.[8] Extending the analysis one step further, expenditures for long-term care (both informal and formal) account for about one-quarter of all health care expenditures in the United States and represent the second largest spending category behind hospital care. While these percentages can only be considered "ballpark" at best, they do underscore the importance of long-term care and illustrate that informal caregivers are the mainstay of the U.S. long-term care health system.

Private Insurance for Long-Term Care

Given the high cost of long-term care, researchers have long wondered why so few individuals, particularly those at or approaching retirement age, have not purchased long-term care insurance. According to the Health Insurance Association of America, over 6.8 million long-term care policies had been sold by the end of 1999. While an impressive number, one has to keep in mind that at the same point in time there were nearly 74 million people at least 50 years of age in the United States. Among the factors contributing to the

---

[8]This figure was arrived at by dividing the total dollar amount of formal and informal care provided in 1997 into the cost of informal care as estimated by Arno, Levine, and Memmott (1999), or $196b/($196b + $119.6b) = 60.7 percent. The amount of formal long-term care provided was assumed to equal the combined value of nursing home expenditures ($85.1b) and home health care expenditures ($34.5b).

relatively small number of long-term insurance policies purchased are adverse selection, moral hazard, Medicaid crowding out, and intertemporal risk (Norton, 2000, and Cutler, 1996).

Adverse selection occurs because there is an asymmetry of information concerning the health status of potential consumers. When this situation develops high-risk individuals have the incentive to withhold information concerning their true health status from insurers and purchase long-term care insurance at premiums based on a pool of subscribers with better health. Over time premiums are driven upward as the high-risk subscribers consume more medical care than their healthier counterparts. Faced with the choice of paying high premiums, low-risk subscribers may elect not to renew their long-term care policies while potential new customers' policies may decide to self-insure and not purchase any long-term care insurance. The problem of adverse selection is particularly difficult in the market for long-term care because the potential population is heterogeneous and a relative lack of claims data make it difficult for insurance companies to accurately assess risk.

For example, Temkin-Greener, Mukamel, and Meimers (2000/2001) estimate that at least one out of seven individuals 65 years of age or older, who have been rejected for long-term care insurance because of poor health, pose no greater financial risk to the insurer than those who have been accepted. Adverse selection also appears to be impacting the demand side of the long-term care market. For example, Sloan and Norton (1997) found that those individuals who reported a high probability that they would need nursing home services in five years were more likely to purchase long-term care insurance, while Mellor (2001) found self-reported poor health to have a significant, yet marginal, impact on the probability of having long-term care insurance.

Moral hazard has also been offered as an explanation for the lack of demand for private long-term care insurance. In a now classic article, Pauly (1990) argues that the elderly prefer to receive care from family in their owns homes rather than from a staff of health care professionals in a nursing home, all else held constant. As a result, the elderly may shy away from purchasing private health insurance because it lowers the out-of-pocket price of formal care and provides their children with an inducement to institutionalize them if and when they need long-term care, or perhaps even prematurely. The incentive to substitute child-provided informal care with formal care results from the relative decrease in the price of formal care that occurs when long-term care insurance is present.

While the preference for informal care on the part of the elderly may decrease the demand for long-term care insurance, the want to protect bequests to family and friends may have just the opposite effect. Long-term care can be quite expensive and even a relatively short stay in a nursing home can wipe out a family's savings. To guard against the potential loss of a desired bequest, a risk-averse individual may purchase long-term health insurance. Thus, the desire to leave a specific bequest in a world where long-term care costs are difficult to project should increase the demand for long-term care insurance.

There is little empirical evidence supporting the notion that the elderly substitute child-provided care for long-term care insurance. For example, Mellor (2001) found the availability of informal caregivers had no statistical impact on whether an elderly person purchased a long-term care insurance policy or intended to purchase one. Sloan and Norton found that the existence of children had no impact on the likelihood of purchasing long-term health insurance. In addition, Sloan and Norton (1997) also found the bequest motive had no impact on the decision to purchase long-term care insurance. Specifically, those elderly who responded that leaving an inheritance was somewhat or very important were no more likely to purchase long-term health insurance than the rest of the sample.

Public support for long-term care through the Medicaid program may also dampen the incentive to purchase private long-term care insurance. Faced with the reduced risk of having to privately pay for long-term care because of the Medicaid program, some consumers may elect to forego the purchase of long-term care insurance. The basic question from an economic perspective is, therefore, whether private long-term care insurance and Medicaid can be considered substitutes. Sloan and Norton (1997) are careful to point out that private insurance and Medicaid can be considered only imperfect substitutes at best. Strict eligibility requirements necessitate that individuals deplete most of their financial assets before becoming eligible for Medicaid coverage. As a result, the Medicaid program offers little opportunity to protect assets that may be consumed in the future or bequeathed to loved ones. Coupled with this, elderly individuals on Medicaid coverage have to contend with the stigma of "going on public assistance."

The empirical evidence appears to support the notion that the demand for long-term care insurance is experiencing at least some degree of crowding out from the Medicaid program. Sloan and Norton (1997) found Medicaid crowding out for individuals over 70 years of age but not for those between the ages of 51 and 64. However, the marginal effects appear rather small, suggesting that we need to look elsewhere for an explanation as to why few people purchase long-term care insurance.

Cutler (1996) points out that the market for long-term care insurance is limited by the intertemporal risk that comes into play when insurers establish premiums. Recall from the earlier discussion on insurance in Chapter 11 that the insurer is responsible for managing the financial risk associated with establishing premiums. Relying on the law of large numbers, the insurer estimates the expected medical costs for a given population over a specified period of time. With that information in hand, the insurer sets the insurance premium to equal the expected benefits to be paid out plus any marketing and administration costs, taxes, and profits. Overall risk, which is reflected in profits in terms of the classic risk return trade-off, is minimized through diversification across a given population of potential policyholders.

With long-term care insurance, insurers are forced to assess risk over an extended period of time where the average cost of an insured event is likely to increase over time.[9] With this increase in cost over time comes increasing risk because the insurer finds it progressively more difficult to predict medical payments well off into the future. The problem is that in this situation the insurer cannot diversify risk across policyholders because everyone faces the same potential increase in costs due to higher input prices. Faced with the inability to lower risk through cross-sectional diversification, the insurer has no alternative but to increase premiums in excess of the expected payout or offer an indemnity type insurance policy. In the first case, the insurer increases the premium to compensate for the added risk of predicting health care costs well into the future by requiring a higher rate of profit. In the second case, the insurer forces policyholders to bear some of the risk of higher health care costs. For example, the policy may call for the insurer to pay up to $200 a day in the event that the policyholder enters a nursing home. If the cost of nursing

---

[9]Take the case of an individual who purchases a long-term health care policy at the age of 55. It may be 25 years or more before benefits are paid out for the first time.

home care is in excess of that amount, then the policyholder must pay the added expense out-of-pocket. To illustrate his point, Cutler notes that for a sample of 73 long-term health care policies in 1991, 72 had indemnity payments. In either case, the demand for long-term care insurance is likely to decrease because of intertemporal risk.

The theoretical and empirical research in this area clearly indicates that the decision to purchase long-term insurance is complex and involves a host of factors. Other variables found to impact the probability of purchasing a long-term health insurance policy include assets, income, age, and education. The positive and significant results for the assets and income variables make sense and suggest that those with greater wealth and income are more likely to purchase insurance because they have a greater incentive to protect against the possibility of spending down to qualify for Medicaid coverage. The positive and significant results for the age variable indicates that as people get older and the possibility of needing long-term care increases, so does the likelihood of purchasing insurance coverage. Finally, more highly educated people are found to be more likely to purchase insurance coverage (Mellor, 2001).

Prices for Nursing Home Services

Unfortunately, a lack of data prevents a detailed examination of the pricing behavior of nursing home and home health care facilities over time. What little information there is can be obtained from the National Nursing Home Survey that is periodically administered by the National Center for Health Statistics. These data appear in table 15–3. According to the survey results, the average monthly charge for all nursing home facilities was $186 in 1963. By 1985 the monthly charge increased almost eightfold to $1,456, and by the middle of the 1990s it topped $3,000. The most recent figures indicate that the average monthly charge for nursing home care equaled $3,891 in 1999, or $46,692 per year.

TABLE 15 – 3

Average Monthly Charge for Nursing Home Care, Selected Years 1963–1999

	1963	1973/74	1977	1985	1995	1997	1999
All Facilities	$186	$479	$ 689	$1,456	$3,135	$3,609	$3,891
Annual Rate of Increase*		9.9%	9.5%	9.8%	8.0%	7.3%	3.8%
Funding Source							
Own Income			$ 690	$1,450	$3,081	$3,643	$3,947
Medicare			$1,167	$2,141	$5,546	$6,037	$5,764
Medicaid			$ 720	$1,504	$2,769	$3,081	$3,505

*This is the average annual rate of increase from the previous period. For 1973/1974 the based year is assumed to be 1973.

SOURCE: Various Issues of *Health, United States* published by the National Center for Health Statistics Health Care Financing Administration. http://www.cms.gov.

The annualized rates of increase, also provided in the table, indicate that price increases for nursing home services were sustained throughout the entire period, hovering at between 9 and 10 percent much of the time. It was not until many of the cost constraints implemented in the mid-1990s began to take hold that the rate of increase began to cool down. By 1999, the average rate of increase fell to a modest 3.8 percent that year.

The information on monthly charges by funding sources in table 15–3 is interesting and merits a brief discussion. During the 1970s and into the 1980s the average rate of reimbursement for Medicaid patients was higher than that of private-pay patients. It was not until somewhere around 1990 that the situation reversed itself and the average monthly charge for private-pay patients exceeded the average charge for Medicaid patients. While these are only average figures and do not consider a number of factors such as the level and quality of care provided, they do appear to confirm the basic premise of the dual market model that private-pay patients pay a higher price for the same nursing home services than Medicaid patients. The high rate of reimbursement for Medicare patients in all likelihood can be attributed to the level of care received by those patients. For Medicare to cover skilled nursing home care, the patient needs to have a qualifying hospital inpatient stay of three consecutive days or more within 30 days of leaving the hospital. The general intent is to cover the cost of rehabilitation for a short period after hospitalization and such care is likely to be more expensive than custodial care, which is provided on a more long-term basis.

Other points of interest generated by the National Nursing Home Survey (2000) are that for-profit nursing homes appear to charge less than their not-for-profit and public counterparts and that the monthly charge for all facilities appears to be positively correlated with the size of the larger nursing home. For example, in 1999 for-profit nursing homes charged an average of $3,698 per month while not-for-profit and public nursing home charged an average of $4,225. At the same time, facilities with less than 50 beds charged $3,808 per month while nursing homes with 200 or more beds charged an average of $4,281. Unfortunately, these figures are difficult to interpret without additional information about the intensity of care provided.

The Utilization of Long-Term Care Facilities

Nursing Homes   Tables 15–4 and 15–5 supply information about the users of nursing home care based on a national survey of nursing homes conducted in 1997 and again in 1999 by the National Center for Health Statistics. Included in table 15–4 is an age profile of nursing home residents in 1999. In general, the data confirm our earlier point that the need for long-term care is heavily concentrated among the elderly population. According to the table more than 9 out of 10 nursing home residents were 65 years old or older, and almost 430 out of every 10,000 elderly persons resided in a nursing home in 1999. To no one's surprise, data in the table also indicate that the need for nursing home care increases rapidly with age among the elderly population. Almost one-half of all nursing home residents were 85 years old or older and more than one of six elderly above the age of 84 resided in a nursing home in 1999.

Table 15–5 provides additional information about the representative nursing home resident in 1997. Approximately three-quarters of all nursing home residents were female. This finding is not surprising given that females tend to outlive their male counterparts and are more likely to require assistance in older age either in nursing homes or in private

T A B L E   1 5 – 4

Distribution of Nursing Home Residents According to Age, 1999

Age Group	Percent of Nursing Home Population
Under 65 Years	9.8%
65 Years and Older	90.3%
65–74 Years	12.0%
75–84 Years	31.8%
85 Years and Older	46.5%

Age Group	Nursing Home Residents per 10,000 Population
All residents	59.1
Under 65 Years	6.6
65 Years and Older	429.2
65–74 Years	108.0
75–84 Years	429.7
85 Years and Older	1825.0

SOURCE: National Center for Health Statistics. *The National Nursing Home Survey: 1999 Summary* (June 2002).

T A B L E   1 5 – 5

Percent Distribution of Nursing Home Residents According
to Gender, Functional Status, and Length of Stay, 1997

	Percent of Nursing Home Population
Gender	
Male	27.8%
Female	72.2%
Functional Status	
Received no help	3.7%
Received help with 1 ADL	7.9%
Received help with 2 or 3 ADLs	49.8%
Received help with more than 3 ADLs	38.7%
Length of Stay Since Admission	
Less than 3 months	17.6%
Between 3 and 12 months	24.5%
1 year to less than 3 years	30.3%
3 years or more	27.6%

SOURCE: National Center for Health Statistics. *The National Nursing Home Survey: 1997 Summary* (July 2000), tables 11, 13, and 20.

residences. In addition, about 90 percent of all residents needed assistance with at least two ADLs. The information on the length of stay since admission is telling because it provides us with an understanding of the extent to which medical care is needed on a long-term basis. At the time when the survey was taken, only 17.8 percent of nursing home residents were at the facility for less than three months. More than half of the residents were in a facility in excess of one year, while more than one in four resided in a nursing home for more than three years. Overall, the average length of stay since admission was 892 days, or slightly more than two years and five months. This is in sharp contrast to a 7.3-day average length of stay for inpatient hospital care in 1997.

While these utilization figures paint an interesting profile of the current users of nursing home services, they do not tell the whole story. There appear to be some interesting trends beginning to emerge that are likely to have a profound impact on the market for long-term care services (Bishop, 1999). First, the extent to which the elderly rely on nursing homes for long-term care is diminishing. According to the most recent figures, while the number of elderly nursing home residents increased from slightly more than 1.32 million in 1985 to 1.47 million in 1999, the proportion of elderly in nursing homes has diminished from 46.2 to 42.9 per 10,000 population over the same time period.[10] Second, the intensity of care provided to nursing home residents has increased because of an increase in disabilities among elderly residents. In 1985, 74.8 percent of the elderly residents had dependent mobility while 40.5 percent had dependent eating. Those percentages grew to 80.4 and 47.4, respectively, in 1999. Bishop (1999) contends that these changes are the result of a decrease in disabilities among the elderly and an increased desire among the elderly to seek care in alternative settings such as home health care, adult day care facilities, or assisted living facilities. According to Cutler (2001), the steady decline in disability among the elderly can be attributed to enhanced medical technology and lifestyle changes. Other contributing factors may be improved socioeconomic status, diminished exposure to diseases, and the development and utilization of medical aids that allow the elderly to live independently for a longer period of time.

Thus, it appears that the nursing home industry has been simultaneously experiencing a significant decline in its patient population and an increase in the disability rate among those patients who require nursing home care. These trends may help explain some of the changes that have taken place in the nursing home industry over the past decades. For example, the increase in the level of care provided may in part explain the significant increase in the price of nursing home services that took place from the mid-1980s to the present. As noted earlier, the average monthly charge for nursing home care increased from $1,456 in 1985 to $3,891 in 1999. The decrease in the proportion of elderly in need of nursing home facilities may also help explain the recent decrease in the occupancy rate for nursing homes. From 1992 to 1999 the occupancy rate for nursing homes fell from 86.0 percent to 82.7 percent. Faced with a shrinking patient base coupled with increased competition from alternative long-term care providers, nursing homes have been forced to provide limited capacity.

Home Health Care and Hospice Care   A variety of demographic characteristics for home health care and hospice patients appear in table 15–6. Over 1.8 million patients utilized some

---

[10]Bishop (1999) points out that there is some evidence to suggest that the average length of stay has also decreased.

TABLE 15 – 6

Home Health Care and Hospice Patient Characteristics, 1998

	Home Health Care Patients	Hospice Patients
Number of Patients	1,881,768	79,837
	Percent Distribution	
Gender		
Male	33.6%	42.7%
Female	66.4%	57.3%
Age Group		
Under 65 Years	31.3%	21.6%
65 Years and Older	68.7%	78.4%
65–74 Years	19.7%	22.7%
75–84 Years	29.9%	32.9%
85 Years and Older	19.1%	22.7%

SOURCE: National Center for Health Statistics. *Health, United States, 2001* (2001), tables 88 and 89.

from of home health care in 1998, which is in sharp contrast to the 2.4 million that received home health care in 1996. This decrease reflects the cost containment and utilization controls mandated by the Balance Budget Act of 1997 for home health care. Only a tiny fraction of that total, 79,837, utilized hospice care in 1998.

In total this means that almost 3.8 million people utilized some type of formal long-term care either from a nursing home, a home health agency, or a hospice facility in the late 1990s. The data also indicate that females utilize formal long-term care more frequently than males, with the degree of gender imbalance being greatest for nursing home care. Finally, it appears that the elderly use formal care most intensively with the heaviest users being between the ages of 75 and 84 for home and hospice care, and over age 84 for nursing home care.

What Do the Demographics Tell Us About the Future of Long-Term Care?

Predicting what the future has in store for the long-term care market is, as you can imagine, a difficult task. However, longer life expectancies coupled with an aging baby boom generation should translate into a substantial increase in the demand for long-term care services.[11] At the turn of the new millennium, between 12 and 13 percent of the total population was 65 years or older and less than 2 percent was 85 years or older. By 2050 the

---

[11]For example, recent population projections estimate that the average life expectancies for males and females are expected to increase from 74.1 and 79.8 in 1999 to 81.2 and 86.7 in 2050, respectively (Hollmann, Mulder, and Kallan, 2000).

number of elderly is projected to make up 20 percent of the total population, with one out of twenty citizens being over the age of 85. Keeping in mind that over 90 percent of nursing home residents were over 65 years old in 1999, these projections indicate that the demand for long-term care is likely to dramatically increase over the next few decades.

These demographic changes notwithstanding, a number of factors may cause the demand for long-term care to increase at a rate lower than otherwise would be the case. For one thing, increased longevity does not appear to have a major impact on health expenditures. Lubitz, Beebe, and Baker (1995) estimated the lifetime Medicare expenses for a sample of beneficiaries and found total health expenditures to be only modestly impacted by longevity. Long-term expenditures are also likely to be impacted by overall health, everything else constant. It stands to reason that long-term care expenses will fall as the proportion of life spent in a relatively healthy state increases. We learned earlier that disability among the elderly has decreased by approximately 1 percent per year over the 1950s. If this trend were to continue into the future, it would have a significant impact on the individual demand for long-term care (Cutler, 2001).

Picking up on this point, Lakdawalla and Philipson (2002) argue that improved health coupled with increased life expectancy will impact the mix of formal and informal care provided along with the total amount spent on formal long-term care. The reason is relatively straightforward: a healthy elderly individual with little demand for medical care may become an informal supplier of health care. What is most interesting, however, is that the authors argue that impact on the supply of informal care depends on the degree to which increases in longevity and health impact men relative to women. If the increase in health and longevity impacts men more than women then the individual demand for long-term care may diminish, on average. If the opposite occurs, the individual demand for long-term care may increase.

Since women live longer than men on average, they generally spend more years alone and, therefore, have a greater need for formal care. Recall from table 15–5 that women made up 72 percent of all nursing home resident in 1997. When the relative supply of healthy men increases, elderly couples stay married longer and husbands become informal suppliers of care. As a result, the demand for formal care among women should diminish. If, on the other, hand, the increase in health and longevity is concentrated among women, the demand for formal long-term care should increase because women will spend even more time alone and without a spouse to provide informal care. Lakdawalla and Philipson test their hypothesis using panel data for 1971 through 1991. Their results generally support the contention that healthy aging is inversely related to the per-capita demand for formal long-term care. Healthy aging decreases the amount of formal care provided directly by "shrinking the base of people who need care, and indirectly, by raising the supply of healthy elderly who can provide care at home" (p. 305).

While improved health and longevity may dampen the individual demand for long-term care,[12] the sheer number of baby boomers reaching retirement age over the next few decades will ensure that the market demand for long-term care increases. One estimate

---

[12]Of course, increased income, enhanced quality, and changes in tastes and preferences may have the opposite effect on the individual demand for long-term care. The increased prevalence of long-term care insurance will also increase demand because it decreases the out-of-pocket price of formal long-term care.

has 76 million baby boomers born between 1946 and 1964 reaching retirement age by 2035 (GAO, 2002). With this anticipated increase in market demand comes a great many challenges concerning the availability of public and private funding and the relative mix of informal and formal care provided.

INSIGHT 15-4

Long-Term Care in Germany

The United States is not the only country wrestling with long-term care issues. In fact, U.S. citizens appear relatively young when compared to individuals residing in other OECD countries. Reinhardt, Hussey, and Anderson (2002) report that the percentage of people aged 65 years and older averaged 14.7 among OECD countries in 1999; the comparable statistic for the United States was only 12.3. Canada (12.4), Germany (16.7), and the United Kingdom (15.7), countries whose health care systems are typically compared to the U.S. System, all face a higher elderly population rate. While industrialized countries around the world face similar problems relating to long-term care, they have taken different paths towards meeting the needs of the elderly. This insight reports on long-term care in Germany, the only OECD country currently mandating universal social insurance for long-term care.

Germany adopted universal social insurance for long-term care in 1994. Prior to that date, Germany had a means-tested program for long-term care similar to that in the United States. Providing support and security to informal caregivers, shifting the balance of long-term care from institutions to home care, increasing attention to quality of care, providing communities with fiscal relief, increasing the supply of long-term providers, and increasing consumer choice were some of the goals behind the reform of long-term care in Germany.

The long-term care program provides extensive coverage for nursing home and home care for people of all ages without regard to their financial status. The social insurance is administered by the sickness funds and is financed by a uniform long-term care insurance premium fixed by law at 1.7 percent of salary. Both employers and employees are responsible for paying an equal share. Retirees pay half of the premium and pension funds pay the other half. To control program expenditures, both revenues and benefits are capped to some degree with revenues fixed by the predetermined contribution rate. Benefits are legislatively determined and therefore do not automatically adjust with inflation. Benefits are fixed by the disability level of individuals and the setting in which the long-term care takes place, as discussed below.

Federal law established the eligibility criteria for long-term benefits, which are the same for both institutional and non-institutional care. People are eligible for long-term care benefits if they have a mental or physical condition requiring a need for assistance that is expected to last at least six months. The minimum threshold for obtaining benefits is assistance with two ADLs and the need for help with some IADLs. Eligible people, at any level of disability, can choose institutional or home care. In 1998, 2.3 percent of the total population participated in the program, including 29.6 percent of the population of age 80 and

(continued)

older. Long-term care in non-institutional settings accounted for about half of all program expenditures. Roughly three quarters of all beneficiaries received care in non-institutional settings.

Expenditures per recipient are capped but the level of payment differs primarily according to disability level and if the care is received at home or in an institutional setting. If home care is received, the maximum expenditure also depends on whether the recipient chooses cash or services. Among those receiving home care benefits, the vast majority choose cash over services. Persons receiving cash benefits, which are much lower than the limits on service benefits, can spend the funds in any way they choose. The common assumption is that recipients give at least some of their cash to informal caregivers. Persons electing formal home care services choose among providers who have contracts with sickness funds. Beneficiaries are responsible for paying any difference between actual charges and the level of benefits received from the program.

Nursing home coverage includes basic care, medical care, and social activities, but not room and board or capital costs. Residents must pay any difference between actual costs and program benefits and are responsible for at least 25 percent of nursing home care costs. Individuals with the highest levels of disability may have the greatest disincentive to live in institutions because they pay a greater proportion of costs given that program costs do not rise as sharply as nursing home costs with respect to disability level. Social assistance, based on means-tested eligibility, is available for individuals unable to afford out-of-pocket costs for either home or institutional care.

Supply appeared adequate to meet need, at least within the first two years of the program. Both the number of home health care providers and nursing homes increased during the first two years. Waiting lists virtually disappeared. The new program, however, has not been very successful at fostering competition. Although communities may not prevent new providers from entering markets, sickness funds must contract with all providers, both not-for-profit and for-profit, that meet minimal standards rather than on the basis of price. Consumers can freely choose among the listed long-term care providers.

Quality of long-term care continues to be an important issue in the German system. Under existing national guidelines, providers are supposed to establish various internal quality assessment and assurance systems. However, many guidelines are vaguely worded and most standards stress structural rather than outcome quality. Although the quality of formal care remains a concern, the quality of informal care is more difficult to monitor and control. For persons receiving cash, the initial medical office assessment and the agency control visits are the primary quality mechanisms for informal care.

While not flawless, experts agree that the long-term care program in Germany has made substantial progress toward achieving its goals. Germany's changing demographics will most likely place great strains on its long-term care system in the future. The percentage of the population aged 90 and older is expected to rise appreciably. Other countries around the world can learn many lessons about instituting a universal long-term care insurance program by more carefully studying the experience in Germany.

SOURCE: This insight is based on Alison E. Cuellar and Joshua M. Wiener. "Can Social Insurance For Long-Term Care Work? The Experience of Germany." *Health Affairs* 19 (May/June 2000), pp. 8–25.

SUMMARY

Monopolistic competition best describes the market structure of the long-term care industry. A large availability of substitute providers exists in the industry and entry barriers are very low. The typical nursing home most likely faces a downward-sloping demand because people prefer convenient locations near former neighbors, relatives, and friends. The buyer side of the market is relatively concentrated with the federal and state governments representing highly influential buyers of both home health care and nursing home care.

Pricing and quality are two important conduct issues pertaining to long-term care. Empirical studies continue to sort the impact of reimbursement policies on the behavior of nursing homes. Recent studies indicate that there may no longer be an excess demand for nursing home services because of the elimination of CON laws and increased availability of alternative ways to acquire long-term care. Research also points out that reimbursement methods faced by nursing homes influence firm behavior because of financial incentives. It appears that more restrictive reimbursement schemes not only lower costs but also adversely impact the quality of care provided. Finally, the empirical evidence also corroborates the property rights theory as for-profit nursing homes appear to produce care at a lower cost than their not-for-profit counterparts but by providing lower quality of care when asymmetrical information exists.

Market competition also appears to impact both the price and quality of nursing home care. While more research needs to be done on the relationship between market competition and price in the nursing home industry before definitive conclusions can be drawn, economic theory suggests that ability of the firm to exercise control over price is dictated by market concentration. The empirical evidence does suggest, however, that greater market concentration is linked to improved quality of nursing home care.

The market for long-term care services has experienced profound changes over the last few decades and these changes are likely to continue into the near future. In the coming years, we are likely to see a significant increase in the demand for long-term care as baby boomers reach retirement age. While improved health and longevity may moderate the overall increase in the demand, the steep increase in the number of retirees will place a significant strain on funding sources for long-term care.

On the supply-side of the market, the delivery system for long-term care has become increasingly more diversified and has an almost endless list of community-based and institutional providers. For example, in recent years a host of community-based long-term care programs have been initiated aimed at augmenting the level of informal care provided by assisting those patients who have difficulty maintaining an independent lifestyle. Meals on wheels, home health care, and adult day care are but three examples of such programs. These community-based programs represent a low-cost alternative to skilled nursing home care because they either delay or avert altogether the decision to institutionalize an individual in need of long-term care. Institutional care is now provided in a number of alternative settings aside from skilled nursing home. For example, assisted living residences and continuing care retirement communities have become very popular in recent years.

While this can only be considered a cursory look at the supply side of the long-term care market, it does indicate that individual providers of long-term care are likely to face increasing competition in the coming years. This increase in competition will likely have an impact on the mix of informal and formal care as well as the total expenditures on long-term care.

REVIEW QUESTIONS AND PROBLEMS

1. Explain the various differences between the demand for long-term care and medical services.
2. List the different providers of long-term care.
3. Explain the profile of the typical informal long-term caregiver.
4. Identify the structural characteristics of the typical nursing home. Think in terms of ownership status, size, chain membership, entry barriers, etc.
5. Who is the main purchaser of nursing home services?
6. Discuss the role that entry barriers play in the nursing home industry.
7. Explain why the number of home health care agencies increased so dramatically in recent years.
8. Who is the largest payer for home health care services?
9. What role does Medicare and Medicaid serve in the home health care industry?
10. What does the empirical evidence suggest about scale economies in the home health care industry?
11. Use the Scanlon model to identify the impact of an increase of the Medicaid reimbursement rate on the private price for nursing home care and the number of private-pay and Medicaid patients.
12. Use the Scanlon model to identify the impact of an increase of the Medicaid reimbursement rate on the private price for nursing home care and the number of private-pay and Medicaid patients given a completely vertical marginal cost curve.
13. Explain theoretically how the method of reimbursement influences costs, quality, and patient case-mix. Note the trade-offs typically involved.
14. Explain why returns to scale are so important when it comes to quality improvements.
15. Discuss theoretically how a nondistribution constraint may influence costs and quality differences among nursing homes with different ownership structures. What are the general findings of studies examining the relation between ownership status and the costs and quality of nursing home care?
16. Explain why the relation between market concentration and the quality of care is theoretically unclear.
17. Identify and explain the intuition behind the Lerner index of monopoly power.
18. Suppose the price elasticity of market demand for nursing home care equals –3 and the individual nursing home's price elasticity of demand equals –6. The Medicaid reimbursement rate facing the nursing home equals $100 per day. Also suppose that because of a few nursing homes in the market and high barriers, the nursing home expects other nursing homes will match its behavior with perfect certainty. Calculate the price charged to private payers by the individual nursing home. How would the results change if the individual nursing home expected offsetting behavior with perfect certainty? How about with a 50 percent probability of off-setting behavior?
19. Discuss the factors that researchers must consider when estimating the cost of informal care.
20. Approximately what fraction of long-term care expenditures is informal care?
21. Identify and explain the reasons why so few people purchase long-term care insurance.

22. Provide a profile of the typical nursing home resident. How is this profile likely to change in the future and why?
23. Discuss the demographic changes taking place that are likely to impact the future of long-term care.

ONLINE RESOURCES

To access Internet links related to the topics in this chapter, please visit our web site at http://santerre.swcollege.com.

REFERENCES

Arling, Greg, and Barry Daneman. "Nursing Home Case-Mix Reimbursement in Mississippi and South Dakota." *Health Services Research* 37 (April 2002), pp. 377–95.

Arno, Peter S., Carol Levine, and Margaret M. Memmott. "The Economic Value of Informal Caregiving." *Health Affairs* 18 (March/April 1999), pp. 182–88.

Bishop, Christine. "Where Are the Missing Elders? The Decline in Nursing Home Use, 1985 and 1995." *Health Affairs* 18 (July/August 1999), pp. 146–55.

Coburn, Andrew F., Richard Fortinsky, Catherine McGuire, and Thomas P. McDonald. "Effect of Prospective Reimbursement on Nursing Home Costs." *Health Services Research* 28 (April 1993), pp. 45–68.

Chattopadhyay, Sajal, and Dennis Heffley. "Are For-Profit Nursing Homes More Efficient? Data Envelope Analysis with a Case-Mix Constraint." *Eastern Economic Journal* 20 (Spring 1994), pp. 171–86.

Chen, Li-Wu, and Dennis G. Shea. "Does Prospective Payment Really Contain Nursing Home Costs?" *Health Services Research* 37 (April 2002), pp. 251–71.

Chou, Shin-Yi. "Asymmetric Information, Ownership and Quality of Care: An Empirical Analysis of Nursing Homes." *Journal of Health Economics* 21 (2002), pp. 293–311.

Cohen, Joel W., and L.C. Dubay. "The Effect of Medicaid Reimbursement Method and Ownership on Nursing Home Costs, Case Mix, and Staffing." *Inquiry* 27 (1990), pp. 183–200.

Cohen, Joel W., and William D. Spector. "The Effect of Medicaid Reimbursement on Quality of Care in Nursing Homes." *Journal of Health Economics* 15 (1996), pp. 23–48.

Cuellar, Allison E., and Joshua Weiner. "Can Social Insurance for Long-Term Care Work? The Experience of Germany." *Health Affairs* 19 (May/June 2000), pp. 8–25.

Cutler, David, M. "Why Don't Markets Insure Long-Term Risk?" Working Paper, *National Bureau of Economic Research* (1996).

———. "Declining Disability Among the Elderly." *Health Affairs* 20 (November/December 2001), pp. 11–27.

Fizel, J., and T. Nunnikhoven. "Technical Efficiency of For-Profit and Non-Profit Nursing Homes." *Managerial and Decision Economics* (September/October 1992), pp. 429–39.

Frech, H.E., and Paul B. Ginsburg. "The Cost of Nursing Home Care in the United States: Government, Financing, Ownership, and Efficiency." In *Health, Economics, and*

Health Economics, ed. J. van der Gang and M. Perlman, North-Holland Publishing Company, 1981.

General Accounting Office. *Long-Term Care Aging Baby Boom Generation Will Increase Demand and Burden on Federal and State Budgets*. Washington, D.C.: March 2002.

———. *Long-Term Care—Baby Boom Generation Presents Financing Challenges*. (Testimony 3/9/98.) Washington, D.C.: April 1998.

———. *Long-Term Care, Current Issues and Future Directions*. Washington, D.C.: April 1995.

Gertler, Paul J. "Subsidies, Quality, and Regulation in Nursing Homes." *Journal of Public Economics* 39 (1989), pp. 33–53.

Gertler, Paul J., and Donald M. Waldman. "Quality-Adjusted Cost Functions and Policy Evaluation in the Nursing Home Industry." *Journal of Political Economy* 100 (1992), pp. 1232–56.

Gonzales, Theresa I. "An Empirical Study of Economies of Scope in Home Healthcare." *Health Services Review* 32 (August 1997), pp. 313–24.

Grabowski, David C. "Medicaid Reimbursement and the Quality of Nursing Home Care." *Journal of Health Economics* 20 (2001), pp. 549–69.

Grabowski, David C., and Richard A. Hirth. "Competitive Spillovers Across Nonprofit and For-profit Nursing Homes." *Journal of Health Economics*, (forthcoming 2002).

Gulley, O. David, and Rexford E. Santerre. "The Effect of Public Policies on the Availability of Nursing Home Care in the United States." *Eastern Economics Journal* 29 (winter 2003), pp. 93–104.

Hannsmann, Henry. *The Ownership of Enterprise* Cambridge: Harvard University Press, 1996.

Harrington, Charlene, James H. Swan., John A. Nyman, and Helen Carrillo. "The Effect of Certificate of Need and Moratoria Policy on Change in Nursing Home Beds in the United States." *Medical Care* 35 (1997), pp. 574–88.

Harrington, Charlene, Steffie Woolhandler, Joseph Mullan, Helen Carrillo, and David U. Himmelstein. "Does Investor Ownership of Nursing Homes Compromise the Quality of Care?" *American Journal of Public Health* 91 (September 2001), pp. 1452–55.

Haupt, Barbara J. "An Overview of Home Health and Hospice Care Patients: 1996 National Home and Hospice Care Survey." U.S. Department of Health and Human Services, National Center for Health Statistics, Advance Data No. 297, April 16, 1998.

Health Insurance Association of America. *Long-Term Care Insurance in 1989-1999 Summary of Study Findings*. Washington, D.C.: 2001.

Holahan, John F., and Joel W. Cohen. "Nursing Home Reimbursement: Implications for Cost Containment, Access, and Quality." *Millbank Quarterly* 65 (1987), pp. 112–47.

Hollmann, Frederick, Tammany J. Mulder, and Jeffrey E. Kallan. *Methodology and Assumptions for the Population Projections of the United States: 1999 to 2000*. U.S. Census Bureau. January 13, 2000.

Kass, D. J. "Economies of Scale and Scope in the Provision of Home Health Services." *Journal of Health Economics* 6 (June 1987), pp. 129–46.

Lakdawalla, Darius, and Tomas Philipson. "The Rise of Old-Age Longevity and the Market for Long-Term Care." *American Economic Review* 92 (March 2002), pp. 295–306.

Lerner, Abba P. "The Concept of Monopoly and the Measurement of Monopoly Power." *Review of Economic Studies* 1 (1934), pp. 157–75.

Levit, Katherine, et al. "Inflation Spurs Health Spending in 2000." *Health Affairs* 21 (January/February 2002), pp. 172–81.

Lubitz, James, James Beebe, and Colin Baker. "Longevity and Medicare Expenditures." *The New England Journal of Medicine* 332 (April 13, 1995), pp. 999–1003.

McNeil, John M. "Preliminary Estimates on Caregiving From Wave 7 of the 1996 Survey of Income and Program Participation." U.S. Department of Commerce, Bureau of the Census. December 1999.

Medicare Payment Advisory Commission, MEDPAC. *Report to The Congress; Medicare Payment Policy*. Washington, D.C.: March 2000.

———. *Report to The Congress; Selected Medicare Issues*. Washington, D.C.: June 1999.

Mellor, Jennifer C. "Long-term Care and Nursing Home Coverage: Are Adult Children Substitutes for Insurance Policies?" *Journal of Health Economics* 20 (2001), pp. 527–47.

Metropolitan Life Insurance Company. *The MetLife Study of Employer Costs for Working Caregivers*. June 1997.

Mukamel, Dana B., and William D. Spector. "The Competitive Nature of the Nursing Home Industry: Price Mark Ups and Demand Elasticities." *Applied Economics* 34 (2002), pp. 413–20.

National Alliance for Caregiving and the American Association of Retired Persons. "Family Caregiving in the U.S. Findings from a National Survey," Bethesda, Maryland, June 1997.

Norton, Edward C. "Long-Term Care." In *Handbook of Health Economics*, Volume 1, ed. A.J. Culyer and J.P. Newhouse, Elsevier Science B.V., 2000.

Nyman, John A. "The Effects of Market Concentration and Excess Demand on the Price of Nursing Home Care." *The Journal of Industrial Economics* 17 (June 1994), pp. 193–204.

———. "Testing for Excess Demand in Nursing Home Care Markets." *Medical Care* 31 (1993), pp. 680–93.

———. "Medicaid Reimbursement, Excess Medicaid Demand, and the Quality of Nursing Home Care." *Journal of Health Economics* 4 (1985), pp. 237–59.

Nyman, John A., and Dennis L. Bricker. "Profit Incentives and Technical Efficiency in the Production of Nursing Home Care." *Review of Economics and Statistics* 71 (November 1989), pp. 586–94.

Nyman, John A., Dennis L. Bricker, and D. Link. "Technical Efficiency in Nursing Homes." *Medical Care* 28 (June 1990), pp. 541–51.

Nyman, John A., and Robert A. Connor. "Do Case-Mix Adjusted Nursing Home Reimbursement Actually Reflects Costs? Minnesota's Experience." *Journal of Health Economics* 13 (1994), pp. 145–62.

Pauly, Mark. "The Rational Nonpurchase of Long-Term-Care Insurance." *Journal of Political Economy* 98 (1990), pp. 153–68.

Pauly, Mark, and M. Satterthwaite. "The Pricing of Primary Care Physician Services: A Test of the Role of Consumer Information." *Bell Journal of Economics* 12 (1981), pp. 488–506.

Reinhardt, Uwe E., Peter S. Hussey, and Gerard F. Anderson. "Cross National Comparisons of Health Systems Using OECD Data, 1999." *Health Affairs* 21 (May/June 2002), pp. 169–81.

Reschovsky, James D. "The Roles of Medicaid and Economic Factors in the Demand for Nursing Home Care." *Health Services Research* 33 (October 1988), pp. 787–813.

Rhoades, Jeffrey, D.E.B. Potter, and Nancy Kraus. "Nursing Homes—Structure and Selected Characteristics, 1996." http://www.meps.ahcpr.gov.

Rosko, Michael D., and Robert W. Broyles. *The Economics of Health Care: A Reference Handbook*. New York: Greenwood Press, 1988.

Scanlon, William J. "A Theory of the Nursing Home Market." *Inquiry* 17 (Spring 1980), pp. 25–41.

Sloan, Frank A., and Edward C. Norton. "Adverse Selection, Bequests, Crowding Out, and Private Demand for Insurance, Evidence from the Long-term Care Insurance Market." *Journal of Risk and Uncertainty* 15 (1997), pp. 201–09.

Temkin-Greener, Helena, Dana B. Mukamel, and Mark R. Meimers. "Long-Term Care Insurance Underwriting: Understanding Eventual Claims Experience." *Inquiry* 37 (Winter 2000/2001), pp. 348–58.

Wagner, Donna A. *Comparative Analysis of Caregiver Data for Caregivers to the Elderly 1987 and 1997*. National Alliance for Caregiving. Bethesda, Maryland, June 1997.

White-Means, Shelly, and Deborah Chollet. "Opportunity Wages and Workforce Adjustments: Understanding the Cost of In-Home Elder Care." *Journal of Gerontology Social Sciences* 51B (1996), pp. S82–S90.

Zinn, Jacqueline S. "Market Competition and the Quality of Nursing Home Care." *Journal of Health Care Politics, Policy and Law* 19 (Fall 1994), pp. 555–82.

PART 4

HEALTH CARE REFORM

CHAPTER 16   Health Care Reform

CHAPTER

16

HEALTH CARE REFORM

Hospital Fees Hit the Middle Class Hard: Present System Favors the Rich and the Poor—Medical Men Suggest Ways to Lower the Cost of Illness—The New York Times

Many people today are dissatisfied with the performance of the U.S. health care system. The cost of health care in the United States is alleged to be higher and rising faster than in any other country. Many worry that the health care monster will continue to devour an increasingly large slice of the economic pie. Moreover, at any one point in time, critics note that one out of every six nonelderly citizens lacks insurance coverage for acute care. Many others in the United States are seriously underinsured or lack proper long-term care insurance coverage.

The title of the newspaper article above captures the U.S. health care system's failure to provide universal coverage and contain health care costs. One indeed might argue (perhaps wrongly) that poor people either receive free care at public institutions or are provided with medical and long-term care coverage through the Medicaid program, while rich individuals can afford to self-insure. Middle-income individuals, then, are hit hardest by hospital fees because they face the prospects of rising copayments, reduced wage income, benefit denial, job lock, or other problems pertaining to private health insurance coverage.

The fascinating thing about the newspaper article cited above is that it originally appeared in The New York Times *75 years ago, proving that the more things change, the more they remain the same.[1] Private health insurance was just barely in its embryonic stage in 1924 when the article was first published. Without health insurance, a large fraction of a middle-class family's income was subject to the vagaries of health status. In fact, at a well-known hospital, the cost of maintaining one patient for one day rose from $2.65 in 1919 to $4.71 in 1929, an average annual increase of nearly 9 percent.[2] The quest for financial security in the 1920s most likely resulted in the eventual birth and growth of private health insurance in the*

---

[1]See Chenery (1924). Incidentally, the next article on the same page was titled "When Russian Empire Tottered—An Inside Picture." Go Figure!

[2]Caldwell (1930), as cited by Stevens (1987). According to Stevens, the 1920s represented the flowering of consumerism in the hospital services industry. Stevens notes that "there was a running joke in the late 1920s that there were two classes of people in hospitals, those who entered poor and those who left poor" (p. 134). Apparently, the joke is still running!

United States. Interestingly enough, William Chenery, the journalist who wrote The New York Times *article, suggested that the United States copy the private health insurance system with which Cuba was experimenting with at the time rather than the British or German social health insurance systems. The U.S. private health insurance industry, in fact, began to emerge about five years later, in 1929, as discussed at the beginning of Chapter 11.*

Today the health care crisis has taken on a different shape. Only a small percentage of the population is currently uninsured compared to the 1920s. However, everyone is affected by the rising cost of health care services, not just the middle-income class. A rising share of compensation going toward health insurance premiums affects employers and employees alike. The poor and elderly populations, as well as the state and federal governments, are affected by Medicaid and Medicare budgets that are being squeezed due to escalating medical costs. Health care analysts and policymakers are searching for ways to improve the American health care system.

Not surprisingly, various groups have advanced a large number of health care reform plans. The plans differ in a number of respects, especially concerning the role the individual, employer, and government play in the financing of medical insurance and the functions the government and marketplace serve in the allocation of health care resources. To help us better understand what health care reform is all about, this chapter

> Summarizes the performance of the U.S. health care system and conducts an international comparison.

> Examines the various proposals for health care reform at the national level.

> Analyzes the experiences of selected states at implementing health care reform.

> Briefly reviews President Clinton's National Health Security Act of 1993.

THE PERFORMANCE OF THE U.S. HEALTH CARE SYSTEM: A SUMMARY AND AN INTERNATIONAL COMPARISON

Thus far, the structure, conduct, and performance of the U.S. health care system has been examined in piecemeal fashion. Chapter 11 analyzed the private health insurance industry, and Chapters 12 through 15 discussed the individual markets for physician services, hospital services, pharmaceutical products, and long-term care. In this section, we summarize what is known about the structure, conduct, and performance of each individual medical care market. After the summary of the individual markets, the aggregate performance of the entire health care economy is assessed and compared to the performance of a select group of health care systems around the world.

Summarizing the Structure, Conduct, and Performance of the Various Medical Care Markets

Private Health Insurance Industry   The structure of the private health insurance industry appears to be reasonably competitive. Although highly concentrated in most geographical markets, a large competitive fringe exists in the industry and large employers face the alternative of self-insurance. These two structural features of the industry help to constrain the conduct of the dominant insurers. Nevertheless, antitrust officials might want to keep a watchful eye on future organizational developments in this market. Barriers to entry appear low so potential competition must be considered by the existing firms, and products appear to be reasonably homogeneous. Consumer information in the group buyer market is relatively complete; however, some information imperfections exist in the market for individual insurance.

As economic theory suggests, the conduct of the insurance industry reflects its competitive structure. The price of medical insurance has tended to decline over the long run, and some firms in the industry have followed undesirable practices because of the intense competition. Benefit denial, cherry-picking, and high premiums charged to the medically indigent are among some of the undesirable practices observed. On the performance side, a large percentage of people remain uninsured in the United States, even after allowing for Medicaid and Medicare coverage. A family without health insurance coverage faces substantial financial insecurity. Overinsurance, underinsurance, and job lock are other problems in the private health insurance industry that impose costs on society.

Physician Services Industry   Because convenience is valued by consumers (and thus the individual demand curves are downward sloping) and given the vast number of sellers in the market, the physician services industry can be considered monopolistically competitive with relatively low barriers to entry. Medical licensure represents the primary barrier to entry into the physician market. The question, from a societal point of view, is whether the benefits of quality improvements resulting from medical licensing outweigh the higher prices from entry restrictions. With the development of large, institutional suppliers of physician services, the necessity of medical licensing may diminish in the future as enterprise liability plays a greater role. The limited nature of the entry barrier has meant that the number of physicians per capita has grown substantially over time. One important structural issue is whether there are too many specialists and not enough primary care givers in the United States. It should not be forgotten that any ability of physicians to raise prices has been seriously compromised, both by MCOs and by the government, which have increasingly used their bargaining powers to extract price concessions from physicians.

The prevalence of an asymmetry of information between patients and physicians has influenced conduct in the physician services market. Health economists continue to analyze if physicians play on the asymmetry of information, especially in competitive markets, by unnecessarily increasing the quantity supplied of their services. This type of behavior was developed and analyzed within the context of the supplier-induced-demand model and the McGuire quantity-setting model. Practice variations have also been observed across geographic regions of the United States (and in other countries as well). Policy analysts continue to sort out the reasons behind practice variations. In terms of performance, the growth in physician prices and expenditures continues to outpace the growth in the general price level and the overall economy, although the differential has moderated in recent years. However, in real terms, physician income growth has stalled in recent years, and the rate of return of physician education is reasonably close to the rates of return observed on comparable types of educational investments.

Hospital Services Industry   Because economies of scale are exhausted at about the 200-bed level, most areas in the United States cannot support more than two or three hospitals. Moreover, people are reluctant to travel far distances for hospital services, so most markets tend to be local in nature. Certificate of need laws, the huge sunk costs of building a hospital, and learning curve effects cause substantial barriers to entry into the hospital services industry. While most hospitals tend to offer standardized products, some large teaching hospitals are often perceived as offering better quality. Given that the out-of-pocket price for hospital services is around 3 cents on the dollar, most patient/consumers tend to be relatively uninformed about price and have little incentive to comparison shop for hospital services. Countervailing these monopoly-like characteristics is the fact that institutional buyers, like MCOs and the government, have taken on a greater buyer role in the hospital services industry. All these considerations suggest that the hospital services industry can best be described structurally as a mild or loose (standardized) oligopoly.

Conduct issues pertaining to the hospital services industry include the effects of ownership and competition on pricing and the charitable function of hospitals. Earlier studies, prior to the 1980s, found that increased competition caused hospitals, especially nonprofit hospitals, to increase quality by adopting new cost-enhancing technologies and thus raising prices. This type of behavior was referred to as the *medical arms race*. Newer studies based on more recent data have tended to find that greater competition has not led to higher hospital prices and, in some cases, has led to lower prices. Given the many complex factors affecting hospital pricing, more careful studies on the effects of competition in this industry are needed before we can comfortably conclude that competition leads to lower hospital prices, however.

The effect of MCOs on the cost of hospital services and the growth of integrated delivery systems (IDSs) are two other important conduct issues concerning the hospital services industry. Studies conclude that MCOs tend to lower hospital costs by about 15 to 20 percent compared to otherwise identical fee-for-service insurance plans. Quality of care in MCOs and in fee-for-service insurance plans is very similar, although some evidence indicates that MCOs may provide poor individuals with inferior care. This is another important area where additional research is required. IDSs, in which physicians, hospitals, and other medical organizations integrate their organizations either legally or by contract, have been evolving over time. These integrated systems have been developing in large part to counteract the powerful institutional buyer side (e.g., MCOs and the government) in the hospital services market. IDSs may offer cost savings and quality of care improvements, but studies have not consistently provided evidence for these benefits.

As far as performance is concerned, hospital expenditures make up a large percentage of GDP. While hospital care expenditures exploded from 1.8 percent of GDP in 1960 to 4.9 percent in 1992, the good news is that the rate has stabilized in recent years and was 4.2 percent in 2000. The hospital price inflation rate continues to outstrip the general price inflation rate, although recent years have witnessed a narrowing of the gap. Staffing ratios at hospitals continue to burgeon, most likely reflecting the more severe case-mix associated with inpatient services, as more people are directed toward outpatient services. Any dramatic attempts at further cost reductions for inpatient hospital services may be futile as a smaller percentage of critically ill patients account for an increasingly greater fraction of costs. Most likely, only rationing of care to the severely ill will further reduce the cost of hospital inpatient services in the future.

Pharmaceutical Industry   Substantial barriers to entry brought on by patents and promotion expenditures, differentiated products resulting from promotion expenditures, and a few dominant firms in the therapeutic markets are the key structural characteristics associated with the pharmaceutical industry. The demand side of the pharmaceutical market has become more concentrated over time due to institutional buyers, but their ability to affect the operation and performance of the industry is still somewhat limited. Recall that consumers' out-of-pocket expenditures currently stand at about 32 percent for drugs compared to less than 3 percent for hospital services. All these characteristics lead to the conclusion that the pharmaceutical industry can be roughly labeled as a tight, differentiated oligopoly.

Despite its oligopolistic nature, there are ample signs of price competition in the pharmaceutical industry. During the patent period, branded drugs often compete against other branded drugs treating the same illness but based on different chemical compositions. After the legal patent period, branded drugs face considerable competition from generic drugs, and generic drugs compete among themselves, as well. Although the price competition is not perfect, it has tended to be much more rigorous since the passing of the Hatch-Waxman Act in 1984. The high promotion expenditures of pharmaceutical companies simultaneously play both an informative and a persuasive role. For example, studies suggest that the promotion expenditures of leading firms tend to preserve their market shares while the promotion expenditures of follower firms reduce the leaders' market shares. Research and development expenditures, the source of product competition among pharmaceutical companies, have been found to depend on cash flows. It appears from the literature that an assortment of firm sizes, some relatively large and some relatively small, are desirable for innovation purposes.

At first blush, the U.S. pharmaceutical industry appears to allocate resources inefficiently. Since the late 1970s, real drug prices have risen, although once again the gap between the drug price inflation rate and the general price inflation rate has narrowed in recent years. In addition, pharmaceutical profit rates are much greater than the manufacturing industry average even after allowing for the amortization of promotion and R&D expenditures. It is interesting to note that these high profits may be financing new drug discoveries because the innovation and commercial introduction of new drugs tend to be risky endeavors. Most pharmaceutical companies have a series of costly misses before a commercial hit. Rather than signal a misallocation of society's resources, the high profits may reflect the high risks and provide the source of financing for R&D ventures. New drug discoveries have increased tremendously in the United States since the late 1970s as a result.

Long-Term Care Industry   The long-term care industry is somewhat unique because of the nature of the care provided and the wide range of organizational settings that offer long-term care. In terms of care, the emphasis is on enhancing the quality of life rather than curing a particular medical problem. Given that long-term medical needs vary widely, a whole range of services are provided in a multitude of organizational settings. For example, long-term care can be provided by a loved one on an informal basis, or on a more formal basis by a home health care agency, at an assisted living facility, or at a skilled nursing home. Overall, the market for long-term care can best be treated as a monopolistically competitive industry with rather modest barriers to entry. On the demand side, estimates indicate that between 12 and 14 million people are currently in need of some type of long-term care. The supply side of the market is composed of an amalgam of health care providers with the three most important being informal providers, nursing homes, and home health care agencies.

Pricing and quantity are two important issues in the market for long-term care. With regard to price, the empirical evidence indicates that the demand for nursing home care appears to be highly elastic with respect to price and that reimbursement policies impact the behavior of nursing homes. Lower reimbursement appears to result in decreased costs and diminished quality. In addition, the market for nursing home care may no longer be characterized by excess demand due to the removal of CON laws and the increased availability of alternative providers. Research also indicates that for-profit nursing homes are more technically efficient and produce at a lower cost than their not-for-profit counterparts, supporting the property rights theory. However, quality of care tends to be higher in not-for-profit settings.

Expenditures on long-term care are substantial and account for approximately one-quarter of all health care outlays when the economic cost of informal care is factored into the equation. Public funding sources play an important role in the market for long-term care, accounting for approximately 60 percent of all formal expenditures. The implication is that the government has considerable power to control prices and affect resource allocation in this industry. Private insurance, however, accounts for less than 10 percent of total formal long-term care expenditures and researchers are somewhat at a loss to explain why so few individuals purchase long-term care insurance. Moral hazard, adverse selection, and Medicaid crowding out are all factors that are likely to come into play.

Overall, the market for long-term care is changing rapidly with a number of demographic and institutional factors coming into play. Market competition is likely to intensify in the future as the number and types of providers diversifies. As a result, the average skilled nursing home is likely to face a highly elastic demand curve for its services and, therefore, have only limited ability to raise price without losing a substantial number of patients. At the same time, the aggregate demand for long-term care is likely to increase as baby boomers reach retirement age in the coming years. However, improved health coupled with longevity may dampen the overall increase.

Overall Health Care Economy   The preceding discussion suggests that the prices and expenditures on various medical services continue to rise, albeit at a slower rate than in the past. The transition to a managed-care health care system has helped to promote some cost savings in various medical care markets but has also resulted in some rationing of care. Choice of physician, physician autonomy and income, hospital inpatient admissions, and selection among pharmaceutical products have all been greatly limited by the movement to a managed-care health care system in the United States. The limitations pertain not only to private managed-care insurance plans but also to managed-care plans under the auspices of the Medicare and Medicaid programs. Whether MCOs have properly curbed the excesses brought on by the unlimited fee-for-service plans of the past or have unnecessarily and unfairly denied care remains a heated issue and an important area for future research. Another issue currently debated is whether the cost savings that can be attributed to the growth in managed care are a one-time phenomenon or the beginning of a long-term trend of lower rates of growth in health care expenditures.

From the preceding discussion, it also seems that competition in the health care sector may have sown the seeds of its own destruction. For example, benefit denial and cherry-picking behavior take place in the private health insurance industry because of competition. Quantity setting behavior in the physician services industry and the medical arms race in the hospital industry are argued to occur because of competition. Indeed, a theory X'er, one who thinks medical care is unique, would certainly subscribe to that opinion. A theory Y'er might argue, however, that competition cannot function properly until more medical firms are organized on a for-profit basis and consumers pay a greater proportion of the price of medical services, two properties of perfect competition that were described at the beginning of Chapter 8.

About the only thing that is clear from this discussion is that the debate over the relative merits of competition in the health care industry is likely to continue in the future.

A portion of that debate is taken up in the remainder of the chapter. Before we tackle that issue, however, let us examine how the U.S. health care system stacks up against other health care systems around the world. For example, we saw in Chapter 4 that the health care systems in Canada, Germany, and the United Kingdom involve a single-payer system rather than a multiple-payer system like that of the United States. Also, their health care systems provide nearly universal access to medical care services and involve a greater financing and regulatory role for the federal government and less reliance on competition in health care matters. Thus it would be interesting and informative to examine how the United States compares to these and other countries in terms of health care expenditures, the utilization of medical care, and health care outcomes. To that we now turn our attention.

The U.S. Health Care Economy: An International Comparison

Table 16–1 compares health care spending, medical utilization, and demographic data for seven of the G-8 countries: Canada, France, Germany, Italy, Japan, the United Kingdom, and the United States. The Federation of Russia is excluded for lack of current data. These countries possess highly developed market economies and share many similar circumstances. (Like the other countries, with the exception of the United States, France and Italy provide nearly universal access to medical services and have a single-payer system.) Data for health care spending on a per capita basis are shown in column 1 of the table. The next four columns contain comparative data on per capita income, the availability of technology, lifestyle (per capita daily calorie intake), and the environment (carbon monoxide emissions). Data for hospital admissions and per capita physician consultations are reported in the last two columns and are intended as measures of medical utilization. All these data are collected and based on definitions established by the Organization for Economic Cooperation and Development (OECD, 2002).

Before discussing the figures in the tables, we should point out that data from different countries may not be directly comparable for several reasons and, therefore, should be accepted with some skepticism. For example, no standard taxonomy exists across countries. Medical authorities in, say, France might distinguish among inpatient and outpatient services differently than do their counterparts in the United States. Also, in practice it is often difficult to draw a line separating medical services, such as acute and long-term care services. In addition, monetary values for health care expenditures and gross domestic product must be converted to a common denominator, such as U.S. dollars, before meaningful comparisons can be made. Any conversion factor, such as purchasing power parities or currency exchange rates, is not without measurement error. Nevertheless, many comparative system analysts believe these data paint a reasonable picture of the health care situation in various countries.

The figures in column 1 suggest that the United States spends more on medical care in absolute and relative terms than do the other countries. Per capita health care spending in the United States ($4,373) was more than double the average of the other six countries in 1999 ($2,150). Three countries, Canada, Italy, and the United Kingdom, had per capita health care expenditures below $2,000. The United States also appears to spend more in relative terms than the other countries on medical care. As a fraction of GDP, medical care expenditures topped 13 percent of GDP in the United States in 1999; this is almost three percentage points higher than Germany, the next largest spender. The remaining five countries held medical expenditures below 10 percent of GDP in 1999, with the United

TABLE 16–1

Comparative Health Care System Statistics for the G-8 Countries Excluding the Russian Federation

	Per Capita Health Care Expenditures (1999)	Per Capita GDP (1999)	MRIs Per Million Persons (1999)	Per Capita Total Calories Intake (1999)	Per Capita Carbon Monoxide Emissions (1997)	Hospital Admissions Per 1,000 Pop. (1998)	Per Capita Physician Consultations (1996)
Canada	$1,939	$22,708	1.8 (1997)	3,161	338	100.6	6.4
France	2,298	21,884	2.8	3,575	142	231.0	6.5
Germany	2,696 (1998)	22,814	6.2 (1997)	3,411	71	226.8	6.5
Italy	1,602	18,500	6.7	3,629	116	180.4	6.6 (1999)
Japan	2,623	37,544	23.2	2,782	30	98.0	16.0
United Kingdom	1,747	23,954	4.5	1,690	88	150.9	6.1
United States	4,373	35,657	8.1	3,754	320	124.9	5.8

SOURCE: Organization for Economic Cooperation and Development. *OECD Health Data 2002.* Paris, France, 2002.

Kingdom spending the smallest fraction of total domestic output on medical care at 7.1 percent of GDP (not shown in the table).

Data in the next six columns provide some explanation for the higher health care spending in the United States. According to the data, per capita income was higher in the United States ($35,657) in 1999 than every other country with the exception of Japan ($37,544). As discussed in Chapter 5, the income elasticity of demand in the aggregate is greater than one, indicating that health care spending is highly responsive to income at the aggregate level. Income (GDP) per capita in the United States is about 45 percent higher than the average of the other countries and, therefore, supports a greater proportion of health care spending.

In addition, we saw in Chapters 7 and 8 that a greater availability of cost-enhancing medical technologies raises the demand and also reduces the supply of medical services. The shifts in demand and supply both lead to a greater amount of spending on health care services, provided both curves are inelastic with respect to price. According to the data in the table, the United States has more MRIs per million persons than all the countries under consideration with the exception of Japan. Data elsewhere suggest that there are also 30 percent more scanners per persons in the United States compared to the average of the other countries (Anderson, 1997). If the availability of technology offers the complete explanation, Japan should also experience high health care costs as there are both more MRIs and scanners in Japan than the United States. That is not the case, however.

We learned in Chapter 2 that lifestyle and environmental factors play an important role in determining the health status and the demand for medical care. People may try to compensate for risky lifestyle behaviors, such as poor diet or excessive drinking, by consuming more health care services. That would cause the demand for medical care to increase and result in an increase in overall expenditures on health care. Per capita total calorie intake shown in column 4 is taken as a crude measure for dietary behavior. According to the figures, the average American consumes more calories on a daily basis (3,754 calories) than residents in any of the other countries and far in excess of that recommended by the medical community. It is generally agreed in the medical community that the average adult female should consume approximately 2,200 calories per day while the average adult male should consume about 2,900 calories. Excessive caloric intake leads to weight gain and could result in a number of medical problems such as high blood pressure and heart failure. While caloric intake may be considered a very simple index of lifestyle at best, it does suggest that lifestyle may play a role in explaining the high medical care costs in the United States.

Environmental factors as measured by per capita carbon monoxide emissions may also play a role in explaining high medical care costs in the United States. According to column 5, carbon monoxide emissions in the United States are far higher than the other six countries with the exception of Canada. Emission levels in the United States are more than twice the levels in France and Italy, and over ten times the level of emissions in Japan. High levels of carbon monoxide emissions inhibit the body's ability to absorb oxygen and can cause a number of medical problems. Most carbon monoxide emissions come from vehicles and it stands to reason that the United States would be high in emission levels. To counter the negative impact of these environmental factors, Americans may consume more medical care than otherwise would be the case, thereby causing an increase in medical care expenditures.

Columns 6 and 7 provide information on medical utilization to see what health dollars may buy besides medical technology. Perhaps the high health care spending in the United States shows up in a relatively large amount of inpatient and physician office visits. An examination of the medical utilization data in the table suggests just the opposite, however. In particular, the United States had only 124.9 hospital admissions per 1,000 population in 1998, compared to 226.8 in Germany and 231.0 in France. Only Japan (98.0) and Canada (100.6) had lower admission rates. The data for physician contacts also allows us to draw a similar conclusion; medical utilization does not explain the high health care cost in the United States.

Comparatively high health care expenditures coupled with low medical utilization rates have led some analysts to believe that medical prices must be significantly higher in the United States than in other countries. Others argue, however, that this may not be a legitimate conclusion to draw from these data due to quality differences in medical services across countries. Specifically, the quality of medical care may be higher in the United States and account for higher medical prices. Unfortunately, good indicators of the quality of care are unavailable because of measurement issues. Anecdotal evidence does suggest that waiting times are short for most medical services in the United States.

Figure 16–1 provides an indication of the level of health in the United States relative to the other countries. The infant mortality rate (deaths per thousand live births) is thought to be highly correlated with other measures of health status, making it a reasonable benchmark for the general state of health of all population segments. The data in the figure imply that all other G-8 countries (excluding Russia) have an infant mortality rate much lower than that of the United States. The discrepancy is not a trivial one. In the United States, about 2.4 more infants out of every 1,000 children born alive never get a chance to blow out the candles on their first birthday cake. Think about that!

In summary, nearly 15 percent of the U.S. population is without health insurance coverage throughout the year. In contrast, nearly universal health insurance coverage exists in the other countries studied. Government in the United States is responsible for financing about 45 percent of all health care spending (but see Insight 16–3). The comparable figure for the other six countries is well over 90 percent (Anderson, 1997). Health care spending as a fraction of GDP is higher, medical utilizations rates are lower, and the infant mortality rate is higher in the United States than in the typical G-8 country (excluding Russia). Many analysts have concluded from such data that health care costs and infant mortality are lower in other countries because the government plays a more dominant role in the health care sector and because there is universal access to health insurance. In fact, many health care policy analysts believe that a similar approach can produce better results in the United States.

AN OVERVIEW OF HEALTH CARE REFORM IN THE UNITED STATES

The debate over health care reform in the United States has been heated, and the volume of the discussion attests to the liveliness of the issue. Facing a bewildering number of proposals and counterproposals from every interest group imaginable, health care professionals and consumers alike have a difficult time keeping abreast of the issues. The debate is further complicated by the vast array of new terminology. Terms with which many of us

FIGURE 16–1
Infant Mortality Rates 1999 (Deaths per 1,000 Live Births)

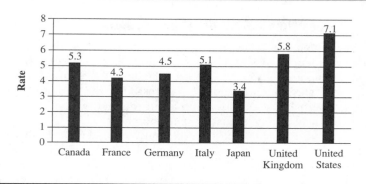

SOURCE: Organization for Economic Cooperation and Development. *OECD Health Data 2002*. Paris, France, 2002.

are unfamiliar, such as *global budgeting*, *health alliances*, and *play-or-pay*, are bandied about regularly. This section attempts to help you sort through this maze by reviewing the efficiency and equity implications of four generic health care reform proposals: medical savings accounts, individual mandates, managed competition, and national health insurance. These four proposals were chosen primarily because they include the basic elements of the majority of the proposals typically considered.

Following this discussion, we examine health care reform at the state level. State governments are a frequently overlooked player in the health care debate. We review the health care reform packages of four states to get a flavor of the various strategies at the state level. Finally, we examine the basic features of the Clinton health care plan, or the National Health Security Act of 1993.

HEALTH CARE REFORM AT THE FEDERAL LEVEL

To bring some consistency to the discussion, each plan is evaluated using four economic criteria:

1. *Universal coverage:* Does the plan achieve universal coverage, and, if so, how?
2. *Financing and budgetary implications:* How is the plan financed, and to what extent does it affect the federal deficit?
3. *Cost containment:* How does the plan contain the growth of medical care expenditures over time?
4. *Employment:* To what extent does the plan influence overall employment opportunities?

Note that the first criterion deals with the issue of vertical equity, while the last two concern efficiency. A summary of how each plan measures up to the four criteria appears in

INSIGHT 16–1

The Federal Employees Health Benefits Program

Did you ever wonder which physician attends to your doctor when she feels ill? Or consider which clinic your dentist goes to when he requires dental care? Or speculate about who provides health insurance coverage to those federal employees overseeing the operation of the Medicare and Medicaid programs in the United States? If so, while we can't help you clear up your wonderment or consideration about the first two questions, this insight offers some information concerning the latter speculation.

Active federal employees, such as those working in the Centers for Medicare and Medicaid Services, receive their health insurance through the Federal Employees Health Benefits Program (FEHBP). The FEHBP is the largest employment-based health benefit plan in the nation, covering over 9 million people, including, in addition to active employees, retired federal employees, dependents of active and retired federal employees, and members of the U.S. Congress. The total cost of the program amounted to $20 billion in 2000. The Office of Personnel Management, a federal agency, runs the FEHBP.

Beginning in 2003, the FEHBP offers enrollees tremendous choice among 188 different plans. The idea is that choice promotes competition among health insurers, which helps to contain costs and spur innovations. Choices include national and regional traditional fee-for-service, PPO, HMO, and POS plans. Each enrollee has at least a dozen fee-for-service options in addition to local HMOs. The federal government pays 75 percent of the plan's premium up to a maximum of 72 percent of the enrollment weighted average of all premiums. The subscriber is responsible for paying any remaining amount above the subsidy cap. Creating consumer cost consciousness is the motivation behind the subsidy cap. To help federal employees make informed decisions, the FEHBP and other organizations distribute information about the various health plans including consumer satisfaction surveys.

The FEHBP has been fairly successful at controlling health insurance premiums. For example, over the period 1992 to 1999, premiums of regional FEHBP plans increased by an annual average of 3.3 percent compared to a 5 percent increase for all private health insurance plans. As another point of comparison, the FEHBP premium increase compared very favorably to the average increase of premiums for CALPERS, the California Public Employees Retirement System, which amounted to 2.8 percent over the same seven-year period. CALPERS is the nation's largest public pension fund and provides health insurance to 1.2 million state and local government employees and their families in California. Moreover, in 2003, premiums of FEHBP plans increased by 11.1 percent, significantly less than the 20 to 25 percent premium increase for CALPER plans.

Many have pointed to the FEHBP as a model for reforming Medicare and a mechanism to expand health insurance coverage. For example, when running for president, Senator Bill Bradley proposed that uninsured individuals should be given income-related vouchers to enroll in the FEHBP. Researchers and policy analysts continue to discuss the merits of broadening enrollment in the FEHBP.

SOURCE: This insight is based on Feldman, Thorpe, and Gray (2002) and information obtained at http://www.opm.gov/insure/health/index.htm.

table 16–2, on the following two pages, which the reader is urged to consult throughout the discussion. In addition, the discussion refers to the generalized model of a health care system discussed in Chapter 4.

Medical Savings Accounts

This plan takes a distinctly market-oriented approach to reforming health care by calling for the development of individual tax-free medical savings accounts (MSAs) to pay for routine medical care. Proponents claim that routine care accounts for a significant fraction of medical expenditures.[3] The program is purely voluntary in that individuals have the option to make yearly contributions to their MSAs up to a specified amount, and any funds left in the account at the end of the year can be carried over to the next year and earn interest. Catastrophic health insurance plans to finance major medical expenses can also be purchased with pretax income. Premiums for the catastrophic plans are generally cheap due to the high deductibles involved.

An example may help to clarify the structure of the MSA proposal. Suppose your employer presently pays $7,000 for your family's major medical and routine care insurance coverage. Under the MSA plan, your employer would purchase catastrophic health insurance coverage worth, say, $3,500 for your family. The catastrophic plan covers expensive major illnesses and has a sizable deductible. In addition, the employer deposits the remaining $3,500 into a tax-free MSA. Your family can use the funds in the MSA to pay for routine care or to finance the deductible on major medical illnesses during the year. The routine care services could be purchased as needed or on a prepaid basis through a health care provider like an HMO. Your family makes the choice by considering relative prices, income, health status, degree of risk aversion, and other demand-side factors. Any unused funds in the MSA are rolled over and used for similar purposes in future years.

The MSA plan does not call for universal health care coverage, but it does give the public freedom of choice. A person can elect to create an MSA and contribute as much as desired up to a preset limit. Because contributions to the MSAs are tax deductible, the price of medical care is reduced, making it affordable for more people. Tax credits also further reduce the price for low-income families, and government subsidies are available for truly needy individuals. Horizontal equity is achieved because all premiums or contributions to the MSAs are tax deductible whether paid by the employee or the employer.[4] Elderly individuals finance health care expenditures with the introduction of medical IRAs. Like traditional IRAs, these accounts grow tax free and can be used to cover medical expenses during retirement. Eventually they will take the place of Medicare.

Under this plan, consumers individually finance a major proportion of medical expenditures by drawing from the MSAs. The impact on the federal deficit is minimal because the current Medicare and Medicaid programs are eventually ended. The increase in the deficit results primarily from forgone tax revenues due to tax credits and subsidies to needy individuals.

Cost containment is achieved through enhanced price competition. Since consumers are directly responsible for payment of most medical care out of their MSAs, they have the

---

[3]This discussion is based on Goodman and Musgrave (1992) and Tripoli (1993). See Heffley and Miceli (1998) for an advanced treatment of the impact of incentive plans on medical care utilization.

[4]If only medical premiums paid by employers are tax deductible, horizontal inequities exist because the price of medical coverage depends on employment status rather than income.

TABLE 16-2

A Summary of the Four Health Care Plans

	Medical Savings Accounts	**Individual Mandates**
Universal coverage	This program is not designed to achieve universal coverage. However, health insurance premiums should become more affordable when they become tax deductible and apply mainly to catastrophic plans. Tax credits and subsidies are used to make health insurance more affordable for poor individuals.	The plan is implemented through mandated insurance coverage and a guarantee by the government that basic medical coverage is available across the country. Tax credits and subsidies are available to make coverage affordable to all. Near-universal coverage is attainable.
Financing	The plan is financed primarily out of individual contributions to medical savings accounts. Because government expenditures on Medicare and Medicaid end, the deficit should diminish.	The plan is financed largely by premium payments by consumers either directly or through employers. A tax increase is necessary, which negatively affects the budget deficit. Medicare and Medicaid programs are ended.
Cost containment	Because consumers pay for most health care expenditures out of their own Medisave accounts, they have the incentive to minimize waste and shop around for competitive prices. A reduction in administrative expenses also translates into cost savings.	Costs are contained through the maintenance of a highly competitive medical insurance market. Private insurance vendors are disciplined by the marketplace to provide competitive prices to consumers.
Employment	Minimal impact because labor market distortions are kept to a minimum.	Minor impact because labor market distortions are kept to a minimum.

incentive to reduce waste and comparison shop. Realizing this, health care providers, such as physicians and hospitals, are forced to provide high-quality, competitively priced medical care. This point is made clear if we look at this plan in terms of the generalized model of a health care system presented in Chapter 4. It is apparent that this plan minimizes the impact of third-party payers because most transactions take place directly between consumers and health care providers. As a result, fewer market distortions occur because third-party payers play a less influential role in the MSA plan. In addition, costs are reduced due to administrative savings. With high deductibles on catastrophic health care

TABLE 16-2

A Summary of the Four Health Care Plans *(continued)*

	Managed Competition	**National Health Insurance**
Universal coverage	Employers are required to provide medical coverage to all full-time workers. Subsidies are provided to make it possible for low-income families to purchase medical insurance. Medicaid and Medicare are maintained. Near-universal coverage is possible.	Universal coverage is achieved through a national health insurance plan that covers all citizens.
Financing	Medical coverage is financed primarily through employer mandates so employees most likely pay through forgone wages. Government expenditures are paid through a payroll tax. The impact on the deficit should not be too significant.	Medical coverage is financed out of an income tax. Also, funds for Medicare and Medicaid are diverted to partially offset the cost of the plan. An employer tax equal to the cost of employer-financed medical insurance is also levied.
Cost containment	Cost containment results from the maintenance of a highly competitive private insurance market. A uniform benefit package is offered, and employers are required to pay for 80 percent of the representative plan. The remaining 20 percent provides an incentive for consumers to shop wisely.	Costs are contained through the utilization of a single-payer system that decreases the administration and billing costs that are the by-product of a multi-payer system. Also, global budgeting is used to establish a constant relation between gross domestic product and health care expenditures.
Employment	Likely to have a significant effect because employer mandates may create substantial distortions in labor markets, especially among low-wage workers.	Employment effects will be concentrated in the private insurance market and health care administration.

plans, insurance companies are no longer bogged down with thousands of small claims that are relatively expensive to process. Managed care is likely to thrive under the MSA plan as health care providers and insurance companies strive to control costs and remain competitive. The employment effect of this plan is minimal because it relies heavily on the market mechanism.

Several criticisms of MSAs have been raised (Tanner, 1995). First, critics claim that consumers are not sufficiently informed to make cost-conscious decisions regarding medical treatments. Opponents argue that due to the lack of information, physicians will continue to induce the demand for their services and health care costs will continue to rise. Second, critics argue that consumers will forgo necessary or preventive care to save money in the MSAs for other purposes. Less medical care, in turn, will lead to poorer health and higher health care costs in the long run. Third, opponents allege that the plan will lead to adverse selection as healthy people select MSAs while sick individuals choose conventional insurance. Eventually, the price of insurance will increase and create financial access problems as more and sicker members enroll in conventional insurance plans. Fourth, critics point out that the deductible on catastrophic insurance will be insufficient to control expenditures on high-cost, low-benefit medicine. That is, once a person is hospitalized for a major illness, the size of the deductible will not matter. Since critically sick patients account for most of the spending on health care, the MSA plan will be ineffective in containing health care costs. Finally, critics argue that an MSA plan is regressive since the benefits will accrue primarily to wealthy individuals.

The advocates of medical saving accounts have responded to each of these criticisms. Basically, proponents point to demand studies showing that consumers are conscious of health care prices, even very small out-of-pocket prices. MSAs will make consumers more responsive and cost conscious, since they will consider the full price of medical services. Further, proponents point to the success of MSA plans currently in use in producing medical cost savings and preventing adverse selection. Finally, advocates claim the current tax break for employer-provided insurance is far more regressive than an MSA plan available for all. The MSA plan has recently become a hot item as the Health Insurance Portability and Accountability Act of 1996 establishes an experiment with MSA plans.

Individual Mandates[5]

Like the MSA plan, the individual mandate plan places the responsibility for medical coverage squarely on the shoulders of consumers. Individuals are required by law to purchase a basic medical insurance plan as defined by the government. They still have the option to purchase more comprehensive coverage, and nothing precludes employers from providing medical insurance to their employees.

Universal coverage is achieved through a combination of mandated medical coverage and the government's guarantee that basic medical coverage is available at a competitive price for those unable to pay for a private plan. Tax credits are offered to ensure affordability, and for those who still cannot afford insurance, government vouchers are available. The Medicaid and Medicare programs are eventually phased out.

To make sure competitively priced medical coverage for the basic plan is available to all, the government solicits bids from private insurance vendors throughout the country. At least one basic plan is offered in every geographic region of the country to serve as "fallback" coverage for any consumer who did not purchase a plan in the private market. The plan also moves toward achieving horizontal equity because tax credits depend on income status rather than employment status.

The plan is financed primarily by individual contributions; however, tax credits and subsidies are available. Although Pauly, Danzon, Feldstein, and Hoff (1991) do not provide figures, they believe a modest tax increase is necessary to extend medical coverage to the

---

[5]This overview is based on Pauly, Danzon, Feldstein, and Hoff (1991).

uninsured. The extent of the increase depends on the magnitude of the tax credits and subsidies provided.

Cost containment is ensured through the maintenance of a highly competitive medical insurance market. Private insurance companies find it in their self-interest to provide high-quality, low-cost insurance to consumers who must purchase and pay for their own medical coverage. Competition is also enhanced because the government plays no role as a third-party insurer since the market for medical insurance is completely private. Employment ramifications are likely to be kept to a minimum. In this type of market environment, managed care is likely to be relied on extensively to control costs.

As with the MSA plan, critics of the individual mandate argue that consumers lack the necessary information to shop wisely. Medical insurance plans contain numerous complex terms and conditions, and therefore are difficult for the average person to comprehend. In addition, some argue that the individual mandate provides less incentive than the MSA plan for consumers to consider the full price of the medical services they buy because third-party payers continue to play an influential role under the individual mandate plan. Finally, critics claim that the individual mandate imposes a serious restraint on an individual's freedom of choice (although it should be kept in mind that Social Security and car insurance in many states are presently mandatory).

Managed Competition[6]

The managed-competition plan has received tremendous publicity primarily because it was used as the basis for the Clinton health care plan. The attractive feature of the plan is that it builds on the existing system of employer-provided medical coverage. Employers are mandated to provide medical coverage for basic medical services and pay, for example, an 8 percent payroll tax on the first $22,500 of wages for employees not covered.[7] Self-employed individuals and early retirees must pay for health care coverage with an 8 percent tax on adjusted income up to a preset maximum. The tax is collected through the income tax system.

The most novel portion of this plan is the creation across the country of government insurance buyer organizations called **health alliances**. These public or not-for-profit agencies use their purchasing power to negotiate competitive prices for health insurance from private insurance companies. Individuals without employer-provided insurance and small employers may purchase competitively priced health insurance through one of these alliances. The alliances also serve as brokers that collect premiums, manage enrollment, and carry out other administrative duties. The intent is to have each alliance offer a number of competing plans to their enrollees.

Universal coverage is ensured through employer mandates and subsidies provided to low-income families to pay for medical coverage. Medicaid and Medicare are maintained and eventually take advantage of the alliances to provide medical coverage. The plan is financed primarily with employer-mandated health insurance premiums and consumer payments. Government expenditures are financed primarily by the payroll tax and other revenues resulting from the plan. The impact on the deficit is not likely to be significant.

---

[6]This discussion is based on Enthoven and Kronick (1989) and Enthoven (1993).
[7]Other health care proposals give employers the option to pay a tax in lieu of providing medical coverage to full-time employees. In the popular literature, this is referred to as the "pay-or-play" option.

Cost containment results from competition among private insurers as they vie for customers through the alliances. This is why the term *managed competition* was coined. The health alliances "manage" the various health care plans to ensure there is sufficient "competition" at the insurance end of the medical care market. To simplify matters for consumers and intensify competition, all plans must offer a uniform benefit package. This puts consumers in a better position to make informed choices. As further encouragement for cost-conscious behavior, employers are required to make a fixed contribution toward medical coverage for each employee equal to 80 percent of the average plan's cost in the area. The remaining 20 percent is the employee's responsibility. A limit is also placed on the tax deduction employees can take for premium payments. This encourages consumers to pick less expensive health plans that provide less generous benefits, since they must pay for more costly plans with after-tax dollars.

One criticism of managed competition is that rural areas may lack enough private insurance companies. The scarcity of suppliers may make it difficult to promote price competition (Kronick, Goodman, Wennberg, and Wagner, 1993). Another complaint is that the government-sponsored health alliances may result in "one-size-fits-all" health insurance plans, and, as a result, consumers will lose the benefits of variety. Finally, one of the more controversial elements of employer mandates is the fact that they create labor market distortions of the type discussed in Insight 11–3. Economic theory suggests that mandated benefits may inhibit employment, particularly among low- or minimum-wage workers, and that the costs of benefits are shared by both employees and employers. Employees pay for mandated benefits through wage reductions.

National Health Insurance[8]

The national health insurance plan calls for the implementation of a national health insurance system similar to the one presently existing in Canada. As such, the current multipayer system in the United States is replaced by a single-payer public medical insurance program. In terms of the generalized model of a health care system, this means the role of third-party payer is completely taken over by the government sector, and the private market for medical insurance is almost completely eliminated (some specific services, such as dental and optical care, may continue to be covered by private insurance).

Universal coverage is guaranteed with this plan because everyone is covered for all necessary medical services, with no coinsurance copayments, or deductibles. The plan achieves vertical equity because it is financed out of general taxes, with a heavy reliance on the income tax system. A tax increase is necessary to provide the additional funding needed to broaden coverage to uninsured individuals. Since currently funded medical programs, such as Medicare and Medicaid, are no longer needed, funds earmarked for these programs would be used to finance a national health insurance program. Employer taxes increase by the amount currently spent on health care benefits. The implication is that employer-provided funds are diverted from the private insurance market to a publicly run health insurance program.

Cost containment is based primarily on the efficiencies associated with using a single-payer system. Billing and administration costs are reduced because health care providers no longer need to contend with the complex set of insurance forms and billing procedures

---

[8]This discussion is based on Himmelstein and Woolhandler (1989).

that result from a multipayer system. In addition, overall expenditures are controlled by establishing a link between gross domestic product and health care costs. Once the proportion between the two is established, overall health care costs are allowed to grow only as fast as the overall economy. Global budgets and simplified fee schedules are utilized to compensate health care providers, such as hospitals and physicians, for services provided. The role of managed care with a national insurance plan is difficult to determine, because most of the impetus for managed care comes from the private health insurance market, which the plan eliminates.

Finally, the employment effects are likely to be most noticeable in the private health insurance market and health care administration. With the elimination of the private health insurance market and the decrease in administrative waste, some job displacement is likely to occur, particularly in the short run.

While the national health insurance plan comes closest to providing universal health insurance, a general criticism has been levied against the plan. The extensive involvement of government and the elimination of private insurers alarm those who believe that government enterprise is monopoly enterprise. Critics claim that the creation of financial innovations to control medical costs would be weakened in a government-run health insurance program. Critics also argue that because a competitive incentive is missing, a public monopoly insurer may offer little variety and be unresponsive to consumer wants.

ATTEMPTS AT STATE HEALTH CARE: SUCCESSES AND FAILURES

Unlike most countries, the United States follows a more decentralized approach to health care policy that allows individual states a certain degree of latitude in developing their own health care policies. The reason is largely historic and has its roots in our federalist form of government, which provides states with limited discretion to govern. Coupled with this tradition has been the general belief in the United States that issues relating to health, education, and poverty are best addressed at the local or community level. A case in point is the Medicaid program, which is jointly financed by the federal and state governments. Since states foot a portion of the bill, they have been given some say as to how those tax dollars are spent. As a result, vastly different Medicaid programs have developed across states over time.

Advocates for a decentralized approach to health care reform point out that this approach is more democratic. This is because states are in a better position than the federal government to address the unique needs of the local population. Another advantage is that states can be seen as "laboratories" or "guinea pigs" where alternative policies can be tried out to see whether they should be adopted at the national level or in other states. Finally, advocates of the decentralized approach are fond of pointing out that the issue of whether health care reform should take place at the state or federal level is largely moot because our system of government allows states to block any major reforms if they desire. All this suggests that states are likely to continue playing a critical role in the formation of U.S. health care policy for years to come.

Confronted with the burden of rising health care costs, a growing number of individuals who lack health care coverage, and a citizenry in no mood for further tax increases, most states have been forced to reexamine their health care programs. Many states are

INSIGHT 16-2

Medical Savings Accounts—The Case of Singapore

The pressure to contain rising health care costs has brought a considerable amount of attention to Singapore's health care system because it relies on medical savings accounts. Current figures indicate that Singapore spends between 3 and 4 percent of GDP on health care. This is a far cry from the 13 percent of GDP the United States currently allocates. Some attribute the ability of Singapore to tame health care spending on the cost containment incentives that come into play with medical savings accounts.

According to Barr (2001), the Singapore health care system is composed of three basic institutional arrangements. The Medisave program is a compulsory savings plan that forms the basis for the individual medical savings accounts. The contribution rates range from 6 to 8 percent of monthly income and are shared between employee and employer. Self-employed individuals must pay the entire amount and caps are placed on monthly contributions, which prohibit more affluent individuals from accumulating unreasonably high savings balances. Medisave accounts are used primarily to finance inpatient hospital care and strict payment schedules are in place to protect the accounts from being depleted too rapidly.

To protect individuals from the financial burden of a major illness, a catastrophic illness insurance plan, called MediShield, is available. This insurance plan is optional and pays for 80 percent of hospital expenses after a rather substantial deductible has been met. The third institutional component of the Singapore health care system is the Medifund, which is an endowment established by the government to finance the health care needs of the poor.

Barr (2001) contends that the ability of the Singapore health care system to contain costs can only partially be explained by the implementation of medical savings accounts. Strict government controls on inputs and prices along with the rationing of medical care have played an even greater role in controlling costs. Other explanations include a relatively young population and the existence of a number of traditional Chinese medical practitioners that are not funded under the government-sponsored health care programs.

SOURCE: Michael D. Barr. "Medical Savings Accounts in Singapore." *Journal of Health Politics, Policy and Law* 26 (August 2001), pp. 709–26.

aggressively investigating various policy options aimed at reforming the financing and delivery of medical care. Naturally, space limitations prohibit a discussion of the health care reform taking place in each state. With this constraint in mind, we now provide a brief overview of the health care reform packages that were adopted in Hawaii, Maryland, Minnesota, and Oregon over the last several years. These states were chosen because they represent the broad spectrum of policies currently under consideration in other states.

Hawaii: The Case of Employer Mandates

Hawaii's health care system achieved a certain level of recognition a few years ago, primarily because it succeeded in achieving near universal health care coverage. Estimates indicated that in 1995 only 5.8 percent of full-time workers between the ages of 18 and 64 and their dependents were without health insurance. That was the lowest rate in the country at that point in time (AARP, 1997). Many years before other states began taking the notion of health care reform seriously, Hawaii passed the Prepaid Health Act of 1974, which mandated, with few exceptions, that employers provide health insurance to all employees. Each medical plan must provide a minimum number of benefits, and the employee's premium contribution is limited to 1.5 percent of monthly salary.

Because a significant proportion of the population remained without medical insurance despite the employer mandate, the State Health Insurance Program of Hawaii (SHIP) was created in 1989. Individuals without insurance who were not eligible for Medicaid or Medicare were able to purchase medical insurance through SHIP. The SHIP program was later rolled into the Hawaii Health QUEST Program that was designed to provide medical insurance for those individuals with incomes up to 300 percent of the poverty level. The premium was based on a sliding scale, with those individuals with incomes at or below the poverty level paying nothing for coverage. In addition, this program provided a standard package of medical benefits. MCOs compete with one another for QUEST contracts (Intergovernment Health Policy Project, 1995).

Unfortunately, however, the uninsured rate has increased significantly in recent years, nearly 10 percent in 2001. A number of factors have been offered to explain this increase. First, the high cost of the QUEST program has forced the state in recent years to tighten eligibility requirements. Second, the state's rather anemic rate of job growth has meant that fewer people are eligible for employer-mandated health insurance benefits. Finally, there is a growing number of employers that provide health insurance only to employees and not their families (*Health Trends in Hawaii*, 2002).

This increase in the number of uninsured individuals coupled with the burden of rising health care costs resulted in an interesting debate concerning whether the state should be granted greater authority to regulate insurance premiums. The debate was exacerbated by the fact that the health insurance market in Hawaii is dominated by the Hawaii Medical Service Association, HMSA, which covers about half of the state's population, and Kaiser Permanente which covers another 20 percent of the population (Cho, 2002). Champions of regulation argue for the need to control premiums and counteract the dominant positions of the two largest insurance carriers, while opponents of the idea argue that the insurance market needs increased competition, not increased regulation. Those in favor of rate regulation eventually prevailed and effective January 1, 2003, the State Insurance Commissioner is granted the authority to review and approve health insurance premium rates (Danninger, 2002).

Maryland: The Case of Regulation

Over the years, the state of Maryland has taken a decidedly regulatory approach to health care policy. Beginning in the 1970s, it implemented an all-payer hospital payment system that is essentially still in place today. Maryland's all-payer payment system regulates the price paid by all buyers of hospital services. Even price discounts to MCOs are limited by the regulation (McDonough, 1997). In 2000 Maryland's hospital payment system went through a significant overhaul. "The goals of the redesign were to provide predictability and stability; be prospective in nature; recognize input cost inflation; be streamlined; and, be reflective of the national experience" (Health Services Cost Review Commission, 2002).

The Maryland Health Care Commission also plays a major role in Maryland's health care system. Of particular importance is the maintenance of the Comprehensive Standard Health Benefit Plan that was established in 1994 to provide small- to medium-sized firms access to health insurance. Any health insurance company doing business in Maryland must offer a standard health insurance package to all businesses employing 50 or fewer workers. Coverage cannot be denied for any medical precondition or frequency of claims submitted. In addition, a community-based rating system has been adopted that allows for only minor adjustments in premiums. To control costs, the average community-rated premium can be no greater than 12 percent of the average wage in the state. However, this legislation does not mandate that employers finance health insurance. The hope is that once employers with few workers have access to reasonably priced medical insurance, they will voluntarily provide it to their employees (Anderson, Heyssel, and Dickler, 1993). Currently, 23 different insurance carriers provide health insurance to nearly 500,000 individuals (Maryland Health Care Commission, 2002).

Minnesota: The Case of Regulated Competition

In contrast to Maryland, Minnesota had taken a more free market approach to health care through the years, except for a relatively brief period in the early 1990s. In 1992 Minnesota approved MinnesotaCare (originally called HealthRight) which addressed the issues of cost containment and access. The cost containment plan placed great emphasis on competition along with some degree of regulation (Blewett, 1994). The competitive aspect focused on integrated service networks (ISNs), which were prepaid health plans that competed on the basis of price and quality. Competition was made possible by the mandatory disclosure of price and quality information and standardization of health benefits coverage.

The regulatory component called for the state commissioner of health to set a cap on the growth of ISN premiums and controlled fees of out-of-network providers through an all-payer rate-setting system. Other cost containment mechanisms included targets for health care expenditure growth, statewide and regional limits on health care spending, health care planning, retrospective review of capital expenditures for new technologies that cost more than $500,000, restrictions on physician referrals, and a ban on balance billing for Medicare charges (Leichter, 1993).

The act addressed the problem of uninsured persons primarily by offering state-subsidized coverage based on a sliding-fee scale to children, their parents, and eventually others not covered by Medicaid. The subsidized insurance was financed through a variety of taxes on health care providers and a 5-cent-per-pack increase in the state cigarette tax. The legislation also called for significant changes in the small-group insurance market similar to those adopted in Maryland. Any insurance company offering health insurance policies in Minnesota must guarantee coverage regardless of health conditions, and policies cannot be canceled due to excessive claims or health reasons. In addition, a modified community rating system was put in place, and small businesses were offered low-cost insurance plans that do not include selected high-cost medical services (Intergovernment Health Policy Project, 1993).

In 1995, the Minnesota legislature began to repeal or modify many of the reforms enacted earlier. For example, the legislature repealed the all-payer rate-setting regulations. In addition, the state curtailed the expansion of MinnesotaCare subsidies to childless households with incomes up to 275 percent of the poverty level (Intergovernment Health Policy Project, 1995). In 1997, the legislature repealed other health care reforms contained in

MinnesotaCare. In particular, the state repealed revenue limits placed on health care providers and changed the growth limits on health care expenditures to cost containment goals that are now voluntary (Minnesota Department of Health, 1998).

Oregon: The Case of Rationing Medicaid Services

Confronted with the conflicting problems of rising Medicaid expenditures and a growing number of people without medical insurance, Oregon developed one of the more controversial health care reform packages. At issue was a plan that rationed medical care to those on Medicaid. The Oregon Health Plan was troubling to many because it represented the first time a government authority had taken such an active role in the explicit rationing of medical services in the United States.

The focal point of the program was a prioritized list of approximately 740 medical procedures. The list was developed after an exhaustive process that measured the relative value of each medical procedure. Each medical procedure was ranked based on its ability to improve health, its cost, and perceived community value. Based on the list, treatment for appendicitis was ranked 12 and medical therapy for a stroke was ranked 287, for example.

Once the legislature has determined the level of funding for the program, the health services commission determines the number of medical procedures the state can finance. According to recent estimates (October 2002), the state covers 566 out of 736 illnesses or disorders. A lack of funds precludes coverage for the remaining 170. For example, any Medicaid recipient in need of a liver transplant because of cancer (ranked number 608) would be denied coverage under the Oregon plan.[9]

Proponents of the Oregon plan argue that the state is trading off comprehensive coverage for a few to make greater access available to many. Prior to the plan, the Oregon Medicaid program covered only individuals with incomes at or below 58 percent of the poverty level as established by the federal government. When the plan was implemented, individuals with incomes at or below 100 percent of the poverty level became eligible for Medicaid coverage. In addition, pregnant women and children below age 6 can also qualify if family income does not exceed 133 percent of the poverty level. For a fixed budget, greater coverage can be achieved only by denying services to a relatively few individuals who need very costly medical care relative to the benefits received. The Oregon Plan also attempted to control cost through the use of managed care (Bodenheimer, 1997).

As you can imagine, criticisms of the program have emanated from all corners of the health care field. From an economic perspective, the program was criticized on both efficiency and equity grounds. Regarding efficiency, there was concern about whether the state can objectively determine the relative values of alternative medical procedures. Tanner (1993) argued that such determination were better left to the marketplace. Equity questions revolved around the fact that the burden of rationing fell exclusively on the poor while those individuals of more affluent means were left untouched.

The desire to control costs and extend health care coverage has resulted in additional changes in the Oregon Plan. Effective February 1, 2003, three different plans, or benefit packages, are available: Oregon Health Plan Plus, Oregon Health Plan Standard, and the Family Health Insurance Assistance Program, FHIAP. The Oregon Health Plan Plus, or OHP

---

[9]This information is available on the Office of Oregon Health Policy and Research web site at http://www.ohppr.state.or.us.

Plus, provides health care coverage to those eligible for Medicaid and other select populations with incomes up to 185 percent of the federal poverty level. The Oregon Health Plan Standard provides fewer benefits than the OHP Plus package but covers individuals who are not eligible for the OHP Plus benefit package and have incomes potentially up to 185 percent of the federal poverty level. Finally, FHIAP provides premium subsidies for the purchasing of private health insurance plans. The ultimate goal is to expand the coverage of the Oregon Health Plan to include up to an additional 60,000 people without any additional outlays from the state.[10]

Before we leave the topic of the health care reform in Oregon, it is interesting to note that in the November 2002 election Oregon voters considered a ballot to have universal health care insurance covering a wide range of medical services, including massages. At a cost of $20 billion the plan was to be financed by increases in the income and payroll taxes along with revenues from the federal, state, and local governments. The proposal was soundly defeated with 79 percent of the voters rejecting the idea (MacDonald, 2002). The implication was that while voters in Oregon were willing to embrace certain health care initiatives that extend coverage to segments of the poor, they were not willing to go so far as to extend health care coverage to all Oregonians.

What Can Be Gained from State Attempts at Health Care Reform?

After reviewing the tremendous diversity in the strategies adopted by states to reform health care, one is left to question what knowledge can be gained from all of this. Barrand and Schroeder (1994) suggest that four basic lessons can be gleaned from health care reform at the state level. First, the tremendous diversity in health care reform reflects the diversity in our health care system across states and the differing views concerning the appropriate role of government. Reform at the national level must be broad enough to consider diversity. Second, attempts at state health care reform reveal that the political process is as complicated at the state level as it is at the federal level. It appears that the political gridlock impeding health care reform at the federal level is also present at the state level. Third, "implementing" health care reform may be more difficult than "designing" reform. With the implementation of such items as new billing procedures, price controls, and quality reviews, states face an enormous set of practical problems in getting the reform up and running. These problems should be kept in mind when changes are made at the federal level. Finally, the need for public education is paramount. Confusion on the part of the public concerning various policies under review only clouds the issue and makes the task of reforming health care even more difficult.

AN OVERVIEW OF THE CLINTON HEALTH CARE PLAN

The National Health Security Act proposed by former President Bill Clinton drew extensively on the managed-competition model of health care reform. Each region of the country would be represented by one not-for-profit health alliance that would utilize its

---

[10]Consult the Oregon Department of Human Services at http://www.omap.hr.state.or.us for further information.

INSIGHT 16 – 3

How Much Health Care Is Tax-Financed in the United States?

According to data published by the Centers for Medicare and Medicaid Services (CMS), government, at all levels, has been responsible for paying for roughly 40 to 45 percent of all health care over the last three decades (http://cms.hhs.gov/statistics/nhe/default.asp). Relative to government, this figure suggests that the private sector has continued to exert greater control over the health care purse strings. Woolhandler and Himmelstein (2002), however, scrutinize the method CMS uses to measure government spending in the national health accounts and show that government has much more control over health care spending than the private sector does in the United States. Readers may be interested to know that Steffie Woolhandler and David Himmelstein are both professors at Harvard Medical School, primary care physicians, and founders of Physicians for a National Health Program, a nationwide group with more than 9,000 members (visit http://www.pnhp.org).

Woolhandler and Himmelstein explain that CMS includes only direct purchasing of medical care for programs such as Medicare, Medicaid, and government-owned hospitals in its measure of government spending. Consequently, public employee benefits, such as the Federal Employees Health Benefits Program, are missing from the reported figure by CMS because although the government supports these public programs with tax financing, private insurers are responsible for writing the actual check because they administer the program on behalf of the government. In addition, Woolhandler and Himmelstein point out that health insurance premiums are exempted from various types of federal, state, and city taxes, so implicitly the government also pays for this portion of health care by granting these tax preferences.

To get a better idea about tax financing of health care, the authors add the direct purchasing of medical care by government, expenditures on public employee health benefits that are tax-financed but administered by the private sector, and the value of the health insurance premium tax preference. In 1999, they showed that direct spending of government equaled 45 percent of all health care spending. Public employees' benefits accounted for another 5.4 percent and the tax subsidy for health insurance premiums amounted to another 9.1 percent. Thus government, at all levels, was responsible for financing nearly 60 percent of all health care costs in the United States, indicating that tax financing accounts for the largest source of health care funds.

On a per capita basis, their estimates for 1999 revealed that the U.S. government spends more on health care than the governments in Switzerland, Canada, Germany, France, Australia, Italy, Japan, Sweden, and the United Kingdom. These are countries where the government traditionally has played a much greater role in the financing and reimbursing of health care. Of course, the much higher overall health care spending in the United States provides part of the explanation for the greater per capita spending figure by the government.

These estimates of Woolhandler and Himmelstein are certainly provocative because they show that tax financing represents the major source of funds for health care in the United States. Indeed, tax financing accounts for an even greater share of health care costs

(continued)

considering that not-for-profit health care organizations such as hospitals and nursing homes are also granted tax preferences. It will be interesting to see how these highly credible estimates of Woolhandler and Himmelstein are interpreted and used in future policy discussions concerning health care reform.

SOURCE: Steffie Woolhandler and David U. Himmelstein. "Paying for National Health Insurance—and Not Getting It." *Health Affairs* 21 (July/August 2002), pp. 88–98.

purchasing power to negotiate premiums for health insurance with private insurance companies. Employers and individuals would be able to purchase health insurance through these alliances at rates that would be lower than those under the present decentralized, fragmented system. Large firms with more than 5,000 employees would be able to form their own corporate alliances.[11]

Universal coverage was to be accomplished primarily through employer-mandated health insurance. Each employer would be required to provide health insurance to its full-time employees and finance at least 80 percent of the premium of the average plan in the health alliance. The remaining portion would be the responsibility of the employee. To make the cost affordable for employers, total premium contributions would be capped at 3.5 to 7.9 percent of total payroll. Additional reductions in premiums would be made available to small firms. Also, adjustments in premiums would be made for unemployed persons, part-time workers, and self-employed individuals.

The plan would be financed from a combination of savings from existing public health insurance programs and additional taxes. Savings from Medicaid would result as that program is merged into the Clinton plan. Presumably, the rate of growth of expenditures for the Medicaid program would diminish over time as the cost containment policies of the Clinton plan take hold. Savings in the Medicare program would emanate from a variety of sources, including more extensive use of managed care and a reduction in payments to providers. There would also be savings from other federal medical programs as they are integrated into the system. Additional taxes would include an increase in the cigarette tax of 75 cents per pack and a 1 percent payroll tax on all corporate alliances.

Cost containment would be achieved primarily through the creation of a national health board. Among other duties, that agency would be responsible for determining the maximum rate of growth of health insurance premiums from year to year. Indirectly, that would give the national health board control over the growth of health care expenditures by allowing it to establish global budgets for each health alliance.

---

[11]The notion of one alliance per region differs slightly from the managed-competition plan developed by Enthoven and Kronick (1989). Under that plan, multiple alliances would be set up in different regions. The argument against multiple alliances is that such an arrangement would add unwanted complexity to the structure. Enthoven and Singer (1995) counter with the argument that health alliances would become too strong under the Clinton plan. Health alliances are meant "to be market makers, not regulating agencies" (p. 89). With only one alliance per region, power may become too concentrated on the demand side and result in numerous mergers on the supply side of the market. The result would be less competition, not more. In addition, with only one health alliance, it may become too easy for interest groups to exert political pressure on the system.

The Collapse of the Clinton Health Care Plan

When former President Clinton unveiled his plan to reform the U.S. health care system on September 22, 1993, public support was initially strong.[12] Early public opinion polls reported twice as many people supporting than opposing the Clinton plan (Rockman, 1995). By the summer of 1994, support for the Clinton plan had dipped to about 40 percent, and it was highly unlikely that any comprehensive health care package would be enacted. The final blow was the election of November 1994, which gave the Republican party control of the House of Representatives. The question now becomes: Why did support for the Clinton health care reform plan erode so rapidly?

The most obvious explanation is that the Clinton health care plan lacked the necessary political support in Congress. Brady and Buckley (1995) utilized the median voter hypothesis to address that possibility. The median position is the middle position at which an equal number is above or below it. As a result, the median position represents the decisive or swing position under a simple majority voting rule (i.e., 51 percent agreement). By observing the characteristics of the median voter, we can identify whether a policy under consideration is likely to pass or fail.

Brady and Buckley ranked each member of the 103d Congress from most to least liberal (or most to least conservative) and argued that the Clinton plan would pass only if it mustered the support of the median voter in each house of Congress. Without the support of those members of Congress, the Clinton health care plan had little or no chance of becoming law. After reviewing the voting records of those legislators at or near the 50th position in the Senate and the 218th position in the House (there are 435 representatives), Brady and Buckley pointed out that the median voters in both the House of Representatives and the Senate represented conservative constituents primarily from southern and border states. Based on the median voter hypothesis, Brady and Buckley concluded that the Clinton plan was politically to the left of the median voter in both houses of Congress and therefore would not be enacted.

Other analysts attribute the demise of the plan to its complexity and the failure of the Clinton administration to articulate the plan to the public in clear and precise terms. Many people found it difficult to understand, and, as debate over reform progressed, they began to worry more about its ill effects than the problem of health care reform. As a result, public support dwindled out of a fear of the unknown.

Steinman and Watts (1995) point to the political institutions in the United States that are biased against reform. Our political system is based on the federalist model, in which political power is fragmented and shared among many groups. This situation "yields enormous power to intransigent interest groups and thus makes efforts" at reform extremely difficult (p. 329). Along similar lines, Morone (1995) states that the U.S. political process is devised "to produce a stalemate" (p. 394). With our system of government, political interest groups had the ability to put pressure on the political process to effectively block any meaningful reform. Also, because the period of debate was so protracted, opponents of reform had time to muster a public relations campaign to turn public opinion against the plan. (Remember the infamous Harry and Louise commercials?)

Navarro (1995) looks at the entire episode from the perspective of class relations. The corporate or capitalist class in the United States rejected the Clinton reform package

---

[12]For a more comprehensive look at why the Clinton plan failed, consult the spring 1995 issues of either *Health Affairs* or the *Journal of Health Politics, Policy and Law.*

because it would weaken their hold over the working class. Any program that guarantees universal medical coverage infringes on the ability of the corporate class to dictate the terms of employment to the working class. To maintain a strong hold, it is preferable that the working class depend on the corporate class for medical coverage rather than on a government entity.

These are just a few of the many reasons being offered to explain why the Clinton health care plan collapsed. It is safe to say that a multitude of social, political, and economic factors contributed to the failure of the plan. Yankelovich (1995) summarizes the entire process best: "Technical experts designed it, special interests argued it, political leaders sold it, journalists more interested in the political ramifications than its contents kibitzed it, and advertising attacked it. There was no way for the average American to understand what it meant for them" (p. 9).

SUMMARY

The advanced state of technology is the greatest strength of the U.S. health care system. Premature babies, sometimes weighing much less than 2 pounds, face a relatively good chance of surviving if they are born in the United States because of the state of technology. A relatively high life expectancy after age 80 is another reflection of the advanced state of health care technology in the United States (OECD, 2002). That is, people 80 years and older in the U.S. tend to live longer than their counterparts in most other countries because of the abundance of advanced medical technologies. Also, the United States continues to be the world leader in pharmaceutical innovation. As mentioned in the text, pharmaceutical products save, extend, and improve the quality of lives.

Unfortunately, the U.S. health care system is not without weaknesses. Its most glaring weakness is exemplified by the fact that nearly 15 percent of the population is without health insurance. The lack of health insurance creates medical access problems and subjects a family's income to the vagaries of health status. The inability to successfully control costs is another major weakness of the U.S. health care system. The growth of health care costs continues unabated, although the pace has slowed in recent years mostly due to the influence of managed-care organizations. Whether managed care can continue to slow the growth of health care costs remains questionable.

Eliminating the weaknesses while maintaining the strengths is a challenge faced by any plan for changing the U.S. health care system. Indeed, much of the debate on health care reform reflects that dilemma. This chapter presented four generic health care reform plans to provide insight into the health care reform debate in the United States. The MSA plan is the most market oriented of the four plans. With this plan, consumers are allowed to contribute to medical savings accounts with pretax income to pay for routine medical expenses. Low-cost catastrophic medical insurance with high deductibles is also available to pay for major medical expenses.

The individual mandate plan also relies heavily on the market mechanism to allocate medical resources. Consumers are required to purchase a private medical insurance plan that covers basic medical care. To make this possible, the government guarantees that basic insurance coverage is available throughout the country at a competitive price through a government-sponsored fallback plan. In addition, tax credits and subsidies are available to further lower the price for those who cannot afford health insurance.

The managed-care plan calls for more government intervention than the previous two plans. The key to this plan is the formation of health alliances, government-sponsored organizations that negotiate with private insurance companies for competitively priced medical insurance. Also, employers are mandated to provide health insurance to employees.

Finally, the national health insurance plan calls for the most extensive level of government involvement in medical markets. With this plan, the government replaces the private insurance market by offering a national health insurance plan that covers all citizens for medical expenses. Furthermore, global budgets and price controls are utilized to contain the growth of medical costs over time.

These four plans capture the essence of the vast majority of the health care reform plans currently being considered. The vast differences among the plans indicate the many opinions that exist concerning what ails the U.S. health care system and what needs to be done to correct those ailments.

We also saw that the states have taken a very active role in health care reform. Almost every state has wrestled with health care reform. Despite the fact that the policies vary immensely across states, the goal is always the same: to simultaneously contain the growth of health care costs while improving access to quality care.

The chapter closed with a basic blueprint of the Clinton health care plan. The Clinton health care plan represents the sixth time during the 20th century that the United States has debated a greatly expanded role for government in health care. Previous debates took place in the late 1910s, the 1930s, the late 1940s, the 1960s, the 1970s, and the 1990s. Only once—during the 1960s, when the Medicaid and Medicare programs were instituted—were proponents of government involvement in medical care successful (Skocpol, 1995).

REVIEW QUESTIONS AND PROBLEMS

1. Discuss the four generic plans for health care reform in terms of the general model of a health care system presented in Chapter 4. Pay particular attention to the role third-party payers play in each plan.
2. Discuss each of the four generic plans for health care reform in terms of theories X and Y as discussed in Chapter 1.
3. Which one of the four generic plans of health care reform appeals to you the most? Substantiate your opinion using economic theory.
4. Which generic health care plan would best correct moral hazard? Why? Which generic plan would best achieve scale economies in health insurance administration? Why? Which plan would provide the most variety? Why?
5. Choose a state other than one of the four discussed in the chapter, and research any basic changes in health care policy that have been made or are currently being considered.
6. Discuss the main features of the Clinton health care reform plan, and provide some reasons why it was not enacted.

ONLINE RESOURCES

To access Internet links related to the topics in this chapter, please visit our web site at http://santerre.swcollege.com.

REFERENCES

American Association of Retired Persons. *Reforming the Health Care System: State Profiles* 1997. Washington, D.C.: 1997.

Anderson, Gerald, Robert Heyssel, and Robert Dickler. "Competition versus Regulation: Its Effect on Hospitals." *Health Affairs* 12 (spring 1993), pp. 70–80.

Anderson, Gerard F. "In Search of Value: An International Comparison of Cost, Access, and Outcomes." *Health Affairs* 16 (November/December 1997), pp. 163–71.

Barr, Michael D. "Medical Savings Accounts in Singapore." *Journal of Health Politics, Policy and Law* 26 (August 2001), pp. 709–26.

Barrand, Nancy L., and Steven Schroeder. "Lessons from the States." *Inquiry* 31 (spring 1994), pp. 10–13.

Blewett, Lynn A. "Reforms in Minnesota: Forging the Path." *Health Affairs* 13 (fall 1994), pp. 200–9.

Bodenheimer, Thomas. "The Oregon Health Plan—Lessons for the Nation." *New England Journal of Medicine* 337 (August 28, 1997), pp. 651–55.

Brady, David W., and Kara M. Buckley. "Health Care Reform in the 103d Congress: A Predictable Failure." *Journal of Health Politics, Policy and Law* 20 (spring 1995), pp. 447–84.

Caldwell, Bert W. "The Cost of Medical Care from the Viewpoint of the Hospital." In *Hospitals and the Cost of Medical Care*. Papers of the American Conference of Hospital Services. Chicago: American Hospital Association, February 18, 1930.

Chenery, William L. "Hospital Fees Hit the Middle Class Hard." *The New York Times*, November 9, 1924, p. 7.

Cho, Frank. "Insurance Rate Control May Not Work For Hawaii." *The Honolulu Advertiser.com*, posted February 10, 2002.

Danninger, Lyn. "Health Insurance Rate Oversight Bills Clears Legislature." *Starbulletin.com*, May 1, 2002.

Enthoven, Alain C. "The History and Principles of Managed Competition." *Health Affairs* (supplement 1993), pp. 24–48.

Enthoven, Alain C., and Richard Kronick. "A Consumer-Choice Health Plan for the 1990s." Parts 1 and 2. *New England Journal of Medicine* 320 (January 5, 1989), pp. 29–37 and (January 12, 1989), pp. 94–101.

Enthoven, Alain C., and Sara J. Singer. "Market-Based Reform: What to Regulate and by Whom?" *Health Affairs* 14 (spring 1995), pp. 105–19.

Feldman, Roger, Kenneth E. Thorpe, and Bradley Gray. "Policy Watch: The Federal Employees Health Benefits Plan." *Journal of Economic Perspectives* 16 (spring 2002), pp. 207–218.

Goodman, John C., and Gerald L. Musgrave. *Patient Power: Solving America's Health Care Crisis*. Washington, D.C.: Cato Institute, 1992.

Health Services Cost Review Commission, 2002. http://www.hscrc.state.md.us/about_us/about_us.htm.

Health Trends in Hawaii. http://www.healthtrends.org (accessed November 22, 2002).

Heffley, Dennis R., and Thomas J. Miceli. "The Economics of Incentive Based Health Plans." *Journal of Risk and Insurance* 65 (September 1998), pp. 445–65.

Himmelstein, David, and Steffie Woolhandler. "A National Health Program for the United States." *New England Journal of Medicine* 320 (January 12, 1989), pp. 102–8.

Intergovernment Health Policy Project. *Profiles of the States and Health Care Reform.* Washington, D.C.: George Washington University, July 1993.

———. *Profiles of the States and Health Care Reform.* Washington, D.C.: George Washington University, October 1995.

Kronick, Richard, David C. Goodman, John Wennberg, and Edward Wagner. "The Marketplace in Health Care Reform: The Demographic Limitations of Managed Competition." *New England Journal of Medicine* 328 (January 14, 1993), pp. 148–52.

Leichter, Howard M. "Minnesota: The Trip from Acrimony to Accommodation." *Health Affairs* 12 (summer 1993), pp. 48–57.

MacDonald, John. "Defeat of Health Care Reform in Oregon Heartens Opponents." *Hartford Courant*, November 7, 2002.

Maryland Health Care Commission, 2002. http://www.mhcc.state.md.us/mhccinfo/objectives.htm.

McDonough, John E. "Tracking the Demise of State Hospital Rate Setting." *Health Affairs* 16 (January/February 1997), pp. 142–49.

Minnesota Department of Health. *MinnesotaCare Interim Growth Limits Changed to Cost Containment.* February 1998.

Morone, James A. "Nativism, Hollow Corporations and Managed Competition: Why the Clinton Health Care Reform Failed." *Journal of Health Politics, Policy and Law* 20 (spring 1995), pp. 394–98.

Navarro, Vincente. "Why Congress Did Not Enact Health Care Reform." *Journal of Health Politics, Policy and Law* 20 (spring 1995), pp. 455–62.

OECD Health Data 2002. Paris, France. Organization for Economic Cooperation and Development, 2002.

Pauly, Mark, Patricia Danzon, Paul Feldstein, and John Hoff. "A Plan for Responsible National Health Insurance." *Health Affairs* 10 (spring 1991), pp. 5–25.

Rockman, Bert A. "The Clinton Presidency and Health Care Reform." *Journal of Health Politics, Policy and Law* 20 (spring 1995), pp. 399–402.

Skocpol, Theda. "The Rise and Resounding Demise of the Clinton Plan." *Journal of Health Politics, Policy and Law* 19 (spring 1995), pp. 86–98.

Steinman, Sven, and Jon Watts. "It's the Institutions, Stupid! Why Comprehensive National Health Insurance Always Fails in America." *Journal of Health Politics, Policy and Law* 19 (spring 1995), pp. 329–72.

Stevens, Rosemary. *In Sickness and in Wealth.* New York: Basic Books, 1987.

Tanner, Michael. "Medical Savings Accounts: Answering the Critics." *Policy Analysis*, no. 228. Washington, D.C.: Cato Institute, May 25, 1995.

———. "Laboratory Failures: States Are No Model for Health Care Reform." *Policy Analysis*, no. 207. Washington, D.C.: Cato Institute, September 23, 1993.

Tripoli, Leigh. "Agoraphobia: What Ails Most of the Conservative Proposals to Reform Health Care." *Business Economics* (April 1993), pp. 30–35.

Woolhandler, Steffie, and David U. Himmelstein. "Paying for National Health Insurance—and Not Getting It." *Health Affairs* 21 (July/August 2002), pp. 89–98.

Yankelovich, Daniel. "The Debate That Wasn't: The Public and the Clinton Plan." *Health Affairs* 14 (spring 1995), pp. 7–23.

actual competition   The level of competition or rivalry as determined by the number of firms currently operating in the market.

adverse selection   Occurs when an individual with poor health acquires low-risk medical insurance meant for healthy consumers. Results when an asymmetry of information develops between the insurer and the subscriber concerning the subscriber's true health status.

advertising   Promotional activities undertaken by a firm to either manipulate the demand for its product or provide more information to consumers. (See *informational advertising, persuasive advertising*, and *reminder advertising*.)

Agency for Health Policy Research   A government agency established to develop outcomes research and medical care guidelines for physician services.

agency theory   A theory that views relationships as a contract between principals and agents. The proper design of the compensation package is an important consideration in agency theory since the interests of the agent are very likely to differ from those of the principal.

allocative efficiency   The condition in which the optimal amount of output is produced given the underlying structure of social benefits and costs. (See *production possibilities curve*.)

American Medical Association (AMA)   A national organization founded in 1897 that represents the collective interests of physicians.

antitrust laws   A body of legislation aimed at promoting competition in the U.S. economy.

applied research   See *technology*.

assignment   A policy under Medicare whereby physicians agree to accept a guaranteed payment for their services and in return forgo the right to balance-bill Medicare patients.

asymmetry of information   The situation where two economic agents in a market transaction have different amounts of relevant information. Asymmetry may allow the agent with more information to practice opportunistic behavior.

average fixed costs   Total fixed costs divided by the quantity of output.

average product   Total output divided by the level of a factor input, such as labor.

average total costs   Total costs divided by the quantity of output.

average variable costs   Total variable costs divided by the quantity of output.

balance billing   A situation where medical care providers bill patients in excess of the price established by a third-party payer.

Balanced Budget Act of 1997 (BBA)   An act passed by Congress in 1997 that significantly expands the role of managed care in the Medicare Program. (See also *Medicare + Choice*.)

Balanced budget refinement act of 1999 (BBRA)   An act passed by Congress in 1999 that allowed health care providers more time to accommodate many of the changes called for in the Balanced Budget Act of 1997.

barrier to entry   An obstacle that prevents firms from costlessly entering a particular market. In the health care field, barriers can exist because of cost structure or legal restrictions.

basic research   See *technology*.

Blue Cross/Blue Shield   A traditionally not-for-profit insurance company that provides medical insurance for hospital (Blue Cross) and physician (Blue Shield) services.

bounded rationality   The notion that people, in general, have a limited ability to formulate and solve problems at a point in time.

boycotting   An agreement among competitors in a given input or output market not to do business with a particular supplier or customer. Boycotting is prohibited by the Sherman Antitrust Act.

brand loyalty advantage   See *first mover*.

capitation payment   A method of payment for medical services whereby medical care providers receive a fixed payment per person in return for providing medical care services regardless of the quantity of medical care delivered.

Centers for Medicare and Medicaid Services Formerly known as the Health Care Financing Administration, this federal agency is responsible for administering the Medicare, Medicaid, and SCHIP programs.

certificate of need (CON) laws State laws requiring health care providers to receive permission from a state agency before making a capital purchase above a stipulated amount.

ceteris paribus A Latin phrase meaning "all other factors remaining constant."

cherry picking A practice by private insurance companies of offering medical insurance to individuals they believe to be healthy while denying coverage to those they believe to be unhealthy.

clinical investigation See *technology*.

clinical need The quantity of medical care that a clinical expert prescribes as though medical care were a free good.

coinsurance A component of a medical insurance plan whereby consumers pay a fixed percentage of the cost of medical care.

collusive oligopoly An oligopolistic-type market structure where all the firms in the industry jointly maximize profits as if they all acted collectively as a monopolist.

community rating A method used by third-party payers to establish insurance premiums based on the average benefits paid out for the total population served. In this case, premiums reflect the average health risk factors for the entire population served.

comparative static analysis A comparison of the initial and new equilibrium points after an external change alters the model.

compensating wage differential The increase in wages needed to attract the marginal worker to a given occupation because there is an added cost to entering the occupation, such as a professional license.

complements Two goods that are used together in consumption. Two goods are complements in consumption if an increase in the price of one good causes a decrease in the demand for the other.

compulsory licensing The situation where one firm is required by law to grant to another firm the opportunity to import or manufacture a patented drug for a royalty.

constant returns to scale Exist when a percentage increase in all factor inputs leads to a proportionately equal increase in output. The long-run average cost curve is horizontal if constant returns to scale exist.

consumer price index (CPI) A price index that measures the cost of purchasing a fixed market basket of consumer goods and services over time. The CPI is used to measure the consumer price inflation rate from one period to the next.

consumer surplus The difference between what consumers are willing to pay for a product and the market clearing price. As such, consumer surplus is represented by the area under the demand curve but above market price.

cost-benefit analysis A method of analysis used for decision making that estimates the total costs and benefits of an activity.

cost effectiveness analysis A method of analysis used for decision making that estimates the total costs of achieving a defined health care objective, such as a life-year saved, from a medical treatment or health behavior.

cost identification study A study that measures the total costs of a particular medical condition. Cost identification considers direct medical costs, direct nonmedical costs and indirect costs.

cost shifting The practice of charging a higher price for a medical service in one market to compensate for a lower price received for the same product in another market.

credence attributes Those characteristics of a good or service that can be assessed only after repeated purchases. Most medical care products possess credence characteristics.

cross-price elasticity An elasticity measure of the extent to which the quantity demanded of one product changes with respect to a change in the price of an alternative product. In precise terms, it equals the percentage change in the quantity demanded of one product divided by the percentage change in the price of another product. If the value of the coefficient is negative, the two products are complements; if the coefficient is positive, the two products are substitutes.

customary, prevailing, and reasonable rate See *usual, customary*, and *reasonable rate*.

data envelopment analysis (DEA) A statistical technique used by researchers to estimate the technical efficiency of organizations.

deadweight loss The social surplus not realized because resources are misallocated.

decreasing returns to scale Exist when a percentage increase in all factor inputs leads to a less than proportional increase in output.

deductible An annual out-of-pocket, lump-sum payment for medical services that a consumer must pay before medical insurance provides reimbursement.

defensive medicine The over utilization of medical services by a health care provider in order to prevent a potential medical malpractice suit.

demand The quantities of a good or service that a consumer is willing and able to purchase at various prices at a specific point in time. The market demand for a product equals the total demand for an entire population.

demand curve A graphical depiction of the relationship between quantity demanded and the price of a good or service. The **market demand curve** equals the horizontal summation of consumers' individual demand curves.

demand function A mathematical expression containing the various factors that influence the quantity demanded of a given product.

dependent variable A variable whose value is influenced by the value of one or more independent variables.

deselection The termination of a health care provider in a medical network based on an established set of criteria.

diagnosis related group (DRG) A reimbursement system developed under Medicare used to compensate hospitals based on the patient's primary diagnosis. (See *prospective payment system*.)

diffusion See *technology*.

discount rate The rate of interest used to discount a future stream of payments. (See *present value*.)

discovery by design The use of scientific knowledge to discover and develop new drugs.

diseconomies of scale Exist when the average cost of production increases with the level of output.

disproportionate share hospital payments Additional reimbursement payments received by states from the federal government for the Medicaid program to defer the high cost of providing medical care to a large number of low-income individuals.

distributive justice (See *horizontal equity* and *vertical equity*.)

drug utilization review Programs that control costs by reviewing the prescribing behavior of physicians to ensure that formularies are followed and inappropriate medicines are not prescribed.

dual-market model An economic model that illustrates how a producer decides to participant or operate in two different market segments.

economic model A simplified depiction of a complex economic phenomenon used by economists to examine economic behavior.

economic profit Total revenues minus total costs, including both explicit and implicit costs.

economies of scale Exist when the average cost of production decreases with the quantity of output.

economies of scope Exist when the total cost of jointly producing two or more products is cheaper than the total cost of producing each product individually.

elastic Describes a situation where the absolute value of the elasticity is greater than 1. This means the percentage change in the dependent variable is greater than the percentage change in the independent variable in absolute value terms.

elasticity A measure economists use to gauge the extent to which one variable changes in response to a change in another variable. It equals the percentage change in a dependent variable divided by the percentage change in an independent variable.

elasticity of input substitution An elasticity measure of the extent to which two inputs can be substituted for each other in the production process. In precise terms, it equals the percentage change in the input rate divided by the percentage change in the marginal products of the two inputs.

employer mandates A health care reform plan that requires employers to provide medical care insurance to employees.

endogenous Describes factors that are determined in the economic model, such as price and quantity in the supply and demand model.

enthusiasm hypothesis The hypothesis that geographic variations in the utilization of certain types of medical procedures reflect differences in medical preferences among physicians.

equilibrium   When there is no tendency for further change. **Market equilibrium** occurs in the supply-and-demand model when quantity demanded equals quantity supplied at the market clearing price.

exclusive provider organization (EPO)   A type of preferred provider organization that provides zero reimbursement to enrollees who acquire medical care from health care providers not included in the network.

exogenous   Describes factors that are determined outside the economic model, such as buyer income or tastes and preferences in the supply and demand model.

experience attributes   Those characteristics of a good or service that can be assessed only after the product has been purchased.

experience rating   A method used by third-party payers to establish insurance premiums based on the expected benefits paid out as a result of individual health risk factors.

explicit costs   Payments made to nonowners of the firm.

externality   Exists when the actions of a market participant affect another participant in either an adverse or a beneficial fashion and no financial compensation takes place. An externality can emanate from either the demand or the supply side of the market.

fee-for-service payment   A method of payment for medical care services whereby a medical care provider receives an individual payment for each medical service provided.

firm   An organization that is responsible for coordinating the transformation of inputs, such as land, labor, capital, and entrepreneurship, into some final output or outputs.

first dollar coverage   A health insurance plan that reimburses an individual for all medical care expenses, beginning with the first dollar spent on medical care.

first mover   A firm that poses a barrier to entry by being the first to introduce a product to a given market. Potential competitors must overcome the problem of name recognition if they wish to enter the market.

fixed costs   Costs of production that remain constant regardless of the level of production.

fixed payment   A payment that is independent of the actual costs or quantity of medical services delivered.

Flexner Report   A report published in 1910 that was highly critical of the medical training physicians received in the United States and Canada. As a result, numerous changes were made in the education and training of physicians.

Food and Drug Administration (FDA)   A government agency that regulates the introduction of new drugs in the United States.

formulary   A list of low-cost pharmaceutical products that physicians are required to prescribe whenever possible. Hospitals and other health care providers use formularies to control costs.

for-profit organization   An organization owned by private individuals. Ownership gives the individuals a claim on any residual profits.

function   A mathematical expression that establishes a relationship between the value of a dependent variable and a set of values for the independent variables.

fuzzy demand curve   A demand curve for medical care reflecting the possibility that the relationship between the price and quantity demanded of medical care may not be exact or precisely known.

gag rules   Rules that prohibit a physician in a managed-care plan from discussing alternative treatment options not covered by the health insurance plan, providing information on the limitations of the plan, and commenting negatively about the plan to patients.

generic drug   A drug that is bioequivalent to a brand named drug.

global budgeting   A method used by third-party payers to control medical care costs by establishing total expenditure limits for medical services over a specified period of time.

group-model health maintenance organization   A health maintenance organization (HMO) that contracts with group physician practices. (See *health maintenance organization*.)

Hatch-Waxman Act of 1984   The Drug Price Competition and Patent Term Restoration Act, which extended the effective life of a new drug product and shortened the approval process for generic drugs.

health   The condition of being of sound body and mind and free of any disease or physical pain.

health alliance   A public agency that uses its bargaining power to negotiate competitive prices for health insurance from the private insurance market. (See *managed competition*.)

Health Care Financing Administration (HCFA) An agency of the U.S. Department of Health and Human Services that is responsible for overseeing the financing and quality control programs for Medicare and the federal portion of Medicaid. The agency has since been renamed the Centers for Medicaid and Medicare Services.

health care system The organizational and institutional structures through which an economy makes choices regarding the production, consumption, and distribution of health care services.

health economics A field of economics that uses economic theory to study how an economy utilizes scarce health care resources to provide and distribute medical care.

Health Insurance Portability and Accountability Act of 1996 An act of Congress that addresses the nonportability of health insurance by making it more difficult for insurers to segment markets and deny individuals or groups health insurance based on health status.

health maintenance organization (HMO) A health care delivery system that combines the insurer and producer functions. HMOs are prepaid and in return provide comprehensive services to enrollees.

Herfindahl-Hirschman index An index used to measure the degree of industry concentration in a given market.

home health care Health care delivered at the home of the patient by a health care provider.

horizontal equity Equity that is achieved when, for example, individuals with similar incomes pay equal amounts of taxes and receive the same amounts of subsidies; in other words, equals are treated equally.

horizontal merger A merger between two firms in the same market.

hospice care Health care provided to a patient who is terminally ill.

human capital approach Equates the value of a human life to the market value of the output produced by an individual over an expected lifetime.

image differentiation The use by a firm of promotional activities to differentiate consumers' perceptions of its product relative to other products in the market.

imperfect consumer information The assumption that consumers lack all the information necessary to make informed decisions concerning the appropriate quantity and type of medical care to consume.

implicit costs Costs that measure the opportunity cost of utilizing resources owned by the firm.

income effect The increase (decrease) in quantity demanded brought about by an increase (a decrease) in real income when the price of a product decreases (increases). The concept is used to derive a downward-sloping demand curve.

income elasticity of demand An elasticity measure of the extent to which the quantity demanded changes with a change in income. In precise terms, it equals the percentage change in the quantity demanded divided by the percentage change in income.

inconsistency See *service*.

increasing returns to scale Exist when a percentage increase in all factor inputs leads to a greater percentage increase in output.

indemnity insurance Medical insurance that reimburses the insured a fixed amount for each type of medical service consumed.

independent provider association (IPA) A type of health maintenance organization that contracts with a number of independent medical care providers to deliver medical services at a discounted price or on a capitation basis.

independent variable A variable whose values are predetermined and influence the value of a dependent variable.

individual mandates A health care reform plan that requires individuals to purchase their own medical insurance. Tax credits and subsidies would be available to those who cannot afford to purchase medical insurance.

inelastic Describes a situation where the absolute value of the elasticity is less than 1, or the percentage change in the dependent variable is less than the percentage change in the independent variable.

inferior good A good for which demand decreases when consumers experience an increase in income.

informational advertising Advertising that provides information to consumers.

inseparability See *service*.

insurance premium The cost of medical insurance. In the private insurance market, it equals the sum of expected benefits paid out, administrative costs, taxes, and profits. (See also *experience rating* and *community rating*.)

intangibility See *service*.

integrated delivery system (IDS) A legal or contractual combination of buyers and suppliers, such as medical organizations producing different medical services, like physician groups, hospitals, and nursing homes.

inventory See *service*.

job lock The situation where an individual cannot change jobs without potentially losing medical care insurance for a given period of time.

law of demand An economic principle stating that the quantity demanded of a good or service is inversely related to its price.

law of diminishing marginal product An economic principle stating that as more and more units of an input are used in production, a point is eventually reached where output increases by a continually smaller and smaller amount. In other words, the **marginal product** of the factor input begins to fall in value.

law of diminishing marginal utility An economic principle stating that as units of a product are consumed, a point is eventually reached where total utility increases at a smaller and smaller rate. In other words, the **marginal utility** of the product begins to fall.

law of increasing opportunity cost An economic principle stating that the **opportunity cost** of an activity increases as more of that activity is undertaken.

law of supply An economic principle stating that the quantity supplied of a good or service increases with its price.

learning-by-doing The economies that result from knowledge or experience gained through the cumulative production of a product.

lifestyle The normal way of life for an individual or population. According to economic theory, how a person or group lives impacts overall health.

limit pricing The practice of pricing a product just below the break-even point of a potential entrant as a way to discourage entry.

loading fee That portion of medical insurance premiums in excess of expected benefits paid out. Its value depends on such items as administrative costs, taxes, and the intensity of competition in the insurance market.

long run A time horizon over which all inputs in the production process are variable.

long-run average cost curve An envelope curve comprising the cost-minimizing points from a series of short-run average cost curves. It represents the lowest cost of producing each unit of output in the long run.

long-term care Health care provided to an individual with one or more disability over an extended period of time for the purpose of enhancing the quality of life rather than curing a particular medical problem.

managed-care organization (MCO) An organization that controls the utilization and cost of medical care by reviewing and monitoring the appropriateness, extensiveness, and costs of medical services.

managed competition A health care reform plan that calls for the establishment of health alliances that would use their bargaining power to negotiate competitively priced medical coverage from a number of alternative private insurance companies.

managerial expense preference model A model of firm behavior positing that managers utilize a portion of the firm's profits to maximize their own utility.

marginal cost The change in total costs brought about by a one-unit change in the production of a product.

marginal product The change in total output brought about by a one-unit change in a factor input.

marginal rate of technical substitution The rate at which one input can be substituted for another in the production process. In precise terms, it equals the ratio of the marginal products of two inputs.

marginal revenue The addition to total revenue brought about by the sale of one more unit of output.

marginal social benefit The change in total social benefit brought about by a one-unit change in the consumption of a good or service.

marginal social cost The change in total social costs resulting from a one-unit change in the production of a good or service.

marginal utility The change in total utility or satisfaction brought about by a one-unit change in the consumption of a good or service.

market allocation   A collusive agreement among rival firms not to compete with one another in a given geographical market. This activity is prohibited by the Sherman Antitrust Act.

market failure   The situation where a market outcome fails to produce the socially optimal quantity of output or distribute income fairly.

McGuire's quantity setting model   An economic model of physician behavior based on monopolistic competition. The model predicts the quantity setting behavior of a physician when physicians are considered imperfect substitutes by consumers.

Medicaid   A jointly financed program between federal and state governments that provides medical insurance to certain segments of the poor population without private health insurance.

medical care   Those goods and services that maintain, improve, or restore an individual's physical or mental well-being.

medical savings accounts   A health care reform plan that allows individuals to establish tax-free savings accounts to finance primary medical care.

Medicare   A federally financed program that provides medical insurance primarily to elderly individuals.

Medicare Payment Advisory Commission (Med-PAC)   An independent federal agency formed by the Balanced Budget Act of 1997 to advise Congress on issues regarding the Medicare Program.

Medicare volume performance standards   A target rate of growth for physician expenditures under Medicare used to establish expenditure limits and contain costs. The targets were enacted under the Omnibus Budget Act of 1989 and later repealed under the Balanced Budget Act of 1997.

Medicare + Choice   Part of the Balanced Budget Act of 1997 that significantly increases the number of insurance plans available to Medicare recipients, along with altering the method in which Medicare pays for those plans.

medigap insurance policies   Private insurance policies purchased by elderly individuals to cover some or all of their medical expenses not paid for by Medicare.

merger   The combining of two or more firms.

merit good   A good provided by the government because it is considered socially desirable.

microeconomics   A field of economics that uses economic theory to study how individual consumers and firms make economic decisions.

molecule manipulation   A method of drug discovery whereby pharmaceutical companies utilize trial and error to determine the therapeutic value of a large number of chemical entities.

monopolistic competition   A product market characterized by numerous sellers, moderate product differentiation, no barriers to entry, and some imperfections in consumer information.

monopoly   A product market characterized by one seller and perfect barriers to entry.

monopoly power   The ability a firm has in a given market to control the price of its product. The degree of monopoly power any firm possesses is inversely related to the level of competition in the market.

monopsony   A market characterized by a single buyer that has the ability to influence market price.

moral hazard   The situation where individuals alter their behavior after they have purchased medical insurance because they are no longer liable for the full cost of their actions.

morbidity rate   The rate at which a given disease is present in a population.

mortality rate   The death rate for a given population measured by the ratio of the number of deaths divided by the average size of the population during a given period.

multihospital system   An organization that is made up of two or more hospitals and is managed by a single corporation.

multipayer system   A system in which health care providers are reimbursed by numerous third-party payers.

multiple regression   A statistical technique used by economists to estimate the relation between a dependent variable and one or more independent variables.

multisource drug   A drug that is no longer under patent protection and is available from alternative suppliers.

national health insurance (NHI)   A government-sponsored health insurance system covering the entire population and financed by tax revenues. Such a system exists in Canada.

national health system (NHS) A health care system directly run by the government and financed by general taxes. Such a system exists in Great Britain.

natural monopoly A firm that faces long-run economies of scale over the entire market demand curve.

net benefit calculus The optimizing rule used by economic agents that looks at the expected net benefits of a given activity, defined as the expected benefits minus the expected costs. When net benefits are greater than zero, the economic agent's well-being is enhanced by choosing the activity in question.

net marginal social benefit The difference between marginal social benefit and marginal social cost.

network health maintenance organization An HMO that provides physician services by contracting with more than one physician group practice.

nominal Describes an economic measure that is expressed in terms of current market prices.

normal good A good for which demand increases when consumers experience an increase in income.

normal profit Occurs when revenues are just enough to cover the opportunity cost of each and every resource used in production of a medical good or service.

normative economic analysis The use of economic theory and empirical analysis to justify whether an economic outcome is desirable.

not-for-profit An organization that is prohibited from distributing profits.

oligopoly A product market that is characterized by a few dominant sellers and substantial barriers to entry.

Omnibus Budget Reconciliation Act of 1989 An act passed by Congress significantly reforming the method by which physicians are compensated under the Medicare program.

opportunistic behavior The situation where a health care provider takes advantage of an asymmetry of information and provides medical care to advance his or her own economic self-interests.

opportunity cost The value of what is given up by not pursuing the next best alternative.

Orphan Drug Act An act providing incentives to pharmaceutical companies to develop drugs to treat rare diseases that are otherwise unprofitable to develop because the potential demand is low.

outcome quality The quality of medical care as measured by its end result, such as patient satisfaction or postcare morbidity or mortality.

out-of-pocket price The price consumers pay for medical care after all third-party payments have been considered.

output maximization See *quantity maximization*.

over-the-counter drug A drug that consumers can purchase without a prescription from a physician.

own-price elasticity of demand An elasticity measure of the responsiveness of quantity demanded to changes in a product's own price. In precise terms, it equals the percentage change in quantity demanded divided by the percentage change in price.

own-price elasticity of supply An elasticity measure of the responsiveness of quantity supplied to changes in price. In precise terms, it equals the percentage change in quantity supplied divided by the percentage change in price.

patent A government document that grants the legal right to an innovating firm to be the sole producer of a product for up to 20 years (in the United States).

patient dumping The situation where a private hospital fails to admit a very sick patient because it fears that the medical bills will exceed a preset limit established by a third-party payer. As a result, the patient is forced to acquire medical care services from a public hospital.

per capita Per unit of the population.

perfect competition A product market characterized by numerous buyers and sellers, a homogeneous product, no barriers to entry, and perfect consumer information.

perfectly elastic The special case where there is an infinite change in the value of the dependent variable when the independent variable changes in value.

perfectly inelastic The special case where the value of the dependent variable is unresponsive to changes in the value of the independent variable.

personal health care expenditures Total expenditures by individuals on medical care goods and services.

persuasive advertising Advertising that aims to convince consumers to purchase the product.

pharmacy benefit management (PMB) companies PMB companies are intermediaries that purchase drugs from manufacturers and pharmacies at a reduced price and resell them to health plans for a fee.

physician payment review commission (PPRC) A commission established in 1985 to advise and make recommendations to Congress regarding physician payment reform. PPRC was replaced by MedPAC.

physician practice hypothesis A hypothesis stating that per capita variations in the use of medical care are explained by systematic differences in clinical opinions concerning the proper type and amount of medical care to prescribe.

physician profiling The process by which a managed-care organization selects and monitors the performance of physicians.

point-of-service (POS) plan A type of managed care insurance plan that requires subscribers who go outside the network for medical care to have higher out-of-pocket expenses. The purpose is to contain costs by encouraging subscribers to acquire medical care from a network of providers.

positive economic analysis The analysis of economic behavior that uses economic theory along with empirical analysis to explain what is or what happened.

potential competition The level of competition as determined by the number the firms that may enter a particular market. Potential competition is determined by the height of any barriers to entry.

practice guideline A statement concerning the known costs, benefits, and risks of using a particular medical intervention to bring about a given medical outcome.

preferred provider organization (PPO) A third-party payer that offers financial incentives, such as low out-of-pocket prices, to enrollees who acquire medical care from a preset list of physicians and hospitals. A PPO is a prepaid type of MCO that combines the insurer and producer functions.

prescription drug A drug that can be purchased only with a physician's prescription.

present value A technique used to determine today's value of a future stream of cash payments.

price ceiling A government-imposed limit on the price of a product.

price discrimination The practice of charging a different price for the same product in two or more markets.

price fixing The practice by rival firms in the same market of acting in a collusive manner and setting prices for the purpose of increasing profits. This practice is prohibited by the Sherman Antitrust Act.

price leadership model An oligopolistic-type market structure where the firms in a given industry agree that one firm will serve as the price leader and the others will follow its pricing and output actions.

primary care Medical care services that deal with the prevention, early detection, and treatment of disease.

primary care physician A physician specializing in family practice, general practice, internal medicine, obstetrics/gynecology, or pediatrics.

process quality The quality of medical care as measured by the quality of treatment.

product differentiation A situation where firms within a given market sell slightly different products.

production efficiency Achieved when one activity (production or consumption) cannot be increased without a reduction in another activity because the maximum level of output is being produced from a finite amount of inputs. (See *production possibilities curve.*)

production function A mathematical expression that shows the maximum level of output that a firm can produce using various quantities of factor inputs.

production possibilities curve (PPC) An economic model that shows the various combinations of goods an economy can produce when **production efficiency** is achieved. **Allocative efficiency** is obtained when society chooses that point on the curve that maximizes overall satisfaction. The model illustrates the economic concepts of scarcity, choice, and opportunity costs.

professional licensure The requirement that a health care professional, such as a doctor or a nurse, obtain a license from the government before being allowed to practice medicine.

profit maximization   A situation where sellers strive to attain the greatest amount of economic profits.

profitability cycle   (see *underwriting cycle*)

progressive redistribution scheme   The situation where net taxes as a fraction of income increase with income.

property rights model   A model hypothesizing that for-profit organizations are more efficient than their not-for-profit counterparts because the owners of for-profit organizations force managers to act in a cost-efficient manner and strive to maximize profits. Managers of not-for-profit organizations do not face such pressure and are free to pursue other objectives, such as quality maximization.

proportional redistribution scheme   The situation where net taxes as a fraction of income remain constant with income.

prospective payment system (PPS)   A method of payment used by third-party payers in which payments are made on a case-by-case basis. Congress adopted a prospective payment system in 1983 when it introduced the DRG system for classifying Medicare patients.

public choice model   A model postulating that public organizations are less efficient than private organizations because bureaucrats and special interest groups cause public organizations to behave inefficiently and overproduce.

public contracting model   A health insurance model whereby the government contracts with various health care providers for medical services on behalf of the general population.

public enterprise   A medical care organization operated by a government authority.

public good   A product has the properties of a public good if it can be consumed simultaneously by more than one consumer and it is costly to exclude nonpayers from consuming the good. Public goods are generally provided by a government entity and funded out of tax revenues.

public interest group theory   A theory of government behavior that hypothesizes that governments intervene in a market-based economy to advance the general interest of its citizens.

quality and quantity maximization   The assumption that a medical care provider jointly determines what quality and quantity of output to produce that maximize utility.

quality differentiation   The situation where firms attempt to differentiate their products based on quality.

quality maximization   Occurs when medical care providers maximize the quality of output produced at the expense of economic profits.

quantity maximization   Occurs when medical care providers maximize the amount of output produced at the expense of economic profits.

quaternary-level care   State-of-the-art medical care.

rationality   The notion that consumers will never purposely make themselves worse off and have the ability to rank preferences and allocate income in a fashion that derives the maximum level of utility.

rationally ignorant   The situation where consumers have less than perfect information concerning a good or service due to the high cost of acquiring additional information.

real   Describes an economic measure that is expressed in base-year prices.

regressive redistribution scheme   The situation where net taxes as a fraction of income decrease with income.

reminder advertising   Advertising that reinforces consumers' knowledge about the product.

required generic substitution   Cost control policies that require physicians and pharmacists to use lower-priced generic drugs whenever medically possible.

resource-based relative value system   A method to compensate physicians that bases the payment on the time and effort of physician services necessary to produce the medical service. This system is currently used by the Medicare program.

risk adjustment   The process of setting the capitation rate for an insurance policy based on the health status and expected medical costs of an individual or group purchasing the plan.

risk assessment   The process of modeling and estimating the expected medical costs of a person or group of people.

risk aversion   The quality of preferring less risk to more, all other things held equal.

risk selection Occurs when a greater share of individuals with either higher or lower expected medical costs enroll in or select a particular medical insurance plan.

rule of reason States that courts should weigh the social desirability of a business practice, such as a merger, when determining if that practice should be allowed to take place. Thus, both the procompetitive and anticompetitive aspects of the business practice are considered.

search attributes Those characteristics of a good or service that are easily evaluated prior to its purchase, such as size, color, or design.

secondary care Medical care that consists of more sophisticated treatments than primary care services.

second opinions A utilization review program in which each decision made by a physician concerning the need for surgery is routinely reviewed by another physician.

selective contracting Occurs when a third-party contracts exclusively with a preselected set of medical care providers.

service A product that exhibits the four characteristics of intangibility, inseparability, inventory, and inconsistency. **Intangibility** means that a medical service cannot be evaluated by the five senses. **Inseparability** means that production takes place at the time of consumption. **Inventory** refers to the fact that it is impossible for health care providers to maintain an inventory of medical services. **Inconsistency** reflects the fact that the composition and quality of medical services vary greatly across points of consumption.

Sherman Antitrust Act A law passed in 1890 prohibiting certain forms of anticompetitive behavior. This act is considered the centerpiece of antitrust legislation in the United States.

short run A time horizon over which the quantity of at least one factor input is fixed in the production process. In this case, output can be altered only by changing the quantity of one or more of the variable inputs utilized in the production process.

short-run economies of scale Exist when average variable costs decline with the level of output.

sickness funds Private, not-for-profit insurance companies in Germany that collect premiums from employees and employers. (See *socialized health insurance*.)

single payer The situation where only one third-party payer is responsible for paying health care providers for medical services.

single-source drug A drug covered by patent protection.

socialized health insurance (SHI) A German-style health care system in which the government mandates that employers and employees jointly finance the cost of medical care insurance.

socioeconomic status The overall position of an individual in a given society based on social and economic factors, such as education and income.

spatial differentiation The situation where firms attempt to differentiate themselves based on location.

special interest group theory A theory of government behavior that hypothesizes that governments intervene in a market-based economy for the purpose of advancing the economic self-interests of a particular interest group.

staff-model health maintenance organization An HMO that directly employs physicians on a salary basis.

Standard Industrial Classification (SIC) system A system, designed by the U.S. Census Bureau, to categorize and code the output of firms into various classes. The code can contain up to seven digits. The four-digit SIC code is considered to represent the industry level. The first digit in the coding system identifies the sector of the economy (0 for agriculture, 2 for manufacturing, 5 for trade). The second digit defines the commodity group in that sector. For example, the two-digit code 28 represents the "chemicals and allied products" group of the manufacturing sector. The third digit represents an industry group. For example, 283 represents the "drugs" industry group and 282 stands for the "plastic materials and synthetics" industry group. The fourth digit identifies a specific segment of an industry group. For example, the four-digit code 2834 represents the "pharmaceutical preparations" industry, and the 2833 stands for the "medicinal chemicals and botanical products" industry.

State children's health insurance program (SCHIP) An act passed by Congress in 1997 that significantly expanded medical insurance coverage to children.

structural quality The quality of medical services as measured by the quality of the inputs used in production, such as credentials of physicians, education of nurses, and vintage and variety of equipment.

structure-conduct-performance paradigm A model used by economists when conducting an industry analysis. It predicts that market structure influences firm conduct, which determines market performance.

substitutes Two goods that are replacements in consumption and fulfill a similar purpose. Two goods are substitutes in consumption if an increase in the price of one good causes an increase in demand for the other.

substitution effect The increase (decrease) in quantity demanded brought about by a relative decrease (increase) in the price of a product. The concept is used to derive a downward-sloping demand curve.

supplier-induced demand model A model of firm behavior that hypothesizes that physicians take advantage of the asymmetry of information about medical care to convince their patients to consume more medical care than is necessary to further their own economic self-interests.

supply The quantity of output a firm is willing and able to produce at various prices during a specific time period. The **market supply** equals the total amount supplied in a given market.

supply curve The short-run supply curve for an individual firm facing a perfectly competitive market equals that part of the short-run marginal cost curve that lies above the average variable cost curve. The market supply curve equals the horizontal summation of the individual firms' supply curves, with adjustments made for factor price changes.

survivor theory Categorizes firms based on size and hypothesizes that any category that includes a growing number of firms over time represents the most efficient producers in comparison to those categories where the number of firms is decreasing.

technical efficiency Achieved when the maximum level of output is produced from a given mix of inputs at a point in time.

technology The development and diffusion of medical technology takes place in four stages. During the **basic research** stage, the investigation of new knowledge is without commercial purpose. In the **applied research** stage, new scientific knowledge is applied to

the solution of a medical problem. The **clinical investigation** stage occurs with testing of new medical technologies on human subjects. The **diffusion** stage marks the commercial introduction and adoption of a new medical technology.

tertiary care Highly complex medical care that involves more sophisticated medical treatments than primary or secondary medical care.

theory X of health economics An economic theory stating that health and disease occur randomly and that economic incentives cannot be called upon to provide quality medical care at low cost. Government intervention is needed to ensure individuals have access to quality medical care.

theory Y of health economics An economic theory stating that individuals have significant control over health through lifestyle choices and that the market mechanism will discipline health care providers to provide high-quality medical care at low cost. There is little need for government intervention in health care markets.

third-party payer An organization that provides medical care insurance to individuals in return for tax or premium payments.

time cost The monetary cost of travel and waiting resulting from the consumption of a good or service.

total costs The sum of **fixed** and **variable** costs associated with the production of a given quantity of output.

total net social benefit The difference between the total social benefit in consuming and total social cost of producing a good or service.

total product curve A curve showing the quantity of output produced by different levels of a specific input, such as labor, given that all other inputs are held constant.

total social benefit The total of the benefits a society receives from the consumption of a particular product. (See *total social surplus*.)

total social cost The total of the costs resulting from the production of a particular product. (See *total social surplus*.)

total social surplus The total social benefit minus the total social cost of producing a given quantity of a good or service.

transaction cost economics The view that contracts may be incomplete and therefore costly to engage in. Transaction costs include the costs of searching out the best price, and the cost associated with the negotiating, writing, and enforcing of contracts.

type I error   Occurs when an outcome is rejected as false when it is true. For example, the FDA rejects an application of a drug even though the drug is truly safe and effective.

type II error   Occurs when an outcome is accepted as true when it is false. For example, the FDA accepts an application of a drug even though the drug is unsafe or ineffective.

underwriting cycle (profitability cycle)   A profit cycle experienced by firms operating in the group health insurance market that includes three consecutive years of underwriting gains followed by three years of underwriting losses.

unitary elasticity   An elasticity with a value of 1 such that the percentage change in the dependent variable equals the percentage change in the independent variable in absolute value terms.

universal coverage   Achieved when an entire population has medical insurance coverage.

usual, customary, and reasonable rate (UCR)   A cost control method utilized by third-party payers to control the fees paid to medical care providers for medical goods and services. The UCR fee is limited to the lowest of the actual charge of the physician, the customary charge, or the prevailing charge in the local area.

utility   The level of satisfaction or pleasure an individual or group receives from consuming a good or service.

utility analysis   A method of analysis used to make policy decisions that considers the quantity as well as the quality of a life saved from a medical intervention. (See also *cost effectiveness analysis*.)

utility function   A mathematical expression that shows the extent to which various factors affect total utility.

utility maximization model   An economic model that assumes people try to attain the highest possible level of satisfaction through their consumption decisions.

utility maximization rule   A rule stating that a consumer's utility is maximized when the marginal utility received from the last dollar spent on each commodity is equal across all goods and services purchased.

utilization review   Programs implemented to control medical costs by evaluating the medical decisions of hospitals and physicians. These programs can be carried out on a prospective, concurrent, or retrospective basis.

value of life   The monetary worth of a human life.

variable costs   Costs of production that vary directly with the quantity of output produced.

variable payment   Reimbursement that increases with higher costs incurred or a greater quantity of services supplied.

vertical equity   Achieved when unequal individuals are treated unequally. For example, people with higher incomes pay higher taxes.

vertical merger   A merger between two firms in a supplier–purchaser relationship.

virtual integration   A contractual combination of buyers and suppliers.

voluntary performance standard   A target rate of growth for physician expenditures financed by the Medicare program. This rate is established by Congress to control the cost of Medicare over time. This cost control method ended in 1997.

willingness-to-pay approach   Determines the value of a human life based on a person's willingness to pay for relatively small reductions in the chance of dying.

community versus,
311–13
Explicit costs, 169
Extensive demand, 118
Externalities, 231
demand-side, 231–34
market solution for,
238–40
negative demand-side,
231
negative supply-side,
234–35
positive demand-side, 231
positive supply-side,
235–36
supply-side, 234–36
taxes and subsidies to
correct, 236–38
Extra billing, 81

Federal Drug Administration,
446–47
Federal Employees Health
Benefits program, 536
Federal Food, Drug and Cos-
metic Act of 1938, 437
Federal Hospital Insurance
Trust Fund, 272
Federal Trade Commission
Act of 1914, 249
Fee-for-service reimburse-
ment, 353
Financial incentives, informed
choices and, 389
Financial incentives and man-
agement strategies
facing consumers/pa-
tients, 150
facing health care
providers, 150–52
First-dollar coverage, 78
First-mover advantage, 445
"Flat-of-the-curve" medicine,
42
Formulary, 151, 440
For-profit health care
providers, differences be-
tween not-for-profit and,
85
Freedom of choice (FOC)
laws, 155
Fuzzy demand curve, 113–14

Gag rules, 153
Generic drugs, 438, 439–40,
441
German health care system
consumer satisfaction
with, 93–94

long-term care in, 515–16
medical technology in,
86–87
physician choice in, 88
production of medical services in, 88
reimbursement in, 82
Sickness Funds, 78, 82
socialized health insurance
(SI), 78
summary of, 88–90
Goldfarb v. Virginia State Bar,
251
Goods
inferior, 104
public, 230
Governance, 411
Government
health outcomes research
by, 280
as producer of health insurance, 264–65
redistribution function of,
254–58
State Children's Health Insurance Program (CHIP)
by, 267–69
See also Medicaid, Medicare
Government intervention
to provide public goods, 230
reasons for, 226–29
taxes and subsidies as corrective instruments,
236–38
types of, 229–58
Government regulations, 241–48
antitrust laws as, 248–52
effects of quality, 246–48
governing public enterprise,
252–54
for human organs market,
245–46
Group model, 148–49

Hatch-Waxman Act of 1984, 445,
465
Hawaii's health care system, 545
Health, 31
determinants of adult, 42–46
determinants of children's,
47–48
empirical evidence on production in U.S., 41–48
marginal utility curve
for, 34
production of good,
35–41
total utility curve for, 33
utility analysis of, 31–33
Health alliances, 541

Health care. *See* Medical care
Health Care Access and Cost
Commission (HCACC),
574–75
Health care expenditures
concentration of, 418–19
distribution of, 257
explaining rising, 201
growth in hospital, 413–15
out-of-pocket (2000),
130–31
in the U.S., 127–31
Health care providers
financial incentives/man-
agement strategies fac-
ing, 150–52
See also Hospitals, Medical firms, Physicians
Health care reform
federal level of, 535–43
individual mandates as,
540–41
managed competition as,
541–42
medical savings accounts
as, 537–40
national health insurance
as, 542–43
National Health Security
Act (Clinton plan),
550–52
overview of, 534–35
state level, 543–50
Health care services. *See* Medical services
Health care systems, 75
Canadian, 78
comparison of national,
88–90
comparison of U.S. and international, 531–34
consumer satisfaction in
selected countries,
93–94
elements of, 75–77
financing of U.S., 90–91
German, 78
Hawaii's, 545
Maryland's, 545–46
Minnesota's, 546–47
model of, 76
Oregon's, 547–48
production of health services, 92
provider choice in U.S., 92
reimbursement in U.S.,
91–92
risk management, reim-
bursement, and con-
sumer cost sharing,
79–84